P9-CCG-082

IDEOLOGIES
SECOND EDITION

IDEOLOGIES

SECOND EDITION

DOUGLAS BALDWIN
Acadia University in Wolfville, Nova Scotia

BOB BERUBE
Strathcona Composite School in Edmonton, Alberta

LARRY BOOI
Strathcona Composite School in Edmonton, Alberta

DAVID JONES
Acadia University in Wolfville, Nova Scotia

DOUGLAS RAMSAY
Calgary Board of Education in Alberta

THOMAS SPIRA
University of P.E.I., Charlottetown, P.E.I.

with

SHARON ADAMS — Central Kings Secondary School, Annapolis Valley, Nova Scotia

WILLIAM CALDER — Dept. of Indian and Native Affairs, Government of Saskatchewan, Regina, Saskatchewan

KLARA SPIRA — Charlottetown, P.E.I.

McGRAW-HILL RYERSON LIMITED
Toronto Montreal New York Auckland Bogotá Caracas Lisbon London
Madrid Mexico Milan New Delhi Paris San Juan Singapore Sydney Tokyo

IDEOLOGIES, Second Edition

ISBN 0-07-551034-0

1 2 3 4 5 6 7 8 9 0 D 1 0 9 8 7 6 5 4 3 2

Sponsoring Editor: Janice Matthews
Permissions Editor: Jacqueline Russell
Associate Editor: Denise Shortt
Senior Supervising Editor: Susan Calvert
Cover and Text Design: Hania Fil
Technical Art: Carole Giguere
Maps: Patricia Code

Printed and bound in Canada by John Deyell Company

Canadian Cataloguing in Publication Data

Main entry under title:

Ideologies

2nd ed.
Includes index.
ISBN 0-07-551034-0

1. Political science. 2. Ideology. I. Baldwin, Douglas, 1944–

JC348.I34 1991 320.5 C91-093119-4

CONTENTS

PREFACE

The world has undergone tremendous changes since *Ideologies* was first published in 1982. The Soviet Union and Eastern Europe are in the process of drastically altering their political and economic institutions. War erupted in the Persian Gulf between Iraq and the American-led "Coalition." The two Germanies have been reunited. The Cold War has ended. South Africa is rethinking apartheid. Islamic fundamentalism now plays a major role in Middle Eastern politics. At home, Canada and the United States have agreed upon free trade. This new edition of *Ideologies* reflects these and other changes. All case studies and statistics have been updated, and the text has been greatly expanded to provide wider coverage of the Third World, environmental issues, women's rights, Asia, Eastern Europe, minority groups, privatization, and South Africa.

This text, however, is not a survey of world history, current politics, or economic decisions. Rather, it is an examination of the major economic and political ideologies of the twentieth century. The case studies provide in-depth examples of these ideologies in practice. We hope that when you have finished studying *Ideologies*, you will have a good grasp of the ideas that have shaped the twentieth century, and that you will have developed the skills necessary to act upon your ideas.

The authors are experienced teachers. Douglas Baldwin is an authority in Canadian and European history. He teaches at Acadia University in Nova Scotia, and has written four other school textbooks. Thomas Spira is professor and chair of the history department at the University of Prince Edward Island. He has written several books on Central Europe, and is editor of the *Canadian Review of Studies in Nationalism*. David Jones is an expert on the Soviet Union, and has addressed committees of the Canadian Senate and the Congress of the United States on the Gorbachev regime. He is professor of Military and Strategic Studies at Acadia University. Bob Berube and Larry Booi teach at Strathcona Composite High School in Edmonton. Larry Booi has co-authored several other school textbooks, and is especially interested in the Third World. Bob Berube is head of the history department. He earned his degree in economics, and has pursued this interest in *Ideologies*. Douglas

Ramsay has a M.A. in the history of Canadian education. He is the social studies specialist for adult education at the Calgary Board of Education. William Calder taught at the University of Alberta before working with the federal and inter-governmental affairs departments in Edmonton and now in Regina. Sharon Adams teaches history at Central Kings Rural High School in Nova Scotia, and has participated in curriculum development task force work for the Nova Scotia Department of Education. Klara Spira is a recent graduate of the University of Prince Edward Island, with expertise in anthropology.

Many people have helped to make this book a success. Steven Bligh McNutt updated the original chapters. Len Brhelle, Heather Carson, Bryan Connors, Marc Keirstead, Orest Melnyk, and Dr. E.A. Mitchner commented upon the second draft and offered many helpful suggestions. Finally, we wish to thank McGraw-Hill Ryerson editors Janice Matthews, Susan Calvert, and Denise Shortt for transforming our rough drafts into their present form.

SECOND EDITION

CHAPTER 1 OVERVIEW

VALUES AND POLITICAL AND ECONOMIC SYSTEMS

Chapter 1 provides an overview of the major themes, content, and approaches of *Ideologies*. It discusses the differences between facts and values and explains what an ideology is and why it is important. A questionnaire helps you to discover your own values and the extent to which you are open-minded. The chapter then previews the major issues and problems that all economic and political systems must address. It concludes with suggestions on how to approach complicated political and economic problems, conduct research, analyse polling statistics, and clearly present the findings of your research.

▶ OBJECTIVES

After reading this chapter, you should be able to:

- ▶ distinguish between facts and values
- ▶ identify the extent of your own open-mindedness
- ▶ define ideology and understand its importance
- ▶ develop an appropriate method for solving problems
- ▶ understand the importance and process of research
- ▶ present your ideas in a clear, logical format
- ▶ analyse polling statistics
- ▶ identify the major issues discussed in *Ideologies*

▶ KEY TERMS

economic system
political system
fact
value
belief
critical thinking
tolerance
ideology
inquiry process

CHAPTER 1

VALUES AND POLITICAL AND ECONOMIC SYSTEMS

World events such as those pictured at the right often occur quite unexpectedly. Although the world is constantly changing, and it is obviously impossible to forecast the future accurately, an understanding of the past enables us to make sense of world events. It is also important to be able to place changing events into proper perspective. This book attempts to provide a better understanding of the past, present, and future by examining the major **economic** and **political systems** of the twentieth century. It also seeks to provide the analytical tools necessary for you to interpret the world and make informed decisions.

This book investigates the major political and economic systems that have shaped the modern Western world and explores Canada's relationship to them. Such a

Mandela arrives—Prime Minister Brian Mulroney welcomes African National Congress leader Nelson Mandela to Canada.
The Bettmann Archive

broad and important field of study is inevitably laden with controversy—in fact, disagreement and controversy are the very essence of politics and economics. Inflation, elections, taxes, and welfare policies are only a few instances of controversial topics. The greatest minds in the world have wrestled with these subjects and have been unable to agree on an answer.

▶ FACTS AND VALUES

Life is not simply a choice between good and bad alternatives. If each dilemma or problem could be solved by referring only to the facts, then it would be a relatively simple task to resolve all conflicts of opinion. In that case, only a lack of knowledge on one or both sides could cause a difference of opinion. Yet we know that this is not always the case. A group of people can be given identical information and still arrive at different conclusions. Some of your classmates, for example, are concerned about the environment, whereas others are not. Varying opinions result from the differing values held by each individual. Values are fundamental ideas about what is important in life. They are standards of conduct that cause people or groups to think and act in certain ways. A **fact** is simply "what is," whereas a **value** is a deeply held conviction or belief. Facts do not change, but people's values may do so. As young people encounter new and different places, ideas, and people, their values are constantly being tested and shaped until the views of some of them become more rigid. When this happens over time, major value changes are much less likely to occur. A disagreement over facts can be resolved, but a dispute over values is much more difficult to settle. Three examples illustrate the problem:

- Edmonton is a beautiful city.
- John Diefenbaker was a great prime minister.
- Emily Carr was Canada's best artist.

These three statements combine fact and value judgments. It is possible to verify the factual statements: Edmonton is a city; John Diefenbaker was a prime minister of Canada; Emily Carr was an artist. The words "beautiful," "great," and "best," however, are value-laden terms. What exactly do "beautiful" and "great" mean? Is the whole city of Edmonton beautiful or just parts of it? Are skyscrapers and large apartment buildings beautiful or do they signify crowded living conditions? Was everything that Diefenbaker did great? Did his policies benefit everyone? Is it possible to compare abstract artists to realist painters? Value-laden statements are almost impossible to prove. To many western Canadians, Diefenbaker was a great man because he was responsible for obtaining more markets for western Canadian wheat. A French Canadian, however, would take a different view because Diefenbaker tended to ignore Quebec's needs. A Calgarian might not think Edmonton is very beautiful simply because of the rivalry between the two cities.

Since it is impossible not to make value judgments, it is important to know and understand your own values and to ensure that they are grounded on a solid base of information. You could, for example, support your **belief** that Edmonton is a beautiful city by referring to the North Saskatchewan River valley or other scenic areas in the city. It is also essential that you examine other people's values and opinions with an open mind. When faced with different choices, people react with selections that vary largely because they possess different values. It seems inconceivable that only one religion, one country, and one lifestyle could be completely correct. Are all the people who hold different values in countries other than ours wrong?

Differing values help to explain the variety of political and economic systems in the world. Each political and economic system is based upon a coherent set of values on such significant decisions as the importance of the individual versus the rights of the state, the degree of government involvement in the economy, and the method of selecting political leaders. Should everyone's income be similar, or should some people be allowed to amass huge fortunes? Should the country's leaders be chosen in free elections, or should an elite group of people make all political and economic decisions? Such questions as these have been debated for centuries. The basic facts have remained constant, but society's values have not. The answer each society selects reflects its underlying values and assumptions.

Informed analysis occurs when a person is asked to evaluate different points of view, arrive at a conclusion, and support it on the basis of facts.

What are your political and economic values? To evaluate them, read the questionnaire on page 6. List the numbers 1 to 20 in your notebook and mark *agree* or *disagree* beside each number. There is no right or wrong answer.

This questionnaire has two purposes. The first is to discover whether your ideas and values change over the course of the year. At the conclusion of this book, return to this questionnaire, answer it, and compare your two sets of responses. The second purpose is to help you discover the extent to which you are open-minded. Add up the *agree*'s you have listed for each even-numbered question (2, 4, 6, 8, etc.). The higher the number of *disagree*'s, the more open-minded you tend to be.

If you value **critical thinking**, and you want to be tolerant of other people and receptive to new ideas, then you must attempt to have an open mind towards controversial issues. **Tolerance** means to recognize and respect the rights and opinions of others whether agreeing with them or not. Permitting someone to follow another religion than your own without condemning him or her is an example of tolerance. Sometimes, however, a society or individual can be too tolerant. Should society permit sexism, racism, murder, and violence? There is often a fine line between the need for toleration and the necessity of imposing restrictions. When, for example, does freedom of speech become libel and when do libel laws become censorship?

People who hold their beliefs so strongly that they will not change them, no matter what, are called closed-minded. This means that their minds are closed to many new and different ideas. Rather than carefully examining information that conflicts with their views, closed-minded people will reject the information without considering its merits. Such people tend to judge issues in black and white terms, and they often evaluate people according to their appearance, occupation, and manner of speaking. Rarely will they question the statements made by figures of authority. As a consequence, they are generally ignorant of the views of those who oppose them.

If democratic governments are to operate effectively, their citizens should be open-minded. Democratic people must be adaptable to change and receptive to different points of view. Tolerance of divergent ideas is basic to democracy, because one of the most important aspects of democracy is the recognition that people are different. Even more important is the acceptance of these differences. In contrast to the open-mindedness of the democratic personality, the authoritarian or closed-minded personality is often intolerant, distrustful, conforming, and rigid.

No individual is completely closed- or open-minded. One of the purposes of this study is to expose you to different ideas. Do not accept anything you read without first questioning it, and do not reject new opinions without first considering their merits. The more open-minded you

QUESTIONNAIRE

▷ 1. People should have a say in determining their fate, and the government should be led by people elected by a majority of the citizens.
▷ 2. Canada and the U.S.S.R. have almost nothing in common.
▷ 3. The Canadian economic system ensures that poverty will be kept to a minimum.
▷ 4. Always compromising with our political opponents is dangerous because it usually leads to a betrayal of our own side.
▷ 5. A socialist economy is designed to benefit the group, rather than the individual.
▷ 6. Even though freedom of speech is a worthwhile goal, it is usually necessary to restrict the freedom of speech of some political groups.
▷ 7. The average Canadian voter is generally well-informed about election issues.
▷ 8. A group that allows much difference of opinion among its members will not exist very long.
▷ 9. One of the beliefs of the private enterprise system is that if all people were free to do exactly as they wanted, then the whole society would benefit.
▷ 10. In this complicated world, the only way we can ensure that the country is governed properly is to rely upon leaders or experts who can be trusted.
▷ 11. The major problem with socialism is that it destroys people's incentive to work.
▷ 12. There are two kinds of people in this world: those who are truthful and those who are not.
▷ 13. There is little difference among socialists, Marxists, and communists.
▷ 14. Among all the different philosophies in the world, there is probably only one that is correct.
▷ 15. A small economic elite has more influence on the Canadian government than the elected representatives (MPs).
▷ 16. Loyal political followers should subscribe only to their party's newspaper.
▷ 17. It is impossible to have democracy in a socialist country.
▷ 18. I wish I could find someone to solve all my problems and tell me what to do.
▷ 19. Dictatorship is not much different from communism.
▷ 20. In the history of the world, there have probably been just a handful of really great thinkers.

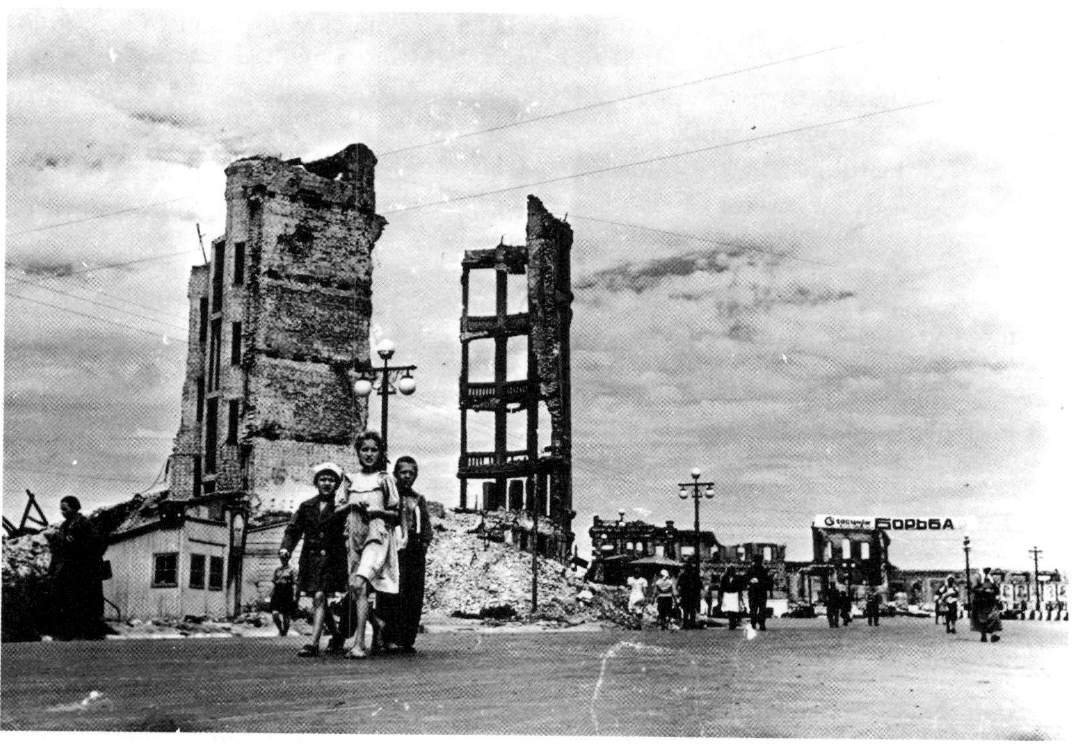

One way to discover your biases is to jot down your reactions to a photograph before reading the caption, and then record your reactions after reading it. How do you react to this photograph? With sympathy? Curiosity? Indifference? Jot down your feelings before reading on.

How does your response change if you discover that the photograph shows:

a) London, England, after a German attack during World War II;
b) Detroit, Michigan, after a riot in 1967;
c) Berlin, Germany, after a combined British-American-Canadian attack in 1945.

Try this test on your friends and family. Then give them the true identity of the photograph, as found on page 14. Record their reactions.
Miller Services

attempt to be, the more you will benefit from this book.

▶ IDEOLOGIES

Our beliefs are influenced by everything we do. As we grow up, we are pushed and pulled in one direction or another by our family, our teachers, and our friends. At times we consciously choose among competing religious, scientific, social, and political ideas, but in most cases, we simply accept certain beliefs without making a conscious choice. Gradually we adopt a set of values that we accept as being true. This set of beliefs about the world is called an **ideology**.

The difference between beliefs and ideologies is that an ideology is a systematic set of beliefs that provides a fairly thorough picture of the world that a group of people accepts as true. Although the word "ideology" has many different definitions and meanings, it generally consists of at least some of the following:

- a set of basic assumptions about human nature and society
- an interpretation of the past
- an explanation of the present
- a vision of the future
- a goal (usually utopian) for which to strive, and a strategy to achieve this goal
- heroes (martyrs, founders, leaders), rituals (pledges, anthems, salutes), and sacred documents (Bibles, manifestos, constitutions)
- a strong emotional appeal that is designed to win converts and encourage action
- a simple, easily understood picture of the world, which it claims is the truth

Although many people are not aware of their own basic beliefs, all contemporary societies have their own ideologies. Few societies, however, are so dominated by a single ideology that there are no alternatives available within the system. Because each ideology is a blend of facts and values and is intended to have an emotional appeal, people often perceive it in terms of black and white, or good and bad, without making the effort to understand what such words as democracy, communism, socialism, nationalism, capitalism, fascism, anarchism, Catholicism, or Protestantism really mean. This is largely due to their unconscious acceptance of one or more of these ideologies.

Ideologies are important because they enable people to understand their environment and order their lives accordingly. An ideology provides a way of judging and evaluating a confusing variety of issues and world events. It makes the future seem more predictable and imparts a feeling of security. An ideology also binds people together by providing them with a common value system and a way of looking at the world, which contribute to a feeling of belonging. Finally, it promises a good life and provides a method of attaining it.

This book examines some of the major economic and political ideologies of the contemporary world. Although it is true that an ideology is not always an accurate depiction of reality, people base their actions upon what they believe is true. It is therefore important to examine the underlying values and assumptions of every political and economic system in order to better understand each country's actions.

▶ POLITICAL AND ECONOMIC SYSTEMS

The fundamental economic and political problems of every country resemble those problems facing every family in the world. Members of each household must decide how their income will be used, who will perform what chores, and how such decisions will be made. In many families with young children, the parents jointly decide what will be done (or one parent makes the major decisions) and the children are told what to do. As the children mature, they are given greater responsibilities, but not always more say in family decisions. A major source of disagreement in many households is how the family's income should be used. Because there almost never seems to be enough money to satisfy everyone's needs, most families choose to budget their income. The purchase of a new automobile might mean fewer restaurant meals and no summer holiday; a new pair of skates might require one member of the family taking a weekend job.

Each country faces similar problems. The family income is equivalent to the production or income derived from such non-human resources as farmland, factories, and minerals, and such human resources as trained scientists, factory workers, and teachers. These factors of production, as they are called, are limited. Each country must decide how best to use them. Should farmland be employed to produce food, or should it be subdivided into suburban housing? Should universities concentrate on training computer programmers or producing surgeons?

The scarcity of human and non-human resources is the central economic problem of the world. It involves making choices and sacrifices. Each country must decide:

- What goods will be produced.
- How they will be produced.
- Who will own the means by which these goods will be produced.
- How these goods will be divided among the people.

As in the family analogy, someone or some group must make these decisions. The central political problem is determining who should govern. A study of a country's political structure must examine who exercises power, how power is maintained, who makes the important decisions, and why these decisions are made.

This book explores the major political and economic systems of the world as they have evolved in the nineteenth and twentieth centuries. The political systems to be examined are dictatorship (rule by one person), oligarchy (rule by a select few), and democracy (rule by the majority). The economic systems to be analysed are private enterprise, the centrally planned economy, and the mixed economy.

All economic and political systems are artificial. They are made by human beings and can be altered by them. The central questions posed in this book are

- How can each country's resources be distributed most efficiently?
- What political system can cater to the needs and wishes of its people most effectively?
- What are the basic values and beliefs of each economic and political system?

Your answers to these three questions will depend upon which goals or values you think are most important. No system is perfect; the more we know about the goals and values of each, as well as the advantages and disadvantages of our own economic and political systems, the better equipped we will be to improve them.

THE INQUIRY PROCESS

It is necessary for you to be aware at the very beginning that this is a ''critical'' book. It does not trumpet the virtues of capitalism and democracy, nor does it overemphasize the benefits of non-democratic governments and the centrally planned economy. Each economic and political system is subjected to a thorough and probing analysis. If a democratic country is to operate effectively, its citizens must understand not only how its institutions operate but also their limitations. Throughout this book you will be asked to analyse different ideas, evaluate opposite points of view, and judge issues based on their merits. To approach such hotly debated topics as political and economic systems in any other way would be indoctrination, not education.

Our lives are constantly complicated by the necessity of choosing between two or more options. We have to solve conflicts where a choice must be made among a variety of ''good'' solutions, rather than simply between good and bad. Every day, problems are becoming more complex and difficult to understand, let alone solve. The ability to make reasoned choices among different competing values and ideas is the mark of an intelligent person. It is also an essential skill for solving the dilemmas and problems of everyday life. One method of dealing with most problems consists of

INQUIRY PROCESS

The Problem: Should Canada belong to NATO?

1. Identify the Problem
    - Define NATO and its basic purpose.
    - Establish the options for Canada.
2. Establish Research Questions
    - What is Canada's role in NATO?
    - What are Canada's obligations to NATO?
    - What are NATO's obligations to Canada?
    - What are the various viewpoints about the problem?
    - How has Canada participated in NATO in the past?
    - What are the strengths and weaknesses of NATO?
    - What has changed since Canada originally joined NATO?
3. Gather and Organize the Information
    - List the members of NATO.
    - Make a map of Europe showing NATO countries.
    - Review the history of NATO and its involvement in Europe.
    - Explore other NATO members' current policies towards the organization.
    - Make a time line of important events concerning NATO from its inception until today.
4. Evaluate the Information
    - Discriminate between relevant and irrelevant information.
    - Judge the reliability and validity of the information.
    - Who is the author of each piece of information?
    - Have the author's statements on other topics been trustworthy?
    - What was the author's motive or purpose for writing?
    - What are the values and assumptions of the author?
    - What is the author's social, political, and economic background?
    - By whom is the author employed?
    - How did the author discover the information?
    - Do the facts support the conclusion?
    - Evaluate the desirability and feasibility of alternative solutions, decisions, or actions.
    - Is more evidence needed?
5. Analyse and Synthesize the Information
    - Recognize underlying assumptions and values of a statement or position.
    - Examine arguments for consistency and contradiction.
    - Distinguish between fact and opinion.
    - Summarize material.
    - Formulate as many solutions as possible.
    - Determine the advantages and disadvantages of each of these solutions.

▷ 6. Resolve the Problem
- Weigh each of the possible alternatives. (What are the probable outcomes of each alternative?)
- Compare the predicted results of each solution.
- Make a decision based upon the evidence.

▷ 7. Apply the Decision
- Become an active participant by writing a letter to your Member of Parliament stating your position on NATO. (petition, organize others, lobby)
- Join the federal political party that most closely agrees with your position on NATO.
- Establish your own party.
- Do nothing.

---

applying seven separate but related operations. This **inquiry process** is illustrated on pages 10 and 11 by approaching the problem of Canada's membership in NATO.

The most time-consuming step is gathering the information. It is also one of the most important aspects of reaching a judicious decision. The researcher is like a detective; in order to discover what happened and why it happened, the researcher must investigate every clue, no matter how small. One bit of information is obtained from a personal interview, another from a government report. Other possible sources include photographs, contemporary novels, newspaper accounts, and private correspondence—the list is almost endless.

After each source has been evaluated and the information analysed, it is time to make a decision. Your thesis, or major argument, will be based not only upon the available evidence but also on your own values. This is because it is almost impossible to discover everything that happened in the past. Individual motives and future developments are equally difficult to determine. Since it is impossible to know everything, social science, by necessity, involves interpretation. Where interpretation is involved, it is almost impossible to reach a definitive answer, since people evaluate or judge the available "facts" according to their own values and upbringing. This, however, does not mean that one interpretation is no better than another. A good thesis must take into account all the known "facts" and must make sure that these "facts" do not contradict each other without a suitable explanation. The ability to uncover the best sources of information and to transfer all these pieces of information into a study that explains both the how and the why is what separates good analysis from bad analysis.

▶ PRESENTING THE RESULTS

The first issue to discover is exactly what type of written assignment your teacher expects—a descriptive account or an analytical evaluation. The former is more a matter of research and organization, and usually requires a chronological approach. The latter involves more critical thinking. It requires you to arrive at a conclusion, or thesis, supported by your research data. The descriptive essay requires the skills of a detective. The analytical essay adds the skills of a lawyer to those of a detective.

After you have selected a topic (for example, Japan's economy), you must establish the purpose of the research. Do you want to show how successful Japan's economy has been in the last forty years, or explain why it has been successful? This is called the thesis question. Your answer is your thesis, and the remainder of the essay should be devoted to proving this conclusion.

One of the best ways to take research notes is to use file cards, recording information only on one side. For each card, list the source of your data (author, title, city of publication, date, and page number). This will help later when preparing footnotes. To avoid the danger of plagiarism (using someone's words or ideas as if they were your own), take point-form notes except where you might want to quote a particularly interesting passage. When you do, present the information in quotation marks (''. . .'').

▶ Organizing

Once the research is completed, it is time to present your results. This must be done clearly and logically. You might have wonderful ideas, but if no one can understand you (awkward writing, too much jargon, etc.), your ideas will never become known. Each section of this book went through four or more different drafts, and benefited from the comments of a half-dozen people. Teachers remarked upon the writing style, vocabulary, and interest level; professors examined the manuscript for accuracy; copy editors improved the grammar; and artists helped with the visuals. The more critical these people were, the better this book became. This is what you need—people who are knowledgeable and not afraid to be frank and honest. It is the end product that is important, not the rough drafts or your ego.

The first step in writing an essay is to prepare an outline. Read through your notes and make a long list of all the topics covered. Now collate them — arrange the information in topics, chronological sequence, or by specific areas. Finally, prepare a point-form outline. A typical outline would include an introduction, thesis development, and a conclusion.

Introduction

This is where you capture the reader's attention and introduce the topic.

- an interesting opening sentence to attract the reader's attention
- the topic of the essay
- the importance of the topic
- your thesis, or major point

This is what the reader sees first, and if your essay is not interesting, it will be discarded. But even if people only read the introduction, they will have read your thesis, which is the unique part of the essay.

Thesis Development

Here you provide proof to support your thesis.

- logical argumentation
- quotations
- statistics
- visuals
- descriptive material
- facts

All information must relate in some way to your thesis. Most writers discard about one-third of their notes because the information does not relate to their thesis. Remember that you are trying to convince the reader that your conclusions are correct, so refer to your thesis after each major section has been completed.

Conclusion

Here you summarize the major points of your essay and restate your thesis. The conclusion is similar to a lawyer's summation in court. It must convince the jury (the readers) that your conclusion is correct.

▶ The Writing

Sort through your research cards and select those cards that pertain to the first topic you wish to write about. Read through them and place the cards around your desk for quick reference. Write quickly. Do not hesitate too long searching for a specific word or worry about spelling. Let the writing flow.

Repeat this procedure for each section. Leave the essay alone for a day or two to allow your mind to contemplate the topic subconsciously. Reread what you have written and edit it. Correct the organization, spelling, and grammar. Now ask a friend to read it—you want this person to be honest and to note each confusing point, every awkward phrasing, all misspellings, and whether your thesis is convincing. Rewrite. Read the paper to someone else to double-check the punctuation, or put it on tape. Revise. Submit.

This is the general procedure we followed in writing *Ideologies*. The skills needed to produce a good research paper are the same as those required to function successfully in our complicated and rapidly changing society. You must know how to find suitable information and how to evaluate and analyse the data before drawing conclusions and acting upon them. This applies just as much to buying a car or voting in an election as it does to performing brain surgery or recommending that a company pursue a particular course of action.

▶ OTHER FORMS OF COMMUNICATION

The methods described above also apply to other forms of communication. Oral reports, video presentations, and artistic displays all need to be well researched, logically organized, and carefully double-checked. Nothing is worse, for example, than listening to someone who never looks at the audience reading a poorly organized report with a monotone voice. To avoid these mistakes it is wise to use cue-cards on which your information is written in point form. This prevents you from reading your report and allows eye contact with the audience. As with any other endeavour, practice makes better.

APPLYING YOUR KNOWLEDGE

1. Give an example of a dilemma where a choice must be made from among several "good" solutions.
2. Choose one of the odd-numbered statements in the Questionnaire (1, 3, 5, etc.) and outline how you would analyse this topic using the Inquiry Process. Use the example of Canada's role in NATO as a guide.
3. Imagine that a magazine writer wanted to publish a story about you. Make a list of all the different kinds of "evidence" (photographs, report cards, etc.) the journalist could examine. What could the reporter learn from each separate source?
4. If you were writing a history of your school, how would your interpretation differ from a similar history written by your principal?

5. To evaluate any piece of information it is important to know who wrote it and why it was written. Imagine that you have just read a pamphlet on where to go for your summer vacation. What might be the major argument of this tract if it were written by:
   a) the federal Department of Industry, Trade and Commerce, Tourism Branch?
   b) the Newfoundland Department of Development, Tourism Branch?
   c) an avid camper?
   d) Air Jamaica?
6. If you wanted to examine the early history of the Social Credit Party of Canada, you might read both the debates in the legislature and contemporary newspapers; you could also interview its present leaders. List three possible sources of information (other than books) for each of the following topics:
   a) a biography of former Prime Minister Lester B. Pearson
   b) the life of a typical western Canadian farmer in the 1880s
   c) the propaganda techniques used in the U.S.S.R. between the two world wars
   d) the extent of poverty in present-day Canada
7. Identify the value judgments and factual statements in the following:
   a) The conquest of New France in 1760 was a tragic occurrence for the French Canadians.
   b) The savage Indians led by Tecumseh fought bravely at the side of the British.
   c) Warning: Smoking reduces life expectancy.
8. Bring three newspaper headlines to class and be prepared to discuss their particular biases.
9. As polls and other statistics become increasingly widespread, it is important to be able to evaluate them critically. Too often, statistics sensationalize, confuse, mislead, over-simplify, or misrepresent information. Survey polls, for example, may be inaccurate because the questions were confusing, or because the interviewed people were not representative of the entire population. When examining statistics, consider these questions:
   - Did the people who performed the research have anything to gain from the results?
   - Who was interviewed?
   - Are the conclusions supported by the figures?
   - Were any questions overlooked?

   a) Read and answer the following questionnaire on Tolerance (Table 1-1). How do your answers compare with those for your province? Explain.
   b) What is being measured in question 1? How might the respondents misinterpret this question? Explain why B.C. differs so much from Alberta.
   c) A good questionnaire will include a few similar questions to check on the respondents' consistency. Did the people reply to question 2 as their responses to question 1 would lead you to expect they would?
   d) What is being measured in question 3 (other than attitudes towards minorities)? What does a comparison of the answers to both questions reveal?

The photograph on page 7 shows Stalingrad, U.S.S.R., at the end of World War II.

Table 1-1
TOLERANCE OF MINORITIES IN CANADA

A new, nationwide poll commissioned by Angus Reid and Southam News asked 1,500 Canadians about minority issues.

The poll, done by telephone, represents a cross-section of adults in all regions of the country.

The size of the Alberta sample was doubled on behalf of the Calgary Herald and the Edmonton Journal.

1. "Some people believe that treating minority groups with generosity is a special part of the Canadian character. Do you personally agree or disagree with this?"

	Total	B.C.	Alberta	Sask./Man.	Ontario	Quebec	Atlantic
Agree	60%	54%	59%	60%	58%	63%	69%
Disagree	32%	38%	37%	34%	32%	32%	19%
Unsure	8%	7%	4%	5%	10%	5%	12%

2. "Buttons are being distributed in the prairie provinces which suggest that Canadian society is being threatened by immigrants. Do you agree or disagree with this claim?"

	Total	B.C.	Alberta	Sask./Man.	Ontario	Quebec	Atlantic
Agree	33%	28%	35%	38%	33%	35%	28%
Disagree	59%	68%	55%	55%	59%	59%	59%
Unsure	8%	5%	9%	7%	8%	6%	12%

3. a) "Overall, what do you think should be a bigger priority for Canada: to encourage Canadians as a whole to try to accept minority groups and their customs and language, or to encourage minority groups to try to change to be more like most Canadians?"

	Total	B.C.	Alberta	Sask./Man.	Ontario	Quebec	Atlantic
Accept minorities	34%	31%	31%	27%	34%	33%	49%
Minorities should change	59%	59%	58%	63%	59%	63%	44%
Unsure	7%	9%	11%	10%	7%	4%	7%

b) "And how do you think the public feels about this? Do you think most Canadians would consider it more important for Canadians as a whole to be more accepting of different minority groups, or for minorities to try to change to be more like most Canadians?"

	Total	B.C.	Alberta	Sask./Man.	Ontario	Quebec	Atlantic
Accept minorities	21%	18%	20%	13%	25%	15%	35%
Minorities should change	67%	71%	70%	82%	64%	72%	48%
Unsure	12%	10%	10%	5%	11%	13%	17%

▸ Source: Angus Reid and Southam News, 1990.

▸ Note: As polls and other statistics become increasingly widespread, it is important to be able to evaluate them critically. Refer to question 9 on page 14.

CHAPTER 2 OVERVIEW

INTRODUCING GOVERNMENT

This chapter examines why we need government, identifies the types of governments, and provides a method for determining which is the "best" system of government. The ideas of three famous philosophers, Thomas Hobbes, John Locke, and Jean Jacques Rousseau, are explored for their views of why humans established governments, the essential nature of moral rights, human nature, and the rights to rebel against authority. The ideas of free will, biological drives, and basic human needs are further explored by examining the conclusions of psychologist Abraham Maslow. Finally, the chapter defines the terms left, right, radical, reactionary, moderate, liberal, and conservative and outlines various methods of classifying political ideologies.

▶ OBJECTIVES

After reading this chapter, you should be able to:

- ▶ understand the major theories concerning why humanity decided to establish government
- ▶ explain Maslow's theory of basic human needs, and place yourself on his pyramid
- ▶ use the various types of political spectrums and terminologies to analyse ideologies and beliefs
- ▶ identify the different viewpoints of what constitutes "good" government
- ▶ evaluate your own political values and justify them in oral and written form

▶ KEY TERMS

absolute power
sovereign
authority
individual's rights
social contract
natural state
radical
moderate
liberal
reactionary
conservative

CHAPTER

2 INTRODUCING GOVERNMENT

Why do governments exist? On the surface, this appears to be an easy question to answer. You might be familiar with the "island analogy" in which some travellers are shipwrecked on a desert island and are faced with the problem of survival. It quickly becomes apparent to them that some form of government is required to solve such problems as theft, defence, and the distribution of chores. However, some of the world's eminent philosophers have disagreed over the purpose and need for government. The following accounts provide brief summaries of the ideas of three such influential men.

▶ THOMAS HOBBES (1588–1679)

In the early days of civilization, there were no laws and no government.[1] Because it is the nature of man to be selfish and to care nothing about others except for how they can aid him, this was a period of complete anarchy, chaos, violence, and destruction.[2] It was a war of all against all, as everyone sought to improve his own material condition of life. The security of an individual depended upon his own strength and intelligence. In this natural state of war, there was no time for beauty, knowledge, fine buildings, art, industry, or culture. There was continual fear and danger of violent death; the life of man was solitary, poor, nasty, brutish, and short.

Men are born with both passions and reason. Their passions bring about this state of war, and their desire for a better life persuades them to seek peace—if only for their own selfish interests. Reason shows man that the only solution is the establishment

▸ [1]This summary is an abridged and modernized version of the major ideas Hobbes proposed in *Leviathan*, published in 1651.

▸ [2]At this time in Western history it was generally believed that women were incapable of participating in government. The writings of Hobbes, Locke, and Rousseau reflect these beliefs as is further evidenced by the use of the masculine pronoun.

of a society with a stable government. But since agreements without the sword are but words, it is necessary that the government be backed by force. The bonds of words are too weak to control man's ambition and greed without the fear of some coercive power. Individual security thus depends upon the formation of an all-powerful government that can curb man's selfish and aggressive nature.

The establishment of a government commences when every man agrees to relinquish his right to govern himself and gives all power to a man (or to a group of men) who will legislate peace and common defence. The people must promise complete obedience in return for order and security. The only choice is between **absolute power** or complete anarchy. Freedom is only possible if the people surrender their liberty to an all-powerful **sovereign**.

The sovereign's power is absolute, whether the sovereign is an individual or a group of men. Self-interest will persist in this new society, but destructiveness, violence, and war will be prevented by fear of the sovereign's power. Society is established and maintained out of fear.

Resistance to the sovereign is almost never justified; obedience must last as long as, and no longer than, the ruler is able to protect the people. The sovereign can only maintain peace if he has complete and unlimited **authority**. If the sovereign loses his power, he ceases to be sovereign and the people are thrown back upon their own devices for self-protection, until they agree to give their obedience (allegiance) to a new sovereign who can protect them.

Thomas Hobbes (1588–1679)
The Bettmann Archive

FOCUS

1. What assumptions does Hobbes make about human beings?
2. How would Hobbes define freedom?
3. How would Hobbes justify the sovereign using force against his subjects?
4. Hobbes wrote *Leviathan* to justify and support the English monarchy (Stuarts), which he believed was the most stable and orderly type of government. At this time, the Stuart monarchy based its rule on the theory of divine right—meaning that the king was chosen by, and responsible only to, God.
   a) Explain why the supporters of the Stuart monarchy believed that Hobbes's writings, which were designed to support the monarchy, were more dangerous than the king's enemies.
   b) Explain how in later centuries thinkers were able to adapt Hobbes's ideas to support a more democratic, albeit monarchical, form of government, which Hobbes opposed.

▶ JOHN LOCKE (1632–1704)

Originally, all men were in the state of nature. They remained so until they voluntarily agreed to become members of a society. Everyone is obliged by the natural moral law (which can be discovered by reason) not to harm another person or take his possessions. This freedom from harm is one of man's natural rights, given to him by God. Fortunately, men are fundamentally reasonable and are inclined to respect these natural rights. Although in theory everyone should obey these laws, it does not follow that everyone will obey them in practice. Some will try to take advantage of others, and sometimes two people, both believing they are right, will come into conflict. In such situations, strength, rather than justice, will prevail. Judges, written laws, and fixed penalties are thus needed to ensure that man's natural rights are preserved.

Society is not unnatural to man. The family, for instance, is natural to man; society is also natural because it fulfills human needs. It is in man's interest to form an organized society in order to protect his property and his other natural rights.

Political society and government must rest on the consent of the people. Because man is by nature free and independent, no one can rule him without his own consent. The purpose of government is to protect and foster the **individual's rights** and liberties. This means that it should interfere as little as possible in man's activities. People are most free when they are left alone. In voluntarily relinquishing the power to protect their own property and maintain their rights, people curtail their liberty. But men relinquish these powers in order to enjoy their liberties more securely, and nobody is obliged to obey unless he has freely agreed to do so.

All laws must rest on the will of the majority, and they must be designed for no other end than for the good of the people. Society can only be dissolved by the agreement of its members. When government does not live up to its trust, rebellion is justified—and the people shall judge when such rebellion is warranted. Government is obligated to rule by the natural and moral laws. Any government that destroys life, liberty, and prosperity has thus forfeited its right to rule.[3]

▸ [3]This is an abridged and modernized version of John Locke's ideas on government as presented in his *Two Treatises of Civil Government*, published in 1690.

FOCUS

1. What assumptions does Locke make about human beings?
2. How does Locke justify the establishment of government?
3. Locke has been criticized for his egoistic view of human behaviour. How could Locke's writings be used to justify the contemporary "me generation"?
4. Hobbes wrote to defend the English monarchy. John Locke's purpose was to justify the English revolution of 1688, which placed William of Orange and Mary Stuart on the throne and strengthened the role of Parliament. Explain how Locke's writings might be used to justify the overthrow of a monarchy.

▶ JEAN JACQUES ROUSSEAU (1712–1778)

Before the existence of society, man roamed the forests and lived like the animals. He drank from the nearby brook and made his bed at the foot of the nearest tree. This man of nature was without speech, culture, and mature thought, yet life was peaceful. There were no wars or suffering because humans generally lived apart from each other and were reluctant to inflict pain upon others. Natural man was neither moral nor vicious; he was not unhappy, but neither was he happy. Selfishness, culture, war, affection, vice, and love can only exist in sociable beings who live together in groups.

Natural man differed from the animals in his ability to improve himself. At some point, men united in a society in order to improve themselves — only within society do men become human, developing their mental and moral abilities, their freedom, and their individuality. Justice is substituted for instinct. Instead of stupid and unimaginative animals, men become intelligent, moral beings.

The problem is to establish a society that will protect everyone, and in which every man will remain as free as he was before. The solution is for all men to conclude a **social contract** and agree to place themselves under the direction of the general will. The general will is always right because it functions in the best interests of the entire group — it stands for the universal good. It follows, therefore, that any government whose object is the good of its people must conform to this general will. A government deserves to be obeyed only if its actions follow the general will.

The general will is simply the common good; it is not necessarily the majority opinion. The will of just one person, for instance, might be the general will if its object was the common good. Those who do not agree with the general will must be forced to obey — they must be forced to be free. The general will is, in reality, the will of everyone (although some might not realize it at the time), and to follow one's own will is to act freely. Therefore, to be forced to conform to one's own will is to be forced to be free. Man serves his own good by serving the common good.[4]

▸ [4]This is an abridged version of Rousseau's ideas. His ideas are difficult to summarize because his two major works, *Discourse on the Origin of Inequality* (1754) and the *Social Contract* (1762), contain many conflicting, or at least paradoxical, statements.

FOCUS

1. What assumptions does Rousseau make about human nature?
2. How does Rousseau justify the establishment of government?
3. How would Rousseau define freedom?
4. What type(s) of political systems could Rousseau's ideas be used to support and justify? Explain.
5. Compare and contrast the ideas of Hobbes, Locke, and Rousseau under the following headings:
   a) human nature
   b) the purpose of government
   c) the role of reason
   d) natural or moral rights
   e) the use of force
6. Write your own analysis of the origins of government. Include in your essay brief

discussions of human nature, whether natural rights exist (and if so, what they are), and the purpose and powers of government.

7. One fundamental question of political theory is, upon what grounds can government be justified? There are at least five different answers to this question.
    - The anarchist's answer is that all governments should be abolished because they all restrict individual freedom. Moral human beings do not need laws. Human goodness will create order.
    - In contrast with anarchism, some people believe that the possession of power is all the justification that government needs. Leaders can compel others to do their bidding by their strength and intelligence alone.
    - Some people justify government on the grounds that it is ordained or sanctioned by God.
    - Government, according to another group of thinkers, is justified because it was established by an agreement among the people to surrender their rights to the government in return for security and order. This is the idea of the social contract.
    - Government can be justified if it works for the general good. Political power is defended on moral grounds and must be obeyed if it lives up to these criteria.

    Rank these five alternatives from the most to the least convincing. Be prepared to justify your ranking.

▶ HUMAN NEEDS

Hobbes, Locke, and Rousseau each reasoned that humanity had once lived in a **natural state** without government. They also believed that people were capable of creating a government that served their interests better than the natural state did. Of course, interests or needs vary from individual to individual. One of the basic philosophical questions is whether humans act according to their own free will, or whether their behaviour is determined by biological drives and instincts. To what extent does reason influence actions? Some human actions are controlled by instinct — an inborn trait rather than a learned response. An infant's behaviour is largely determined by basic biological needs — children cry when they are hungry, cold, or in pain. As the child grows, new needs appear that have been acquired from interacting with other people and the environment. These include such needs as a search for security, as well as acceptance and approval from friends.

Psychologist Abraham Maslow classified human needs into seven groups and arranged them from basic biological needs at birth to complex psychological needs that emerge only after the basic needs have been satisfied. At each developmental level, needs must be at least partly fulfilled before the requirements at the next level become important. Physiological needs are at the base of this hierarchy. Humans need food, shelter, water, and sleep for survival. Unless these needs are satisfied, we do not have the time or the motivation to proceed to the next stage. Once these physiological needs are satisfied, the next concern is safety. This is perhaps more important for children than for adults, who can usually rely upon help from such agencies as the fire department and the police. Safety needs dominate during times of crisis, war, and natural disaster.

The third step for human beings is the need for belonging and love. Maslow believed that humans are social beings. We need to belong, to be accepted, to have friends, and to love and be loved. This need

Figure 2–1
MASLOW'S HIERARCHY OF NEEDS

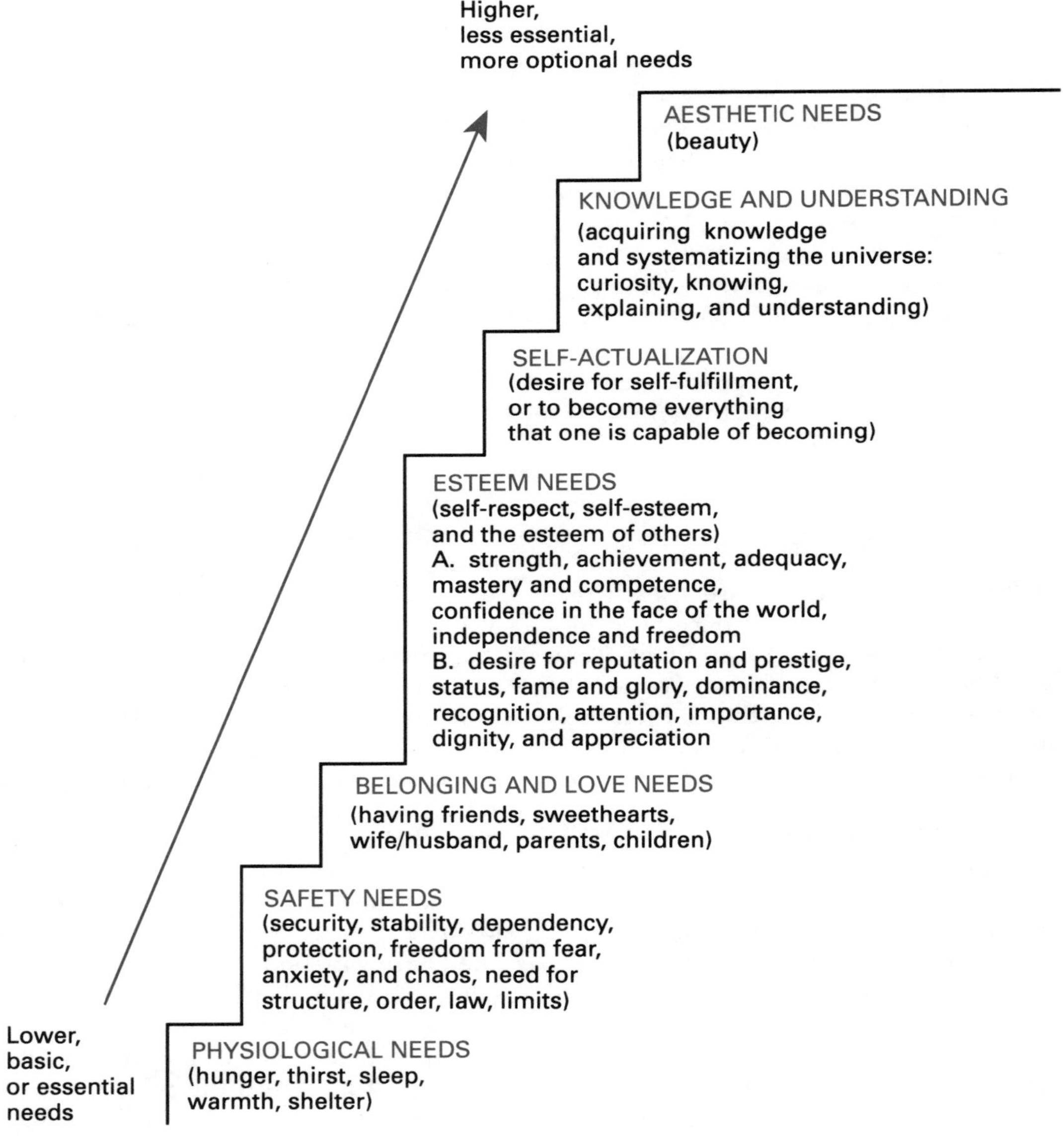

▸ Source: Diagram of ''Maslow's Hierarchy of Needs'' from *Understanding Interpersonal Communication*, 4/e, by Richard L. Weaver II.

Abraham Maslow, psychologist
The Bettmann Archive

can be fulfilled through marriage, by having children, and via membership in clubs and work-related associations.

Maslow divided esteem needs into the drive for achievement and success and the need to have the respect of others. People seek awards, compliments, and promotions for their abilities and actions. Humans clamour for recognition and to be appreciated.

Only a few people can reach the self-actualization category. Self-actualized individuals develop themselves to their highest potential. They are open, creative, and spontaneous; possess a sense of humour; and are capable of deep reflection.

Higher-level needs include people's need for knowledge and understanding. People need to learn, experiment, inquire, and philosophize.

Finally, humans have aesthetic needs. They need to surround themselves with beautiful objects.

Although Maslow's theories, which he believed were relevant to individuals in all cultures, are not accepted by everyone, they are widely used as a way of explaining people's actions, be it voting behaviour, employee job satisfaction, or aggressive conduct.

▶ THE POLITICAL SPECTRUM

Another method of classifying governments depends upon the distinction between "left" and "right." These words were first used as political labels shortly after the French Revolution in 1789. In the French Assembly, those members who

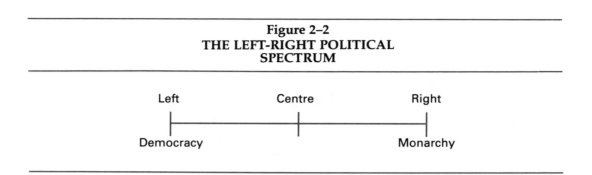

Figure 2–2
THE LEFT-RIGHT POLITICAL SPECTRUM

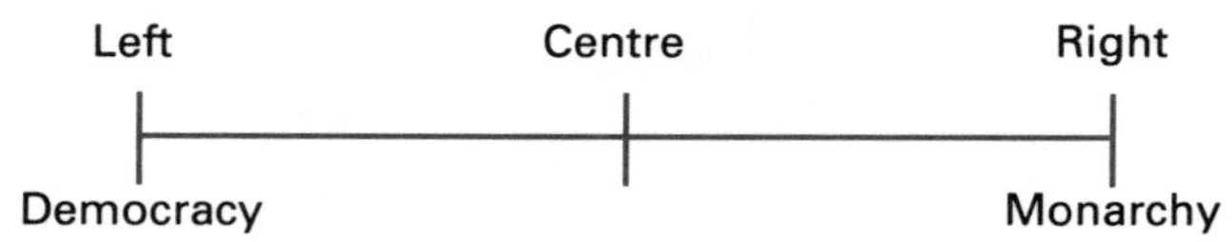

favoured a strong monarchy sat on the right-hand side of the chamber, and members who wanted democratic government sat on the left. The extreme right believed that God conferred all political power to the monarch through heredity, whereas the extreme left argued that all power came from the people. Those people in the centre sought a compromise. Figure 2-2 indicates such a classification.

▶ Economic-Political Spectrum

In the nineteenth century, as socialism and economic democracy became more prominent, this left-right classification shifted. Figure 2-3 illustrates this new spectrum, based upon economic beliefs. The Marxist Communist motto was "from each according to his ability, to each according to his needs." Social democrats sought equality of opportunity, especially for the lower classes. Liberals also desired equality of opportunity but emphasized the middle classes. Conservatives staunchly defended private property and supported private charity. Fascists believed that abilities were inherited, and equality was thus impossible—as well as undesirable.

Political ideologies may also be classified according to how much control the government has over the economy and society in general. As Figure 2-4 shows, communists and fascists favour total government control, whereas anarchists believe that society can best exist without government. Liberals desire active government regulation in order to promote greater economic and social equality. Socialists believe in government control of vital industries and agencies, and conservatives want to limit government controls to only essential activities.

Figure 2–3
AN ECONOMIC SPECTRUM

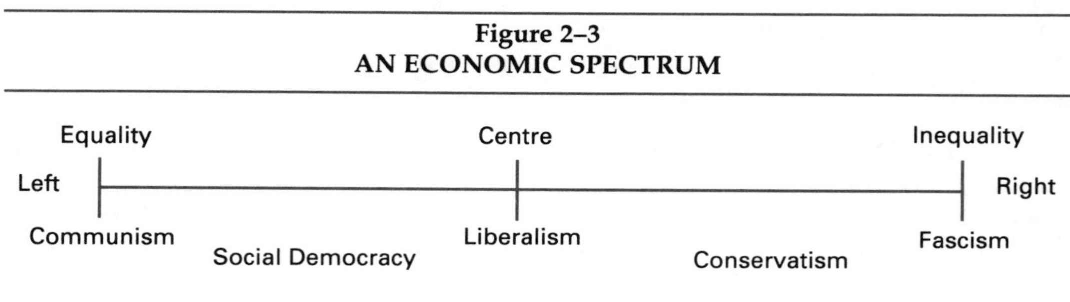

Figure 2–4
GOVERNMENT REGULATION

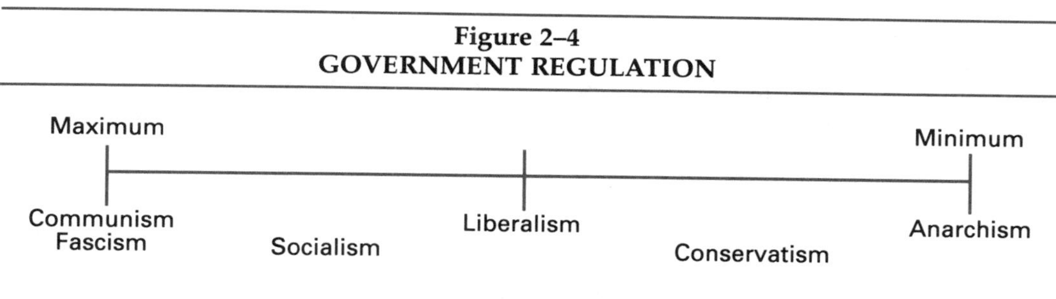

The conventional left-right spectrum does not apply to all issues. Left and right are only convenient labels. They should not be substitutes for a detailed understanding of each group's point of view. In many cases, the extremes of the spectrum end up working together — although for different reasons and objectives.

▶ Change and the Political Spectrum

"She's a radical feminist."

"Isn't there a more moderate solution?"

"That's too liberal for me."

"If he was any more reactionary, he'd be Attila the Hun."

"That's a rather conservative comment."

These terms—**radical**, **moderate**, **liberal**, **reactionary**, and **conservative**—are among the most commonly used words in politics. Unfortunately, they are also the most misunderstood and misused terms in political science. In everyday language, these terms usually have a value attached to them, but in political analysis they are value-free. Figure 2-5 indicates their location on the left-right spectrum.

This classification examines people's attitudes towards change in the political system. Almost every group desires change. Those people who wish to adopt new political institutions or values can be placed on the left of the status quo (the existing state of affairs), and individuals who want to return to past ways are to the right of the status quo. The extent of the desired change is also important in this spectrum. The further people find themselves from the status quo, the more dissatisfied they are with the existing situation and the more drastic their proposed changes. Such people are more likely to demand immediate, revolutionary "improvements."

Figure 2–5
THE POLITICAL SPECTRUM

Ultra Left | Radical | Liberal | Moderate | Conservative | Reactionary | Ultra Right

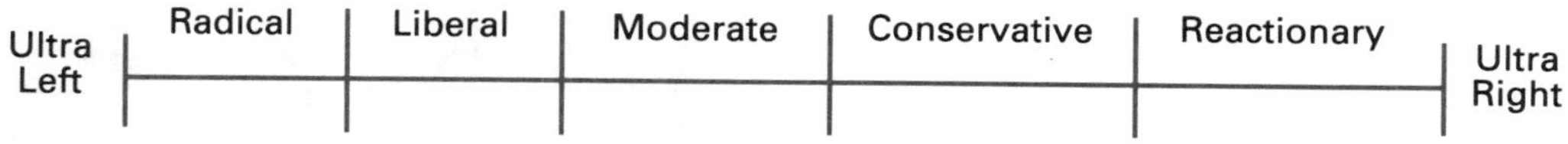

Radicals are extremely unhappy with the status quo and favour instant, fundamental change in society. Radicals on the extreme left end of the political spectrum believe that society is so corrupt that it can only be cured through violence. Compromise is impossible! Radicals a little further to the right are also frustrated with the system, but prefer relatively peaceful methods where possible. Political scientist Leon Baradat suggests that such famous political activists as Mahatma Gandhi and Martin Luther King, Jr. can be found at the far right of the radical group. They proposed immediate and profound changes in India and the United States, but opposed violence.

Liberals are less dissatisfied with the existing political system, and generally abide by the law, seeking change only by legal methods. They do, however, advocate rapid and far-reaching changes if the status quo is of the extremist type. The word "liberal" comes from the Latin word *liber*, meaning "free." Liberals are optimistic about people's ability to solve their own problems. They believe in the power of reason. Since nothing is sacred, theoretically, everything can be changed for the better. As a result, the ideals and objectives of liberalism have changed over the last three centuries. In the seventeenth and eighteenth centuries, such original liberals as John Locke, Adam Smith, and Thomas Jefferson argued for personal freedom and fewer government restrictions, and in favour of private property. Today, such ideas are associated with conservatism. Liberals viewed people as being essentially good and were optimistic about humanity's ability to improve the world. Contemporary liberals still maintain these ideals, but prefer to use the government to improve society, even if this means restrictions on how much private property one person can control.

Moderates are generally satisfied with the status quo. Some changes, they believe, are needed, but they are only minor adjustments that should be gradually adopted. Conservatives also support the status quo, although for different reasons. Conservatives are cautious of change. They speak of upholding tradition. As a result, changes tend to be both gradual and minimal. Conservatives tend to be less optimistic than liberals of people's abilities to solve their own problems. They thus tend to prefer authoritarian rule to democracy. In the eighteenth century, Edmund Burke provided a philosophical base for conservatism. In a well-governed society, Burke stated, everyone knew his or her place. The wealthy, intelligent, and the "well-born" should govern in the best interests of everyone, while the people of lower rank should recognize their betters and submit to their rules.

Modern conservatives believe that government should intervene as little as possible in human affairs. Compulsory seat-belt legislation is the type of regulation conservatives oppose as being an invasion of

Sir Edmund Burke (1729–1797)
National Archives of Canada, Neg. No. C 100389

individual freedom. Conservatives believe strongly in the rights of private property, prefer political order, and tend to be elitist and authoritarian.

Only reactionaries desire to return to an earlier autocratic time. They are just as frustrated by the status quo as are the radicals, but instead of proposing a brand new world, they seek to replace the present system with former institutions and values. As with radicals, reactionaries range from those who believe in the necessity of violence to the more peaceable proponents of traditional government.

Few people retain the same viewpoint on the political spectrum on every issue. Most people are happy with at least some aspects of society and do not want to change them (conservative), but can think of several areas that need adjustment (liberal). In general, however, it is possible to locate individuals in one of these five positions on the spectrum. The "left" believes in rational thought and human equality, whereas the "right" does not believe that the average person bases decisions on rational reasons and admires elitist societies. On the far left, Karl Marx's communist theories were termed "scientific socialism." Marx envisioned a future society in which ordinary people held all political power and shared equally in material goods. On the far right, fascist leader Benito Mussolini appealed to people's emotions and declared, "Feel, don't think!" The masses were expected to obey their leader without question.

▶ POLITICAL VALUES AND THE AMERICAN REVOLUTION

In 1775, the thirteen British colonies to the south of present-day Canada went to war with Great Britain to win their political independence. Those who sought freedom did so for a variety of motives, and not all Americans agreed with the war. Many of those people who opposed independence escaped to Canada when the proponents of warfare gained control of the colonies' governments. The victorious Americans termed them "Tories," whereas the British called them "Loyalists." Although the following discussion is fiction, it attempts to accurately represent the ideas and conditions that existed in the thirteen colonies (parts of the present-day United States) in 1773. As you read this fictional narrative, think about what type of government each person wished to have.

One careful look at George Watkins told you a lot about the man. He was tall, erect, and broadshouldered. He wore carefully tailored trousers and a waistcoat. His shoes were slightly worn but carefully polished. Here was a man of taste and character who had known wealth.

George took a table in the room reserved for the more prosperous, well-educated people. He ordered a mug of ale from the barmaid.

"And the English," he thought to himself, "do they respect private property?" He was bitter about the English. Ten years before, early in 1763, George had put almost all his money into land west of the Allegheny Mountains. He had expected to sell the land later at a good profit. Then the English announced the Proclamation of 1763, forbidding any Englishman to settle west of the Alleghenies. The land he bought was, for all practical purposes, taken away from him. He could not sell it. It didn't seem that the English government respected the right to property any more than the radicals.

As Watkins sat in deep thought, Dr. Soame Johnson came to his table. Watkins and Johnson had been friends for many years, but of late they argued more and more over the English treatment of the colonies.

"I've been thinking, Soame," said Watkins, "our people in England just don't seem to

understand our problems. I'm not sure they want to understand them. We seem to have lost our voices. I wonder if this Sam Adams might not have something when he speaks up about independence.''

Dr. Johnson looked startled. ''There are few of us who don't think King George needs a lesson in how to run his colonies. But I certainly cannot go along with fire-breathers like Hancock and Adams. We should do what we must, calmly and legally.''

''But England doesn't even seem to want to meet us halfway,'' said Watkins. ''And fellows like Adams and Hancock are in this thing so deep now, they've either got to have a fight or lose their shirts. They look to be in fighting trim, too.''

Dr. Johnson's voice rose: ''We both know Hancock is a convicted smuggler who'll cut his country's throat just to save himself from jail! If this fuss ends, John will have to pay 100,000 pounds to England for the smuggling he's done. Do we want a war just so a man can get away with breaking the law?''

''But Hancock was only forced to smuggle because England was worrying more about herself than about us,'' said Watkins. ''And Hancock is too good a businessman and shipper to foot the bill for England's trouble.''

Johnson's face flushed. ''George, are you defending a common criminal? Hancock was found guilty and fined. You don't deny that?''

''No.''

''And if you're willing to defend a criminal, why not defend Sam Adams, too? You and I both know Sam Adams wants to fight England and turn this country into a slaughterhouse because he hates kings and noblemen. No matter what's offered him now, he'll never be satisfied. Look at the kind of man he is. He was at the bottom of his class at Harvard. His father was poor. Because of that he hates everyone who isn't poor—and that includes you, George. He can't make money or keep it so he argues that everyone who can must be dishonest. He was made tax collector of Boston and lost his job because he was behind in his accounts. Now he hates the government that ousted him. Sam Adams is powerful in the colonies because he tells the dissatisfied, the lazy, the idle that they're the only honest people. I tell you we can't have war, no matter what, because if men like Adams start running the show there won't be a decent businessman or doctor or lawyer or any man of property left at all in America. And the country will be governed by riffraff out of the gutters.''

Dr. Johnson puffed with the effort of his speech.

Watkins replied very slowly, ''You know, Soame, I can't help but agree with much of what you say. But are you sure you're painting the whole picture? The English have not governed us very well. And I am not sure that they can govern well. Just yesterday I received a letter from Joshua Tuttle, who is in England right now. He is convinced that the English government is corrupt. Enormous salaries, pensions, bribes, quarrels, padded accounts, illegal contracts, and illegal jobs—all using up the tax money. Maybe England is more of a stone around our necks than a protector of our rights.''

Johnson rose to his feet, leaned forward, and pounded on the table.

''Open your eyes! Do you know what Sam Adams and his gutter crowd are doing? They have mobbed and beaten ministers, lawyers, and doctors who have done nothing more than express their opinions. Yes, the finest men we've got have been thrown out of every town in the colony. Those rebels say they are fighting for freedom. Yet they do not permit anyone the freedom to disagree with them.

''And what are you going to do, Watkins? Join those guttersnipes and rabblerousers? I say, let's stand up for our rights and be counted—as good Englishmen—to protect our rights to property and liberty.''

Johnson got up and stamped out of the room. A wry smile came over Watkins' face. He thought of Johnson's last statement—''protect . . . property and liberty.'' England's Proclamation had taken almost all his property.

His musing was broken by loud voices com-

ing from the barroom, where the common people drank and talked. He caught several words, "smuggling . . . Stamp Act . . . stupid Englishmen." Watkins arose and walked over to the doorway. A tall, dark sailor was speaking in loud tones. And Dr. Johnson, interrupted in his flight, stood bristling at the sailor's words.

"So what are these laws supposed to do, these Trade and Navigation Acts? They're supposed to strangle our trade and make us servants of our royal master, His Majesty George the Third. Has George ever been to America? Has he ever worked aboard a trading ship? He calls it smuggling when honest merchants and self-respecting sailors try to make a living. I say it's not American smuggling that's the cause of this trouble, it's English tyranny."

Dr. Johnson snorted back at him. "I don't care what's at the heart of this trouble—call it tyranny if you will—but smuggling is lawbreaking, and that's not good no matter who does it. You seamen and your masters have taken the law into your own hands too long. Right now the English laws are our laws, and most of us are Englishmen. If you'll break the laws of your government when that government is England, who's to say you'll obey them if we set up a government of our own? Or do you want no government, so you won't have to pay any taxes or obey any laws at all?"

The tall sailor banged his glass on the bar, straightened up to full height, and glared down at Johnson: "The difference is, my fine fat fellow, that American shippers are willing to pay American taxes to pay for things that help America. But American shippers ain't goin' to stuff the bellies of a bunch of English lords."

Johnson's face reddened. He stormed for the door.

The sailor shouted after him, "Why don't you go back to your king, then, and kiss his boots and pay him tribute? Because that's the law. I say law is what men say is fair and just and right for all the people, not what some king dreams up three thousand miles away."

There was a shout of approval from the little crowd at the bar. But several men who had kept silent throughout the argument quickly left the inn.

▲ ▲ ▲ ▲

Meeting at Lincoln. *George Watkins tasted the crisp fall evening air as he rode to Lincoln. He felt a tingle of excitement. Tonight he would finally see and hear Sam Adams.*

When he dismounted from his horse, he could see that there was already a crowd in front of the meetinghouse, talking, laughing, grumbling, arguing. Rawboned farmers had come from all corners of Lincoln, Concord, Lexington, and adjoining towns to hear the great Sam Adams.

The babble suddenly quieted. Watkins looked back down the dirt road as he hitched his horse. He knew it must be Sam Adams coming. So here was the man the poor loved and cheered, and Watkins both feared and admired.

Sam Adams climbed down from his horse, tied it, and threaded his way through the groups of men in front of the meetinghouse. He mounted the steps, turned, and raised his hands. Dead silence fell over the crowd.

"Friends and fellow countrymen," he began. "We have been subjected to greater tyranny and injustice than any people has ever endured. The crops which we have raised with much sweat and toil are taxed without our consent. Our ships can no longer trade. The rights and privileges which we have always had are denied us. Our people are murdered by the King's soldiers . . ."

Adams went on, talked of his favorite organization, the Sons of Liberty, and how it was linked to similar groups by Committees of Correspondence.

As he continued speaking, denouncing the king and demanding "the rights of free men," wave after wave of excitement swept over the crowd. It reached a fever pitch, then almost a frenzy. George Watkins felt the excitement despite himself. Yet, as the farmers shouted and cheered and drew closer to the speaker,

Watkins and others like him drew farther toward the outskirts of the crowd.

Suddenly a voice rose against Adams. The crowd stirred angrily. But Adams carefully stopped. "No, my fellow countrymen," he said softly, "let this gentleman speak."

The dissident turned out to be James Cartwright, a widely known Lincoln minister. He mounted the meetinghouse steps and shouted, "My fellow Englishmen, my fellow townsmen, this man Adams who stands before you and seizes your reason . . . is a godless traitor. Worthy people of high character have warned me against him. He is preaching treason. Friends, have you forgotten that without England our fathers could never have settled this land? You shout against British soldiers but your memories are short. Ten years ago you cheered these same soldiers when they saved your wives and children from . . . Indians. You speak against the laws of England. But if it were not for England we would all be slaves of an irresponsible French King. May God protect our beloved England that has struggled so long to protect the lives and property of all her countrymen."

The crowd had been confused. Then a murmur of protest grew into a roar. Deacon Cartwright's words were drowned in a sea of angry voices.

Sam Adams rose again to the highest step of the meetinghouse. His clear, slow voice cut through the tumult. "Here is a defender of tyranny, an enemy of the Sons of Liberty right in our midst. Need I speak more of the dangers that stalk our homes and firesides!"

The crowd jostled Cartwright and spit on him as he went down the steps. Someone pushed him to the ground. He scrambled to his feet and dashed blindly into a tree on the outskirts of the crowd. The crowd laughed. A voice shouted, "Let's get him, boys. Let's show him what happens to kinglovers." The crowd began to move after him.

George Watkins suddenly found his voice in the confusion. "No." Watkins shouted as loud as he could. "Let him go. Let's hear Sam Adams out. He has something more important to say."

The crowd began to mill back toward the meetinghouse steps. Sam Adams went on.

What, Watkins wondered to himself, had possessed him to enter the brawl, to join this mad crowd? Had he really wanted to save the deacon? Or was he really interested in more of what Sam Adams had to say? If the time came to fight, if war came with England, would he be running with Deacon Cartwright, or fighting beside Sam Adams?[5]

Table 2-1
BELIEFS ABOUT "GOOD" GOVERNMENT

1. It would be wrong to change the system of government we have inherited. It has the benefits of long experience.
2. A leader is not finally responsible to the people, but only to God, from whom authority is received.
3. Fair decisions can be made only by impartial leaders who have no special interest whatsoever at stake. Only these people should be allowed to govern.
4. Leaders should not bow to the prejudiced interests of the people, but should be guided by a sense of law. Legal rights and the general welfare should be their only guidelines.
5. All people should have a say in determining their own fate. Thus the government should be run by representatives chosen by a majority of the people.
6. A country belongs to those people who own property in it, and they should govern.
7. Power should be separated and divided among several ruling groups. Centralized power often brings tragic mistakes.
8. The power to govern should be given to the most capable people, to those who have demonstrated intelligence and skill. Most people do not have enough skill to govern the country.
9. Life is naturally a struggle. Those strong enough to seize power earn the right to govern.
10. Time, money, and effort are saved when a small, unified group runs the government. It is inefficient and wasteful to split power among groups who will bicker and delay decisions.

▸ [5]Special reprint permission granted by Field Publications. Copyright © 1967 by Field Publications.

FOCUS

1. Match the following categorizations to the ten statements in Table 2-1.
   a) competence and know-how
   b) tradition or familiar customs
   c) religion, belief in a supreme being
   d) law, the written and spoken rules of the society
   e) separated power
   f) strength—"might makes right"
   g) property ownership
   h) impartiality
   i) majority rule
   j) efficiency
2. With which of the ten statements would each of the following people most agree?
   a) George Watkins
   b) Soame Johnson
   c) John Hancock
   d) Sam Adams
   e) James Cartwright
3. Place the men in question 2 on a left-right spectrum.
4. Prepare to participate in a mock debate among these men.
5. Select two of these men and explain why their political values differed.

▶ WHY STUDY GOVERNMENT?

Government is an integral part of every society. It makes laws, interprets them, and carries them out. Government affects almost every aspect of our lives — from taxes and transportation to schools and traffic lights. It can prevent us from achieving our most cherished goals, and it can require us to sacrifice our lives in time of war. The political system might therefore be viewed as the master control system of society. The economy is affected by government laws restricting unfair employment practices, regulating labour relations, and establishing tariffs. Family activities are limited by school regulations, medical requirements, and marriage laws. The rules of a society can range from a few simple traditions, passed down orally from one generation to another, to a complex, bureaucratic state.

The study of politics, which is usually called political science, was born when people began to speculate about the rules of society. Should these rules be obeyed? Why do different countries have dissimilar governments? Is there one set of rules that every society should adopt? This inquiry has been going on for thousands of years.

Each generation is faced with deciding whether to accept the rules made or accepted by the previous generation, or whether to modify or replace them with others. The ordinary citizen, faced with the decision of voting for a political party, may be trying to answer the question that Greek philosophers tried to answer over two thousand years ago: what is the best form of government? Of course, ordinary citizens are more likely to attempt merely to decide which party will help them the most. Even so, the voter is really asking a similar question: what is the best form of government for me?

▶ GOVERNMENT AND POWER

Monarchy, democracy, dictatorship, fascism, theocracy, constitutional monarchy, communism, aristocracy, oligarchy — the number of different types of governments seems endless. In the fourth century B.C., Greek philosopher Aristotle attempted to simplify the choice by classifying governments according to their distribution of political power. Governments where only one person ruled were termed monarchies. Aristocracies were political systems in which more than one, but not many, ruled. And in democracies the majority of the people administered the state. Although the distribution of power is only one method of categorizing governments, power is an essential ingredient in almost every type of organization. In particular, it is the way in which governments gain and use their power that distinguishes them. An absolute monarch does not usually have to listen to the wishes of his subjects. When King Louis XIV of France said "I am the State," what he really meant was "I am the Government and what I say goes." In a democracy, the people themselves, through their elected representatives, decide how the government should use its power.

The principle of one-person rule is rooted in a philosophy or ideology that supports and justifies the use of power. A street gang in Calgary or Vancouver, for example, may be controlled by one person to whom all swear obedience and loyalty. A successful assumption of power is thought to show that the leader is superior to other people. Organized crime is only one example of the success of this philosophy.

The leadership principle, however, is too limited to attract or hold many followers for a long period of time. Ideas are needed to recruit supporters and encourage loyalty. Hitler did this by adopting the belief that the German people were the master race. In North America, the Ku Klux Klan's ideology states that its members are ordained by God to protect Protestant White society from Catholics, Blacks, and Jews. Historically, most governments based their power upon religion. This was true of the Egyptian pharaohs, the Russian tsars, and the Chinese emperors. Communist states justify their actions by reference to the doctrine of class warfare against capitalists and to the belief that under communism all property will be administered for the benefit of the working class. In like manner, the belief in the "rule of the majority" is employed by democratic governments to justify their use of power.

Which is the best system of government? To answer this question we must examine the ideology or system of beliefs of the various available choices. The important questions to ask are

- Who controls power?
- How is power maintained and passed on from generation to generation?
- Upon what basis are decisions made?
- What are the government's goals and ideals?
- What role does the individual citizen play in the political system?

In the next two chapters we will examine the strengths and weaknesses of various democratic and non-democratic systems of government. At the conclusion of this section of the book you will be asked to evaluate these political systems and to design your own ideal political system.

APPLYING YOUR KNOWLEDGE

1. Draw up a complete record of everything you did yesterday. Identify those activities you did (or did not do) that were affected by government regulations.
2. Explain the importance of ideas or ideology to the maintenance of political power.

3. a) List two countries, past or present, for each of Aristotle's categories.
   b) What are some of the problems you encountered in trying to apply Aristotle's classification scheme to the real world?
   c) How else might governments be categorized?
4. Re-read the ideas of Hobbes, Locke, and Rousseau and decide which of Aristotle's categories each philosopher would have liked the best. Explain your choices.
5. Provide two examples of instinctive behaviour.
6. Where would you locate yourself on Maslow's hierarchy of needs?
7. Where would you locate yourself in Figures 2-2, 2-3, and 2-4? Provide an example of one historical individual for each category in Figure 2-5.
8. Explain how various left-right groups might combine on an issue such as abortion or euthanasia.
9. Select a contemporary social, economic, or political issue and explain the probable position of a radical, a reactionary, a liberal, a conservative, and a moderate.

FURTHER RESEARCH

1. Read William Golding's *Lord of the Flies*.
   a) Discuss the society created by the boys, the major problems they encounter, and the ultimate result.
   b) Whose ideas (Locke's, Hobbes's, or Rousseau's) does Golding adhere to most closely? Explain.
2. Role-play a debate among Hobbes, Locke, and Rousseau.
3. Working in groups, determine what each of these men would say about your school's form of government.
4. Prepare your own spectrum for political parties and locate the Canadian, American, and British parties on it. For this project, you will have to decide what beliefs or values to evaluate, and then research each party's position on them.
5. Research the ideas of one of the following people on motivation and report on their findings:
   a) B.F. Skinner
   b) Sigmund Freud
   c) Alfred Adler
6. Working in groups, devise your own questionnaire to examine the left-right spectrum of values in your school.

CHAPTER 3 OVERVIEW

THE WORLD'S POLITICAL SYSTEMS: THE IDEALS OF DEMOCRACY

This chapter examines democracy. It explains the growth of the idea of democracy until the present, evaluates the extent of democracy in the world today, and explores the changing definitions of democracy over time and from one country to another. The chapter also discusses the conditions necessary for democracy to operate effectively, the importance of natural or fundamental human rights, and the need for minority guarantees. It concludes with a discussion of the advantages and disadvantages of democracy.

▶ OBJECTIVES

After reading this chapter, you should be able to:

- ▶ understand the reasons for the growth of democracy in the last century
- ▶ devise your own definition of democracy
- ▶ describe the conditions necessary for democracy to flourish
- ▶ understand the importance of minority rights
- ▶ apply Gastil's methodology to any country in the world
- ▶ summarize the advantages and drawbacks of democracy
- ▶ develop your own ideal political constitution
- ▶ create, carry out, and analyse your own questionnaire
- ▶ conduct research on a variety of political topics

▶ KEY TERMS

democracy
formal democracy
polis
direct democracy
representative democracy
universal suffrage
natural rights
human rights
tyranny of the majority
bureaucracy

CHAPTER 3

THE WORLD'S POLITICAL SYSTEMS: THE IDEALS OF DEMOCRACY

Democracy! Over the centuries people have struggled to implement it, wars have been fought in its name, and many have died for it. Since the defeat of Nazi Germany and Fascist Italy in World War II, almost every country describes itself as democratic. "Probably for the first time in history," a United Nations survey stated in 1951, "democracy is claimed as the proper ideal description of all systems of political and social organization." Even military regimes frequently seek to justify their assumption of power by promising to restore democracy when the time is right.

It wasn't always this way. Except for a brief democratic experiment in Athens, Greece, before the birth of Christ, the idea remained unpopular until the nineteenth century. Men of wealth and culture usually rejected democracy because they thought it would destroy their power. Aristotle, for example, argued that since democracy was the rule of the many, and because in all societies the many are the poor, democracy was the rule of the poor. Another ancient Greek philosopher, Plato, added that since the poor were uneducated, they were incapable of making good laws and would discriminate against the intelligent and wealthy people who were in the minority. Other critics argued that the poor were incapable of understanding what was in their own best interests, and that government should be left to the educated and wealthy citizens who could govern in the real interest of the entire community.

These basic criticisms of democracy were accepted by nearly every educated person from the earliest historical times down to the second half of the nineteenth century. Then, with the flourishing of capitalism in the eighteenth and nineteenth centuries, democracy gradually became an acceptable system of government. Today, most countries claim to be democratic.

Even non-democratic governments call themselves democracies. Communist countries employ terms such as "people's democracies" and "democratic centralism." President Sukarno of Indonesia called his dictatorship a "democracy with leadership," Nasser's Egypt was a "democratic dictatorship," and Castro's Cuba is a "true democracy."

▶ A DEFINITION OF DEMOCRACY

The fact that such politically different countries as South Africa, Canada, Cuba, Germany, the United States, and the Soviet Union all claim to be democratic indicates that democracy has an ambiguous meaning. According to communist theory, democracy is rule by and for the working class. Under communist control the country's resources will be shared equally, and private property — the source of class exploitation—will be abolished. In communist terms, democracy means material equality, not necessarily political liberty. If the state must restrict individual freedom in order to achieve an equal distribution of the country's wealth, then it should do so. Communists use the term **formal democracy** for such democratic ideas as freedom of speech, press, and association and equality before the law. In their view, real democracy means economic equality. Western liberal democracies, on the other hand, place the highest value on civil liberties.

To clear up the confusion concerning the meaning of democracy, George Bernard Shaw once suggested that the world's leading scholars and thinkers be brought together to settle the issue once and for all. However, the root of the problem lies much deeper. Disagreements about the meaning of democracy reflect fundamental differences in values and ways of life. Democracy is also a very broad concept. Viewed as a political system, it is a method of conducting government and making laws. As a decision-making process, it is a way of reaching policy decisions in which all adult citizens are entitled to participate. As a social system, it exists to promote and protect individual freedom and equality. But democracy is much more than this—it is a vision of a way of life in which all people are free to develop their potential as human beings.

Supporters of democracy believe that people are by nature rational, moral, and just. Given a chance, they can live in peace, discuss issues rationally, make wise decisions, and improve the world.

The word "democracy" is a combination of the Greek words *demos* (the people) and *kratein* (to rule), meaning rule by the people. This book defines democracy as a political system that provides a free and open competition for power among various individuals and groups, as well as a significant degree of accountability to the people by those who hold the formal positions of power.

▶ DIRECT AND REPRESENTATIVE DEMOCRACY

The genesis of democracy took place many centuries ago in the **polis** of Athens, Greece. A polis consisted of a small town and its immediate surrounding countryside. It had to be large enough to be self-sufficient, but small enough that everyone would know each other by sight. Because of its size, every citizen had the opportunity to participate in government decisions.[1] In an average year, approximately fifteen to twenty percent of the populace served in some governmental capacity. These positions were usually filled by drawing lots. The most important government jobs were rotated every year or two. Once a week (or when it was necessary) the citizens gathered to decide upon matters of policy. All citizens had the opportunity to speak their minds and then a decision was reached by majority vote.

▸ [1]Only *sons* of citizens who had been born in the polis were allowed to participate in government. Women and slaves were excluded.

This method of government is called **direct democracy**, because the people themselves make the laws. Today, although several New England towns in the United States and some Swiss cantons practice it, no country has adopted direct democracy.

Although democracy is defined as government by the people, no country has ever allowed all its inhabitants to participate in decision-making. At different times, age, sex, literacy, wealth, colour, ethnicity, and religion have been used to prevent certain people from voting or holding public office. Today, some of these restrictions, such as not allowing children and the legally insane to vote, seem logical. However, at one time

Figure 3–1
PERCENTAGE OF ADULTS HAVING THE RIGHT TO VOTE IN GREAT BRITAIN

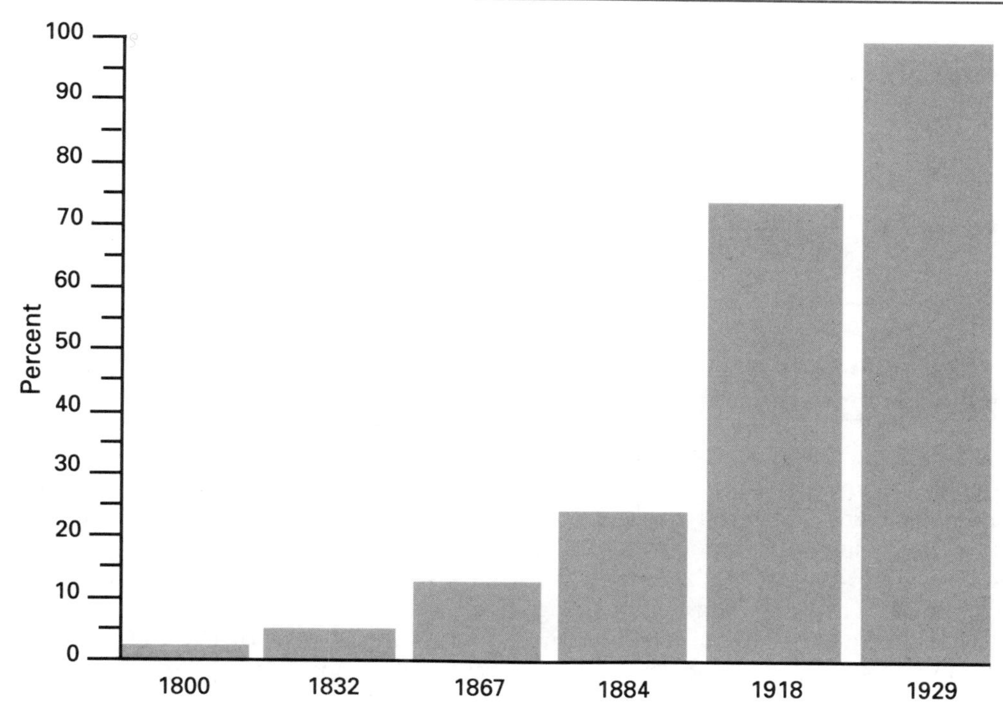

or another, society considered each of the preceding limitations as self-evident. In the nineteenth century, every country took it for granted that women should not be allowed to vote. In Great Britain, women did not have full suffrage until 1929, French women gained the vote only in 1945, and Swiss women had to wait until 1971. For a long time, the United States limited the political rights of Blacks. In Canada, Japanese-Canadians, native Indians, Roman Catholics, and the poor were denied the vote at various times. Yet these countries have long been recognized as democracies.

As times change, so too does the definition of democracy. Beliefs that were inconceivable in one period of history are taken for granted at a later time. Not so long ago, Canadians under twenty-one years of age were not allowed to vote. The age limit is now eighteen. What might it be thirty years in the future? Such changes are evident almost everywhere. In the nineteenth century, most people defined democracy solely in terms of political and legal equality. Today, governments place more importance on curbing economic and social inequalities.

Canada, like most other Western countries, is a **representative democracy**. This means that the citizens elect people to represent their interests. These elected representatives then meet and pass laws on behalf of the whole country. Figure 3-2 illustrates the differences between these two forms of democracy.

Figure 3–2

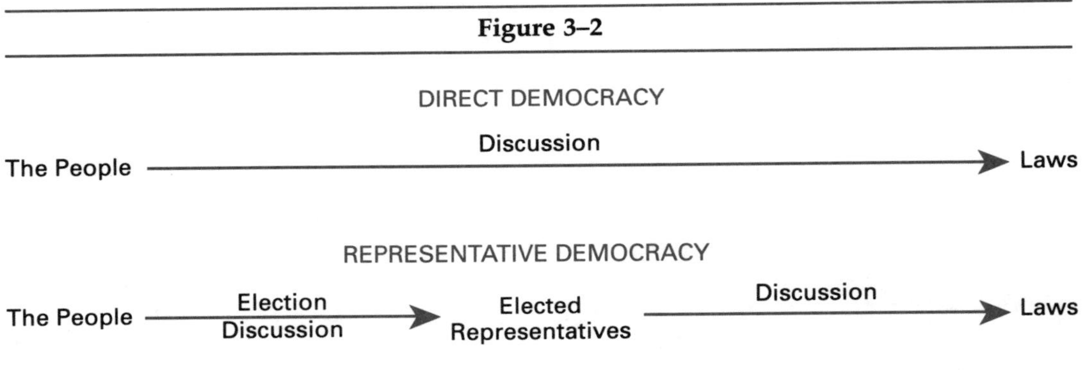

▶ THE PREREQUISITES OF DEMOCRACY

In the representative system of democracy, the people are one step removed from government decisions. Western representative democracies believe that a political system is democratic if the people have effective control over their representatives. During the last two centuries, liberal reformers in such countries as Great Britain, France, Germany, Sweden, Switzerland, Italy, Canada, and the United States have succeeded in gaining a reasonable degree of control over their governments. Just what constitutes a "reasonable degree of control," however, has been a matter of debate.

One such debate centres around the role of the elected representative. Should the representatives make decisions according to their own independent judgments or according to the wishes of their constituents? Supporters of the first viewpoint argue that most of the people are not interested in the issues, and if legislators make unpopular decisions they can be voted out of office at the next election. This ensures that the representatives are accountable to the public. Liberal cabinet minister C.G. Power defended this view in the Canadian House of Commons:

A member of Parliament, when he is elected by his constituency . . . is elected, not to be the mouthpiece or delegate of any group or class in his constituency, but to represent in this House the whole people of Canada. He comes here to give his best judgment upon the questions which are put before him — not to give a decision upon instructions he may have received from people thousands of miles away who know nothing of the question under discussion. . . . I do not believe in that kind of democracy.

The second viewpoint asserts that the representatives are the people's agents. The legislators, according to this argument, are obligated to discover their constituents' views and to act upon them. This position was expressed in the House of Commons by Opposition member W.M. Good:

I fully recognize that the average elector has neither the time nor the facilities for securing information which will enable him to decide wisely on many complicated questions of legislation. But that does not mean that I would deprive the people themselves of that ultimate authority which I think they ought to have. I employ technical advisers myself—lawyers, doctors, engineers and so forth; but I do not give them blank cheques, nor do they presume to take the attitude common among politicians under the party system.

No matter which viewpoint you favour, several conditions are necessary in order to ensure popular control over government decisions. These include:

▸ **1.** The people should be able to remove their leaders and replace them with more suitable representatives. This requires that:
   a) Elections be held at relatively frequent and guaranteed intervals.

Voters line up to cast their ballots in an Alberta provincial general election. To what extent does the right to vote help to ensure that Canadian politicians are accountable to the people? What other institutions and mechanisms exist to ensure accountability? If you were attempting to measure the effectiveness of all these mechanisms in achieving accountability, how would you do so?
Provincial Archives of Alberta, Edmonton Journal Collection, J.4488/3

b) There is a real choice among different candidates and parties.
c) Elections are reasonably free of fraud, bribery, and intimidation. This usually implies the use of a secret ballot to protect voters from being punished for their political opinions.
d) There is **universal suffrage**. The larger the franchise, the greater the degree of democracy.
e) Freedom of association prevails. It would be impossible to present the electorate with an effective alternative unless those people who want to run for election had the freedom to organize.

▸ **2.** Formal equality before the law. Every citizen has similar political and legal rights.

▸ **3.** To insure legal equality, judges should be free from political or other control.

▸ **4.** Such civil liberties as freedom of speech, freedom of the media, protection for minority groups, and freedom from arbitrary arrest and prosecution must be guaranteed.

▶ FUNDAMENTAL RIGHTS

All democratic countries believe that certain human rights are essential to the full development of the individual's personality. Some rights have been considered so essential that they are called **natural rights**, meaning that they are beyond argument. In seventeenth-century England, for example, John Locke stated that humanity's fundamental natural rights included protection of private property and the right not to be destroyed or enslaved. The United States Declaration of Independence in 1776 stated:

We hold these truths to be self-evident, that all men are created equal, that they are endowed by their Creator with certain unalienable Rights, that among these are Life, Liberty, and the pursuit of Happiness.

The obvious assumption behind this statement is that human nature is similar everywhere. Whether or not one accepts this assumption, it is true that what one country believes are fundamental rights are not necessarily the beliefs of another country. The French Declaration of Rights, for instance, was written only thirteen years after the American Revolution, but it contained no mention of the ''pursuit of Happiness.'' Instead, it dealt with the need to protect liberty and property, to prevent arbitrary arrest, and to limit excessive taxation. The differences between the countries, of course, was more a reflection of the specific needs and historical development of the United States and France than a difference in human nature.

Natural rights not only have different meanings to different people, but they have also changed with the times. In the eighteenth century, rights were discussed almost exclusively in political terms. A number of social or economic rights, which today are believed to be natural or normal, were not even thought of a century and a half ago. The United Nations' Universal Declaration of Human Rights, for example, acknowledges the right of an individual to work for a living, to earn equal pay for equal work, to join a trade union, to obtain education, and to be cared for by the state in times of sickness. Most Western countries now assume that political rights alone cannot achieve individual equality and liberty.

The concept of fundamental rights is therefore subjective. Rights are ''self-evident'' only in their own time and place, and even then they are often interpreted in widely different ways.

▶ HUMAN AND MINORITY RIGHTS

Over 100 000 teenagers, clad in T-shirts and jeans, screamed at the top of their lungs as Bruce Springsteen belted out "Born in the U.S.A." This was no ordinary rock concert. It was the beginning of a fifteen-country tour in 1988, designed to promote the fortieth anniversary of the United Nations' Universal Declaration of Human Rights. The thirty articles in this document basically state that every person in the world should be treated with dignity and respect. The Declaration includes the right to life, liberty, and security; the right not to be held in slavery, tortured, or arbitrarily arrested; and the right to freedom of thought, religion, and expression. Although many countries have agreed to these ideas, **human rights** are still ignored in many areas of the world. According to the 1985 Amnesty International Report, governments around the world were killing, torturing, and imprisoning their citizens. In Iraq, political prisoners were burned with cigarettes and administered electric shocks. In Guatemala, three church workers were tortured and killed for assisting refugees to escape the country. In Cameroon, eight captives were allowed to die of malnutrition. In Burma, the army used enemy civilians as minesweepers. In the Soviet Union, dissenters were committed to psychiatric hospitals. And in Northern Ireland, residents were shot by the Irish Republican Army (I.R.A.) and by British security forces.

Democracies must be particularly alert to ensure that the rights of their minorities are protected. When a minority comes to believe that the majority is continually treating it unfairly, the minority will ultimately refuse to abide by government laws. Faced with the threat of disturbance, anarchy, or even civil war, the state will be tempted to resort to repressive measures. Democracies thus need to operate on the bases of consensus and compromise. Majority rule is most effective when the minority agrees with its decisions. Majority rule (fifty percent plus one) is not a synonym for democracy. According to the Equality Rights section of the Canadian Charter of Rights and Freedoms, "Every individual is equal before and under the law and has the right to the equal protection and equal benefit of the law without discrimination and, in particular, without discrimination based on race, national or ethnic origin, colour, religion, sex, age or mental or physical disability."

▶ THE ADVANTAGES OF DEMOCRACY

Because democracy can be defined in many different ways, the arguments in its favour have been posed in a variety of guises. One of the most persistent defences of democracy is that government policies will be made in the interest of the people. The argument is as follows: the rule of a few will produce a government that passes laws for the benefit of the few. The rule of the many will create a government that legislates on behalf of the majority. In other words, those people who hold political power will use it for their own benefit. Therefore, if the wishes of the entire community are to be followed, all must rule. Government of the people is most likely to be government for the people.

Another argument in favour of democracy emphasizes its ability to safeguard individual liberties. Free competition among contending political parties provides a check against possible governmental tyranny and oppression, just as periodic elections provide a powerful antidote to the corrupting effect of political power. This essentially negative view of democracy assumes that democratic government will be less arbitrary in its actions than will other political systems.

In 1974, Pauline Tremblay was not allowed to play soccer in the all-male B.C. Juvenile Soccer Association. She is shown here with her mother, leaving the courthouse in Vancouver after seeking a court injunction that would allow her to play soccer. To what extent can the court system in a democracy defend individual rights?
Vancouver Province *Photo*

Another group of political theorists asserts that democracy is more than just a method of arriving at decisions. To them, the democratic process is a means of developing or moulding a democratic-minded citizenry. The democratic environment, they assume, will promote the creation of self-governing, confident, inquiring, intelligent human beings who are willing to compromise and are respectful of different opinions and values. Because decision-making in a democracy relies upon voluntary co-operation and the arts of verbal and written persuasion, physical violence is replaced by peaceful coercion, and force is replaced by intelligence. By actively taking part in elections and voluntary organizations, citizens will develop a co-operative, public-spirited character that will place the good of the entire society above narrow, self-interested goals.

▶ DEFINING DEMOCRACY IN PRACTICE

Since the early 1970s political scientist Raymond D. Gastil has been involved in monitoring the extent of democracy in the world. To determine how democratic each country is, he rates its performance in adhering to both political and civil rights on a scale from one (best rating) to seven (worst). Gastil's checklist for political rights includes:

- Has there been a recent election?
- Is there more than one political party?
- Are the elections run fairly?
- Is there an effective opposition?
- Are the candidates freely selected?
- What role does the military play in the political process?
- To what extent do other countries control the government?
- Do minority groups have a say in government?
- Are there periodic changes in the ruling party?
- How wide is the franchise?

Since political liberties cannot exist without civil rights, Gastil evaluates each country according to some of the following criteria:

- Is the media free of political censorship?
- Is there freedom of association and religion?
- Is the judiciary free of corruption?

- Is there freedom from torture and arbitrary imprisonment?
- Does the government ever lose in court in political cases?
- Is there freedom to join a trade union?
- Is there freedom to travel, own property, and marry?
- What is the degree of economic inequality?

Not surprisingly, Gastil discovered that countries that had a high degree of civil liberties also provided full political rights. Of the 175 countries he surveyed in 1984, only thirty-six percent received ratings of either one or two in both categories; forty-two percent were rated as six or seven. This means that about fifty-one countries, approximately thirty percent of the world's population, could reasonably be considered democratic. Since Gastil first began this study in 1973, some parts of the world have exhibited frequent changes. However, worldwide the percentage of people living in freedom had changed very little by 1984.

Table 3-1
MEASURES OF DEMOCRACY IN 1984

Country	Political Rights	Civil Liberties	Country	Political Rights	Civil Liberties
Albania	7	7	Argentina	2	3
Australia	1	1	Austria	1	1
Bahamas	2	2	Botswana	2	3
Brazil	3	3	Burma	7	7
Canada	1	1	Chile	6	5
China	6	6	Costa Rica	1	1
Denmark	1	1	Egypt	5	5
Gambia	3	4	India	2	3
France	1	2	Bulgaria	7	7
Great Britain	1	1	Pakistan	7	5
Iraq	6	7	Japan	1	1
Kenya	5	5	Kuwait	4	4
Mexico	3	4	Nigeria	7	5
Paraguay	5	5	Peru	2	3
Portugal	1	2	South Africa	5	6
Sweden	1	1	South Korea	5	6
Sudan	5	5	Ivory Coast	5	5
Turkey	4	5	Uganda	4	5
U.S.S.R.	6	7	Uruguay	5	4
Venezuela	1	2	Zimbabwe	4	5

- Source: Published by permission of the *Journal of International Affairs* and the Trustees of Columbia University in the City of New York.

FOCUS

1. What do the highly rated (or lowly rated) countries have in common?
2. Research one of the non-democratic countries to ascertain why Gastil rated it as he did.
3. What countries have probably changed their rating since 1984? Explain.
4. Working in groups of three, rank Gastil's questions in order from most to least important.

▶ BECOMING DEMOCRATIC

Today, as country after country seems to be adopting democracy, it should be remembered that many of the African and South American countries that have tried democracy since World War II have reverted to authoritarian rule. For democracy to work, the people must be familiar with their democratic rights and willing to fight for them. Democracy usually requires high literacy rates; national unity; a consensus on national goals and values; relative economic equality; and the absence of passionate religious, racial, ethnic, or political differences. Many of the countries without democratic governments are educationally and economically less developed. In Asia, South America, and Africa (the three areas with the least amount of democracy), there is no significant middle class, and the people are polarized between the wealthy and the poverty-stricken. It should also be remembered that the evolution of democracy in Western Europe took centuries and was frequently accompanied by revolutions.

Democracy cannot be achieved overnight. Citizens must have faith in the system and be ready to defend it.

▶ SOME DRAWBACKS TO DEMOCRACY

Several years ago, an influential British member of Parliament visiting Canada stated, "What is wrong in my country — and I have a suspicion it is wrong over here as well—is the contrast between the reality of how we politicians behave, and the legend of how we behave." Textbooks are full of descriptions about how democracy works. According to popular belief, there is an all-competent citizenry that is capable of settling any public problem. The free press provides people with all the facts, and after people listen to the pros and cons of each issue they make up their minds. Proper machinery is then provided to enable citizens to elect those candidates who will do their bidding. The contrast between this assumption and the actual reality of politics has undermined the ordinary citizen's confidence in democratic government and in the integrity of leaders.

To admit that there is a difference between the theory and practice of democracy does not mean that democracy is a sham or that we should discard it completely. This admission, in fact, should help strengthen our democratic system of government, because we can then concentrate our efforts upon improving its defects. The remainder of this introduction will outline some of the major criticisms of democracy. Case studies will explore some of these criticisms in greater depth.

▶ Tyranny of the Majority

Most democracies rely upon a simple parliamentary majority (fifty percent plus one) in making policy decisions. This is based on the dual assumption that the majority is more likely to be correct than the minority, and that the majority is entitled to have its own way. Unfortunately, this has frequently led to what is called the **tyranny of the majority,** which means that the minority is deprived of its rights. Historical examples of such tyranny include White domination of Blacks in the southern United States, the mistreatment of native Indian populations in Canada and the United States, and Protestant oppression of Roman Catholics in Northern Ireland. Apartheid in South Africa is an example of tyranny by the minority.

▶ Inefficiency

Some critics claim that technology has progressed too fast for democracy to cope with it effectively. The phenomenal growth of economic, scientific, and technical information makes it impossible for the average person to remain well-informed. Members of Parliament are in most cases poorly equipped to cope with the increasing size and complexity of government activities. As a result, democratic government is too slow and inefficient to meet the demands of a rapidly changing world. Here the critics might point to the snail-like pace of Canada in patriating the Constitution, or in devising a method of amending it, to substantiate their point of view.

▶ Elite Groups

Some political scientists argue that in all large organizations, power and political influence gradually fall into the hands of a few leaders who soon lose touch with the rank and file. As a result, the minority imposes its opinion upon the majority. Democratic governments, they argue, are no exception. In Western democracies, this minority usually consists of wealthy citizens who have the time, influence, and money to ensure that their needs are catered to by the government.

Another form of undue influence is the existence of lobbies and pressure groups which put enormous political pressure upon the government in power to do their bidding. Examples include the Canadian Manufacturers' Association, Greenpeace, pro- and anti-gun lobbies, pro- and anti-abortionists, labour unions, and pollution and nuclear disarmament organizations.

According to some writers, however, the existence of such interest groups within society actually serves to strengthen democracy, because these groups enable concerned citizens to express their opinions about any legislation that directly affects them. In theory, competition between interest groups representing different concerns allows people to exert greater control over decisions of the government. This theory is called pluralism.

There are, however, several serious criticisms of pluralism. As Figure 3-3 illustrates, the people are another step further removed from the decision-making process. Active participation in pressure groups requires more time, money, and knowledge than most people possess. Many citizens do not have organizations to represent their interests, nor is every pressure group equal in terms of finances, power, or access to influential people. As a result, some critics believe that Canada and other Western democracies are ruled by a small number of people who control the economy and influence government decisions.

Figure 3–3

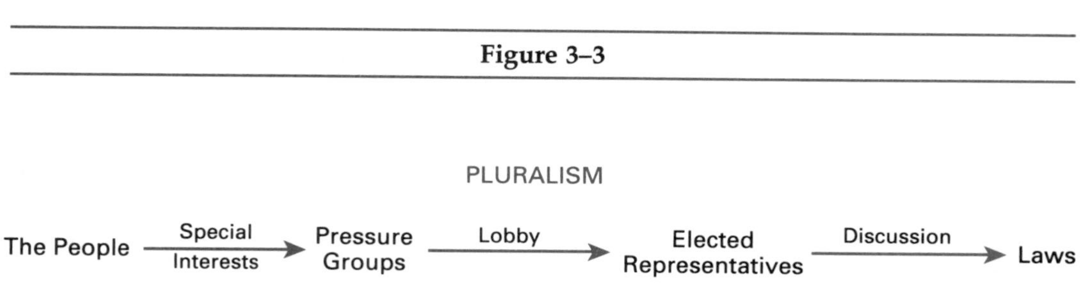

▶ The Uninterested Electorate

According to some critics, democracy expects too much from the citizen. Democratic reformers, they argue, have concentrated so much of their effort on providing democratic institutions that they have forgotten that most people are more interested in sports, movies, or their work, than they are in politics. This lack of interest is aggravated by the growing size and complexity of government — and the civil service — which leaves the average citizen feeling powerless and alienated from government.

▶ Bureaucracy

As democratic governments expanded the scope of their activities in the twentieth century, the civil service, or **bureaucracy**, became enlarged to handle the increased, and more technical, workload. In 1900, there was one public official in the United States for every 300 Americans. Today, the figure is about one to fifteen. In Canada, if the military is included, about twelve percent of the labour force are government employees. The bureaucracy's role is to advise elected government officials and to administer the laws and policies decided upon by the government. In theory, politicians make choices from the options presented them by trained and specialized civil servants. The central problem is to ensure that the bureaucracy is accountable to the people through their elected representatives. Civil servants are relatively permanent; politicians regularly come and go. And, whereas bureaucrats soon come to possess a specialized knowledge of their area, cabinet ministers are constantly switched from one portfolio to another. Since politicians depend upon the advice of their experts, civil servants wield a great deal of power and may dominate elected members who do not have the needed technical knowledge.

The civil service places another barrier between the people and their elected representatives and often increases the voters' sense of remoteness from the decision-making process. In addition, some people fear that the bureaucracy has too much political clout. In recent years, governments have appointed ombudsmen to investigate claims by individual citizens that the bureaucracy has treated them unfairly. Originating in Sweden in 1809, the office of ombudsman was adopted by Finland in 1919, Denmark in 1953, and Norway in 1962. Almost every Canadian province has appointed its own ombudsman. Investigative news reporting, the courts, and well-organized interest groups can also mount effective opposition to unpopular bureaucratic measures. Despite these criticisms of government bureaucracy, the government could not operate effectively without a trained, efficient civil service.

▶ CONCLUSION

Democracy is founded on faith in the people. Its future rests on the citizens' commitment to making it work. This means ensuring that the democratic machinery is functioning properly and that the needs of the majority and the minority are respected. As British Prime Minister Winston Churchill declared, "It has been said that democracy is the worst form of government except all those other forms that have been tried from time to time."

In this introduction to democracy, we have examined its origins, goals, prerequisites, and fundamental principles. In the real world, each democratic country has adopted its own variation of democracy, based upon its own history, culture, values, and goals. It is unrealistic to believe that one particular political system can satisfy every country's needs, just as it is unrealistic to believe that any one method of government is without flaws.

The following case studies examine the political institutions of Canada, the United States, Sweden, France, and Mexico, before we turn to several important issues that challenge the ultimate viability of democracy. Although democratic governments vary from place to place, they can be evaluated according to the extent to which:

- government decisions are subject to popular control
- the ordinary citizen is involved in the running of the country
- individual liberties are upheld

The choice of appropriate institutions to achieve political goals will depend upon what the citizens want from democracy. The intention of the rest of this chapter is to explore some of the criticisms of democracy with a view towards improving, rather than destroying, the system. What changes, if any, would you like to see implemented in Canada?

APPLYING YOUR KNOWLEDGE

1. Why do you think that countries that are not democratic in nature claim to be democracies?
2. Explain why it is difficult to define democracy.
3. In the past, direct democracy was generally considered impractical because of distance and the number of people involved. Technology has now advanced sufficiently to enable everyone to listen to debates in the House of Commons and to immediately express an opinion on every government policy.
   a) What changes might it produce in our system of government?
   b) Would these be beneficial?
4. In the past, Canadian governments have occasionally asked people for their opinions on important questions before reaching a final decision. At the turn of the century, the Laurier government conducted a referendum to discover the general attitude to prohibition of alcohol; during World War II, the Mackenzie King government asked the people if they would release the government from election promises it had made; more recently, the Quebec government asked its citizens for permission to negotiate a new constitution with the federal government.
   a) Do you think referendums should be used more frequently? Explain.
   b) Should the government be required to act upon referendum results? Explain.
   c) Research one of these referendums and report on the issue, the result, and the government's decision.
5. Explain why freedom of speech and freedom of the media are important prerequisites of democracy.
6. Explain why many countries now believe that political rights alone cannot achieve equality and individual liberty.
7. a) Discuss how living in a democracy might promote the development of inquiring, tolerant people.
   b) Is there such a thing as inalienable rights? If so, what are they? Explain.
8. Should prisoners be allowed to vote? Explain your decision in a mock letter to your elected representative.

9. Should the voting age be lowered; if so, to what age? Explain.
10. What percentage of the parents of your classmates are civil servants?
11. In 1983, a nation-wide opinion poll revealed that fifty percent of Canadians thought that a member of Parliament should vote as the constituents wanted, thirty-eight percent believed members should vote according to their conscience, and twelve percent thought that members should vote as the party required. Since this is not how Parliament works, what should be done?
12. If you were shipwrecked on a deserted island with thirty people, what rules would be required, and how would these rules be enforced?

FURTHER RESEARCH

1. Select one of the following topics. Research it (either in the library or by conducting a survey) and write an essay on the topic. This essay should include the pro and con arguments, and it should arrive at a well-reasoned conclusion. Use the problem-solving techniques outlined in Chapter 1 to prepare your essay.
   a) In a democracy, everyone should be forced to vote in elections.
   b) Political parties that advocate non-democratic systems of government should be prohibited.
   c) Everyone should be required to pass a political knowledge and current events test before being allowed to vote.
   d) Elections should be held no more than one or two years apart.
   e) Elected representatives should act according to their own consciences, not according to the desires of their constituents.
2. Divide into small groups to do this question. Imagine that there will be an election for the student council. Your group has been appointed to prepare a list of rules and regulations for this election. Draw up a document explaining who can vote (teachers?), what campaign practices will be prohibited, how the voting will be conducted, and how you will ensure that the class representatives will act in the best interests of their classmates after they are elected.
3. Design a constitution for your school, defining the rights of the students and the extent and limits of the teachers' powers. What are the goals or purposes of this constitution?
4. Investigate and report to the class on how to contact an ombudsman.
5. Make a list of ten government agencies that affect your life. Obtain information from one of these bodies that outlines what it does and how best to appeal one of its decisions. For a list of these bodies and their phone numbers and addresses, see the most recent edition of the *Canada Year Book*.
6. Research Canada's decision not to allow the franchise to either Japanese-Canadians or native Indians. Why was this decision made, and why was it subsequently changed?
7. Between 1982 and 1984, over 14 000 Canadian students in grades 7, 10, and 12 were polled about their attitudes concerning some of the following issues.

Statement	Strongly Agree			Strongly Disagree		
	Grade 7	10	12	Grade 7	10	12
Native groups should be allowed to keep their own way of life.	80	88	73	10	12	12
Canadian citizens should have the right to criticize the policies of their government.	71	87	89	12	5	4
Everyone in Canada should have the right to free speech.	87	93	91	6	3	3
The right of Canadian workers to strike should be taken away.	25	19	18	54	60	59
Political leaders do not care what people like me want.	59	57	48	21	23	27
The Canadian system of justice is fair.	46	51	40	20	19	16
Immigrants should be allowed to keep their own culture and traditions.	69	64	63	12	20	17

▸ Source: Kristian John Kirkwood et al., "Is Canadian Studies Working?" *History and Social Science Teacher*, Summer 1987. By permission of Kristian John Kirkwood (1991).

a) Investigate whether age made a difference to the answers and explain the results.
b) Compare the responses to the first and last questions and explain the different results.
c) What does this chart reveal about the democratic nature of the people surveyed?
d) Conduct your own poll and compare the results with those of this study.

8. Some native peoples believe that their societal structure influenced the development of democracy in the United States. Research the democratic beliefs and practices of some of the native peoples of North America. What parallels can be drawn?

Case Study 1 Overview

Democratic Institutions in Canada and the United States

This case study begins by exploring the different types of democracies in the world and classifies them according to unitary or federal systems of government. The Canadian variety of democracy is then examined, including such government bodies and practices as responsible government, the House of Commons, the Senate, the prime minister and cabinet, the office of governor general, and the role of the individual member of Parliament. The process by which a government bill becomes law is outlined. Then, the case study describes the United States' variety of democracy, with its separation of powers, president, Supreme Court, Senate, and House of Representatives. The case study concludes with a comparison of the Canadian and American systems and a discussion of the strengths and weaknesses of each.

▶ OBJECTIVES

After reading this case study, you should be able to:

- ▶ better understand how the Canadian government operates
- ▶ compare the Canadian and American systems of government and explain which features of each you prefer
- ▶ devise your own ideal system of government
- ▶ debate the advantages of either system
- ▶ understand American politics

▶ KEY TERMS

bicameral
unitary system
federal system
executive
minority government
coalition government
responsible government
legislative power
judicial power
checks and balances

Case Study

1 Democratic Institutions in Canada and the United States

Democratic governments are based upon the principle that the wishes of the people should be law. This means that the legislature must be accountable to the electorate. Although few people differ with the theory, almost every country disagrees on the best method of achieving it. Some democracies are parliamentary monarchies, others are republics. Most governments have a **bicameral** legislature (an upper house and a lower house), but a few countries have only one house. In the United States, both houses have considerable political power, but in Canada the House of Commons dominates the Senate.

Elected officials are usually chosen for periods ranging between two and five years. The members of the House of Representatives in the United States remain for two years, whereas members of Parliament (MPs) in the Canadian House of Commons are elected for a maximum of five years. The time between elections varies from fixed terms (as in the United States and Sweden) to variable terms subject to change (as in Canada and Great Britain). It is impossible to prove which of these systems is the best. History, tradition, and convenience have often had more to do with the choice of options than have logic or political theories.

Governments can be classified according to their degree of centralization. In a **unitary system**, law-making power is concentrated in one central government. There might be municipal, regional, or other governments, but the central body can veto their actions. The vast majority of countries has a unitary government, including France, Japan, Great Britain, Sweden, and Colombia. In a **federal system**, government powers are divided between the central government and regional or provincial governments. A written constitution assigns different functions to each governing body. The central government usually has control over such national concerns as defence, foreign affairs, postal service, and currency. Regional governments are responsible for such local matters as education, roads, and hospitals. A constitutional or supreme court is required to arbitrate disputes between the two areas of government and interpret the constitution.

Although there are fewer than twenty federal governments in the world, five of the six largest countries by area are federal. (China is the exception.) The American Constitution of 1789 created the first modern federal government. This model was later copied and modified by Brazil, Canada, Mexico, Australia, Czechoslovakia, Austria, Argentina, India, West Germany, the U.S.S.R., Switzerland, and Indonesia. Federal systems are usually created in geographically large countries and in states with a variety of culturally distinct groups. Switzerland is geographically small, but it has a diverse religious and linguistic population. Canada opted for a federal system in 1867 to allow Quebec to retain its cultural distinctiveness, and because the Maritime colonies did not want local matters to be decided by Ottawa. One of the reasons why the United States created a federal system was to ensure that one level of government could act as a check on the other and to prevent any one body from becoming too powerful.

Practically all federal governments have a bicameral legislature (two houses) to ensure that each regional government has a voice in the central government. In most cases, each region has equal representation in the upper house. The selection of the regional representatives ranges between appointment by the central government and popular election, and their powers vary from powerlessness to equality with the lower house. Canada's first prime minister, John A. Macdonald, desired a weak Senate partly because he believed that the American Civil War in the 1860s had been caused by the individual states having too much power.

The most important question democracies have to decide upon is the relationship among the legislature (which makes the laws), the **executive** (which carries out the laws), and the judiciary (which enforces the laws). In deciding this question, democracies have adopted either the British parliamentary system or the American presidential or republican form of government. This is the major difference between the Canadian and American governments.

▶ THE CANADIAN GOVERNMENT

The British monarch is Canada's head of state and is represented by the governor general. The head of state has little political power and serves more of a symbolic than a political role. The governor general, for example, is selected by the government in power, must act on the advice of the cabinet, and performs such ceremonial duties as greeting visiting dignitaries and signing all legislation. Only in times of emergency, when the government is deadlocked, can the governor general act on his or her own initiative.

The most important component of the parliamentary system is the House of Commons. It is the effective ruling body. Following a federal election, the leader of the political party with the majority of elected representatives in the House of Commons becomes prime minister. If no party wins a majority, then the leader who can gather a majority of the MPs' support becomes prime minister. Such a situation leads to the formation of a **minority government**, or a **coalition government**, in which two or more parties temporarily unite to achieve a majority. The most important group within the House of Commons is the cabinet. It consists of the prime minister and the heads of such government departments as finance, national defence, and immigration. Using the civil service as a source of information and advice, the cabinet draws up bills and submits them to the House for approval. Solidarity prevents cabinet members from criticizing government bills in public or disclosing private cabinet discussions. Individual members of Parliament may introduce bills, but since they do not have the undivided support of the government, few succeed. Although the cabinet is extremely powerful, it is ultimately responsible to the House of Commons. If the cabinet loses the support of the majority of members in the House, then the prime minister and the executive must resign. In such cases, there is either an election or another party will attempt to gain majority support, in which case its leader becomes the new prime minister. This system is called **responsible government**—the prime minister and cabinet are responsible to the elected representatives in the House of Commons and must resign if they lose this support. This is the major difference between the American and Canadian political systems.

This is the theory. In practice, the immense control exerted by political parties generally prevents individual MPs from voting against their party's policies. To date, the only examples of a government losing office as the result of a defeat in the House occurred in 1873, when Alexander Mackenzie defeated John A. Macdonald as a result of the Pacific Railway Scandal; in 1926, when W.L. Mackenzie King defeated Arthur Meighen; and in 1979, when the combined vote of the Liberals and the N.D.P. overthrew Joe Clark's government on the budget issue. In the last two cases, the defeat was made possible by the presence of a minority government.

▶ Creating A New Law

A new policy or law is usually devised by a cabinet minister in conjunction with the members of that particular department. This proposal is then submitted to the cabinet for discussion. If the idea is approved, the cabinet committee on legislation drafts the bill and resubmits it to the cabinet for final approval. Only now is the bill presented to the House, where it must pass through three readings. (All bills that require the expenditure of public moneys must originate in the House of Commons.) During the first reading, the title of the bill is announced to House members, and the text of the proposed legislation is distributed to them. During the second reading, the members debate and vote on the principle of the bill. From here, a parliamentary committee examines the bill clause by clause. It might invite expert witnesses and interested groups to comment upon the proposal. The membership in these committees is based upon each political party's strength in the House. Although the governing party thus controls each committee, the latter sometimes amends a proposal before returning it to the House. During the second and third readings, the opposition parties have the opportunity to criticize and amend the proposed legislation. The bill is then introduced into the Senate, where it goes through a similar process of three readings and committee reports. When the Senate does not object to the principle of the proposal, it will often process the bill at the same time as it is being examined in the lower house. Amendments made by the Senate must receive approval by the House of Commons. When the governor general signs the bill it becomes law.

Since the government must maintain the confidence of the House of Commons to remain in office, loyalty to the party usually takes precedence over the MPs' personal beliefs. Party members, however, have the opportunity to influence government bills

Figure 1
OVERVIEW OF THE LEGISLATIVE PROCESS

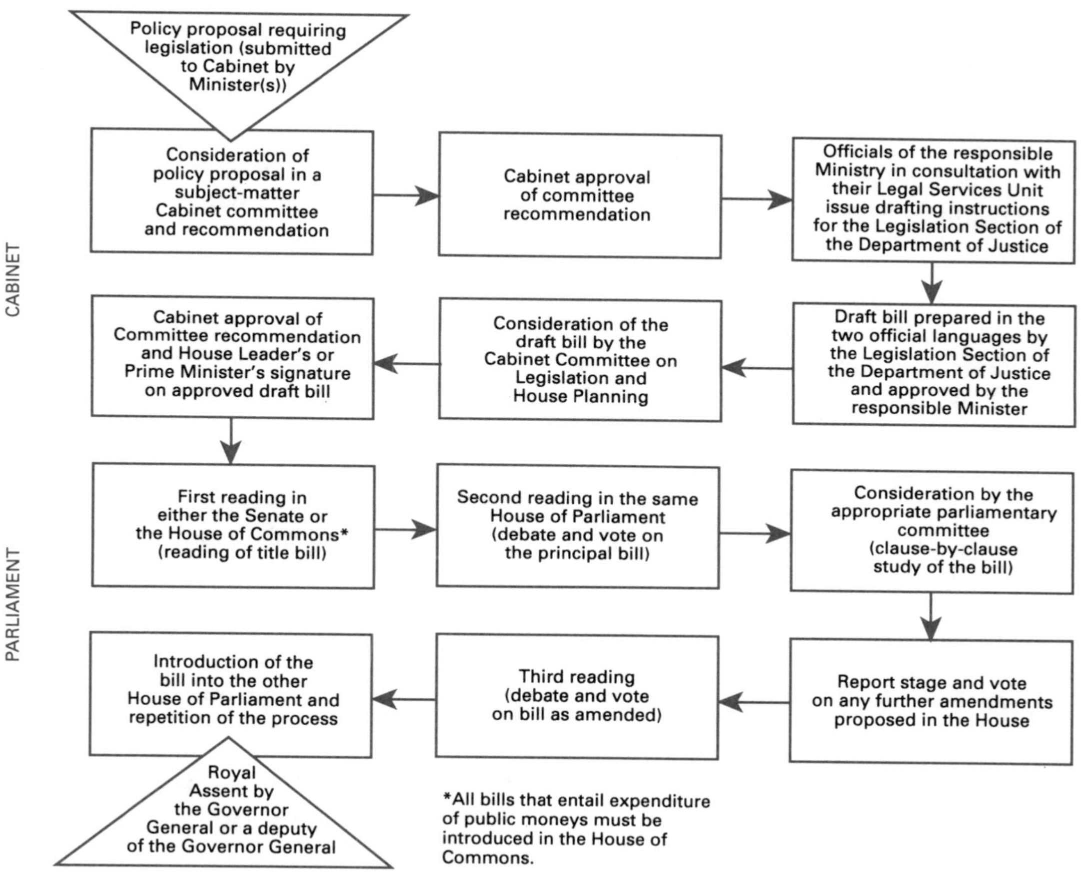
CABINET
Policy proposal requiring legislation (submitted to Cabinet by Minister(s))
Consideration of policy proposal in a subject-matter Cabinet committee and recommendation
Cabinet approval of committee recommendation
Officials of the responsible Ministry in consultation with their Legal Services Unit issue drafting instructions for the Legislation Section of the Department of Justice
Draft bill prepared in the two official languages by the Legislation Section of the Department of Justice and approved by the responsible Minister
Consideration of the draft bill by the Cabinet Committee on Legislation and House Planning
Cabinet approval of Committee recommendation and House Leader's or Prime Minister's signature on approved draft bill
PARLIAMENT
First reading in either the Senate or the House of Commons* (reading of title bill)
Second reading in the same House of Parliament (debate and vote on the principal bill)
Consideration by the appropriate parliamentary committee (clause-by-clause study of the bill)
Report stage and vote on any further amendments proposed in the House
Third reading (debate and vote on bill as amended)
Introduction of the bill into the other House of Parliament and repetition of the process
Royal Assent by the Governor General or a deputy of the Governor General
*All bills that entail expenditure of public moneys must be introduced in the House of Commons.

▸ Source: Statistics Canada.

and policies at party caucus meetings, at which times the prime minister informs and consults all elected party members. In reality, when a government measure reaches the floor of the House of Commons, it is almost certain of success. This explains why the debates in the House often take place before a half-empty chamber.

▶ The Upper House

Another important component of the Canadian parliamentary system is the Senate. Although its members supposedly represent the interests of the provinces, senators are appointed by the federal government. Senators must be at least thirty years old and live in the province they represent. They may serve until they reach the age of seventy-five, or miss two consecutive sessions of Parliament. Although the Senate can amend bills and delay legislation (except money bills), it cannot permanently stop government measures. Various influential people and most provinces have suggested radical changes to the composition, powers, and selection of senators. The comments range from abolishing the Senate to greatly expanding its powers, and from popular election to provincial control over appointments. Alberta Premier Donald Getty, for example, has championed the Triple E Senate — an *e*lected Senate with *e*ffective powers and *e*qual provincial representation. The basic debate is whether senators should be elected or appointed (and by whom); what regions, groups, or people they should represent, and what powers they should have.

In September 1990, the question of Senate reform once again emerged in the forefront of Canadian politics. When the Liberal-dominated Senate refused to approve the Goods and Services Tax (GST) that had been passed by the Conservative-dominated House of Commons, Prime Minister Brian Mulroney successfully appealed to Queen Elizabeth under section 26 of the British North America Act to create eight new Senate seats. The new senators all supported the GST. Although the Conservative party now had a majority in the Senate, the Liberal members blocked a final vote on the GST. The prime minister claimed that the Senate was acting undemocratically. An appointed body, he argued, should not block the wishes of the elected House of Commons. Liberal Senators, however, pointed to opinion polls that indicated that the majority of Canadians opposed the GST and supported the Senate's actions. Before deciding what type of Senate you think Canada should have, let us first examine how the United States has distributed political power.

▶ THE UNITED STATES GOVERNMENT

In Washington, D.C., there are three famous buildings that symbolize the government of the United States of America: the White House is the residence of the president (the executive power); on "the Hill," a little distance from the White House, is the Capitol building, which is the home of the Senate and the House of Representatives (the **legislative power**); still higher on the Hill is the Supreme Court building (the **judicial power**). The existence of these separate buildings symbolizes the division among the executive, legislative, and judicial branches of the U.S. government. In order to prevent any one group or party from becoming too powerful, the American Constitution divided the powers of government among these three branches and established a system of checks and balances designed to prevent any one group from controlling the state. This separation of executive, legislative, and judicial powers is one of the most important differences between the Canadian and American governments.

▶ The Executive Branch in Canada and the United States

In the United States, the chief executive is the president, who is responsible for the enforcement of laws and for the negotiation of treaties with foreign countries. The president is commander-in-chief of the armed forces and appoints federal judges and government ambassadors (subject to the approval of the Senate). The president recommends laws to Congress (Senate and House of Representatives) and signs or vetoes measures passed by Congress.

There are two major differences between the American congressional system of exec-

Figure 2

THE EXECUTIVE	
CANADA	UNITED STATES
PRIME MINISTER	PRESIDENT
➤ Leader of the political party that has the support of the House of Commons. ➤ Member of Parliament. ➤ Term up to five years. ➤ May be re-elected indefinitely.	➤ Leader of a political party. ➤ Not a member of Congress. ➤ Elected for a four-year term. ➤ May be re-elected only once.
Powers ➤ Proposes policies for the country. ➤ Chooses cabinet. ➤ Must resign if loses support of the House of Commons.	Powers ➤ Proposes policies for the country. ➤ Chooses cabinet. ➤ Retains position even when proposals are defeated by the legislature. ➤ Signs or vetoes bills passed by Congress. ➤ Commander-in-Chief of the armed forces.

utive power and the parliamentary system of executive power. In the American government, the executive power is in the hands of one person, the president. The executive power in Canada is controlled by the cabinet and the prime minister, who are jointly responsible for government decisions.[1]

▸ [1]American cabinet ministers are appointed by the president and are not members of Congress, nor are they responsible to it.

The second difference is even more significant. In the parliamentary system, cabinet ministers are members of Parliament and they retain their office only as long as they have the support of the majority of the House of Commons. The executive is therefore responsible to the elected members of Parliament. The president, on the other hand, is not a member of Congress and is not responsible to that body. The chief executive is elected for a four-year period and holds office for the duration of this term despite the fact that his or her party may not have a majority in Congress. This executive independence was founded on the belief that the president should not be a servant of the two houses of Congress. The prime minister's position, on the other hand, is based upon the belief that the executive should be responsible to the House of Commons.

This difference is illustrated by the manner in which each is elected. Presidential elections are held on the Tuesday following the first Monday in November of any year that can be divided evenly by four — such as 1984, 1988, 1992, and 1996. A president cannot be elected for more than two consecutive terms. In Canada, a national election must be called within five years of a government attaining office, but it can be held at any time within the five-year period. The prime minister is not elected separately but is the leader of the political party with the largest number of supporters in the House of Commons, and can retain that position as long as the support of Parliament is secured.

In the United States, the president is both the head of state and the head of the government. These positions in Canada are filled by two individuals — the governor general and the prime minister. The head of state is the governor general, while the head of government is the prime minister, who is elected by the people. Because in the United States the president represents both of these positions, Americans may revere the office of the president but may not politically support the person in that office. Consequently, the American flag has come to symbolize the country itself.

▶ The Legislative Branch

One of the first observations that a Canadian visitor to the American Congress would make is that the seating arrangement is quite different from that of the House of Commons. Examine the two photographs shown opposite and describe the differences in seating and other physical arrangements. What do they illustrate about the differences between government and opposition in Canada and the United States?

In a parliamentary system, most of the important bills are drawn up by the cabinet and are introduced into the House of Commons as "government measures," which means that the executive must resign if a bill is defeated. In the American government, the president recommends legislation, but Congress does not have to pass it. In fact, each house usually writes its own bills and then holds extensive negotiations with each other before reaching a final agreement.

The legislative branches in both countries consist of two houses. The American Senate, however, is far more important than the Canadian Senate, and is more powerful than the House of Representatives. This is because it has the right to approve or reject the president's appointments of judges to the Supreme Court, ambassadors to foreign states, and all cabinet ministers. Treaties made by the president with other countries must also be ratified by a two-thirds majority of the Senate. Each state elects two senators for six-year terms. To ensure a greater element of democracy in the American Senate, one-third of the Sen-

The Canadian House of Commons
Canapress Photo Service

The U.S. House of Representatives
Courtesy U.S. Information Services

ate positions come up for re-election every two years.

The House of Representatives is elected for a two-year term, whereas the House of Commons has a flexible term of up to five years. Both lower houses may initiate bills dealing with money matters. The House of Representatives, in co-operation with the Senate, can override the president's veto if a two-thirds majority of both houses is secured. The House of Commons, however, can reverse any executive decision by a simple majority vote and may also remove the cabinet if it wishes.

▶ The Judicial Branch

The most important court in both countries is the Supreme Court. Its judges are appointed by the executive and hold their positions until retirement. The Supreme Courts in the United States and Canada are the final courts of appeal.

Because the United States is governed by a written constitution, compared to Canada's partly-written, partly-by-custom constitution, the American Supreme Court has had a tremendous influence on the country's development. It is the Supreme Court that is responsible for interpreting the Constitution and deciding whether a government law or practice is constitutional or not — it has the last word.

▶ Checks and Balances in the U.S.

It should now be evident what Americans mean by the terms separation of powers and **checks and balances**. Each of the three branches of government acts as a check on the freedom of the others. The president commands the armed forces, but only Congress may declare war or vote money for troops. All bills passed by Congress must be signed by the president before they become law; Congress, however, can override the president's veto by passing the same bill again with a two-thirds majority in each house. Congress can also refuse to vote the money required by the president to implement policies. The Supreme Court, through its right to interpret the Constitution, can check both the executive and legislative branches by declaring a law unconstitutional. Yet even the Supreme Court's powers are not absolute — new judges can be appointed by the president with the Senate's approval, and the existing judges can be impeached by the House of Representatives.

Canada and the United States are just two examples of democracies. Approximately one country in every four has a democratic government, although each differs in some way from the other.

A country's system of government is a product of its history, values, and goals. The differences between Canada and the United States, for instance, are partly the result of their different relationships with Great Britain. Both were colonies of Great Britain, but the United States had to fight for its freedom, whereas Canada achieved it peacefully. No wonder Canada's government more closely resembles the British system.

▶ STRENGTHS AND WEAKNESSES OF THE TWO SYSTEMS

In the United States, the staggered terms of office reduce popular control of elected officials. House members serve for two years, the president for four years, and senators for six years. It thus takes at least six years to completely change the government. The fact that these terms of office are fixed and almost unchangeable further reduces the electorate's control over the government. Direct control is limited to election day. As a result, the government does not change suddenly during times of

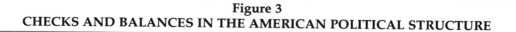

Figure 3
CHECKS AND BALANCES IN THE AMERICAN POLITICAL STRUCTURE

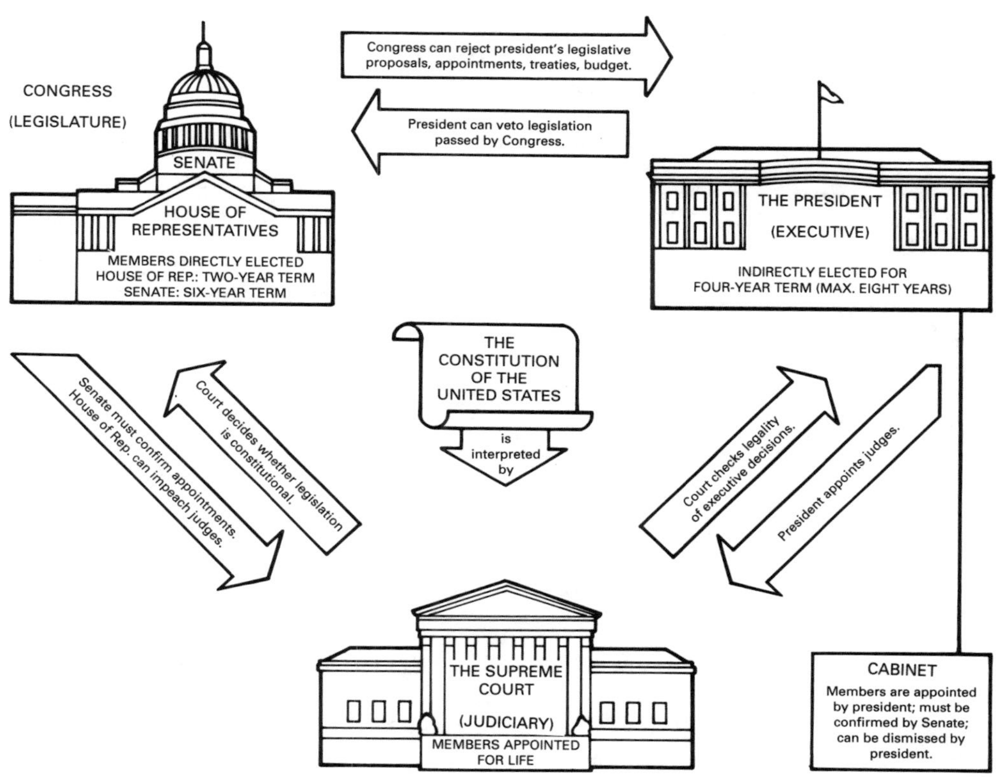

crisis. Whereas some people consider this stability an advantage, critics argue that it fosters an unresponsive government.

Another possible problem is the checks and balances system. Although it prevents one government body from becoming too powerful, it can also lead to political deadlock when the president's political party does not control the Congress. If the Democratic and Republican parties are divided along ideological lines, then the possibility exists for long-term instability. In addition, since the legislature cannot topple the executive by a vote of non-confidence, there is no need for party solidarity, and no reason for the president's fellow party members to support the executive's proposed bills. This freedom does, however, allow elected representatives to vote according to their conscience, or their constituents' wishes.

The Canadian principle of responsible government, on the other hand, can lead to successive changes in government and instability. This is particularly true for a minority government. Critics also claim that the need for party discipline and the dominance of the House of Commons has made the cabinet much too powerful, and that it is in danger of becoming a cabinet autocracy. Indeed, want of confidence motions have overturned the government only three times in Canadian history.

Some political scientists rate the American system as more liberal, and the Canadian system as more democratic. By more liberal, they mean that it is difficult for one group of people to control the government. By more democratic, they mean that the parliamentary system more effectively expresses the will of the majority.

APPLYING YOUR KNOWLEDGE

1. Define the following terms: responsible government, federalism, Congress, checks and balances, minority government, coalition government, bicameral, and impeachment.
2. Using Figure 3 as a guide, devise your own chart for the legislative branch of government for Canada and the United States.
3. Which system do you think is more democratic? Explain your choice.
4. Write a short answer to the following question: should the prime minister be selected in the Canadian manner or elected separately (as in the United States)?
5. What is the ideal length of time between elections? Explain.
6. How important should party loyalty be? Explain.

FURTHER RESEARCH

1. If Parliament is meeting, follow the process of one particular bill through the House. Or attend sessions of your local government.
2. Prepare for a debate on the topic: Canada's system of government is preferable to the American system of government.
3. Using the techniques outlined in Chapter 1, research and write an essay on one of the following topics:
   a) The Senate—Should it be abolished?
   b) The monarchy—Should it be abolished in Canada?
   c) Federal union (Canada and the United States) versus legislative union (Great Britain)—Explain why Canada or the United States did not follow Great Britain's example.
   d) Compare the division of powers in Canada, the United States, or Switzerland between the central government and the regional governments.
   e) The role and importance of the civil service in Canada.
4. Research the process of how the Canadian and American constitutions are amended.

5. In 1867, the Canadian Fathers of Confederation intended that the federal government be much more powerful than provincial governments. Since then, the federal government's powers have ebbed and flowed. Working in groups, brainstorm the impact that world wars and economic depressions would have on federal powers relative to provincial powers.
6. Working in groups, write a one-act play or videotape a class debate on a current political issue.

Case Study 2 Overview

Democracy in Sweden

This case study examines Sweden's system of government. It describes the political similarities and differences between Canada and Sweden, briefly discusses Sweden's political parties, explores the importance of the general consensus that exists among the various political parties and non-government organizations, and outlines how an idea becomes a law in Sweden. The case study concentrates on how Sweden employs a system of proportional representation to elect its members of Parliament, discusses the strengths and weaknesses of this method, and explores the impact proportional representation would have on the Canadian government.

▶ OBJECTIVES

After reading this case study, you should be able to:

- ▶ understand and explain Sweden's system of government
- ▶ evaluate the benefits and weaknesses of proportional representation
- ▶ summarize the similarities and differences between the Canadian and Swedish systems of government
- ▶ apply the Swedish system of proportional representation to Canada
- ▶ debate the benefits of the Swedish ''politics of compromise''

▶ KEY TERMS

Riksdag
interest groups
proportional representation
electoral district
multi-member constituencies

Case Study 2

Democracy in Sweden

In many ways, Sweden's government is similar to Canada's. Both countries are constitutional monarchies in which the monarchs have so little effective power that they perform more of a public relations function than anything else. The genuine power lies with the **Riksdag** (Parliament), the prime minister, and the council of state (cabinet). In 1971, Sweden abolished its upper house. In most other matters, however, the Swedish government functions resemble those of its Canadian counterpart. The prime minister is the leader of the political party that has the support of a majority of the elected members of the Riksdag. The prime minister and the appointed cabinet can be voted out of office by Parliament, although (as in Canada) party solidarity prevents this from happening very often. Each cabinet minister is in charge of a separate department, such as finance or national defence, and is responsible for preparing legislation for the approval of the Riksdag. Thus, unlike in the American system of separation of powers, the governing political party in Sweden combines both executive and legislative functions.

Sweden has six major political parties. The Social Democratic Labour party is the largest. It favours social welfare policies and draws most of its support from the blue- and white-collar workers. The Centre party, which appeals to the farmers, has generally opposed the high taxes needed to fund the country's comprehensive welfare policies. The Conservative party has close ties with big business and with people in upper-income brackets. The Liberal party is struggling to retain its middle-class support, whereas the Communist party gets scattered votes from those workers who believe in nationalizing industry and erasing all class differences. The Green party, formed in the 1980s, attracts voters concerned with industrial pollution and other environmental problems. Despite these differences, political discussions and parliamentary debates lack the fire and the conflict of Canadian or American politics. The following account by an American political scientist describes the politics of compromise in Sweden:

On a Saturday morning in the university city of Uppsala, on a pedestrian mall in front of a modern supermarket (actually a consumers' cooperative), gather students of the major political persuasions plus adherents to half a dozen ultraleft grouplets. They hold up banners and placards, distribute leaflets, and sell party newspapers. Three young Conservatives take turns speaking through a small public address system they have set up, explaining that they are not reactionaries (indeed, they call themselves "moderates"), but that taxes, centralization, and planning have gone too far in Sweden and are driving out individual initiative and freedom. Facing them are the banners of Trotskyists and Maoists, demanding a total reconstruction of Sweden's society. The Conservatives finish speaking, there is scattered applause (not, of course, from the Trotskyists and Maoists). There are no catcalls, no attempts to interrupt, and nothing is thrown. Instead, the members of the various groups circulate politely, passing out their literature, and occasionally explain what they stand for. The visiting American, familiar with other parts of Europe and with U.S. campuses . . . is slightly amazed. Why aren't they hitting each other, shouting down their opponents, heckling the speakers? Why aren't police patrolling the area? The answer is simple: such is not the Swedish way. Swedes are so thoroughly civil that even when they disagree with each other—and their disagreements are serious—they stick to the norms of polite society. Violence is out of the question.[1]

The opposition parties do not oppose the government as much as they negotiate, bargain, and compromise with it. The Social Democratic Labour party, for example, held power continuously from 1932 to 1976, yet only twice did it have a majority of the seats in the Riksdag. All members of the Riksdag, even those in opposition, can introduce a proposition that requires government action. Trained specialists within the civil service are then assigned the task of researching and designing needed legislation. Part of this research involves consultation with all the groups that might be affected by the legislation. The final draft is submitted to these interest groups for their comments, and then the draft and the comments proceed to the Riksdag for discussion.

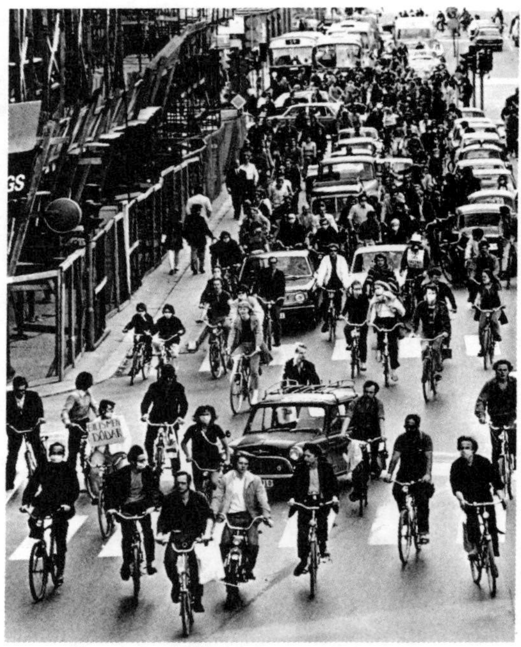

A political demonstration with a difference: to protest motor traffic and its effects in downtown Stockholm, Swedish cyclists obstruct traffic. They belong to a political movement called Alternative City. Some are wearing masks to dramatize their concern about automobile exhaust fumes.
Canapress Photo Service

[1]Michael Roskin, *Other Governments of Europe: Sweden, Spain, Italy, Yugoslavia, and East Germany*, © 1977, pp. 23–24. Reprinted by permission of Prentice-Hall, Inc., Englewood Cliffs, N.J.

Parliament itself consists of an aggregation of **interest groups**. Most of the important labour leaders, business people, and representatives from other important segments in society are elected to the Riksdag. This multi-level office-holding blurs the distinction between public and private interests in Sweden and provides another check on unpopular legislation. In Sweden, politics are thought of in terms of co-operation rather than conflict.

▶ PROPORTIONAL REPRESENTATION

Another major difference from North American governments is the method by which the triennial Riksdag is elected. The Swedes believe that single-member constituencies like those in Canada and Great Britain result in wasted votes, and can create parliaments that do not accurately reflect the nationwide strength of each party. The Canadian election statistics reproduced in Table 1 illustrate this point. Using the percentage of the popular vote received by each party, compute the number of seats each party should have gained.

Sweden's solution to these problems is **proportional representation**. Each constituency is allotted several seats and the voters cast their ballots for the political party (not the candidate) of their choice. Within every **electoral district**, the parties may nominate as many candidates as the number of seats in the riding. The party then ranks these representatives in order of preference. If the party wins three seats, then the first three names on its slate of candidates are elected to the Riksdag.[2] These seats are won according to the proportion of the vote received by each party. In this way, 310 members are elected to Parliament. Another thirty-nine seats are allotted to the parties on the basis of their total votes obtained nationally. This compensates for any differences between the percentage of seats held by the parties and their general popularity. To prevent a proliferation of smaller political groups, a party must obtain at least twelve percent of the total vote in a single riding, or four percent of the nation-wide vote, to obtain representation in the Riksdag. Somewhat similar systems are used in Holland, Israel, Denmark, and Norway.

One criticism of Sweden's system of proportional representation is that the political party can exert more control over its members than is possible in a single-member constituency. The candidates are chosen by the local party leaders, and if they do not

▸ [2]Members are elected for a three-year term. Almost ninety percent of all eligible voters cast their ballots at each election.

Table 1
CANADIAN FEDERAL ELECTION RESULTS, 1974–1988

Election Year	Total Seats	Conservative party Total Seats	Conservative party % Popular Vote	Liberal party Total Seats	Liberal party % Popular Vote	New Democratic party Total Seats	New Democratic party % Popular Vote
1974	264	95	35	141	43	16	15
1979	282	136	36	114	40	26	18
1980	282	103	33	146	44	32	20
1984	282	211	50	40	28	30	19
1988	295	169	43	83	32	43	20

1. To what extent does the percent of seats gained by each party reflect popular support?
2. What effect does the Canadian single-member constituency have on third party success?

''tow the line,'' they might be listed at the bottom of the slate of candidates, thereby virtually ending all chances of election. Swedish electors vote for a party rather than a candidate.

There are several alternatives to Sweden's system of proportional representation. Canada uses single-member constituencies. The candidate who obtains the most votes wins the parliamentary seat being contested. In Japan, most constituencies are served by two to six representatives. The maximum number of candidates that each party may run in each constituency equals the number of members to be elected. However, since each person can vote for only one candidate, the Japanese electoral system sometimes encourages competition among members of the same party. The candidates with the most pop-

Table 2
SASKATCHEWAN FEDERAL ELECTION RESULTS
1988

Constituency / Candidate	Votes
Kindersley-Lloydminster	
McKnight, Bill, PC	15 089
Whitmore, Grant, NDP	11 198
Kaufman, Bev, L	5 039
Hermanson, Elwin, RP	2 217
Mackenzie	
Althouse, Vic, NDP	15 931
Scowen, Jack, PC	12 649
Lutz, Garfield, L	4 988
Froese, John, RP	689
Moose Jaw-Lake Centre	
Laporte, Rod, NDP	15 916
Gottselig, Bill, PC	15 508
Boxall, Linda, L	5 936
Appenheimer, Eldwin, CRWP	287
Prince Albert-Churchill River	
Funk, Ray, NDP	17 915
Cennon, J.J., PC	8 234
Kingsmill, Peter, L	5 007
Suitor, Ken, RP	490
Richardt, Mary, CRWP	105
Regina-Lumsden	
Benjamin, Leo, NDP	21 593
Richardson, Sam, PC	9 934
McGregor, Don, L	5 840
Rands, Brian, NIL	139
Regina-Qu'Appelle	
deJong, Simon, NDP	18 608
Hicke, Wm. Lawrence, PC	10 854
Smith, Larry, L	5 028
Regina-Wascana	
Schneider, Larry, PC	15 339
Bailey, Dickson, NDP	14 829
Goodale, Ralph, L	14 804
Caribou, Kimball, Comm	76
Madsen, Ian, Libert	65
Saskatoon-Clark's Crossing	
Axworthy, Chris, NDP	19 889
Hnatyshyn, Ray, PC	14 847
Patrick, Bill, L	6 554
Morwick, Keith, GP	222
Saskatoon-Dundurn	
Fisher, Ron, NDP	20 986
Bryden, Grant, PC	13 859
Ferguson, Debra, L	8 389
Knutson, Elmer, CRWP	384
Quesnel, Harold, CW	51
Saskatoon-Humboldt	
Hovdebo, Stan, NDP	17 703
Ravis, Don, PC	14 793
Williams, C.M. Red, L	8 442
Souris-Moose Mountain	
Gustafson, Len, PC	17 200
Sample, Jeff, NDP	11 924
Bauche, Mike, L	6 965
Rutten, Kelvin, CRWP	652
Swift Current-Maple Creek-Assiniboine	
Wilson, Jeff, PC	15 944
Balas, Laura, NDP	11 827
Lewans, Paul, L	7 958
The Battlefords-Meadow Lake	
Taylor, Len, NDP	14 516
Gormley, John, PC	13 804
Currie, Neil, L	5 152
Quist, Ted, RP	461
Langley, Connie, CRWP	197
Yorkton-Melville	
Nystrom, Lorne, NDP	18 523
Battiste, Virginia, PC	12 543
Autumn, J. Robert, L	5 149

Note: PC—Progressive Conservative party; L—Liberal party; NDP—New Democratic party; RP—Reform party; CRWP—Confederation of Regions Western party; Comm—Communist party; GP—Green party; Libert—Libertarian party; CW—Commonwealth party; NIL—No Affiliation ular support are successful. For instance, in a five-member constituency, the individuals with the five highest vote totals are elected members of Parliament. In Ireland, which also has **multi-member constituencies**, the voters rank the people running for office in order of preference. Candidates who are the first choice of only a few electors may still be able to gain a seat in Parliament if they are ranked second or third by a sizeable portion of the constituency's voters.

Table 3
ALLOCATION OF SEATS IN SWEDEN

	Party A	**Party B**	**Party C**	**Party D**	**Party E**	**Seat Awarded to Party**
Total Vote Polled	$\frac{13\,000}{1.4}$ =	$\frac{10\,200}{1.4}$ =	$\frac{30\,300}{1.4}$ =	$\frac{52\,500}{1.4}$ =	$\frac{4\,000}{1.4}$ =	
Seat 1	9 286	7 285	21 643	37 500	2 857	D
				$\frac{52\,500}{3}$ =		
Seat 2	9 286	7 285	21 643	17 500	2 857	C
			$\frac{30\,300}{3}$ =			
Seat 3	9 286	7 285	10 100	17 500	2 857	D
				$\frac{52\,500}{5}$ =		
Seat 4	9 286	7 285	10 100	10 500	2 857	D
				$\frac{52\,500}{7}$ =		
Seat 5	9 286	7 285	10 100	7 500	2 857	C
			$\frac{30\,300}{5}$ =			
Seat 6	9 286	7 285	6 060	7 500	2 857	A
	$\frac{13\,000}{3}$ =					
Seat 7	4 333	7 285	6 060	7 500	2 857	D

The allocation of seats in Sweden is determined in the following manner:

1. The total vote for each party is divided by 1.4. The party with the highest total is awarded the first seat.
2. The total vote for the winning party is then divided by three, and this new figure is compared to the total the other parties received after dividing it by 1.4. The party with the highest total is awarded the second seat.
3. The party that won the second seat has its original vote divided by three, and this new figure is then compared to the other parties' totals as listed in step 2. The highest total is awarded the third seat.
4. Once a party has won twice, its total vote is divided by five. After its third seat, the total is divided by seven.

▸ Source: Figures adapted from Allan Ingelson, *Så regeras Sverige*, Stockholm: Bonniers, 1965, p. 31.

APPLYING YOUR KNOWLEDGE

1. Make a list of the similarities and the differences between the Swedish and Canadian systems of government.
2. Table 2 shows the outcome of the 1988 federal election in Saskatchewan.
   a) How many seats did each party win?
   b) What percentage of the total vote did each party receive?
   c) Compare your answers for a) and b) and devise a fairer system.
   d) Working in groups, devise an appropriate proportional representation scheme for Saskatchewan.
   e) Critique another group's scheme. (Are there too many parties? Will stability be possible? etc.)
3. Apply the Swedish system (Table 3) to the Saskatchewan results.
4. What are the benefits of single-member constituencies as they exist in Canada?

   One way to organize your thoughts is to brainstorm with others. For a specific question, quickly list all the ideas as they come to mind. Focus on quantity rather than quality. The advantage of this method, especially in group situations, is that one thought usually leads to another and another, as everyone builds on the original thought. After all the suggestions have been made, the answers can be grouped together and analysed.

   Thought-webbing, or mind-mapping, uses a similar technique to provide a visual image of your ideas. Write the question to be solved in the middle of the page and draw a circle around it. The answers fill the rest of the page and are connected to the question, and to similar ideas, by lines. Thought-webbing aids in making connections among ideas, in showing relationships, and in organizing and categorizing ideas. The thought-web on page 71 illustrates this procedure. The plus signs (+) represent the advantages of proportional representation, and the minus signs (–) are for its disadvantages. As you can see, some ideas could be interpreted either way, depending upon your viewpoint or values.

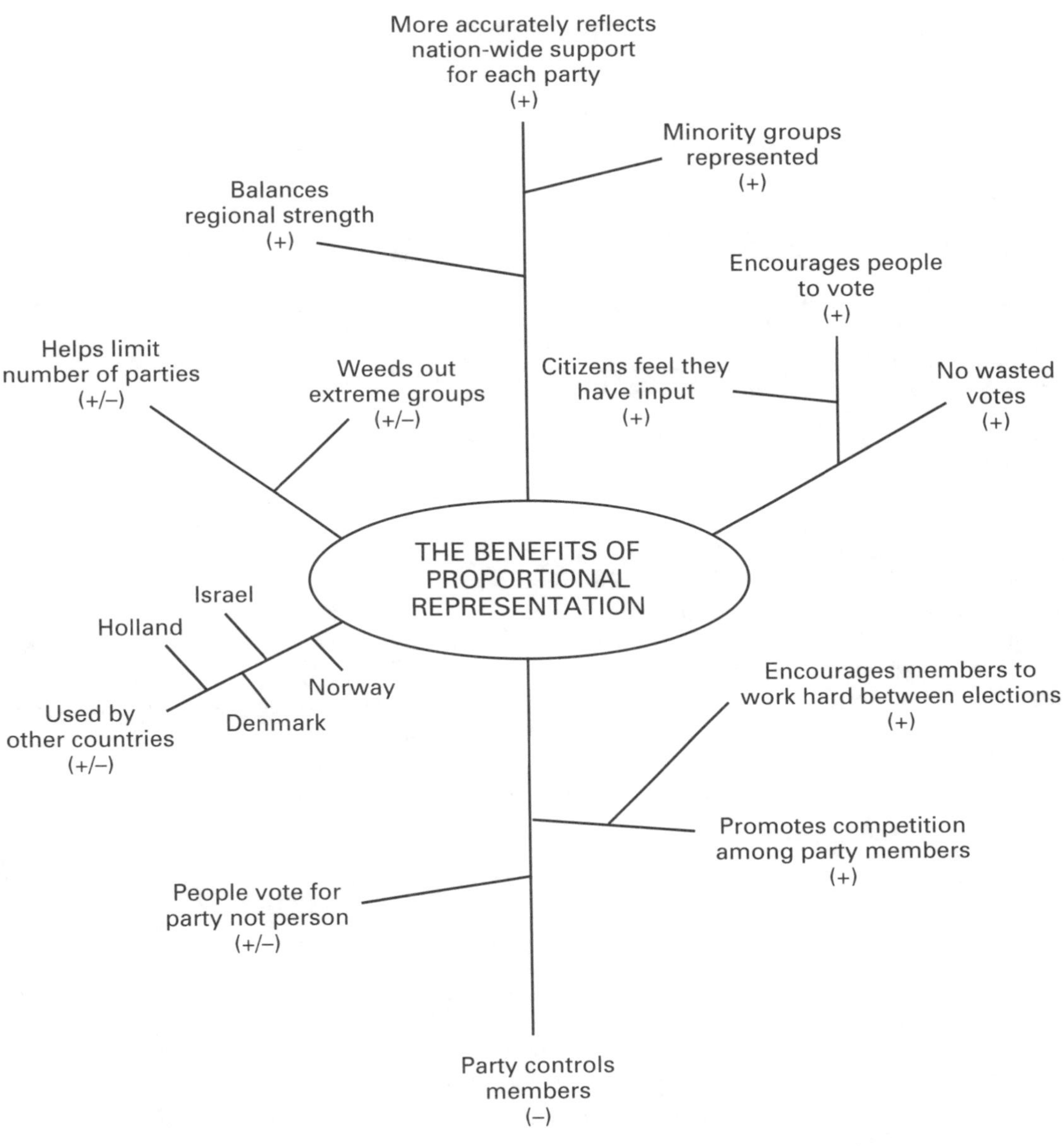
More accurately reflects nation-wide support for each party (+)
Minority groups represented (+)
Balances regional strength (+)
Encourages people to vote (+)
Helps limit number of parties (+/–)
Weeds out extreme groups (+/–)
Citizens feel they have input (+)
No wasted votes (+)
THE BENEFITS OF PROPORTIONAL REPRESENTATION
Israel
Holland
Norway
Used by other countries (+/–)
Denmark
Encourages members to work hard between elections (+)
Promotes competition among party members (+)
People vote for party not person (+/–)
Party controls members (–)
(+) Positive
(–) Negative

Case Study 3 Overview

France: Combining Parliamentary and Presidential Systems

This case study describes France's political system and compares it to the American and Canadian systems. The case study begins with a brief history of French politics and the reasons behind the present French constitution established by Charles de Gaulle in 1959. The French government, with its president and prime minister, is a combination of the American presidential and the British parliamentary systems. This case study outlines the functions and responsibilities of the French Senate, National Assembly, prime minister, and president, and comments on why France selected a different form of government. The case study concludes with a discussion of some of the problems still facing France today.

▶ OBJECTIVES

After reading this case study, you should be able to:

- ▶ explain the similarities among the French, Canadian, and American systems of government
- ▶ debate the advantages of the French system
- ▶ explain why France adopted its present constitution
- ▶ devise a diagram that compares the French, Canadian, American, and Swedish political systems
- ▶ evaluate the advantages of a strong central government
- ▶ discuss what Canada could learn from France

▶ KEY TERMS

written constitutions
splinter parties
consensus
referendums
non-confidence vote

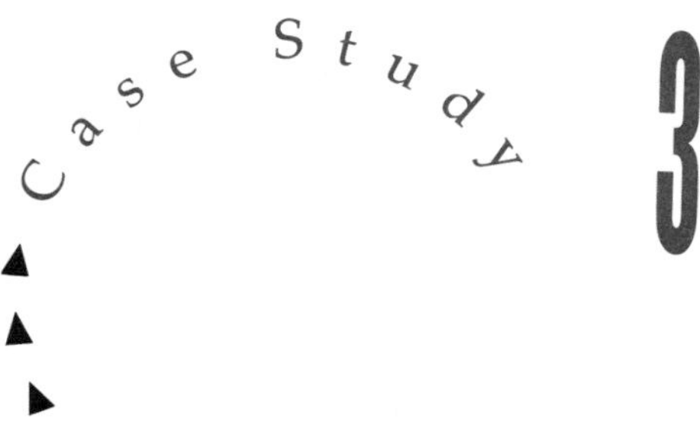

France: Combining Parliamentary and Presidential Systems

▶ HISTORICAL BACKGROUND

The French political system differs markedly from that used by the world's other democratic states. According to a noted expert on French politics, "France is, without doubt, the most mysterious of the Western countries. . . . her people refuse, almost doggedly, to fit the framework of the rest of Western Europe and the Atlantic world."[1] France, the first of continental Europe's democracies, shares many characteristics with its sister democracies in Canada, the United States, Sweden, Great Britain, and elsewhere; yet the dissimilarities are as diverse and striking as the resemblances.

▸ [1]M. Curtis, *Introduction to Comparative Government*, 2nd ed., New York: Harper & Row, 1990, p. 105.

Until 1789, France was one of Europe's leading monarchies. It was thought that the king derived his power directly from God, and therefore his word was law. Consequently, a constitution was unnecessary. After the 1789 Revolution, the king lost his absolute power and the country's new revolutionary leaders devised a written constitution to spell out the government's duties and obligations to the people.

Since then, France has adopted and discarded a large number of **written constitutions**. It has seen regimes of various ideological types come and go at an average rate of one every twelve years. Before the Fourth Republic (1946–1958) ended, France had had about twenty constitutions. Two of these were never adopted, and only one, that of the Third Republic (1870–1940), lasted over two decades. (See Table 1 for a listing of France's five republics.)

Table 1
FRANCE'S REPUBLICS

First Republic	1792–1799
Second Republic	1848–1852
Third Republic	1870–1940
Fourth Republic	1946–1958
Fifth Republic	1958–

▶ THE FOURTH REPUBLIC

Following World War II, persistent problems plagued the Fourth Republic. One of the difficulties was the presence of too many **splinter parties**. These represented varying shades of political and ideological viewpoints, ranging from the extreme right to the extreme left. France had six major groups represented in Parliament, each with conflicting demands. Communists and Socialists might agree on the need to nationalize major industries, but not on wage controls or foreign policy. Socialists and the *Mouvement Républicain Populaire* (MRP), a coalition consisting of middle-of-the-road Liberals and Roman Catholics, both favoured European political and economic integration, but generally disagreed on state aid to Catholic schools. The Radicals agreed with the Socialists regarding education, but disagreed over how to deal with nationalist movements in France's worldwide colonial possessions.

In view of these constant disputes, French prime ministers found it virtually impossible to preside over stable governments and carry out their programs. This lack of **consensus** in matters of social, educational, and foreign policy paralysed the political process. Parties were unable to capture majorities, only pluralities (less than half of the parliamentary membership). In order to form the government, a party leader had to negotiate coalition agreements with parties of different ideological beliefs. Such partners proved invariably unreliable and unco-operative, and frequently brought down the government on a motion of non-confidence in the Chamber of Deputies (the lower house, similar to the Canadian House of Commons). In the twelve years following World War II, France went through twenty governments. Some lasted only two days. Only a stable and competent professional civil service kept the country from lapsing into anarchy and chaos.

The most serious and prolonged crisis to strike the Fourth Republic was a civil war in Algeria that pitted Algeria's Arab Muslims against the French settlers and the army; a cruelly fought struggle on both sides that threatened to spill over into France. The Chamber of Deputies responded to this challenge by granting Charles de Gaulle, a war hero, emergency powers for six months.

▶ THE FIFTH REPUBLIC

De Gaulle accepted the challenge, relying on his public prestige, army support, and favourable public opinion throughout Europe. De Gaulle disappointed his army backers by negotiating to relinquish Algeria to the Algerian Arab revolutionaries. This process was completed in 1962. In the meantime, de Gaulle restored order in France and presided over the drafting of a new constitution that created the Fifth Republic in 1958.

This presidentially dominated government has been France's most stable regime to date. The new constitution effectively resolved the difficult question of who wields the supreme political authority in the country. In the past, prime ministers had seen their programs paralysed by non-confidence motions in the Chamber of Deputies. In the process, democracy became lost in a welter of private parliamentary manoeuvrings.

Former French President Charles de Gaulle
The Bettmann Archive

De Gaulle's new constitution drastically altered those aspects of the country's parliamentary system that had not worked in the past. France's new president created a two-level governmental structure that retained elements of the earlier parliamentary system, complete with prime minister and cabinet. To this he added a powerful, American-style, popularly elected president, who was not responsible to the legislative branch of the government. This freedom from parliamentary control has enabled French presidents to direct the affairs of the country without interference.

Such power could easily deteriorate into a dictatorship. However, the higher courts have some authority to protect the public interest. Furthermore, French voters can exercise their franchise every seven years and elect a new president if they desire.

▶ The President

As chief of state, the popularly elected president is invested with nearly monarchical powers for a seven-year renewable term. The president selects the prime minister and with the advice of the latter appoints all cabinet members, military officers, political advisers, and some members of the judiciary. The president signs bills, ratifies treaties with foreign countries, passes laws, and presides over cabinet sessions. The president cannot veto bills, but can ask Parliament to re-examine bills considered objectionable. The president has the right to go to the people with direct popular **referendums** if Parliament refuses to co-operate. Between 1961 and 1972, the Fifth Republic conducted five referendums. After one parliamentary year has elapsed, the president can dissolve the National Assembly before the expiration of its five-year mandate and call for new elections. The president can also rule the country for up to six months by decree. The president has to consult with the prime minister and the speakers of the Assembly and Senate, but need not take their advice.

The chief success of the de Gaulle constitution rests on the fact that, as in the United States, the people vote for the president. As a result, French presidents have grown immensely in prestige and authority since 1958. They have become towering government figures, exceeding even the American presidents in political power. French presidents have almost always enjoyed disciplined, obedient majorities in the National Assembly, which can never remove a president from office.

French Prime Minister Jacques Chirac (right) greets President François Mitterrand at Paris Roissy Airport.
The Bettmann Archive

▶ The Prime Minister

Although the prime minister exercises a number of functions that conflict and overlap with the president's responsibilities on matters of national security, the prime minister is helpless before a president who wishes to assert his or her authority. A prime minister's appointment requires no official approval by Parliament, and he or she does not even have to belong to a political party. The prime minister may be dismissed by both the Assembly and by the president. As of 1990, the president replaced six of the last seven prime ministers while they still enjoyed the confidence of the Assembly.

In view of these and numerous other limitations, mainly having to do with presidential power, the prime minister plays but a small formal role in the French government. Most prime ministers in the Fifth Republic have accepted their position as being largely ceremonial, or for the sake of appearances, or for reasons of ambition, primarily view their offices as a stepping stone to the presidency.

▶ The National Assembly and Senate

The National Assembly consists of 577 popularly elected deputies. They serve five-year terms. If no one candidate captures a majority of the vote, the top two nominees have a run-off election. Senators are chosen for nine-year terms. Two-thirds of the members are popularly elected and one-third are appointed by a variety of national and local associations. One-third of the Senate's membership is renewed every three years. Theoretically, the Senate and Assembly have equal powers. Bills must be passed jointly. Budgets must always be submitted to the Assembly first, however, and only the Assembly may oust the government (that is, the prime minister and the cabinet) on a **non-confidence vote**. Parliament's decision-making powers are limited. The president, through his or her overwhelming powers, can easily override the wishes of the Senate and Assembly.

The French legislature suffers several other limitations and restrictions. It meets only 150 days each year. Although it has jurisdiction over taxation, the judicial system, education, social security, rules governing elections, and the establishment of public institutions, the president can bypass or ignore the Parliament on these issues. The most important matters in the Fifth Republic are regulated by presidential decree. Although the National Assembly can express its displeasure with, and can even remove, the prime minister and the cabinet, in practice this action is so difficult that it has never succeeded. Not only must the majority of the deputies (counting even the absent ones) be included in the vote, but the government must declare that it is staking its survival on the passage of the bill in question.

The French National Assembly

▶ The Fifth Republic: A Success Story

De Gaulle's constitution successfully merged the principles of presidential and parliamentary government to give France stability. Most French people are apparently content with the compromise solution, because it maintains the semblance of the earlier republics, but places overwhelming power, prestige, and responsibility in the hands of the popularly elected president. Only a relatively few extreme leftists and rightists have opposed the new system. De Gaulle's constitutional system has systematically whittled down the number of extremist deputies in the National Assembly from about thirty-three percent in 1956 to under five percent in 1988. Since members of these extremist groups had contributed mostly to bring about France's instability, their curtailment through constitutional means has been a favourable by-product of de Gaulle's constitution.

The de Gaulle constitution enjoys considerable success with the public because it simplifies the passage of controversial legislation. In the past, conservative senators used to delay or block the passage of progressive laws in France. Now, the Senate has been deprived of that power. One-third of the senators are still chosen by local and national officials and by members of the Assembly. This would seem to give non-elected senators too much power, were it not for the fact that the Senate enjoys only a shadow of the authority possessed by the elected National Assembly, the prime minister, and the president. Figure 1 illustrates the distribution of power among these governmental branches.

The French people appreciate the fact that all branches of the government must obey their elected president. If, for example, the Senate and Assembly cannot agree on a certain item of legislation, the president can refer such bills to the electorate for a referendum, as de Gaulle did during the Algerian crisis and several times thereafter. In 1972, President Georges Pompidou conducted a referendum that approved British membership in the Common Market.

▶ WHY IS FRANCE DIFFERENT?

In order to comprehend why France has a different political system than other democracies, we must examine certain circumstances that have set it apart. There are numerous vital issues on which the French people are sharply divided, with no compromise or consensus in sight. Some of these controversies strike at the very heart of French national unity, and therefore require the presence of a firm executive to mediate these issues.

▶ Issues Dividing France

- France's centralized bureaucracy is determined to carry out the government's economic and social plans among a diverse population composed of people with minds of their own. This has fuelled tensions, thwarted governmental objectives, and caused passive and at times aggressive resistance.
- French citizens disagree on the question of whether big business, such as chain stores, supermarkets, and shopping malls should prevail over the traditional, small, neighbourhood, family-owned store.
- The French public is uncertain to a larger degree than other peoples on whether to have the government nationalize vital industries or whether to privatize all businesses.
- France is increasingly divided on issues of race and religion. Since the end of

Figure 1
PARLIAMENTARY VERSUS PRESIDENTIAL SYSTEMS

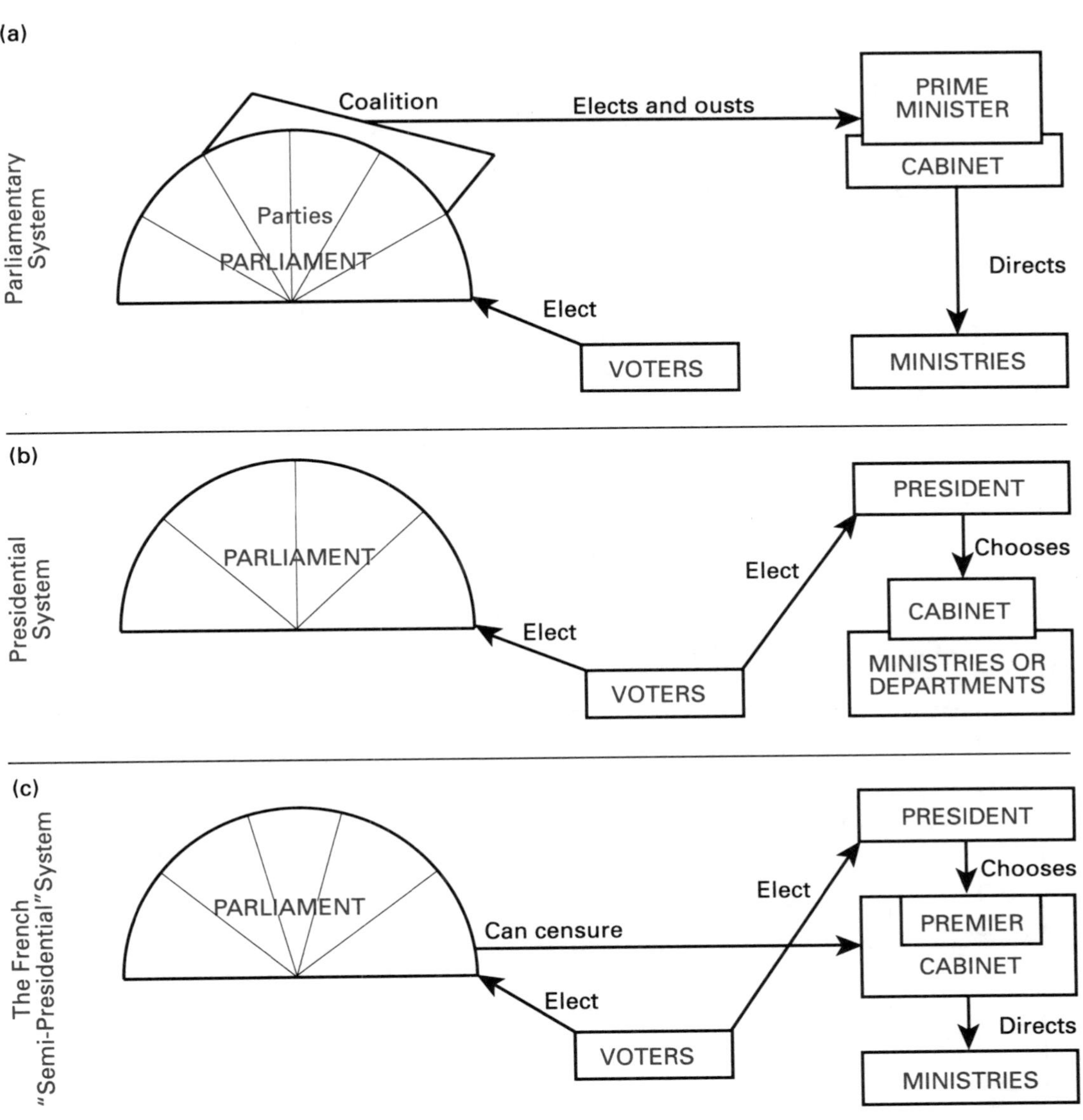

Source: Michael G. Roskin, *Countries and Concepts: An Introduction to Comparative Politics*, 3rd ed., © 1989, p. 7 and p. 87. Adapted by permission of Prentice-Hall Inc., Englewood Cliffs, N.J., 07632.

Figure 2
THE GOVERNMENT IN THE FIFTH REPUBLIC

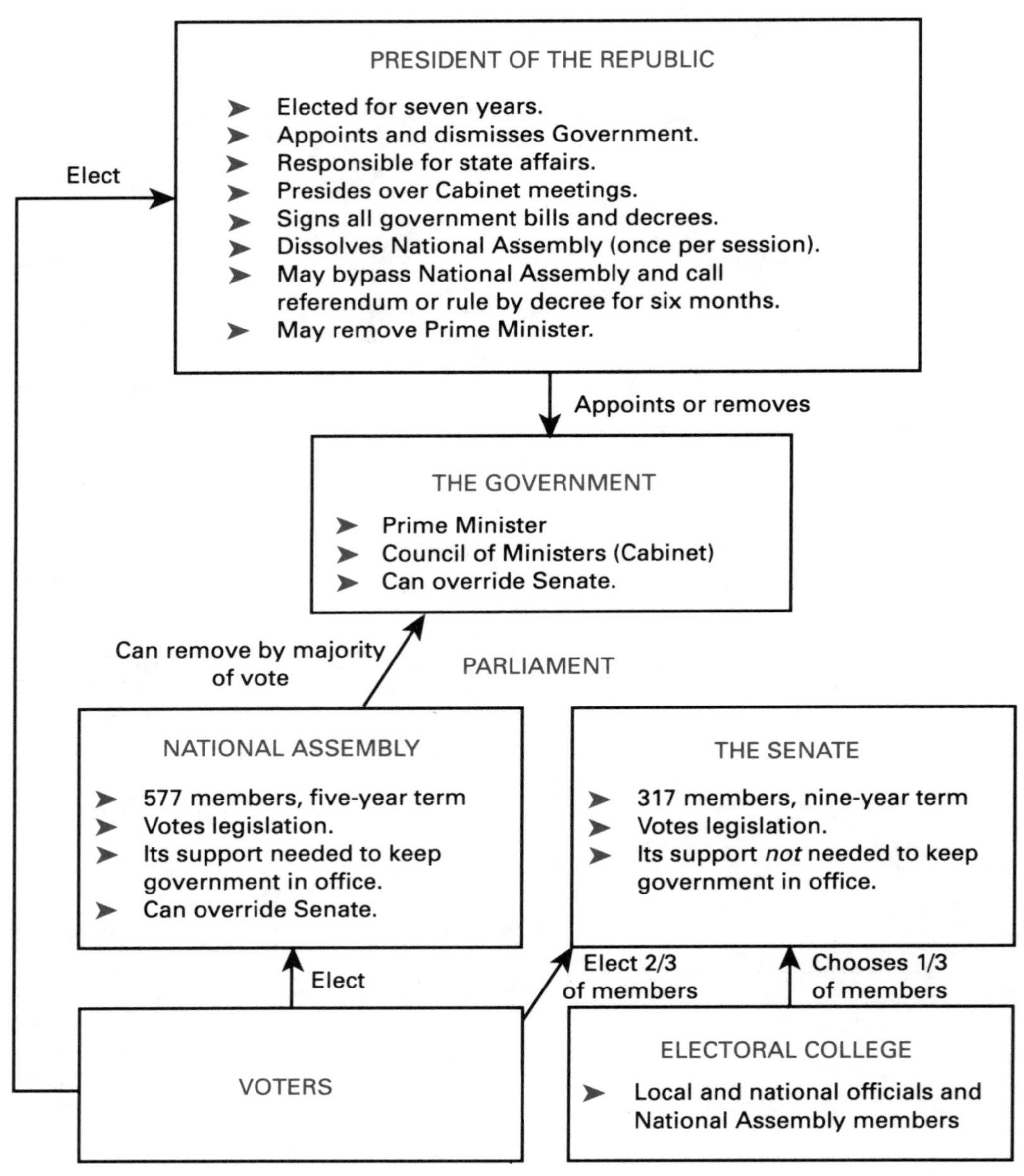

PRESIDENT OF THE REPUBLIC
➤ Elected for seven years.
➤ Appoints and dismisses Government.
➤ Responsible for state affairs.
➤ Presides over Cabinet meetings.
➤ Signs all government bills and decrees.
➤ Dissolves National Assembly (once per session).
➤ May bypass National Assembly and call referendum or rule by decree for six months.
➤ May remove Prime Minister.
Elect
Appoints or removes
THE GOVERNMENT
➤ Prime Minister
➤ Council of Ministers (Cabinet)
➤ Can override Senate.
Can remove by majority of vote
PARLIAMENT
NATIONAL ASSEMBLY
➤ 577 members, five-year term
➤ Votes legislation.
➤ Its support needed to keep government in office.
➤ Can override Senate.
THE SENATE
➤ 317 members, nine-year term
➤ Votes legislation.
➤ Its support *not* needed to keep government in office.
Elect
Elect 2/3 of members
Chooses 1/3 of members
VOTERS
ELECTORAL COLLEGE
➤ Local and national officials and National Assembly members

‣ Source: Diagram adapted from *Comparative Politics: Diverse States in an Interdependent World* by David F. Roth, Paul V. Warwick, and David W. Paul.

World War II, the country has lost its nearly one hundred percent French, Roman Catholic, White population. Millions of French citizens today have come from all parts of the world and represent a multitude of religions and ethnic backgrounds.

- These population changes in France have encouraged the formation of extreme right-wing nationalist political parties. The public is undecided on how to deal with these latter-day fascist-type challengers to France's democratic order. The French are also uncertain whether to permit the alien peoples living in their midst to practice their unique customs or whether to force them to integrate into the French cultural and linguistic stream. To complicate matters, France's immigrants are also split on the issue of whether to integrate or whether to preserve their ancestral customs and languages.

▶ CONCLUSIONS

It has been said that in France any democratic political system would prove successful, provided that the country was free from external threat or economic calamity. The Third Republic (1870–1940) stood the test of time. It proved conclusively that there might be some truth in this assertion. It survived World War I, a conflict won at the cost of enormous human and material sacrifices. The Third Republic, however, crumbled under the combined weights of economic adversity and domestic ideological and political strife, plus the overwhelming military onslaught by Nazi Germany. The Fifth Republic has functioned well since 1958 because conditions in France have been relatively favourable. It has yet to be tested by a series of multiple adversities at home and abroad, which also brought down the Fourth Republic (1946–1958).

APPLYING YOUR KNOWLEDGE

1. Compare the method of senatorial selection in France to senatorial selection in Canada and the United States.
2. A French president may rule by decree for six months. How would you feel if our country introduced such an arrangement? Explain your answer.
3. In France, the president is elected by popular vote. Do you believe that this system is sufficient to protect democracy? Why or why not?
4. Make separate lists comparing the similarities and differences of the governments of France, Canada, and the United States.
5. a) Explain why France has a powerful presidency.
   b) Working in groups, draw a left-right continuum (see Chapter 2) and place Canada, the United States, and France on it.
6. Debate the advantages of France's political system versus that of Canada or the United States.
7. Which features of France's political system might be successful in Canada? Explain your answer.

Case Study 4 Overview

Mexico: A Strong Presidential System

Mexican politics is dominated by one political party, the Institutional Revolutionary party (P.R.I.), which is the focus of this case study. It describes the reasons behind this one-party dominance and explains how the P.R.I. has been able to maintain power for so long. Also discussed are Mexico's form of proportional representation, the P.R.I.'s treatment of other parties, the president's powers and method of selection, and how the system has managed to change with the times. The case study concludes with an examination of whether or not the system is democratic.

▶ OBJECTIVES

After reading this case study, you should be able to:

- ▶ explain the origins and success of Mexico's one-party government
- ▶ understand how the Mexican government operates
- ▶ compare the Mexican and Swedish systems of proportional representation
- ▶ evaluate whether Mexico has a democratic government
- ▶ explain how the P.R.I. has been able to retain power for so long

▶ KEY TERMS

Institutional Revolutionary party (P.R.I.)

oligarchy

republican democracy

Case Study

4 Mexico: A Strong Presidential System

Most residents of Canada, the United States, Great Britain, Sweden, and most other democracies take it for granted that the only way a democratic country can function properly is by having one or more effective opposition parties to keep the incumbent government responsive to the electorate and provide alternative ideas. This is not true of Mexico, which is an unusual democratic country. For the last fifty years or so, the **Institutional Revolutionary party** (P.R.I.) has been virtually the only effective political party in Mexico, yet the country has not sunk into the type of tyranny in which opponents of the regime must either hide or live in fear for their lives. The P.R.I. is so confident of its power that it has even permitted selected opposition parties to function openly. The P.R.I. has built-in safeguards and procedural mechanisms both to keep opposition parties in check and to prevent Mexico from leaving the ranks of the world's democracies. This latter point is essential if the P.R.I. wishes to retain the good will of its American neighbours. This case study investigates a mixed political system that could be described as both dictatorial and democratic.

▶ HOW THE PRESENT SYSTEM FUNCTIONS

The present system of government in Mexico followed the Revolution of 1910–1917 that vanquished the conservative coalition of large landowners and the Roman Catholic Church. The Constitution of 1917, which has been amended several times, established a federal form of government and adopted the American system of separation of executive, legislative, and judicial powers — at least in theory. It also established a strong centralized state with a powerful chief executive to dominate all branches of government. (See Figure 1.)

It took seventeen years for several strong presidents to solidify the system as a one-party **oligarchy** functioning under a president, but maintaining Mexico's stance as a

Figure 1

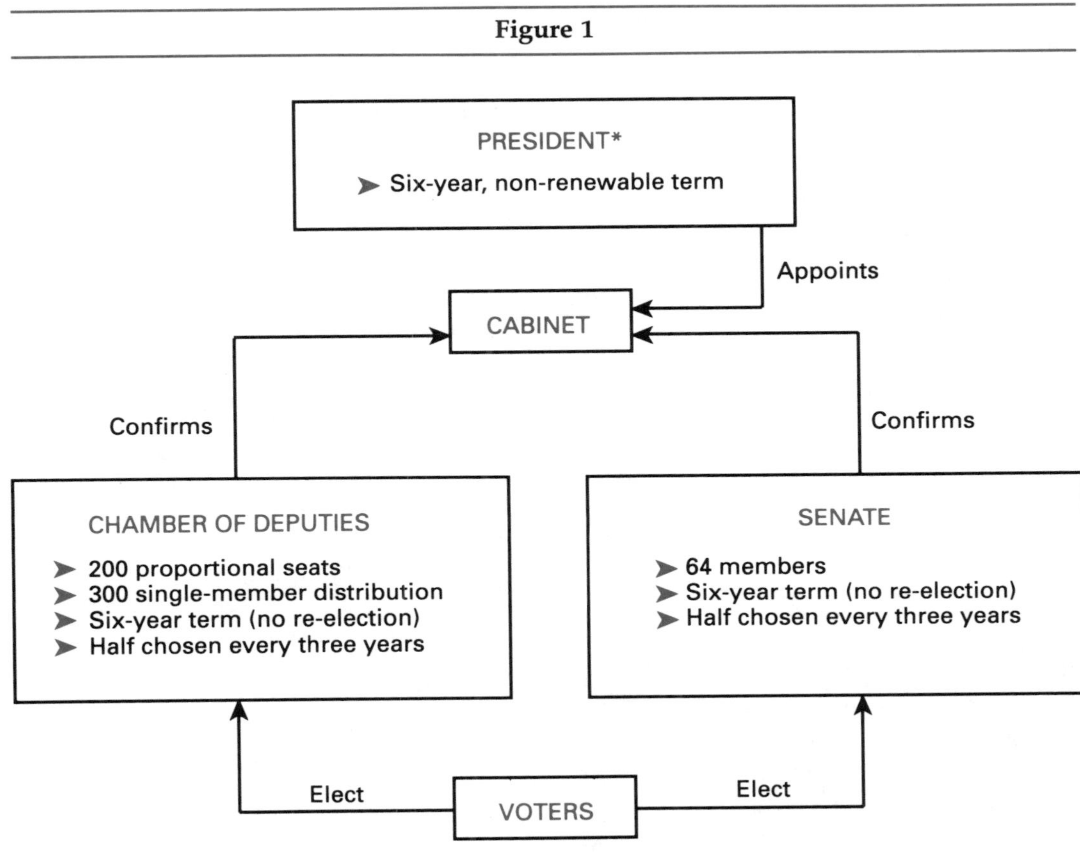

* As in the United States, the President of Mexico is the head of the party.

multi-party presidential democracy. The P.R.I. became the core around which this system operated. General Lázaro Cárdenas (1934–1940) paved the way for the P.R.I. by organizing Mexico's principal classes into the Mexican Revolutionary party (P.R.M.). This precursor of the P.R.I. was an alliance of most segments of the population, including labour, the peasantry, teachers' unions, government white-collar workers, professional associations, as well as private farmers and small-business people. For a few years, Cárdenas also included the armed forces as a separate interest group in the party, but his successors abolished this unpopular arrangement a few years later. The P.R.M.'s organization encompassed the vast majority of Mexico's population and excluded only a small minority consisting of large landowners, industrialists, and the Roman Catholic hierarchy.

Political observers have regarded the Mexican semi-democratic presidential system as a success. Mexico does not allow presidents to be re-elected. This permits a degree of flexibility that has enabled the system to respond to the popular will every six years. Incoming presidents immediately attempt to defuse tensions and dissatisfactions accumulated under their predecessors' rule by making concessions to the groups most dissatisfied with their predecessors' policies.

In practice, this system of ever-changing leadership has functioned well. Manuel Avila Camacho (1940–1946), the founder of P.R.I., pursued a moderate policy. He reduced the political role of the army, and, although he slowed the pace of land reforms and ceased nationalizing large industries, he also began a limited social security system for workers. He made peace with the Catholic Church and fostered good relations with the United States, which made it possible for Mexico's excess labour to enter the U.S.A. The re-organization of the P.R.M. into the P.R.I. was merely a streamlining and modernization operation. Its smooth functioning proved to the outside world that Mexico had become a mature, responsible, and stable democracy that was worthy of investments by the international banking and industrial community.

One important sign of the maturity of the Mexican political system was the fact that Camacho was the last army general to serve as Mexico's president. Since 1946, civilian presidents have governed Mexico without fear of army intervention. They have supported a centrist (neither socialist nor excessively capitalist) economic system and favoured peaceful coexistence with the Roman Catholic Church and the United States.

Mexican President Carlos Salinas de Gortari
Press Office, Embassy of Mexico, Washington, D.C.

▶ HOW THE P.R.I. MANAGES THE POLITICAL PROCESS

The P.R.I. dominates Mexico's political system, while maintaining openness and apparent democratic procedure. The party has attempted to highlight opposition groups' weaknesses and foibles. A few decades ago, the opposition party to the right, the National Action party (P.A.N.), frequently threatened violence to achieve its aims, and hence enjoyed little voter confidence. In the 1970s, the party renounced violence and began attracting voters. By 1988, it became the largest single opposition party in Mexico. The P.R.I. deliberately exaggerated the importance of the P.A.N. by associating it with the forces that had opposed the Mexican Revolution. Indirectly, the P.R.I. thus advertised itself as the defender of the Revolution. By reminding the public of the possibility of right-wing violence, the government succeeded in undermining the P.A.N.

The P.R.I. used moderation with small leftist opposition parties. As long as these groups did not publicly condemn government policies, they would receive financial support from the P.R.I., and their members would be left in peace. This is how the P.R.I. assured itself of having a loyal opposition and of minimizing vocal dissenters.

Eventually these political ploys became "legalized." At first, the P.R.I. influenced selected opposition candidates by offering them seats in the Chamber of Deputies that were actually won by P.R.I. candidates. President López Mateos (1958–1964) later put this system on a constitutional basis. He introduced a proportional representation system similar to Sweden's. This virtually guaranteed the smaller parties a share in the Chamber of Deputies on the basis of their total percentage of the national vote. Presidents José López Portillo (1976–1982) and Miguel de la Madrid (1982–1988) further refined this provision, so that 200 of the 500 seats in the Chamber of Deputies would always be awarded on a proportional basis to parties other than the P.R.I. Should the P.R.I. ever win fewer than 260 of the remaining 300 seats during an election, then it would be entitled to share in the proportional seats. Whatever the outcome of a federal election, the P.R.I. could never have fewer than 260 deputies in the Chamber of Deputies. This gives the P.R.I. permanent control of the Chamber, and the party is always able to choose the president.

According to political scientist Martin C. Needler, the P.R.I. has been successful because it is attuned to the sentiments of the Mexican electorate. University students are some of its most enthusiastic supporters. The government makes certain that graduates are given preferential treatment in hiring practices and offered leadership positions in the party. By controlling most of the news and commentary that appears on television, radio, and in the daily press, the government is able to influence the masses. In general, the government caters to the financial and economic demands of most of Mexico's occupation groups. The government generally treats even hard-core opponents gently and avoids the use of police brutality and harassment. As a last resort, political offenders may be subjected to highly publicized legal proceedings to set an example.

The P.R.I. has numerous political advantages. By competing in elections, the minor parties in effect signify their support and affirm that the political system is legitimate and just. Under this system, the P.R.I. enjoys the best of two possible worlds. In many single-party police states or dictatorial regimes, the ruling party is always forced to minimize opposition. It dominates a resentful population by brute force. Under the Mexican form of government, the P.R.I. is certain to retain political power. Therefore, it can allow its opposition representation and not resort to oppressive tactics.

▶ THE MEXICAN PRESIDENT—CHIEF EXECUTIVE

The P.R.I. is able to remain strong and prestigious because its candidates always win the presidency. In Mexico, the president is the chief political figure, the prime mover, and inspirer of all government activities. As the leader of the governing party, the president appoints personnel to chief government positions, plans political strategy, and sets the moral tone of the administration. The disciplined political machinery of the P.R.I. responds to the wishes of the president, and P.R.I. members of the two legislative bodies seldom fail to support the president.

The power of the Mexican president is all-encompassing. The president appoints cabinet members; supervises their activities and those of their respective ministries; controls the choice of party nominations for

Former Mexican President General Avila Camacho, pictured at his desk in the Capitol Building.
The Bettmann Archive

the Senate, Chamber of Deputies, and state governors; supervises the work of the legislature; and issues decrees. Occasionally, presidents have proclaimed laws that proved unconstitutional. President López Portillo (1976–1982) nationalized the banks by decree, an action that was challenged by the Supreme Court. The bill had to be legalized by a prepared legislative measure passed by the two legislatures.

The Mexican government has the appearance of a democracy in many respects. The people cast their ballots for senators and deputies selected by the president. The president is pre-selected by the incumbent president about one year prior to the end of the term in office. As a public relations strategy, the P.R.I. releases the names of several pre-candidates and invites the public and the press to critique them. It would appear, however, that the party, following the president's wishes, has already decided who the candidate will be. Still, the party holds a convention, which confirms the choice already made by the president and the P.R.I. leadership.

The election of the P.R.I.'s presidential candidate is virtually assured in Mexico, even though the individual must win the majority of the votes. In the 1988 presidential election, Carlos Salinas de Gortari had trouble gaining a majority. At the time, the government's position was precarious. The economy was faltering, and an important P.R.I. politician, C. Cárdenas, defected and ran as an independent backed by three small parties, which had hitherto always supported the P.R.I. The people gave Salinas 50.36 percent of the vote. Some political observers suspected that the P.R.I. had "adjusted" the count to prevent a run-off election for its candidate. None of the opposition parties seriously challenged the outcome.

▶ HOW DEMOCRATIC IS MEXICAN "DEMOCRACY"?

The Mexican political system serves as a good example of a dictatorship with many of the characteristics of a **republican democracy** responsive to all sectors of the country. The P.R.I. publicizes itself as the defender of Mexico's "little people" and brands opponents of the regime as the enemies of the popular Revolution of 1910–1917. The government has yet to overcome the types of problems that attend all rapidly changing societies. The Mexican cities are over-populated, the population is underemployed, and many urban dwellers live in unhygienic shanty towns. But the Mexicans are a peaceful people, and they appreciate their government's determination to avoid all appearances of intimidation and violence directed against enemies of the regime.

Mexico's political system is living proof that every rule must have an exception. Technically, Mexico belongs among the world's democratic multi-party states. In fact, however, Mexico's multi-party system is always controlled by a single party, the P.R.I. One might argue that since Mexicans are willing participants in this system of government, democracy is alive and well in Mexico. The counter-argument might be, however, that anyone who refuses to co-operate with the P.R.I. faces an uncertain political future in Mexico. Joining the P.R.I. is the only alternative a Mexican has of becoming a member of the country's ruling elite. Co-operating with the P.R.I. makes it possible for an opposition member to at least participate in the political proc-

Table 1
MEMBERSHIP OF THE CHAMBER OF DEPUTIES 1988–1991

Party	Seats won in single-member districts	Seats won by proportional representation	Total
P.R.I.	235	26	261
P.A.N.	38	64	102
P.P.S.	4	32	36
P.A.R.M.	7	25	32
P.F.C.R.N.	5	26	31
P.R.D.	9	17	26
Independent Group	2	10	12
Total	300	200	500

▸ Note: P.R.I. — Institutional Revolutionary Party; P.A.N. — National Action Party; P.P.S. — Popular Socialist Party; P.A.R.M. — Authentic Party of the Mexican Revolution; P.F.C.R.N. — Party of the Cardenista Front for National Reconstruction; P.R.D. — Party of the Democratic Revolution.

▸ Source: Press Office, Embassy of Mexico, Washington, D.C.

Defying the P.R.I. publicly means permanent exile to the political wilderness.

Since the P.R.I. dominates the Chamber of Deputies and is the only party able to elect a president, the word "democracy" has no conventional meaning in Mexico, except for members of the P.R.I. and their supporters. According to our definition of the term "democracy," a country's dissenters must be able to participate in the political process, even if their involvement results in the overthrow of the ruling party's domination of the country's political system.

APPLYING YOUR KNOWLEDGE

1. Construct charts to illustrate the differences and similarities among the political systems of Mexico, the United States, Canada, Sweden, and France.
2. Debate the advantages of a non-renewable, six-year presidential system.
3. Would you describe Mexico as a democracy? Explain your answer.
4. Why did the P.R.I. adopt proportional representation, even though this system helped the opposition parties? (See Table 1.)
5. Debate the advantages and disadvantages of Mexico's proportional representation system.
6. If you were a large landowner in Mexico, how would you go about ensuring that your economic interests were being safeguarded?
7. How do you think the average Canadian would respond to living under Mexico's political system?
8. Stage a debate between a P.R.I. spokesperson and members of the large landowning groups who are dissatisfied with the government's relationship with other interest groups.
9. Devise your own legislative system for Mexico that would represent all factions and interest groups.
10. Arrange a make-believe peace conference among all of Mexico's dissident groups and the P.R.I. Try to reach some sort of compromise that would accommodate everyone's needs.

Case Study 5 Overview

The Role of Political Parties in a Democracy

This case study examines the extent to which Canadian political parties are accountable to the people for their actions. The origins of Canadian political parties are examined, as is the growing power and dominance of the party over individual members of Parliament. The case study then discusses the strengths and weaknesses of one-party, two-party, and multi-party systems and evaluates which method provides the greatest degree of accountability to the electorate. The role of the party caucus is also evaluated. The case study concludes with an analysis of the functions, strengths, and weaknesses of the Canadian political party system.

▶ OBJECTIVES

After reading this case study, you should be able to:

- ▶ debate the ideal number of political parties
- ▶ discuss the strengths and weaknesses of the Canadian party system
- ▶ outline the functions of political parties
- ▶ evaluate the extent to which Canadian political parties are accountable to the people for their actions
- ▶ explain the origins of parties in Canada
- ▶ role-play a typical election campaign
- ▶ write a reasoned, well-researched essay on an aspect of Canadian political parties

▶ KEY TERMS

political parties
one-party system
two-party system
multi-party system
caucus
party loyalty
party discipline

Case Study

5 The Role of Political Parties in a Democracy

Earlier we defined democracy as a political system in which there is a free and open competition for power among various individuals and groups, with a significant degree of accountability to the people by those who hold formal positions of power. This case study examines the extent to which Canadian **political parties** are accountable to the people for their actions.

▶ DEFINITION AND ORIGIN

A political party is a group of people who have joined together to accomplish specific goals. In order to achieve these goals, the party attempts to elect sufficient members to public office to gain control of the government.

Although it is difficult for us to imagine democratic politics without organized political parties, they are essentially a modern phenomenon. Parties existed in Great Britain as early as the eighteenth century, but organized political parties were not fully established in England until the early nineteenth century. The first Canadian political parties began to emerge in central Canada in the 1820s and 1830s, but since the governor and his appointed councils were the real decision-makers in the British North American colonies, organized political parties did not emerge until after responsible government was granted in the 1840s.

Responsible government basically meant that the governor would have to sign the bills passed by the executive council,[1] which was now controlled by the elected representatives of the people. Political parties emerged to ensure that the executive council would do what members of the party wanted it to do. However, party ties

▸ [1]Members of the executive council played much the same role in government as cabinet ministers do today.

remained loose for another half-century. The secret ballot was not adopted until 1874 and simultaneous balloting was not completely established until 1908. With open balloting and non-simultaneous elections, candidates did not need to commit themselves to a party until it became evident who would win. Before the western provinces went to the polls, for example, they usually knew which party would win the election. To assure themselves of some influence in the government, they often voted for this party.

Until the beginning of the twentieth century, candidates often knew all the voters personally, and because the population was small, they could canvass the people without outside help. As a result, they had less need for the support of a party. All this was changed with the extension of the franchise to women and the poor in the early twentieth century.

At Confederation, each MP represented approximately 750 voters; 120 years later, the average MP represented 86 000 citizens. Candidates can no longer canvass more than a small proportion of the people, yet the votes of these citizens are necessary for victory. The obvious solution is to rely upon a party to supply scores of tireless workers, campaign literature, and media coverage.

Another reason for the growing reliance on political parties has been the rise in campaign costs. In the 1988 general election, for example, the average Conservative, Liberal, and N.D.P. candidate spent over $32 000 in campaign expenses. One unsuccessful candidate in Ontario spent $64 000. Of course, these figures pale in comparison with the cost of political contests in the United States. It is not unusual for an individual running for a seat in the American Senate to spend millions of dollars. None-

Table 1
TELLING STATISTICS, 1988

	Canada	United States
Percentage of incumbent federal legislators who were re-elected in the last campaign	72.5	97.9
Average cost of individual election campaigns for federal legislators	$29 512	Senate: $2 million House: $267 966
Maximum amount that could be spent by a candidate in the last federal election campaign	Ceiling varies per riding (in 1988, highest was York North, Ont., at $65 258)	No limit (limit ruled unconstitutional by the U.S. Supreme Court in 1976)
Basic salary of an elected federal legislator	$62 100	$89 500 (U.S.)
Maximum allowable honorariums, fees, and other employment	No limit	House of Representatives: a maximum of 30 percent of salary may be earned from other sources, including outside employment Senate: a maximum of 40 percent of salary, but not permitted to earn income through outside employment

▸ Source: *Maclean's*, July 3, 1989, pp. 59–60. Reprinted by permission from *Maclean's*.

Which system most favours the wealthy candidate? Explain.

theless, and despite laws in this country designed to reduce the amount of money each candidate may spend on election campaigns, the costs of becoming an MP are still beyond the limits of most Canadians. It is the modern political party with its national organization and tireless fundraisers that provides the money needed to get elected. With this kind of potential power, how is the political party accountable to the people?

▶ One-Party Versus Two-Party Versus Multi-Party Systems

What is the ideal number of political parties needed to ensure the largest degree of accountability to the people? The three basic types of party systems are one-party (see Case Study 4 on Mexico), two-party (as in the United States), and multi-party (as in Italy). A possible fourth type of party system is a combination of two strong parties with one or more weaker, yet still significant, parties (as in Canada).[2]

On the surface, it appears that a **one-party system** is incompatible with democracy because it doesn't present the electorate with a real choice between candidates or policies. However, such a system can perhaps be called democratic if no one is excluded from membership, if everyone is permitted to express an opinion within the party, and if members are free to organize themselves within the party to push for particular policies.

The supporters of the **two-party system** claim that it is superior to other systems because it presents voters with a definite, clear-cut alternative that allows them to evaluate how well the party of their choice did in carrying out its promises. The counter-argument, however, is that the two-party system reduces the alternatives presented to the voters. In addition, the two parties also tend to become alike on important matters of policy. Let us use the issue of capital punishment (the death sentence) as an example. Assume that public opinion is evenly divided between those who support capital punishment and those who oppose it. If one party moderately favours capital punishment (point A in the first diagram), the other party merely has to position itself at point B in order to attract enough support to win power. Assuming that the first party is willing to modify its beliefs in order to gain power, it would now have to move to point C in order to win. Ultimately, the drive to find the middle ground will reduce the differences between the two parties.

Opinions on Capital Punishment

Oppose C B A **Support**

Supporters of the two-party system claim that this argument is based upon the erroneous assumptions that both parties will do anything to win and that they have no firm, unshakable beliefs of their own. Furthermore, they maintain, any party that constantly changes its opinions would soon lose the confidence of the electorate.

The same pressures towards conformity do not operate in a **multi-party system**. As the following diagram illustrates, a move to the right or the left by any party might result in a loss of part of its original support to the party it moves away from. For example, if party C moves to point X, it might steal some of party B's support, but it also runs the risk of losing followers to party D.

Opinions on Capital Punishment

Oppose A B X C D E **Support**

[2] The following discussion has been abridged and adapted from Jack Lively, *Democracy*, Oxford: Basil Blackwell, 1975, pp. 44–49.

In a multi-party system, therefore, the parties maintain their distinctiveness, which allows them to present the electorate with a clear choice of policy alternatives.

The disadvantage of multi-parties is that one party seldom wins a majority and the government usually consists of a coalition of two or more parties. This makes it less easy for the voters to know which party is responsible for the government's actions. Even if a party is part of the ruling coalition, it can deny responsibility for individual governmental policies. Coalition government may force the parties either to compromise their principles or to withdraw their support, thus causing a series of unstable governments.

A hybrid of the two-party and multiparty system is the existence of significant third parties within the two-party system. Third parties arise because one segment of the electorate believes that neither of the two parties is concerned with its special needs. Certainly, it seems virtually impossible for two political parties continuously to satisfy the varied demands and interests of modern countries, which are often separated by geographic boundaries, language, religion, ethnicity, and conflicting economic interests. In Canada, the N.D.P. has been the most prominent third party. From the 1930s until the late 1970s, the Social Credit party also held a number of seats in Parliament.

Although third parties strive to win, it has been argued that their significance in the past has been primarily to keep the other two parties on their toes. They help to bring fresh ideas into politics, and if these ideas prove popular, they are usually adopted by the older parties, such as the adoption of the C.C.F.'s social welfare policies in Canada after World War II. New parties also allow neglected and frustrated people to vent their grievances and bring their demands to the attention of the country. Finally, by stirring up popular interest, third parties tend to bring democracy closer to more of the people.

▶ THE CAUCUS

Once elected, representatives are expected to look after the interests of their constituencies; this includes voting on proposed legislation and discussing policies in the party **caucus**. In parliamentary democracies such as the United Kingdom and Canada, the House of Commons is considered the major democratic agency in the government because it has final say on all laws and can force the executive to resign. It is in this body that the country's different ethnic groups, occupations, and classes are represented. ''No Cabinet which keeps in constant touch with this body,'' argues R.M. Dawson in *The Government of Canada*, ''can be very far removed from fluctuations in public opinion, for the House is always acting as an interpreter . . . conversely, a Cabinet which grows out of touch with the Commons is courting disaster.''

Within the governing political party, the caucus provides another forum for individual members of Parliament to exert their influence. At these meetings, the party discusses general policies and strategy, and the cabinet submits its proposed legislation for general approval. The meetings are private and the members are expected to express their views without restraint. It is at this time that they are able to modify government policies to reflect the interests of their constituencies. As Canadian Prime Minister W.L. Mackenzie King told the House of Commons in 1923:

> *[The caucus] is the means whereby a Government can ascertain through its following what the views and opinions of the public as represented by their various constituencies may be. It is not a means of over-riding Parliament. It is a means of discovering the will of the people through their representatives. . . . After all, what a Government has*

to keep before it, if it is to be worthy of the name of a Government, is, first of all, the support it will receive in the country for the measures it introduces; secondly, the support it will receive in Parliament. . . . [The caucus] is simply coming into closer consultation with the people's representatives in a manner that permits of the greatest freedom of expression on their part.

Lester Pearson (prime minister from 1963 to 1968) also believed that the caucus performed an important role in the governing process:

MR. PEARSON: I used to take caucus meetings very seriously and I was always available to members of the caucus for discussion. I never missed a caucus meeting if it was possible to be there. Not all of my predecessors or all my colleagues felt that way.

MR. HOCKIN: Did you ever chair caucus as Prime Minister?

MR. PEARSON: No, a private member is chairman of the caucus, but I was always there and I used to subject myself—as my colleagues did—to every kind of examination. I used to encourage the frankest kind of questioning, however critical.[3]

In return for this opportunity to express their feelings, the elected party members agree to accept the decisions of the caucus as final and to support these government measures when they come before the House of Commons for approval.

▶ THE STRENGTHS OF POLITICAL PARTIES IN CANADA

Political parties, state their defenders, fulfill a variety of important functions in a democracy. Firstly, they provide a degree of popular control over the government. Political parties provide a channel of communication between the people and the government. In order to compete for the electorate's support, each party must attempt to discover what the people want, and then try to satisfy these wishes when elected. By offering candidates for re-election, the party provides the people with a way of expressing their opinions and of holding the governing party accountable for its actions.

Secondly, they recruit and train political leaders. Parties interest people in politics, persuade them to accept minor political offices, choose candidates to run for elections, and provide them with financial and organizational support.

Political parties organize and educate the public and provide alternate choices for the electorate. In their attempts to win elections, political parties propose a series of social, economic, and political policies (the party platform) designed to gain broad support. The election campaign then attempts to mobilize citizens to vote for these platforms. Between elections, parties keep the electorate informed about government actions — either to gain support for them, or to convince the people not to vote for the government at the next election. Parties not in power thus provide a useful check on government actions.

Successful political parties limit conflict and help to unify the country. In order to achieve power in a country such as Canada, a political party must obtain substantial support from a population that is divided by ethnicity, religion, income levels, values, and regional differences. Faced with divisions, a party must be flexible; it must avoid issues that divide the country and soften those that do exist. It is no mere coincidence that the two Canadian party leaders with the longest terms in office — John A. Macdonald and W.L. Mackenzie King— were always willing and able to make concessions, to postpone contentious deci-

▸ [3]Thomas A. Hockin (ed.), *Apex of Power*, Toronto: Prentice-Hall, 1977, pp. 257–258.

In addition to promoting national unity, political leaders must maintain the support of their own parties. This cartoon indicates that although Joe Clark, former leader of the Progressive Conservative party, was leading in the public opinion polls in 1981, some members of his party were trying to replace him. Since 1896, the Liberal party governed Canada for sixty-five years and the Conservative party for twenty-six years. Find out how many leaders each party has had during this period, and draw your own conclusions.
Blaine/The Hamilton Spectator

sions, and to bring people of divergent beliefs together.

Finally, parties provide a method for changing leaders peacefully, and create a forum for dissent. Dissatisfied citizens can attempt to change the direction of government by organizing their own political parties.

▶ THE WEAKNESSES OF POLITICAL PARTIES IN CANADA

The most sweeping criticism of Canadian political parties concerns their relationship with elected representatives. The first loyalty of the representatives, critics charge, is to the party rather than to the people who elected them. In other words, political parties make government less accountable to the people.

This has arisen, critics argue, because of the rapid growth in the size of the electorate. Because the average MP now represents nearly 90 000 citizens and requires tens of thousands of dollars to get elected, he or she must rely on a party organization to provide the canvassing and money necessary to run a successful campaign. This has tended to increase party control over candidates who run for political office. A survey of first-term MPs revealed that the

Figure 1
PARLIAMENTARY PAYOUTS

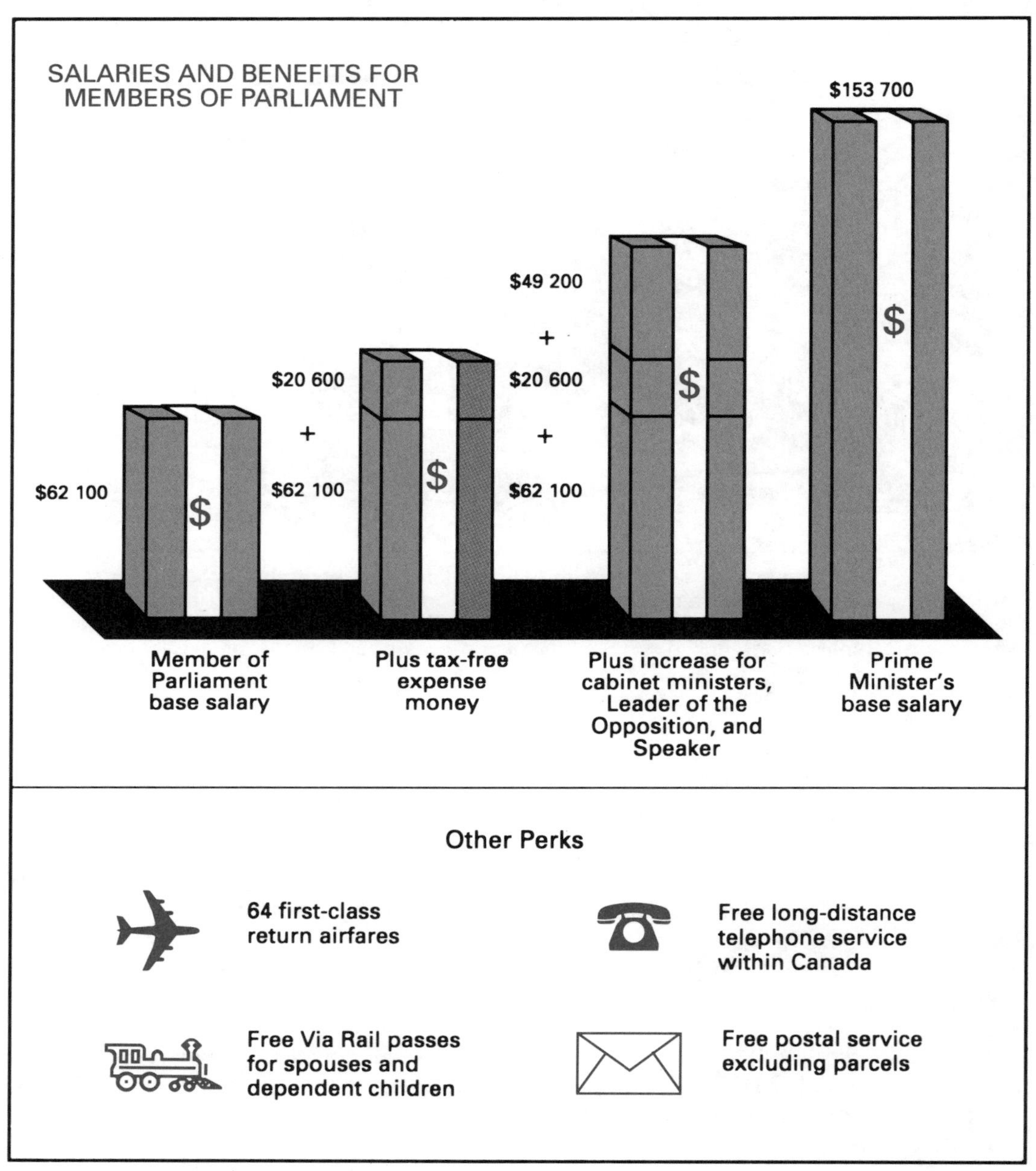

Source: Adapted from Canapress/Sylvie Caron.

Do you think that Canadian MPs receive too much money? Explain.

vast majority of them believed they would not have been elected had they run as independents. The decision to allow a party to place its name on the ballot opposite its candidate's name has further diminished the chances of independent candidates.

As a result, individual MPs have become increasingly more dependent upon the party and its leader. After an election, say the critics, **party loyalty** becomes a prime political virtue for successful candidates. All members are expected to support their leader, whether or not they agree with the party's policies. Canadian MPs almost never vote against their own party, lest they run the risk of being expelled from the party caucus. Occasionally, on issues such as capital punishment and abortion, party discipline is relaxed so that MPs may vote according to their conscience.

Party members have a natural tendency and willingness to accept the control of their leader, whom they selected at a party convention. Sometimes, it is said, the only glue holding a party together is its allegiance to the leader. The media has also increasingly concentrated its attention on party leaders, and in many cases, individual members owe their victory directly to their leader's popularity. This serves to reduce members' independence. In addition, a prime minister has at least one hundred important positions, such as cabinet posts, to distribute among the party faithful. An MP who votes contrary to party instructions will have little hope of political advancement. As a last resort, the prime minister can call a new election and withdraw the party's support from a recalcitrant member.

According to some critics, the belief that the people's representatives have ultimate control over government legislation is a myth. Laws, they argue, are decided upon by the cabinet and then passed seemingly without question by a government majority in the House of Commons. The only substantial criticism comes from opposition parties, and they generally have too few members to prevent a bill from passing. The House of Commons merely refines the legislation; it polishes but does not control policy.

Critics also charge that the caucus, which is traditionally depicted as an agency in which individual members can propose and influence government legislation, has become merely a place for the cabinet to inform backbenchers of what it is planning to do. The influence MPs might have on policy decisions varies according to their

Margaret Thatcher, prime minister of Great Britain in the 1980s. Why has there never been a female prime minister of Canada?
Canapress Photo Service

prestige and knowledge. But because almost one-half of the members habitually lose their bid for re-election, and since first-year representatives often lack the time and the expertise to effectively critique legislation drawn up by cabinet ministers (who have whole departments of experts to advise them), the people's representatives usually have little control over public policies.

In some democracies, representatives are less restricted by party discipline than are Canadian MPs. American politicians usually owe their first loyalty to their constituency rather than the party. While the citizen may be better represented by such a system, this lack of **party discipline** also slows the pace at which legislation is passed and implemented. In the United States, there are few restrictions on how much money a candidate may spend during an election campaign. Politicians may even use their own money. This reduces the control that American parties have over their candidates, and encourages only the extremely wealthy to participate in politics.

APPLYING YOUR KNOWLEDGE

1. How well does the Canadian party system work in practice?
   a) Draw up separate lists of its advantages and disadvantages.
   b) Upon what criteria or values is each list based?
   c) What is your opinion? Explain your answer.
2. Explain the following statement: "The two-party system is likely to work best when there are more than two parties."
3. The revised version of the 1982 Elections Expenses Act
   - limited each candidate to spending no more than one dollar for each of the first 15 000 voters in the constituency, fifty cents for each of the next 10 000 voters, and twenty-five cents for the remaining voters;
   - allowed candidates in sparsely populated constituencies an additional fifteen cents per kilometre travelling money;
   - allowed campaign spending limits to increase with inflation;
   - limited the national party organizations to thirty cents for each voter, with adjustments made for inflation;
   - designated part of each candidate's travelling and postage expenses to be paid for through taxes;
   - stipulated that the names of all donors who contributed more than one hundred dollars be made public.

   Critics of this act argue that it is not fair to taxpayers and donors, nor is it equally fair to all of the parties.
   a) What are the grounds to support each criticism?
   b) What is your opinion of this bill?
4. Discuss the following quotation:
   "The evils in the party system are not peculiar to it but are the outcome of general human frailties. Indeed, it is hard to see how the parties that must woo the electorate with success can do other than reflect its virtues and its vices. Perhaps it is people as much as institutions that need to be reformed."
5. What is the ideal number of political parties needed to ensure accountability? Give reasons for your choice.

6. Explain how the inclusion of a party's name beside its candidate's name on the ballot might reduce an independent candidate's possibility of winning.
7. Using the diagram ''Opinions on Capital Punishment'' as a guide, devise a hypothetical distribution of opinion that would prevent the parties in a two-party system from offering almost identical policies.
8. Would you like to see Canadian MPs given more freedom to vote against their parties? Why?

FURTHER RESEARCH

1. Write a short fictional story that describes what changes might take place in elections if political parties were banned.
2. Choosing either the Liberal or the Conservative party, prepare a short report on its origins. Include an explanation of how, if at all, its general ideology differs from that of the other major party. Use the inquiry techniques outlined in Chapter 1 to assist you in preparing this report.
3. Select one of the following third parties and write an essay explaining why it arose and the extent of its success.
   a) Social Credit in Alberta in 1935
   b) The C.C.F. in Saskatchewan in 1944
   c) The New Democratic Party
   d) The Progressive Party in 1921.
4. Invite a federal or provincial member of the government to speak to the class about party organization, campaigning, and the role of the individual representative in the government.
5. Prepare for a class debate on one of the following statements:
   a) ''It doesn't matter which of the two major parties I vote for, they're both the same.''
   b) ''There's no point in voting for one of the third parties because they don't have a chance of winning.''
   c) ''A multi-party system is preferable to the two-party system.''
   d) ''The Canadian party system is as democratic as possible, given the frailties of human beings.''
6. Role-play an election campaign or a government caucus meeting on the issue of the death penalty.

Case Study 6 Overview

Voting Behaviour: Rational or Irrational?

How well does the theory of democracy work in practice? Elections, considered the life blood of democracy, are based upon the assumption that people vote on the basis of rational decision-making. This case study employs statistical analysis to determine how important such variables as occupation, social class, ethnicity, religion, and regionalism are in predicting how people will vote. It then examines the importance of the media and public opinion polls in influencing the electorate and evaluates their benefits and disadvantages. The case study concludes with a discussion of the importance of elections and the need for citizen participation in the democratic process.

▶ OBJECTIVES

After reading this case study, you should be able to:

- ▶ analyse and evaluate election statistics
- ▶ design, administer, and analyse your own survey
- ▶ decide whether the average voter casts his or her ballot for "rational" reasons
- ▶ discuss the importance of the media and public opinion polls in influencing the electorate
- ▶ appreciate the need for active citizen involvement in the democratic process
- ▶ conduct research using newspapers and other media

▶ KEY TERMS

electorate	bias	electoral process
ethnic orgin	pollsters	political apathy
opinion poll		

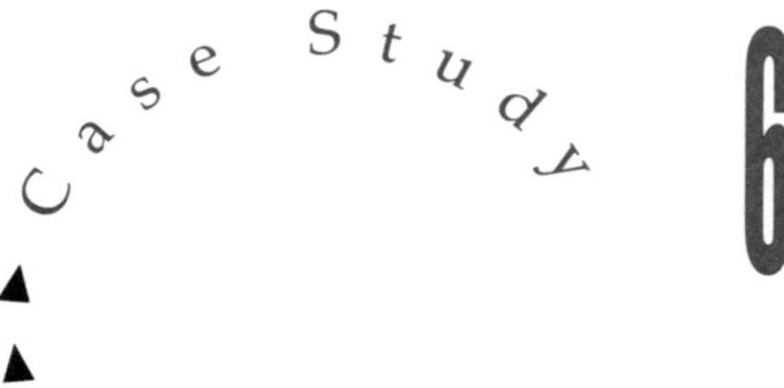

6 Voting Behaviour: Rational or Irrational?

The word democracy means "rule by the people." The fundamental belief of democracy is that ultimate political power is vested in the people as a whole. Although elections are not the only methods of discovering citizens' desires — referendums and public meetings are two alternatives— they are the most visible and important. In fact, elections are generally considered the lifeblood of democracy.

Prior to an election, competing political parties decide upon their policies and nominate candidates to run in the contest. In casting ballots, the **electorate** decides not only which people (or party) it wants to direct the government but also what policies it wants the new government to implement. The victorious party is thus assumed to have a mandate to carry out its platform. Elected representatives know that if their actions while in power do not please the majority, they will not be re-elected; thus they are loath to pass unpopular measures and will attempt to implement their election promises. This power to reward and punish decision-makers is the guarantee that ultimate political power rests in the hands of the people.

This is the theory of democracy. How well does it work in practice? If the government is to carry out the wishes of the people, it must first discover these wishes. That is one of the purposes of holding periodic elections. For the electoral process to work effectively, voters must be well informed about the platform of each party and know what it has done since the preceding election.

One of the assumptions underlying the importance of elections is that the average voter is "rational." This implies that voters understand the major campaign issues; are aware of the relationship of the issues to themselves; know each candidate's stand on these issues; and finally, vote for that candidate or party which comes closest to their own beliefs.

In the last several decades, political scientists in Canada, France, Great Britain, and the United States have employed election statistics, questionnaires, and sample surveys to determine why people vote as they do. In many cases their results have been startling. Rather than presenting their conclusions (which are still being debated), we will let you analyse the data and reach your own conclusions. The major issue in this case study is whether or not average Canadians are rational in their voting behaviour. A supplementary question for you to keep in mind is the extent to which a rational and informed electorate is necessary to maintain democracy.

▶ POLITICAL CHOICE: A STATISTICAL APPROACH

If you could vote in the next election, which party would you support? Why? You can probably think of several reasons — you admire the ideas or personality of the candidate in your riding, you prefer the candidate's party or the party leader, you agree with what the party did in the House of Commons, or you think that you will personally benefit if the party wins the election. These are all valid reasons. They also imply that you make rational decisions based upon the available evidence.

Can you remember when you first began to favour a political party? One study has shown that approximately one in three Canadians had formed a political attachment by the time they had reached grade 4, and nearly sixty percent had identified themselves with a political party by the time they entered grade 8. These students knew very little about politics and were generally unable to name the leaders of each political party, yet they had formed an attachment to a particular party.

Why do people support a particular party? The answer is not as simple as you may think. It involves a combination of many inputs, from what voters hear on television to their religion and occupation. Figure 1 illustrates some of these forces.

In recent years, some political scientists have argued that electoral behaviour is more closely related to the voter's social and economic position in society than to the election issues. Ethnicity, religion, occupation, place of residence, education, and social class, they argue, largely deter-

Figure 1

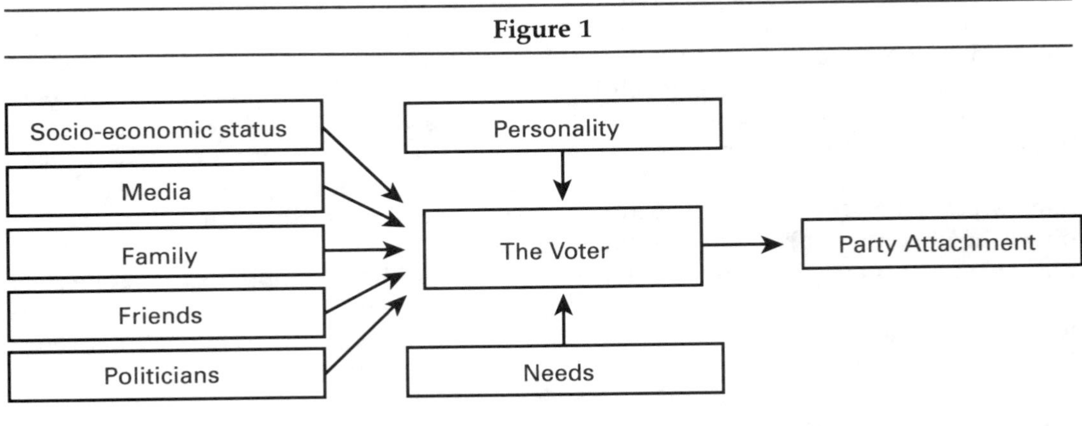

mine how people vote. Does this imply that voters do not base their electoral actions upon the available evidence and are irrational when it comes to casting their ballots?

To help answer this question, let us examine the federal elections of 1968 and 1974. Prior to each election, a cross-section of the electorate was interviewed, and each person's religion, **ethnic origin**, occupation, social class, and voting intention were recorded. Figures 2 to 5 compare these characteristics. Figures 2 and 3 examine ethnicity and religion as they relate to voting intentions.

In Great Britain, one of the most important determinants of voting behaviour is social class—most blue-collar workers support the Labour party, and the majority of white-collar workers vote for the Conservative party. There are several ways of determining a person's social class. Individuals may be categorized according to their occupation, education, and income—this is the usual method of determining social class because it is easy to use. Another method of classifying social class is to ask individuals to what class they think they belong. A poorly educated railway worker, for instance, might consider himself to be in the upper-middle class because he has a son who is a lawyer and a daughter who is studying to be a doctor. Figures 4 and 5 examine the relationship of occupation and social class to electoral behaviour in Canada.

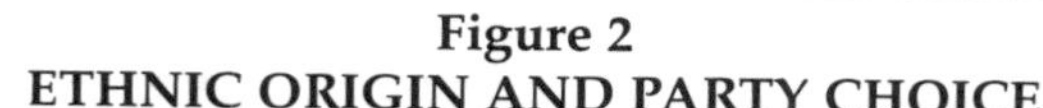
Figure 2
ETHNIC ORIGIN AND PARTY CHOICE

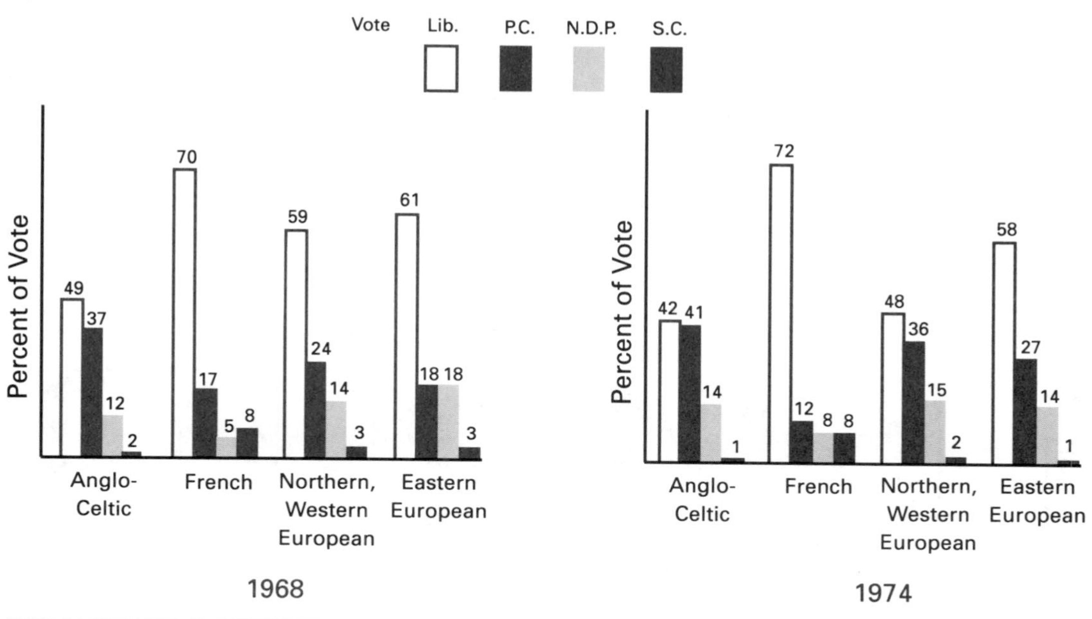

‣ Source: This graph and those shown in Figures 3, 4, and 5 are adapted from Harold D. Clark et al., *Political Choice in Canada*. Toronto: McGraw-Hill Ryerson Limited, 1979. Reprinted by permission of McGraw-Hill Ryerson Limited.

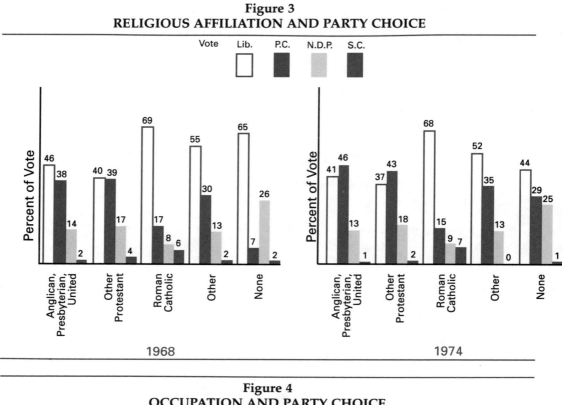

Figure 3
RELIGIOUS AFFILIATION AND PARTY CHOICE

Vote: Lib. | P.C. | N.D.P. | S.C.

Percent of Vote

1968

	Lib.	P.C.	N.D.P.	S.C.
Anglican, Presbyterian, United	46	38	14	2
Other Protestant	40	39	17	4
Roman Catholic	69	17	8	6
Other	55	30	13	2
None	65	7	26	2

1974

	Lib.	P.C.	N.D.P.	S.C.
Anglican, Presbyterian, United	41	46	13	1
Other Protestant	37	43	18	2
Roman Catholic	68	15	9	7
Other	52	35	13	0
None	44	29	25	1

Figure 4
OCCUPATION AND PARTY CHOICE

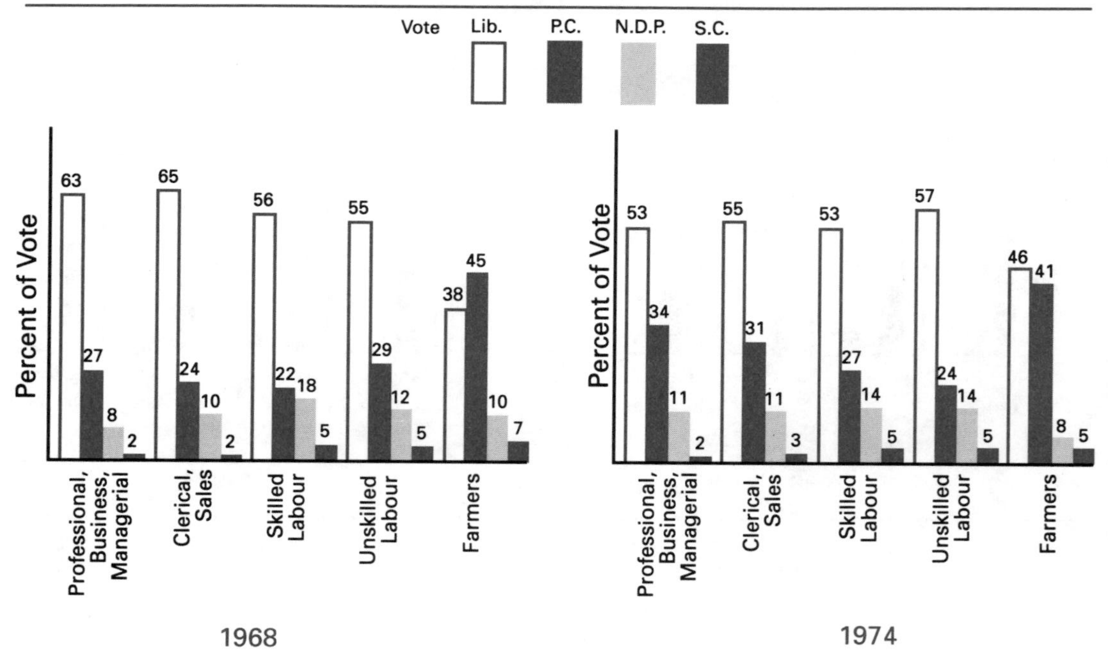

Figure 5
SELF-DECLARED SOCIAL CLASS AND PARTY CHOICE

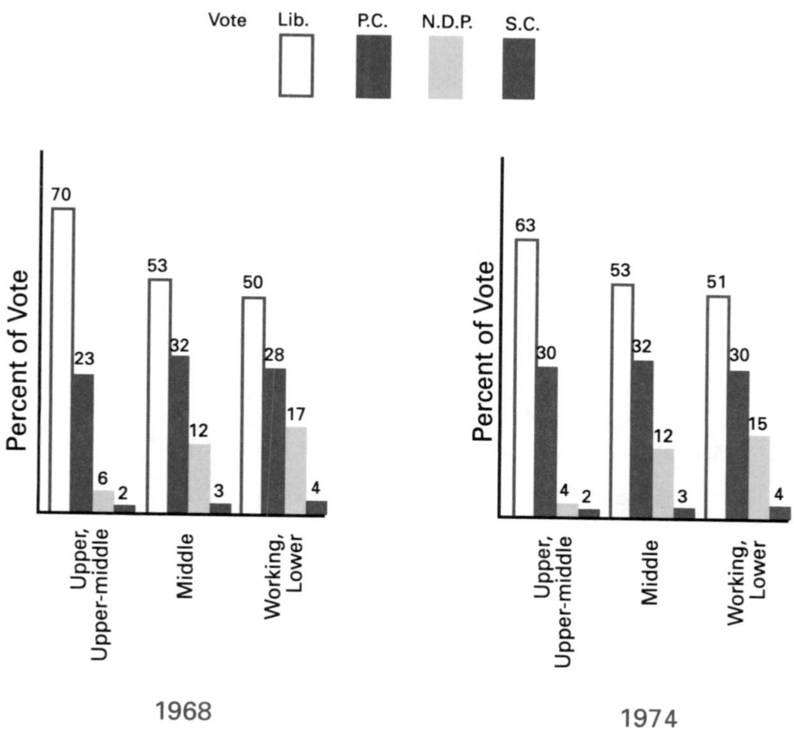

▶ Regionalism and Party Choice

In addition to being divided along ethnic and religious lines, Canada is also fragmented into separate geographical and political regions. The Atlantic provinces, which are divided from central Canada by the narrow Gaspé Peninsula, rely heavily upon natural resources (rather than manufacturing) and generally have a lower standard of living than central Canada. Quebec is separated from Ontario by religion, language, culture, and ethnic origin. Ontario is set off from the prairie provinces by its rocky terrain north of Lake Superior, its lack of petroleum, and its greater industrial development. British Columbia is isolated by the Rocky Mountains.

How important is this regionalism to Canadian electoral behaviour? Do French Canadians in Quebec vote as do French Canadians in the rest of Canada? Do British Columbians usually vote differently than Ontarians? Is the province in which people live a greater determinant of their voting behaviour than are their socio-economic characteristics? To help ascertain the answers to these questions, examine the results of an **opinion poll** conducted prior to the 1968 federal election, shown in Table 1. (The Social Credit party, which received support from only four percent of the sample, has been excluded.)

Table 1
VOTER PREFERENCE IN THE 1968 FEDERAL ELECTION (in percent)

Region	Total	Religion		Self-Declared Class			Origin		Occupation				
		Roman Catholic	Non-Catholic	Upper	Middle	Lower	British	French	Pro-fessional	Clerical	Skilled Labour	Unskilled Labour	Farmer
Atlantic Provinces													
Liberal	45	67	35	38	48	46	40	73	44	50	47	50	40
Conservative	54	32	63	63	49	52	59	23	56	50	51	50	60
N.D.P.	2	1	2	—	3	2	1	3	—	—	3	—	—
Quebec													
Liberal	68	66	86	68	72	62	83	65	76	78	68	56	49
Conservative	18	19	12	17	16	22	14	20	14	10	17	26	27
N.D.P.	5	5	2	12	4	4	2	5	7	6	4	6	—
Ontario													
Liberal	57	80	47	70	60	52	49	83	58	63	54	58	55
Conservative	28	7	36	27	29	24	34	7	33	26	22	23	38
N.D.P.	16	13	17	3	11	24	17	10	10	11	24	19	6
Prairie Provinces													
Liberal	44	57	41	82	44	41	43	76	59	52	50	44	21
Conservative	38	25	41	14	44	33	45	12	32	35	32	25	54
N.D.P.	15	13	16	5	10	23	11	4	9	12	16	25	19
British Columbia													
Liberal	58	76	55	75	62	45	51	38	69	68	50	48	71
Conservative	13	—	15	19	14	11	17	—	15	20	3	20	14
N.D.P.	18	16	18	—	14	30	20	50	8	8	29	24	—

▸ Source: Data from John Meisel, *Working Papers on Canadian Politics*, 2nd Enl. ed. Montreal: McGill-Queen's University Press, 1975, Table 2.

FOCUS

1. In 1972, the decennial census revealed that 45 percent of Canada's population was of Anglo-Celtic origin and 29 percent claimed French ancestry; 46 percent of the population was Roman Catholic and 40 percent Protestant; 48 percent had fewer than nine years of formal education and only 8 percent had attended university or college; 7 percent were farmers, 24 percent held professional or managerial positions, and 33 percent engaged in clerical occupations. Assuming that people voted as they said they would, use this data and Figures 2 to 5 to estimate the percentage of the popular vote likely to be received by each political party in either 1968 or 1974. For example, in 1968, 69 percent of Canada's Roman Catholic voters indicated they would vote Liberal. Since Catholics constituted 46 percent of the population, the Liberals received an estimated 69 percent of 46 percent—that is, 32 percent. When the same computations are carried out for each religion, the total projected Liberal vote will be known.
2. a) Using Figures 2 to 5, rank the Liberals' source of strength in 1968 in order from most to least important.
   b) What criteria did you use to determine which was the Liberals' most important source of strength? Did you use the data provided in question 1?
   c) Is it fair to term the Liberals a middle-of-the-road party—that is, a party that draws a large measure of support from almost every sector of society? Explain.
3. Among what sectors of the population did:
   a) the Conservatives gain support between 1968 and 1974?
   b) the N.D.P. lose support between 1968 and 1974?
4. Which of the socio-economic characteristics (religion, ethnic origin, or social class) that we have examined varies the most from party to party and from election to election? How might this be explained?
5. In the 1988 federal election, the Progressive Conservative party won most of the seats in the province of Quebec. How does the increased Conservative support in Quebec alter traditional patterns of party support among ethnic and religious groups?
6. Conduct your own survey to determine whether voting patterns have changed since 1974.
7. Examine opinion polls conducted prior to the most recent federal election. Compare the results to those in Table 1.
8. Use back issues of *Maclean's* and daily newspapers to analyse the election results in the most recent provincial or federal election.

▶ THE MEDIA AND THE ELECTORATE

The ability of the electorate to make a meaningful choice between party platforms hinges on its knowledge of contemporary politics. The voter receives information from such institutions as family, school, and interest groups, as well as through party activities and participation in the community. The media, however, plays an indispensable role in disseminating news about political events.

What role does the media play in the choices that voters make? Does the media act as an impartial observer of political events, or does it attempt to influence people's political views? In other words, are voters presented with enough impartial information to make an informed decision, or are their choices ill-informed because they are based on inadequate or biased information? Let us examine some evidence bearing on these questions.

Critics charge that the growing role of the media in election campaigns has accentuated public relations, physical appearance, and personality over party platforms and campaign issues. During the last fifty years, politicians have had to develop new techniques to keep pace with the invention of the radio in the 1920s, and television in the 1940s. In Canada, William Aberhart demonstrated the effectiveness of radio campaigning when he became premier of Alberta in 1935 — after entering politics only two years earlier. Twenty-two years later, John Diefenbaker effectively used television to capture the prime ministership of Canada. Other party leaders, such as Joe Clark and John Turner, were much less successful in using the media to their political advantage. Clark's chin and Turner's speaking quality often seemed to be the main focus of media attention.

The benefits and pitfalls of television campaigning are vividly portrayed in the following synopsis of the first televised leadership debate in North America:

In 1960, two candidates for the U.S. Presidency, John Kennedy and Richard Nixon, made history when they appeared face-to-face in live television debates. The election vote was extremely close (Kennedy eventually winning by 0.2 percent) and most observers agree that the televised debates made the difference. However, there are indications that Kennedy came out on top not so much because of what he said but because of how he ''performed.''

Just before the first debate, Nixon learned that Kennedy was not going to use makeup. Nixon decided he would also go in front of the cameras without makeup. Kennedy, supporting a deep suntan, did not need makeup, but Nixon who was extremely tired after campaigning and had a fever, did. A good makeup job could have masked Nixon's pale, drawn appearance. Nixon also suffered from a tendency to perspire, and the beads of sweat on his face made him look nervous and ill-at-ease.

All of this affected the viewers' image of the two men. Kennedy, an accomplished television performer, appeared cool, self-assured and confident. Nixon appeared nervous and under pressure.

When analyzing the reaction of the estimated 101 million viewers, researchers found that Kennedy came out of the debates a clear winner. However, some people who only listened to the debates on radio, and therefore did not see Nixon's haggard appearance, thought Nixon was the winner.

Following the TV debates, many undecided voters made their choice of candidate. The Gallup Poll showed that Kennedy picked up three percentage points, while Nixon only got one point. The net effect was that Kennedy picked up just enough votes to win the election.

The merit of the live television debate is that voters are able to see how candidates react under intense pressure, and in situations they can not control or anticipate. The danger is that an accomplished television performer can easily defeat a more able, honest and potentially better, leader who is uncomfortable in front of the cameras.[1]

To ensure that they ''perform'' well, each party has a team of public relations people who are skilled in the arts of communication. Jingles, cartoons, and sophisticated advertising techniques have taken the centre stage. Politicians recognize that television provides many people with much of their campaign information, so they plan campaigns with careful attention to the

▸ [1]Reprinted with the permission of *Canada & the World* Magazine, Oakville, Ontario.

media. Newspapers are no different — a study of the newspaper coverage of the 1974 election, for instance, revealed that 42 percent of newspaper reports dealt exclusively with party leaders, and only 12 percent discussed the issues.

▶ Re-making Stanfield

In 1972, *Maclean's* asked a noted hair stylist, whose advice had previously been sought by several prominent politicians, to analyse the television appearance of Robert Stanfield, the Conservative party leader, and to suggest improvements. Here is his initial assessment:

Robert Stanfield is the example of a man who has strong characteristics that he has not yet taken advantage of. In fact his dogmatic, conservative, almost upper-class British image doesn't do his political position justice. The high forehead caused by balding is distracting on camera (a light reflection always seems to bounce off one side causing the viewer to lose concentration on what he's saying). The bushy eyebrows are too severe and don't lend themselves to natural expression. The clothes accentuate his severity. The problem is to soften his hard image and make his personality more appealing.

The hair stylist explained the first makeover in this way:

Mr. Stanfield's most positive feature is his eyes. They are reassuring, contemplative and, in the right mood, even kind. But the bushy eyebrows distract [sic] these characteristics and so do the crow's feet at the corners of his eyes. It will take cosmetics to deal with the crow's feet and for the moment I'll concern myself only with the eyebrows by clipping them slightly. My main concern here is to defeat the school-principal severity his brow projects. I

The real Stanfield
Christopher Beacom

A different Stanfield
Christopher Beacom

Another Stanfield
Christopher Beacom

felt that by giving the leader longer and fuller sideburns and a fuller style with more body on the sides and back of his head I could create a softer appearance. The color of the hair would therefore contain more highlights and texture. Next the nose; nicely shaped but too prominent and disconcerting. I decided to add a Ronald Colman type moustache to deal with this sharp feature and also camouflage the slight droop at the corner of his mouth. On occasion I have seen this droop come across as a sneer. Add to this redesign a colored shirt, striped tie and vest and there is an over-all effect of quiet distinction.

The designer was not satisfied with the new image so he tried again:

The eyebrows are still too heavy. I clipped and reshaped them. I took base makeup and erased those annoying crow's feet. It works. His eyes no longer conceal themselves. He is immediately more communicable and the TV viewer can relate to the feelings his eyes now freely express. The bald head isn't distinguished after all, and so in these days when hair extensions are as common as false teeth I gave him a full head of hair. This was no easy task. It took some experimenting before I came to a natural style. The hairpiece relieved the leader of his gaunt look. But it also made the moustache seem gratuitous. I dropped it, and by applying cosmetics I lifted the top lip and lightened the cleft chin. Next I noticed that his Adam's apple looked too prominent and his clothes didn't suit the new image. I selected a coloured shirt with a higher collar to cover the Adam's apple. Got rid of the old school tie and replaced it with a wider, more contemporary knit. I made sure that the knot suited the elegance of the tie. . . .[2]

These comments illustrate the extent to which it is possible to shape an image of what is assumed to be voter preference. Reread the hair stylist's account and imagine the arguments that might have been used by Stanfield's advisers in support of these comments. Why do you think the changes were not adopted?

▶ Are Media Biased?

Canadians obtain the vast majority of their potential information from the media. Ninety-nine percent of Canadian households have at least one radio and one television. In 1985, there were 115 daily newspapers and 929 weekly papers printed in Canada. Since the media provides us with what we know about current politics, it is important that the media be as unbiased as possible, that it presents all sides of an issue in a balanced way. Newspapers, television, and radio stations, however, are owned and operated by business people whose primary aim is to earn profits. Wealthy advertisers thus carry more influ-

▸ [2]*Maclean's*, May 1972, pp. 21–25. Reprinted by permission from *Maclean's*.

ence with media owners than do the poor. Some critics point to the fact that two corporations (Southam and Thomson) control almost one-half of all Canadian daily newspapers and argue that "the freedom of the press belongs to those who own one." The media, on the other hand, claims to be as unbiased as possible and points to the fact that the CBC, although it is government-owned, is an additional source of bias-free news.

▶ POLLS AND THE ELECTORATE

Opinion polls play an increasingly important role in Canadian election campaigns. Governments use them to help decide when to call elections. During the actual campaign, parties utilise private polls to determine which policies voters prefer. The media deluges the public daily with polls dealing with party popularity.

There is debate over whether polls taken during election campaigns assist or hinder the democratic process. Proponents of polls claim that they give citizens greater input into party policy. Polls are a means by which voters may express their favour or displeasure with a party's platform or actions. Most parties are extremely wary of supporting measures that are broadly opposed by the general public. Although they are not a substitute for direct democracy, polls are one of the few means by which the Canadian public can make its collective will known to the politicians.

Polls are much more accurate today than they were years ago. In the 1936 election, for instance, several newspapers in the United States predicted that Alf Landon would win a landslide victory over Franklin Roosevelt in the presidential election, and some erroneously announced the morning of the election that Landon had won. The actual result was quite the contrary. The problem was that **pollsters** had limited their surveys to those individuals who owned telephones. Since few Americans during the Depression could afford telephones, the polls predicting a Landon victory reflected only the opinions of the wealthy citizens. Today, pollsters use more scientific and accurate means to measure public opinion. Even if one poll during an election campaign is inaccurate, other polls will generally rectify this situation.

Polls may, in certain circumstances, encourage voters to participate in elections. If poll results indicate that the election outcome will be close, voters will feel that their vote is of magnified significance, and they will make a special effort to vote. Also, some political analysts claim that if a particular party is trailing badly in the polls, its supporters will be more likely to cast ballots. In this way, polls may have a positive influence on the operation of democracy.

However, many political analysts and politicians claim that polls have a detrimental impact on the **electoral process**. They suggest that polls be banned or severely restricted during election campaigns. A standard nation-wide poll uses a sample of one thousand people. These randomly selected individuals are supposed to be representative of the entire Canadian population. In reality, this is not always the case. A poll based on 1000 interviews is accurate within plus or minus four percentage points nineteen out of twenty times. If 30 percent of Canadians actually support a particular policy or party, then 19 out of 20 polls should have results between 26 and 34 percent. One poll would not fall within this range.

This margin of error may substantially alter poll results. Suppose that an opinion poll measured party preference as follows: Liberal — 38 percent, Conservative — 35 percent, and N.D.P. — 27 percent. Liberal support could actually range from 34 to 42 percent, Conservative support from 31 to

39 percent, and N.D.P. support from 23 to 31 percent. Thus, the Liberal advantage over the N.D.P. could be as high as 19 percent or as low as 3 percent. Polls are seldom ever completely accurate. Rather, they provide only a general indication of public opinion.

During election campaigns, according to some political experts, voters might support a particular party because it is leading in the polls. Such individuals would rather vote for a winner than a loser. This tendency for parties to benefit from their leading position in the polls is known as the bandwagon effect. In this way, polls may contribute to landslide election victories.

Polls measure public opinion only at a particular point of time. Sometimes, public opinion may be simply a momentary reaction to a particular event. After John Turner's successful performance in the 1988 federal election leadership debate, the Liberal party surged to the lead in most public opinion polls. However, Liberal support dropped significantly only a few weeks later. The argument can be made that voters were responding favourably to a single event. Also, it should be remembered that polls only measure voter intention. They cannot predict how individuals will actually vote. There is a great difference between voters telling a pollster that they intend to vote for a particular party and actually voting for that party.

Some politicians and parties may manipulate polls to their political advantage. For instance, a party that favoured higher taxes might produce a poll result, according to which 62 percent of Canadians would be willing to pay more taxes. Although this would seem to be an indication of widespread support for the party's policy, such is not necessarily the case. Sixty-two percent of Canadians may be willing to pay higher taxes, but for what purpose? Would they support a 20 percent tax increase in order to raise the salaries of MPs and senators? Perhaps 32 percent of the voters favoured new taxes only if the money was used for social programs, while the remaining 30 percent of the supporters of higher taxes vehemently opposed such programs. In other words, polls often fail to measure the different reasons why people may support a particular policy.

Some polling firms that produce polls for the media are also employed by political parties. Are poll results biased towards a particular party? Recently, some politicians complained that this is the case. On one hand, it seems difficult to imagine that professional pollsters would risk their reputation by deliberately favouring one political party. On the other hand, some polling firms do consistently give a particular party higher support than it receives in other opinion polls.

As you can see, many of the arguments concerning the usefulness of polls are contradictory. There is no real evidence to say conclusively that voter rationality is or is not affected by public opinion polls. Further studies are required before the impact of polls during election time can be better understood.

▶ FINAL WORD: A CASE FOR THE DEFENCE

Even if the election campaign does little to change most people's minds, it does interest citizens in its outcome and encourages them to vote. In search of maximum electoral support, each party is alert to new issues that will catch the imagination of the people. While it might be true that many voters know very little about campaign issues, it does not mean that people do not know what they like. Politicians are notorious for failing to implement election promises. As a result, the electorate judges parties on their past performances rather than on their present promises. Has the government done a good job under the circumstances, or has it performed badly? This is how voters make their decisions.

Certainly, politicians, journalists, and historians have few doubts about voter rationality. Politicians spend a great deal of their time trying to convince citizens of their party's merits, and journalists attempt to explain election results and public opinion polls according to party policies.

It is sometimes suggested that voters' **political apathy** (approximately twenty-five percent of the people do not vote in national elections) is a sign that they are alienated by the system and feel politically powerless. According to a study of over 1200 Canadians, only fifty-two percent believed that the government cared about what they thought, fifty-six percent thought that they had no say in what the government does, sixty-seven percent believed that members of Parliament soon lose touch with the people who elected them, and sixty-seven percent stated that government and politics are too complicated for them to understand.

This does not mean, however, that rational political choices are impossible to make. The only way to develop the skills and attitudes needed for good citizenship is through meaningful political participation. Experiments in the business world have shown that factories that permit workers to participate in production decisions have a more responsible work force. Meaningful participation will help create citizens who have self-esteem, tolerance, and self-reliance. By encouraging greater participation in the electoral process, we could encourage more meaningful voter choice.

APPLYING YOUR KNOWLEDGE

1. To what extent does the media accurately portray campaign issues? (Incorporate your own personal experiences in the answer.)
2. a) Discuss Mr. Stanfield's personality as depicted in each of the photographs.
   b) How would you expect each "new" Mr. Stanfield to behave in front of a crowd?
   c) Would you advise Mr. Stanfield to change his image? Explain your reasons.
3. Are you in favour of televised leadership debates? Explain your answer.
4. Based on the evidence provided in this case study, and on other evidence of which you are aware, give a carefully reasoned answer to the following question: what role does the media play in the choices that voters make?
5. Do you favour banning polls during election campaigns? Why?
6. Define "meaningful participation" and explain how this might be achieved.
7. a) Do average Canadian voters base their decisions on a reasoned analysis of the political and economic issues as presented in the election campaign? Explain.
   b) Is this important? Why?

FURTHER RESEARCH

1. Examine a local newspaper and the television news for examples of what some commentators term "the cult of personality."
2. Canada has had several "leadership debates" in the past. Ask your parents for their impressions of one of these debates and be prepared to discuss the importance of issues as compared to personality.

3. Working in groups, conduct a content analysis of the national news of different daily newspapers (or the news on different channels). Examine both the amount of space (or time) given to each national topic and the emphasis or bias in the report.
4. Examine a daily newspaper for the amount of articles supplied by such international news agencies as C.P. and U.P.I.
5. Invite a representative from an advertising agency (or a political party) to talk to the class about planning a political campaign.
6. Divide into small groups, prepare a questionnaire, and conduct a survey of the student body of your school on one of the following topics:
   a) knowledge of politics
   b) long-term party loyalty
   c) party loyalty as a function of parents' political affiliation
   d) importance of religion, ethnicity, class, or gender, on party preferences
7. Debate the merits of opinion polls during election campaigns.
8. Research the promises made by a victorious party leader and discuss whether the leader followed through on these promises.

Case Study 7 Overview

Individual Freedom Versus Group Welfare

This case study explores the delicate balance between individual freedom and the need to obey the law. How much control should a democratic government have over an individual's freedom of action? American President J.F. Kennedy's argument that all citizens are obligated to obey the law is contrasted with Martin Luther King, Jr.'s statement that civil disobedience is sometimes justified. The case study concludes with an examination of the life of Indian leader Mohandas Gandhi and his ideas and activities regarding civil disobedience.

▶ OBJECTIVES

After reading this case study, you should be able to:

- ▶ appreciate the problems related to preserving order in a democratic society
- ▶ decide upon how much control the government should have over its citizens
- ▶ debate the issue of public order versus individual freedom
- ▶ demonstrate your understanding of the philosophy behind non-violent protest
- ▶ discuss the merits of civil disobedience

▶ KEY TERMS

individual freedom
public order
civil disobedience
non-violent protest
passive resistance

Case Study 7

Individual Freedom Versus Group Welfare

In the spring of 1974, a group of police officers conducted a drug raid in a small Fort Erie hotel. By the time they finished, they had searched virtually all of the 115 patrons on the premises; in the case of the 35 women patrons, the police had them herded into washrooms, stripped, and subjected to [comprehensive physical] examinations.

Despite all of the searching, stripping, and inspecting, the police found nothing more incriminating than a few grains of marijuana. And most of these few grains were found not on articles of clothing or within body orifices, but rather on the floor and tables of the lounge.

The ensuing public outrage forced the government of Ontario to create a special Royal Commission to assess the propriety of the raid. After listening to the evidence of the police, the patrons, and other interested parties, the Commission issued the inevitable verdict: the intrusive aspects of the raid were described as ''foolish'' and ''unnecessary,'' but, cautioned the Commission, they were not unlawful.

Under the Narcotic Control Act, if the police have reasonable grounds to believe that places other than dwelling houses contain illicit drugs, they are entitled, without warrant, to enter forcibly and conduct a search. . . . According to the Commission's interpretation of the Act, the police, in such circumstances, may search everyone found on the premises whether or not each search is accompanied by reasonable suspicion. All it takes to render a person lawfully vulnerable to such intrusions is the coincidence of being innocently present on suspicious premises. . . .[1]

[1]Reprinted with permission from *When Freedoms Collide: The Case For Civil Liberties* by Alan Borovoy, published by Lester & Orpen Dennys Ltd., copyright © 1988 A. Alan Borovoy.

▶ DEMOCRACY AND FREEDOM

This unfortunate incident illustrates the theme of this case study—how much control should a democratic government have over an individual's freedom of action? Democratic societies are based on the belief that people should decide for themselves how to worship; what to read, write and say; where to work; and with whom to associate. This is one of the basic differences between a democratic and a non-democratic state. In a dictatorship, the ruler usually decides how the citizens should live, whereas in a democracy, the objective is for the citizens to decide for themselves how they will live.

The survival of the democratic system depends upon the preservation of these freedoms. Many democratic countries (as we shall see in Chapter 4) have been turned into dictatorships, without the shedding of a drop of blood, when people no longer cared enough to preserve their freedom. It is often easier to let someone else make the decisions that we ourselves ought to make as responsible citizens, and it is never easy to regain what has been lost through carelessness. Perhaps the most eloquent warning of the perils to freedom emerged from the ruins of World War II. Recounting his experience with the Nazi regime in his country, Reverend Martin Niemöller, a German Protestant clergyman, made the following statement:

First they arrested the Communists—but I was not a Communist, so I did nothing. Then they came for the Social Democrats—but I was not a Social Democrat, so I did nothing. Then they arrested the trade unionists—and I did nothing because I was not one. And then they came for the Jews and then the Catholics, but I was neither a Jew nor a Catholic and I did nothing. At last they came and arrested me—and there was no one left to do anything about it.

Here is the everlasting problem of democracy: the very freedoms that democracy gives us—such as freedom of speech—can be used against democracy by its enemies. Yet we cannot preserve freedoms by destroying them—if freedoms are denied to one person or one group, they can just as readily be taken away from every citizen.

▶ THE NEED FOR ORDER

If freedom is defined as the absence of restraint, then freedom is impossible. We are constantly restricted and controlled by the religious and moral beliefs of society, by government rules and regulations, by our need to make a living, and by the actions of other individuals. These and other restrictions prevent us from always doing what we want—even Robinson Crusoe was limited by his environment and his own abilities.

There are two aspects of freedom: the first is the freedom to do what one wants, and the second is the freedom from being interfered with by others. Together, these two aspects of freedom present a paradox—does individual freedom include the right to kill and maim others? If so, then the victims have been deprived of their rights. This is the paradox: the victim and the attacker cannot both have absolute freedom of choice. If cigarette smokers have the right to smoke, do they also have the right to contaminate the air in an elevator? If a chemical company has the freedom to operate as it wants, does it have the right to pollute the rivers and destroy the livelihood of the fishers who depend upon these rivers? Similarly, the freedom to let your front lawn become overgrown conflicts with your neighbour's freedom not to have to contend with dandelions or an unpleasant view from the front window.

The preamble to the Canadian Bill of Rights states that "men and institutions remain free only when freedom is founded upon respect for moral and spiritual values and the rule of law.'' The state, in other words, protects your freedom by restraining mine. If I steal your car, the state will put me in jail and I will lose my freedom because I restricted your freedom to drive your car. An important problem that each democratic society must solve is achieving the proper balance between **public order** and individual freedom. How much power should the state have over the individual? A balance must be struck between our freedom to associate with whomever we wish and to speak, write, and worship as we please, and the government's duty to preserve the peace and protect the general welfare. To what extent should the individual be bound by the law? Are there circumstances under which a citizen is justified in disobeying the law? This is an issue that has been debated for centuries. The following are the arguments that are frequently used for each side of this dispute.

▶ The Obligation to Obey the Law

Violence is not justified in a democracy because a democracy offers alternatives to it. Violence is counter-productive because it nourishes repression, not justice. American democracy, declared President J.F. Kennedy,

. . . is founded on the principle that observance of the law is the eternal safeguard of liberty and defiance of the law is the surest road to tyranny. . . . Americans are free, in short, to disagree with the law, but not to disobey it. For in a government of laws and not of men, no man, however prominent or powerful, and no mob, however unruly or boisterous, is entitled to defy a court of law.

If this country should ever reach the point where any man or group of men, by force or threat of force, could long deny the commands of our court and our Constitution, then no law would stand free from doubt, no judge would be sure of his writ and no citizen would be safe from his neighbours.

According to this argument, individuals in a democracy are not justified in disobeying a law because there is no guarantee that they will disobey only unjust laws. This, in turn, will undermine the willingness to obey all laws, and the collapse of society will follow. Furthermore, if one person is allowed to disobey one law, everyone must then be allowed to disobey other laws when the circumstances seem to be justified. This will only make the situation worse—as soon as we entrust the right of disobedience to everyone, we can be sure that many just laws will be disobeyed. The choice is between social order and chaos.

▶ The Right to Disobey the Law: A Counter-Argument

Although disobedience should not usually be condoned, there are times when it is justified. Disobedience, for better or worse, does settle some problems, often for the better. The best example is the success of the civil rights movement in the United States during the 1960s. The theory of non-violent **civil disobedience** was expressed by Martin Luther King, Jr. in his famous letter from an Alabama jail on April 16, 1963:

I have almost reached the regrettable conclusion that the Negro's great stumbling block in his stride toward freedom is not the White Citizen's Councilor or the Ku Klux Klanner, but the white moderate, who is more devoted to ''order'' than to justice. . . . I had hoped that the white moderate would understand that law and order exist for the purpose of establishing justice and that when they fail in this purpose they become the dangerously structured dams that block the flow of social progress. I had hoped that the white moderate would understand that the present tension in the South is a necessary phase of the transition

Dr. Martin Luther King, Jr. (1929–1968)
Canapress Photo Service

from an obnoxious negative peace, in which the Negro passively accepted his unjust plight, to a substantive and positive peace, in which all men will respect the dignity and worth of human personality. Actually, we who engage in nonviolent direct action are not the creators of tension. We merely bring to the surface the hidden tension that is already alive. We bring it out in the open, where it can be seen and dealt with. Like a boil that can never be cured so long as it is covered up but must be opened with all its ugliness to the natural medicines of air and light, injustice must be exposed, with all the tension its exposure creates, to the light of human conscience and the air of national opinion before it can be cured.[2]

▶ MOHANDAS GANDHI AND NON-VIOLENCE

The civil rights movement in the United States based its **non-violent protest** activities on the actions of Mohandas Gandhi, who successfully used non-violent political protests in India and South Africa to counter colonialism, racism, poverty, religious bigotry, and economic exploitation. The remainder of this case study examines Gandhi's career as a social activist and focuses on the importance an individual can have on world events.

Gandhi was born in India in 1869. To achieve his ambition of becoming a lawyer, he went to school in England at the age of seventeen. After several years of lonely study, Gandhi returned to India and was later called to the bar. As a debater in court, however, he was a failure. Once he even broke down in court, cried, and was unable to proceed. Just when it appeared that his life as a lawyer was a failure, the Indian government sent Gandhi to South Africa to represent an Indian firm in a legal dispute with the South African government. Here, Gandhi was moved by the injustices that his compatriots endured. Asians were denied legal status in South Africa. They were registered and fingerprinted, had to pay a special tax for living in the country, and could not be legally married. Gandhi spent much of the next twenty-one years attempting to improve their position.

Influenced by the writings of Russian reformer Leo Tolstoy, and drawing upon Christian, Jain, and Hindu beliefs, Gandhi gave up all worldly ambitions and began a campaign of **passive resistance** in South Africa. Although the government had Gandhi and some of his Indian followers arrested and thrown into jail, the agitation they had created forced the authorities to grant limited legal status to Indians in South Africa.

Returning to India in 1914, Gandhi took up the cause of overworked and underpaid Indian mill workers who lived in terrible squalor. When a labour strike failed, Gandhi refused to eat until the owners remedied the workers' grievances. Gandhi

▸ [2]Excerpt from *Why We Can't Wait* by Martin Luther King, Jr. Copyright © 1963, 1964 by Martin Luther King, Jr. Copyright © 1991 renewed. Reprinted by permission of HarperCollins Publishers Inc.

got thinner and thinner, until the mill owners finally gave in and granted his requests. At this time, Gandhi acquired the title "Mahatma" (Great Soul), for championing the causes of the poor and the oppressed.

In 1920, Gandhi turned his attention to improving the lot of India under British rule. Since 1857, Great Britain had ruled India mainly for its own economic advantage. Although the British united the country, introduced democracy, and improved India's economy, they were so arrogant and racist in their supposed superiority that leaders such as Gandhi and Jawaharlal Nehru sought self-rule and independence for India.

The Mahatma organized a non-co-operation movement. He encouraged all Indians not to work for the British in any capacity. No one was to pay taxes or attend government schools, hospitals, or law courts. Police officers and soldiers were not to go to work. Although Great Britain granted some reforms, it still denied India self-rule. Following a series of bloody riots in 1921, for which Gandhi spent two years in jail, the Mahatma decided that Indians were not yet trained for non-violence and began to teach the virtues of peaceful opposition. He preached self-restraint even in the face of the worst form of provocation. Gandhi instructed protestors to act calmly and cheerfully despite beatings, shootings, and imprisonment. Non-violence was not meant to be passive. When faced with cowardice or violence, Gandhi recommended action. "When my eldest son asked me what he should have done, had he been present when I was almost fatally assaulted in 1908, whether he should have run away and seen me killed or whether he should have used his physical force which he could and wanted to use, and defended me, I told him that it was his duty to defend me even by using violence. . . ."

In the mid-1920s, Gandhi decided to protest against the British tax on salt, which

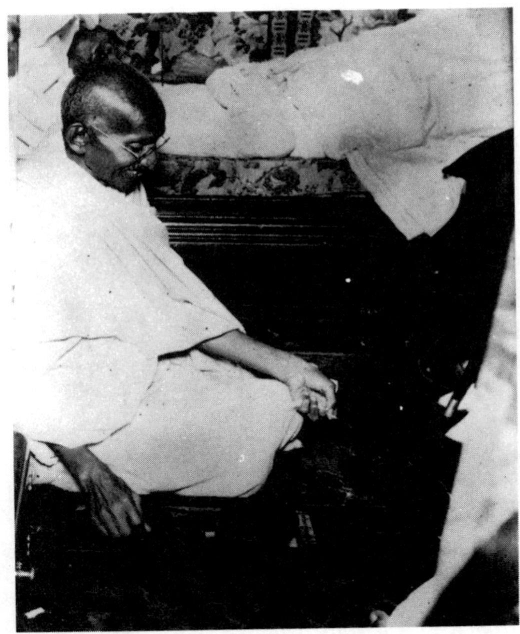

Mohandas Karamchand Gandhi, later called Mahatma, or Great Soul.
The Bettmann Archive

weighed particularly heavily on the poorer classes, and the law that forbade people from making their own salt from sea-water. In a 386 km symbolic march to the coast, Gandhi was joined by thousands of supporters. As he passed through villages, Indian officials quit their jobs, although this action meant a loss of their lands. To quell the growing opposition, the British government arrested Gandhi once again. When the civil disobedience continued, the British released Gandhi from jail and allowed him to participate in negotiations with British officials in England. When these discussions failed, the Mahatma, who was now back in jail, announced that he would "fast unto death," unless his demands were met. Gandhi was now in his early sixties and many people feared that another fast might kill him. Anxious crowds waited outside the prison day and night for news of his condition. Several days later, the government agreed to compromise, and Gandhi broke his fast.

Gandhi now decided to abandon mass disobedience because he believed that the Indian people were not yet ready for it. He now adopted individual disobedience and began a country-wide march throughout India with his followers. Once again, the British imprisoned him. He fasted once more, and the British released him.

Frail and thin, with large eyes, and wearing only a loincloth, Gandhi was hardly a visually striking person. He was nevertheless tenacious when basic principles were at stake. Non-violence was one such belief. "War with all its glorification of brute force is essentially a degrading thing," Gandhi wrote. "It demoralizes those who are trained for it. It brutalizes men of naturally gentle character. Its path of glory is foul with the passions of lust, and red with the blood of murder. This is not the pathway to our goal. . . . Self-restraint, unselfishness, patience, gentleness, these are the flowers, which spring beneath the feet of those who accept but refuse to impose suffering. . . ."

At a prayer meeting in Delhi in 1948, Nathuram Godse, a Hindu extremist, sat in the front row of the congregation with a small pistol in his pocket. "I actually wished him well and bowed to him in reverence," Godse recalled at his trial. Gandhi now touched his palms together, smiled, and blessed the congregation. At this moment, Godse pulled the trigger, killing Gandhi. Indian Prime Minister Jawaharlal Nehru declared over the radio, "The light has gone out of our lives and there is darkness everywhere."

APPLYING YOUR KNOWLEDGE

1. Half of the class will write a fictional story describing what life would be like in Canada if there were no restrictions on individual freedoms. The other half will write a fictional story describing what life would be like if there were no restrictions on police powers. Compare the stories.
2. Is a democratic government ever justified in suspending democratic rights in order to defend democracy? Describe a situation in which this might occur.
3. Describe situations in which freedom of the press, freedom of association, and freedom of speech might need to be restrained.
4. Write a short essay based on the statement, "A threat to the freedom of one Canadian is a threat to the freedom of all Canadians."
5. What alternatives to violence are available in Canada?
6. a) Make a list of the laws you believe to be unfair and explain your reasoning.
   b) What might happen if everyone broke these laws?
   c) Do you agree with Martin Luther King, Jr.'s letter? Explain.
   d) Would you agree with King if he advocated violence? Explain.
7. Write a short essay or prepare for a debate, based on one of the following statements:
   a) The police should be allowed to break the law in order to preserve national security.
   b) No one, including the police, should be above the law.

8. a) To what extent do democratic states need some form of emergency legislation that will give the police extraordinary powers in times of national peril?
   b) Who will decide when the country is in peril?
   c) Which individual freedoms should be safeguarded, and how can they be protected?
9. To what extent would Gandhi's tactics have succeeded against a more ruthless government?
10. Comment on the argument that Gandhian non-violence encourages evil by not resisting evil with appropriate means.
11. Police consider wiretapping and other forms of electronic surveillance necessary to prevent crime. This justification has three major aspects: firstly, crime is on the increase and we need every reasonable technique at our command to combat it; secondly, fighting organized crime (such as the Mafia) presents the police with very different problems than does apprehending the individual criminal; thirdly, criminals will use technology to aid their endeavours, and the police should not be handicapped by having its use denied to them.

    The demand for greater police powers is commonly justified by the claim that only criminals have anything to fear; wider police wiretapping powers, it is argued, will only be used against organized crime. However, neither the police nor the justice system is infallible. Even with the best intentions, it is impossible to ensure that law enforcement efforts are directed only towards those who are guilty of crimes.

    Set forth your view on the subject outlined above.

FURTHER RESEARCH

1. Research the physical problems associated with prolonged fasting.
2. Divide into small groups and prepare a solution for the following dilemma: how can society limit police activity without hampering the police in its law enforcement duties?
3. Research and report on one of the following topics:
   a) In 1937, the Social Credit government of Alberta passed "An Act to Ensure the Publication of Accurate News and Information." This amounted to more than simple censorship of the news. The government was given the power to force newspapers to carry any information the government demanded. The government, not the news media, had the power to determine what was accurate news. This attack on the freedom of the press was so widely denounced that the act never became law.
   b) The defection of Igor Gouzenko from the Soviet embassy at Ottawa in September 1945, revealed widespread Russian spy activities against Western democracies. As a result of Gouzenko's information, the Canadian government seized a number of suspected spies and traitors. An order-in-council (a law that does not need Parliament's approval) empowered the minister of justice to hold suspects indefinitely, and to deny them legal advice. This was a clear breach of the right of *habeas corpus*, and it set a precedent that worried many people. If an order-in-council could be based on one occasion to suspend a freedom by overruling the accepted laws of the land, what is to prevent another government from doing the same whenever it pleases?

4. Prepare for a debate on one of the following topics:
   a) the rights of non-smokers
   b) the right to erect billboards on one's own front yard
   c) the right of police officers to search suspects
   d) the right of a democratically elected Parliament to legislate democracy out of existence
5. A 1989 *Maclean's* poll of 1000 Canadians and 1000 Americans provided the following results. Debate this question.

In times of crisis, do you believe government should or should not have the power to declare a national emergency and remove all civil rights?

	Canada	**United States**
Should not	49%	56%
Should	48%	41%
No opinion	3%	3%

▸ Source: *Maclean's*, July 3, 1989, p. 48. Reprinted by permission from *Maclean's*.

Case Study 8 Overview

Pressure Groups, Lobbyists, and Democracy in Canada

This case study examines the role and importance of pressure groups and lobbyists in the democratic decision-making process. The case study begins by outlining what pressure groups are, their objectives, and how they attempt to influence government policies. This is followed by an evaluation of the strengths and weaknesses of pressure groups in general. The most important lobby groups in Canada are then examined. The case study concludes with an examination of the goals, methods, and results of the environmental organization, Greenpeace.

▶ OBJECTIVES

After reading this case study, you should be able to:

- ▶ identify the variety of pressure groups operating in Canada
- ▶ explain why the Canadian government passed the Lobbyist Registration Act in 1989
- ▶ evaluate the advantages and disadvantages of pressure groups
- ▶ design your own pressure group
- ▶ debate whether pressure groups are beneficial in a democracy

▶ KEY TERMS

pressure groups | lobbyist | civil servant

Pressure Groups, Lobbyists, and Democracy in Canada

A group of people with a common interest or cause, voluntarily collaborating to influence the government to adopt a specific policy, is known as a pressure group. This case study examines how **pressure groups** operate and evaluates their power within the Canadian political system. To what extent do pressure groups influence government actions between election campaigns? Do pressure groups exert too much influence on government? Are pressure groups beneficial to the workings of democracy?

▶ OBJECTIVES AND FUNCTIONS

The following excerpts from the constitutions of several Canadian associations provide an insight into both their objectives and the areas in which they might influence government policies. The Canadian Textiles Institute exists, it states, ''entirely for the purpose of supporting the efforts of members to develop, maintain and extend a favourable business climate in which to operate.'' The Montreal Board of Trade similarly ''voices the outlook of business in matters of public concern, encourages active exchange of ideas and opinions among businesspeople, provides information on government legislation and regulations, and seeks equitable conditions should the latter be unduly restrictive or burdensome.'' The Toronto Musicians' Association seeks to ''unite into one organization all persons who become members, to secure for the members improved wages, hours, working conditions, and other economic advantages through collective negotiations and bargaining.''

High among the priorities of such organizations is a mandate to represent the group's interest before the government. This function is emphasized in association publications. A Canadian Mining Association brochure, for example, states that its "main role is to project the views of the industry on a national scale and co-ordinate its efforts with those of government departments in regard to policies affecting exploration, mining and processing, and the development of exports."[1]

Logo of Canadians A.G.A.S.T. (Against Goods and Services Tax)

▶ METHODS OF INFLUENCING GOVERNMENT POLICIES

Pressure groups attempt to influence government policy either directly through contact with the government or indirectly by influencing public opinion, which in turn might affect government decisions.

▶ Direct Methods

Direct influence by pressure groups can be accomplished in many ways. They may, for example, have their members write letters to the prime minister, send petitions to a local member of Parliament, submit briefs to government committees, conduct protest marches, establish contact with important civil servants and politicians, or write letters to newspapers.

Probably the most effective means of directly influencing the government is by working quietly within the government bureaucracy behind closed doors. Knowing the right people and how to use them is one of the most important ways of getting an organization's point of view across to civil servants and politicians. This process is called lobbying. Pressure groups want to know who the decision-makers are, how and when to approach them, and how to maintain this contact. Because organizations wanting to pressure the government usually lack the expertise to answer these questions themselves, they often hire a **lobbyist** to do it for them. Lobbying has become a big business. Private organizations spend millions of dollars to get a particular concern or viewpoint heard by some important government member or civil servant.

Many major companies do not need lobbyists the way smaller companies or individuals do. John Chenier, co-publisher of the *Lobby Digest* and *Lobby Monitor* states, "If you are the president of any important national or regional company, you don't have any problem getting in to see people."

As a rule, Canadian lobbyists focus their attention on the civil service and the cabinet, rather than on the individual member of Parliament. The reason why the civil service is a primary target for pressure groups is explained by a prominent senior **civil servant**:

▸ [1]Adapted from Robert Presthus, *Elite Accommodation in Canadian Politics*, Cambridge: Cambridge University Press, 1973, pp. 101–102.

People who really want to guide and influence government policy are wasting their time dealing with Members of Parliament, senators and, usually, even ministers. If you want results—rather than just the satisfaction of talking to the prominent—you deal with us, and at various levels. . . . To produce results you need to see the key planners, who may be way down in the system, and you see them early enough to push for changes in policy before it is politically embarrassing to make them.

This view is supported by a highly successful lobbyist.

Really, most new ideas begin deep in the civil service machine. The person in charge of some special office . . . writes a memo suggesting a new policy on this or that. It works its way slowly up and up. At that stage civil servants are delighted, just delighted, to talk quietly to people like us, people representing this or that corporation or industry directly involved. That is the time to slip in good ideas. Later it oozes up to the politicians and becomes policy. By the time it is a government bill it is the very devil to change it. Then you have real trouble.[2]

Cabinet ministers are also important targets for lobbyists, because they are known to exercise influence on final policy decisions. Individual back-benchers usually agree with the cabinet's decisions and concentrate more on the needs of their constituents than on important policy issues. When a bill has reached the House of Commons, it can be radically amended only after considerable embarrassment to the government.

Pressure groups rarely employ just one tactic at a time. When the Consumers' Association of Canada began its campaign to ban the use of trading stamps in supermarkets, it requested its members to write letters to their members of Parliament; presented briefs to federal and provincial attorneys-general; made submissions to the prime minister and the minister of justice; recruited the support of such organizations as the Retail Merchants' Federation, the Canadian Labour Congress, and the Canadian Federation of Agriculture; and distributed material to the media in order to publicize its position. It is important to note, however, that the Consumers' Association did not completely succeed in this impressive attempt to influence government policy.

▶ Indirect Methods

Indirect influence by pressure groups on government policy is becoming more significant. Politicians are very aware of public opinion polls, and the major political parties in Canada use their own public opinion companies to provide feedback on how Canadians feel about various issues. Pressure groups know this and many of them spend a great deal of time and effort to influence public opinion. How important is this strategy for an organization? According to *Law Now*,

Many votes are close, so even a small group concerned with issues can have a large influence on an election. Also, political parties almost always use issues as the medium through which they project themselves, so hot issues and the way political parties stand on them, can be a very important part of future government policy. Still, an interest group must make its concern a popular issue and the election must be relatively close for that issue to influence the outcome of the election and the platform of the winner. These fragmented interest groups can then only have a questionable influence at best over government policy, although they have had some grand successes. For example, the reversal of the decision to de-index old age security and pension payments, or the temporary suspension of the baby seal

▸ [2]Quoted in W.T. Stanbury, *Business Interests and the Reform of Canadian Competition Policy, 1971–1975*, Toronto: Carswell/Methuen, 1977, p. 20.

hunt. These successes are greatly outnumbered by the causes and ideas constantly being forwarded.[3]

Successful or not, many pressure groups continue to try and influence government opinion, both between and during elections. According to a survey of 134 federal MPs, fifty-six percent of them considered that "mobilizing public opinion" was the most effective method of influencing government policy.

When governments have to make decisions, they often find that more than one pressure group is after a favourable decision. For example, conflicting interests can occur when a company wants to build a manufacturing plant that may disrupt part of the environment. The company may lobby the government directly to gain permission to build the plant. An environmental group may indirectly try to stop the plant by launching a media campaign or by holding rallies against the plant's construction. This use of public pressure, the environmentalists hope, will force the government to rule in their favour.

▶ Pressure Groups—For Better or Worse

Pressure groups are a fact of life in the Canadian democratic process. They are the principal mechanism by which interested people make their preferences known to government policy-makers. Some people argue that pressure groups provide a necessary communications link between the governed and the governors. Pressure groups provide decision-makers with information about the "real world," including technical information as well as an assessment of the feelings and attitudes of the organization's members. In this way, pressure groups provide opportunities for meaningful political activity and help government to identify areas of dissatisfaction.

The communication flow is two-way. Governments often use pressure groups as a means of testing their proposals before taking them to Parliament. They will request advice and assistance before finalizing their policies. Pressure groups are also utilized to help explain government policies to the public and to obtain support for them. Finally, lobbyists act as a check on the government, advising, warning, and providing alternate courses of action for the legislators.

The basic flaw in this theory, according to some political scientists, is that some segments of society are better organized than others and can mobilize greater resources in support of their interests. These resources include money, available time, organizational skills, and political connections. In fact, some areas of society remain unorganized or poorly organized at best. By and large, the most active pressure groups represent producers rather than consumers; although there are many labour unions, consumer associations, charitable societies, and church groups, the most influential pressure groups represent business. In addition to their contacts with the media, business groups maintain continuous contact with important government agencies. As a result, when the desires of a multinational oil company (to take one example) come into conflict with an environmental group, the oil company has the advantage.

The very fact that pressure groups work behind closed doors, argue their detractors, means that at best they are subverting the idea of open government. At worst, they have something to hide. Civil servants and politicians naturally wish to work with the most powerful pressure groups because they do not want to antagonize these groups and jeopardize important political support. What tends to happen is

▸ [3]Doug Kennedy is a partner in the Alberta law firm of Parlee McLaws.

that wealthy groups, which can afford to hire teams of lawyers, lobbyists, and publicists, are more able to influence government decisions. There are always more poor people than rich people, yet the existence of pressure groups enables the minority to dominate the majority — the very antithesis of democracy.

FOCUS

1. a) Make a list of five organizations, clubs, or groups to which you or your family belong.
   b) Briefly list the purpose of each of these organizations.
2. a) How do pressure groups differ from the organizations to which you belong?
   b) Describe a situation in which one of your organizations might temporarily become a pressure group.
   c) Discuss the tactics your group might choose to present its case.
   d) What are the chances for success? Explain.
   e) To what extent would your chance of success rest upon the organization's size or influence?
3. Explain why civil servants are the prime targets of pressure groups. To what extent does this undermine the function of the House of Commons?

Who Lobbies Whom?

Since 1989, lobbyists have had to register under the Lobbyists' Registration Act. Who is lobbying whom is now public information. The act requires the name and address of the individual doing the lobbying, the name of the client for whom the lobbying is being done, the subject matter of the lobbying, and, if the client is a corporation, the names of all related corporations. The following two documents provide an example of the type of information available through the registry.

Document 1

THE TOP LOBBYING FIRMS

This ranking list refers only to the number of clients for whom lobbyists are doing "registerable" activity. Some firms may be lobbying for only 15 clients, but have dozens of others who have hired them for advice, strategic planning or other help.

This list, provided by the Lobbyists' Registration Office, includes all clients registered since the office opened at the end of September, 1989, to the end of February [1990].

Government Consultants International has more registrations than other firms because each of their partners registers for each client.

1. Public Affairs International (PAI), Ottawa and Toronto; now owned by Hill and Knowlton, Inc., owned in turn by British firm, WPP Group: 54 clients/112 registrations.
2. Government Consultants International (GCI), Ottawa: 50 clients/493 registrations.

3. Fred Doucet Consulting International, Inc. (FDCI), Ottawa: 35 clients/111 registrations.
4. Osler Hoskin and Harcourt, Toronto: 33 clients/48 registrations.
5. S.A. Murray, Toronto and Ottawa: 27 clients/118 registrations.
6. McMillan Binch, Toronto: 27 clients/36 registrations.
7. Government Policy Consultants, Ottawa: 17 clients/60 registrations.
8. Lundrigan Consulting Services, St. John's: 17 clients/34 registrations.
9. Intercon Consultants, Ottawa: 15 clients/38 registrations.
10. Executive Consultants Ltd., Ottawa: 15 clients/19 registrations.

According to figures released by the Lobbyists' Registration Branch, the following are the top subject matters [of lobbyists].

1. International Trade (1946)
2. Regional Economic (1928)
3. Industry (1873)
4. Government Procurement (1838)
5. Science and Technology (1609)
6. Corporate Affairs (1579)
7. Consumer Issues (1472)
8. Transportation (1408)
9. Investment (1377)
10. Environment (1313)

Source: *The Globe and Mail*, March 10, 1990, p. D2.

Document 2

This document is a list of some of the leading lobbyists in Ottawa in 1990, their previous government associations, and their clients.

Former Staff of Brian Mulroney

FRED DOUCET, Fred Doucet Consulting Intl. Inc.:

▷ Chief of staff for opposition leader Brian Mulroney in 1983; senior policy adviser in the PMO (Prime Minister's Office), 1984–1987; organizer for economic summits, 1987–1989; set up his own lobbying firm in 1989 in association with his brother, Gerald, a founding partner at GCI.

▷ Key clients: International Aviation Terminals Inc., John Labatt Limited, Bearhead Industries Ltd., Albert Energy Co. Ltd., Brascan Ltd., T.C.C. Beverages Ltd. (Coca-Cola), Le Groupe MIL Inc., Paramount Pictures Corp., Central Capital Corp., Polaroid Canada Inc., Bitove Corp., Pocklington Financial Corp., OCR Holdings Ltd., Toronto Olympic Organizing Committee 1996 Inc., Noranda Inc., Merrill Lynch Canada Inc., Seabeco Group Corp., Sather-Allen Holdings, Royal Trustco Ltd.

PATRICK MACADAM, Government Consultants Intl. Inc.

▷ Caucus liaison office, PMO, 1984–1987; minister-counsellor at Canadian High Commission, London, 1987–1989.

▷ Key clients: Irving Pulp and Paper, Inc., Advanced Fibreoptics Technologies Corp., Airport Development Corp., Huang & Danczkay Ltd., Anheuser-Busch Companies Inc., ASEA Brown Boveri Inc., Bearhead Industries Ltd., Bell Canada, British Aerospace PLC, Buck Werke GmbH & Co., Canadian Liquid Air Ltd., Canadian Marconi Co., Clearwater Fine Foods Inc., enRoute Card Inc., Ernst & Young, GEC Canada Ltd., Harbour Grace Fishing Co. Ltd., Hiram Walker-Gooderham & Worts Ltd., MBB Helicopter Canada Ltd., Merck Frosst Canada Inc., Microtel (SI) Inc., Petrowest Petroleum Ltd., Pharmaceutical Manufacturers Association of Canada, Saint John

Shipbuilding Ltd., Squibb Canada Inc., Upjohn Company of Canada, Aerocar Quebec Ltd. William Fox, Earnscliffe Strategy Group Inc., Fox Communications Consultants

WILLIAM FOX, Earnscliffe Strategy Group Inc.; Fox Communications Consultants

▷ Press secretary, PMO, 1984–1987.

▷ Key clients: Power Corp. of Canada, The Portage Program, Ballet Opera House Corp., Canadian Centre for Arms Control and Disarmament, Fletcher Challenge Canada Ltd., Walker and Duncan Gordon Charitable Foundation, Canadian Business Aircraft Assoc., Varity Corp.

Mulroney Political Supporters

FRANK MOORES, Government Consultants Intl.

▷ Former Tory premier of Newfoundland nominated Mr. Mulroney for Conservative leader in 1976, a key Mulroney leadership organizer from 1979 to 1983.

▷ Key Clients: See list for Patrick MacAdam.

GERALD DOUCET, Doucet Associates Consulting, Fred Doucet Consulting Intl. Inc.

▷ Former Nova Scotia cabinet minister, long-time Mulroney friend from St. Francis Xavier University, founding partner of Government Consultants Intl.

▷ Key clients: shares many clients with his brother, Fred, but also lobbies for Halifax Dartmouth Industries Ltd., Champlain Pipeline Operating Co. Inc., Harrison & Associates Assurance Inc., Novatron Information Corp., Pathways Inc.

Conservative Party Advisers and Organizers

HARRY NEAR, Earnsliffe Policy Group, Near Consultants and Associates Ltd.

▷ PC Campaign Director, 1988 federal campaign; former chief of staff to Pat Carney when she was energy minister.

▷ Key clients: Adecon Inc., Varity Corp., Canadian Business Aircraft Assoc., Arthur Andersen & Co., Blackhawk Technology Corp., Canadian Soft Drink Association, Foothills Pipe Lines Ltd., Gordon Capital Corp., Huang & Danczkay Ltd., McCarthy Securities Ltd., The MIL Group, Polysar Ltd., Progras Ltd., Westcoast Energy Inc.

JOHN H. TORY, Tory Tory Deslauriers and Binnington

▷ Senior advisor on the 1988 campaign, travelling with Mr. Mulroney.

▷ Key clients: Blyth & Co., Canadian Football League, Canadian Independent Adjusters, International Thompson Ltd., National Tobacco Co. Ltd.

Former Cabinet Ministers, MPs and Senior Political Staff

STEWART MCINNES, McInnes Cooper & Robinson

▷ Former minister of supply and services and public works, defeated in 1988 election.

- ▷ Key Clients: Zeus Mineral Corp. Ltd., Nova Aqua Smolt Ltd., Donna Rae Ltd., four persons on immigration matters; Halifax-Dartmouth Industries Ltd.

RONALD ATKEY, Osler Hoskin & Harcourt

- ▷ Former minister of employment and immigration in 1979 Joe Clark government, former chairman of Canadian Security and Intelligence Review Committee.
- ▷ Key Clients: Amway of Canada Ltd., Bow Valley Industries Ltd., British Gas (Canada) Ltd., Lancaster Financial Inc., Daiwa Bani Canada, Quorum Funding Corporation, Warner Bros. Canada.

Former Senior Bureaucrats

SIMON REISMAN, Reiscar Ltd., Reisman and Grandy Ltd., Trade and Investment Advisory Group (TIAG)

- ▷ Former free trade negotiator for Canada in Canada-U.S. agreement, former deputy minister.
- ▷ Key clients: Loblaw International Merchants, William Neilsen Ltd., Ranger Oil Ltd., Beatrice Foods Inc.

RAYMOND HESSION, Arvess Management Services Corp.; president, Paxport Management Inc.

- ▷ Former secretary to the Treasury Board
- ▷ Key clients: Atlantic Research Canada, Inc., Gandaif Technologies Inc., Hughes Aircraft of Canada Ltd., Senstar Corp.

Source: *The Globe and Mail*, March 10, 1990, p. D2.

FOCUS

1. Use Documents 1 and 2 to explain why some companies have more clients than other firms.
2. Explain why these people went into the lobbying business.
3. If you were part of the following pressure groups, which lobbyist would you choose and why?
   a) a small oil company
   b) an anti-pollution group
   c) a pulp and paper company
   d) a multinational manufacturing company
   e) a save the whale committee
4. Why do you think there is more interest in lobbying for international trade matters than for environmental concerns?
5. Should there be laws regarding who can/cannot be lobbyists? Explain.
6. As previously mentioned, the information from Documents 1 and 2 is available to the public. Do you think this is a good idea? Explain.

Greenpeace and the Environment Lobby

In 1970, a Vancouver committee known as Greenpeace protested the detonation of a nuclear bomb in the Pacific Ocean. From this initial protest, an international environmental organization evolved that has become one of the most well-known and successful pressure groups in the world. Since 1970 Greenpeace has been involved in protest campaigns against toxic waste, acid rain, nuclear weapons, whaling, sealing, and kangaroo slaughter. It has national organizations in over seventeen countries in North America, Europe, and South America.

On page 136 there is a chronology of some of the activities Greenpeace has been involved in during the 1980s. It is only a sample of the numerous causes and tactics employed by this international pressure group. As you read through this chronology, answer the following questions:

▸ **1.** Using a blank map of the world, indicate where the various protests occurred.

▸ **2.** Greenpeace is a good example of a pressure group that uses a variety of methods to put direct or indirect pressure on governments and com-

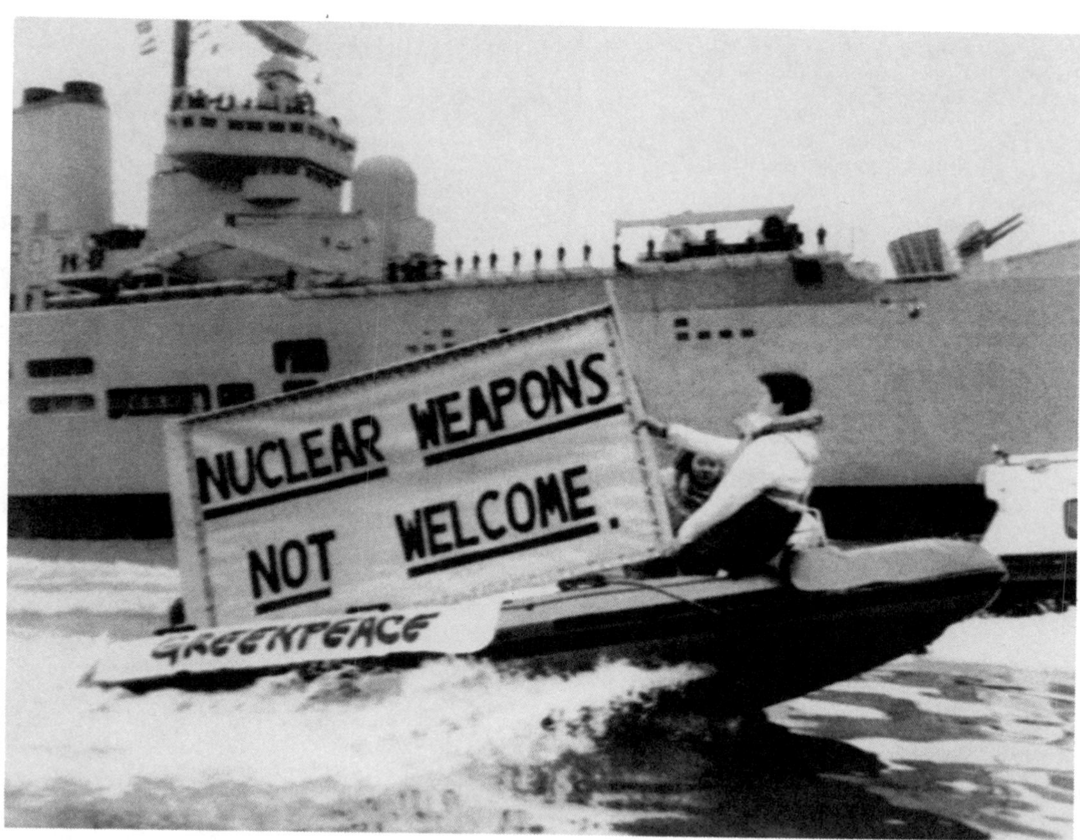

Members of Greenpeace, an environmental protection group, hold up an anti-nuclear protest sign in front of the aircraft carrier HMS *Ark Royal* in Portsmouth, England, December 15, 1988.
The Bettmann Archive

GREENPEACE THROUGH THE 1980s

1982

Country	United States
Protest	Failure of United States Environmental Protection Agency to act in the best interest of the environment
Action	Two Greenpeace activists climbed down within fifteen metres of Niagara Falls and hung a banner reading "E.P.A. Protecting the Environment or Industry?" The two were charged with disorderly conduct.

1983

Country	Norway
Protest	Norwegians hunting seal pups
Action	Global campaign against hunting seal pups. Norway stopped seal pup hunting and limited number of ships hunting adult seals.
Country	Australia
Protest	Australian uranium mining
Action	Blockade in Great Victoria Desert of largest uranium mine in the world. Two hundred and sixty arrests including fifty Greenpeace members.
Country	Norway
Protest	Stop Norwegians from whaling
Action	Organized consumer boycott of Norwegian fish exports. Norway agreed to stop whaling in 1986.

1984

Country	Canada
Protest	Stop Canada from allowing the United States to test its cruise missiles on Canadian territory
Action	Demonstrations outside missile range at Cold Lake, Alberta, including a net to trap the missile. Tests continued throughout the decade.
Continent	Antarctica
Protest	Preserve Antarctica as a world park with no industrial development
Action	Two Greenpeace protestors occupied mooring lines of an Antarctic research vessel in New Zealand. This vessel was equipped to explore for oil in Antarctica. No action resulted.

1985

Country	Belgium
Protest	Protest dumping of titanium dioxide waste into the North Sea
Action	Greenpeace twice blocked passage of dump ship. Belgian government announced an end to the dumping of titanium in 1987.

1985 cont'd.

Country	International
Protest	Against the establishment of turtle farms
Action	Opposed turtle farms at the convention of International Trade in Endangered Species. Along with the Centre for Environmental Education, Greenpeace was successful in stopping the five turtle farms.

1986

Country	United States
Protest	Against the burning of hazardous waste
Action	Two Greenpeace protestors climbed a sixty metre smoke-stack in Indiana. They opposed the plan to build a hazardous waste incinerator in the area. Health authorities banned the construction of the plant.
Country	Australia
Protest	Against French nuclear testing in the South Pacific
Action	Two Greenpeace workers climbed to the top of the Sydney Opera House and hung anti-French nuclear test banners. Nuclear tests continued.

1987

Country	United States
Protest	Against acid rain from American industry
Action	Four Greenpeace workers hung a banner on Mount Rushmore in South Dakota. The four were sentenced to ninety days in jail, two years probation, and $3000 in fines.

1988

Country	Denmark
Protest	Encourage an international approach to Europe's environmental problems
Action	Greenpeace "action bus" embarked upon a ten-week tour of countries on the Baltic Sea.

1989

Country	Soviet Union
Protest	Awareness campaign to introduce Greenpeace to the people of the Soviet Union
Action	Release of the double album "Greenpeace: Breakthrough" (with twenty-four leading rock musicians and bands). This was the biggest release of a Western rock album in the U.S.S.R.

panies. Examine any five protests and determine which of the following strategies Greenpeace used to exert pressure. (Note: it may have used more than one strategy at the same time.)
a) media support
b) confrontation
c) publicity tactics
d) government co-operation
Which of these did it use the most?

▸ **3.** What do you think has made Greenpeace successful?

▸ **4.** Greenpeace believes in using any non-violent means to achieve its goals. Do you think a pressure group is correct in using a philosophy of "the end justifies the means"?

▸ **5.** Research a recent Greenpeace operation. Explain the issue, the tactics, and the results.

▸ **6.** Prepare for a mock debate on one of these issues.

APPLYING YOUR KNOWLEDGE

1. Read your local newspaper for two days and make a list of all the interest groups mentioned. Which groups are attempting to influence government policies? What tactics are they using? How many of these groups represent the wealthy and influential members of society?
2. Prepare for a debate (or write an essay) on the topic: "Pressure groups are essential (or detrimental) to the proper working of democracy."
3. Write an essay stating what this case study reveals to you about the power and influence of pressure groups in Canadian politics.
4. Write an essay explaining why pressure groups arise and what functions they perform.
5. Is the existence of pressure groups in Canada inevitable? Explain your view.
6. Would Canadians as a whole be better off if political pressure groups were forbidden? Explain.
7. Prepare for a mock interview with a lobbyist, or invite a member of a pressure group to speak to your class.

Case Study 9 Overview

The Struggle for Political Equality—Female Suffrage

Women's struggle for political equality combines many of the themes of the previous case studies, including voting behaviour, non-violent disobedience, and lobbying. This case study begins with an examination of the different treatment afforded women in developed versus developing countries, and then focuses upon women's struggle for the franchise in Great Britain and Canada. In both countries the obstacles to gaining the vote are outlined, as are the women's methods of achieving change and their success. In Great Britain, male opposition forced women to use more violent means than were needed in Canada. The case study concludes with an overview of the problems facing Canadian women today.

▶ OBJECTIVES

After reading this case study, you should be able to:

- ▶ outline and compare the methods used by British and Canadian women to achieve the franchise
- ▶ contrast the position of women in developed and developing countries
- ▶ evaluate the present demands of the women's movement
- ▶ discuss the reasons behind the opposition to giving women the vote
- ▶ interview family members about past attitudes
- ▶ analyse newspapers and other forms of media for evidence of sexism

▶ KEY TERMS

political equality | suffrage | societal norms

The Struggle for Political Equality—Female Suffrage

The previous case study examined lobbying as a way of changing opinions and policies. Women have utilized this technique in their long struggle for **political equality**. There was a time when society considered women too weak, emotional, and irrational to vote in elections. An analysis of women's struggle for political equality illustrates the major themes developed in the previous four case studies.

▶ DEFINITION AND ORIGINS

Women have been seeking political equality since the mid-1800s. The definition of equality, however, varies from country to country and over time. In some countries, gaining the vote symbolizes equality to women. Elsewhere, equality means equal access to political positions. Even in countries once headed by a female leader, such as India and Pakistan, women lack political and economic equality. Political equality, like democracy, reflects fundamental differences in values and ways of life. Although the definition varies, female suffrage is an important first step in the political arena. This case study examines how women achieved the right to vote and to run for public office in Great Britain and Canada.

Women around the world did not achieve the franchise simultaneously. They gained this right depending upon the political, economic, and social climate of the time. The chart on page 140 reveals that in most countries women now have the right to vote.

In developed countries, many women are actively involved in politics. They do a great deal of "behind-the-scenes" work, which brings success to the leader and ultimately to the party. Although they make important contributions in the areas of

Table 1
EQUAL VOTING RIGHTS FOR WOMEN

1893 New Zealand
1902 Australia
1906 Finland
1913 Norway
1915 Denmark
1915 Iceland
1917 U.S.S.R.
1918 Luxembourg
1918 Poland
1919 Austria
1919 Czechoslovakia
1919 Germany
1919 Netherlands
1919 Sweden
1920 Canada
1920 U.S.A.
1922 Ireland
1924 Mongolia
1928 United Kingdom
1929 Ecuador
1930 South Africa*
1931 Spain
1932 Brazil
1932 Thailand
1932 Uruguay
1934 Cuba
1934 Sri Lanka (Ceylon)
1934 Turkey
1935 Burma
1937 Philippines
1942 Dominican Republic
1944 France
1944 Jamaica
1945 Japan
1945 Indonesia
1945 Italy
1946 Albania
1946 Korea (N. and S.)
1946 Liberia
1946 Panama
1946 Trinidad and Tobago
1947 Bulgaria
1947 China
1947 Malta
1948 Belgium
1948 Israel
1948 Romania
1949 Chile
1949 Costa Rica
1949 India
1949 Syria
1950 El Salvador
1950 Haiti
1951 Barbados
1951 Nepal
1952 Bolivia
1952 Greece
1953 Mexico
1954 Nigeria
1955 Ethiopia
1955 Ghana
1955 Honduras
1955 Nicaragua
1955 Peru
1956 Benin
1956 Burkina Faso (Upper Volta)
1956 Cameroon
1956 Central African Republic
1956 Congo
1956 Gabon
1956 Guinea
1956 Ivory Coast
1956 Kampuchea (Cambodia)
1956 Laos
1956 Madagascar (Malagasy Republic)
1956 Mali
1956 Mauritania
1956 Monaco
1956 Niger
1956 Pakistan
1956 Senegal
1956 Vietnam
1957 Colombia
1957 Lebanon
1957 Malaysia
1958 Algeria
1958 Somalia
1959 Cyprus
1959 Morocco
1959 Tunisia
1961 Burundi
1961 Gambia
1961 Paraguay
1961 Sierra Leone
1962 Kuwait
1962 Rwanda
1962 Samoa
1962 Uganda
1963 Kenya
1963 Libya
1963 Iran
1964 Afghanistan
1964 Iraq
1964 Malawi
1964 Zambia
1965 Guatemala
1965 Singapore
1965 Sudan
1966 Botswana
1966 Guyana
1966 Lesotho
1970 South Yemen
1971 Switzerland
1975 Angola
1975 Cape Verde
1975 Mozambique
1975 Papua New Guinea
1975 Portugal
1980 Zimbabwe
1982 Jordan

*White women

▸ Source: Joni Seager and Ann Olson, *Women in the World: An International Atlas*. London and Sydney: Pan Books, 1986.

human relations and often hold the position of secretary, few women are involved at the upper level of politics and they receive fewer rewards. Women constitute more than fifty percent of the population, yet they continue to be under-represented in politics. In 1989, of the 284 members in the Canadian House of Commons, only thirty-nine were women. In Canada and the United States, government legislation on abortion, pay equity, and divorce are critical issues affecting women, but where male politicians generally make the final decisions.

The situation in developing countries is different. Here, the only opportunities for women outside of the areas of child and house care involve low paying jobs. Women have less power, money, and autonomy and are burdened with more responsibility than men — they not only work outside the home but are also responsible for nearly all the household chores. These women are concerned about effective contraception and the healthy birth and life of their children. They find themselves in a situation of dependency. For example, in India women received the vote in 1949, and Indira Gandhi was the prime minister from 1966 to 1977 and from 1980 to 1984. Yet in daily life, Indian women's opinions are not sought, and women are not considered the equals of men. The fact that a woman brings a dowry to her marriage suggests that she is considered a piece of property. In Indian cities the status of women is changing rapidly. Many parties prefer female politicians because they tend to gain female support. But in the countryside, traditional customs continue. A woman is highly respected in her home, but secluded from public interaction.

▶ GAINING THE VOTE IN DEVELOPED COUNTRIES

Mirroring the varied definitions of political equality are the ways in which women established a political voice in their country. In the 1800s, the social standing of a woman depended on her father's or husband's status. Middle- and upper-class women concentrated on the religious and emotional needs of their families, decorated their homes, and dressed lavishly. As they recognized specific problems that needed to be addressed, they lobbied for reform. Industrialization increased opportunities to work outside the home, but the factories were exploitive, had abominable working conditions, and paid little. Women demanded changes. Their sense of a shared identity had begun to emerge. Once their united voice brought factory reforms, women sought redress on many other issues. But women usually lost out in their attempts to gain these reforms. Therefore, to get reforms on such matters as child labour, prohibition, and morality issues (prostitution), women sought the vote.

In each country, women organized to fight for the right to vote. Their methods and success varied according to the political atmosphere of the time. In Great Britain, women organized protest marches and forced male politicians to grant them the vote. In Canada, women used peaceful and constitutional means to help them attain the vote.

▶ THE SUFFRAGE MOVEMENT IN GREAT BRITAIN

In Great Britain, women began to demand suffrage near the end of the nineteenth century. Women faced two main obstacles: the Victorian attitudes held by men and women, and the firmly entrenched power structures. At this time, society focused on women as physical objects. Women were to be attractive and pleasant but were considered too irrational and emotional to participate in the world outside the home. It is interesting to note that there was a distinction made between a lady and a woman. A female who was a wife or daughter of a gentleman was called a "lady." A female who was a wife or daughter of a working man was called a "woman." Women were thus defined according to their relationship with a man. Using this definition, it was "ladies" who led the suffrage movement. Lord Tennyson penned words that were widely accepted during this time:

Man to command and women to obey.
All else is confusion.

This was not only a time of harsh and repressive sexual puritanism but also of rampant pornography. Christabel Pankhurst, a vocal suffragette (a woman who advocated female suffrage), believed that male sexual lust was the real reason why men resisted giving women the vote. In her view, men were afraid that if women voted, prostitution and sexual abuse against women would be outlawed. Other arguments against giving women the vote included:

- It is unwomanly to vote.
- Women would not vote if they had the opportunity.
- Women do not wish to vote.
- Bad women will vote.
- Politics will degrade and corrupt women.
- Wives might vote against their own husbands and thus destroy the harmony of the home.
- Wives would usually vote as their husbands wished, so the result would not be materially changed.
- Women are fairly represented by men. Their fathers and brothers vote.
- Women's brains are not as large as men's, therefore they should not vote.
- Brainwork is more exhausting for women than for men.
- Women are more nervous than men, and the excitement of elections would undermine their constitutions and tend to unbalance them.
- The strain of political life would prevent motherhood.
- If women were allowed to vote, there would be too many voters.

Ladies' demands were labelled "militant." Violent and oppressive behaviour was not considered acceptable for females. At this time, asking a question in a public meeting — anything against the norm — was considered aggressive. Society believed that women were the weaker sex and that they were controlled by the monthly changes in their bodies. The fury with which society reacted to the suffragettes' methods demonstrates that when people are afraid of something they often respond irrationally.

Most of the British "militants" were models of late Victorian uprightness. They were upper middle-class ladies. They practiced the Quaker or Unitarian religion and were well-educated. At first, they used energy, intelligence, and persistence to present their cause. But they soon realized that rational, peaceful methods would not be rewarded. They were tired of being laughed at and of being the focus of such music hall comic songs as the following:

Put me upon an island where the girls are few
Put me among the most ferocious lions in the zoo
You can put me on a treadmill, and I'll never, never fret
But for pity's sake, don't put me near a Suffragette.

The suffragettes soon began to use violence to focus attention on their cause. No one was listening to them, so they used physical means to achieve their goals. As their anger increased, so did the examples and frequency of what was called "violent" behaviour. In October 1905, Sir Edward Grey addressed a Liberal audience in Manchester. Christabel Pankhurst and Annie Kenney, both suffragette leaders, attempted to force Grey to state the Liberal government's position on granting women the vote. Grey refused to answer their questions. They persisted. Finally, they were forcibly ejected and arrested when they tried to talk to the crowd. Witnesses later said that the young women were mauled by the Liberal stewards who threw them out. But it was the women who were charged with obstruction and assault of a police officer. She had her hands tied behind her, so it was impossible for her to be violent. The suffragettes responded by heckling all Liberal speakers in an attempt

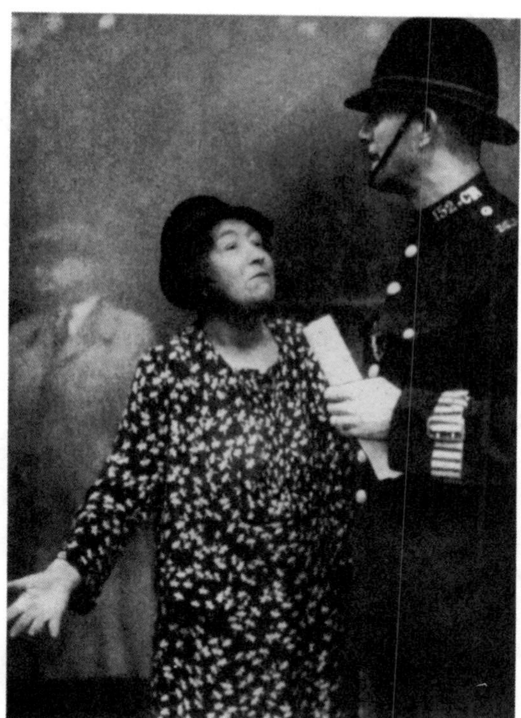

Many suffragettes met opposition from Victorian police.
National Archives of Canada/Neg. No. C8870

to force the party to adopt female suffrage. They also sent deputations to the House of Commons. From this point on, the press described them as "militant."

In January 1906, a group of women, tired of waiting to be heard in Parliament, announced that they were willing to go to prison to get the vote. Emmeline Pankhurst told women that they had to be violent and risk arrest. On February 13, 1907, the suffragettes marched on Parliament. An all-day battle developed, and sixty women were arrested. The police officers were so violent that many women were injured. The women tried again that night to get into Parliament, but the police stoned them.

When the vote was still withheld, the suffragettes increased their opposition. The police became more violent. There were isolated cases reported of stone throwing in June 1908. In November 1909, Mrs. Pankhurst was charged with assaulting a police officer. She had hit the officer repeatedly, but only so that she herself would be arrested, and the police would stop its brutality against the more vulnerable members of her group.

After Black Friday, November 18, 1910, the women became committed to violence. On this day, many were arrested after a stone-throwing episode. Once in jail, some women went on hunger strikes. The government retaliated and had them force-fed. In this very painful procedure, a tube was forced down their throat. Several women got infections and some died.

The women's militancy made the cause of suffrage noteworthy. Publicity was the aim. These women knew the power of the printed word. They also became violent in reaction to being provoked. It is important to note that some men did speak out in favour of the women's cause. Robert J. Richardson, for example, wrote a pamphlet clearly stating that women contributed a great deal to society and should be viewed as equals. John Stuart Mill (1806–1873), another famous male champion of women's rights, sought to get the vote for women when he was elected to Parliament in 1865.

In 1918, married women over the age of thirty were allowed to vote. The voting laws had been changed to enfranchise soldiers who could not vote under the existing system, and some women were included in this legislation. But it was not until the Equal Franchise Act of 1928 that all women over the age of twenty-one were placed in the same position as men and allowed to vote in parliamentary and local elections. British suffragettes had won this right

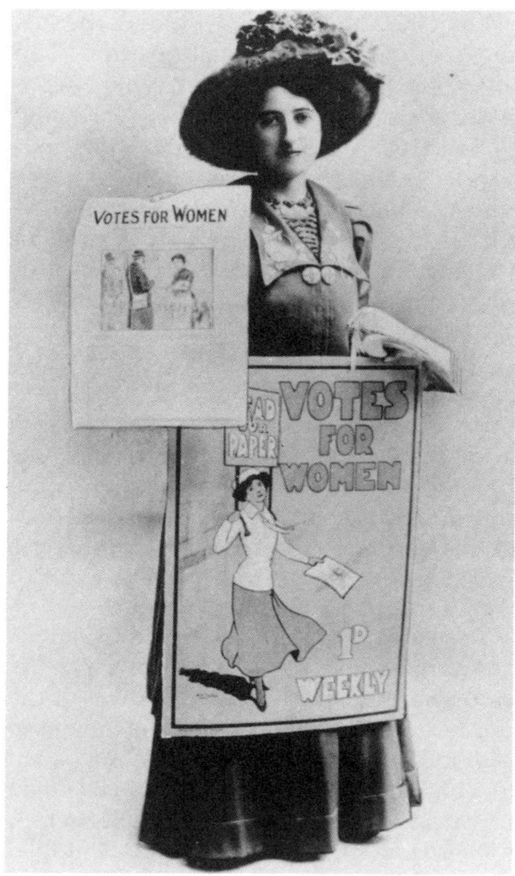

National Archives of Canada/Neg. No. PA 143958

through persistent lobbying at all levels of government.

▶ SOCIAL AND POLITICAL FEMINISM— THE CANADIAN ALTERNATIVE

The suffrage movement in Canada was not nationally organized until 1889. Women were hampered by the restrictive attitudes of the time, their lack of unity across the country, and the opposition from the media and government. Each province had unique conditions that had to be overcome before the vote was secured. Individual women lobbied actively for the vote and others worked together as a group to lobby within the political framework. The leaders were Protestant, elite, urban professionals who had leisure time to fight for reforms.

Women were officially excluded from politics. During most of the nineteenth and early twentieth centuries, women were not allowed to serve on juries or attend university. A woman was not considered to have political merit. If she spoke out for the vote, she was considered aggressive and bold.

Women were encouraged to remain apart from the evils of politics. Between 1908 and 1909, the French-Canadian newspaper *Journal de françoise* conducted a plebiscite among prominent women about their feelings regarding women getting the vote. Of the published replies, nineteen favoured suffrage, while thirty-five opposed it. The wife of the former lieutenant-governor of the province of Quebec wrote:

I consider that the role of a woman is to govern her home and to direct the education of her family. In my opinion she would gain nothing by descending into the political arena in becoming an elector.

Such narrow attitudes concerning women were prevalent among males *and* females. Consider these facts about the political and educational position of women at the turn of the century:

- **1.** No woman had the right to vote. The Election Act of the Dominion of Canada stated that "no woman, idiot, lunatic, or criminal shall vote."
- **2.** No woman could be elected to federal or provincial government offices.

- **3.** Wives had to obey their husbands and could legally be beaten.
- **4.** It was a commonly accepted fact that the chief function of a woman was to keep house for her husband and to bear his children. One out of every five women in Canada died in childbirth.

Women in English and French Canada worked within different environments to activate change. Women in Quebec received the vote later than in the other provinces because the Roman Catholic church, which dictated **societal norms**, opposed female franchise. They were to be dominated by men and excluded from political and professional life.

Canadian women entered the power sphere by speaking out on such social issues as child labour, prostitution, tuberculosis, poverty, and slums. Dr. Emily Stowe of Toronto was one of the first people to speak out on behalf of women's rights in Canada. She attended school in the United States because no Canadian medical school accepted female students. In 1876, Dr. Stowe and her friends formed the Toronto Women's Literary Club. The name was misleading. The club's main concern was getting women the vote. Gradually, other women's groups were formed throughout Canada. These suffrage clubs joined in 1889 to form the Dominion Women's Enfranchisement Association. "Votes for Women!" was the cry. The battle was on!

The demand for the vote was linked with the desire to improve society. Factory conditions were terrible. Young boys and girls worked twelve hours a day in crowded, unhealthy factories. Juvenile delinquency and crime were growing at an alarming rate. The urban poor lived in slums infested with rats and lice. Women were particularly concerned with the drinking problem. Alcoholic husbands spent their earnings on liquor and left their families without food or shelter. All too frequently they returned home to mistreat their wives and children. The suffragettes believed that if women were given the vote they would purify politics, pass laws to improve working conditions, and ban alcohol.

Perhaps the most important figure in the suffragette movement was Nellie McClung. Born in Ontario and raised on a Manitoba farm, Nellie McClung started her career as a school teacher. She gained national attention in 1908 when her novel *Sowing Seeds in Danny* became a best seller. She was a fighter almost from the start of her life. "I went to the one outhouse in the schoolyard," an old schoolfriend recalled, "flung open the door and got the surprise of my life. A quick, hard, well-placed kick to the stomach knocked me back reeling." Years later, while she was speaking against liquor at a temperance meeting, a heckler yelled, "Don't you wish you were a man right now, Nellie?" She quickly replied, "Don't you wish you were?" A fiery, eloquent speaker, Nellie devoted herself to getting women the right to vote.

Sir Rodmond Roblin was the premier of Manitoba in 1914. He opposed the suffragettes. "I don't want a hyena in petticoats talking politics to me," he once told Nellie, "I want a nice gentle creature to bring me my slippers." Later, the premier addressed a delegation of female suffragettes.

Let it be known that it is the opinion of the Roblin government that woman suffrage is illogical and absurd as far as Manitoba is concerned. Placing women on a political equality with men would cause domestic strife. Sex antagonism would be aroused. It is an easy flame to fan. I believe that woman suffrage will break up the home. It will throw the children into the arms of servant girls. The majority of women are emotional, and if given the franchise they would be a menace rather than an aid.

The next evening the ladies staged a mock Parliament in the Walker Theatre. This time, however, the women were the politicians and the men were pleading for the vote. Nellie played the premier's role. Copying Sir Rodmond's gestures, she proclaimed:

The trouble is that if men started to vote, they will vote too much. Politics unsettles men, and unsettled men means broken furniture, broken vows, and divorce. If men were to get into the habit of voting—who knows what might happen—it's hard enough to keep them home now. History is full of unhappy examples of men in public life—Nero, Herod, King John.

Her performance ''brought the house down'' and probably convinced many in the audience of the justice of her cause.

A year later, Sir Rodmond was defeated by the Liberals under T.C. Norris. The suffragettes had campaigned for Norris, and thus in January 1916, Manitoba became the first province to grant women the vote. Saskatchewan and Alberta passed similar laws

Nellie McClung (right) and Emmeline Pankhurst
Glenbow Archives, Calgary, Alberta, NC-6-1746

that year. Ontario and British Columbia followed suit in 1917. The next step was to convince the federal government.

Table 2
A TIMETABLE FOR WOMEN'S POLITICAL EQUALITY

Province	Suffrage
Manitoba	1916
Saskatchewan	1916
Alberta	1916
British Columbia	1917
Ontario	1918
Nova Scotia	1918
New Brunswick	1919
Prince Edward Island	1922
Newfoundland	1925
Quebec	1940
Canada	1917 (limited) 1920 (all women)

▶ WHY THE WESTERN PROVINCES GRANTED WOMEN THE FRANCHISE—A DEBATE

History is interpretation. ''Facts'' are only important for what you do with them. As a result, historians often differ. They write conflicting interpretations of the same event, often using the same ''facts.'' One topic of disagreement is why the western provinces granted women suffrage before the eastern provinces did. Read the following actual debate between two historians and decide for yourself.

One View:

The author is way off target. According to the author, women in the west were the first to get the vote because they worked alongside the men on the farm, and thus proved their worth.

This is a load of bunkum. The women in the Maritimes and in Upper and Lower Canada also worked alongside the men on the farm. Women made an enormous contribution in the settlement of Canada, but it has nothing to do with the issue of them getting the vote.

The reason why Manitoba was the first province to get the vote is very obvious if the facts are considered:

1. *There was the enormous reputation of Manitoba editor Cora Hind.*
2. *There was Nellie McClung, the catalyst who made it happen.*

In my view, the actual personalities were the key. In Ontario, the suffrage movement was headed by Emily Stowe. She was an aggressive woman who had more or less declared war on men. The only men she could put up with were those who, like her husband, did what they were told. She antagonized males because she took out the verbal knife and slashed them to pieces. By contrast, the western suffragettes gained great support in many male areas. For starters, the leaders were intelligent women, and they gathered many male admirers. They were not so silly as to confront men, making it a male-female issue. They simply stated the facts. Cora Hind, the agricultural editor of the Manitoba Free Press, *proved that she could do her job better than any man had done. Farmers, grain dealers, and many others admired her for this. Nellie McClung also gained terrific support, even though her outspokenness created several male and female enemies.*

But it was the individuals who did it. People can create changes if they care enough.

A Rebuttal:

This interpretation ignores several important factors. During the pioneer period in the Maritimes and central Canada there were no laws against women voting. Women were not legally denied the franchise until society became more settled. Women were not officially granted the vote during this period because few people even considered the topic. The question did not arise until the 1870s, and then it was aided by American and British examples. By this time, the east was no longer a pioneer community. The western provinces first granted women the vote because pioneer farming involved the entire family. Women worked side-by-side with men. Some females even pulled the ploughs when there was not enough money for a horse. Because the west was more recently settled, it was easier to effect changes. Western farmers thought that Ottawa and central Canada controlled their lives too much. They wanted reforms. The farmers demanded a more democratic government. Female suffrage was a democratic reform.

FOCUS

1. What is your position on this debate?

▶ WORLD WAR I AND THE SUFFRAGE MOVEMENT

World War I was the single most important event in promoting women's suffrage. Great Britain, France, and Russia went to war against Germany and Austria-Hungary in 1914. As a British colony, Canada was also at war. Most Canadians believed that this was a fight between democracy and dictatorship. If this were true, argued the suffragettes, how would Canadians justify losing thousands of lives in Europe trying to bring democracy to Germany, when half the population at home was denied the right to vote?

The war also created new opportunities and responsibilities for women. As young men volunteered for the army, their places were taken by women. Factory jobs normally held by men were now performed by women—and done efficiently. Farm wives were left to run the homestead themselves and succeeded. Women knitted socks for the soldiers, raised money for the war, and served as nurses. They had earned the right to vote.

The most important reason for the federal enfranchisement of women, however, was party politics. A federal election was due to be held in 1917. Conservative Prime Minister Robert L. Borden was worried that his party would lose to the Liberal party led by Wilfrid Laurier. Many people were unhappy with the Conservative government. In western Canada, the farmers were dissatisfied with high freight costs and low wheat prices. Urban workers were also discontented. The cost of food had risen faster than wages. Many workers believed that their bosses were taking advantage of the war situation to make very large profits. The worst discontent was in Quebec. French Canadians objected to fighting in a war that they thought did not concern Canada.

The Borden government was thus in trouble. To make matters worse, the Canadian troops in Europe were receiving insufficient reinforcements. In the spring of 1917, for example, more than 20 000 Canadian soldiers were killed or injured, but only 3000 new men were added to the forces.

The prime minister decided to conscript Canadians to fight overseas. The Liberals opposed conscription, but Borden was convinced that this law was essential to win the war. He was also determined to win the election at any cost. The Military Voters Act was passed in August 1917, and the Wartime Elections Act was introduced in September. The first law gave the vote to all members of the Canadian armed forces, male or female, no matter how long they had lived in Canada. The second act granted the vote to all mothers, wives, sisters, and daughters of Canadian soldiers. It also took the vote away from immigrants born in enemy countries who had settled in Canada after 1902, as well as from all people who refused to fight for religious reasons.

The intention of these bills was obvious. As one politician remarked, "It would have been more direct and at the same time more honest, if the bill simply stated that all who did not pledge themselves to vote Conservative would be disfranchised." The Conservatives won the 1917 election. The next year, all women twenty-one years of age and over received the vote.

▶ PROBLEMS FOR CANADIAN WOMEN IN OFFICE

After the war, women tried to balance a family and a career, break into newly available professions, fight discrimination, and have a political voice. In 1921, four women, or 0.6 percent of the total candidates, were nominated to run in the federal election. Agnes Macphail was the only woman elected to the House of Commons. This thirty-one-year-old school teacher represented the United Farmers of Ontario party in South East Grey, an area in rural Ontario. Macphail defeated ten men to win the nomination and then spent two months convincing her constituents that her gender would not diminish the quality of her representation. She recorded her feelings of isolation in the House of Commons in "Men Want To Hog Everything":

I couldn't open my mouth to say the simplest thing without it appearing in the papers. I was a curiosity, a freak. And you know the way the world treats freaks.

Her success mirrored the fortunes of the suffrage movement. Her constituents did not always share her concerns, and not all women backed her ideas. When she supported Glace Bay miners in their attempts for better working conditions, several women's groups spoke out against her. This was another example of the fragmentation within the suffrage movement. It seemed that women needed a single evil to combat in order to eliminate splinter groups. It was only in 1931, when the question of electing a woman to the Senate became an issue, that internal differences among feminists were briefly overcome.

▶ POLITICAL EQUALITY REVIEWED

Women's struggle to receive the vote was marked by opposition from many men and women. Although the vote has been awarded, women still face barriers that hinder social, political, and economic equality. The majority of women in developing countries face overwhelming daily concerns for sufficient food and sanitation that seem more important than demands for equal representation in government. In developed countries, there are still major obstacles to be overcome by women in politics. Negative male attitudes, lack of time and money, and male networking continue to deter women from seeking political leadership. Women continue to be under-represented, except in pink-collar roles. This means that they hold secretarial-type jobs but are rarely the boss. Although the number of women elected to the House of Commons increased from four in 1921 to thirty-seven in 1990, it will take another 210 years at this rate to achieve equal representation at the federal level. However, women are becoming more visible leaders. In 1989, the federal New Democratic party elected Audrey McLaughlin as its leader. Although this suggests that women can and will be taken seriously as future leaders of this country, it is still just one more step towards their acceptance as persons. In 1915, Nellie McClung penned words that might have been written today:

At the present time there is much discontent among women and many people are seriously alarmed about it. They say women are no longer contented with woman's sphere and woman's work. We may as well admit that discontent is not necessarily wicked. Discontent may mean the stirring of ambition, the desire to spread out, to improve and grow. Discontent is a sign of life, corresponding to growing pains in a healthy child.

In the late nineteenth century, discontented women began to activate a change. If women still experience this discontent today, the world must be prepared for more changes.

In 1989, Audrey McLaughlin became the first female leader of a Canadian federal government party.
Canada Wide/Tim McKenna

APPLYING YOUR KNOWLEDGE

1. Examine Table 1 and categorize the type of countries that first granted female suffrage. Which were the slowest? Provide a possible reason for this.
2. For each of the reasons given why women should not vote, devise a counter-argument. Which reasons are contradictory?
3. What was the importance of World War I to the suffragette cause in Canada?
4. The only other occasion the British Parliament used force-feeding on a person in jail was against conscientious objectors. Can you recognize any similarities between the behaviour of the suffragettes and these men?
5. Why did British women use violence? Was it justified?

FURTHER RESEARCH

1. Research the "Persons Case" and the question of Senate eligibility. What similarities existed between this case and the struggle for the franchise?
2. Interview your grandmother or any woman over the age of sixty-five. Discover her impressions of women working outside the home. Speak to a young female friend about the same situation. If the two interviews are very different, suggest reasons for this.
3. Interview several women on the major issues affecting them. Ask them to outline their feelings of groups such as REAL Women and ardent feminists.
4. Research the struggle that Canadian native peoples endured to get the vote and compare their methods with those that women used. Pay special attention to the problems of native women.
5. Imagine that the year is 1912. Prepare for a mock debate on whether women should have the vote. The females in the class will argue no, the males will argue in favour of women getting the vote.
6. Nellie McClung once declared:

   When a newspaper wishes to disprove a woman's contention or demolish her theories, it draws ugly pictures of her. If it can show that she has big feet or red hands or wears unbecoming clothes, that certainly settles the case and puts her where she belongs.

   Examine newspapers to determine whether the media still focuses on women's appearance rather than on what these individuals say or do.

CHAPTER 4 OVERVIEW

THE WORLD'S POLITICAL SYSTEMS: AUTHORITARIAN FORMS OF GOVERNMENT

This chapter examines the basic principles underlying authoritarian states. It discusses the origins and variety of authoritarian governments; reviews the writings of Carlyle, Nietzsche, Arendt, Hitler, and Machiavelli; and explores the ''Great Man'' theory, divine right, dictatorship, military coups, fascism, and totalitarian regimes. The chapter outlines the major characteristics of totalitarian and fascist states and evaluates the various theories that explain the attractiveness and success of such regimes. The conclusion compares fascism and communism and provides a critique of authoritarianism.

▶ OBJECTIVES

After reading this chapter, you should be able to:

- ▶ compare the similarities and differences among the various types of authoritarian regimes
- ▶ understand the reasons for the rise and success of authoritarian states
- ▶ evaluate the underlying beliefs of authoritarian ideologies
- ▶ outline the methods used by dictatorial leaders in gaining and maintaining power
- ▶ analyse the various theories proposed in support of totalitarian regimes

▶ KEY TERMS

authoritarian governments
totalitarian
autocrats
coup d'etat
civil liberties
crisis theory
charismatic; charisma (n.)
authoritarian personality

THE WORLD'S POLITICAL SYSTEMS: AUTHORITARIAN FORMS OF GOVERNMENT

We have defined democracy as a system of government under which the ultimate power rests with the people, who elect lawmakers and other representatives from among themselves. Elections are held either at the end of a legally defined term of office (as in the United States) or when an administration or cabinet chooses to dissolve government or loses the support of the majority of the elected lawmakers (as in Canada or Great Britain). The government thus derives its authority from the "will of the people" as expressed through elections.

Abuse of governmental authority is limited by the fact that all citizens enjoy a number of basic "civil rights" or individual liberties. These are guaranteed either by tradition (common law) or by a bill of rights. The concept of such "rights" and the belief that the protection of the individual enjoying them is a prime responsibility of the state have become hallmarks of the ideology of modern liberalism and of liberal democratic forms of government.

Leaders of **authoritarian governments** see matters differently. They tell the people what to do and expect the people to obey. This obedience is usually justified in the name of some higher value (crown, state, or race) to which an individual's interests and rights may be sacrificed. Such governments are commonly termed authoritarian and represent the opposite extreme to a pure democracy.

Just as there are different types and

degrees of democracy, there are also different versions of authoritarian regimes. In some cases, they may be simple one-person (often military) dictatorships, ruled by an authoritarian parental figure. Such countries may permit the expression of a broad range of dissenting views. In others, the leader may demand total submission to the views of the party or government. Authoritarian governments that seek to dominate and control all facets of society are generally referred to as **totalitarian**. Under this type of rule, all opposition is banned and the citizens surrender all civil rights to the ruling dictator, elite, or party.

The following discussion examines the basic principles underlying authoritarian states, as well as the major ideologies (fascism and communism) that have evolved to justify this form of rule. But remember, not only are these principles imposed more rigorously in some countries than in others, but they have also been implemented with varying degrees of rigor at different times in the same country.

▶ THE "GREAT MAN" THEORY

Most authoritarian regimes throughout history have been based on the belief that a small elite is best able to govern a country. In the nineteenth century, many political thinkers, impressed with Napoleon Bonaparte's reforms in France, advocated rule by a talented and "enlightened" leader. The English writer Thomas Carlyle, for example, claimed that perfect government demanded rule by such a "great man." As a conservative, Carlyle detested democracy because it threatened to destroy the stratified, traditional social and economic order he so admired in Great Britain, and substitute it with rule by the masses. According to Carlyle:

The history of what man has accomplished in this world is at bottom the history of the Great Men who have worked here. They were the leaders of men, these great ones; the modellers, patterners, and in a wide sense creators of whatever the general mass of men contrived to do or to attain.

By the early twentieth century, many other political theorists had popularized such ideas. Especially influential were the views of German philosopher Friedrich Nietzsche, who envisaged a future society in which a "superman" (*Übermensch*) would be free to devise his own code of conduct and create his own destiny. Nietzsche believed that, while democracy created equality for all, it also bred conditions in which the spirits of superior people were crushed in the interests of the mediocre. This was a disaster, he argued, because only the superior person could achieve anything worthwhile. Such views, usually simplified, influenced many people. They included Adolf Hitler, who claimed:

In all ages it was not democracy that created values, it was individuals. However, it was always democracy that ruined and destroyed individuality. It is madness to think and criminal to proclaim that a majority can suddenly replace the accomplishment of a man of genius. . . . Every people must see in its most capable men the greatest national value, for this is the most lasting value there is. . . . The will of the nation . . . is of most use when its most capable minds are brought forth. They form the representative leaders of a nation, they alone can be the pride of a nation—certainly never the parliamentary politician who is the product of the ballot box and thinks only in terms of votes. . . . [1]

In 1933, after ten years of struggle, Hitler became chancellor of Germany and,

▸ [1]Quoted in T. Hoy (ed.), *Politics and Power: Who Should Rule?*, New York: Putnam's, 1968, pp. 254–255.

inspired by these convictions, immediately began transforming that country into the *Third Reich*, one of the most powerful totalitarian states of the modern world.

▶ DICTATORSHIP

The idea of dictatorship, or rule by one person of superior strength and abilities, is very old. In the ancient world, one-person rule usually took the form of an absolute monarchy, headed by the ruler as priest-king. For example, in about 3000 B.C. a single king or pharaoh emerged in Egypt. By conquering smaller territories, he forcibly united the region along the Nile River into a single state under his absolute rule. His authority, and that of his successor pharaohs, was strengthened by the claim that they were gods. Their power was symbolized by the massive pyramids built to house the pharaohs' bodies after death.

Similar developments occurred in China, the Middle East, and India. In China, the emperors were viewed as the ''sons of heaven.'' The first Shang ruler, who united China in the late 200s and built the famous Great Wall, left behind him a burial tomb that rivalled anything found in Egypt. All such regimes were non-democratic and were dominated by powerful individuals holding political, military, and religious powers. Such states were typical of the ancient world. The democracies of Athens and the Roman Republic stand as marked exceptions. Even in Athens, the philosopher Plato argued for rule by an oligarchy of elite ''guardians,'' and Rome eventually abandoned its one-thousand-year-old republican principles for rule by an emperor, or priest-king.

European monarchs continued to enjoy religious and political authority throughout the Middle Ages. In the seventeenth century, for example, Russian rulers claimed

The Great Wall of China
Consulate General of the People's Republic of China in Toronto

complete power as tsars and **autocrats**. Western European political thinkers also developed theories of the ''divine right'' of kings. Monarchs, they claimed, were appointed by God and were responsible to God alone. Their subjects, therefore, were duty-bound to obey them unquestioningly. God's will was present in the birth of a new monarch, and any rebellion was thus a revolt against God. (See Chapter 2.)

Liberal democratic ideas arose in opposition to monarchical rule. Although their initial victories came in the English revolutions of the 1600s, the American Revolution (1775–1783), and the French Revolution (1789–1799), it was only in the latter 1800s that democratic forms of government became common throughout Western Europe. The end of World War I in 1918 was widely regarded as marking the victory of the liberal democratic ideal, the principles of which spread into East-Central Europe. But this liberal triumph was short-lived. During the 1920s and 1930s, many democratic regimes — both old and new — rapidly reverted to authoritarian forms of rule, as citizens grappled with the economic collapse and political instability that followed World War I and were intensified by the Great Depression (1929–1939). Hungary, Italy, Poland, Germany, and Spain, along with Japan and many Latin American countries, turned to dictatorial forms of government. In Russia, meanwhile, Vladimir Lenin's ''dictatorship of the proletariat'' had been transformed into the personal dictatorship of Joseph Stalin.

Unlike most pharaohs and monarchs of the past, the new dictators of the twentieth century were not chosen because of a blood tie with past rulers. Rather, their power depended on the support of important segments of society, and usually of the army.

The term dictator comes from ancient Rome, where it referred to a position created to deal with national emergencies. When the Roman Republic was threatened by an invasion or other crisis that the regular authorities could not solve, one man was appointed with absolute powers to rule the republic until the emergency was over. At that point, his authority reverted to the republic and he himself again became a private citizen. In the modern world, however, few dictators have shown a willingness to relinquish their powers voluntarily.

Joseph Stalin
Canapress Photo Service

LATIN AMERICAN DICTATORSHIPS BETWEEN THE WARS

The Great Depression spawned dictatorships throughout Latin America. Only seven South American countries escaped dictatorial rule during the interwar period. In Central America and the Caribbean, dictatorships thrived in a number of countries: Cuba, the Dominican Republic, Guatemala, Honduras, El Salvador, and Nicaragua.

Bolivia — Alternated between civilian and military dictatorships
Brazil — G. Vargas, 1930
Cuba — F. Batista, 1933
Dominican Republic — R. Trujillo, 1930
Ecuador — Political turmoil, 1931
El Salvador — M. Martinez, 1932
Guatemala — J. Ubico, 1930
Honduras — T. Andino, 1932
Nicaragua — A. Somoza Garcia, 1936
Peru — A. Leguia, 1919

In many ways, the behaviour of the majority of modern dictators was accurately forecast by Niccolò Machiavelli, an Italian politician of the sixteenth century. Basing his conclusions on the actions and intrigues of the petty Italian princes and despots of his own times, he described how a ruler should best manage his affairs to retain and increase his power. According to Machiavelli:

A man who wishes to make a profession of goodness in everything must necessarily come to grief among so many who are not good. Therefore it is necessary for a prince, who wishes to maintain himself, to learn how not to be good and to use this knowledge and not use it, according to the necessity of the case. . . . A prince, then, should have no other thought or object so much at heart . . . as the art of war and the organization and discipline of his army; for that is the only art that is expected of him who commands. . . . This then gives rise to the question "whether it be better to be beloved than feared, or to be feared than beloved." It will naturally be answered that it would be desirable to be both the one and the other; but as it is difficult to be both at the same time, it is much more safe to be feared than to be loved. . . . It must be evident to everyone that it is more praiseworthy for a prince always to maintain good faith, and practice integrity rather than craft and deceit. And yet the experience of our own times has shown that those princes have achieved great things who made small account of good faith, and who understood by cunning to circumvent the intelligence of others; and that in the end they got the better of those whose actions were dictated by loyalty and good faith. . . . A sagacious prince then cannot and should not fulfill his pledges when their observance is contrary to his interests, and when the causes that induced him to pledge his faith no longer exist. If men were all good, then indeed this precept would be bad; but as men are naturally bad, and will not observe their faith toward you, you must in the same way not observe yours to them. . . . And therefore it is necessary that he should have a versatile mind, capable of changing readily, according as the winds and changes of fortune bid him; and, as has been said above, not to swerve from the good if possible, but to know how to resort to evil if necessity demands it.[2]

▶ MILITARY COUPS

Approximately one-fifth of the world's governments are military dictatorships. In most of these countries the leaders gained their positions of power by a ***coup d'etat***. "I came in on a tank," said Saddam Hussein of Iraq, "and only a tank will evict me." Or, as Salvador Allende declared prior to the 1973 coup in Chile, "It won't cost you much to get a military man in. But by heaven, it will cost you something to get him out."

A *coup d'etat* is a violent or illegal change in government. The leaders of a coup are usually public officials who infiltrate the army and then use the armed forces to seize power. In order for a coup to be successful, the leaders must gain the support of the army officers. Officers with similar ethnic or religious affiliations or political views may be most easily swayed. The leaders may also look for officers with frustrated career ambitions who may be eager to participate in forming a new order. If the officers cannot be won over, the leaders may attempt to immobilize the army, or at least distract it, while the coup is being executed. The essential elements of a successful takeover include: seizing the presidential palace, if only for symbolic reasons; disrupting communications and transportation by seizing or jamming the government radio, closing the airport, and setting up roadblocks around the capital; and arresting important political opponents.

Once the coup leaders have gained power, or at least control of communications, they will want to address the people. Depending on what the previous regime was like, they may promise equality to all, an end to political terrorism, the dawn of a new era, or freedom from external control. When the leaders have consolidated their power, there is no need to fulfill these promises. Further consolidation depends upon both local support and international recognition. American support might be won by promising to maintain trade relations and protect private property. Soviet recognition might be gained by talking about the rights of the workers. In either case, it will be possible to play one superpower against the other. The winner will provide the new regime with economic aid. The final step will be to transform the regime from a military to a quasi-democratic government. As political scientist Luttawak wrote in 1969, generals who fail to become politicians very soon cease to be either.

Iraqi President Saddam Hussein
Canapress Photo Service

▸ [2]Niccolò Machiavelli, *The Prince*, New York: Airmont Publishing Co., 1965, pp. 72, 81–82, 85, 86–87.

FOCUS

1. Investigate any revolution and compare the tactics to those described in this case study.
2. a) Why do you think non-democratic governments have been so pervasive in world history? What can they do that democracies cannot?
   b) What advantages might they have over democratic regimes?
3. Do great people change history, or do they simply reflect the dominant ideas of their society?
4. a) Re-read the views of Hobbes, Locke, and Rousseau in Chapter 2 and compare their views of human nature with those of Machiavelli.
   b) Explain how Machiavelli viewed human nature and how this influenced his advice.
   c) Would his advice be useful to a democratically elected leader? Explain.
5. Research and evaluate the political system in either Sparta, Greece; Louis XIV's France; or the Russia of Peter the Great.
6. Divide into small groups. Devise a non-democratic system that will ensure, as much as possible, that the state will be governed fairly and effectively. Include provisions for succession. Present your system to the rest of the class. You might consult Plato's *Republic* and Thomas More's *Utopia* for examples.

▶ TOTALITARIANISM AND IDEOLOGY

In the wake of World War II, a number of American political scientists, among whom Karl Friedrich and Hannah Arendt were prominent, developed the theory of totalitarianism to explain the successes of authoritarian regimes such as Mussolini's Fascist Italy, Hitler's Nazi Germany, and Stalin's Soviet Union. They believed that these and similar governments were unique in terms of the degree of control the state exercised over its citizens. The term totalitarian referred to these regimes' apparent desire to control totally all aspects of human life. This goal, they argued, was made possible by the advances in communications (radio, cinema, telegraph, airplanes, railroads, automobiles) achieved during the nineteenth and twentieth centuries. These changes enabled the state to control almost all access to information and thereby attempt a systematic indoctrination of the populace.

Modern totalitarian states differed from earlier non-democratic states insofar as this indoctrination was pursued in accord with an ideological vision of the world and a program for restructuring society. This propaganda allowed a totalitarian leadership to strengthen its hold on the state, limit opposition, promote mass solidarity, and prepare for war. In this effort, the rulers devoted special attention to the youth, because if the system were to endure, it had to prepare future leaders who believed in the regime's methods and ideology.

In this context, the term ideology means a prescribed set of beliefs about human nature, society, and the ideal state. Older anti-democratic leaders, as well as some modern ones, usually were content to maintain the status quo. As long as their authority and desires remained unthreatened, they frequently left the people alone to act and think as they chose. But the ideologies inspiring modern totalitarian leaders — whether of the left or right — more often than not condemn the existing order as selfish and corrupt and seek to replace it with a morally and spiritually more satisfying social and economic system. To achieve this ultimate goal, the regime uses its monopoly of education and the media to convert the citizenry to its beliefs. In the process, liberal-democratic individual rights are regarded as obstacles to building the new and perfect world.

▶ Origins of Totalitarianism

Why, we may ask, would the citizens of a democratic state give up their voice in government and surrender their **civil liberties**? One common answer is that they simply had no choice. From the start, most dictatorships enjoyed at least the passive support of the police and armed forces, which permitted them to use violence against their opponents. Once in power, totalitarian leaders usually escalated the levels of terror and violence to consolidate their rule and expand their authority throughout all levels of society. In an environment of censorship, secret police, death squads, and concentration camps are used to exert physical and psychological control over the populace. This fear helps to promote conformity with the regime's directives. In Hitler's Germany, for example, the secret police (Gestapo), the Nazi party's private army of Brownshirts (SA), and the elite guards (SS) performed these functions. In the Soviet Union, this was the work of such state agencies as the KGB (Committee for State Security) and the "Bluecaps" or Internal Troops of the Ministry of the Interior (MVD).

Chile provides a typical example of the use of terror by a right-wing regime. In 1973, the democratically elected socialist government of President Salvador Allende was overthrown by a military coup that brought General Augusto Pinochet to power. To ensure continued dominance, the military immediately launched a campaign of terror. During the first year of Pinochet's rule, some 60 000 people were arrested and held for at least twenty-four hours for interrogation. Some of these people were subsequently tortured, executed, or simply "disappeared." As an international commission that investigated this situation reported:

> *The original mass arrests were directed not only against persons suspected of having illegal possession of arms, but against all who were believed to hold left-wing views, including members of the deposed government, political party leaders, leaders of trade unions, of the urban and rural poor and of students, as well as outstanding journalists, artists or intellectuals. Many other people of no particular importance or influence were arrested through denunciation or as a result of "military operations," i.e. search and arrest operations aimed at ensuring complete control by the military authorities. . . . Methods of torture employed . . . included electric shock, blows, beatings, burning with acid or cigarettes, prolonged standing, prolonged hooding and isolation in solitary confinement, extraction of nails, . . . immersion in water, hanging, simulated executions, insults, threats, and compelling attendance at the torture of others. A number of people . . . died under torture and others . . . suffered permanent mental and nervous disabilities. . . .*
>
> *The object of the torture appears to be threefold: to obtain "confessions" to serve as the basis for subsequent prosecution; to obtain information about associates and activities; and to intimidate . . . the victim, his associates, and the public in general.*[3]

▸ [3]International Commission of Jurists, *Final Report of the Mission to Chile, to Study the Legal System and the Protection of Human Rights*, April 1974, pp. 19–20, 24–25. Reprinted with the permission of The International Commission of Jurists, Geneva.

Even admitting the effectiveness of terror, it is clear that totalitarian regimes cannot exist without substantial willing support from the populace. Pinochet came to power at a time when there was considerable discontent with Allende; Mussolini was revered by numerous Italians. Many Germans remember the first years of Hitler's rule as the best years of their lives, and one can still hear Russians mourning the days when "Boss" Stalin maintained order with an iron-fist. The question remains: why have authoritarian and totalitarian ideas been so attractive to so many people in the modern era?

▶ Theories of Causation

One widely accepted explanation for totalitarianism is the **crisis theory**.[4] This theory states that conditions of acute distress, such as economic depression or war, may give rise to such intense feelings of resentment, frustration, insecurity, and outright fear that people are willing to accept drastic political solutions. Since the existing order seems incapable of adequately coping with their anxieties, people turn to totalitarianism with its **charismatic** and dominating leaders, emphasis on action, and compelling promises of future well-being and glory. A number of historical examples seem to support this explanation: Mussolini took power in 1922 when Italy seemed on the brink of civil war brought about by social, political, and economic tensions; Stalin consolidated his power between 1928 and 1930 in an atmosphere of foreign threats and economic crisis; and Hitler emerged victorious in 1933 during the depths of the Great Depression.

▸ [4]The following examination of totalitarianism was derived largely from Reo. M. Christenson et al., *Ideologies and Modern Politics*. New York: Harper and Row, 1981, Chapters 3, 4.

Not all countries have sought escape from their problems by turning to totalitarianism. So we again face the question of why some countries are less immune to the lures of such ideologies. There is no universal agreement on this issue. Some people have suggested that a crisis must be accompanied by a social climate that is conducive to totalitarian thought. American political sociologist Seymour M. Lipset identified fascist appeal with the middle classes and communist appeal with the lower classes. He argued that in 1932 the average follower of Hitler "was a middle-class self-employed Protestant who lived either on a farm or in a small community, and who [was] previously . . . strongly opposed to the power and influence of big business and big labor." Isolated and insecure, they were driven by their anxiety to Nazism, which promised both security and a renewal of national glory.

Lipset also argued that the lower classes were basically predisposed towards authoritarian and totalitarian values. Their lack of education, he believed, prepared them for action rather than words, and towards accepting simple, uncomplicated answers. Since the lower classes also earned lower wages, they were more likely to be dissatisfied and willing to blame their problems on others (the capitalists in Russia or the Jews in Germany). Other scholars have argued that the lifestyles in lower-class families, which are often characterized by frustration and friction, produce authoritarian parent-child relationships, which further predispose workers to totalitarian appeals.

Psychologist T.W. Adorno identified a personality type that he believed to be especially susceptible to totalitarian values. In his view, authoritarian parent-child relationships tend to produce adults who blame others for their misfortunes. They become dependent upon others for their strength, while simultaneously scorning those whom they consider to be inferior. A person possessing an **authoritarian personality** is characterized by stereotyped thinking, conformism, an idealization of power and strength, a desire to punish "evil," a tendency to see people in terms of black and white, and a willingness to be satisfied with superficial solutions to problems. Such people, he maintained, are prime candidates for the lures of totalitarianism. (See the questionnaire in Chapter 1.)

These theories, as well as the concept of totalitarianism itself, assume the existence of a modern, industrial, and largely urban social structure. As many sociologists and psychologists have pointed out, however, this form of society often tends to create a sense of personal isolation and powerlessness that are for the most part absent in pre-industrial, agricultural, and traditional social orders. Whatever its drawbacks, the pre-industrial order is generally regarded as providing individuals with a secure sense of place within their group, so that many people find the burden of individualism under modern conditions to be profoundly confusing and deeply alienating. As a result, they are often driven to seek refuge in the more secure environment promised by the prophets of totalitarianism.

According to psychologist Erich Fromm, it is these feelings of alienation that cause some people to recoil from the responsibilities of freedom and make them yearn for direction from a strong leader who will give meaning to their lives and rescue them from their sense of uncertainty and helplessness. "The principal avenues of escape in our time," he wrote, "are the submission to a leader, as has happened in fascist countries, and the compulsive conforming as is prevalent in our own democracy." In other words, according to Fromm, a "fear of freedom" is a modern phenomenon. It can be explained largely by the competitive individualism introduced by political and economic liberalism.

▶ Critique of Totalitarianism

The explanations for modern anti-democratic movements examined thus far have concentrated largely on psychological motives. While such studies have their place, they still tell us very little about the nature and goals of the movements. According to recent scholarship, the theory of totalitarianism over-simplifies reality and minimizes the real differences among the various dictatorships. Early writers assumed that the control amassed by totalitarian dictatorships made them more efficient than their democratic rivals. More recent research has demonstrated that the efforts to ensure such control in fact led to large-scale corruption and the growth of massive bureaucracies. More frequently than not, the right hand had little or no idea of what the left hand was doing. In addition, the same studies have suggested that the differences among dictatorial regimes are as numerous as the similarities.

Even so, all modern totalitarian regimes appear to share a number of similar characteristics. Among these are a desire to control and shape society; the dominance of a single political party, based on a mass movement and controlled by a charismatic leader; the abolition of individual rights and a developed system of internal repression; full censorship of the media, combined with an extensive network of propaganda agencies that pay special attention to youth; the subordination of the economy to the needs of the state and its rulers; the militarization of society in the sense of stressing military values and the need to prepare for war; and the spread of an ideological doctrine that both justifies and sustains all these measures.

These ideologies reject liberal-democratic beliefs in favour of a different form of ideal system. In so doing, they also reject the respect for the individual inherent in the liberal tradition. They regard the nation as a living organism in which the individual is only a single cell. Each person has value only as a part of the larger whole and therefore can be sacrificed freely for the greater good of the social organism. Totalitarian ideologies justify the need for such sacrifices by maintaining a perpetual atmosphere of crisis, which demands continued vigilance to ensure that an unscrupulous enemy does not somehow rob the group of its pre-ordained victory in the struggle between good and evil. This same sense of ongoing struggle, along with the biological view of the nation as a living organism, demands activist and expansionist policies. The leaders regard the social organism as being healthy only as long as it is growing and expanding. The only alternative is decline and eventual death.

▶ FASCISM

Although the term fascism refers specifically to Benito Mussolini's totalitarian movement, it is not inappropriate to consider most of these new credos under this general label. A common feature of all fascist regimes is their acceptance of the organic view of the nation. Membership is acquired by birth alone. In this manner, they seek to overcome the sense of personal loneliness and alienation of modern liberal-democratic societies by creating the all-embracing family of the nation. This may take the form of a racial doctrine. According to Hitler, the Germans were the true representatives of the superior Aryan race, and all other races were either degenerate (the Latins), primitive (the Slavs), or criminal brutes (the Jews).

For Mussolini, birth in the Italian cultural family was enough and, until he came under Hitler's influence in the late 1930s, Jews held high office in his Fascist party. Italian workers were first and foremost Italians. They acted instinctively and emotionally (not rationally) as Italians and so needed direction from a charismatic leader (the Duce) who best understood and represented the Italian nation's characteristics and goals. The same was true of a German worker. Like all other Aryans, he was expected to follow his Führer unquestioningly, even if it meant his death for the sake of the health of the German nation.

In this context, the Marxists were obvious foes. Not only were they rivals for support from the masses, but their doctrine of class warfare and workers' internationalism was a clear threat to national unity. In addition, the Marxists' claim of rationalism threatened the very basis of the fascists' irrational nationalisms.

One final aspect of fascism also deserves close attention. Many fascists seek to turn the clock back and hold up as an ideal a period of past national grandeur. Mussolini copied the customs of ancient Rome and sought to create a social-economic system modelled on medieval guilds. Hitler favoured a new religion based on such Norse gods as Odin and Thor.

▶ SUMMARY

As the above discussion suggests, we would be mistaken to equate Communist Russia with Nazi Germany. It is true that Soviet Russia, especially under the rule of Joseph Stalin, shared many totalitarian traits with the fascist dictatorships. All were regimes based on mass movements, dominated by a single leader who attempted to exert total control over the populace by propaganda and terror. The same may be said of theocratic regimes such as the fundamentalist Shiite Muslim government in Iran.

There are vast ideological differences among the various fascist, Marxist, and theocratic dictatorships of our century. Fascism motivates people by myths, emotions, and hate rather than reason; looks to the past for its models; and rejects reason and science as a means of solving social and economic problems. As a result, fascist regimes tend to maintain themselves by a restless activism that leads to external expansion. Theocratic Iran seems to share many of these traits, but proclaims an ideology based on a more deeply-rooted religious doctrine that has a wide appeal beyond that country's borders. Communists, on the other hand, believe in human rationality and hail technology and the physical sciences as the means to build a brighter future. This belief, as well as their commitment to reason, encourages internal change and has allowed the Soviet Union to progress slowly from the Stalinist police state to the less autocratic state of Mikhail Gorbachev.

The authoritarian challenge did not end with the defeat of Hitler in 1945 or with the death of Stalin in 1953. Aspects of totalitarianism exist in a number of countries, especially in the Third World. Such ideas are also advocated by small Nazi or White supremacist parties in Canada, the United States, Western Europe, and elsewhere, as well as by groups such as the Ku Klux Klan. Indeed, it seems likely that as long as severe social and economic problems continue to plague large parts of the globe, especially areas where the roots of liberal

Group of hooded Ku Klux Klansmen at Freeport, Long Island
The Bettmann Archive

democracy have been newly planted, the challenge of totalitarian ideologies will continue to confront the world. Japan gave proof of this in the 1930s, and China is a current example. But as Iran demonstrated, these may draw their inspiration from sources very different from those found in Europe.

APPLYING YOUR KNOWLEDGE

1. a) Explain why totalitarian states attempt to dictate musical tastes, architectural styles, and literary themes.
   b) Discuss the importance of physical repression in the maintenance of political power.
2. What features of modern life might make a person feel isolated and powerless?
3. Which of the following theories best explain the origins of totalitarianism: the crisis theory, the ideas of S.M. Lipset, the theories of T.W. Adorno, or the writings of Erich Fromm? Explain.
4. Prepare a chart that illustrates the similarities and differences between fascism and communism.
5. Outline a hypothetical situation in which many Canadians might advocate an authoritarian government.

FURTHER RESEARCH

1. Prepare for a debate on one of the following topics:
   a) Most people prefer to be told what to do rather than to assume responsibility for their own decisions.
   b) The parent-child relationship is the most important factor in determining a child's basic personality. Authoritarian parents create authoritarian children.
2. a) Write an essay that deals only with the advantages of authoritarian government.
   b) Criticize a classmate's essay from the viewpoint of a supporter of democracy.
3. Stage a debate between a make-believe communist and a make-believe fascist on the nature of humanity and society.

Case Study 10 Overview

The Government of the Union of Soviet Socialist Republics

This case study traces the evolution of the government of the U.S.S.R. from the Russian Revolution of 1917 to the present. The first section examines the pre-Gorbachev governmental structure and compares how the political system was supposed to operate in theory with how it worked in practice. It discusses the origins of the Communist party, its membership and functions, the purposes of election campaigns in the Soviet Union, and the role of such government bodies as the Council of Ministers, the Supreme Soviet, and the office of General Secretary. The final section discusses Gorbachev's political reforms, his ''democratization'' of the Communist party, and his liberalization of the political system. The case study concludes with an analysis of the strengths and weaknesses of the growing power of the president and what this signifies for the future.

▶ OBJECTIVES

After reading this case study, you should be able to:

- ▶ evaluate the difference between theory and practice in the Soviet Union
- ▶ draw a schematic diagram of the present political structure
- ▶ compare the pre-Gorbachev system with the present political structure
- ▶ debate the merits and future directions of the Soviet government

▶ KEY TERMS

one-party state
C.P.S.U.
proletariat class
democratic centralism
Politburo
perestroika
glasnost
Congress of People's Deputies

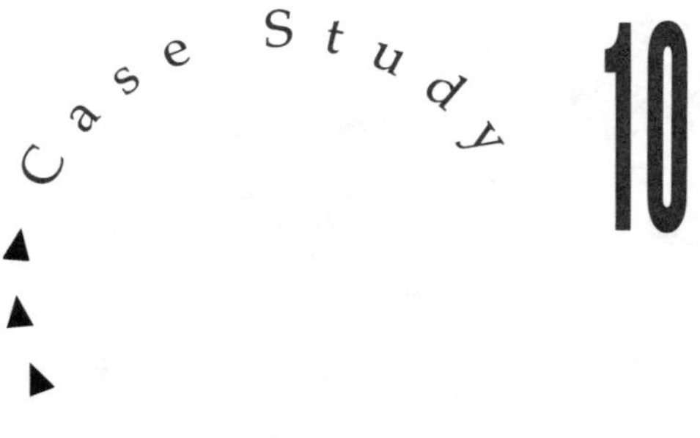

The Government of the Union of Soviet Socialist Republics

Chapter 4 noted the wide variation in types of authoritarian regimes. The historical record contains numerous examples of dictatorships, monarchies, oligarchies, and military juntas, as well as the more recent fascist and communist totalitarian police states. There are more models of anti-democratic than of democratic states, and we should not assume that the record to date is complete.

Indeed, recent events suggest that even the totalitarian state created by Joseph Stalin may be capable of evolving into a system that contains many of the hallmarks of the existing liberal democracies. This case study examines the evolution of the Soviet system of government. As you read it, keep the following questions in mind: Who makes the decisions? How are decisions made? What are the basic values and assumptions of this system of government? How and why has this system evolved since Stalin's death?

▶ EVOLUTION OF THE SOVIET CONSTITUTION

In theory, the Soviet government has always been a democracy. Article 2 of the present constitution reads:

All power in the Soviet Union belongs to the people.

The people exercise state power through Soviets of People's Deputies, which constitute the political foundation of the U.S.S.R.

All other state bodies are under the control of, and accountable to, the Soviets of People's Deputies.

Sovet is simply the Russian word for "council." The first modern soviet appeared as a strike council in St. Petersburg (now Leningrad) during the 1905 revolution. Similar "grass roots" councils sprang up throughout Russia after the fall of the monarchy in February/March 1917. These bodies were truly democratic in nature and they began coordinating policies through country-wide congresses, which elected a national committee to represent them between meetings. It was by seizing power in the name of the second of these national congresses in October/November 1917 that the Bolshevik party, led by Vladimir Lenin and Leon Trotsky, formed the first Soviet government. Since then, soviets have been an important element of the official revolutionary myth that the Communist party has used to justify its tenure in power.

In January 1918, the national congress of soviets proclaimed Russia to be a "republic of the Soviets of Workers', Peasants', and Soldiers' Deputies. All power in the center and the localities belongs to these Soviets." A companion decree made the Congress of Soviets "the highest organ of power within the borders" of what became the Russian Socialist Federated Soviet Republic (R.S.F.S.R.). A Central Executive Committee managed its affairs between sessions, while a Council of People's Commissars, also elected by the congresses, served as the federation's cabinet or executive.

When the Union of Soviet Socialist Republics was created as a federal state in 1922, the other republics adopted this same structure. Similarly, the Congresses of Soviets of the U.S.S.R., along with their Central Executive Committees, became the highest legislative body, and a Council of People's Commissars (later Council of Ministers) of the U.S.S.R. emerged as the supreme executive body. Although subsequently renamed, these three institutions (congress, executive committee, and ministerial council) remained in place until Mikhail Gorbachev's constitutional reforms of 1988/1989.

The democratic essence of the soviets was undermined immediately by the creation of a **one-party state**. Under the pressure of civil war and internal reconstruction, Lenin and his colleagues became increasingly intolerant of opposition. By 1922, the Communist party had become the sole political organization in the U.S.S.R. The Constitution of 1977 still declared:

The Communist Party of the Soviet Union [C.P.S.U.] is the leading and guiding force of Soviet society and the nucleus of its political system, of all state organizations and public organizations. The C.P.S.U. exists for the people and serves the people.

The Communist Party, armed with Marxist-Leninism, determines the general perspectives of the development of society and the course of the internal and the foreign policy of the U.S.S.R., directs the great constructive work of the Soviet people, and imparts a planned, systematic, and theoretically substantiated character to their struggle for the victory of Communism.

▶ THE COMMUNIST PARTY

Marxist-Leninists have justified the monopoly of power by the **C.P.S.U.** by two basic arguments. Firstly, since Marxism taught that political parties represent the interests of economic classes (the bourgeoisie, proletariat, etc.), a state with only a **proletariat class** needs but a single party. Secondly, Lenin viewed the Communist party as the "vanguard of the proletariat," the custodian of the "true" doctrine of communism, and hence the only body capable of interpreting this doctrine in modern conditions. This being the case, the presence of other political parties was at best an unnecessary irritation, and at worst a dangerous obstacle to the proper development of Soviet society. For these reasons, communist thinkers considered the U.S.S.R. a one-party "people's democracy."

It is essential to bear these concepts in mind when attempting to understand the function and organization of the Communist party. Also, remember that its purpose is quite different from that of North American political parties. The party is responsible for supplying leaders for almost every organization in the country, for providing political and economic guidelines for mobilizing the people to fulfill the party's directives, and for public indoctrination.

Given these responsibilities, membership in the party is theoretically restricted only to those who are worthy in terms of political consciousness, honesty, ability, and dedication. As a result, only about twenty percent of those over eighteen are full members. As of January 1989, the C.P.S.U. had 18 975 725 full members and 512 097 candidate members (out of a total population of 286 717 000). As communists, they are expected to set an example of dedication, accept the party's right to make basic decisions affecting their lives, undertake whatever tasks are given them, and adhere to strict rules of personal conduct. Members who fail to meet these standards, or who disobey C.P.S.U. directives, are "purged" from the party. Although

Soviet leader Mikhail Gorbachev exchanges a few words with the then Foreign Minister Andrei Gromyko during a Kremlin rally marking the 115th anniversary of Lenin's birth.
The Bettmann Archive

this happens to tens of thousands of people each year, the privileges that come with party membership, and its value for career advancements, encourage a steady stream of new recruits.

The Communist party represents the educated elite. Factory directors are communists, as are journal editors and almost all army and naval officers. So too are most judges, attorneys, high-ranking security police officers, forty percent of engineers, and roughly half of the U.S.S.R.'s scholars. Nonetheless, the party takes pride in stressing that the majority of its members are employed in industry or agriculture (72 percent in 1989). Of these, the overwhelming mass were urban workers (45 percent), not peasants (11 percent). Similarly, women are underrepresented (30 percent), as are the non-Slav nationalities (Balts, Caucasians, Central Asians, etc.). In 1989, 59 percent were Great Russians, 16 percent were Ukrainians, 4 percent were Belorussians, 2 percent were Kazakh, 1.5 percent Georgian, and 0.4 percent were Latvian. Very few of the non-Slavs held high positions in the party which, like the government, remained dominated by Great Russians.

▶ THEORY VERSUS PRACTICE

As with the soviets, the Communist party theoretically is democratic in nature (see Figure 1). Indeed, in its early period it was a truly democratic organization in which various factions competed under Lenin's overall leadership. But the party emerged from the civil war with its leaders in no mood to permit internal squabbling. In 1921, Lenin therefore banned "factions" and affirmed the principle of **democratic centralism**. Issues were to be thoroughly discussed from the bottom up until they were resolved at the top by a party congress. This done and a clear policy adopted, all discussion and dissent were to cease, and all party members were expected to obey and implement the policy without further questions.

Once Stalin had concentrated power in his hands, democratic centralism became the justification for stifling all opposition and ensuring his complete personal control over the party. Subsequent leaders have possessed similar powers. As a result, the party's general secretary has been the most powerful public figure in the U.S.S.R. In February 1990, the C.P.S.U. openly admitted the errors of the Stalinist regime:

> *The authoritarian regime has had an extremely negative effect on the Party, its role in society and its methods of work. Much harm has been done by over-centralization, the suppression of free thought, and the purges. The Party's prestige was greatly damaged because of ideological and moral degeneration.*

In its Stalinist form (Figure 2), the party's policies were made by the small group of leaders in the **Politburo**, under the supervision of the Secretariat. The Politburo was, in practice, the country's supreme policy-making body, and its deliberations were almost invariably kept secret. Although its membership has fluctuated, the Politburo normally consists of fifteen leading party (and often state) members, presided over by the general secretary.

Through a framework of commissions and departments, the general secretary and his assistants supervise all government and state appointments and implement policies throughout the entire country. As of 1989, General Secretary Gorbachev had at his disposal in the Secretariat six commissions and twenty-nine departments, including those responsible for agriculture, defence, ideology, transport and communications, culture, the chemical industry, and propaganda.

Figure 1
THEORETICAL STRUCTURE OF THE COMMUNIST PARTY

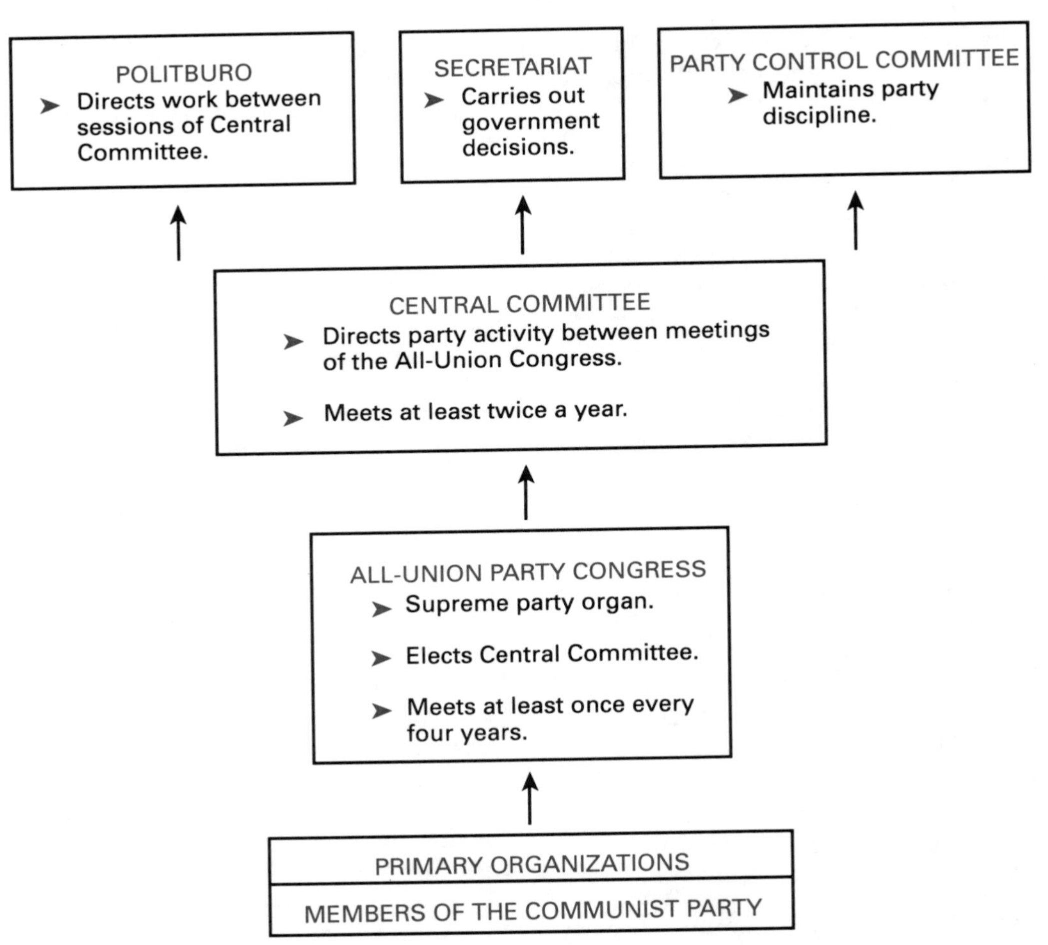
(arrows indicate appointment or election)
POLITBURO
➤ Directs work between sessions of Central Committee.
SECRETARIAT
➤ Carries out government decisions.
PARTY CONTROL COMMITTEE
➤ Maintains party discipline.
CENTRAL COMMITTEE
➤ Directs party activity between meetings of the All-Union Congress.
➤ Meets at least twice a year.
ALL-UNION PARTY CONGRESS
➤ Supreme party organ.
➤ Elects Central Committee.
➤ Meets at least once every four years.
PRIMARY ORGANIZATIONS
MEMBERS OF THE COMMUNIST PARTY

Despite the rules against factions, the C.P.S.U. remains the major arena for the discussion of different viewpoints within the Soviet Union. Competing groups within the party continue to push for specific policies and programs. They either seek to gain the ear of the top leadership or, at times of changes in leadership, to ensure the victory of a sympathetic candidate. Indeed, major policy changes in the U.S.S.R. have often parallelled changes in leadership. But once a victor emerged, the principle of democratic centralism ensured the apparent adoption of the new orthodoxy all the way down the line.

Figure 2
STRUCTURE OF THE COMMUNIST PARTY IN PRACTICE

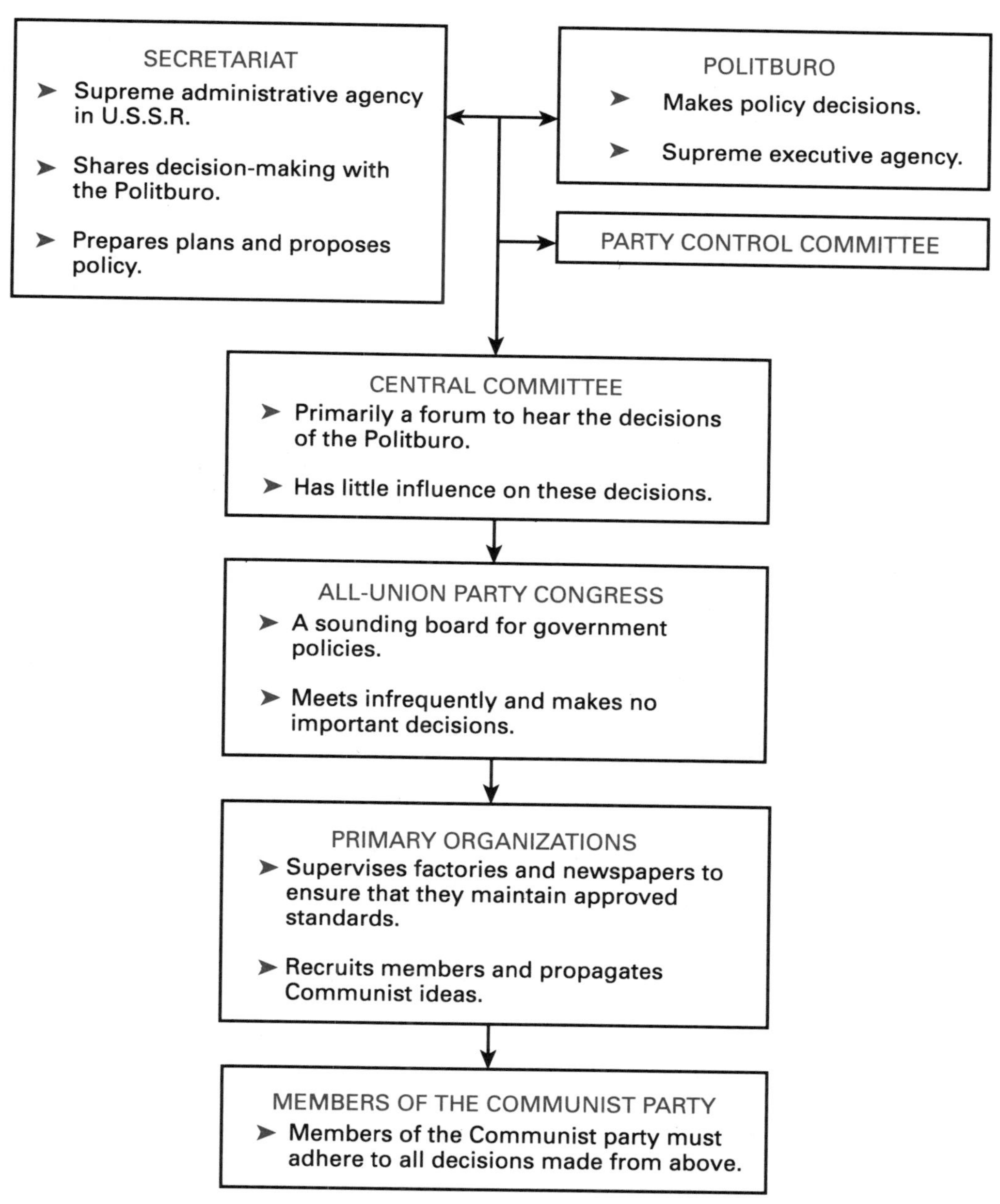

▶ THE GOVERNMENT STRUCTURE TO 1988

As Figure 3 demonstrates, until recently the U.S.S.R.'s government retained all the basic institutions present in October 1917. The Constitutions of 1936 and 1977 gave "exclusive" legislative power to a parliament known as the Supreme Soviet of the U.S.S.R. A direct descendent of the Congresses of Soviets, this body consisted of two co-equal houses, the Soviet of the Union and the Soviet of Nationalities. Yet the Supreme Soviet seldom met more than twice a year, and then only for a few days. The real decision-making occurred elsewhere. The Presidium passed the majority of laws, which were later approved and applauded by the Supreme Soviet. The Presidium was elected by a joint session of both houses of the Supreme Soviet. A joint session of the Supreme Soviet also elected a Council of Ministers (formerly Council of People's Commissars) to act as "the highest executive and administrative organ of state power." It was headed by a first minister or premier, who theoretically was the most powerful figure in the state. The Chairman of the Supreme Soviet's Presidium acted as president, a largely ornamental head of state.

Like Canada, the U.S.S.R. was and remains a federal state. Although the problems of federalism are detailed in Case Study 14, here we should note that each of the fifty-three separate regimes in the U.S.S.R. had a similar form of government. Each of these units had a designated number of deputies in the Council of Nationalities, making it somewhat similar to the American Senate. This gave the Soviet Union a system of government that in theory was federal and democratic. But in practice, the authority of these lower governing bodies was significantly limited by both the powers granted the central authorities in Moscow and by the pervasive influence of the C.P.S.U.

The real purpose of the Supreme Soviet was not to maintain a careful watch over the executive (as is the case in Canada), but to help spread its messages. Since the reports of its proceedings received wide coverage in the media, its sessions served as publicity events for the unveiling of new laws. Although it officially formed an independent and parallel organization to the government, the party transformed the Supreme Soviet into an agency of the C.P.S.U. Indeed, in many respects the two were integrated, and it was the C.P.S.U. that made government policies. In practice, the C.P.S.U.'s control of the government was even tighter than this suggests. The overwhelming majority of ministers and senior state officials were party members, and subject to its discipline. As well, the leaders of party and government have tended to be interchangeable.

Traditionally, then, the Soviet system was designed to allow a small group of people to control the government. Given the ban on other political parties and the C.P.S.U.'s control over internal security, organized opposition from below was virtually impossible. Until recently, therefore, Soviet elections were ritualistic affairs. Like sessions of the Supreme Soviet, they were often occasions for propagandizing new policy "lines" rather than opportunities for the people to make a meaningful choice among various leaders and policies. When Soviet voters went to the polls, they were told to put an "X" through every name on the secret ballot except the one they supported. As there was seldom more than one name on the ballot, there was no real choice. Even in local elections, the C.P.S.U. nominated sixty percent of the candidates.

Despite the fact that the results of such elections were a foregone conclusion, the party traditionally made vigorous efforts to ensure a high voter turn-out. In districts in which prominent political figures ran, special efforts were made to meet local griev-

Figure 3
THEORETICAL STRUCTURE OF THE SOVIET NATIONAL GOVERNMENT

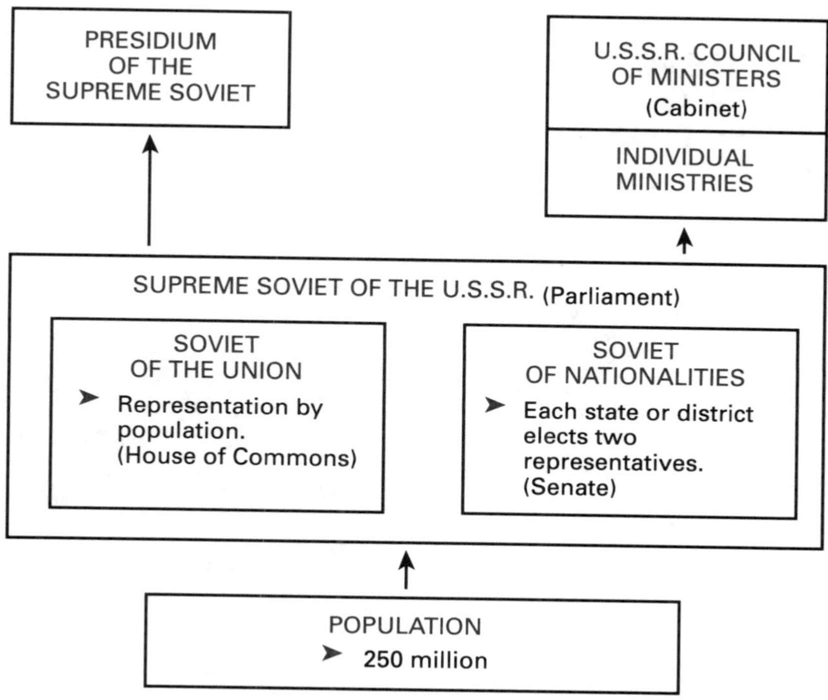

ances (for a new bridge, for example). Elsewhere, local party leaders made frequent speeches, party workers distributed pamphlets and conducted door-to-door canvassing, invalids were transported to polling booths, and so on. As a result, the U.S.S.R. long boasted a 99.8 percent voter turnout. These activities were designed largely to rally the people, demonstrate unity, publicize the government's achievements, and simultaneously provide the illusion of a real democracy.

Other considerations cast further doubt on the Soviets' claims that the U.S.S.R. was a constitutional democracy. In theory, there seemed much to justify the boast that the Stalin Constitution of 1936 was "the most democratic constitution in the world." It included a bill of rights that guaranteed freedom of speech, association, religion, organization, and of the press. Other provisions promised gender equality, as well as protection against arbitrary arrest. All discrimination was forbidden and everyone was granted the right to employment, education, leisure time, and support in the case of sickness and old age. Unfortunately, as critics were quick to point out, the constitution did not establish a means to enforce these rights, nor did it limit the government's power over citizens. Further, along with the list of citizens' rights, there were also citizens' obligations, which included the duties to abide by the law, maintain labour discipline, perform all public duties honestly, and safeguard public socialist property.

▶ GORBACHEV'S PROGRAM OF CONSTITUTIONAL REFORM

By the mid-1970s, the Stalinist system was showing signs of strain. New ideas and programs began to surface among the Soviet elite. Yet little could be done under the geriatric rule of Leonid Brezhnev, during what is now called the "period of stagnation" (1964–1982). Signs of change subsequently became evident during the brief rules of Yuri Andropov and Konstantin Chernenko. But a full program of "restructuring" (***perestroika***) only became possible with the election of Mikhail Gorbachev as General Secretary of the C.P.S.U. in the spring of 1985.

While economic restructuring was the essential aspect of Gorbachev's effort, he recognized that the momentum necessary for economic growth was impossible to achieve without an initial "democratization" of government. Nonetheless, his first steps in these directions were occasional and hesitant, as he manoeuvered to consolidate his position within the C.P.S.U. In 1987, he passed laws promoting public discussion of major political issues and reinforcing citizen's rights of appeal against unjust government decisions and violations of civil rights. More significant, perhaps, was the unprecedented openness (***glasnost***) devoted to both the debates within the C.P.S.U. and the activities of the Supreme Soviet of the U.S.S.R.

Major political reform came in 1988, which included enforcing the rule of law, giving greater protection for civil liberties, clearly separating the functions of party and government, and introducing policies "to ensure the full authority of the Soviets of Peoples' Deputies as the basis of the socialist state system." To achieve this last goal Gorbachev demanded the establishment of an active Supreme Soviet that would function under an elected president. A second group of proposed measures dealt with the party. It was also to be "democratized" to allow "the free discussion of all topical questions of policy and practice." Other resolutions suggested the possibility of a multi-party system emerging in the future.

Gorbachev has been trying to gain the support of two extreme factions in the Communist party; those who support Stalin's harsh policies and those who condemn Stalin as a butcher. Gorbachev criticizes Stalin's "mistakes," but praises the wartime achievements and modernization measures of the former leader.
Canada Wide/Craig Robertson

▶ THE SOVIET GOVERNMENTAL SYSTEM TODAY

By the end of 1988, Gorbachev had successfully introduced the first phase of this re-organization. He had also emerged as President of the U.S.S.R., as well as General Secretary of the C.P.S.U. The Supreme Soviet quickly gave its approval to these innovations. The new president was secure enough by the end of 1988 to introduce a number of amendments to the constitution that, once adopted, radically restructured both the electoral system and the structure of the central government.

As Figure 4 illustrates, the **Congress of People's Deputies** became the most important political body. Its 2250 members represent an increase of one-third over its

Figure 4
HIGHER BODIES OF STATE AUTHORITY AND ADMINISTRATION OF THE U.S.S.R.

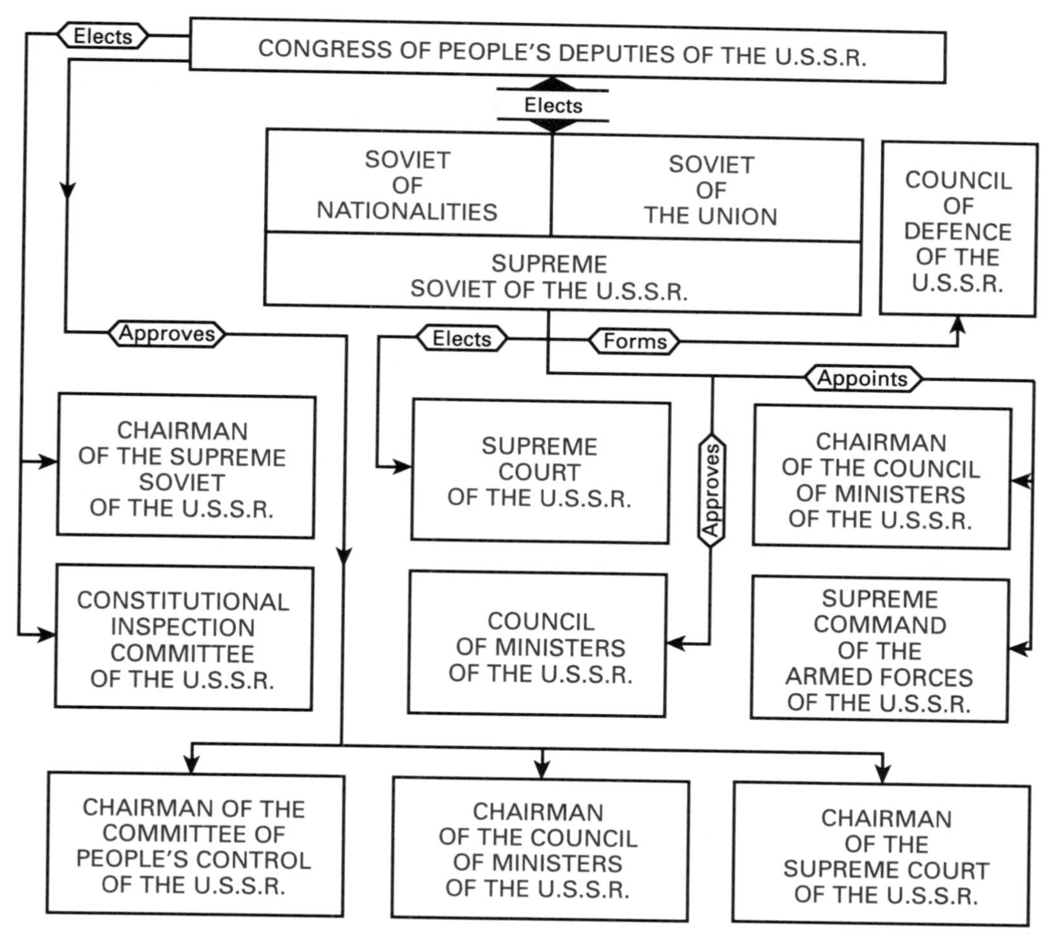

predecessor, and they are elected for five-year terms. One-third of its members are elected from Canadian-type electoral constituencies; a second third of the candidates from ethnic-territorial districts; and a final third are elected by national public organizations such as the C.P.S.U., the Young Communist League, unions, academic institutions, the stamp collectors' society, and so on. This Congress normally meets once a year and can amend or adopt a new constitution; revoke legislation of the Supreme Soviet; redraw the U.S.S.R.'s borders, as well as those of the union republics; resolve matters of jurisdiction among the various levels of government; approve the general course of foreign and domestic policies; and hold referendums when necessary. The new legislative body comprises two houses, each with 271 popularly elected members. The Soviet of Nationalities represents the federalist nature of the U.S.S.R. and includes deputies from each republic and autonomous region or area. The Congress of People's Deputies elects one-fifth of both houses, as well as the Supreme Soviet and the President.

The new Supreme Soviet acts as a more or less permanent legislative body. Apart from legislation in general, its responsibilities include electing a Presidium to manage its business (under the Chairman) between sessions; appointing the Chairman of the Council of Ministers (the premier) and approving that body's membership; establishing internal borders; examining the annual budget and longer-range economic plans; creating the Defence Council of the U.S.S.R., as well as a number of standing commissions and committees; approving all leading military, diplomatic, and judicial appointments; ordering mobilizations, declaring war, and ratifying treaties; calling and overseeing national elections; and so on (see Figure 5).

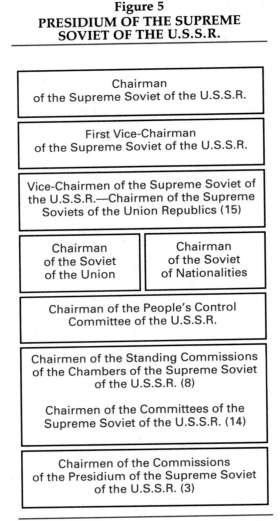

Figure 5
PRESIDIUM OF THE SUPREME SOVIET OF THE U.S.S.R.

Chairman of the Supreme Soviet of the U.S.S.R.	
First Vice-Chairman of the Supreme Soviet of the U.S.S.R.	
Vice-Chairmen of the Supreme Soviet of the U.S.S.R.—Chairmen of the Supreme Soviets of the Union Republics (15)	
Chairman of the Soviet of the Union	Chairman of the Soviet of Nationalities
Chairman of the People's Control Committee of the U.S.S.R.	
Chairmen of the Standing Commissions of the Chambers of the Supreme Soviet of the U.S.S.R. (8) Chairmen of the Committees of the Supreme Soviet of the U.S.S.R. (14)	
Chairmen of the Commissions of the Presidium of the Supreme Soviet of the U.S.S.R. (3)	

The public's interest in the newly elected bodies was indicated by the fact that during the first six months of 1989 the government received some 680 000 letters and telegrams. The Supreme Soviet itself was swamped by 38 000 visitors. Nonetheless, Gorbachev clearly remained dissatisfied with the rate of progress and won approval early in 1990 for a further program of reform. This new program set as its objective the complete transfer of real power from the C.P.S.U. to the government. To this end, the party was to surrender its privileged position and compete against other political parties. A true separation of executive, legislative, and judicial government functions was also to be instituted.

At first glance, these changes seem to point to the introduction of liberal democratic ideals into the U.S.S.R.'s political system. But in reality, the Communist party is still far from powerless. Even with the abolition of Article 6 of the constitution (which preserves the C.P.S.U.'s privileged position), the new system nonetheless offers the party elite distinct advantages. For example, as a "public organization" of some twenty million Soviet citizens, the C.P.S.U. has significant representation in the Congress and Supreme Soviet. The same is true of related groups, such as the Young Communist League, the armed forces, and trade unions. Indeed, of the 2 250 People's Deputies elected in 1989, 1 957 were Party members, and only 160 deputies could be called "non-party." True, membership now is becoming less attractive as liberal factions leave the party to join other political groupings in challenging its dominance. Even so, the C.P.S.U. is in no immediate danger of being swept from the Soviet political stage, and Gorbachev still wields considerable authority as general secretary.

▶ THE EXECUTIVE PRESIDENCY

The real threat to the C.P.S.U.'s continued dominance, and perhaps to the growth of liberal democracy as well, is the increasing power of Gorbachev's presidency. When he became President of the U.S.S.R. in late 1988, the position was still largely honorific. Under the constitutional amendments adopted at the end of that year, much of the general secretary's authority passed to the head of state. The president now heads the Defence Council, which makes him the effective commander-in-chief of the armed forces, and not just a figure-head. The same is true in a number of other executive areas as well. Faced with growing ethnic violence, economic discontent, and political opposition, Gorbachev resolved to further strengthen his position. In March 1990, the Third Congress of People's Deputies passed a law establishing an "executive" president who "will have the powers of a U.S. president, the Canadian prime minister, and the governor-general all rolled into one." (Although Gorbachev was elected to this position by the Congress, all future elections will be conducted by direct popular suffrage.)

Gorbachev's powers include the right to introduce legislation; veto other bills; appoint prime ministers, ministers, and senior judicial figures; declare war and martial law; negotiate treaties; and grant political asylum. The Congress of People's Deputies, however, must approve all presidential decrees and appointments, and it can override his veto or fire him by a two-thirds vote. As general secretary and president, Gorbachev has amassed more *de facto* power than any Soviet leader since Stalin.

The extent to which the party has lost ground was evident at the C.P.S.U. Congress in July 1990. Armed with his new powers, Gorbachev faced down a hostile majority of delegates. Despite the dislike most delegates felt for many aspects of these reforms, Gorbachev's foremost opponents failed to win election to the Secretariat. Given his presidential powers, the delegates had little alternative but to leave him in charge of the party and the state apparatus.

While Gorbachev has undermined the party's monopoly on state power, the extent to which the recent reforms will promote a growth of liberal democracy is questionable. A number of Soviet commentators have debated the extent to which Gorbachev can carry out a major social and economic transformation while simultaneously introducing truly demo-

SOVIET LEADERS SINCE STALIN

▸ Georgi M. Malenkov	Premier	1953–1955
▸ Nikita S. Khrushchev	General Secretary	1953–1964
	Premier	1958–1964
▸ Nikolai A. Bulganin	Premier	1955–1958
▸ Leonid I. Brezhnev	General Secretary	1964–1982
▸ Aleksei N. Kosygin	Premier	1964–1979
▸ Yuri V. Andropov	General Secretary	1982–1984
▸ Konstantin U. Chernenko	General Secretary	1984–1985
▸ Mikhail S. Gorbachev	General Secretary	1985–
	President	1988–

cratic institutions. Instead, they argue, society must undergo an ''authoritarian'' period while the requirements for democracy are put in place. Gorbachev's close advisor and long-time Ambassador to Canada, Aleksandr Yakovlev, has indicated that the Soviets' vision of a democratic regime may well differ from Western concepts of government. Yakovlev's image of a president is that of a figure who is above parties and factions and acts as a conciliator among them.

▶ PROGNOSIS

The future of the Soviet Union's infant democracy is uncertain. To some extent, of course, its fate will depend on events beyond Gorbachev's immediate control—the ease with which he can implement his economic restructuring, the extent of nationalist rebellion, and so on. He has amassed great power to deal with such problems. But to date, apart from one law banning political attacks on the president, he has shown little inclination to employ his authority outside of the normal constitutional processes. He has also done much to ''democratize'' the Soviets' traditional political institutions and continues to give an impression of being seriously committed to further ''democratization.'' Even so, events may yet convince him that a further ''authoritization'' phase is necessary for safeguarding true economic reform and maintaining of the U.S.S.R.'s political-territorial integrity.

APPLYING YOUR KNOWLEDGE

1. What was the traditional difference between the theory and practice of democracy in the Soviet government?
2. What is ''democratic centralism'' and what role did it play in the life of the Communist party?
3. Draw a diagram showing how you think the Soviet system of government operated before Gorbachev.
4. Debate the benefits of one-party government.

5. Explain the major differences between the C.P.S.U. and Canadian political parties both before and since Gorbachev.
6. What were the advantages and disadvantages of the pre-Gorbachev system of Soviet government?
7. On the basis of the information in this case study, how would you answer the following questions for the pre- and post-Gorbachev periods.
   a) Who makes the decisions in the U.S.S.R.?
   b) How are these decisions made?
   c) What appear to be the basic values and assumptions of this system of government?

FURTHER RESEARCH

1. On the basis of this case and Case Studies 14 and 21, write a speech for a delegate to a C.P.S.U. Congress defending the Gorbachev regime.
2. Explain whether the most recent Soviet government is closer to the Canadian or the American model.
3. Discuss whether Gorbachev's position is that of an enlightened dictator.
4. Prepare to debate the advantages of having an enlightened dictator.

Case Study 11 Overview

How Authoritarian Governments Achieve Power: Mussolini, Mao, Batista, and Castro

This case study examines how four authoritarian leaders achieved power. Mussolini's success in Italy in the 1920s is attributed to a combination of the political and economic turmoil in the country after World War I; the problems faced by the Italian government; and Mussolini's personality, fascist ideology, and tactics. Mao's success in China after World War II is similarly explained by the country's political and economic situation and by Mao's philosophy and strategy. The case study concludes with an examination of the success of the Batista regime in Cuba and the successful revolution led by Fidel Castro.

▶ OBJECTIVES

After reading this case study, you should be able to:

- ▶ analyse the relative importance of personality, ideology, tactics, strategy, and the political and economic situation to the success of revolutionary regimes
- ▶ compare the theories outlined in the previous chapter to four actual case study situations
- ▶ evaluate the underlying beliefs of revolutionary groups
- ▶ compare the methods used to gain power by these four individuals
- ▶ extrapolate what you have learned in this case study to help in examining other countries

▶ KEY TERMS

guerrilla warfare
puppet dictatorships
Il Duce
fascism
communists
the Long March
Platt Amendment

Case Study

11 How Authoritarian Governments Achieve Power: Mussolini, Mao, Batista, and Castro

Non-democratic governments have achieved power in a variety of ways. Such fascist leaders as Benito Mussolini in Italy and Adolf Hitler in Germany employed the democratic electoral process in the 1920s and 1930s to gain political office, and once in power, used their position to impose one-party rule. In a monarchy, power is peacefully passed on through inheritance. Most non-democratic leaders, however, gain power by such violent means as revolutions, **guerrilla warfare**, and military *coup d'états*; it is also not unusual for such countries to install **puppet dictatorships** in conquered countries.

Historical and contemporary examples of non-democratic regimes are almost endless. Dictatorships continue to flourish in Latin America, Africa, and Asia; in the twentieth century, communist regimes emerged in Asia, Europe, and some Third World countries. More often than not, one dictatorship has merely replaced another non-democratic government, but in several instances, democracies fell victim to non-democratic regimes.

One of the best methods of analysing the underlying beliefs of a political system is to examine how political power is achieved and what provisions are made for the continuance of the regime. Are the people consulted? To what extent are individual rights and freedom subordinated to the demands of the state? Who are the political leaders? What role does the individual citizen play in the political system? Keep these questions in mind as you read the following accounts of the rise to power of Benito Mussolini, Mao, Fulgencio Batista, and Fidel Castro.

▶ THE DECLINE OF DEMOCRACY

Immediately following World War I, democracy appeared ready to sweep through Europe. During the 1920s and 1930s, however, country after country turned to some type of authoritarian or dictatorial rule. In Turkey, Poland, and Iran, military officers assumed control. Yugoslavia, Romania, and Albania established monarchical dictatorships. Dictatorships also emerged in Bulgaria, Greece, Austria, the three Baltic states, Portugal, and Spain.

The peace treaty was partly to blame for this situation. Its harsh terms angered the defeated countries, and even left two countries on the victorious side, Italy and Japan, particularly unhappy. The hard economic times following the war and the terrible depression of the 1930s also served to discredit democracy. Confused, bitter, and unemployed, many people turned to energetic and dynamic men who promised to solve their problems. Unhappiness seemed to exist everywhere. During the 1930s, Japan witnessed the assassination of two prime ministers, two failed military coups, and the rise of military personnel to key political positions. In the Caribbean and South and Central America, many countries fell under dictatorial rule between the 1920s and the 1950s. This case study examines the methods that Mussolini, Batista, Mao, and Castro used to gain power.

▶ ITALY AFTER WORLD WAR I

World War I (1914–1918) had a traumatic effect upon Europe, and Italy was no exception. Soldiers returned from the battle front to find that there were no jobs available because munitions factories and other war industries had been closed. The continued decline of Italy's gross national production and a decrease in overseas trade resulting from the war added to the economic problems. Unemployment rose from 90 000 in the summer of 1920 to over half a million by the end of the next year. The cost of living increased by fifty percent, and the middle classes soon found that their meagre savings were consumed by the inflationary spiral. For example, a family that had managed to save 10 000 lire before the war, soon discovered that a lira in 1919 could buy one-tenth of the amount of food it had in 1913. Most urban workers and rural peasants had no savings to lose and remained mired in poverty.

What made the situation so bad was that Italian politicians had promised the people prosperity after the war. Disillusionment now began to set in, and many Italians became increasingly unhappy with the country's rulers. In the countryside, rich landlords had their houses burned and their livestock slaughtered when they opposed several left-wing groups attempting to redistribute their land among the poorer peasants. Although not much land actually changed hands, the mayhem convinced large landholders that stronger government action was necessary.

In the large industrial cities, strikes became more and more frequent. Industrial strife reached a peak in the fall of 1920, when workers seized 600 factories in a series of sit-in strikes. Although the crisis soon passed and the factories were ultimately returned to their owners, sporadic strikes continued to disrupt Italian industry. These rural and urban conflicts revealed the weakness of the government. Paralyzed by divisions within Parliament, the government lacked the power to intervene and re-establish order.

Figure 1
ITALY AND SURROUNDING COUNTRIES

One of the Italian government's promises to the people had been that participation in World War I would bring national honour to the country. Italy, in fact, had entered the war to secure additional territory and had emerged from the war with high hopes of obtaining the western part of Yugoslavia, including the ports of Trieste and Fiume, a strip of Dalmatia on the eastern Adriatic shore, and some of Germany's colonies in Africa.[1] The failure of Italy to secure most of these possessions was viewed by the middle and upper classes as a blow to her national prestige. Once again, the government was accused of inaction and ineffectiveness.

▶ The Italian Government

Italy at this time was a constitutional monarchy. As in Great Britain, the king had limited powers and the Chamber of Deputies, similar to the Canadian House of Commons, was the most important legislative branch of government. Unlike in Canada or Great Britain, clearly defined political parties had been slow to emerge in Italy, partly because it had only become a unified country in 1870, and partly because the people were not used to democratic procedures. Italy had a parliament, but no parliamentary traditions. The party system, for example, was extremely fragmented. There were at least ten different political parties, and the two largest ones — the Socialists and the Christian Democrats — were unable to work together because of ideological differences. In addition, elected representatives frequently switched from one party to another.

The result was chronic political instability. On the average, governing coalitions changed every year and a half. When the people turned to the government for help, they saw a divided Parliament engaged in endless debates, bickering, name-calling,

▸ [1]Italy's lack of ideological commitment to the war was evident when the country chose the winning side part way through the conflict in return for promised territorial gains.

Austrian prisoners at the end of World War I under guard by Italian mounted soldiers. Italians believed that their success during the war would lead to prosperity afterwards. Their disillusionment helped to set the stage for Mussolini's success.
Canapress Photo Service

"buck passing," and procrastination. Faith in democracy began to dwindle as the political regime seemed incapable of defending Italy's interests abroad; solving the country's economic woes; or of providing law, order, and efficient government at home. To fill this vacuum, the people turned to more charismatic and dominant leaders. The problems persisted. Into this confused situation stepped Benito Mussolini.

▶ MUSSOLINI

Benito Amilcare Andrea Mussolini was born in northern Italy in 1883, the eldest in a family of three children. His father was a blacksmith with socialist beliefs that he tried to instill in his children. Mussolini, in fact, was named after the Mexican revolutionary Benito Juarez, and his middle names were taken from two prominent Italian socialists.

Although the Mussolini family was poor, Benito was sent to a Catholic school. Here, in his second year, he was expelled for stabbing a rich schoolmate with his penknife. Despite another knifing incident at the next school, Mussolini graduated in 1902 with an elementary school teaching certificate. A year later, he travelled to Switzerland to further his education, but soon became so involved in encouraging strikes and establishing trade unions that he was deported. Returning to Italy, Mussolini continued his socialist preachings and in 1908 was imprisoned as a dangerous revolutionary. Once out of prison, Mussolini became editor of *Avanti* (Forward), the official newspaper of the Italian Socialist party, and for the next few years he threw himself behind the socialist cause with total commitment.

When World War I erupted in 1914, Mussolini termed it a middle-class war and urged Italy to remain neutral—which was acceptable socialist doctrine. It was not long, however, before he changed his mind and began urging Italy to participate. As a result, Mussolini was forced to resign from *Avanti* and break with the Socialist party. A short while later, he was drafted into the army, where he was wounded, discharged, and exempted from further duty. Mussolini was then ready to begin a new phase in his career.

▶ Mussolini—The Man

Before describing Mussolini's rise to power, let us first examine the character of the man who was to rule Italy for over two decades. Mussolini did not cut an imposing figure—only slightly over 150 cm tall, he was below average height. His hairline was rapidly receding and his round face was marked by a jutting jaw, a large mouth, and dark protuberant eyes. To disguise his short stature, Mussolini always stood ramrod straight, pushed out his lower lip and jaw, and tilted his head back so that he always seemed to be looking down at the person to whom he was talking. Once in power, he enjoyed standing next to the king, whom he dwarfed in size.

Mussolini and the Fascists sought to epitomize virility and strength. Poor health and an ulcer, which prevented Mussolini from eating meat and drinking wine, were therefore hidden from the public. Likewise, his fondness for playing the violin, which was considered effeminate, was seldom mentioned. Instead, he was pictured as a horseman, a pilot, and a driver of fast cars. Although Mussolini also liked to pretend that he was a cultured, well-read intellectual, he had little interest in art, and he usually skimmed a book as quickly as possible to obtain its highlights. His one love was politics, and his goal was to achieve power and influence.

In personal relationships, ***Il Duce*** (The Leader, as he liked to be called) was a vain egotist who was insensitive to the feelings of those around him. His only real friends were his father and brother. He was ready to sacrifice everyone else, including his wife who bore him five children, and his many mistresses, in his pursuit of power.

Clearly, Mussolini suffered from an inferiority complex. In times of crisis, he was afraid to take action. Lacking self-confidence, he tended to follow the advice of whoever spoke to him last. Complex problems were ignored or reduced to a simple matter of black and white—which perhaps accounts for his ability to move from socialism to fascism.

Rhetorical skill was Mussolini's major asset. With a voice that was both powerful and flexible, *Il Duce* was able to establish a rapport with a crowd—and stimulate it to action. He spoke in a series of sharp, often unconnected statements. In short, he had charisma. Following World War I, he was ready to put his talents and his ambition to work.

▶ Mussolini's Philosophy

It takes more than rhetorical skill and charisma to win the support of a country. A successful leader must also have an ideology or a set of objectives that are appropriate to the period and to the people. Mussolini's set of ideas (confusing as they sometimes were) was called **fascism**.

"Our program is simple," stated Mussolini, "we wish to govern Italy. They ask us for programs, but there are already too many. It is not programs that are wanting for the salvation of Italy, but men and will power." He saw life as a struggle in which positive action and discipline were needed for success; democracy and socialism were too passive and sentimental to survive in a world of conflict and struggle. Democracy was flawed because it exalted the individual and did not acknowledge that most people are irrational. Majority rule therefore meant that the country was reduced to the level of the lowest common denominator.

Individuals, according to Mussolini, were first and foremost members of a nation to which they gave all their loyalty and love. In his view, the whole was greater than the sum of its individual parts. Only by subordinating themselves to the will of the state could people reach their fullest potential. This appeal to nationalism gave many Italians a sense of belonging, security, and self-worth. They were part of a larger whole, and that larger whole, Mussolini promised, would soon be one of the most powerful nations in the world.

Fascism also glorified the leader. People owed absolute obedience to their immediate superior; and everyone was ultimately subordinate to the national leader. Just as there were some classes in society better able to rule than others (that is, the Fascist party), only one person, Mussolini stated, was qualified to govern the Italian nation. Only he (it was assumed that the leader would be male) knew the real needs of the state, and therefore had to be given total obedience. The leader's will was indistinguishable from the collective national will, and was infallible. In a moment of vanity, Mussolini once declared: "Fascism is Mussolinism . . . what would Fascism be if I had not been?"

Fascism appealed to nationalists, to those who wanted efficient leadership and a restoration of law and order, to authoritarian-minded people, to anti-communists, and to those who gloried in war and feats of courage. It offered hope to confused people and it promised national greatness.

▶ Mussolini's Rise to Power

In March 1919, Mussolini began to gather around him a small group of ex-socialists and former armed service men who were having difficulty adjusting to civilian life. Initially, the movement was nationalistic, anticlerical, and anticapitalist. Attempting to appeal to the workers, Mussolini advocated an eight-hour work day, universal suffrage, and an end to class privileges. In the election of that year, however, his party received fewer than 5000 votes, and his old socialist friends paraded in front of his house carrying a coffin bearing Mussolini's name.

Mussolini changed course once again. Rather than continue to appeal to the apparently unresponsive lower classes, he decided to cater to wealthy businesspeople. He drafted a less radical platform that offered something for everyone. This sudden reversal did not appear to bother Mussolini, and he subsequently told the people, "we permit ourselves the luxury of being aristocratic and democratic, conservative and progressive, reactionary and revolutionary, legalist and illegalist, according to the circumstances of the moment, the place and the environment." In 1920, following an abortive attempt by workers to seize the factories, *Il Duce* threw his whole weight against the socialists and the **communists**. Groups of young men called *squadristi* were outfitted in black shirts and sent into the streets to combat the communists. They broke strikes, raided trade union offices, vandalized left-wing newspapers, and terrorized anyone who opposed them. It was not long before this violence spread throughout Italy. If, as sometimes happened, a fascist member was murdered, within hours truckloads of fascists would come rumbling into town on a punitive expedition. The government, which also disliked left-wing groups, did nothing to stop the violence. In fact, it quietly supplied the fascists with weapons and gave them free railroad transportation. The police, too, would often either aid them in their battles against the leftists, or do nothing to stop them. The *squadristi* attacks created a sense of camaraderie among Mussolini's supporters. More important, they helped to mobilize widespread support. In the process, a private army, answerable only to Mussolini, was created.

▶ The March on Rome

In the 1921 general election, Mussolini's party captured thirty-five seats in Parliament, and party membership grew to 300 000. This was an indication of the growing success of Mussolini's tactics. By the next year, almost every segment of society was ready to co-operate with the fascists. Merchants, skilled workers, professionals, and intellectuals all wanted a strong leader who could rebuild Italy's national prestige and restore law and order in the streets. To landowners, fascism meant protection against further land seizures. To employers, it meant fewer strikes and the possibility of lower wages. Mussolini's deliberate attempts to increase violence and anarchy in the streets served to keep property owners in a state of alarm. With the government unable to do anything, fascism seemed the only solution. Moreover, the Socialist party's success in appealing to the labouring class made the middle and upper classes uneasy. Mussolini played on their fears by prophesying that a communist revolution similar to the 1917 revolution in Russia would happen in Italy if he were not elected.

Although *Il Duce* had been anticlerical and antimonarchist, by 1922 he was on cordial terms with Pope Pius XI, and the Queen Mother herself was an avid fascist. The Pope, distrusting the parliamentary system which he thought was incapable of preventing the growth of socialism, believed he could work with Mussolini. King Victor Emmanuel's younger brother supported the fascists, who he hoped would put him on the throne. The fear that the fascists might replace Victor Emmanuel with his brother was enough to keep the king from obstructing the spread of fascism. Finally, the civil service and many politicians supported *Il Duce* because they believed they could control his actions. Given power, Mussolini would become more responsible — or so they thought.

By 1922, Mussolini felt strong enough to challenge the government. When the government ignored his threat to seize control of the state if he was not given power immediately, he ordered the *squadristi* to isolate the government offices in Rome from the rest of Italy by capturing strategic railway and telegraph offices. At the same time, the fascists, approximately 26 000 strong, began their march on Rome.

After a period of indecision and confusion, the government decided to call out the army. In retrospect, this was the correct decision. The fascists were outnumbered and had no cannons; some of the insurgents were armed only with clubs. They were trained for street fighting, not for a full-scale military campaign. In fact, the fascist troops were instructed to avoid conflict with the army, and where the authorities did offer resistance, the marchers fell back without putting up a fight. The king, however, did not know this. He used his authority to cancel the government's order to call out the army. Two days later, the king invited Mussolini to become the new premier — the change in government was thus constitutional.

▶ The Fascist Government

For the first few years, *Il Duce* lived up to the expectations of the upper and middle classes. He took lessons in protocol and manners. He wore conventional clothes for public appearances, and he reported twice weekly to the king. In Parliament, Mussolini established a conventional ministry and was given a vote of confidence by the Chamber of Deputies. It is true that he demanded and was granted dictatorial powers until the end of 1923, but this was not unusual in Italy at this time, and was perfectly legal.

Gradually, Mussolini gained more and more power. Although the Chamber of Deputies continued to function, the Fascist party selected all candidates and presented them to the electorate for approval. The ballot read: "Do you approve of the list of deputies chosen by the Fascist Grand Council?" Civil servants who disagreed with the fascist philosophy were dismissed. *Il Duce* was given permanent control of the military forces, which swore personal allegiance to him. Local municipal elections were abolished and municipal officials were appointed by the government in Rome. Newspapers were censored. Socialist and Catholic trade unions were prohibited. "Italy wants peace and quiet, and calm in which to work," Mussolini declared, "This we shall give her, by love if possible, by force if need be."

By the end of 1926, Mussolini was the undisputed fascist dictator of Italy. He would remain so until his dismissal in July 1943. (Two years later, he was caught by his enemies and hanged.) In the interval, Benito Mussolini helped bring about the bloodiest war in the history of the world.

FOCUS

1. There are two general ways to explain Mussolini's rise to power. The first is to attribute *Il Duce*'s success to the man himself. This follows the "great man" theory of history, which states that every so often, a strong and dynamic person will

appear, who by the very force of his personality, drive, and intelligence will shape the environment to suit his purposes. The second explanation is that Mussolini's success was a direct outgrowth of Italian history. According to this theory, the environment shaped Mussolini's rise, not the reverse. Fascism triumphed because it responded to the needs of society. Select one of these two explanations, or develop your own theory, and defend it.

2. Explain how the Italian government could have prevented Mussolini's rise to power.
3. How do you think power would have been transferred in fascist Italy if Mussolini had died while he was still at the height of his power in 1943?
4. What does this case study reveal about the underlying beliefs of the fascist regime? Discuss under the following headings: individual rights, the power of the state, might makes right, the end justifies the means.
5. a) What does this case study reveal about the potential weaknesses of democracy? (Use the inquiry techniques outlined in Chapter 1.)
   b) What can be done to avoid these problems?
6. Italy was not the only country in Europe to turn to totalitarianism between the two world wars. Again using the inquiry techniques outlined in Chapter 1, research and write an essay explaining why *either* Adolf Hitler rose to power in Germany or General Franco gained control of Spain. Organize your essay in a similar manner to the case study on Mussolini. Discuss the reasons for discontent, the personality of the man, and the way he used the situation to achieve power.

▶ THE CHINESE REVOLUTION

In 1911, the Kuomintang party toppled the increasingly inept Manchu dynasty from power in China. Dr. Sun Yat-sen, the new leader, was an idealistic man who wished to restore China's national pride and economy after years of foreign domination. Convinced that only large-scale reforms would achieve this goal, Sun Yat-sen based his government upon a three-fold program of nationalism (the unification of China and the expulsion of all "foreign devils"), democracy (a popularly elected government), and socialism (nationalization of all basic industries and redistribution of land to the starving peasants). However, Sun Yat-sen failed to gain complete control of the army, and warlords in every province continued to dominate and oppress the people.

When Sun died in 1925, the Kuomintang comprised two major groups. He was succeeded by his lieutenant, Chiang Kai-shek, who led the conservative faction. The Communist party formed the second group. Having failed to successfully incite revolution in Europe, Stalin and Lenin aided in the creation of the Chinese Communist party in 1921, and suggested that the party ally itself temporarily with the Kuomintang. In 1927, however, Chiang Kai-shek broke with the Communist party and attempted to destroy it. His troops killed thousands of communist supporters, including all the labour leaders. The survivors fled from the cities and hid in the countryside.

Chiang's suppression of communist activity in the cities, and China's small urban and industrial base, forced leaders such as Mao Zedong to modify Lenin's and Marx's reliance on the industrial workers for help. Following the 1927 disasters, Mao retreated into the countryside and turned to the peasants, who, he wrote, were like the "raging winds and driving rain. . . . No force can stand in their way. . . . They will bury beneath them all forces of imperialism, militarism, corrupt officialdom, village bosses and evil landlords." This "mighty storm" would sweep all opposition before it. Mao thus insisted that the civilian population be treated with respect. Force was only to be used on the enemy. In their mountain strongholds, the communists redistributed the land to the people; reduced taxes; eliminated child slavery, prostitution, and opium smoking; and began mass political education programs. Since the "richest source of power to wage war lies in the masses of the people," Mao issued the following instructions to his men:

- **1.** Speak politely.
- **2.** Pay fairly for what you buy.
- **3.** Return everything you borrow.
- **4.** Pay for anything you damage.
- **5.** Don't hit or swear at people.
- **6.** Don't damage crops.
- **7.** Don't take liberties with women.
- **8.** Don't ill-treat captives.

As the peasantry became friendlier, Mao's ragged band of followers grew larger, and Mao expanded his bases.

Mao's other major contribution to Marxist-Leninist revolutionary theory was the belief in guerrilla warfare. *Guerra* is the Spanish word for war, and "guerrilla" means "little warrior." Lenin believed that power must be achieved at a single stroke, in as little time as possible. Chiang's immense power, and China's tremendous size, however, meant that any revolutionary struggle would take many years. Mao argued that the communists would have to become mobile and harass their enemy, rather than engage in major conflicts. They should confuse their foes, disrupt their lines of communications, force them to disperse their strength, and most important, undermine their morale. Never destroyed, the guerrillas would provide the appearance of invincibility and would thus humiliate those who could not defeat them. To Mao, guerrilla warfare meant: "The enemy advances, we retreat; the enemy camps, we harass; the enemy tires, we attack; the enemy retreats, we pursue."

During the first phase of the guerrilla warfare, Mao's soldiers were to concentrate on securing safe bases for rest and training. No other territory was worth losing men over. In the second phase, numerous small groups were to ambush and otherwise harass the enemy. "The first law of war," Mao wrote, "is to preserve ourselves and destroy the enemy." The final phase would begin only when victory was certain and involved conventional warfare with large troop movements.

In 1930, Chiang mobilized his forces against the communists, and four years later his larger and better-equipped army had surrounded them. Faced with destruction, Mao's Red Army left its mountain base, broke through Chiang's lines, and fled northward. Thus began one of the twentieth century's most dramatic adventures — **the Long March**. For over a year, Mao and some 130 000 supporters trudged through uncharted territory, crossed eighteen mountain ranges, and fought ten warlords before establishing a separate base in Yenan. Their snake-like route was the equivalent of crossing Canada on foot from Halifax to Vancouver and returning to Winnipeg. Since it was more a running battle than a march, only about 35 000 people survived. The hardships of the journey caused a leadership struggle within the party, from which Mao emerged victorious. From 1949 until the early 1980s, almost every important Chinese leader was a survivor of the Long March.

When Japan attacked China in 1937, Chiang reluctantly agreed to join forces with Mao to fight their common enemy. In fact, Chiang only agreed to a truce after he had been kidnapped by one of his own officers. Their combined forces were overwhelmed by the Japanese, who gained control over most of China's cities by 1939. Several times their uneasy truce broke down and the two Chinese forces fought each other rather than the Japanese. Whenever possible, Chiang's forces held back and allowed the Red Army to bear the brunt of the fighting, while they carefully stockpiled American weapons in preparation for the final battle with Mao. This allowed Mao to portray himself as a patriotic leader, and Chiang as a traitor to China. Corruption within Chiang's government, its brutal and overpaid officers, and its reluctance to fight the enemy, increased communist support. While Chiang's forces deteriorated from inactivity, Mao built respect for the Red Army.

Following the United States victory over Japan in 1945, the two forces engaged in a final struggle for control of China. The Soviet Union and the United States tried to convince the combatants to form a coalition government, but both sides were confident of victory. Fair treatment of the peasantry now paid dividends. Mao's cause was also aided by Chiang's inept and corrupt dictatorship, which was by now quite unpopular. Mao's promises to restore China's pride and revive an economy that was in tatters found fertile ground. Eventually, although the United States supported Chiang, Mao forced Chiang to retreat to the island of Taiwan (Formosa) in 1949, and Mao proclaimed the creation of the People's Republic of China.

Following this victory, Mao hoped to export his brand of revolutionary communism to other countries in Asia, Africa, and Latin America—all of which suffered from uneven economic development and ruthless governments. According to Mao, success depended upon establishing bases in the most rugged areas, protracted military conflict, peasant guerrilla warfare, winning the support of the local population, and appealing to the people's patriotism or nationalism. Communist parties in Burma, Cambodia, Laos, Malaysia, the Philippines, and Thailand copied Mao's liberation policies. In Vietnam and Korea, Chinese military assistance helped establish new communist states.

Chinese communist leader Mao Zedong (1893–1976), also spelled Mao Tse-tung, became the ruler of mainland China in 1949.
Canapress Photo Service

FOCUS

1. Explain how Mao adjusted traditional Marxist revolutionary theory to fit Chinese conditions.
2. Research and write a biographical sketch of Mao similar to the sketch of Mussolini in this case study.
3. If Canada was captured by an enemy country, how successful would guerrilla warfare be in overthrowing the new government?
4. Research the success of Mao's tactics in North Vietnam.
5. Mao believed in continuous revolution. Examine his goals, methods, and success in any one of the following periods: the anti-landlord campaign (1949–1952), the First Five-Year Plan (1953–1957), the Hundred Flowers Movement (1957), the Great Leap Forward (1958–1960), or the Great Cultural Revolution (1966–1976).

▶ THE CUBAN REVOLUTION

Cuba is the largest island in the West Indies. From end to end, it measures 1245 km, and its width varies from 35 km to 208 km. The island is located in the entrance to the Gulf of Mexico, only 150 km off the Florida coast. Because of its size and strategic location in Latin America, Spain colonized Cuba and enslaved the natives shortly after Cuba's discovery by Christopher Columbus. During the following four centuries, Cuba remained a dependency of Spain, which profited from the island's abundant sugar plantations.

Cuban nationalistic feelings erupted in 1868. The next thirty years were filled with bitterness, despair, bloodshed, and terror, as the Cuban people attempted to free themselves from Spanish control. Finally, with the help of the United States, the Spanish forces were defeated in 1898. No sooner had Cuba achieved independence from Spain than it fell under the control of the United States.

▶ Americans in Cuba

The United States had considered annexing Cuba for strategic reasons as early as 1808, but it was not until the rapid expansion of the American industrial revolution that annexation became a realistic proposition. By the 1890s, the aggressive American business community had expanded its influence into Hawaii, the Philippines, Mexico, China, Nicaragua, Venezuela, Cuba, Samoa, and the Midway Islands. These countries provided a market for America's agricultural and industrial products. Although Cuba was controlled by Spain, American investments in the island totalled over thirty-three million dollars in 1898. In addition, there was a prosperous two-way trade in flour, sugar, and manufactured goods, although the almost continuous warfare between Spain and the Cuban rebels interrupted this trade. Many businessmen began to believe that if Spain could not protect American property and provide a stable government on the island, then in the interest of commerce, the United States should intervene. When an American battleship moored in a Cuban harbour was allegedly blown up by Spain in 1898, Washington decided to intervene on Cuba's behalf in what became the Spanish-American War. This decision was based on a combination of popular sympathy for the Cuban rebels, outrage at Spanish atrocities committed in Cuba, the desire to eliminate European power from the western hemisphere, and the need to secure the

Figure 2
CUBA AND SURROUNDING AREA

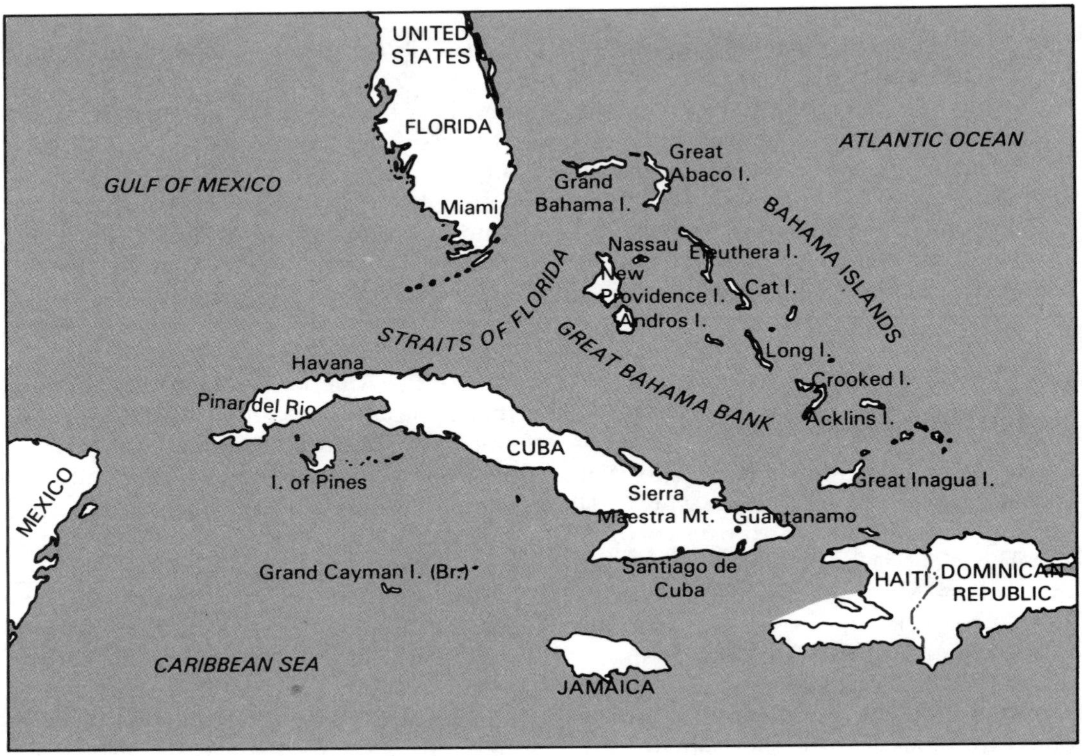

safety of American investments on the island. Following the defeat of Spain, American troops remained in Cuba for four years. During this time, the United States ran the government and American businesspeople took the opportunity to consolidate their holdings and acquire more property.

On May 20, 1902, American troops were withdrawn. A new Cuban constitution granted universal male suffrage and provided for a popularly elected, but all-powerful president who could serve for a maximum of two consecutive four-year terms. National happiness, however, was tinged by humiliation and a feeling of impotence. The United States had made its withdrawal of troops contingent upon Cuba's acceptance of the **Platt Amendment**. This document literally made Cuba an American protectorate. It allowed the United States to intervene in Cuban affairs for "the preservation of Cuban independence, the maintenance of a government adequate for the protection of life, property and individual liberty." The amendment also restricted Cuba's authority to make treaties or to borrow money from abroad. The United States navy was given specified coaling and naval stations; American control over the island's public utilities was consolidated; and a trade agreement was passed that opened Cuba to American agricultural and industrial products.

The Platt Amendment remained in force until 1934. Prior to that time, the United States interfered several times to maintain order in Cuba. Almost all the influential Cuban leaders during this period had close ties with American businesses and politicians. Unfortunately, the knowledge that the United States would intervene to protect Cuba from attack or to solve its internal political problems kept Cubans from learning how to run their own affairs. This attitude has been called the ''Platt Amendment mentality.''

▶ The Revolution of 1933

Soon after the American withdrawal, dissatisfaction with Cuban politics turned into strikes, protest marches, and riots, the president took harsh measures. Anti-government newspapers were shut down and the university and high schools were closed. Hired killers roamed the streets. A few small uprisings were brutally crushed and political prisoners were tortured.

By 1933, it was obvious that something had to be done. In an attempt to find a peaceful solution, the United States sent Ambassador Sumner Welles to Cuba to mediate between the government and the opposition. Welles made little headway — near the end of July 1933, a nation-wide strike brought industry and communications to a standstill. When several revolts within the army broke out a few days later, President Machado resigned.

The public went wild with delight. Revenge-crazed mobs roamed the streets looting, stealing, and killing Machado's supporters — some were literally hacked to pieces in public squares. Students demanded radical social and economic reforms, as well as political independence from the United States. One popular slogan read: ''Cuba for the Cubans.''

Once again, however, the people were frustrated. The army allied with politicians to appoint Carlos Manuel de Céspedes as president. Céspedes was a conservative politician who had the support of the United States and was unwilling to do any more than end the blatant brutality of the Machado regime.

The violence continued. On September 4, rank and file soldiers led by Sergeant Fulgencio Batista rebelled against their officers. The soldiers had been upset by a proposed reduction in their salaries and by an order restricting promotion within the army. Although the army by that time had full control of the government, it needed civilian support. After a meeting with university students, a junta of five men formed a provisional government. Former university professor Ramón Grau San Martin headed the government, and Batista (now a colonel) remained in control of the army.

Once again, however, the government was overthrown by the army. After only 120 days in office, Grau was removed by the Batista-led army and replaced by Carlos Mendieta, a supporter of Batista. During his short period in power, Grau had proposed agrarian reforms, attempted to nationalize the sugar and mining industries, tried to cancel the Platt Amendment, and proposed to set the maximum working day at eight hours. These ideas naturally aroused the hostility of both the United States and the island's industrial and commercial leaders. At the same time, the reformism of Grau did not go far enough to satisfy the students, and he lost their support as well. Batista took advantage of this situation to elevate himself to the most powerful position in Cuba.

The failure of Grau to gain American endorsement of his regime had kept alive the hopes of his opponents. When the ambitious Batista forced Grau to resign on January 14, 1934, the United States almost immediately recognized the new regime, which promised to protect foreign investments and provide a stable, ordered government. In order to buttress the Mendieta-Batista regime, the United States agreed to renounce the Platt Amendment (although it retained control of the port at Guantanamo), lower the tariff on raw Cuban sugar, and guarantee Cuba twenty-eight percent of the American sugar market. These terms were calculated to soothe Cuban nationalistic feelings, bolster the island's economy, and enhance the reputation of the new Cuban government.

The plan was successful. Not only had the reformers lost their chance to rebuild the social and economic institutions of the country, but the 1933 revolution also marked the entry of the army into politics. From this point onwards, every civilian regime lay at the mercy of military leaders.

▶ The Batista Era

Fulgencio Batista was twenty years old when he joined the army in 1921. Since he was poorly educated and came from the lower classes, Batista started at the bottom. During the next decade he rose slowly but steadily. Always ambitious and industrious, he learned to type, studied law, dealt in real estate, managed a farm, sold fruit and vegetables, and taught commercial subjects at night school. After he rose to power, Batista hired instructors to teach him and his wife proper social graces. An avid reader, he collected material on Benito Mussolini, whom he admired. In person, Batista was a charming, persuasive talker who always seemed to have a smile on his lips.

From 1934 to 1940 Batista, as head of the army, ruled Cuba through a series of puppet presidents. Realizing that it would be impossible to maintain power by force alone, he formed a series of separate alliances with the propertied classes; the Communist party; the workers; and the old, traditional political parties. At the same time, he sponsored a series of reforms designed to improve living conditions: legislation was passed in the areas of health, sanitation, education, and pensions; a minimum wage was set; and tenants on small sugar plantations were protected from arbitrary eviction. In this way, Batista broadened the base of his support.

Ultimately, however, the regime relied on the army as its source of power. During this period, the army was enlarged and modernized, and its living standards were greatly improved. The United States supplied the army with the best in weaponry and trained many of the Cuban officers. It was this army that Batista employed to rout his enemies. During the general strike of 1935, for example, hundreds of people were injured, union offices were raided and destroyed, and opposition newspapers were closed. The strike was ruthlessly suppressed. Although this kind of terrorism did not continue for very long, the Batista-controlled government reinstated the repression and corruption that had been symptomatic of pre-1933 Cuba. The army shared in the fruits of this corruption. In fact, the rank and file were recruited from demoralized Cuban youth who had no compunction about joining in the spoils of office.

After the adoption of a new, more democratic constitution in 1940, Batista ran for the presidency and was successful. This was the first time he was the official head of Cuba. In the following election, Batista defeated by Ramón Grau San Martin. Fearing reprisals, he fled to Florida. Grau's autocratic rule was not much better than Batista's. Patronage, corruption, and embezzlement of public funds were widespread. Disillusionment led to cynicism — politicians, the people came to believe, could not be trusted.

Cuban leader Fulgencio Batista with his family.

Batista returned to Cuba in 1948. Four years later, he decided to run once again for the presidency. When it became obvious that he would not win, Batista used his influence with the army to overthrow the regime on March 10, 1952. The ease with which the coup was carried out, and the lack of opposition to it, illustrated the weakness of Cuba's political institutions. The people were too demoralized to resist. Besides, how could Batista be any worse than the previous "democratic" politicians? Cuban propertied classes and American businesspeople supported the coup because they hoped that the new dictator would impose law and order after so many years of chaos.

This time, Batista was less willing to compromise. His despotic, gangster-like tactics and his increasing reliance on corruption soon alienated the propertied classes that had originally welcomed him. Although the Cuban economy was generally prosperous during the late 1940s and early 1950s, the increased wealth of plantation owners, ranchers, hotel owners, and utility companies was not passed on to the workers, who had one of the lowest standards of living and the highest illiteracy rates in Latin America. Outside of Havana, for example, there were very few medical doctors. Unemployment, which reached a high of sixteen percent in 1957, became a chronic problem. The workers had no institutions through which they might express their frustration, or in which to organize their discontent with the system. The most obvious source of help would have been the trade unions, but Batista had won their leaders over to his side through bribery and intimidation.

The Roman Catholic Church, which played an important role in the overthrow of several other Latin American dictatorships, was generally conservative in nature and did not oppose Batista until 1958. Even then, the church had no deep roots in Cuban society because most of the priests were still Spanish, and because the church catered largely to the urban middle class.

Opposition to the regime was thus disorganized and leaderless. There was no credible alternative around which the people could unite. Several attempts at opposition were met with fierce brutality, and Batista's opponents were jailed and exiled. The Communist party was driven underground. Appeal to the United States appeared hopeless because Washington had just granted recognition to several other Latin American dictatorships. Help from the army was highly unlikely, as it had become a mercenary institution allied to Batista and generally isolated from the rest of society.

FOCUS

1. Explain the meaning of the phrase "the Platt Amendment mentality."
2. Using the 1933 Cuban Revolution as an example, discuss the ingredients needed for a successful overthrow of government.
3. What are the similarities and the differences between Mussolini's rise to power and Batista's success?
4. Explain the reasons behind Washington's continued support of non-democratic regimes in Cuba.
5. Imagine that you are living in Cuba in 1958 and that you oppose Batista. Based on what you have read about the difficulties of opposing the dictator, how would you attempt to change the government?

▶ FIDEL CASTRO

From 1952 to 1956, the burden of opposition was carried by university students. Dissent took the form of student demonstrations, terrorism, armed assaults on military garrisons, and assassination attempts on Batista's life. Although this opposition was defeated, the flame was kept alive. Unfortunately, there was no charismatic national leader around whom the students could unite. Certainly, the older generation of politicians had proven itself unworthy of trust.

Opposition to Batista's regime also came from recent graduates from the University of Havana—one of these was Fidel Castro. Born in 1926, Castro came from a wealthy landowning family. He was brought up in the country, where his playmates were children of the poorer families in the area. Castro attended a Catholic high school in Santiago where he obtained good marks and was named Cuba's best school athlete in 1944. Tall, good-looking, athletic, and articulate, he entered into politics as soon as he began university. Although he was a good debater and a courageous, active thorn in the side of the Batista regime, Castro was never the leader of more than a handful of followers. In 1950, he graduated from law school and joined a small law firm but was never very happy as a lawyer and took little interest in the firm. Most of his clients were poor widows or labourers whom he charged very little.

▶ Castro's Rise to Power

When it became apparent that Batista could not be deposed by legal action, Castro decided to organize an armed uprising. His first target was the army barracks in Santiago de Cuba. Success here would provide his men with badly needed weapons and,

Castro hoped, act as a catalyst in arousing Cubans to take up arms against the reactionary regime.

Security was a prerequisite: Castro divided his supporters into cells of about ten each; no one was told where the target was or when they would strike. Contact among the cells involved only cell leaders, and then only through intermediaries. The date of the uprising was set for July 26, 1952, at 5:30 a.m. This was carnival night, and a large group of strangers would likely go unnoticed. Success depended upon surprise.

Despite meticulous planning, the raid ended in failure and Castro was forced to flee. Many of those who were caught in the raid were tortured and murdered. Five days later, Castro and the rest of the conspirators were apprehended, and Castro was given a fifteen-year prison sentence.

Despite its failure, the attack captured the imagination of Cubans, and gave Castro national publicity and prestige. While in prison, he worked out the strategy and tactics he would later use to overthrow Batista. He also wrote articles for a popular Cuban magazine and succeeded in having 10 000 copies of *History Will Absolve Me* (a reprint of his defence in court) printed. This material was smuggled out of prison in match boxes with false bottoms, or by using lemon juice to write between the lines of his regular letters.

Castro was freed from prison in May 1955, as part of a general amnesty designed to improve Batista's public image. He had been offered freedom earlier, in exchange for a promise not to cause any more problems, but the prisoner apparently replied: "We do not want amnesty at the price of dishonour. . . . Better a thousand years in prison before the sacrifice of integrity." Shortly after he was released, Castro became convinced that the government was plotting his assassination, and he fled to Mexico.

Cuban leader Fidel Castro on his release from prison on May 16, 1955.
Canapress Photo Service

In Mexico, Castro met Dr. Ernesto ("Ché") Guevara, who had fought against the Guatemalan and Argentinian dictators and was now searching for another Latin-American war of liberation in which he could participate. Castro began to plan for an invasion of Cuba. The liberation movement had begun. Despite harassment from the Mexican authorities, some eighty men were trained in guerrilla warfare. They were taught how to shoot, make bombs, use camouflage, attack, withdraw, disappear, and attack again. When Castro thought that his men were ready, he announced that he would return to Cuba in 1956. "I want everyone in Cuba to know I am coming," Castro replied to one of his men who questioned the wisdom of disclosing their plans. "I want them to have faith in the 26th of July Movement.

It is a peculiarity all my own although I know that militarily it might be harmful. It is psychological warfare.'' When Castro proved true to his word, the movement gained a great deal of political currency in a country used to broken promises and disappointments.

The invasion was planned for November 30, 1956. It was to coincide with a wave of locally organized sabotage in Cuba, and with an attack on the island's military installations. The two forces were then to join to overthrow the government.

It didn't work that way. Rough seas, an over-crowded, leaking boat, and seasickness combined to delay Castro's landing by two days. By the time the boat arrived, the uprising had been crushed and most of its leaders were dead or in jail. The rebels would have to fend for themselves. To make matters worse, the ship landed off course and the eighty-two revolutionaries had to wade through two miles of swamp and quagmire. By that time, a government plane was flying over their heads and a naval vessel began to fire into the surrounding bush. A short while later, a group of soldiers surprised them, killing twenty-one men. The surviving members divided into small groups and headed for the rugged Sierra Maestra mountain range. Two weeks later they re-formed in the mountains. Besides Castro, his brother Raul, and Ché Guevara, only nine members survived the trip. Although they were physically exhausted and without weapons, Castro announced, ''and now we're going to win.''

The first rebel victory was in La Plata, where a small army post of about twelve soldiers was seized early in 1957. Castro now had more weapons than men, but this problem was partially solved in February of that year, when Herbert Matthews of the *New York Times* was invited to the Sierra Maestras to interview Castro. The Cuban government had reported that Castro had been killed, and the interview was arranged to let Cubans know that he was alive and fighting. While Matthews was interviewing Castro, his brother paraded back and forth with the same men, to give the impression that they had more men than the eighteen they did have. When the interview was published, it created a sensation. Castro was pictured as a romantic figure combating a wicked tyrant. This won him the sympathy of many Americans as well as the support of the Cuban people.

Batista ordered the army to destroy the guerrillas, but army action served only to reinforce Matthews's newspaper account of Castro as a formidable force. Unable to capture the rebels, the army decided to remove the farmers in the Sierra foothills from their homes and then bomb the depopulated area—a tactic that also failed.

The number of volunteers grew with each success. Peasants lent their assistance partly because the friendly and considerate guerrilla force was quite different from the arrogant and brutal soldiers; also, the rebels paid for everything, provided free medical care, and promised to redistribute land once they overthrew the government. The high standard of morality maintained by the guerrillas helped to shake people's cynicism.

By April 1957, the guerrilla camp had grown to approximately eighty men, and Castro was ready to expand his attacks. Enemy detachments were ambushed and small army posts were attacked. In May, a stunning victory in the Battle of Uvero proved the rebels' fighting ability. In December, army troops were pulled out of the Sierra Maestra and a ring of army posts were erected to surround Castro's headquarters in the mountains. If the government could not destroy the rebels, perhaps it could quarantine them.

In the summer of the following year, the guerrillas broke out of the encirclement and moved farther west. By winter, they controlled almost the whole eastern half of the island, and this with fewer than two thousand fighters. The army had not been trained in guerrilla warfare and was no match for the rebels. As desertions increased, the army became demoralized. Corruption and brutality, not warfare, were their strong points. By December, they were in no mood to resist the guerrillas.

Part of Castro's strategy was to keep the people constantly informed of his progress. Early in 1958, *Radio Rebelde* began broadcasting. Its policy was to tell the truth, which contrasted markedly with government propaganda. Castro's followers also proved to be apt propagandists. They placed a two-page advertisement for cigarettes in Havana newspapers, showing a man with a pack of cigarettes in one hand and a book entitled *High Fidelity* in the other.

The army's reprisals were so violent that Batista lost the loyalty of many of his supporters, and citizens were repulsed by the sight of the bullet-riddled bodies of young men left in the streets with bombs tied to them as a warning to the rebels. Batista's picture on movie screens began to provoke catcalls, and when musicians played the dictator's favourite song at dances, couples stood still.

The government's morale was further weakened by the decision of the United States to stop all shipments of weapons and munitions to Cuba. Although these supplies were not of crucial military importance, the action indicated that Washington was losing patience with the regime. Castro, on the other hand, was careful not to alienate America. He promised to protect foreign investments, maintain the private enterprise system, and promote freedom. In fact, Castro was successful partly because no one knew his future plans. The period of hostilities had been so brief that he had not alienated any large group from his movement.

Batista's regime was built on terror and fear. Once Castro showed that he had a good chance of defeating the dictator, the people—particularly peasants who wanted the land reforms Castro promised — flocked to the guerrillas. The government finally collapsed and Batista fled the country, leaving the capital open to the guerrillas. In December 1958, thirty-three-year-old Fidel Castro became the leader of Cuba.

Although Castro was influenced by such Marxists as Ché Guevara, he did not become a communist until after the revolution. American hostility apparently drove Castro into Soviet arms. Although Castro hoped to export his revolutionary techniques to other Latin American states, the absence of suitable mountainous terrain in most of these countries made rural guerrilla warfare almost impossible. Castro's success, however, showed that revolutionary leaders need not begin as committed communists to be successful.

APPLYING YOUR KNOWLEDGE

1. Investigate the 1978–1979 Khomeini revolution in Iran, and compare its tactics to those described in this case study.
2. Compare your answer for question 2 on page 200 with this account of Castro's rise to power. Rewrite your answer to incorporate this new information.
3. To what extent was Castro's victory a product of Batista's ineptness, and to what extent was it due to Castro's own abilities?

4. What are the major causes of revolutions? Many people believe that it is poverty and exploitation, yet if this were so, the poor of the world would be in a constant state of rebellion. Other writers believe that revolutions are caused by ideas, or by great leaders. What is your view? Explain your choice.
5. Non-democratic governments, as we have seen, rely heavily on the army for support. How can the role of the army in politics best be restricted?
6. a) Imagine that your goal is to seize control of a democratic government. Explain how you might best achieve this goal.
   b) What would be the government's best defence against your plan? Why?
   c) To what extent (if at all) must a democratic government adopt non-democratic means to prevent a coup d'état? Is it then democratic? Explain.

FURTHER RESEARCH

1. Prepare for a debate on the question: are violent revolutions ever justified?
2. Research the history of Castro's regime since 1959 and report on one of the following topics:
   a) the democratic nature of the Castro regime
   b) its relationship with the Soviet Union
   c) its relationship with the United States
   d) its economic policies
3. Divide into four groups and choose either Europe, Asia, Africa, or Latin America and make a list of those countries that are basically democratic and those that are not. For each non-democratic country, briefly explain how the present regime gained power.

Case Study 12 Overview

How Authoritarian Governments Maintain Power: Nazi Germany

This case study examines how Hitler was able to retain power in Germany throughout the 1930s. After briefly outlining Hitler's rise to power, the case study employs primary documents to explore how he was able to maintain his control over Germany. Hitler's methods included control of the legal and judiciary system; positive economic achievements; extensive propaganda; indoctrination of young people through youth groups and education; his magnetic personality; and the use of violence, terror, and internal purges. The case study concludes with the attitudes of two teenagers who grew up during the Hitler years and the reasons why one man reluctantly co-operated with the Nazis.

▶ OBJECTIVES

After reading this case study, you should be able to:

- recognize the value of original documents
- analyse primary documents
- explain why Hitler was able to maintain power
- write an essay evaluating the different techniques Hitler used to keep power
- understand why so few people opposed Hitler's regime
- identify the major tactics used by authoritarian states once in power and the importance of propaganda and control of the media

▶ KEY TERMS

Weimar Republic
Putsch
Nazi party
Storm Troopers
Reichstag
Führer
plebiscites
Mein Kampf
Third Reich

Case Study 12

How Authoritarian Governments Maintain Power: Nazi Germany

Up to this point, we have examined how several non-democratic governments achieved power, and we noticed that violence and extra-legal tactics were common practice. Most authoritarian regimes, however, must rely upon methods other than force and intimidation if they hope to remain in power. This case study analyses how Adolf Hitler maintained the support of the German people in the 1930s.

▶ THE RISE OF ADOLF HITLER

In many ways, Hitler's rise to power in Germany resembled Mussolini's success in Italy a decade earlier. Both countries had only recently been unified, and neither had a long tradition of democratic government before they were overthrown by a semi-legal coup. The results of World War I left Italy and Germany unhappy, and this disillusionment was turned against the governing democratic regime that had signed the peace treaty. Hitler and Mussolini used economic problems and fear of a communist revolution to further their own ends.

At the end of World War I, after centuries of autocratic rule, a democratic government (the **Weimar Republic**) was established in Germany. Unfortunately, the leaders of the new Weimar Republic had signed a peace treaty (which many Germans believed imposed unjust measures on their country) for which the kaiser's autocratic government escaped blame. Because the German people had not seen the approaching collapse of the army at the front, they deluded themselves into believing that the Liberals and Socialists had betrayed them. As a

"Our Last Hope." What emotions did this poster hope to arouse?
Imperial War Museum

result, many people still associated the glories of Germany with the kaiser's autocratic regime and its military might.

The Weimar government was soon threatened by both left- and right-wing groups that wished to overthrow it. In 1919, a Marxist group failed in an attempt to establish a communist regime, and four years later, Adolf Hitler's rebellion (the Munich Beer Hall ***Putsch***) was equally unsuccessful.

Despite the large number of political parties competing for power, the Weimar Republic limped on until the Great Depression hit the Western world in 1929. When the government proved incapable of solving the country's economic problems, Adolf Hitler's National Socialist German Workers' party (the **Nazi party**) took advantage of the situation to seize the reigns of power.

Hitler had used the period after his unsuccessful *Putsch* in 1923 to raise a private army (the **Storm Troopers**, or S.A.) patterned after Mussolini's Black Shirts. Financed by wealthy industrialists who feared a communist revolution, the Nazi party made rapid political gains. From only seven seats (out of 608) in the 1928 **Reichstag** (lower house), the party gained 230 seats in the 1932 election. Political chaos continued as Nazi and left-wing groups fought in the streets. When the Nazis' electoral support dropped in the 1932 election, conservative elements in the government calculated that they would be able to control Hitler. In January 1933 they persuaded President Hindenburg to appoint the Nazi leader as chancellor.

They miscalculated. Hitler quickly outmanoeuvred the moderates and called a snap election for March 1933. A month before the election, the Reichstag building was destroyed by a fire that Hitler blamed on the Communists — although many historians suspect that Hitler was responsible. Jails were filled with the Nazis' left-wing opponents, and Hitler subsequently won a majority in the Reichstag. The Nazis had consolidated their power.

But this case study is not about how Hitler achieved power, rather it examines how one totalitarian state was able to maintain control over the country. The following documents illustrate some (but not all) of the methods employed by the Nazis that enabled them to rule Germany for twelve years — a period during which Hitler threatened the very survival of Western European civilization, and heaped death, destruction, and terror on Germany and its European neighbours. At the conclusion of this case study, you will be asked to write an in-depth essay explaining how Hitler retained control over Germany. The questions at the end of each section are designed to help you analyse the documents.

Hitler talking to a young girl at his mountain retreat near Berchtesgaden. Note how the photograph presents him as the "Viennese Gentleman."
Daily Mail/*Solo, London*

▶ The Use of the Law

The following three acts reveal how Hitler legally established his control over the German government and sought to maintain it:[1]

1. **Decree of the Reich's President for the Protection of the People and State —February 28, 1933**

   In virtue of Section 48(2) of the German Constitution, the following is decreed as a defensive measure against Communist acts of violence endangering the state:
   Article 1

   Sections 114, 115, 117, 118, 123, 124, and 153 of the Constitution of the German Reich are suspended until further notice. Thus, restrictions on personal liberty, on the right of free expression of opinion, including freedom of the press, on the right of assembly and the right of association, and violations of the privacy of postal, telegraphic, and telephonic communications, and warrants for house-searches, orders for confiscations as well as restrictions on property, are also permissible beyond the legal limits otherwise prescribed.

2. **Law Against the New Establishment of Parties—July 14, 1933**

   The German Cabinet has resolved the following law. . . .

   (1) The National Socialist German Workers' Party [The Nazi Party] constitutes the only political party in Germany.

   (2) Whoever undertakes to maintain the organizational structure of another political party or to form a new political party will be punished with penal servitude up to three years or with imprisonment of from six months to three years, if the deed is not subject to a greater penalty according to other regulations.

3. **Law to Safeguard the Unity of Party and State—December 1, 1933**

   The German Cabinet has resolved the following law. . . .

▸ [1]*Nuremberg Documents.*

(1) After the victory of the National Socialist revolution, the National Socialist Workers' Party is the bearer of the German state-idea and indissolubly joined to the state.

(2) The ***Führer*** *determines its statutes.*

During the first few years after his assumption of power, Hitler held a series of elections and **plebiscites** to show that the people approved of his actions. The results were usually close to 100 percent in his favour. The following document illustrates one method that was used to achieve these results.

Police supervision of plebiscites. Subject: Plebiscite of 10 April 1938

Copy of a schedule is attached herewith enumerating the persons who cast "No" votes or invalid votes at Kappel, district of Simmern. The invalid votes are listed first, ending with —; thereafter come the "No" votes.

The control was effected in the following way: some members of the election committee marked all the ballot papers with numbers. During the ballot itself, a voters' list was made up. The ballot papers were handed out in numerical order, therefore it was possible afterwards with the aid of this list to find out the persons who cast "No" votes or invalid votes. One sample of these marked ballot papers is enclosed. The marking was done on the back of the ballot papers with skimmed milk.

The ballot cast by the Protestant parson Alfred Wolferts is also enclosed.

The identification of two persons was impossible because there are several persons of the same name in the village and it was impossible to ascertain the actual voter.[2]

▸ [2]Jeremy Noakes, Geoffrey Pridham, *Documents on Nazism, 1919–1945*. London: Jonathan Cape, 1974, p. 292. Reprinted by permission of the Peters Fraser & Dunlop Group Ltd.

FOCUS

1. Explain how Hitler was able to ensure the appearance of popular support for his actions.
2. How might these contrived elections and plebiscites help Hitler maintain political power?

▶ Promises and Fulfillment

Hitler promised the German people that he would defeat the depression that had crippled the country's economy and build Germany into a world power once again. The extracts that follow outline his economic policies.

In 1936 Hitler summed up the success of the Nazi party since 1933:

And what has National Socialism in these four years made of Germany? . . .

How [our enemies] would have jeered if on the 30th of January, 1933 I had declared that within four years Germany would have reduced its six million unemployed to one million!

That the receipts from German agriculture would be higher than in any previous year in time of peace.

That the total national income would be raised from 41 milliards annually to over 56 milliards.

That trade would once more recover.

That German ports would no more resemble ship grave-yards.

That in 1936 on German wharves alone over 640 000 tons of shipping would be under construction.

That countless manufactories would not

merely double but treble and quadruple the number of their workmen. And that in less than four years innumerable others would be rebuilt.

That to the German Reich would be given roads such that since the beginnings of human civilization they have never had their match for size and beauty: and that of the first 7000 kilometres which were planned already after not quite four years 1000 kilometres would be in use and over 4000 kilometres would be in course of construction.

But we did it![3]

Hitler had this to say about Germany's economic growth:

I am further convinced that our people itself will continuously grow more healthy with this sober, clear, and decent political and economic leadership. I say 'political leadership', for these successes are not due primarily to economics, but to the political leadership. Clever economists, one may presume, there are elsewhere, and I do not believe that German economists have grown clever only since the 30th of January 1933. If, before that date, there was no progress, that was because the political leadership and the formation of our people were at fault. The change is due to the National Socialist Party![4]

▸ [3]From *The Speeches of Adolf Hitler*, translated and edited by Norman H. Baynes, published by Oxford University Press for the Royal Institute of International Affairs, 1942.

▸ [4]*Ibid.*, pp. 651–652.

FOCUS

1. Using these two extracts, explain why Hitler became popular in Germany.
2. Discuss how Hitler used words to manipulate people's feelings.

▶ The Purge

The following description reveals how Hitler dealt with insubordination within the Nazi party:

As early as 1934, disgruntled party members began to conspire against Hitler himself. They were led by one of Hitler's most intimate friends, Roehm, the leader of the SA. Their general complaint was that Hitler had not gone far enough in his reforms and that a "second revolution" was in order. Hitler tried vainly to placate this group, not only on grounds of political disagreement but because the Army, whose support was essential to Hitler, had made it clear that no such extremism could be tolerated. When all entreaties had failed, Hitler struck with a ruthlessness and a rapidity which sickened the outside world, not yet inured to seeing the head of a state himself supervising the murder of his friends. The purge of June 30, 1934, had a double effect: it recreated unity in the Nazi ranks and sealed the alliance between Hitler and the Army. From then on most of the Army leaders—even if they did not share the popular fanatic trust in Hitler—recognized him for what he was: the man under whose leadership the military strength of Germany would be rebuilt. It is not by accident that Hitler began at the time to compare himself more and more frequently with Frederick the Great and Bismarck and to claim that he was their true heir. Nothing could appeal more strongly to the spirit and tradition of the German Army.[5]

▸ [5]Raoul de Roussy de Sales, *Adolf Hitler: My New Order*. New York: Hitchcock, 1942, pp. 135–136.

FOCUS

1. Explain how Hitler used the S.A. revolt to strengthen his control over Germany.
2. How would a similar disagreement be treated in a democratic country?

▶ The Portrait of a Dictator

How much of Hitler's success was due to personality and charisma? The following extracts help to answer this question:

Physically, Hitler weighed about 150 pounds and was five feet nine inches in height. His skin was pale, and his physique generally unprepossessing. . . .

In his own private circle, Hitler's behaviour was generally genial. No one crossed him, and he was liked by his intimates for the usual reasons—kindliness and cordiality. He was especially friendly toward children and older people. He had a great understanding for the little pleasures and in his dealings with women displayed a positive charm.

Everyone who discussed this point with me mentioned that Hitler behaved like "a Viennese gentleman"—a German character similar to our "Southern gentleman." This behaviour not only included the usual social amenities but an exaggeration of grace. For instance, Hitler made it a point to kiss the hand of any woman to whom he was introduced. . . .

As an orator Hitler had obvious faults. The timbre of his voice was harsh, very different from the beautiful quality of Goebbels'. He spoke at too great length; was often repetitive and verbose; lacked lucidity and frequently lost himself in cloudy phrases. These shortcomings, however, mattered little beside the extraordinary impression of force, the immediacy of passion, the intensity of hatred, fury, and menace conveyed by the sound of the voice alone without regard to what he said.

One of the secrets of his mastery over a great audience was his instinctive sensitivity to the mood of a crowd, a flair for divining the hidden passions, resentments and longings in their minds. . . .

One of his most bitter critics, Otto Strasser, wrote:

I have been asked many times what is the secret of Hitler's extraordinary power as a speaker. I can only attribute it to his uncanny intuition, which infallibly diagnoses the ills from which his audience is suffering. . . . Adolf Hitler enters a hall. He sniffs the air. For a minute he gropes, feels his way, senses the atmosphere. Suddenly he bursts forth. His words go like an arrow to their target, he touches each private wound on the raw, liberating the mass unconscious, expressing its

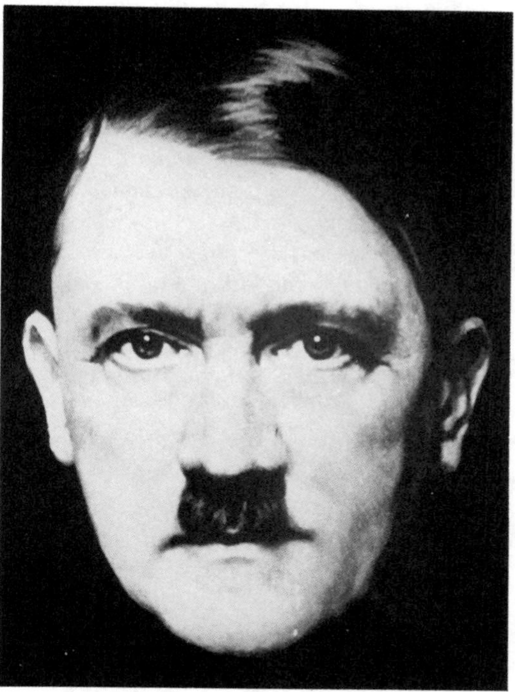

This photograph was often used in Nazi propaganda posters. What effect would this picture have on the viewer, and how is this affect achieved?
Canapress Photo Service

innermost aspirations, telling it what it most wants to hear. . . .

When he wanted to persuade or win someone over he could display great charm. Until the last days of his life he retained an uncanny gift of personal magnetism which defies analysis, but which many who met him have described. This was connected with the curious power of his eyes, which are persistently said to have had some sort of hypnotic quality. Similarly, when he wanted to frighten or shock, he showed himself a master of brutal and threatening language. . . .[6]

▸ [6]From *22 Cells in Nuremberg* by Douglas M. Kelley. Copyright 1947 by the author. Reprinted with the permission of the publisher, Chilton Book Company, Radnor, P.A.; *Hitler: A Study in Tyranny* by Alan Bullock (first published by Odhaus Press), reprinted by permission of Paul Hamlyn Publishing, part of Reed International Books Ltd.

FOCUS

1. a) Discuss those personality aspects that most contributed to Hitler's success.
   b) To what extent would Hitler have been successful in a democratic country? Why?

▶ Justice in the Third Reich

Judges were often reminded of what the regime expected of them. The following command is a typical example of Nazi attitudes towards justice:

The National Socialist ideology, especially as expressed in the Party programme and in the speeches of our Führer, is the basis for interpreting legal sources.

The judge has no right to scrutinize decisions made by the Führer and issued in the form of a law or a decree. The judge is also bound by any other decision of the Führer which clearly expresses the intention of establishing law.

In the following extract, a German defence attorney describes the problems of gaining a fair trial in Nazi Germany.

At that moment I intervened and asked permission to question the defendant, before the hearing of evidence, about . . . whether he had been beaten by the officers of the Secret State Police in connexion with the signing of these statements.

I had hardly finished the question when the State prosecutor jumped up excitedly and asked the president of the court to protect the officers of the Secret State Police against such attacks by the defence.

Appeal Judge—rose from his chair, leant on his hands on the court table and said to me: ''Council for the defence, I must draw your attention to the fact that even though the trial here is conducted in camera *[in secret] a question such as you have asked can lead to your being arrested in the courtroom and taken into custody. Do you wish to sustain the question or not?''*

These details are still fresh in my memory because they made an extraordinary impression on me. Also, subsequently I have repeatedly discussed this case because it seemed to me typical of National Socialist justice.[7]

▸ [7]Noakes, *Documents*, pp. 273, 275. Reprinted by permission of the Peters Fraser & Dunlop Group Ltd.

FOCUS

1. a) Discuss the importance of controlling the legal system in a non-democratic regime.

b) What were the basic assumptions behind the Nazis' control over the judiciary?
c) What do these documents reveal about the importance of an impartial legal system for the maintenance of democracy?

▶ Propaganda

Hitler appointed Joseph Goebbels as Minister for Propaganda and Public Enlightenment. This included control over art, moving pictures, sports, the celebration of national holidays, radio, newspapers, music, museums, tourism, the post office, libraries, and the national anthem. The documents that follow illustrate the purpose and activities of the Propaganda Ministry.

These selections are typical instructions to Germany's newspapers:

General Instruction No. 674

In the next issue there must be a lead article, featured as prominently as possible, in which the decision of the Führer, no matter what it will be, will be discussed as the only correct one for Germany. . . .

What is necessary is that the press blindly follow the basic principle: The leadership is always right! Gentlemen, we all must claim the privilege of being allowed to make mistakes. Newspaper people aren't exempt from that danger either. But we all can survive only if, as we face the world, we do not put the spotlight on each other's mistakes, but on positive things instead. What this means in other words is that it is essential—without in principle denying the possibility of mistakes or of discussion—that it is essential always to stress the basic correctness of the leadership. That is the decisive point. . . .

The Propaganda Ministry asks us to put to editors-in-chief the following requests, which must be observed in future with particular care:

Photos showing members of the Reich Government at dining tables in front of rows of bottles must not be published in future, particularly since it is known that a large number of the Cabinet are abstemious. Ministers take part in social events for reasons of international etiquette and for strictly official purposes, which they regard merely as a duty and not as a pleasure. Recently, because of a great number of photos, the utterly absurd impression has been created among the public that members of the Government are living it up. News pictures must therefore change in this respect.[8]

In this selection, Hitler discusses the psychological importance of evoking the public's emotions through the use of mass demonstrations:

The mass meeting is also necessary for the reason that in it the individual, who at first, while becoming a supporter of a young movement, feels lonely and easily succumbs to the fear of being alone, for the first time gets the picture of a larger community, which in most people has a strengthening, encouraging effect. The same man, within a company or a battalion, surrounded by all his comrades, would set out on an attack with a lighter heart than if left entirely on his own. In the crowd he always feels somewhat sheltered, even if a thousand reasons actually argue against it.

But the community of the great demonstration not only strengthens the individual, it also unites and helps create an esprit de corps*. . . . When from his little workshop or big factory, in which he feels very small, he steps for the first time into a mass meeting and has thousands and thousands of people of the same opinions around him, he is swept away by three or four thousand others into the*

▸ [8]Noakes, *Documents*, p. 335, reprinted by permission of the Peters Fraser & Dunlop Group Ltd.; Joachim Remak, *The Nazi Years: A Documentary History*, pp. 87, 88. Copyright © 1969 by Simon & Schuster, Inc. Reprinted by permission of Simon & Schuster, Inc.

mighty effect of suggestive intoxication and enthusiasm, when the visible success and agreement of thousands confirm to him the rightness of the new doctrine and for the first time arouse doubt in the truth of his previous conviction—then he himself has succumbed to the magic influence of what we designate as ''mass suggestion''.[9]

The following excerpt is from the writings of Ernst Huber, one of the leading political ideologists of the Nazi party:

[The Reich] is founded on the recognition that the true will of the people cannot be disclosed through parliamentary votes and plebiscites but that the will of the people in its pure and uncorrupted form can only be expressed through the Führer. Thus a distinction must be drawn between the supposed will of the people in a parliamentary democracy, which merely reflects the conflict of the various social interests, and the true will of the people in the Führer-state, in which the collective will of the real political unit is manifested.

▸ [9]Adolf Hitler, *Mein Kampf*, translated by Ralph Manheim, published by Hutchinson.

FOCUS

1. Using Hitler's instructions to the press as an example, outline the instructions that you think might have been given to:
   (a) artists,
   (b) libraries,
   (c) movie producers.
2. a) Paraphrase Ernst Huber's message.
   b) How would Huber's writings help sustain the Nazi government?
3. Locate photographs of the Nazi rallies at Nuremberg, especially those in Albert Speer, *Inside the Third Reich*, Macmillan, 1970. From the photos, describe the atmosphere created by these rallies and discuss how they were designed to win the support of the people. Remember to look at such small details as the armbands and the seating arrangements, as well as the total picture.

▶ Education

Schools were considered important agents in the creation of proper citizens, and thus in maintaining power. In the first account, a brother and sister recall their early school days in Nazi Germany. In the second reading, a critic of the regime remembers his feelings about Nazi education.

Every subject was now presented from the National Socialist point of view. Most of the old lecture books were replaced by new ones which had been written, compiled, and censored by government officials. Adolf Hitler's Mein Kampf *became the textbook for our history lessons. We read and discussed it with our master, chapter by chapter, and when we had finished we started again from the beginning. Even though we were supposed to know the contents of the book almost by heart nothing much ever stuck in my mind. . . .*

Our school had always been run on very conservative lines and I am sure the situation was difficult for our teachers. Most of them had been doubtful about Hitler, but unless they wanted to lose their jobs they had to make a violent turn in his direction. Even if they sympathized with my attitude towards politics, they could not afford to let me get away with it. Some of the children in each class would not hesitate to act as informers. The Government was probing into the past history of every teacher, exploring his political background. Many were dismissed and it was dangerous to act as anything but a National Socialist.[10]

This excerpt was taken from a Nazi history textbook that was compulsory reading for German high school students:

The Aryan: The Creative Force in Human History

In the second millennium B.C. the Aryans (the Nordic race) invaded India and established Aryan culture there. A branch related to the Aryans created the foundations for the power and flowering of the Persian empire. Ancient Hellenic culture likewise is traceable to the blood of Nordic immigrants. . . .

The Roman Empire was founded by the Italics, who were related to the Celts. With the vanishing of the Nordic component—that is, with the disappearance of Nordic blood—the fate of these proud empires was sealed. The Goths, Franks, Vandals, and Normans, too, were peoples of Nordic blood. A renaissance took place only in the Western Roman Empire, not in its eastern counterpart, because in the west, Nordic blood developed its creative power in the form of the Longobards. Remnants of the western Goths created a Spanish empire. The spread of Christianity in northern and eastern Europe was in the main supported by Nordic people, and the Nordic longing for freedom of the spirit found powerful expression in the Reformation. It was Nordic energy and boldness that were responsible for the power and prestige enjoyed by small nations such as the Netherlands and Sweden. . . . Everywhere Nordic creative power has built mighty empires with high-minded ideas, and to this very day Aryan languages and cultural values are spread over a large part of the world, though the creative Nordic blood has long since vanished in many places. Ethnological historical research has proved that the Nordic race has produced a great many more highly talented people than any other race.

Nordic boldness not only is a precondition for the martial exploits of nations of Nordic origin, but it is also a prerequisite for the courageous profession of new, great ideas.[11]

German students were required to recite the following prayers at lunch:

Before Meals:

Führer, my Führer, bequeathed to me by the Lord,
Protect and preserve me as long as I live!
Thou hast rescued Germany from deepest distress,
I thank thee today for my daily bread.
Abideth thou along with me, forsaketh me not,
Führer, my Führer, my faith and my light!
Heil, mein Führer!

After Meals:

Thank thee for this bountiful meal,
Protector of youth and friend of the aged!
I know thou hast cares, but worry not,
I am with thee by day and by night.
Lay thy head in my lap.
Be assured, my Führer, that thou art great.
Heil, mein Führer![12]

▸ [10]George L. Mosse, *Nazi Culture*. New York: Grosset & Dunlop, 1968, p. 278.

▸ [11]Mosse, *Nazi Culture*, pp. 79–81.

▸ [12]*Ibid.*, p. 241.

FOCUS

1. Discuss the purpose and assumptions behind the Nazi educational system.
2. Explain why the history books emphasized the greatness of the Nordic race.
3. a) Discuss the purpose of the prayers. What feelings were they designed to evoke?

b) Why did the Nazis place such an important emphasis on educating the youth of Germany?

4. To what extent do you think education is important to the maintenance of democracy?

▶ Youth

Hitler Youth clubs were established to assert greater control over the country's youth. In 1935, only those people who had participated in such clubs were eligible to enter the civil service, and the following year, membership in the Hitler Youth was made compulsory. The following speech was read to new members when they joined the youth club:

Dear boy!/Dear girl!

This hour in which you are to be received into the great community of the Hitler Youth is a very happy one and at the same time will introduce you into a new period of your lives. Today for the first time you swear allegiance to the Führer which will bind you to him for all time.

And every one of you, my young comrades, enters at this moment into the community of all German boys and girls. With your vow and your commitment you now become a bearer of German spirit and German honour. Every one, every single one, now becomes the foundation for an eternal Reich of all Germans.

When you too now march in step with the youngest soldiers, then bear in mind that this march is to train you to be a National Socialist conscious of the future and faithful to his duty.

And the Führer demands of you and of us that we train ourselves to a life of service and duty, of loyalty and comradeship. You, ten-year-old cub, and you, lass, are not too young nor too small to practise obedience and discipline, to integrate yourself into the community and show yourself to be a comrade. Like you, millions of young Germans are today swearing allegiance to the Führer and it is a proud picture of unity which German youth today presents to the whole world. So today you make a vow to your Führer and here, before your parents, the Party and your comrades, we now receive you into our great community of loyalty. Your motto will always be:

"Führer, command—we follow!"

(The cubs are asked to rise.) *Now say after me: "I promise always to do my duty in the Hitler Youth in love and loyalty to the Führer and to our flag."*[13]

▸ [13]*Ibid.*, p. 357.

FOCUS

1. a) What feelings towards Hitler and Germany was this speech designed to evoke?
   b) How would such speeches help maintain Hitler in power?

▶ Violence

Hitler wrote in ***Mein Kampf*** that government authority must rely upon popularity, tradition, and power. The following historical account written in 1964 illustrates how Hitler used violence to maintain his regime:

It was not due to either negligence or accident that concentration camps continued to exist past the time when people no longer had any reason to fear the "Red danger." They formed a well-calculated part of the system. To quote Hitler:

Terrorism is an effective political tool. I shall not deprive myself of it merely because these simple-minded bourgeois "softies" take offense. These so-called atrocities render it unnecessary for me to conduct hundreds of thousands of individual raids against mutinous and dissatisfied people. People will think twice before opposing us, if they know what awaits them in the camps.

The exact fate of these unfortunate victims—the political opponents, the trade-union leaders, the clergymen, the monks, Jehovah's Witnesses, and pacifists—was only hinted at among people in the ***Third Reich****. Those who returned from these hells had to keep silent to avoid renewed danger to themselves. In all probability, their stories would not even have been believed. Yet, it was known, or could have been known, that prisoners were sent to camps without a trial and for indefinite periods, and that there was no right of appeal.*

In this day, the trials before German courts of former concentration camp commandants and guards have given all of us an insight into the grisly realities of these camps. Hundreds of witnesses have revealed how limitless power unleashed evil instincts. "In the camps, everything human disappeared. We were merely objects. No normal mortal can imagine how we were treated," said one of the witnesses. Blows, beatings, and kickings were part of the daily routine, so much so that one of the accused camp-torturers declared during his trial that such measures did not constitute mistreatment! Prisoners had to do "gymnastics" until they fainted with exhaustion, or, for hours on end, had to give the Saxon salute, i.e. remain in a deep knee-bend with arms laced behind their heads. These were merely the harmless "jokes" indulged in by the camp guards. Prisoners were whipped for the slightest offense—or for none at all; they were strapped on a rack, and ordered to execute knee-bends after being whipped; no less frequently prisoners were trussed up with hands tied behind their backs.

The life of a prisoner counted for nothing. Prisoners disliked by the guards were arbitrarily selected for injections (abgespritzt)*, which means they were murdered through injections of Phenol or Evipan, only one of a number of methods of killing. Prisoners were often trampled to death with nailed boots, or drowned in cesspools, or driven into the electrically charged barbed-wire fences of the camps, or, in an especially bestial manner, hosed to death with high-pressure water hoses. Innumerable witnesses have placed all these ghastly details on court records during many months of trials, and the defendants have admitted them.*

In this system human beings had turned into "things" to such an extent that the administrative S.S. bureaus concerned "calculated the profitability" of prisoners. A prisoner was expected to live on average for nine months. During this time, according to calculations, the productivity of each prisoner was calculated to yield 1,631 Marks for the Nazi state (the total includes the profit gained from the "careful utilization of the corpse").

. . . While all these horrors took place, only a few people knew about the full extent of the atrocities. Yet, the mere two letters KL (Konzentrations-Lager)*—the abbreviation used by the S.S., instead of the popular KZ—inspired terror, exactly as Hitler had wanted it, as his own words bear testimony. The terror threatened anybody who dared to offer even the slightest resistance to the two main doctrines. Those ready—or at least pretending—to believe that "the Jews are our misfortune," and that "the Fuhrer can do no wrong," were able to stay out of danger.*[14]

[14]Hannah Vogt, *The Burden of Guilt: A Short History of Germany, 1914–1945*. New York: Oxford University Press, 1964, pp. 220–223.

FOCUS

1. a) Explain why the use of terror and brutality would intimidate rather than anger the German people.
   b) To what extent is the use of terror an important tool for the maintenance of power in a non-democratic regime?

▶ A PERSONAL VIEW

We have now examined some of the methods used by the Nazi regime to ensure continued support. How did the people react to these measures?

Two German teenagers recall their feelings after Hitler's assumption of power in 1933:

One morning, on the school steps, I heard a girl from my class tell another: "Hitler has just taken over the government." And the radio and all the newspapers proclaimed: "Now everything will improve in Germany. Hitler has seized the helm."

Hans at the time was fifteen years old; Sophie was twelve. We heard a great deal of talk about Fatherland, comradeship, community of the Volk, and love of homeland. All this impressed us, and we listened with enthusiasm whenever we heard anyone speak of these things in school or on the street. For we loved our homeland very much. . . . We loved it, but were hardly able to say why. Until that time we had never lost many words over it. But now it was written large, in blazing letters in the sky. And Hitler, as we heard everywhere, Hitler wanted to bring greatness, happiness, and well-being to this Fatherland; he wanted to see to it that everyone had work and bread; he would not rest or relax until every single German was an independent, free, and happy man in his Fatherland. We found this good, and in whatever might come to pass we were determined to help to the best of our ability. But there was yet one more thing that attracted us with a mysterious force and pulled us along—namely, the compact columns of marching youths with waving flags, eyes looking straight ahead, and the beat of drums and singing. Was it not overwhelming, this fellowship? Thus it was no wonder that all of us—Hans and Sophie and the rest of us—joined the Hitler Youth.[15]

The following account outlines the choices available to the individual German after Hitler assumed power:

Albrecht Haushofer was confronted with a serious dilemma when the Nazis came to power. There were three possibilities open to him. He could oppose Nazism openly, and run the risk of being killed and of causing persecution to his family. He could flee the country and express himself without let or hindrance from abroad; or he could work for the regime in one capacity or another, in the hope of influencing the course of events in a peaceful direction.

He never seriously thought of open opposition to the Nazi regime, since any hostility might have produced a violent reaction, and have landed him in a concentration camp. Albrecht knew how ruthless the Nazis could be, and he had no reason to believe that the matter would be left there. At the very least his internment and fate would have caused great embarrassment to his family, especially to his half-Jewish mother, of whom he was very fond. He did not wish to take risks which might involve harm to her, physical or otherwise. This left him with the choice of either leaving Germany or of working for the Third Reich. The possibility of emigration was

▸ [15]Mosse, *Nazi Culture*, p. 275.

carefully considered, but it did not appeal to him, as he felt that he would be running away, and that outside Germany he would not be in a position to alter the actions of the German leaders.

The third course, that of working for the regime in the hope that he might tone it down, was an option more in accordance with his temperament and outlook. His intellectual vanity was such that he imagined he might be able to manipulate those with authority in the Reich.[16]

▸ [16]James Douglas-Hamilton, *Motive For A Mission: The Story Behind Hess's Flight to Britain*. London: Macmillan, St. Martin's Press, pp. 38, 48.

APPLYING YOUR KNOWLEDGE

1. Explain why Hans and Sophie joined the Hitler Youth.
2. What comparisons can be made between the motives of Hans and Sophie and those of Albrecht Haushofer for endorsing the Nazis?
3. Put yourself in Haushofer's position and explain what you would have done and why.

FURTHER RESEARCH

1. Using appropriate inquiry techniques (from Chapter 1), write an in-depth essay explaining how Hitler retained control over the German people.
2. Compare Hitler's authoritarian regime with one other authoritarian government and account for the differences.
3. Using Canada as an example, discuss
   a) techniques used by democratic governments to retain power,
   b) similarities to and differences from the methods used by Hitler,
   c) the existing safeguards that prevent the excesses of the Hitler regime.
4. Research and write an essay on *one* of the following topics:
   a) How Hitler's foreign policy between 1935 and 1939 increased support within Germany for Hitler
   b) Hitler's personality and retention of power
   c) The reasons for Hitler's rise to power
   d) The development of Nazi policy towards the Jews
   e) The use of propaganda in stereotyping the Jewish people
5. Research and discuss the implications of the Holocaust for present and future generations. You might consider the consequences of tolerance of persecution, indifference, and the abuse of power as well as the notions of conscience, personal responsibility, and courage.

Case Study 13 Overview

The Republic of South Africa: Government for Some?

This case study examines the history of South Africa's political system and its apartheid policies. It begins with a brief discussion of the present situation of the Blacks in South Africa before outlining the early history of South Africa. After exploring the changes in the political system from 1948 until the present, the case study examines the government's policy of apartheid, including its origins, purpose, development, and practice. The various White, Black, and ''Brown'' political parties are described and their goals outlined. The homelands policy of the government is explained; and the case study concludes with several primary documents that portray what it is like to live in South Africa if your skin is not white.

▶ OBJECTIVES

After reading this case study, you should be able to:

- ▶ understand why the government adopted its apartheid policies and why they are opposed
- ▶ outline the complexities of the situation in South Africa
- ▶ debate the wisdom of apartheid and propose alternative courses of action
- ▶ evaluate primary documents
- ▶ determine your own stand on the issues raised in this case study

▶ KEY TERMS

apartheid
Afrikaners
Boers
Bantustans
homelands
Coloureds
Great Trek
segregated
African National Congress (ANC)
Pan Africanist Congress (PAC)
Inkatha

13 The Republic of South Africa: Government for Some?

This case study examines the history of the eighty-year-old Republic of South Africa and explains how and why the country failed to follow the examples of other former British colonies such as Australia, New Zealand, and Canada. It also investigates how **apartheid** originated, how it operates, and whom it benefits. The fundamental question to keep in mind is whether South Africa's policies have any legal, moral, or ethical merit.

▶ THE HISTORICAL BACKGROUND

Despite some favourable gestures in the recent past, the Republic of South Africa is still the world's last stronghold for a relatively small White minority that dominates a non-White majority. (See Table 1.)

Table 1
1989 TOTAL POPULATION = 35 625 000

Blacks	69%
Whites	18%
Asians (Indians)	3%
Mixed Races (Coloureds)	10%
Total	100%

The Whites consist mainly of **Afrikaners** or **Boers**, the descendants of seventeenth-century Dutch settlers, and the offspring of nineteenth-century British colonists. The government grants these and all other Caucasians (Whites) the franchise. Asians, mainly from India, and Coloureds (people of mixed races) enjoy a narrow, practically meaningless franchise and few liberties. The vast Black majority is denied not only the franchise but all freedoms. Theoreti-

Figure 1
SOUTH AFRICA

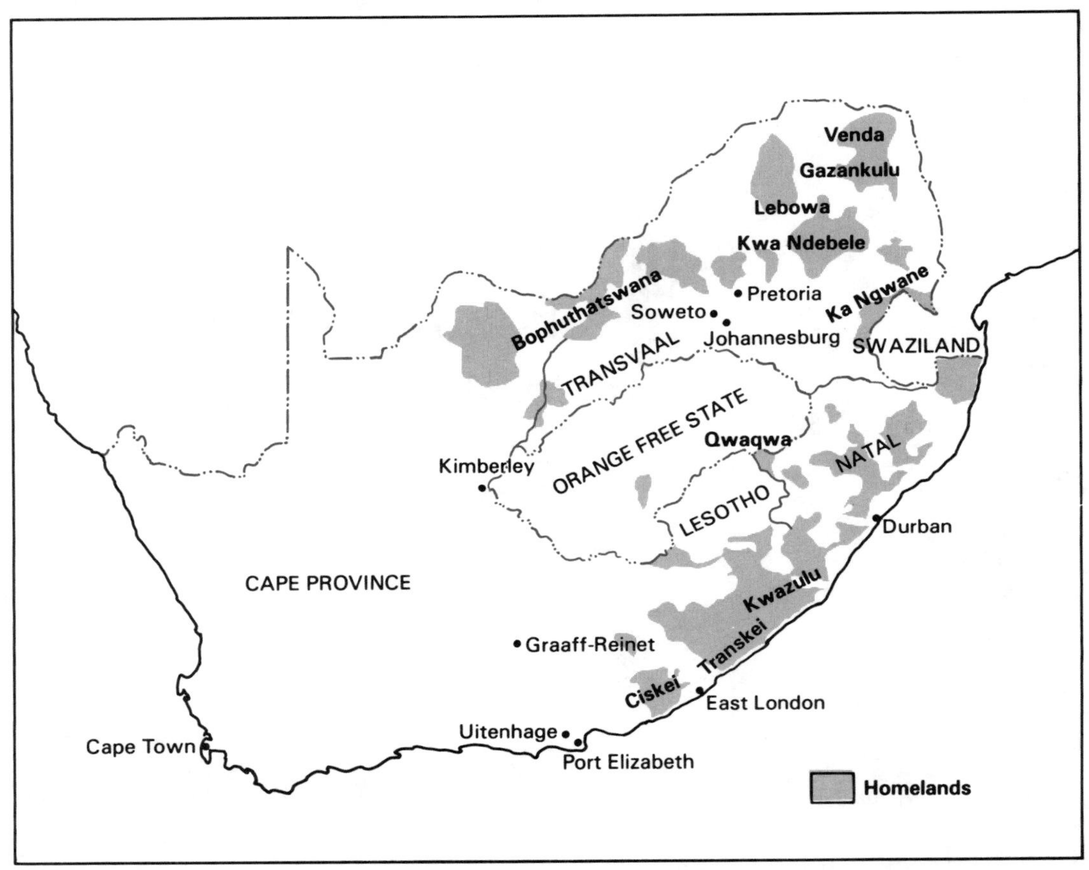

cally, they are not citizens of the Republic, but foreign ''visitors'' supplied with working passes. After working hours, they must return to their allocated native **Bantustans**, or tribal **homelands.**

The history of the land now occupied by the Republic of South Africa helps to explain the current government situation. Most Afrikaners claim that the land their ancestors colonized in the mid-seventeenth century was an unpopulated barren wasteland. This is a half-truth. The land had been occupied sporadically by a succession of different native tribes prior to White explorations. The ancestors of those tribes had established large native kingdoms from the fifteenth century to the seventeenth century in the Transvaal and Transkei regions. (See map of South Africa.)

In 1652, the Dutch East India Company founded Cape Town at the Cape of Good Hope as a depot for the company's Indian trade. The town attracted Dutch settlers as well as numerous other European adventurers. These European settlers encountered tribes of Black Hottentots, a branch of Bushmen and Bantus. The Dutch enslaved these natives and brought additional slaves from the East Indies and Madagascar. The resultant mixture produced the Cape **Coloureds**, who are one of the three major racial groups in the Republic.

By the end of the seventeenth century, the restless Dutch settlers moved northward. In a series of wars lasting a few centuries, they defeated the Black tribes who barred their way. The Boers evolved the notion that the land belonged to them, because African natives lacked the European concept of individual land ownership. The natives occasionally concluded treaties with the Boers to permit the temporary use of their land. The Boers, however, disregarded these provisions and settled disputes by killing the natives.

During the Revolutionary Wars (1792–1815), the Dutch lost the Cape Colony to the British. In 1815, Great Britain incorporated the Cape Colony into its empire, which resulted in a large influx of British settlers. A steady migration of Muslim and Hindu immigrants from Great Britain's Indian colony further diversified South Africa's racial composition. The Boers could not tolerate these changes. Between 1836 and 1838, they undertook the **Great Trek** into the interior. The survivors eventually founded two small republics — Transvaal and Orange Free State. Here, they practised their Dutch Reform (Protestant) religion and developed Afrikaans, a unique new language based on Dutch. British settlers established a colony at Natal. The Afrikaner Boers lived in an uneasy truce with their British neighbours for four decades.

The discovery of diamonds and gold led to tensions when British adventurers overran the Dutch territories. In two wars (1881–1882 and 1899–1902), the British defeated the Boers, incorporated their territories into British South Africa, and in 1910 proclaimed the Union of South Africa. In 1934, South Africa became a self-governing state. After a referendum in 1961, the Union became the Republic of South Africa and withdrew from the British Commonwealth. This entire period was marked with tension between Afrikaners and the British. They agreed on one point, however. Neither side wanted non-Whites to participate in the government.

▶ THE AFRIKANER NATIONAL PARTY

In 1948, Daniel F. Malan's Afrikaner National party won the elections and formed a government based on racial policies. Apartheid now became South Africa's guiding principle. Each person was assigned to one of four racial groups: Whites, pure Blacks, Coloureds, and Asians. Each group was physically **segregated** and given its own political institu-

South African Parliament in session
Bureau For Information

tions. Mixed neighbourhoods, inter-racial marriage, and common drinking and bathing facilities were forbidden. Blacks, in particular, could not engage in certain occupations, and they were paid less than Whites for performing similar work.

The South African government also implemented its so-called tribal homeland policy. The country's Black residents had their citizenship revoked and transferred to areas called Bantustans, selected arbitrarily by the government. The goal was ultimately to grant separate political independence to Whites, Bantus (Blacks), Asians, and Coloureds. These homelands were first created in 1959, and about thirteen percent of South Africa's poorest land was allocated for this scheme. Ten Black homelands were established, but not a single one has been recognized as an independent country by any state except South Africa. The United Nations has no plans to consider their applications for membership. In actual fact, all of these "states" are governed by leaders handpicked by the South African government, although they are increasingly being challenged by the Black residents. Since the South African government does not trust the loyalty of these "governments," their only effective law enforcement consists of the South African armed forces and police.

In 1978, Nationalist leader Pieter Willem Botha became Prime Minister of South Africa. South Africa faced numerous extraordinary domestic and external problems that required unique solutions. The international oil crisis of the 1970s considerably reduced the country's industrial profits by making manufactured products more expensive. A sharp drop in the price of gold between 1979 and 1981 and the increased cost of imports resulted in double-digit inflation and high interest rates. The high interest rates ensured the seepage of capital abroad, but it made borrowing more expensive for consumers and entrepreneurs alike. On one hand, the public's buying power declined, whereas the producer's expenses increased. Many businesses could not afford to pay higher wages and maintain large inventories, and had to be content with lower profits. Numerous businesses went bankrupt, putting thousands of people out of work. This further reduced the public's ability to purchase goods and added to the general pessimism about the country's future. Botha faced massive opposition from the business community, which was still predominately English, and from the farming community largely managed by the Afrikaners. The danger of large-scale riots and uprisings by unemployed non-Whites became a frightening possibility.

Botha reacted by trying to gain the support of educated Coloured and Asian South Africans and by creating an urban Black middle class that would identify with big business and industry rather than pursue radical politics. If these groups could be won over, the Coloured, Black, and Asiatic masses might be deprived of capable leadership. This technique is termed "co-opting."

Some of Botha's reforms were merely cosmetic. "Separate development" replaced the word "apartheid." "Influx control" (the prohibition of Black settlement in White cities) became "orderly urbanization," and "passbooks" became "identity documents." This merely made Blacks angrier than ever and raised tensions to a higher pitch.

A few reforms, however, were more meaningful and effective. The government pledged to abolish favouritism in employment, segregation in public facilities, and legal obstacles to racial mixing. Non-Whites would gain a larger share in the economy and in decision-making. Programs sought to improve housing for Blacks in the segregated townships. Blacks could form trade unions and strike for higher wages and other economic gains. Blacks wanting to start or expand businesses would be able to apply for generous loans, and educational loans would enable Blacks to be better trained.

Although Botha had no intention of dismantling the Bantustan system—the chief feature of apartheid—his reforms offended many members of the White community, particularly the English-speaking business people and the ultra-conservative rural Afrikaners. These individuals felt betrayed, and numerous right-wing members of the National party quit to form new opposition parties. The Nationalists, who had dominated South African politics since 1948, were in danger of being ousted by a determined White extremist coalition.

Botha saw the need to change South Africa's existing political system in order to prevent the possibility of being overthrown. Until 1983, South Africa had been structured politically along British lines — the ''Westminster Model.'' The all-White House of Assembly chose the leader of the majority party as prime minister, who could be defeated by a motion of non-confidence by that Assembly.

Botha decided to change this system. In a 1983 referendum, the White voters ratified a new constitution that enabled Botha to turn South Africa from a parliamentary to a presidential republic. Botha became president for a five-year term without being responsible to the new tricameral (three houses) Parliament that had elected him. He created one legislative chamber for Whites, one for Coloureds, and one for Asians. Under the new constitution, if the tricameral Parliament was deadlocked, the president could govern South Africa without it with his handpicked council. The new system gave the president overwhelming political power, because he could not be ousted from his position. (See Figures 2 and 3.)

Since the Constitution of 1983, the President's Council has allowed the president to govern the state without restrictions. The Council serves as a powerful tool for

Figure 2
REPUBLICAN CONSTITUTION, 1961

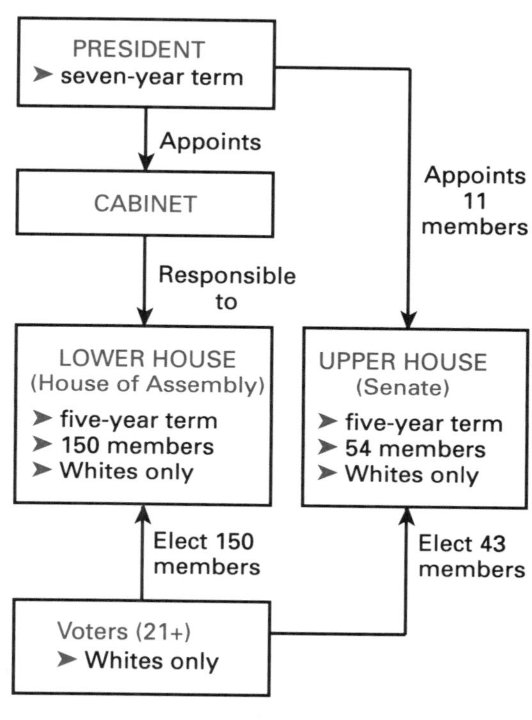

the president, especially when he is deadlocked in the tricameral legislature. An example of this occurred under President Botha in 1986, when the government introduced two stringent security bills. The White Chamber, dominated by the National party, voted for the bills. The Coloured and Asian Chambers voted against them. In the three chambers combined, 159 deputies, including several dozen White Liberals in the White Chamber, voted against the measures. Only 146 voted in favour of the bills. But in South Africa, Coloured and Asian legislators' votes do not have the same weight as the votes cast by Whites. If the three chambers cannot agree, then bills may be sent to the President's Council, which is dominated by the president. In this instance, the

Figure 3
REPUBLICAN CONSTITUTION OF 1983

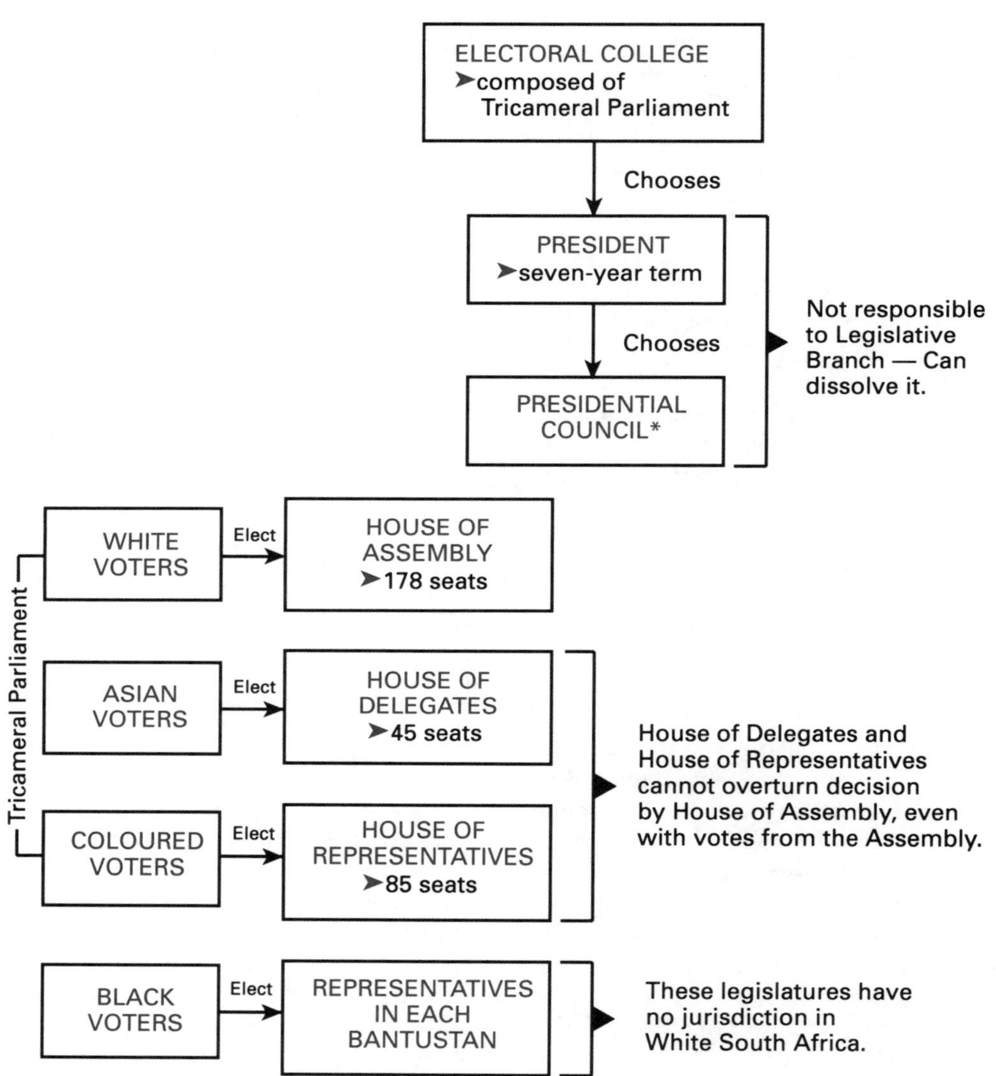

*60 Presidential Council Members are selected as follows:

- ➤White House of Assembly elects 20 members,
- ➤Asian House of Delegates elects 5 members,
- ➤Coloured House of Representatives elects 10 members.

The president selects 25 members. (He may select non-Whites.)

Council approved the bills. But even if the Council had defied the president's wishes, its powers are not binding, only consultative.

▶ WHITE PARTIES

It is important to understand how the South African government manages to maintain a virtual dictatorship despite the presence of parties representing varied shades of opinion.

The National party has dominated South Africa since 1948. Originally it was a purely Afrikaner (Boer) party, but over time, it attracted numerous English-speaking Whites. Apartheid is the creation and life force of the "Nats." The party favours government control over the economy rather than a free market, and it makes no secret of the fact that the economy is manipulated to secure a job for every White person, especially Afrikaner, who desires to work.

The Progressive Federal party (Progs) has its voting strength in English-speaking cities such as Johannesburg, Cape Town, and Durban. The Progs would abolish apartheid and devise a power-sharing formula with Blacks, Asians, and Coloureds, although even they do not favour a one-person, one-vote franchise. The Progs are American-style, classical economists and favour private industry in a free market.

In 1982, a right-wing faction of the National party formed the Conservative party and captured many seats in the rural areas where the National party had been dominant. The Conservative party believes that the country's future lies in maintaining apartheid without change or concessions.

The Herstigte Nasionale party (HNP), founded in the mid-1980s, won a few seats, then lost its only one in 1987. Even further to the right is the tiny Afrikaner Resistance Movement, which is a Nazi-style party that vows to preserve the White race in power through violent action. One of these groups, probably the Afrikaner Resistance Movement, planned but failed to assassinate President F. W. de Klerk, several cabinet ministers, Nelson Mandela, and Joe Slovo, head of the South African Communist party, in June 1990.

South African President F.W. de Klerk
Bureau For Information

▶ BLACK PARTIES

In 1960, there were no legally sanctioned Black political parties in south Africa. In 1989, the de Klerk government released Nelson Mandela from his twenty-seven-year house arrest and legalized his party, the **African National Congress (ANC)**. When it was originally founded in 1912, the ANC pledged to achieve freedom through non-violent protest. In response to government persecution, the ANC adopted violence as a means of fighting apartheid. In 1964, the government convicted its leaders of plotting revolution and sentenced them to life imprisonment. The ANC chose exile in neighbouring Black countries and carried on guerrilla warfare and sabotage inside South Africa. With the release of Mandela and the legalization of the ANC, the party has pledged to resume peaceful negotiations.

The ANC's eighteen-member National Executive Committee is still based in Lusaka, Zambia, and until 1990 had a military arm called the "Spear of the Nation." The ANC defines itself as a multi-racial party, and some of its leaders are White, for example, Communist party leader Joe Slovo. Apart from the insignificant Communist party, it is the only credible organization that is avowedly multi-racial and hence able to claim to represent the entire South African constituency. It remains to be seen whether this multi-racial approach has a chance of paying political dividends.

South African Black leader Nelson Mandela waves his fist in the ANC salute during a visit to Toronto.
Canada Wide/Stan Behal

A small extremist faction, the **Pan Africanist Congress (PAC)** has been fighting underground and in exile since 1958 for a new "Azania," a South Africa that would be governed by the Black majority.

It is interesting to note that both the principal White and Black parties have spawned extremist groups that have further widened the gap between the two races.

▶ THE "BROWN" PARTIES

The Labour party, which dominates the Coloured Chamber, has tried to embarrass the regime into change. Its leader, the Reverend Allan Hendrickse, who served in President Pieter W. Botha's cabinet, participated in a Coloured "swim-in" at a Whites' only beach. He dared Botha to fire him from the cabinet or have him arrested. Botha did neither. He had no intention of antagonizing the Coloured community that was seething with resentment as it was. With each challenge, the Nationalists and apartheid have suffered a loss of prestige and credibility. In themselves, however, such actions have been insufficient to weaken the well-entrenched segregation system.

In 1983, Coloureds organized a multi-racial alliance, the United Democratic Front to oppose the new constitution. Composed of some 850 community, church, and labour groups with a total membership of two million, the UDF almost at once became the Coloureds' chief resistance group to apartheid. The government retaliated by accusing the UDF of being a branch of the outlawed ANC and jailed UDF leaders on charges of treason. In 1988, the UDF was banned and rendered ineffective.

The Indians and Coloureds, collectively known as the "Browns," are in the worst position in South Africa. They are the two smallest minorities, and they do not co-operate with each other. The Asians prefer to ignore national politics and are content with self-government within the Asian community. As a result, fewer than one out of five Asians vote in elections. The Coloureds lack both numbers and economic or political clout. They have attacked apartheid by becoming increasingly violent against the White authorities.

▶ THE ROLE OF A LEGAL BLACK PARTY

South Africa has had one legalized Black party that must be seriously considered as a contender for a possible peaceful solution in this divided land. ***Inkatha***, a Zulu cultural movement launched in the 1970s, was never outlawed by the government. This one-million strong party has a government-approved territorial base and a popular and charismatic leader, Zulu Chief Gatsha Buthelezi. The chief wishes to liberate all of South Africa's Blacks. The White regime would not agree to this. Another problem plaguing Buthelezi is that his movement attracts very few non-Zulu Blacks. In fact, many radical Blacks despise Buthelezi for allegedly being a sell-out and a ''fascist.'' In Natal, *Inkatha* supporters and the UDF have been killing each other in a bitter rivalry. This increasingly raises the spectre of Blacks fighting Blacks instead of jointly opposing apartheid and the White regime. Still, Buthelezi has the advantages of being legal; of having a secure home base; and of ruling over a large, loyal, and highly disciplined Zulu following.

▶ THE HOMELANDS

All plans for South African unification may be spoiled by the government's ''homeland'' policy. If it succeeds, then a White-Black settlement will be beyond the realm of possibility. The fate of the Browns would become intolerable in an overwhelmingly White-dominated society. Originally, the homelands were native reserves strongly resembling American and Canadian native peoples' reserves. These reserves emerged in the wake of the last Kaffir Wars of the nineteenth century. The present government wishes to place all South African Blacks in the ten ''homelands,'' and thereby deny them South African citizenship. One problem has to do with the poor quality and small size of these territories. A mere thirteen percent of South Africa is supposed to hold some twenty-five million Blacks, most of whom have never seen these lands and have no desire to leave the White areas of the country. The army, however, is empowered to deport all individuals whose skills are not needed in the White areas to a homeland. There they would have to live in squalor under native leaders appointed by the South African government. Thus far, some 3.5 million Blacks have been deported, mostly against their will. One authority has called these homelands ''simply storage bins for humans.''

FOCUS

1. Write a fictional story of South Africa's immediate future if the ANC or Buthelezi achieve power from the viewpoint of
   a) an Afrikaner,
   b) an English South African,
   c) a Black citizen, or
   d) an Asian citizen.

2. Devise your own legislative system for South Africa.
3. Based on what you have read on South Africa, do you believe that a truly democratic system can work in this country? Explain.
4. Do you believe that the following measures would help or hurt apartheid? Explain your reasons.
   a) economic boycott of South Africa
   b) athletic boycott of South Africa
   c) expelling South Africa from the United Nations
   d) arming the non-Whites of South Africa
   e) organizing South Africa's Black neighbours to attack South Africa
5. Organize a debate on the topic: Integrated South Africa versus racial division of the country. Which is the better solution for peace?
6. Divide the class into two groups and debate the following question: Since the 1983 Constitution, is the president of South Africa a democratic leader or is he a dictator?
7. In an essay, explain why South Africa did not follow the ''Westminster Model'' of constitutional development.
8. Arrange a debate on the question: To whom does the land of South Africa belong?
9. Does the 1983 Constitution have any legal, moral, or ethical merit? Explain.
10. Compare South Africa's treatment of its native population to Canada's handling of native peoples.

Following are selected interviews of Black South Africans. No attempt has been made to edit these. They speak for themselves. The article from *National Geographic*, on the other hand, is a polished report that more or less verifies the oral statements in the previous interviews.

In 1985, four South African revolutionaries (A to D) were interviewed about life in the townships and Bantustans.

A

You cannot contain your anger because everyday you are reminded that someone else is running your life, that someone else is sending you off to the mines to dig for gold and diamonds and there is no return for you or your family and your people. So you are this volcano that is ready to erupt. Physically even the houses in the different townships are different. Just by looking at them you see the steps of legal status of the people. if you go to the white areas you have some of the most beautiful mansions. They do have houses for poor whites and they have the same kind of uniformity that you see in our townships, but they are much bigger than anything you will find in the townships. In the Indian and Coloured areas you will find smaller houses but they still have greater facilities than the African townships, things like water systems and electricity. . . .

B

The structure of the cities is such that the rich whites live the farthest away from everybody else. These are the suburbs and then there are the downtown areas and shopping areas. Poor whites live around these areas. Then you have a distance of about eight miles [13 km] from the downtown and this is where the Indians live. About five to eight miles [8 km to 13 km] away from the city is where the Coloureds live—also separate from the Indians. Furthest away are the Africans. African townships, which are not cities because only whites can live in cities, are 15 to 20 miles [24 km to 32 km] away from the cities and those rich areas.

C

Violence is another part of township life. In part it comes from alcohol. But mainly it comes from the oppression itself, having so many people in a clamped-down area. South African youth become very politicised. You belong to groups like a dance club, a karate club or a civic group and they are all actually political groups, or they are often political groups.

Getting Socialised

D

You get socialised to your situation as a black person very early. You are black and because of that you live in this township. There are certain things you are told from a very young age—you cannot sit there, that's a white man's place and you can't go in there, that's a white man's place—you are told these things by your own mother even before the white man tells you. So from a very young age you become aware of the political situation. I mean to the extent that you don't even say anything to a white kid that goes by. You are even scared at some stages, a white kid could slap you and the first thing that strikes your mind is that if I slap him back I will be arrested. You will feel that way as a five-year-old. . . .

Source: Reprinted from "A World to Win," 27, Old Gloucester Street, London WC1N 3XX.

GROWING UP ANGRY

What is "daily life" in South Africa?

A

Daily life means seeing your parents helpless when their children are being chased by the police in and out. It means seeing your door kicked in at early hours of the morning, seeing your kids picked up and beaten in front of you, seeing your parents being abused and called names—your mother being called bitch and you father called this and that and assaulted.

B

Growing up in that society is knowing that maybe your mother won't come home because when she came home there was a police van at the station and people were being asked to show their passbook. Growing up in that society means that if your mother is picked up at the bus station or the train station you have no way of finding out what happened to her until three days or a week when you will either hear a neighbor say that your mother has been picked up or hear from someone just released from jail that they actually saw your mother in prison. . . . This is growing up in that system—your parents are never sure that when you leave in the morning you will be back at night.

Source: Reprinted from "A World to Win," 27, Old Gloucester Street, London WC1N 3XX.

A POET'S VIEW OF THE MINES

An uncompromising picture of the plight of the African mineworker is given in an impressive poem by the great Zulu poet B. W. Vilakazi, who died in 1947. Two stanzas of this poem, "In the Gold Mines," translated from the Zulu "Ezinkomponi," appear below.

Roar, without rest, machines of the mines,
Roar from dawn till darkness falls;
I shall wake, oh, let me be!
Roar, machines, continue deaf
To black men groaning as they labor—
Tortured by their aching muscles,
Gasping in the fetid air,
Reeking from the dirt and sweat—
Shaking themselves without effect.

My brother is with me, carrying
His pick and shovel on his shoulder,
And, on his feet, are heavy boots.
He follows me toward the shaft:
The earth will swallow us who burrow,
And, if I die there, underground,
What does it matter? Who am I?
Dear Lord! All round me, every day,
I see men stumble, fall and die.

Source: Reprinted from "A World to Win," 27, Old Gloucester Street, London WC1N 3XX.

Without warning South African police in an armored vehicle leveled shotguns at a crowd that gathered after the funeral of a woman run over by a police truck in a black township this past July. The mourners turned and ran. Free-lance photographer Peter Magubane took five frames of the fleeing crowd, then began running too. He did not realize that he had been shot in the feet and backs of his legs. Helped into his car, he went for private treatment, for by appearing at a public hospital he, the victim, would likely have been charged with "public violence."

With 17 pellets of lead shot still embedded in him, one wound still oozing, he pressed on to complete his coverage for *National Geographic* of the Ndebele people.

Such dangers have often confronted the 54-year-old South African photojournalist. In June 1969, while working for the *Rand Daily Mail*, Magubane was arrested for allegedly conspiring to overthrow the state. When first jailed, he was forced to stand with each foot on a stack of bricks while police interrogated him—day and night for five days. He was held without bail in solitary confinement in Pretoria Central Prison until September 14, 1970.

Though twice acquitted of the charges, he was "banned" within his own country for five years. He was forbidden to attend gatherings, associate with more than one person at a time, leave Johannesburg without permission, or pursue his profession.

He survived mainly by buying goods at auction and reselling them.

Yet he never put his cameras away and has published seven books, including two on Soweto, the giant black township outside Johannesburg. His *Magubane's South Africa* was banned in South Africa for seven years.

Now based in New York City, Magubane returned to South Africa last November to cover the continuing violence. New restrictions had been placed on the press, but whatever rapport he had from years of dealings with the police promised little help. "The senior officers know me, but they are not where the trouble is; they're behind desks. So I'm just another photographer."

Source: *National Geographic Magazine*, February 1986.

Table 2
TIME CHART

	South Africa's Road to Apartheid		Domestic and Foreign Opposition to Apartheid
1815	Civil rights only to Whites	1893 to 1914	Indian leader Mohandas Gandhi, a lawyer, leads Indian residents in unsuccessful quest for full citizenship (see Case Study 7)
1912	ANC banned by authorities	1912	African National Congress (ANC)
1919	Asiatics forbidden to acquire property		
1920	Segregation Act legalizes total restriction of Blacks		
1926 +	Blacks denied the right to practise certain skilled occupations	1926 +	Widespread Black opposition prevents government from introducing additional segregation measures
		1945	South Africa joins United Nations—is questioned on racial policies
1949	Mixed marriages banned		
1950	Group Areas Act provides for the segregation of four racial groups	1950	Disorders and passive resistance erupts among Blacks
	Suppression of Communism Act authorizes minister of justice to declare illegal any organization promoting communism; the act also defines communism as opposition to apartheid		United Nations names special commission to conduct inquiries into racial discrimination in South Africa; South Africa withdraws its delegate from U.N. as a protest
1951	Coloured voters removed from the White register; they had been voting with Whites since 1852	1951	Worst riots in Cape Town history
1953	Bantu Education Act introduces apartheid in all educational institutions		
		1958	South Africa returns its delegate to the U.N.
1959	Limited self-government in Black "homelands"		
1960	Black political organizations opposed to apartheid banned		
		1961	British Commonwealth rejects South Africa's application for membership
1962	Self-governing Black Bantustans (Native Territories) within the Republic; all forms of opposition to the regime and its policies outlawed	1962	U.N. declares economic sanctions against South Africa

1963	Law permits the jailing of suspects without a warrant and the indefinite detention of political prisoners		
1964	First Bantustan (Transkei) established	1964	U.N. Security Council approves a resolution condemning apartheid and plans further economic sanctions against South Africa
		1976	Uprising in Soweto
1983	South Africa switches from parliamentary to presidential system, which strengthens apartheid	1983 to 1984	Black uprisings led by African National Union (ANU) grow in intensity
1985	Government declares state of emergency to counter demonstrations	1985	Economic and political pressures from abroad continue
1986 May	South African troops attack ANC bases in Zambia, Zimbabwe, and Botswana	1986	Government abolishes pass laws and promises limited Black participation in government; Bishop Desmond Tutu addresses U.N. and demands renewed sanctions
June	South African security forces gain almost unlimited authority to crush strike by 16 000 non-White railway workers		
1986 to 1987	Increased fighting rages between hostile Black factions	1987	U.S.A. plans to cease investments in South Africa
1988 June	Government proclaims new restrictive labour laws and bans political activity by trade unions and anti-apartheid groups	1988	Two million Black workers stage three-day strike to protest government regulations
		1989	Nelson Mandela released from twenty-seven-year home detention
		1990	South African Parliament repeals 1953 segregation law (apartheid)—Separate Amenities Act
		June/ July	Nelson Mandela goes on world tour to preach against apartheid; insists on continued economic sanctions

APPLYING YOUR KNOWLEDGE

1. Study the time chart (Table 2) and answer the following questions:
   a) Thus far, have sanctions against South Africa proven effective in improving the condition of non-Whites? Cite examples.
   b) Identify the most active decade of apartheid activity by the South African government.
   c) Identify the most active decade of anti-apartheid activity by non-Whites in South Africa.
   d) Explain why Desmond Tutu was not satisfied with promises of limited Black participation in South Africa's government.
2. From the interviews, answer the following questions:
   a) What do you see as the main sources of Black anger and despair. List your answers in the order of their importance.
   b) How is the structured view of Afrikaners regarding society reflected in the way the various races and income groups are located?
   c) What does it mean to ''get socialised to your situation as a black person very early''? Explain and give examples.

3. From the *National Geographic* report, answer the following questions:
   a) Why do you think the police shot Magubane? Was it a chance shot or was it aimed at him? Explain your reasons.
   b) Would a democracy acquit a person twice, yet ''ban'' him for five years? Prepare a defence *and* a condemnation of the South African government's handling of the Magubane case, based on what you now know about South Africa.

Case Study 14 Overview

The Nationalities Problem in the Soviet Union

This case study examines how one authoritarian regime, the Soviet Union, deals with the problem of minority rights. The case study begins with an examination of pre-revolutionary treatment of Russia's numerous ethnic groups, and then outlines the multicultural policies of the Soviet regime, distinguishes between theory and practice, and the reasons behind repression by the Soviet regime of its ethnic minorities. The present situation is then examined, including the ethnic composition of the U.S.S.R., the location of the major groups, and Gorbachev's policies and actions. The case study concludes with several primary documents that outline the situation, concerns, and desires of several ethnic groups.

▶ OBJECTIVES

After reading this case study, you should be able to:

- ▶ explain the historical treatment of minority groups in the U.S.S.R.
- ▶ analyse primary documents
- ▶ identify and understand the minority problems in the U.S.S.R.
- ▶ evaluate Gorbachev's policies and compare Canada's treatment of minority ethnic groups with the actions of the U.S.S.R.
- ▶ analyse maps and statistical data
- ▶ identify alternative courses of action and propose solutions

▶ KEY TERMS

self-determination	Russianization	autonomous
federalism	(Russianized)	

Case Study

14 The Nationalities Problem in the Soviet Union

SOVIET CITY PUT UNDER NEW CURFEW AS RIOTERS BURN HOMES, CARS

Toronto *Globe and Mail*, September 22, 1988.

RAMPAGING MOBS KILL THREE SOVIET SOLDIERS

Halifax *Chronicle Herald*, November 24, 1988

THOUSANDS FLEE HOMES IN ARMENIA, AZERBAIJAN

New York Times, December 2, 1988.

Throughout 1988 headlines such as these made Canadians suddenly aware of a small, far-off Caucasian district known as Nagornyi-Karabakh. Although religious, ethnic, linguistic, and nationalist competition and strife are commonplace in today's world, until recently, few appreciated the destructive potential such forces had for the U.S.S.R. Most recently, events in the Baltic republics, the western Ukraine, the Caucasus, Central Asia, and elsewhere have demonstrated that an explosive mixture of nationalist, ethnic, and religious resentments and hatreds seethe beneath the seeming conformity of Soviet life. These divisions separate the many smaller ethnic groups from the dominant Great Russians and from each other. Nagornyi-Karabakh, a Caucasian region over which the Azeris (Azerbaijanis) and Armenians have recently fought with each other, as well as with the Russian troops sent to restore order, is but one example. This case study examines how one authoritarian regime deals with the problem of minority rights. It also illustrates the importance of examining actions as well as constitutions and grandiose statements. As you read this study, keep in mind Canada's experiences with its various ethnic groups.

▶ THE TSARIST "PRISON" OF NATIONS

The roots of the Soviet problem pre-dated the Revolution of 1917. The Muscovite rulers incorporated the first groups of non-Slavic subjects into their realm in the late 1400s. Today, the Soviet Union is in fact the world's last-surviving multinational empire. By 1897, the date of the first Russian census, the empire's population was distributed as follows:

Table 1
NATIONAL COMPOSITION OF IMPERIAL RUSSIA, 1897

Great Russians	44.3%	Turkic Peoples	10.8%
Belorussians	4.7%	Jews	4.0%
Ukrainians	17.8%	Poles	6.3%
Total East Slavs	66.8%	Finnish Peoples	2.8%
Latvians/Lithuanians	2.5%	Germans	1.5%
Caucasian Tribes	1.3%	Georgians	1.1%
Armenians	0.9%	Iranians	0.6%
Mongolians	0.4%	Others	1.0%

There was also a great deal of religious diversity. The Russian Orthodox church claimed the allegiance of 70 percent of the populace; Muslims, 11 percent; Roman Catholics, 9 percent; Protestants, 5 percent; and Jews, 4 percent. Despite official attempts to "Russify" the non-Slavs, many of these nationalities rose in violent rebellion during the revolutions of 1905–1906 and 1917–1920. On both occasions only the armed intervention of the central government ended bloody Azeri-Armenian hostility.

▶ SOVIET NATIONAL SELF-DETERMINATION IN THEORY

Such acts of repression and pacification earned the empire the reputation as a "prison of nations." Ethically, no 1917 revolutionary could reject a peoples' right to "national **self-determination**," and tactically, nationalist rebellion was a useful means of undermining the established order. From the first, therefore, Vladimir Lenin solemnly advocated the "rights of all nations in the state to self-determination." On gaining power, his Soviet government took steps to implement this policy by decreeing:

- **1.** The equality and sovereignty of the nations of Russia;
- **2.** The right of the nations of Russia to self-determination, including the right to secede and form independent states;
- **3.** The abolition of all special national and national-religious restrictions and privileges of every kind; and
- **4.** Freedom for the development of all the national minorities and ethnic groups inhabiting Russia.

Article 4 of the 1924 Constitution asserted that "each of the union republics preserves the right to freely secede from the Union." Article 17 of the "Stalin Constitution" of 1936 repeated this statement, as did Article 72 of Leonid Brezhnev's in 1977. Today's U.S.S.R. is declared to be a federal, multinational state formed "as a result of the free self-determination of nations and the voluntary association of equal rights Soviet Socialist Republics."

▶ SOVIET NATIONAL SELF-DETERMINATION IN PRACTICE

Despite these fine sentiments, since 1918, no Soviet government has willingly permitted any region to secede from the U.S.S.R. Those parts of the Tsarist empire that did escape (part of Poland and Finland) did so by force of arms. Others had a less-lasting success: the Ukraine was regained by 1920 and the Caucasus in 1923, and the remaining Baltic states (Lithuania, Latvia, and Estonia), along with Moldavia were reabsorbed as union republics in 1940. In each of these cases, Moscow employed force or the threat of force, as well as terror, to ensure the region's ''voluntary'' union in the Soviet federation. How, we may well ask, can this be balanced with the theory outlined on page 239?

The answer lies in the Marxist attitude towards nationalism. Lenin and his followers accepted nationalist self-determination only as a half-way stage in social development. As Marxists, they believed that capitalists promoted national conflicts to prevent the workers from uniting in favour of better wages and working conditions. With the final defeat of capitalism, nationalist appeals would lose their effectiveness. As Lenin himself put it:

We demand the free right of self-determination . . . not because we dream of a system of small economic entities, or of the ideal of small states but, on the contrary, because we desire very large states, and a drawing together, even a merging of nations, but on a truly democratic, truly international basis. . . .

Stalin also insisted that the

principle of self-determination should be limited in such a way as to make it applicable only to toilers [workers], and not to the bourgeoisie [capitalists]. Self-determination must be a means of attaining socialism. . . .

In this manner, the slogan of ''self-determination of nations'' was transformed into the ''self-determination of the toiling masses.'' Not surprisingly, Lenin and Stalin had little hesitation in branding nationalists within and outside the Russian empire as enemies of the revolution.

Most of the early Soviet leaders did attempt to implement the principles of democratic **federalism** within the new state. Under Stalin, however, these principles were violated frequently. The autonomy of the regional areas was eroded continually in favour of the central government in Moscow. This process accelerated with Stalin's purges in the late 1930s, and, in some cases, Stalin destroyed the U.S.S.R.'s national and ethnic leaderships. They were replaced by trusted agents who were either Great Russians or **Russianized**. In addition, whole nationalities were simply uprooted from their historical homelands and transplanted elsewhere. In 1944, for example, the Crimean Tatars, who then made up twenty percent of the peninsula's populace, were forcibly moved to central Asia.

In this manner, Stalin (a Georgian) transformed the U.S.S.R. into a repressive multinational empire. The main instruments of integration and assimilation were the state bureaucracy, the Communist party, the centralized industrial system, the armed forces, and the ''organs of state security.'' The fact that Russian remained the language of higher education, national politics, and military command ensured the Russification of non-Russians seeking careers outside of their immediate home region. The advantage that this gave the major Slav groups meant that the empire inherited by Gorbachev was dominated by Great Russians or their Russianized Slav cousins. Today, they still hold the overwhelming majority of top positions in the party, government, security services, and so on. In the armed forces, for example, national representation (by percent) in the all-important General Staff in 1989 was as follows: Great Russians, 85; Ukrainians, 10; Belorussians, 3; and Others, 2.

▶ POLITICAL-NATIONAL FRAMEWORK OF THE U.S.S.R. IN 1990

The existence of the central government in Moscow is based on a treaty signed by each of the fifteen union republics. In accord with this pact, each of the republics relinquished certain powers (external affairs, defence, control of overall economic planning, the overall direction of the justice and police systems, etc.) to the "all-union" government but retains all remaining authority for its own administration. In particular, each is to enjoy complete independence in solving questions connected with the republic's internal life, such as economic management in its territory, ensuring the rights and freedoms of its citizens, and promoting social and cultural development. These union republics, therefore, are the basic building blocks of the Soviet state and are theoretically the fundamental means of protecting the individual identities of the major national groups. The existing union republics are detailed in Table 2 below.

Within these larger units, a number of smaller groupings of nationalities are protected by the existence of twenty **autonomous** republics, eight autonomous regions, and ten autonomous areas. As in the case of the republics, this scheme of regional self-government is officially intended to permit these smaller nations "to develop their statehood with due consideration for their national and other peculiarities and way of life" by granting them "their own economic and government bodies to develop the judicial system, press, schools, theatre and other cultural establishments in their native tongue." With their own parliaments and administrations, these areas are in many ways embryonic states in their own right. But sometimes, as with Nagornyi-Karabakh, an autonomous region may be formed to protect a segment of national minority (in this case the Armenians) that has its own union republic elsewhere but finds itself marooned in an alien national republic (Azerbaijan).

Although these lesser political units vary widely in size and population, they are often far from insignificant. But, of course, neither numerous inhabitants nor extensive territory is required for the development of a national consciousness. Thus the

Table 2
UNION REPUBLICS AND POPULATIONS, 1989

Regional/Ethnic Grouping	Republic	Capital	Area (000 km²)	Population, 1989 Census (000 000)
Slav	Great Russian (R.S.F.S.R.)	Moscow	17 075.4	147 386
	Ukrainian	Kiev	603.7	51 704
	Belorussian	Minsk	207.6	10 200
Balts	Lithuanian	Vilnius	65.2	3 690
	Latvian	Riga	63.7	2 681
	Estonian	Tallinn	45.1	1 573
Romanian	Moldavian	Kishinev	33.7	4 341
Caucasian	Georgian	Tbilisi	69.7	5 449
	Armenian	Erevan	29.8	3 283
	Azerbaijan	Baku	86.6	7 029
Central Asian	Uzbek	Tashkent	447.4	19 906
	Kazakh	Alma Ata	2 717.3	16 538
	Kirghiz	Frunze	198.6	4 291
	Tajik	Dushanbe	143.1	5 112
	Turkmen	Ashkabad	488.1	3 534

Figure 1
ADMINISTRATIVE–TERRITORIAL DISTRIBUTION OF THE NATIONS AND NATIONALITIES OF THE U.S.S.R.

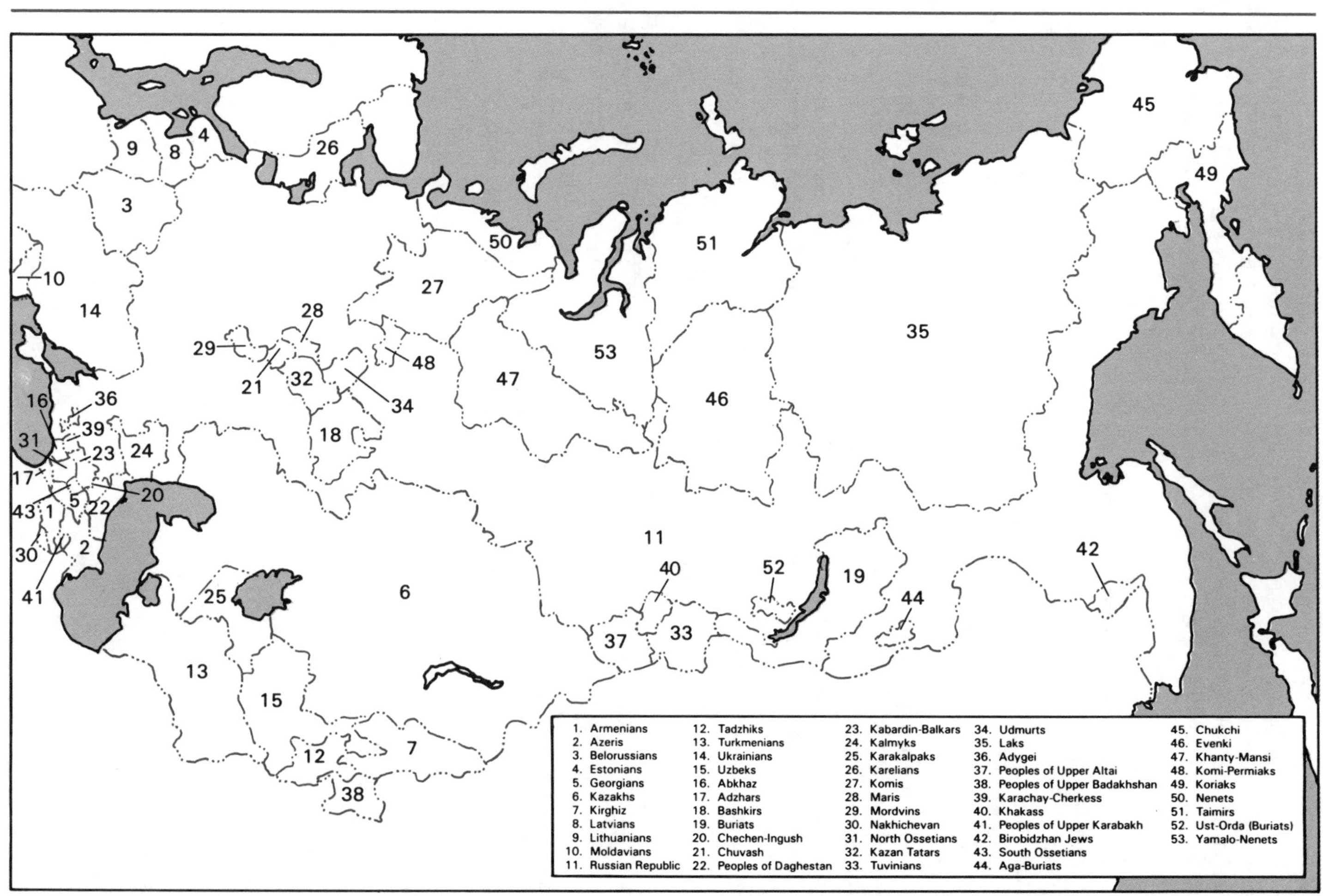

Figure 2
THE FEDERATED REPUBLICS OF THE U.S.S.R.

Abkhaz A.S.S.R., a section of the Georgian S.S.R. that borders the Black Sea and was the scene of violence in early 1989, is a mere 3000 square kilometres in size and has only 386 000 inhabitants. Of these, Abkhazians comprise 17 percent, Georgians 50 percent, and Russians and Armenians roughly 16.5 percent each. Since 1978, Abkhaz nationalists have established their own university and television and publishing programs. Now, faced by a Georgian backlash, they feel fully justified in demanding that the Abkhaz A.S.S.R., despite its minute size and diverse populace, be separated from Georgia and promoted to the status of full republic.

▶ THE SOVIET MOSAIC

The geographically distinct national entities just described represent only the tip of the Soviet ethnic iceberg. The U.S.S.R. contains some 400 nationality groups whose members speak ninety-six distinct languages. Its citizens use seventy-five distinct alphabets and receive school instruction in thirty-nine languages (a drop from the 1930s).

One other aspect of the Soviet mosaic that deserves attention is the changing balance of the major population groups. The birth rate among the major Slavic groups has dropped rapidly in recent decades, while that of Muslims has risen. Between 1984 and 1986, for instance, the rate of natural population increase in the R.S.F.S.R. was 9.3 percent, as compared to an average of 26.6 percent in the Muslim republics of central Asia. As a result, demographers predict that the Great Russian population proportion will decline from 52.4 percent in 1979 to perhaps as low as 46 percent by the year 2000. These demographic trends have numerous implications for future Soviet policies, especially those concerning industrial and military strength.

▶ SOVIET "MULTICULTURALISM"

Although the nature of ethnic demands in today's U.S.S.R. ranges from outright separatism in the Baltic Republics to expanded linguistic rights in more remote areas, the underlying causes of discontent are evident in the following letter from a Caucasian nationalist written in early 1990. First, there is the purely cultural concern:

. . . The Kabardinian language has been virtually excluded from the intellectual sphere and relegated to the "kitchen-sink." Russian is used for meetings, conferences and business correspondence. Many now believe that to speak Russian makes one an internationalist, while to speak one's own language is to commit the sin of nationalism. This attitude has depleted the native vocabulary of a people that no longer knows its own language or its own culture. . . . A big handicap in teaching local languages is the Cyrillic alphabet, introduced in the 1930s. All attempts to improve it have met with vigorous opposition.

The Republic's intellectuals are very worried about the rapidly diminishing numbers of people who speak their own language fluently. Some parents don't even want their children to learn it, thinking that they can only succeed in Russian. . . . The local teachers' school does not have classes in Kabardinian. . . . None of the nurseries or the schools in the capital of Nalchik teaches the native language.

In our Republic, the national composition of people in executive positions does not correspond to the national composition, which is more than 50 percent indigenous. The First Secretary of the Regional C.P.S.U. [Communist party] committee, the secretary of the Regional Party Committee in charge of the law-enforcement bodies, the First Secretary of the Nalchik City Party Committee, the Minister of Internal Affairs, the Attorney General, the K.G.B. Chairman, and the Chairman of Agriculture do not belong to our indigenous nationalities. The list goes on. This policy depresses the indigenous people, making them feel like "second-class" citizens. . . . [1]

▶ THE NATIONALITIES PROBLEM UNDER GORBACHEV

The rise of Mikhail Gorbachev and his policies of *glasnost* (openness) and democratization opened the floodgates of nationalist violence. This first became evident in the December 1986 riots in Alma Ata, the Kazakh S.S.R.'s capital, when the central authorities replaced a Kazakh with a Russian as chief of the local party. During 1987, nationalists throughout the U.S.S.R. formed their own "movements," and in early 1988 violence again erupted, this time in Nagornyi-Karabakh. But while all uprisings shared common concerns, their aims ranged from demands for total separation from the U.S.S.R. (Lithuania, Latvia, and Estonia) to greater political status (the Abkhazians), to the restoration of lost homelands (the Volga Germans, Crimean Tatars), and to the demand by Armenians that Nagornyi-Karabakh be transferred to their jurisdiction from that of Azerbaijan A.S.S.R.

Beyond this, however, demands are made for ecological and cultural guarantees. As in Canada, numerous native peoples in the Russian north find themselves threatened by economic progress, especially by oil exploitation. In the words of one of their deputies:

We earnestly ask the government to save our small nation before it is too late. To leave us the living space along the Bolshoi Yugan and Mali Yugan rivers. To stop oil production on these rivers. No settlements, oil derricks or oil pipelines should be built beyond the village of Ugut up the river. Let there remain at least one distinctive corner of our land. Our settlements should be declared a national preserve. The Khant people hopefully expect that our government will take time from global problems to see our problems, and finally decide to preserve our small nations.

In view of the Soviet Union's past harsh treatment of national minorities, the West tends to sympathize with their demands. Indeed, the United States has never recognized the incorporation of the Baltic Republics into the U.S.S.R. and officially still regards them as captive "nations." Nonetheless, demographic data suggest that their claims for separation from the Soviet Union may not be quite as simple as they appear. Although it is true that in 1982 Lithuania, which has been the most resolute Baltic Republic in pushing for full independence, was populated by some eighty percent native Lithuanians, its neighbours are in a somewhat more ambiguous position. For example, Estonians made up only sixty-five percent of their republic's population, and Latvians comprised a mere fifty-three percent of their republic. Russians, meanwhile, made up nine percent, twenty-eight percent, and thirty-three percent of these republics, respectively.

Similar figures could be quoted for other regions. Thanks to the internal migration brought about by Stalin's policies, by 1979 one-fifth of the U.S.S.R.'s citizens lived outside of their ethnic and cultural homelands. Another perhaps unintended result of these policies was ethnically mixed marriages, which by the early 1980s represented almost ten million Soviet families. All these factors considerably complicate the U.S.S.R.'s ethnic situation and, in most cases, preclude simple solutions.

In dealing with these problems, Gorbachev has had to adopt a multi-faceted approach. To begin with, he has reaffirmed

▸ [1]*Moscow News*, January 1990, #4, p. 6.

the theoretical right of secession as guaranteed by the constitution. But when faced with Lithuania's declared intention to separate, he first stood firm, ordered military demonstrations, imposed a gasoline embargo, and then showed flexibility in negotiations. In Alma Ata, Baku, and Tiflis, he used military force to maintain and impose order, and in Nagornyi-Karabakh he resorted to direct rule from Moscow. Yet he has taken action only when forced to do so, and to date he has virtually ignored the declarations of sovereignty by a number of regions. Equally important are the numerous, less dramatic steps being taken to defuse ethnic discontent — steps that include such seemingly unimportant initiatives as the establishment of a "Fund of Culture" in Lithuania to protect cultural monuments, the creation of a German cultural centre and Korean theatre in Kazakhstan, the launching of a new Jewish newspaper in the Far East, and publication of a teach-yourself-Yiddish text, as well as new school books for the Crimean Tatars.

By themselves, such measures will hardly solve the nationalist crisis in the U.S.S.R. More important for the future are the extensive powers with which Gorbachev is endowed as president. These permit him to issue decrees that are binding throughout the U.S.S.R.; to declare a state of emergency or martial law; to ban demonstrations, strikes, publications, parties, and movements that seem likely to disturb the public order; and to impose direct "temporary presidential rule" over particular republics and regions, with the right to revoke their legislation, remove their governments, suspend their Parliaments, and assume the appropriate judicial functions. While these powers may serve their purpose in the short term, only the success of Gorbachev's more general social and economic reforms seem likely to create a climate suitable for a lasting settlement of many ethnic complaints. And even then some problems, like that of Nagornyi-Karabakh, may still prove insoluble and continue to provoke bitter conflicts.

The following comments about secession and national unity were printed in *Time* early in 1990. Identify the theme or message of each Russian, and evaluate the argument supporting the message.

A CHORUS OF COMPLAINTS FROM OUTSIDE MOSCOW

All the placards demand greater freedom from the Kremlin. But the grievances differ from one republic to the next, and freedom sometimes means secession, sometimes not

BELORUSSIA

OLEG CHERNYSHEV
Stage Designer

"Belorussia is industrially strong, so that means we contribute much more to Moscow than we get in return. Belorussians also work harder than people in all the other republics. Our national front is seeking independence, but I'm not so sure. All the republics can help each other. We have good farming, so if we secede, we will be fine. But those republics that do not have rich earth will not be able to survive on their own."

TURKMENISTAN

MARAL AMANOVA
Biologist

"We don't discuss secession in our republic, and ethnic conflict does not exist. Our misfortune is that Moscow kept making us grow more and more cotton. We didn't even have room to raise cattle. Can a republic that produces only oil, gas and cotton really feed itself?

"I am for a more independent republic but within the framework of a union. This way we can make agreements with other republics: you give us cotton and we give you meat. Otherwise, if we have a market economy and each republic can sell abroad or to another republic, we will not get enough meat."

ESTONIA

IGOR GRYAZIN
Lawyer

"Sovereignty is a fiction in the U.S.S.R. As before, the Moscow center holds its monopoly, especially over the economy. It refuses those economic forms of life Estonians prefer: private property and farming on a cooperative basis, the development of light industry and food production, with a minimum of heavy industry.

"Secession is now irreversible. All of Moscow's decisions for democracy came too late. Two years ago, I supported a confederation and was blamed for nationalism. Today, my idea is old. This is idiocy—the Estonians say they are being robbed, the Russians and the Uzbeks say they are being robbed. Nobody wins. But the mechanisms of Soviet power is that we all produce and give it to Moscow and Moscow reallocates while everyone loses."

ARMENIA

LYUDMILA ARUTYUNYAN
Sociologist

"Our country was founded on taboos, and one of them was that you could not leave the union. Armenia is on the border of Turkey, our historic enemy. That fact did not allow us to think about secession. But in the past two years, we have had a crisis of faith in Moscow as the Azerbaijanis continue to harass us. Our appeals to the center were answered with formal notes, requests for calm and rationality. They should have said, 'Let's figure out a compromise between Armenians, Azerbaijanis and the federation.' If the union does not defend the people of Nagorno-Karabakh [an Armenian enclave within Azerbaijan] against violence, then the question arises, Can we be a part of the Soviet Union? The center must fulfill those functions that make it attractive to stay."

GEORGIA

TARAS SHAMBA
Law professor

"I come from Abkhazia, an autonomous republic within Georgia. For 42 days in 1918 we were an independent state. Then Georgia destroyed the Abkhaz government and subjugated us. Today, we want to make an agreement on an equal basis with Georgia and with Russia and create our own small republic. We want this to preserve our language, our culture, our history, so the people will not disappear."

TADZHIKISTAN

BIKHODZHAL RAKHIMOVA
Mechanical engineer

"Our republic was created in 1924, and in all these years we've had nothing. We were a distant Czarist outpost. Tadzhikistan had been part of the Great Silk Road, and this trade left its traces in the northern part of our country, which is better off. But without the Soviet Union today we won't advance. Compared with the Baltics, we are a milk cow for raw materials. To build enterprises we need equipment, and where will we get it if we separate?"

Source: *Time*, March 12, 1990. Abridged.

APPLYING YOUR KNOWLEDGE

1. Outline the changes made in Soviet policies on the national question since 1917.
2. Which union republic has the greatest/least population density?
3. Compare the federal structure of the U.S.S.R. to Canada's. What similarities are there between Canada's guarantees of ''provincial'' rights and the U.S.S.R.'s for the protection of national/ethnic rights?
4. To what extent are the concerns of nationalists within the U.S.S.R. typical of those found elsewhere in the world and to what extent are they specifically Soviet problems?
5. On the basis of this case study and the chapter on Soviet government, describe the powers enjoyed by President Gorbachev.

FURTHER RESEARCH

1. Compare the material and legal position of the Canadian Inuit with that of the tribes inhabiting the Soviet North. Or compare Quebec's situation with Lithuania's.
2. Working in groups, devise a solution to the problems outlined in this study.
3. Prepare for a debate on whether the Baltic Republics should be allowed to secede.

Case Study 15 Overview

The Process of Change: Eastern Europe

This case study explores those factors that affect political change by examining the recent revolutions in Eastern Europe. To understand Eastern Europe, it is essential to study the region, its sub-regions, and the individual states. Regionally, the area has many common features. The most important aspects affecting the development of Eastern Europe were the competing imperial rivalries and the ethnic tensions within the region. From a sub-regional approach, the most significant difference is the division between the northern and southern states. The policies of the Soviet Union have always played a key role in determining the actions within each country. The case study concludes with a discussion of the origins and events of the 1989–1990 revolutions in Eastern Europe and their implications for the future.

▶ OBJECTIVES

After reading this case study, you should be able to:

- ▶ discuss those factors that promote and retard political change
- ▶ work in a group to devise a possible solution to the issues raised in this case study
- ▶ understand the importance of studying a country from both a regional and a sub-regional approach
- ▶ recognize the importance of the U.S.S.R. in the area
- ▶ evaluate the significance of ethnic differences in Eastern Europe

▶ KEY TERMS

Stalin's Russia
Tsarist Russia
imperial rivalries
De-Stalinization
Hungarian uprising of 1956
Prague Spring (1968)
democratization

Case Study

15 The Process of Change: Eastern Europe

So far we have discussed political and economic systems in specific countries as if they never changed. Ideas and institutions, however, are constantly changing. Rather than viewing the past as a series of photographic slides, it can best be seen by three slide projectors, all sending their images onto the same screen. One projector shows current values, another the ideas of the past, and a third the newly emerging values. Change is thus a major component of world events. What factors initiate and retard change? This case study examines the history of Eastern Europe in order to identify some of these factors.

▶ LEVELS OF ANALYSIS

The year 1989 brought changes to Eastern Europe that future historians may well compare to those brought to Western Europe by the French Revolution of 1789. Popular movements suddenly overthrew one Communist regime after another. The result has had implications that go far beyond the borders of Eastern Europe. Indeed, what we have witnessed has been the destruction of the general European order as it has existed since 1945. This in turn has brought the reunification of East and West Germany and a frantic search for a new order that will guarantee future European security and stability. In many ways, success in this last venture will depend upon the extent to which those involved understand the dynamics that are transforming the region once called "the powder-keg of Europe."

The study of Eastern Europe can be approached at the regional, sub-regional, and individual levels. The first level considers the region as a whole, in the same way that we might approach Latin America or

South-East Asia. This highlights the many similarities imposed on the region by its geography and history. Yet this regional approach obscures many of the distinct national characteristics of the individual states involved. A full understanding can therefore be achieved only by examining the region at all three levels.

▶ The Regional Approach

Since 1945, Eastern Europe has usually included Poland, East Germany, Czechoslovakia, Hungary, Romania, Bulgaria, Yugoslavia, and Albania. The common denominator uniting them was that each of these countries emerged from World War II with Communist regimes that were modelled on **Stalin's Russia**. But a glance at the accompanying maps indicates that at different times other countries were associated with the region. Before 1914, for example, most scholars would have excluded eastern Germany but added Austria (the Hapsburg empire), **Tsarist Russia**, Greece, and European Turkey.

All of this is, of course, very confusing. But the point is that since 1800 the definition of what comprised Eastern Europe has varied considerably, since this region has been in a constant flux with shifting frontiers. Indeed, the years 1945 to 1988 repre-

Figure 1
TERRITORIAL CHANGES IN EUROPE SINCE 1715

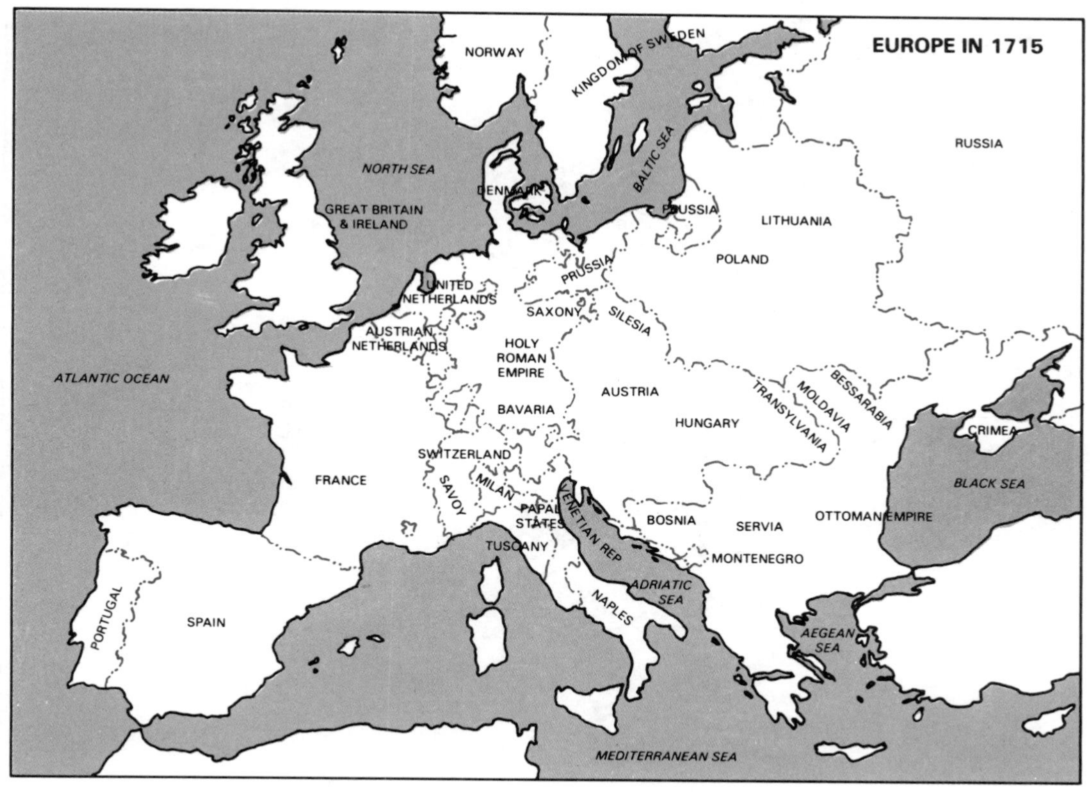

sent the longest period of stability that this region had known over the last two centuries. The fact that this stability was imposed by the U.S.S.R.'s military might is also indicative of one of the root causes of the chronic instability. These are, quite simply, the imperial rivalries of the great powers bordering the region and the rise of nationalist passions within the region.

Imperial Rivalries

First, let us examine the impact of **imperial rivalries**. Until 1918, the influences exerted by the Hapsburg (Austro-Hungarian), Ottoman (Turkish), Tsarist (Russian), and German empires affected the fates of the region's smaller states.

Until the late 1800s, the northern part of Eastern Europe was effectively controlled by Russian, Hapsburg, and Prussian (later German) rule. Power in the south, on the other hand, was divided between the Hapsburg and Ottoman empires, with Russia acting as an interested spectator. This relatively stable order was disrupted by two factors: the decline in power first of the Turkish empire, then of the Hapsburg empire, and the nationalism unleashed across Europe by the wars of Napoleon Bonaparte, which began to disturb the Balkans in the early 1800s. First the Serbs (Yugoslavs); then the Greeks; and finally the Romanians, Bulgarians, and other nationalities raised the banner of revolt against the Turks. The resulting Balkan Wars of 1912–1913 had a number of important consequences for the region. Firstly, they effectively weakened Ottoman rule and eventually forced Turkey from all but a toe-hold in Europe. Secondly, the decline

of Turkish power in the Balkans created a vacuum that sparked Austro-Hungarian, Italian, and Russian political rivalries in the area.

Equally important to understanding the area is a knowledge of the region's ethnic diversity. Eastern Europe includes West Slavs (Czechs, Slovaks, and Poles), South Slavs (Serbs, Croats, and Slovenes), Turkic Albanians, Latin Romanians, Greeks, Bulgars, Hungarians, and so on. In terms of religion, the area is divided among Protestants, Roman Catholics, Greek and Russian Orthodox, and Muslims. Not only do these religious differences add fuel to nationalist tensions but they have also had immense cultural significance. Those influenced by the Orthodox faiths (Serbs, Bulgarians, Macedonians, and Greeks) use a Cyrillic alphabet, as opposed to the Latin script employed by those subjected to Catholic influences (Hungarians, Czechs, Poles, Slovaks, Croats, and Slovenes). The various ethnic groups have also intermixed and often intermarried, and their national "homelands" frequently overlap one another.

All this makes it difficult, if not impossible, to draw firm frontiers along clearly defined ethnic lines. The result is the continual presence of numerous territorial issues around which agitators can rouse nationalist passions, such as those that ignited World War I when, in June 1914, a Serbian nationalist assassinated Francis Ferdinand, the Hapsburg heir to the throne of Austria-Hungary. While that conflict largely liberated the Eastern European

countries, it did not remove the threat of outside domination or regional conflict. Indeed, recent events have demonstrated that regional and ethnic disputes still play a major role in the Balkans.

Despite nationalist hatreds, Eastern European countries still tend to share a number of cultural characteristics. Throughout the region, industrialization has been concentrated in small, well-defined pockets; society has long remained dominated by large, often aristocratic landowners; and anti-Semitism has retained considerable popular appeal. Although hostility and a sense of superiority to the Soviet Union are often cited as other common features, these attitudes are far from universal. Indeed, while neighbours such as Poland, Hungary, and Romania have exhibited considerable anti-Russian sentiments, Bulgaria, Czechoslovakia, and Yugoslavia have traditionally regarded Russia (and at times, even the U.S.S.R.) as a natural Slav ally in their efforts to gain and maintain national independence.

▶ The Sub-regional Approach

Even during the period of Soviet domination, Western analysts recognized that Communist Eastern Europe could usefully be divided into two sub-groups: a "Northern Tier" of Poland, East Germany, and Czechoslovakia and a "Southern Tier" comprising Hungary, Bulgaria, and Romania. In many ways, this division naturally emerged from the region's history. The Northern Tier states under German and Hapsburg control were exposed to significant influences from Western Europe. They underwent varying degrees of industrialization and had some experience with constitutional rule. Even so, apart from Czechoslovakia, liberal democratic traditions were weak and, along with the Baltic Republics, all had authoritarian governments by 1939.

In the Southern Tier, only Hungary witnessed some industrialization and had limited experience with constitutional rule. Bulgaria, Romania, Albania, and much of Greece and Yugoslavia had long lived under the rule of the Ottoman Turks and had been largely insulated from the main currents of Western liberalism. Like the Ottomans, they had a legacy of despotic governments, heavy taxation, corrupt bureaucracies, political and economic underdevelopment, and in times of crises, racial and religious intolerance. This legacy helps to explain the authoritarian regimes and fascist movements that appeared in Yugoslavia, Greece, and Turkey during the 1920s and 1930s.

▶ The Individual State Approach

Historians quite rightly stress that only a national history can explain a country's adoption of a particular course of action. History makes each country unique. The most striking deviation from the Soviet norm is perhaps the role of the various churches. In East Germany, the Lutherans often played a leading role. To some extent, the same is true of the Catholic Church in Hungary. In Poland, the power of the Catholic Church has been superior to the Communist party in the eyes of the people and has been an enduring symbol of national identity and unity. Since 1953, similar variations have been observed in such matters as land-holding, economic policies, cultural liberty, foreign relations, and so on.

▶ FACTORS OF INSTABILITY AND CHANGE

The same national ambitions and characteristics that promote internal changes within a country's own borders will, more often than not, simultaneously undermine efforts to achieve sub-regional and regional stability. This may explain why, to date, any stability at these levels has been imposed from the outside upon Eastern Europeans. And if these small countries "have often been victims of their larger neighbors' ambitions," as one observer has noted, "history shows that when they have had the power and opportunity they, too, have exhibited imperialistic tendencies and have been just as ready to seize *their* neighbors' land."

The record suggests that in Eastern Europe the success achieved by internal forces for change has been directly dependent upon the actions of the surrounding great powers. Major transformations have occurred only when this was done with their permission, or when the great powers were prevented from imposing their will. In other words, local proponents of change can only succeed if the sub-regional and regional environments favour such local initiative.

▶ THE SOVIET EASTERN EUROPEAN EMPIRE

Germany's collapse following World War II left the Red Army in undisputed control of the whole region north of the Greek frontier. Meanwhile, the political leaders of the individual Eastern European countries had either been exterminated, forced into exile, or completely discredited through their collaboration with Hitler. The only exceptions were Albania and Yugoslavia, both of which were ruled by victorious Communist leaders. As a result, Stalin faced little opposition as he installed co-operative regimes throughout the ''liberated'' region.

In the West, most people have tended to regard the Eastern European situation as being largely static until the upheaval of 1989. Yet beneath the surface it was in considerable turmoil, even if the signs of this upheaval only occasionally broke through. This turmoil resulted partly from the continuing tension that existed due to the obedience of local Communist leaders to Soviet economic policies (COMECON) and military control (Warsaw Pact).

While the impulse for change remained alive and well in each Eastern European country, such impulses could find expression only when changes in the Soviet Union brought shifts in the regional environment.

A brief glance at a chronology of Eastern European politics since 1945 clearly demonstrates this interaction between regional and national factors. The major events of the postwar period occurred in clusters that parallelled major turns in Soviet domestic and external policies. For example, in 1947/1948, a suspicious Stalin was convinced of the need to counter Western initiatives by tightening his hold on Eastern Europe and the Soviet Union. The results were new purges at home, the formation of the Communist Information Bureau (Cominform) and CMEA, the coup in Czechoslovakia, and the blockade of Berlin. Similarly, growing international tensions led to the building of the Berlin Wall in 1961.

On the other hand, thaws in the Soviet domestic situation, such as that brought about by Stalin's death in 1953 or by Khrushchev's program of **De-Stalinization** in 1956, were frequently interpreted by Eastern Europeans as signals for national upheavals at home. Stalin's death was followed by riots in East Berlin, strikes in Poland, and the **Hungarian uprising of 1956**. The same is true of decreased international tensions. Moves towards a Soviet-American detente between 1968 and 1970 were accompanied by Dubček's **Prague Spring (1968)**, the Soviet invasion of Czechoslovakia, and strikes in Poland that led to a change of leadership in early 1971.

▶ THE EASTERN EUROPEAN REVOLUTIONS OF 1989

In retrospect, the roots of 1989 are obvious in the sub-surface tensions. In particular, the continuing struggle of the Polish Solidarity trade union movement and the Hungarian Communist party's cautious moves towards introducing market mechanisms in the late 1980s served as a prologue. But these individual national developments remained muted until the regional environment changed drastically thanks to the impact of Mikhail Gorbachev's program of internal *perestroika* (or ''restructuring'').

Having launched his internal program, Gorbachev quickly realized that his goals could be achieved only in an atmosphere of reduced international tensions. In this context, a withdrawal of Soviet forces from East Germany, Poland, Czechoslovakia, and Hungary could bring major political benefits by reducing European tensions and by cutting expenditures abroad. In addition, maintenance of the Eastern European empire, which was supported by Soviet oil and grain exports, was itself a major drain on Moscow's resources. When these practical considerations were combined with **democratization**, which Gor-

Tens of thousands of pro-democracy demonstrators gather peacefully in Eastern Europe.
Canapress Photo Service

bachev had made an essential part of his internal program, a change in the U.S.S.R.'s Eastern European policies seemed inevitable. Signals of this new attitude came in the withdrawal of Soviet troops from Afghanistan in January 1988. When the spirit of rebellion began sweeping through Eastern Europe in earnest, the Soviet leader either expressed mild support or remained passive.

Moscow's new policies at long last gave the region's nationalist impulses free reign. Nonetheless, as 1989 dawned, there seemed little indication that it would be a year of radical transformations. Appropriately enough, the first step towards toppling Eastern Europe's regimes came in Poland, where a deteriorating economic situation had provoked a series of strikes in 1988. As a result, President Jaruzelski agreed to negotiate directly with Solidarity, which had been outlawed for seven years, and on February 6, 1989, a series of roundtable talks got underway. Much to the world's (and the Poles') surprise, on April 18, these discussions resulted in a historic pact that legalized Solidarity and promised free elections. These elections proved a disaster for the Polish Communist party as Solidarity swept to victory and, after further negotiations with Jaruzelski, formed Eastern Europe's first non-Communist government since 1948.

In the Southern Tier, the impetus for change came in Hungary. Throughout the 1960s and 1970s this country had prospered relative to its neighbours, thanks to the government's more liberal internal policies. But an economic crisis in the mid-1980s had shaken confidence in this regime. By 1987 there were widespread demands for change, and in May 1988 János Kádár was ousted from power. Although 1989 opened quietly, demands for change continued, and by late March the Communist Minister of Justice openly admitted that the country was ready for free elections and a democratic constitution. Humiliated by the large turn-out enjoyed by the opposition on May Day, the splintered Hungarian Communists finally voted to transform themselves into the Hungarian Socialist party and opened the way to free elections. This was the first time the ruling party in a Communist country had formally abandoned communism.

Space precludes examining the other national revolutions of 1989 in similar detail. Suffice it to say that if the processes of change in Poland and Hungary were plotted with some care and ended in orderly elections, changes elsewhere in Eastern Europe began unexpectedly on the streets. Emboldened by Gorbachev's attitude and the events in Poland and Hungary, mass movements forced the resignation of East Germany's hardline Communist regime, broke down the Berlin Wall in early November, forced the resignation of the Czechoslovak Communist

Berliners welcome East Germans crossing the wall into West Berlin.
Canapress Photo Service

government in early December, and overthrew the dictatorship of the Ceauşescu family in Romania after a bloody rebellion in December 1989/January 1990. Only in Bulgaria, where Party leader Todor Zhivkov resigned after thirty-five years in power, did change come without overwhelming pressure from below.

▶ IMPLICATIONS AND PROGNOSIS

While the West greeted the collapse of the Soviet empire with evident satisfaction, grave problems remain. As the *New York Times* explained it, the year 1989 "produced a new map, where the sense of regional identity is more fragile [than earlier]. It is an Eastern Europe defined not by ideology but by national character, and one in which the flames of nationalism continue to burn throughout the region." The strength of these nationalisms is evident from the Bulgarians' harsh treatment of the Turkish minorities, the Romanians' hostility to the Transylvanian Hungarians, the renewed friction between Czechs and Slovaks, the ethnic turmoil in Yugoslavia, the Poles' and Czechs' worries about the two countries' German frontiers, and so on. Whereas Hungary and the Northern Tier countries have rejected their old Communist parties, the Romanians and, more clearly, the Bulgarians, have elected the old leaderships in different guises. At the same time, a common regional economic crisis has made some form of economic integration an urgent necessity. It remains to be seen to what extent these needs can overcome older national hatreds.

Externally, the international constraints affecting the region are still ill-defined. Faced with Gorbachev's withdrawal, the limited willingness and capabilities of the United States and Western Europe to provide economic help, and the likely economic and political power of a newly unified Germany, the region now finds itself in international limbo. The consequences of this situation go far beyond the immediate economic problems of these Eastern European countries. Indeed, the collapse of the Warsaw Pact represents the end of the European balance and makes the creation of a new European security system a matter of urgency. Without such a system, Eastern Europe may once again become an economically backward region in which nationalist passions are fanned by outsiders for their own power and profit and again become an international hot spot.

APPLYING YOUR KNOWLEDGE

1. Describe and illustrate the three levels at which Eastern European politics can be studied.
2. On the basis of further research, trace the rise and fall of communism in one Eastern European country.
3. Outline the basic differences among the countries in the so-called Northern and Southern tiers.
4. Prepare a map of the region showing clearly the boundary between the sub-regions.
5. Examine the events of 1989 in one Eastern European country and explain the fall of its Communist regime.
6. Prepare for a debate on the future of Eastern Europe.
7. Outline those factors that retarded change in Eastern Europe.

8. Working in small groups, devise a solution for the ethnic/national problems in the region.
9. What factors initiated change in Eastern Europe?
10. Project two events that might alter Canada's economic or political systems. Explain how they might change.

Case Study 16 Overview

Political Systems in Developing Countries: Costa Rica and Zimbabwe

This case study examines the political development of two very different developing countries — Costa Rica and Zimbabwe. There is a wide range among the Third World countries in terms of their economic situation and political systems. Costa Rica is a democracy that has survived because it has few class and racial divisions and a well-educated populace. Zimbabwe has one-party rule. The case study outlines each country's early history, political development, and present political situation. Profiles are included of Costa Rica's Sánchez and Zimbabwe's Mugabe. The case study concludes by asking whether one-party rule or democracy is best suited to developing countries.

▶ OBJECTIVES

After reading this case study, you should be able to:

- ▶ compare the ideologies, political systems, and history of Zimbabwe and Costa Rica
- ▶ analyse the leadership styles of Mugabe and Sánchez
- ▶ discuss the range of Third World countries
- ▶ evaluate and compare statistical data
- ▶ debate the benefits of one-party rule
- ▶ develop a suitable research plan for examining another Third World country
- ▶ understand the problems of developing countries

▶ KEY TERMS

South
North
military juntas
Non-Aligned Movement

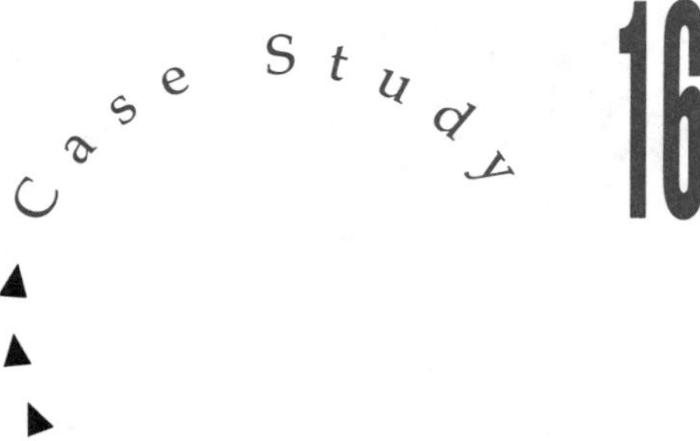

Political Systems in Developing Countries: Costa Rica and Zimbabwe

People in the Third World or the "**South**" face political problems that are similar to those of people in the more developed world. Someone has to make the rules or laws for the society; someone has to carry out these rules; and there must be some way of determining what the rules mean, whether they have been broken, and what penalties to prescribe. In this general sense, their political problems and tasks are similar to those of Canada and other more developed countries of the "**North.**"

In other ways, the situation in less developed countries is substantially different. Almost all of these countries were once controlled by colonial powers. This colonial heritage has had an enormous impact on their development, both political and economic. At the same time that each country achieved independence and had to decide upon a suitable political system, it had to cope with such economic problems as large international debts, falling prices for commodity exports, rapidly rising populations, and a world economy dominated by the increasingly sophisticated economies in the North. In many cases, these new political units emerged in societies where literacy levels were low, formal political experience was limited, and local divisions were deeply entrenched.

The range of social and economic conditions that exist both within and among the countries of the South is enormous. At one extreme are oil-rich countries such as the United Arab Emirates (GNP—$15 720). At the opposite extreme are the world's poorest countries such as Ethiopia (GNP—$120), Malawi, and Tanzania (GNP—$160 for each). India has people speaking over 1600 dialects, and its constitution recognizes regional languages. Indonesia has approximately 300 ethnic groups. In South Korea, on the other hand, virtually the entire population is of Korean origin. China has a population in excess of 1.1 billion, whereas almost forty Southern countries have fewer than one million people each.

These vast contrasts have created political systems in the South that are quite diverse. India is a federal parliamentary democracy. Ethiopia is governed as a Marxist single-party peoples' republic. Argentina has alternated between attempts at democracy and **military juntas**.

Keep these questions in mind as you read the following profiles of Costa Rica and Zimbabwe:

- What elements of democracy and authoritarianism are present?
- What values, beliefs, and ideologies support the existing political system?
- To what extent is the political system the result of particular conditions within the country?
- What factors have caused the country's political system to change over time?
- What solutions, if any, would you suggest?

COSTA RICA

Table 1
BASIC DATA—COSTA RICA

Geography	Area in Square Kilometres: 51 022 Capital (Population): San José (800 000) Climate: tropical and semi-tropical	**Military**	Number of Armed Forces: about 7200; army replaced by civil guard in 1948 Military Expenditures (% of Central Government Expenditures): 1.1% (1986)
People	Ethnic Makeup of Population: 96% White (including a few *Mestizos*); 3% Black: 1% Indian Religion(s): 95% Roman Catholic; 5% others Adult Literacy Rate: 93%	**Economy**	Currency ($ U.S. Equivalent): 58 colones = $1 (1986) Natural Resources: hydroelectric power Agriculture: coffee; bananas; sugarcane; rice; corn; cocoa; livestock products Industry: food processing; textiles and clothing; construction materials; fertilizer
Communication	Televisions: 470 000 (1987) Telephones: 292 000 (11.8/100) Newspapers: 4 dailies		
Transportation	Highways—Kilometres: 15 400 Railroads—Kilometres: 800 Usable Airfields: 188		
Labour Force	32% agricultural; 25% industry and commerce; 38% services and government	**Foreign Trade**	Imports: $1.4 billion (1988) Exports: $1.3 billion (1988) Main Partner: U.S.A., 41%

- Sources: Paul B. Goodwin, Jr., *Global Studies: Latin America*, 3rd ed. Guilford, Conn.: The Dushkin Publishing Group Inc., 1988.
The Canadian World Almanac and Book of Facts 1990. Global Press, 1989.

Table 2
THE WORLD, LATIN AMERICA, AND COSTA RICA: BASIC INDICATORS

Region or Country	Population Estimate mid-1990 (millions)	Birth Rate (per 1000 pop.)	Death Rate (per 1000 pop.)	Natural Increase (annual, %)	Population "Doubling Time" in Years (at current rate)	Infant Mortality Rate	Total Fertility Rate	Life Expectancy at Birth (years)	Urban Population (%)	Per Capita GNP, 1988 (U.S. $)
World	**5 321**	**27**	**10**	**1.8**	**39**	**73**	**3.5**	**64**	**41**	**$ 3 470**
More Developed	**1 214**	**15**	**9**	**0.5**	**128**	**16**	**2.0**	**74**	**73**	**15 830**
Less Developed	**4 107**	**31**	**10**	**2.1**	**33**	**81**	**4.0**	**61**	**32**	**710**
Less Devel. (Excl. China)	**2 987**	**35**	**11**	**2.4**	**29**	**91**	**4.6**	**59**	**36**	**870**
Latin America	**447**	**28**	**7**	**2.1**	**33**	**54**	**3.5**	**67**	**69**	**1 930**
Central America	**118**	**32**	**6**	**2.5**	**27**	**51**	**4.1**	**67**	**61**	**1 640**
Belize	0.2	37	6	3.1	22	36	5.0	69	50	1 460
Costa Rica	3.0	29	4	2.5	28	17.4	3.3	76	45	1 760
El Salvador	5.3	35	8	2.7	26	54	4.4	62	43	950
Guatemala	9.2	40	9	3.1	23	59	5.6	63	40	880
Honduras	5.1	39	8	3.1	23	63	5.3	63	42	850
Mexico	88.6	30	6	2.4	29	50	3.8	68	66	1 820
Nicaragua	3.9	42	9	3.3	21	69	5.5	62	57	830
Panama	2.4	27	5	2.2	32	23	3.1	72	52	2 240
North America	**278**	**16**	**9**	**0.7**	**93**	**9**	**2.0**	**75**	**74**	**19 490**
Canada	26.6	14	7	0.7	96	7.3	1.7	77	77	16 760
United States	251.4	16	9	0.8	92	9.7	2.0	75	74	19 780

▸ Source: Population Reference Bureau, Inc., *1990 World Population Data Sheet*, Washington, D.C.: Population Reference Bureau, Inc., 1990.

FOCUS

1. Which of the Central American countries is the best off and which is the worst off economically? Explain.
2. Using the present population data, the birth and death rates, and the infant mortality and total fertility rates, estimate the population of Costa Rica in the year 2020.

▶ Political History

Despite the name "Rich Coast," Costa Rica lacked the gold and silver that the Spanish *conquistadores* desired, so it was generally ignored after its discovery by Columbus in 1502. Since there were very few local native Indians, Spanish settlers had to work the land themselves. The settlers farmed the interior plateau and had little contact with the outside world. They lived in poverty, and there were few differences among

Figure 1
COSTA RICA

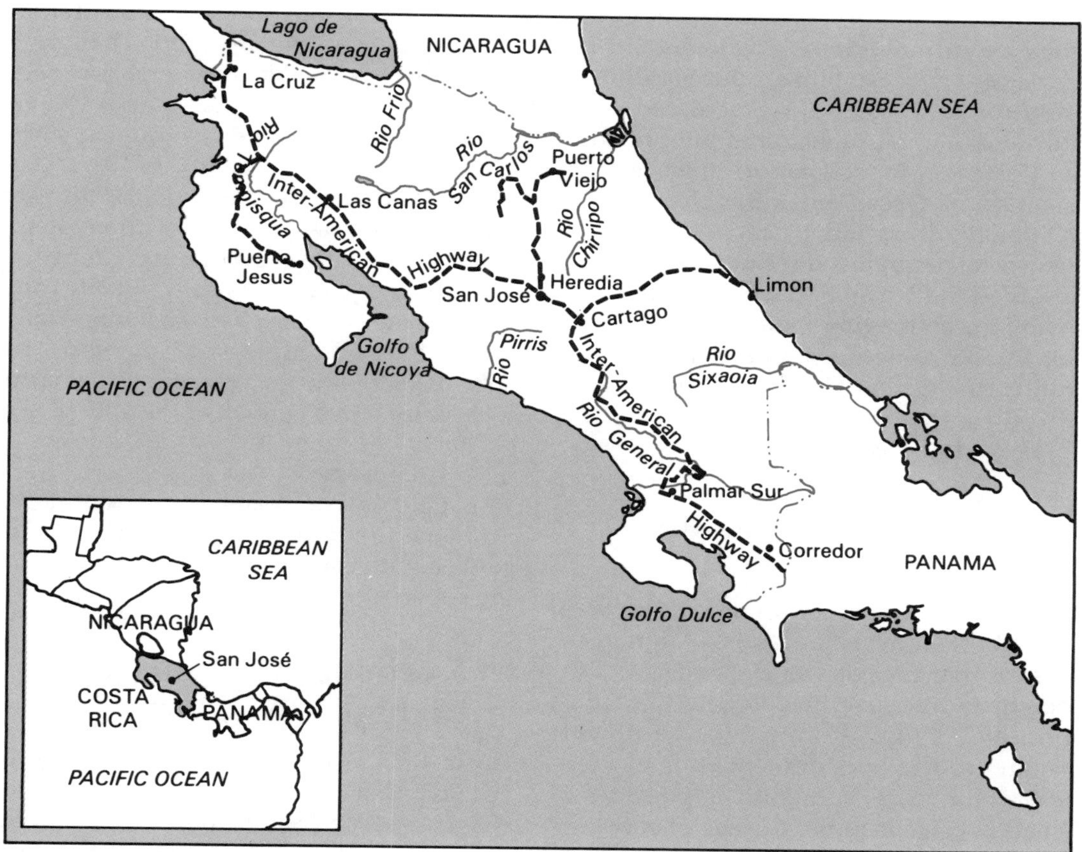

them. These factors, according to some historians, contributed to the tradition of democracy that emerged.

Along with much of Central America, Costa Rica gained its independence from Spain in 1821. After a brief period of membership in the United Provinces of Central America, Costa Rica became a separate republic in 1838. Following a half century of disorder and dictators, Costa Rica held the first truly democratic election in Central America, followed rapidly by free and compulsory education for all children. After this event, democracy in Costa Rica was interrupted on only two occasions. In 1948, José Figueres Ferrer led a successful civilian uprising to depose Rafael Calderón Guardia, who had refused to accept the presidential election results. Figueres restored constitutional government, abolished the country's armed forces, and confirmed Costa Rican neutrality as a foreign policy. Figueres, who became president of Costa Rica (1953–1957 and 1970–1974), tried to create a "modern welfare state." The giant American-controlled United Fruit Company agreed to give Costa Rica one-third of its profits, which encouraged the government to become heavily involved in promoting the growth of industry.

Following the victory of the left-wing Sandinistas in Nicaragua in 1979, Costa Rica's neutrality was threatened. In its attempts to "destabilize" the Sandinista government, including aid to the "Contras," the United States put pressure on Costa Rica for assistance. However, the election of Oscar Arias Sánchez of the National Liberation party resulted in a return to neutrality. President Arias was awarded the Nobel Peace Prize in 1987 for his efforts in bringing about a "peace plan" for Central America. Rafael Angel Calderon of the Social Christian Unity party (PUSC) succeeded Arias as president in 1990 in a free election.

▶ The Political System

The Executive

Costa Rica's system of division of powers and checks and balances is designed to ensure that no one person or group can dominate the government. The Constitution of 1949 gave the executive power mainly to the president, who is elected every four years. Voting is compulsory for all adult citizens under the age of seventy. Failure to vote is punishable by fines. The president and two vice-presidents must receive at least forty percent of the votes cast, or a runoff election is held between the two leading candidates. The president appoints the cabinet.

The president's power is limited in a number of ways. The president's veto power over legislation can be over-ridden by the Assembly, and the Supreme Court can review the president's administrative acts. More importantly, the president is limited to one term of four years, although he or she may be re-elected after being out of office for eight years. The president has no military force because a national army has been outlawed.

The Legislature

The unicameral Legislative Assembly consists of fifty-seven members who are elected by proportional representation every four years. The constitution limits the Assembly's power. A considerable variety of parties exists, but two parties have tended to dominate the government since 1948.

The Supreme Electoral Tribunal, consisting of three magistrates and three alternates selected by the Supreme Court for six-year staggered terms has complete control over the elections. This guarantees fairness. Party campaign expenses are subsidized by the government if the party wins at least five percent of the vote.

The Judiciary

The Legislative Assembly appoints a Supreme Court of seventeen judges, who serve eight-year terms, usually after gaining experience on the court of appeal.

▶ Freedom and Human Rights

Costa Rica is usually referred to as the country that best exemplifies maximum civil and political rights to its people. Freedoms of speech, press, religion, and assembly have not been curtailed in recent times. People are free to join labour movements, bargain collectively, and strike. Equal wages must be paid for equal work, regardless of race or gender. Illness, disability, maternity, and old age are covered by social insurance.

▶ Democracy and Costa Rica

Costa Rica has problems. It has a substantial foreign debt, an expensive social welfare program, a sensitive relationship with the United States, a high sales tax that falls heavily on the poor, and a rising unemployment rate. However, its democratic features have survived, despite the turmoil that exists elsewhere in Central America.

The following observations help explain why democracy has continued to prosper in Costa Rica. Firstly, Costa Rica has been isolated from world affairs. Secondly, because it lacked both a subservient non-White population and a large landowner class, more small- and medium-sized farming operations were created, which led to increased economic equality. As a result, the country tends to have few class and racial divisions. Thirdly, since the government has promoted education, the population is more literate than the people of other Central American countries. Fourthly, Costa Rican governments have been consistently committed to the social welfare of the inhabitants and have taken an active role in the economy and in the redistribution of income.

In addition, authoritarianism has been prevented partly by limiting and then by abolishing the military. As a result, Costa Rica has a tradition of politics of consensus. Accommodation, participation, and free expression have tended to defuse antagonisms. Human rights are respected, and political competition is open, so that the grievances that plague many other countries are not a problem in Costa Rica. Finally, Costa Rica's traditional neutrality has helped to keep the country out of disputes and wars and the problems that accompany them.

Costa Rican President Oscar Arias Sánchez
Cindy Karp, Time *Magazine*

▶ Profile: Oscar Arias Sánchez

Arias served as president of Costa Rica from 1986 to 1990. He was born into one of Costa Rica's wealthiest and most influential coffee-growing families in 1941. He read widely as a child, especially during periods of debilitating asthma. In his high-school yearbook, Arias stated that he wanted to become president of Costa Rica. While studying at Boston University, he became fascinated by the Nixon-Kennedy presidential debates and Kennedy became his role model. He went on to further studies in economics and political science in Great Britain and became a professor of political science at the University of Costa Rica in 1969.

Arias became known for his accomplished literary style and was directly involved with politics in 1970 when José Figueres Ferrer returned to the presidency. Arias served on the government's economic council and then became minister of planning, where he directed programs that promoted economic growth in Costa Rica. He was elected to the Legislative Assembly in 1978. As a leading social democrat, he represented Costa Rica at meetings of the Socialist International throughout this period.

Arias captured his party's nomination for president and won the 1986 election as a "peace candidate." Within Costa Rica, Arias tried to promote the growth of consumer and producer co-operatives as alternatives to private and government enterprise and as a way of increasing grassroots democracy through direct citizen involvement. However, he had difficulty in solving Costa Rica's economic problems.

Arias's success was mainly in foreign policy. The United States continued to undermine the Nicaraguan Sandinista government by supporting the contras, a rebel force that occasionally operated from Costa Rican soil. While Arias criticized Sandinista policies, he expelled the contras from Costa Rica, a policy that angered the United States.

Arias's chief contribution to humanity came in a "peace summit" meeting with Honduras, Guatemala, Nicaragua, and El Salvador in August 1987. The leaders approved the Arias plan, which was based on periodic free elections; an end to outside military aid to insurrectionist forces, including the contras; ceasefire negotiations; amnesties; reductions in armed forces; and the promotion of democracy. Despite opposition from the United States, the plan provided the basis for peace in the region, particularly in Nicaragua. Arias was awarded the Nobel Peace Prize for his 1987 peace plan, which he accepted on behalf of all Central America.

Former President Arias accepts congratulations for his Nobel Peace Prize.
Bill Gentile/SIPA Press

The following is an excerpt from an interview with President Arias as he left office in 1990:

Q. You won the Nobel Peace Prize for your Central American pacification program in 1987. Was the award premature?

A. Well, most people reacted very favorably. I know of only a few Reagan advisers who didn't like it. . . . The Nobel Prize helped us a lot because we captured the attention of the world, and it became more difficult for the Reagan Administration to continue with its war policies in the area.

Q. Costa Rica still enjoys peace and relative prosperity. What is your secret?

A. That we have no army; that the money we saved when we abolished it in 1948 has been spent on education. I think it stems from the wisdom of our 19th century statesmen, who decided that no project was more important than free and compulsory education for everybody; and also from the decision in the early 1940s to build a welfare state and not a garrison state.

Q. Less than a week before leaving office, you signed an agreement with major private banks wiping out 64%, or about $1 billion, of Costa Rica's private foreign debt. You must have been very persuasive.

A. It was the best agreement ever signed with crediting banks. [U.S. Deputy Treasury Secretary] David Mulford told me that it was due to two factors: the success of Costa Rica's economic policy over the past years, which allowed a real growth average of 5% during my administration; and the goodwill earned by Costa Rica with its peace program for Central America, and the desire of the international community to help us more and more. The message is clear: Peace pays.

Source: "Violence Leads to No Solution," *Time*, May 21, 1990.

▶ ZIMBABWE

The name Zimbabwe was derived from ruins called the "Great Zimbabwe," the large stone remnants of an earlier iron-age civilization that flourished before the coming of the Europeans in the 1500s and 1600s. As a British colony in the late 1800s, the area was called Southern Rhodesia, after the British imperialist Cecil Rhodes, who helped defeat the Shona and Ndebele tribes in order to gain control over the region's mineral wealth for Great Britain. Effective rule over the territory fell increasingly into the hands of the White settlers, rather than those of the British government. During the colonial period, the Whites created racial barriers and increased their control over the Blacks by preventing them from establishing labour unions and learning skilled occupations. The Whites also restricted African movement by enacting "Pass" laws.

The White minority dominated Zimbabwe. In 1965, after refusing Great Britain's requests to offer concessions to Black nationalists, Ian Smith's conservative White minority government unilaterally declared its independence from Great Britain. The United Nations sponsored eco-

Figure 2
ZIMBABWE

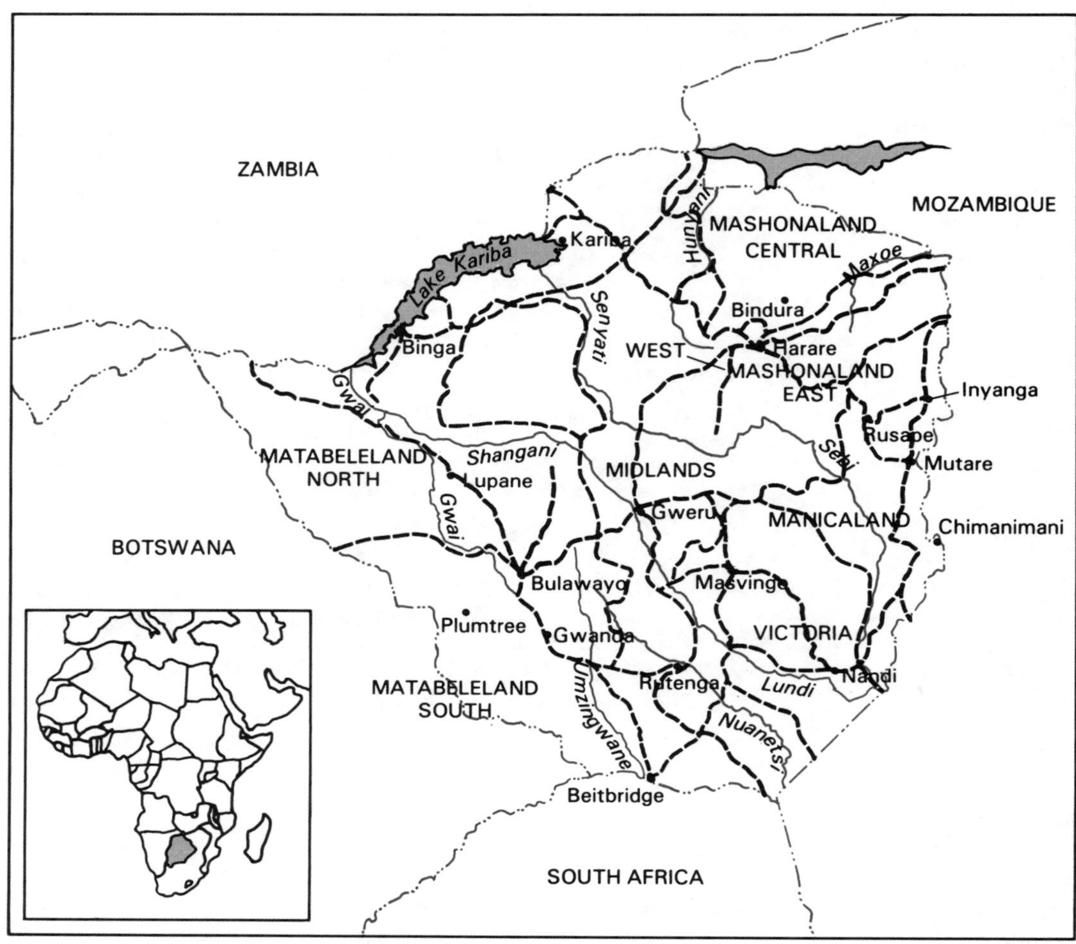

nomic and arms embargoes against Rhodesia, and Zimbabwe nationalists turned to armed struggle in order to achieve Black majority rule. Guerrilla conflict raged throughout the 1970s. The left-wing government of neighbouring Mozambique and other Black states supported the rebels. South Africa supported Rhodesia. Whites began to flee the country at the rate of about 1000 per month in 1977, and the economy suffered.

After many failed attempts at compromise, the two sides reached an agreement at Lancaster House in London in 1979 that led first to a ceasefire and then to an election the next year. Guerrilla groups led by Robert Mugabe, which had enjoyed a loose alliance since 1976, dominated the voting. The moderate party of Joshua Nkomo, the Zimbabwe African People's Union (ZAPU), had Ndebele support and won twenty-three of the eighty seats reserved

Table 3
BASIC DATA—ZIMBABWE

Geography	Area in Square Kilometres: 390 759 Capital (Population): Harare (730 000) Climate: subtropical	**Military**	Number of Armed Forces: 41 000 Military Expenditures (% of Central Government Expenditures): $464 800 000 (6.2%)
People	Ethnic Makeup of Population: 71% Shona; 16% Ndebele; 2% White; 11% others Languages: Official: English; others Spoken: Shona, Ndebele, others Religions: 75% Christian; 24% traditional indigenous; 1% Muslim Adult Literacy Rate: 50%	**Economy**	Currency ($ U.S. Equivalent): 1.72 Zimbabwe dollars = $1 Inflation Rate: 16.2% Natural Resources: gold; chrome ore; coal; copper; nickel; iron ore; silver; asbestos Agriculture: tobacco; corn; sugar; cotton; livestock Industry: mining; steel; textiles
Communication	Televisions: 112 000 Telephones: 214 000 Newspapers: 2	**Foreign Trade**	Imports: $1.2 billion (1987) Exports: $1.4 billion (1987) Main Partners: South Africa 22%; West Germany 8%; United Kingdom 7%
Transportation	Highways—Kilometres: 85 237 Railroads—Kilometres: 2743 Commercial Airports: 2		
Labour Force	35% agricultural; 30% industry and commerce; 20% services, 15% government		

▸ Sources: Dr. Jo Sullivan, *Global Studies: Africa*, 3rd ed. Guilford, Conn.: The Dushkin Publishing Group Inc., 1989.
The Canadian World Almanac and Book of Facts 1990. Global Press, 1989.

for Blacks. Ian Smith's Rhodesian Front won all twenty White seats.

The new government, with self-styled Marxist Robert Mugabe as prime minister, faced formidable economic, social, and political problems. Inter-tribal strife threatened the country. South Africa, a country that was important to Zimbabwe's economy, appeared potentially hostile. Segregation dominated society. As a result, facilities for Africans were inferior, and Whites still controlled over half the land. Yet, if the Whites left in large numbers, the economy would be devastated. In addition, an earlier agreement limited the government's actions by partially protecting the privileged status of Whites. Zimbabwe had to create a government structure to accommodate these factors.

▶ The Political System

Zimbabwe has been independent since 1980, but as circumstances have altered, its system of government has undergone substantial changes. Robert Mugabe has gradually worked closer to his often-stated goal of a one-party state.

The Early Structure

Zimbabwe adopted a parliamentary system in 1980. As in Canada, the prime minister commanded a majority in the House of Assembly. The president had little power and was chosen by an electoral college composed of the members of both houses of Parliament (the forty-member Senate and the 100-member House of Assembly). The prime minister chose the cabinet, mostly

Table 4
EASTERN AFRICA AND ZIMBABWE—BASIC INDICATORS

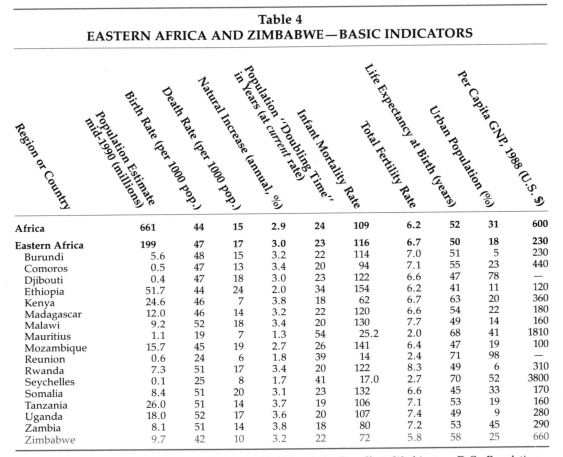

Region or Country	Population Estimate mid-1990 (millions)	Birth Rate (per 1000 pop.)	Death Rate (per 1000 pop.)	Natural Increase (annual, %)	Population "Doubling Time" in Years (at *current* rate)	Infant Mortality Rate	Total Fertility Rate	Life Expectancy at Birth (years)	Urban Population (%)	Per Capita GNP, 1988 (U.S. $)
Africa	**661**	**44**	**15**	**2.9**	**24**	**109**	**6.2**	**52**	**31**	**600**
Eastern Africa	**199**	**47**	**17**	**3.0**	**23**	**116**	**6.7**	**50**	**18**	**230**
Burundi	5.6	48	15	3.2	22	114	7.0	51	5	230
Comoros	0.5	47	13	3.4	20	94	7.1	55	23	440
Djibouti	0.4	47	18	3.0	23	122	6.6	47	78	—
Ethiopia	51.7	44	24	2.0	34	154	6.2	41	11	120
Kenya	24.6	46	7	3.8	18	62	6.7	63	20	360
Madagascar	12.0	46	14	3.2	22	120	6.6	54	22	180
Malawi	9.2	52	18	3.4	20	130	7.7	49	14	160
Mauritius	1.1	19	7	1.3	54	25.2	2.0	68	41	1810
Mozambique	15.7	45	19	2.7	26	141	6.4	47	19	100
Reunion	0.6	24	6	1.8	39	14	2.4	71	98	—
Rwanda	7.3	51	17	3.4	20	122	8.3	49	6	310
Seychelles	0.1	25	8	1.7	41	17.0	2.7	70	52	3800
Somalia	8.4	51	20	3.1	23	132	6.6	45	33	170
Tanzania	26.0	51	14	3.7	19	106	7.1	53	19	160
Uganda	18.0	52	17	3.6	20	107	7.4	49	9	280
Zambia	8.1	51	14	3.8	18	80	7.2	53	45	290
Zimbabwe	9.7	42	10	3.2	22	72	5.8	58	25	660

▸ Source: Population Reference Bureau, Inc., *1990 World Population Data Sheet*, Washington, D.C.: Population Reference Bureau, Inc., 1990.

FOCUS

1. Compare Central American countries to East African countries under the following headings: population increase, wealth, and standard of living.

from the House of Assembly, but occasionally from the Senate. As in most parliamentary systems, the prime minister and cabinet would have to resign if they lost the support of the majority in the Assembly.

In the House of Assembly, Black voters directly elected eighty representatives, whereas twenty members were elected by Whites and the small numbers of Asian and mixed-race voters.

In the White constituencies, candidates were ranked so that if a candidate did not gain a majority in the first vote, additional elections were held until one person obtained a majority. The Black constituencies used proportional representation. People voted for ranked party lists, rather than for individual candidates, and seats were distributed according to the proportion of votes won.

The structure of the Senate reflected the desire to provide for the interests of minorities, especially the Whites and the traditional chiefs. Black MPs selected fourteen senators, and the White MPs chose ten senators. Five more were Shona chiefs, and five were Ndebele chiefs chosen by the chiefs themselves. The prime minister selected the other six. These tended to be elder leaders or representatives of small minorities. In addition, Whites were given an effective veto over changes to the structure of Parliament until 1989.

Changes in the Late 1980s

Robert Mugabe had long ago made it clear that he intended to seek "socialism . . . built on the basis of Marxist-Leninist principles that take account of our historical, cultural, and social experiences."[1] In order to achieve this objective, he favoured a one-party state, partly because multi-party systems in Africa tended to split along tribal lines, which often triggered civil war. A one-party system with mass participation, he believed, was more appropriate to Zimbabwe's needs. It could provide effective representation for all groups, while promoting badly needed national unity and orderly development.

▸ [1]Virginia Curtin Knight, "Zimbabwe A Decade After Independence," *Current History*, May 1990, p. 204.

After the 1980 election, Joshua Nkomo and three other ZAPU members accepted roles in the Mugabe government but were ousted in 1982 for plotting to overthrow the government. The elections of 1985 split along tribal lines, with Mugabe's ZANU obtaining sixty-three seats and Nkomo's ZAPU receiving fifteen seats.

The key change came in December 1987 when the ZANU and ZAPU agreed to merge into one party after years of political wrangling and guerrilla activity in the Ndebele areas of the south. In 1989 the merger was completed. With his new domination of the Assembly and the expiry of the Lancaster House agreement, Mugabe moved to revise the country's political structure. Special White constituencies were eliminated. A new 140-member Assembly was chosen with 120 directly elected members and twenty appointed by the president (in order to deal with minority concerns). The Senate was abolished, and a new executive presidency was established that largely combined the offices of president and prime minister. Mugabe became executive president, and Nkomo accepted a key post in the new government.

▶ Zimbabwe's One-Party State: Two Views

The benefits of a one-party government in Zimbabwe have been frequently debated. In the following excerpts, two authors discuss its strengths and weaknesses. How do the writers justify their viewpoints?

A. Zimbabwe's Accomplishments

The difficulties Zimbabwe faces should not overshadow its accomplishments. First, the success of the war created an unprecedented sense of public confidence in the possibility of developing a democracy. Second, in a short time Zimbabwe has succeeded in providing a minimum of welfare benefits—notably in health and education—to the majority of its people. Finally, Zimbabwe has so far been able to offer to its racially mixed population a peaceful nonracist solution to the bitter conflict between the "two nations." The majority of white citizens remain in the country, although their numbers diminished after independence.

ZANU and Mugabe see the one-party state as the solution for problems of unity and development. If political unity can be fostered, economic growth sustained, and South African aggression and destabilization checked, Zimbabwe can move toward the equitable society promised during the revolutionary struggle.

Source: From *Global Studies: Africa*, 3rd ed., 1989.

B. Get Rid of the Dictators

Our states are still young and fragile, of course. Our populations are still largely illiterate. So, when democratic political competition begins, there is the risk that the electorate will split not according to ideas, but according to ethnic, religious, or regional origin. That is an unquestionable weakness for African societies tempted by the adventure of democratic pluralism. Following independence, the demons of regionalism—egged on by foreign interests—engulfed certain states, and not unimportant ones, in secession and chaos.

Is that any reason to lock ourselves forever into single-party regimentation? While the rest of the world is moving toward greater democracy and more pluralism, can Africa be burdened with institutions that will soon exist nowhere else? Our non-aligned partners in Latin America and in Asia have made considerable progress recently in this respect. . . .

The truth is that, despite our handicaps, our peoples are perfectly capable of taking the shock of democratic pluralism, as long as it is introduced gradually. There have been successful examples of this both north and south of the Sahara. One is Burkina Faso [formerly Upper Volta], the poorest of the poor. Under the regime of Gen. Aboubakar Sangoulé Lamizana in the 1960s and 1970s, political parties contended several times, with no major incidents. Despite dire poverty and a lack of education, and despite ethnic, cultural, linguistic, and religious differences, the peasants of Burkina Faso showed sound political judgment in their choices. . . .

To set up legal and institutional systems that are in tune with the times and more responsive to human aspirations, we have to devise forms of government that guarantee participation for all citizens in the management of public affairs, through the free exchange of opinions. And we must come up with acceptable approaches that make it possible to assume power and, if need be, to leave power without clashes and violence. These goals are all the more imperative because democracy is the driving force behind economic development—an area in which Africa has a long road to travel.

▸ Source: Siradiou Diallo, *Jeune Afrique* in *World Press Review*, May 1989, p. 64.

▶ Profile: Robert Mugabe

A member of the Shona tribe, Mugabe was born in 1924. His father was a carpenter, his mother a teacher. He was educated by Jesuits and became a teacher. In 1950, he attended the South Africa All-Black University of Fort Hare, which was a training ground for Black political leaders. There, he earned the first of his six university degrees. (His degrees are in education, administration, economics, and law.) He later said: "My hatred and revulsion for the colonial system had started at Fort Hare, and . . . it grew. I decided I would fight to overthrow it."[2]

Throughout the 1950s, the involvement of Mugabe in Black nationalist activities increased. In 1960, he joined Joshua Nkomo's organization as information minister but bolted from the party and helped to form ZANU in 1963. As a result of his organizational activities, Mugabe was first restricted and then imprisoned. He remained in detention from 1964 to 1974. When his only child, a four-year-old son, died in Ghana in 1966, the White-dominated government refused him permission to attend the funeral. During this time, he earned advanced degrees by correspondence, tutored fellow prisoners, and became a Marxist.

After his release, Mugabe turned to armed struggle. He directed ZANU's guerrilla raids from Mozambique into Rhodesia with support from China. He consistently resisted the Rhodesian government's attempts to settle with Black moderates in what Mugabe regarded as token and inadequate reforms. He instead held out for full majority rule and continued to co-operate with Nkomo's ZAPU in the Patriotic Front.

In 1979, Mugabe agreed to some protection of the White minority for a ten-year period and to supervised elections. This ended the fighting. When his party won the election, his career as Zimbabwe's first prime minister (1980–1988) and executive president (1988–) followed. As prime minister he faced the enormous tasks of reconciliation and nation-building.

Despite his Marxist views, Mugabe is generally viewed as having been cautious and pragmatic in his approach to power. The government has not forcibly nationalized companies and has instead gradually tried to increase its ownership of some key private enterprises. It has also attempted to attract more foreign investment. There have been substantial improvements in agriculture and in public health and welfare programs. He has made peace with the White community and has walked a fine line in his relations with South Africa, on which land-locked Zimbabwe depends for trade and transportation links to the outside world. At the same time, he has been a leader in supporting other neighbouring Black countries, especially Mozambique, in their struggles. Mugabe became chairperson of the **Non-Aligned Movement** in 1986 and is generally regarded as having great personal integrity and no interest in amassing personal wealth.

▸ [2]Peter M. Gareffa, ed., *Newsmakers 88*. Detroit: Gale Research Inc. Book Tower, p. 291.

▶ CONCLUSION

Although the less developed world is quite diverse, it generally has high birth rates, relies on agriculture, suffers mass poverty, and endures marked economic inequalities. United Nations' official Paul Hoffman once wrote: "Everyone knows an underdeveloped country when they see one. They are characterized by poverty, with beggars in the cities and villages eking [out] a bare subsistence in the rural areas. They usually have insufficient roads and railways . . . few hospitals . . . most of its people cannot read or write . . . many have isolated islands of wealth . . . and exports to other countries usually consist almost entirely of raw materials. . . .''

What government system can best resolve these problems? The previous discussion has outlined how two less developed countries have restructured their governments. Is a one-party state the better solution or can democracy succeed?

APPLYING YOUR KNOWLEDGE

1. How are less developed and more developed countries similar and how are they different in their political problems and tasks?
2. a) To what extent is it possible for the rest of Latin America to copy Costa Rica's approach? Why?
   b) Would it be desirable? Why?
3. a) To what extent is the form of government in Zimbabwe an outgrowth of its struggle for independence?
   b) To what extent does it reflect the problem of ethnic differences?
4. Evaluate Mugabe's idea of a one-party system for Zimbabwe. What are its strengths and weaknesses?
5. What factors have contributed to Mugabe's success as a political leader?
6. a) Compare the political systems of Zimbabwe and Costa Rica. How are they similar and how are they different? What factors account for those similarities and differences?
   b) Compare the careers of Arias and Mugabe in terms of background, goals, methods, and accomplishments.
7. To what extent do you think that these two political systems are ''appropriate'' to their respective societies? Explain the judgments that led you to your conclusions.

FURTHER RESEARCH

1. What elements of Costa Rica's government are similar to those of the other countries studied in this text. Make a chart.
2. Choose five countries at random from each of Latin America, Africa, and Asia. Using the most recent figures available, compare the three areas on the basis of birth rate, death rate, natural increase rate, infant mortality rate, fertility rate, percent of urban population, and per capita Gross National Product (GNP).
   a) What conclusions can you draw from these data?
   b) What limitations do your conclusions have?
   c) How do your conclusions compare with those of other students (who have chosen different countries)?
3. a) Investigate what has happened recently in Costa Rica and Zimbabwe. To what extent have conditions changed? Summarize your conclusions in an essay.

b) Find out more about the contra war in Nicaragua and the guerrilla war that led to Zimbabwe's independence. In what ways were they similar and different?

4. Choose a less developed country and compare its political system to that of Costa Rica or Zimbabwe.

CHAPTER 5 OVERVIEW

MAJOR POLITICAL SYSTEMS: A SUMMARY

This chapter reviews the major differences between authoritarian and democratic beliefs and explores the political values in Saudi Arabia to indicate the wide range of political systems that exist outside the Western world. After examining the importance of studying each country's political ideology, the chapter summarizes the recent political changes in the world; conjectures about the future of communism; and discusses the growing importance of Muslim fundamentalism, multinational corporations, and environmental political parties and organizations. It concludes with a discussion of the importance of understanding different ideologies and beliefs before rejecting them and the significance of keeping an open mind.

▶ OBJECTIVES

After reading this chapter, you should be able to:

- ▶ discuss the recent political changes in the world
- ▶ work in groups to design your own ideal political system
- ▶ research and present an oral report to the class
- ▶ appreciate the importance of maintaining an open mind when evaluating politics
- ▶ hypothesize about future political directions
- ▶ understand that the values of the Western world are not held by every country

▶ KEY TERMS

hereditary monarch
Balkans
Greens
multinational corporation
Shiite Muslims

CHAPTER

5 MAJOR POLITICAL SYSTEMS: A SUMMARY

Our study of political ideologies has concentrated on the relationship between people and their leaders. In an ideal democracy, government functions in obedience to the desires of the governed. In an authoritarian state, however, government functions in obedience to the desires of the rulers, and the people must respect and obey this authority.

In the real world, governments lie somewhere between the two ends of this spectrum. Even the most democratic government demands a certain obedience to authority for the protection of everyone, whereas in an authoritarian state the government must take care not to demand more of its citizens than they are prepared to give.

We should remember that the concepts of authoritarianism and democracy that we have been examining were formulated in Western Europe or by the descendants of Europeans in other parts of the world. These concepts fit most easily when we examine governments influenced by Western civilization. Although it is useful to analyse all governments in relation to these concepts, it must be done with care to avoid applying inappropriate categories to non-Western governments.

Let us briefly consider one example of this potential danger. Saudi Arabia is ruled by a **hereditary monarch** assisted by an extensive network of hereditary princes. Even so, any male citizen can approach the monarch directly with a personal petition. Certain times and places are set aside to allow people access to the ruler, who is required by custom to listen to the lengthy recital of his subjects' needs and might well decide to investigate the matter personally and remedy the situation.

On the surface, it appears as though the Saudi citizen has more effective access to his government than does the citizen of Canada, who has difficulty getting the attention of government clerks. However, Saudi women have no right to launch political petitions, and the monarchy is not required to do what the male citizens ask. In addition, the monarch and his princes make all major government decisions without consulting the people. Some analysts suggest that an understanding of Saudi government can better be gained by examining the traditions of desert nomads, from which the political system came, than by comparing it to Western forms of government. The Saudi government, they suggest, is a traditional government superficially adapted to twentieth-century conditions.

Many Third World governments need to be examined individually, in the light of their history and their present political and economic situation in the world. A study of many African countries, for example, should probably pay attention to tribal alliances that hold them together or threaten to split them apart. Sometimes, Third World countries can adopt Western ideologies (see Case Studies 4, 16, and 24), but often they try to avoid being identified with any of them.

How, then, can studying ideologies help us when we are examining governments? In the first place, an ideology explains the basis on which all governments exist. An examination of ideologies introduces us to the study of government at its fundamental level. Once we have thought about government in general, we are in a better position to examine specific governments.

In the second place, the study of ideologies can provide some tools in problem solving. Suppose that we have studied a particular government and discovered that large groups of people are so frustrated with the way the system operates that they might rise up against the government and overthrow it. To what extent does the democratic ideal of citizen participation in government offer a potential solution in this particular situation? Is the solution appropriate, given the circumstances and the nature of the country in question?

Ideologies can also be used to evaluate our own governments. Assuming that no government is ever a perfect expression of the ideology it sets forth, political ideals can be used to suggest ways for improvement. Ideologies give us a target at which to aim.

Finally, a careful study of ideologies helps us to identify our most deeply held values and enables us to maintain or change our standards depending on the norms embraced by the people of other countries throughout the world.

This brings us to the most recent changes in the world. In response to popular demands, country after country has cast off dictatorships in favour of multi-party systems and free elections. This revolution occurred gradually in Latin America, which has finally rid itself of generals and military juntas in favour of democratic governments. The process began in Ecuador in 1979, spread to Peru (1980), and then emerged in Bolivia (1982), Argentina (1983), Uruguay (1984), and Brazil (1985). Since then, several other countries in Central America, as well as Chile and Paraguay, have experienced democratic triumphs. As of 1991 Cuba is the only country remaining defiantly communist and retaining a non-compromising one-party state system in Latin America.

In Black Africa, the trend against Marxist one-party states and in favour of multi-party democratic systems has become popular, most particularly in former Portuguese colonies, where Soviet aid became the major prop of native communist governments. Soviet assistance has dried up everywhere, and the former client states are adopting Western-style governments and seeking subsidies from the capitalist world. Kenya, a non-Marxist authoritarian country with a rigid one-party government is an exception. It insists on retaining its traditional system. Its intimate links with the British Commonwealth and fairly good civil rights record have enabled it to defy the democratic trend, at least for the present.

In East-Central Europe and the **Balkans**, an area until recently dominated by the Soviet Union, the collapse of communist, one-party, totalitarian governments was unexpected, sudden, and convincing. It was associated with the Soviet Union's weakness caused by the unsettling economic consequences of *perestroika* (restructuring of the Soviet economy) under Gorbachev. By 1990, every country in the Soviet bloc — East Germany, Czechoslovakia, Poland, Hungary, Romania, and Bulgaria — had experienced grass roots democratic revolutions that easily overthrew the incumbent communist regimes. Only in Romania and Bulgaria did the former communists retain a toehold, but at the heavy price of abandoning their communist labels and democratizing their party programs to permit opposition groups to compete in the political marketplace. Only Albania, an independent Marxist state, has thus far refused to abandon its dictatorial and repressive communist ways.

An important consequence of the recent peoples' revolution was the East Germans' wish to reunify with West Germany. This

About 300 000 people crowd a Leipzig street in a huge pro-democracy demonstration on the eve of the election of the new East German leader.
Canapress Photo Service

impulse was so powerful that neither the Western allies nor the Soviet Union, with its 350 000 troops stationed on East German soil, could stop or slow German reunification. Total reunion became a reality in October 1990.

A vitally important by-product of the worldwide democratic revolution has been the threatened fragmentation of the Soviet Union, where dozens of nationalistic and numerous religious forces play a great part. Of the fifteen Soviet republics, only one is overwhelmingly Russian in nationality. The other republics are inhabited by a vast number of non-Russian peoples. Combined, they make up nearly one-half of the U.S.S.R.'s total population. Secession has reared its head in the three Baltic republics of Lithuania, Latvia, and Estonia, as well as in some of the Soviet Union's Asiatic republics inhabited by Christians and Muslims. The latter are caught in the grips of a worldwide Muslim fundamentalist revival. Whatever the outcome of this struggle, the Soviet Union will for some time to come be unable to exert its global power as it had for the past few decades.

Still another recent development, especially in the advanced industrial states, has been the growing power and activities of environmental groups. People realized that unchecked industrialism was polluting our bodies of water, making our air toxic, and rendering our land unusable. Some experts warn that life as we know it might soon terminate, unless the authorities do something to halt harmful economic activities.

This crisis has spawned many powerful political groups in all Western countries. Although they are called by different names in different places, they are generally labelled **Greens**. It is possible that in the near future these environmental reformers might attempt to seize the political initiative in their respective states and force governments to rectify the damages done to nature in the name of "progress."

About 3500 people gather on Ottawa's Parliament Hill to celebrate the twentieth anniversary of the first Earth Day.
Canapress Photo Service

When it comes to a combination of conservation, responsible economic management, and effective government, the world has an excellent model to follow. Sweden's government is in the forefront of the fight against pollution and its harmful by-products. Jonathan Power, a London-based journalist, wrote that in Göteborg, a major Swedish port and industrial centre with a population of nearly half a million, "there are no expressways slicing up the neighbourhoods. Transportation is by fast, non-polluting streetcars first, bicycles second, and cars third. . . . There are no slums. Nor are there any homeless, and there is barely any unemployment." Power described Sweden's government as "capitalist vigour at its best, capitalism without vulgarity, with a social conscience and an artistic vision."[1] The governments of capitalist democracies the world over could learn excellent lessons from the Swedish government, which simply refuses to surrender to the profit motive. Observers would find similar attitudes and conditions in the other Scandinavian countries of Norway, Denmark, and Finland.

The developed industrial world is apparently on the threshold of adopting new political practices, based upon a new political ideology. On the eve of the Industrial Revolution, the contemporary ideology proclaimed that the government that governed least, governed best. In practice, this meant that governments confined their activities to political and diplomatic topics and permitted the economy to function without interference. The abuses of industrialism forced governments in the nineteenth and twentieth centuries to regulate the worst offences of the economic sector. More recently, **multinational corporations** have begun to influence governments. These companies have unlimited finances, control the resources of poor countries, and lobby successfully in the larger countries. These corporate giants, in fact, behave like sovereign governments. The time may not be far off when multinational corporations might openly force the world's governments to do their economic bidding, based upon the belief that the economic experts employed by the multinational corporations know how to govern a state best.

The recent spread of another political ideology further clouds the future. When the Ayatollah Khomeini, the spiritual leader of the **Shiite Muslims** in Iran overthrew the Shah in 1979, he revived an old ideology. Iran became a theocracy and eliminated the Shah's extensive Westernization measures. Today, Iran is governed by mullahs, or religious leaders, who conduct the affairs of state along strict Muslim fundamentalist principles.

According to this ideology, religious authorities in Muslim states should regulate the political, economic, social, and moral activities of the people. Iran has tried to export this way of life to other parts of the Islamic world. It has fought a long, bitter, and bloody war with Iraq. (Although Iraq's 1990 seizure of Kuwait was motivated by political and economic factors, Muslim solidarity poses additional problems in this area.) In Lebanon, there has been escalating fighting among ethnic and religious factions. In the Gulf states, there have been riots and large losses of life in holy shrines such as Mecca.

The fundamental religious ideology guiding political affairs in Muslim states has important consequences for world prosperity and peace. Muslim countries control most of the world's petroleum supplies. Should the Shiite fundamentalists seize control of the oil-rich Arab states, then it is not too far-fetched to envision a stoppage of fuel deliveries to Western countries that enjoy friendly relations with Israel, a country ideologically opposed to the Muslim fundamentalists. The world might re-experience the events of the first Arab oil embargo of 1973. How would the West react to a second major disruption of its economic well-being caused by regions possessing an entirely different ideology?

In order to accept or reject these ideologies, it is essential that we first understand them. This entails keeping an open mind, learning about contemporary world affairs, analysing the issues, and separating fact from opinion. It is equally important that we understand the beliefs, practices, and institutions of our own country. It is difficult to chart future directions without knowing where we have been.

▸ [1]Jonathan Power, "Who Will Get the Peace Dividend? Make Civilization, Not War," *World Press Review*, June 1990, pp. 21–22.

APPLYING YOUR KNOWLEDGE

1. Choose one of the following countries and present a report to the class that briefly outlines its political structure and what you consider to be its major strengths: Switzerland, Germany, the People's Republic of China, Yugoslavia, Japan, or a country of your choice.
2. Imagine that Canada has adopted a totalitarian form of government. Write a fictional account of the life of a typical grade 12 student under this totalitarian regime. Remember to include some of its benefits and disadvantages. Two sources of information to aid you are James D. Forman, *Fascism*, Chapter 1, New York: Dell, 1974 and George Orwell, *Nineteen Eighty-Four*, New York: Harcourt Brace, 1949.
3. Totalitarian leaders would argue that their systems of government are superior to democracy because they act more quickly and effectively in times of emergency. Prepare for a debate on this topic.
4. a) Write an essay explaining which aspects of Canada's political system you agree with and which aspects you would like to change. Explain your selection.
   b) If you would like to make changes, what could you do to promote them?
5. Divide into small groups and design your own ideal political system. Your answer should include a discussion of how decisions are made, how the decision-makers are chosen, what rights people should have, and how these rights can be protected. You might also design a flag, write a national anthem with appropriate music, or decide upon a suitable currency. Explain your choices.
6. Do multi-party systems and free elections necessarily guarantee individual rights? Explain.
7. In your view, will the world integrate under one major philosophy, or will it splinter into interest groups, as before? Explain.

CHAPTER 6 OVERVIEW

AN INTRODUCTION TO ECONOMIC SYSTEMS

This chapter introduces the importance of economic systems and discusses the three most important economic questions that each country must answer: What should be produced? How should it be produced? How should these goods be divided among the people? There are four ways of answering these questions: by traditional methods, through central direction, by the market forces of supply and demand, and through a mixture of central planning and the market economy. The chapter examines the traditional economy through the use of primary documents that outline how the Inuit lived. It concludes with a discussion of such economic terms and concepts as GNP, capital, and global interdependence.

▶ OBJECTIVES

After reading this chapter, you should be able to:

- ▶ understand the basic concepts of economics
- ▶ distinguish among the various types of economic systems
- ▶ evaluate primary documents
- ▶ analyse statistical charts and graphs
- ▶ explain GNP, the importance of scarcity and productivity, and the extent of global economic interdependence
- ▶ discuss the significance of the three basic economic questions

▶ KEY TERMS

scarcity
traditional economy
market economy
centrally planned economy
productivity
Gross National Product
interdependence

AN INTRODUCTION TO ECONOMIC SYSTEMS

Every day we make hundreds of economic decisions that affect our own lives and the lives of thousands of people we don't even know. Did you have cereal or eggs for breakfast? Did you watch television last night or go to a movie? What clothes did you wear to school today?

If you chose eggs, then in some small way you have encouraged farmers to raise chickens rather than plant cereal crops. By going to the movies, you contributed money to the theatre owner, the movie producer, the actors, the ushers, and probably to the popcorn and soft drink industries.

Similarly, we are affected by the economic decisions of others, which are beyond our personal control. The construction of a large shopping mall in the suburbs might undercut your family's downtown business and result in bankruptcy and the loss of your car and home. An increase in the price of gasoline might reduce your summer trips to the cottage and lead to the purchase of a wood-burning stove.

Besides affecting personal affairs, economic issues constitute an important part of most political decisions. Should the government delay repairing roads in order to reduce taxes? How can unemployment be reduced and inflation lowered? Can working conditions be improved? Are welfare payments necessary? What role should the government play in the economy? The answers to such questions are extremely important not only in themselves but also because, as history has shown, economic depression and unemployment have contributed to discontent, revolution, and wars.

▶ SCARCITY

Despite a rapid improvement in the standard of living in the Western world during the last century, most people still do not have everything they desire. You might find, for example, that when you look at your own bank account, you do not have enough money to buy a CD player or to purchase a new wardrobe. In other words, when it comes to satisfying all your desires, you don't have enough money. There are never enough available resources to satisfy everyone's demands. This scarcity is a fundamental fact of economics — it is the fact from which the study of economics originates. According to one popular definition, economics "is the science that investigates problems arising from the **scarcity** of resources and goods that can be used to satisfy human wants. It studies how people allocate and develop their scarce resources

Figure 6–1
THE PROBLEM OF SCARCITY

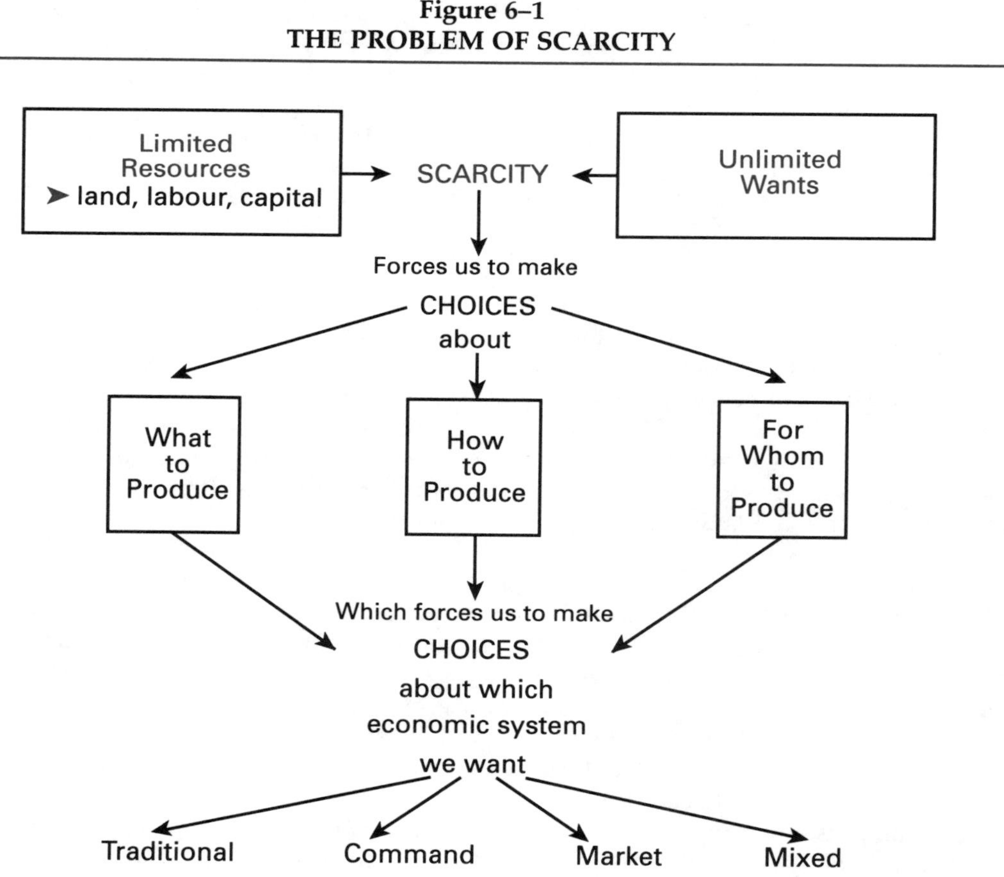

‣ Source: Adapted from P. Saunders, L. Silk, and A.H. MacDonald, *The World of Economics*, 2nd Cdn. ed. Toronto: McGraw-Hill Ryerson Limited, 1979, p. 24.

to satisfy their wants and needs in a way that is compatible with the basic values of their societies.''[1]

Scarcity is, of course, a relative term. For many people in Asia, Africa, and South America, it can mean not having enough food to eat, whereas for many North Americans, it can simply mean not having a video cassette recorder. Most Canadians have the basic necessities of life (food, shelter, and clothes); what they desire are more consumer goods, such as stereos, cameras, stylish clothes, and automobiles. Because of the discrepancy between these desires and the resources necessary to supply them, people must choose which goods they want. Hence, economics is also called the science of choice.

[1] P. Saunders, L. Silk, and A.H. MacDonald, *The World of Economics*, 2nd Cdn. ed., Scarborough: McGraw-Hill Ryerson, 1979, p. 24.

▶ BASIC ECONOMIC QUESTIONS

To satisfy their wants, people must decide how best to use their time and energy, what to purchase, how much money to save for future needs, and how to increase their incomes. Similarly, because no society can avoid the problems created by the scarcity of resources, each country must decide how its limited resources can best be used to meet its needs. Every society must confront these three questions:

1. *What goods should be produced?* Should we grow wheat, manufacture machinery, educate the populace, or defend the country?

Figure 6–2
THE SCIENCE OF CHOICE

- 2. *How should these goods be produced?* By what people, using which resources and what techniques, will goods be produced? Who should farm? Who will work in the factories? Should we grow wheat with few people and many machines, or should we use more people and machinery, but less land?
- 3. *How much should everyone get of what is produced?* In Canada, there are not enough homes for every family. Who should have them? Should a few people receive most of the goods, or should the country's resources be divided evenly?

Canada, Sweden, the U.S.S.R., Cuba—indeed, every country in the world—must solve the three basic economic problems of "what," "how," and "how much." The institutions and practices that each country establishes to meet these questions form an economic system. Although many methods have been used in the past to organize an economy, three broad categories can be distinguished: economies run by tradition, economies run by central direction, and economies run by the market. Although none of these three types exists in pure, undiluted form, it is useful to examine the workings of each system.

In traditional economic systems (such as practised in many tribal societies), the customs and natural environment of the people determine how society will function. To the question of what to produce, the **traditional economy** answers, "produce what has always been produced." Similarly, a traditional economy solves the question of how by replying, "as we have always done it." Children, for example, are expected to follow in their parents' footsteps. The distribution of goods is also determined by customs and force of habit.

The **market economy**, on the other hand, solves the problems of production and distribution by allowing individuals to make their own economic decisions. In this system—also called private enterprise or capitalism — the country's resources are privately owned and government does not intervene in the economy. (See Chapter 7.)

In a **centrally planned economy** — often called a socialist, communist, or command system — the country's resources are owned and controlled by the government, which makes all major economic decisions. (See Chapter 8.)

No society relies exclusively on the traditional, central direction, or market system, although most societies depend more heavily on one type than on the other two. In most modern industrial countries, the market and the centrally planned systems have merged into a hybrid form called the mixed economy. (See Chapter 9.) In Canada, for example, the country's resources are generally privately owned, but the government often intervenes in the economy to try to rectify such social ills as unemployment and poverty.

While it is useful to establish categories, it is not an easy task to label the different economic systems existing in the world today. In the real world, economies are complex and dynamic; every country's economic system has undergone tremendous changes over the last century. Moreover, capitalism in Canada is not the same as capitalism in Japan, the United States, or Great Britain, and Cuban communism differs from Chinese communism. Finally, the values or ideology of each economic system affect all aspects of a society, tending to become confused with politics and political ideologies. It is impossible to completely separate political systems from economic systems.

Before examining the problems and economic issues more closely associated with industrialized countries, let us first examine how traditional societies decide the three basic economic questions.

▶ THE TRADITIONAL ECONOMY: THE INUIT

In traditional economies, time-tested beliefs and practices, based on knowledge and adaptation to the natural environment, answer the three basic economic questions. Traditions and customs are the result of generations of trial and error and are deeply rooted in the culture's history. Most traditional economies are found in Africa and Latin America. The Canadian Inuit's economy was also largely based upon traditional practices. Although the Inuit's culture is rapidly changing because of the growth of White culture, we need not go back too far in Inuit history to witness the workings of a traditional economy.

The land of the Inuit stretches north of the treeline across the top of North America from Alaska to Greenland. There are about

Figure 6–3
INUIT GROUPS

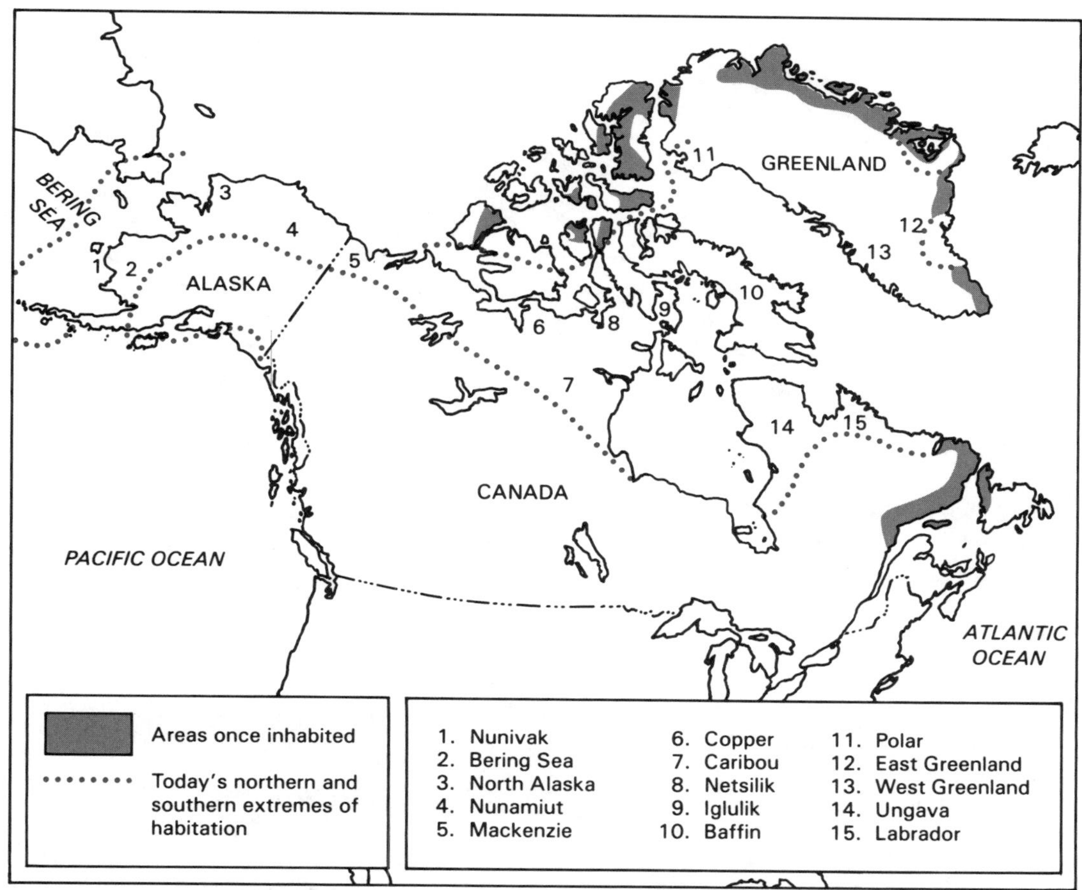

▸ Source: Adapted from Heather Smith Siska, *People of the Ice*. Vancouver: Douglas & McIntyre Ltd., 1980, pp. 6–8.

100 000 Inuits in the world. Those living in Canada number approximately 25 000. The most northerly part of their habitat is the Arctic, which is a cold polar desert, covered with snow for nine months of the year. Temperatures reach −60°C. Winters are long and cold, and summers are short. The growing season in the most southerly regions is sometimes only forty days. The topography is characterized by massive icebergs, glaciers, mountainous islands, and deep-cut fiords. Farther south, rolling plains and treeless tundra are found.

▶ What to Produce

The geography of the Inuit habitat is so severe that the "what" question stresses basic needs of food, clothing, and shelter. The following eyewitness account of the Inuit in 1913 illustrates how the people decided the three economic questions.

WHAT TO PRODUCE: THE SEAL OR THE CARIBOU

The Noahanirgmiut [no-a-ha-NEERG-me-ut] were still living on seal meat and were making no attempt to kill any of the numerous caribou that were continually migrating past . . . [they] had never hunted caribou on the ice and had not considered it possible. It would in fact be a fairly hopeless thing for them to try it; and while no doubt some of them might occasionally secure an animal, they would waste so much time that the number of pounds [kilograms] of meat they obtained in a week's hunt that way would be but a small fraction of the amount of seal meat they might have secured in the same time. Besides that, this is the season which the Eskimo give up to the accumulation of blubber for the coming year. . . . By getting seals in the spring . . . they secure an agreeable article of diet for the coming autumn and provide themselves as well with a sort of insurance against hard luck in the fall hunt. Each family will in the spring be able to lay away from three to seven bags of oil. Such a bag consists of the whole skin of the common seal. The animal has been skinned through the mouth in such a way that the few necessary openings in the skin can be easily sewed up or tied up with a thong. This makes a bag which will hold about three hundred pounds [140 kg] of blubber, so that a single family's store of oil for the fall will run from nine hundred [400 kg] to two thousand pounds [900 kg].

Source: This excerpt and the two following are from Vilhjalmur Stefansson, *My Life with the Eskimo*. New York: The Macmillan Company, 1913, pp. 264–265, as they appeared in Edward Fenton (ed.), *Comparative Economics*.

HOW TO PRODUCE IT: CATCHING A SEAL

The whole principle of successfully stalking a seal is just in realizing from the first that he is bound to see you and that your only hope is in pretending that you are also a seal. If you act and look so as to convince him from the first that you are a brother seal, he will regard you with unconcern. [Imitating] a seal well enough to deceive a seal is not difficult, for, to begin with, we know from experience that his eyesight is poor. You can walk up without taking any special precautions until . . . you are within two hundred and fifty or three hundred yards [230 m to 275 m]. Then you have to begin to be more careful. You move ahead while he is asleep, and when he wakes up you stop motionless. You can safely proceed on all fours until within something less than two hundred yards [180 m], but after that you will have to play seal more faithfully. Your method of locomotion will then have to be that of the seal, which does not differ very materially from that of a snake, and which therefore has its disadvantages at a season of the year when the surface of the ice is covered with puddles of water anywhere from an inch to twenty inches [2.5 cm to 50 cm] in depth, as it is in spring and early summer. You must not only crawl ahead, seal-fashion, but you must be careful to always present a side view of your body to the seal, for a man coming head-on does not look particularly like a seal.

Until you are within a hundred yards [90 m] or so the seal is not likely to notice you, but somewhere between the hundred yard [90 m] and the seventy-five yard [70 m] mark his attention will suddenly be attracted to you, and instead of going to sleep at the end of his ordinary short period of wakefulness, he will remain awake and stare at you steadily. The seal knows, exactly as well as the seal hunter knows, that no seal in this world will sleep continuously for as much as four minutes at a time. If you lie still that long, he will know you are no seal, and up will go his tail and down he will slide into the water in the twinkling of an eye.

When the seal . . . has been watching you carefully for twenty or thirty seconds, you must raise your head twelve or fifteen inches [30 cm or 40 cm] above the ice, look around seal-fashion, so that your eyes will sweep the whole circle of the horizon, and drop your head again upon the ice. By the time he has seen you repeat this process two or three times in the space of five or six minutes he will be convinced that you are a seal, and all his worries will be gone. From then on you can proceed more rapidly, crawling ahead while he sleeps and stopping while he remains awake, never doing anything unbecoming a seal. In this way you can crawl within five or ten yards [4 m or 9 m] of him if you like, and as a matter of fact I have known of expert seal hunters who under emergencies would go after a seal without any ordinary weapon and crawl so near him that they could seize him by a flipper, pull him away from his hole, and club or stab him.

FOR WHOM TO PRODUCE IT: DIVIDING THE SEAL

When we had entered the house the boiled pieces of seal meat had already been taken out of the pot and lay steaming on a sideboard. . . . My hostess picked out for me the lower joint of a seal's foreleg, squeezed it firmly between her hands to make sure nothing should later drip from it, and handed it to me, along with her own copper-bladed knife; the next most desirable piece was similarly squeezed and handed to her husband, and others in turn to the rest of the family. When this had been done, one extra piece was set aside in case I should want a second helping, and the rest of the boiled meat was divided into four portions, with the explanation to me that there were four families in the village who had no fresh seal meat.

The little adopted daughter of the house, a girl of seven or eight, had not begun to eat with the rest of us, for it was her task to take a small wooden platter and carry the four [small] pieces of boiled meat to the four families who had none of their own to cook. . . . Every house in the village in which any cooking was done had likewise sent four portions. . . . During our meal presents of food were also brought us from other houses; each housewife apparently knew exactly what the others had put in their pots, and whoever had anything to offer that was a little bit different would send some of that to the others, so that every minute or two a small girl messenger appeared in our door with a platter of something to contribute to our meal.

. . . [Many years ago, a certain Eskimo caught a huge bearded seal. Until he had killed it,] he had not thought of the other hunters, but now he looked around and saw that they were all far away. . . . [He] felt sure that none of them had any idea what kind of a seal he had caught. (The hunters' law does not require that the hunters within sight be summoned to share at the cutting up of a common, small seal.) When a bearded seal is killed all the hunters within view must be called in to share the prize.

It had occurred to him that by keeping the thing secret (by pretending this was a common seal), he might keep the animal to himself, and especially the skin, for he knew that he could sell pieces of it to a neighboring tribe who seldom catch bearded seals, for numerous articles of value. Accordingly, he secretly cut the animal up, gave out the story that he had killed only a small seal, and pledged his wife to secrecy; but the story leaked out as such stories will. People came to him and took away from him both the skin and the meat and reproached him bitterly. He now repented his act and felt crushed by the disapproval of his people, but his punishment was to be made even heavier, for within a year he began to lose his eyesight and in another year he was stone blind. Since then he, poor miserable man, has been blind and a charge upon the community. Thus it was sure to go with those who did wicked things; and while he felt sure that I was a good man, nevertheless to know his story would do me no harm, and he wished I would pass it on to others, warning them to avoid selfish ways.

FOCUS

1. What evidence is there that the decisions of traditional societies are strongly influenced by nature?
2. How does the Inuit concept of ''saving'' differ from that of a southern Canadian?
3. How did they decide what to produce?
4. a) Explain how the ''how'' question is answered.
   b) What ''tools'' might the Inuit be using?
   c) Speculate about how the introduction of a high-powered rifle might revolutionize Inuit life. What would be some disadvantages to the use of this ''tool''?
5. How did the Inuit learn to catch seals?
6. How did the Inuit decide the ''for whom'' question?
7. The hunter who killed the bearded seal was acting on the basis of self-interest.
   a) Why was it not applicable here?
   b) How did the decision of the tribe support tradition and show resistance to change?
8. How was the tradition of sharing enforced?

▶ PRODUCTIVITY

A car salesperson closes a deal at 10:00 a.m. in suburban St. Albert, Alberta. At the same time off the coast of Lunenburg, Nova Scotia, a small fishing boat returns with the morning's catch. Both of these activities are examples of production. Production is the major purpose of all economies. Economies must produce goods such as radios or fish or provide services such as those of the car salesperson in order to satisfy the needs and wants of the population. How many cars are sold and how many fish are caught is called productivity. More formally, productivity is an individual's output over a specific span of time, most commonly per hour.

Productivity = Output per Work Hour

Productivity is a simple way to measure how many goods and services a firm or a country is producing, and whether it is improving or not. Normally, when productivity increases, the economy is considered to be growing and therefore healthy. The rate of that growth is important, too.

Productivity allows business and government to compare one firm or country with other firms or countries. By examining which country can produce the most in a given time, it is possible to obtain some insight into the possible efficiency of that economy. Since economic efficiency is related to how well one country is able to compete with another, productivity helps us to determine competitiveness. Figure 6-4 compares Canada's manufacturing competitiveness, or efficiency, with that of three other countries.

Figure 6–4
MEASURES OF COMPETITIVENESS IN MANUFACTURING, FOUR INDUSTRIALIZED COUNTRIES, 1980–1987

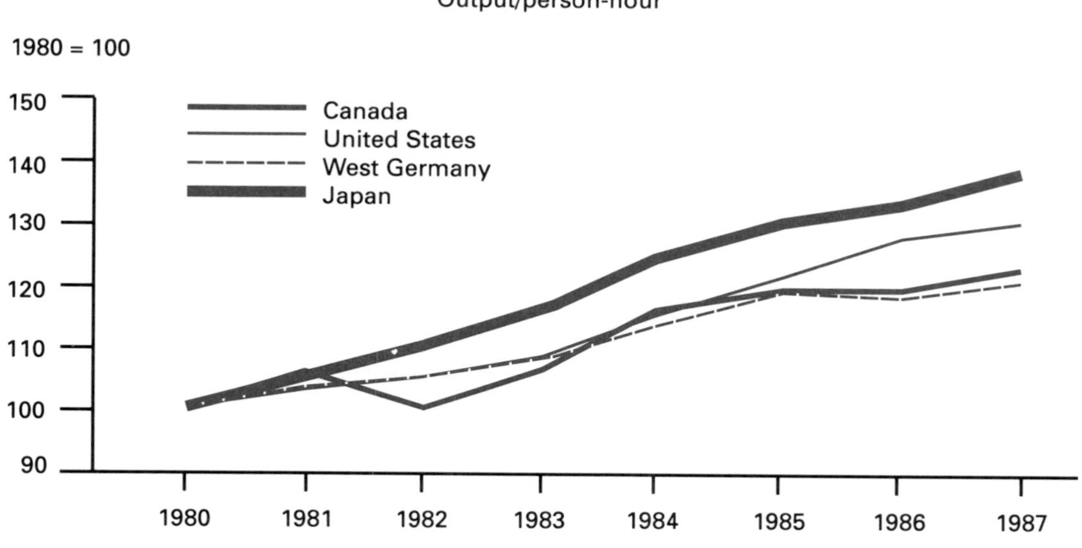

‣ Source: Economic Council of Canada, *Legacies*, Twenty-Sixth Annual Review, 1989, p. 14.

FOCUS

1. Which country is in the best/worst competitive position? Why?
2. Why are some countries more productive than others?

▶ GROSS NATIONAL PRODUCT

The car salesperson and the fisher are examples of individual productivity. When dealing with an entire economy, the government must consider everything that is produced by all its work force. The **Gross National Product (GNP)** of a country is the value of all goods and services produced in a given year. Productivity and GNP are very closely related. The better the productivity of individual workers, the greater the GNP. This is considered a positive situation because it indicates that the economy is growing. Because productivity differs in each country, so too does the GNP. Table 6-1 shows the value of GNP for selected countries.

Table 6-1
GROSS NATIONAL PRODUCT/PERSON/YEAR IN U.S. $ (1984)

Canada	11 400
U.S.A.	12 820
Sweden	14 870
South Korea	1 700
Taiwan	1 300
Japan	10 080
India	260
Niger	330
El Salvador	650

▸ Source: United Nations Educational Scientific Cultural Organization (UNESCO), *Statistical Yearbook, 1983*.

▶ PRODUCTIVITY AND CAPITAL

Capital is anything that increases an individual's ability to perform economically useful work. For example, the stone that early humans used to kill their prey was an early form of capital. Capital helps make human labour more productive. Modern forms of capital include all manner of technology and knowledge. Machinery helps workers produce goods more quickly. In one day, modern workers produce as much as their counterparts of 1900 did in a week. It is not surprising then that governments and industry strive to introduce more technology, since after the initial cost of installation, machines are cheaper than human labour.

▶ INTERDEPENDENCE

Although countries have different economic systems, they find it necessary to interact through trade. In this global age, all economies are dependent in some way on others. Since few countries possess all the resources that they need, they are forced to trade with other states to obtain them. Japan is a good example of this situation. Although highly industrialized and producing goods that are in great demand around the world, Japan is poor in resources and energy. Table 6-2 verifies this fact.

Table 6-2
JAPANESE IMPORTS BY COMMODITY (1984)

Percentage of Total Imports	
Fuels	44.8
Industrial supplies	29.7
Food and beverages	11.2
Machinery	6.3
Consumer goods	4.9
Others	3.1

▸ Source: Reprinted from *Canada and Its Pacific Neighbours* by Adrian Seaborne and David Evans, with permission of Weigl Educational Publishers Limited.

Figure 6–5
FORD'S TRANSNATIONAL INVOLVEMENT

UNITED KINGDOM
Carburetor, rocker arm, clutch, ignition, exhaust, oil pump, distributor, cylinder bolt, cylinder head, flywheel ring gear, heater, speedometer, battery, rear wheel spindle, intake manifold, fuel tank, switches, lamps, front disc, steering wheel, steering column, glass, weatherstrips, locks

SPAIN
Wiring harness, radiator and heater hoses, fork clutch release, air filter, battery, mirrors

BELGIUM
Tires, tubes, seat pads, brakes, trim

FEDERAL REPUBLIC OF GERMANY
Locks, pistons, exhaust, ignition, switches, front disc, distributor, weatherstrips, rocker arm, speedometer, fuel tank, cylinder bolt, cylinder head gasket, front wheel knuckles, rear wheel spindle, transmission cases, clutch cases, clutch, steering, column, battery, glass

AUSTRIA
Tires, radiator and heater hoses

CANADA
Glass, radio

SWEDEN
Hose clamps, cylinder bolt, exhaust down pipes, pressings, hardware

NORWAY
Exhaust flangs, tires

UNITED STATES
EGR valves, wheel nuts, hydraulic tappet, glass

ITALY
Cylinder head, carburetor, glass, lamps, defroster grills

DENMARK
Fan belt

JAPAN
Starter, alternator, cone and roller bearings, wind-screen washer pump

FRANCE
Alternator, cylinder head, master cylinder, brakes, underbody coating, weatherstrips, clutch release bearings, steering shaft and joints, seat pads and frames, transmission cases, clutch cases, tires, suspension bushes, ventilation units, heater, hose clamps, sealers, hardware

NETHERLANDS
Tires, paints, hardware

SWITZERLAND
Underbody coating, speedometer gears

Note: Final assembly takes place in the United Kingdom and the Federal Republic of Germany.

▸ Source: Adapted from Alyn Mitchner and R.J. Tuffs, *One World*. Edmonton: Reidmore Books, 1989, p. 32. Photo courtesy the Ford Motor Company.

A country wishing to obtain or maintain a high standard of living for its people seeks world markets for its products. Canada, for example, depends a great deal on world markets because its domestic market is too small (25 million people) to generate enough wealth to maintain the standard of living to which most Canadians aspire.

Another factor promoting **interdependence** is the growth of multinational corporations. These are large corporations that have their head offices in one country but possess branch plants in other countries around the world. They promote trade by establishing factories in many different countries and shipping their product to markets around the world.

What happens in one country can have repercussions around the world. There is no better example of this than oil. The modern industrial state requires oil to power its transportation; lubricate its machinery; and provide numerous by-products such as cosmetics, medicines, and plastics. The Western world used to take its oil supply for granted, probably because such Western firms as British Petroleum, Texaco, and Shell controlled the world's oil production. This monopoly ended in 1959 when Venezuela and several Arab oil-producing countries met in Cairo to sign an informal agreement regulating the supply of oil. This agreement created the Organization of Petroleum Exporting Countries, or OPEC. When OPEC imposed an oil embargo in 1973 against Israel's allies, the world, especially countries in North America and Europe, suddenly realized how dependent it was on oil. Oil prices quadrupled in 1973 and doubled again in 1979. In response, North Americans and Europeans began rationing gasoline, and people who used oil to heat their homes became more conservation-minded. In fact, conservation became the buzzword at all levels of the economy. Dependent on outside oil sources, Japan searched for alternative sources of energy, boosted its use of coal, developed nuclear energy, and sought alternative energy supplies.

For the non-industrial developing world the high fuel prices were devastating because energy costs made up a high portion of the cost of the products they produced. Higher energy prices meant that these countries had to increase the price of their exports in a world market that was already too competitive. This was the beginning of the great debt crises to come.

For oil-producing countries, most of which are Arab, there was unprecedented wealth. This windfall resulted in ambitious public projects such as universities, hospitals, highways, water systems, and many other forms of social improvement, as well as greater military expenditures.

But what goes up must come down. Oil prices plummeted in the 1980s. By 1986, the price of oil had declined from $40.00 to $10.00 per barrel. This reflected the effectiveness of conservation, the search for alternative supplies such as Great Britain's off-shore oil discoveries, and the difficulty OPEC encountered in controlling its own members. Getting all its members to agree on limiting their respective oil supplies became OPEC's greatest problem. Members such as Iran and Iraq, which needed oil revenues to finance a bloody religious war with each other, were reluctant to limit oil sales. Once again, these effects were felt around the globe. The interdependence map on page 299 illustrates the relationship among oil producers, oil consumers, and the spin-off trade.

Figure 6–6
WORLD INTERDEPENDENCE—THE EXAMPLE OF OIL

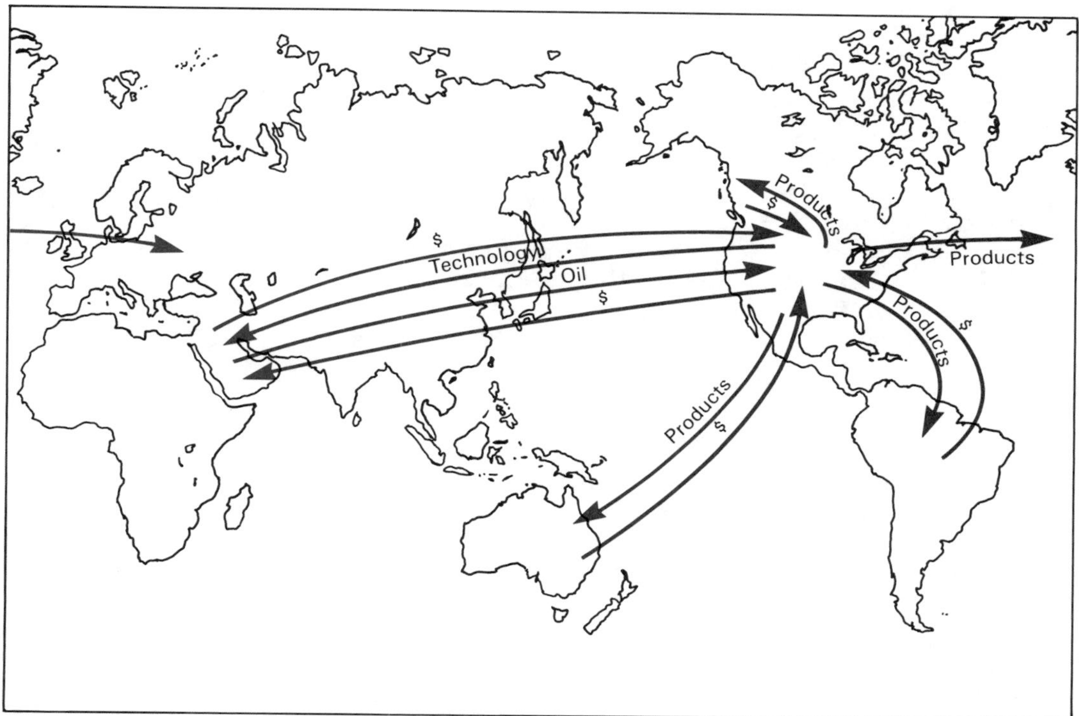

APPLYING YOUR KNOWLEDGE

1. Pretend that each person in the class has won $100 in a lottery.
   a) Compare what each student would do with this income.
   b) Why did the decisions vary?
   c) How do these differences help explain the variety of economic systems?
2. How would you measure the productivity of each of the following: a student, a teacher, a lawyer, a politician?
3. Is productivity and GNP the best way to compare economies? Explain.
4. Check all your clothing, jewelry, and school supplies for country of origin.
   a) List these countries and locate them on a map.
   b) Why are these items not all made in Canada?

CHAPTER 7 OVERVIEW

THE WORLD'S ECONOMIES: PRIVATE ENTERPRISE

This chapter outlines how the private enterprise system works in theory and how it solves the three basic economic questions discussed in the previous chapter. It begins with a brief history of the origins and growth of capitalism, including the ideas of A. Smith, D. Hume, D. Ricardo, T. Malthus, and C. Darwin. Concrete examples then illustrate the role of prices, competition, supply and demand, and profits in the functioning of private enterprise. The major values and beliefs of capitalism are summarized. The chapter concludes with several primary documents that discuss the theoretical merits of the private enterprise system.

▶ OBJECTIVES

After reading this chapter, you should be able to:

- ▶ explain how the private enterprise system operates
- ▶ debate the merits of capitalism
- ▶ evaluate the major values of private enterprise
- ▶ discuss the origins of capitalism
- ▶ provide examples of how prices, competition, and supply and demand operate in the private enterprise system
- ▶ outline the major characteristics of capitalism
- ▶ summarize the ideas of the major proponents of capitalism

▶ KEY TERMS

private enterprise
capitalism
mercantilism
protective tariffs
laissez-faire
free enterprise
invisible hand
social Darwinism
private enterprise system
competition
profit motive

CHAPTER 7

THE WORLD'S ECONOMIES: PRIVATE ENTERPRISE

As we pointed out in Chapter 6, each country must decide which goods it would most like to have, what resources will be used in their production, and how these goods will be distributed among the people. These decisions are difficult to make because each one opens up a whole range of overlapping problems that must be coordinated for the economy to run smoothly and efficiently. What type of work should each Canadian do? What will their salaries be? How many automobiles should be produced, and what proportion of them should be station-wagons? Should Prince Edward Island concentrate on growing wheat or potatoes or on raising livestock? This chapter describes how, in theory, the economic system known as **private enterprise** solves these three basic problems. It also examines some of the criticisms levelled at **capitalism**.

▶ THE ORIGINS OF CAPITALISM

The prevailing economic system in Europe prior to the nineteenth century was **mercantilism**. According to this economic theory, a country's international strength was directly related to its supply of gold and silver. Individual states thus controlled their economies in order to accumulate precious metals and thereby become more powerful. To achieve this objective, countries always sought to export more goods than they imported. Since a self-sufficient state produced everything it needed within its own borders, each country geared its economy to achieve this end. Economic activity was believed to be too important to be left to the discretion of individuals. Politics were thus joined to economics. Mercantilist governments regulated almost every aspect of their economies (although they seldom owned any enterprises). They enacted **protective tariffs** to limit imports from other countries and protect local industries. The British, for example, forbade the purchase of French and Italian silks, and France prohibited the importation of cottons from Great Britain. For similar reasons, skilled workers were forbidden to leave their countries. Government restrictions were everywhere. The state fixed the size, weight, and quality of many goods. Overseas colonies were created to supply raw materials for the mother country and to provide a market for manufactured products. Goods produced in the colonies could be exported only to the mother country, and then only in ships belonging to that state. The government gave local monopolies, or even entire overseas colonies, to individuals. In 1670, for example, Great Britain gave much of present-day Northern Ontario, Quebec, Saskatchewan, Manitoba, and Alberta to the Hudsons Bay Company. Craft guilds controlled specific trades in every town. These guilds limited competition by controlling who and how many could enter a trade. They also regulated prices and quality.

During this time the Roman Catholic Church condemned usury (lending money at high interest rates), sought to set a ''just price'' for every commodity and service, and took a dim view of commercial professions. Under these conditions, commercial banks and large-scale business enterprises had difficulty developing.

In the sixteenth century, the discovery of minerals in the Americas and riches in China and India provided more capital for enterprising businesspeople. The expanding population and improved transportation system created new markets for consumer goods such as textiles, spices, and furs. Entrepreneurs emerged to buy and sell goods from foreign lands. They kept themselves informed of changes in fashion and fluctuations in demand from year to year, and were always ready to switch their priorities according to the supply and demand for goods. Rather than seeking to restrict trade, they favoured free trade.

The Protestant Reformation in the sixteenth century slowly changed the negative image of business. The Calvinists, in particular, glorified the qualities needed for capitalism by stressing the value of hard work, thrift, and material growth. They believed that profits should not be spent on high living but reinvested in the business; that wealth should be used to produce more wealth; and that prosperity attained by honest means brought divine reward in heaven.

Towards the end of the seventeenth century, merchants in Holland, France, and England began to complain about their governments' economic restrictions. So too did American colonists who wished freedom to operate their own economy. Mercantilism also ran counter to the newly emerging ideas of liberalism. (See Chapter 2.) Liberals believed that the economy, like the state, should be free to follow natural laws, not the arbitrary rules of governments. In their view, a free economy in which private enterprise was unimpeded by government regulations was as important to business interests as political freedom was to the well-being of individuals. They believed that when people were motivated by self-interest, they worked harder and achieved better results. Competition spurred economic activity. To them, the best government was one that interfered as little as possible with the economic activities of its citizens.

▶ ADAM SMITH

In the late eighteenth century, British philosopher David Hume insisted that government should not interfere with foreign trade. Simultaneously, in France, a school of economic philosophers called the physiocrats developed the slogan ***laissez-faire***, meaning "hands off," or "let the government leave the economy alone." The culmination of *laissez-faire* thinking came when a Scottish professor named Adam Smith published *An Inquiry into the Nature and Causes of the Wealth of Nations* (1776).

Although many people have disagreed with Smith's ideas, his book remains one of the great classics of economic thought. Two centuries later, the model of an economic system he described in 1776 is still defended by many economists. Reacting to the restrictive economic laws, Smith advanced this novel viewpoint:

Every individual is continually exerting himself to find the most advantageous employment for whatever capital he can command. It is his own advantage, indeed, and not that of society, which he has in view. But the study of his own advantage naturally, or rather necessarily, leads him to prefer that employment which is most advantageous to the society. . . . In this case, as in many other cases, he is led by an invisible hand to promote an end which was no part of his intention. I have never known much good done by those who affected to trade for the public good.

Unlike mercantilist supporters, Smith declared that the strength of a country rested on the value of the goods it produced, not on the amount of gold and silver it possessed. He claimed that government laws and restrictions hindered, rather than promoted, economic growth. There was no need to plan the economy. If people were free to pursue their own self-interest (which Smith believed to be a basic psychological drive), the sum of their individual actions would automatically work for the betterment of society. To ensure that such a "natural" economic law would operate effectively, government was not to interfere in the economy. The government's role would be restricted to protecting the country against foreign enemies, ensuring competition, maintaining law and order, and protecting individual property rights.

Adam Smith (1723–1790)
National Archives of Canada, Neg. No. C7186

This was the doctrine of private enterprise — an economic system based upon private property, competition, profit, and the freedom to buy and sell.[1] It was another

▸ [1]The term *private enterprise* refers to the fact that most economic concerns are operated by private groups rather than by government agencies. This system is also called *free enterprise* (because the individual is free to conduct business without interference), *capitalism* (because individuals are allowed to own capital goods), and the *price system* or *market economy* for reasons which will soon be evident.

generation before the British government slowly adopted the doctrines of *laissez-faire*.

The development of modern capitalism is usually associated with the Industrial Revolution and the emergence of large-scale factory production. By 1860, Great Britain was the workshop of the world, retaining few traces of the old economic order. With the success of British capitalists and inventors, the ideas of free enterprise soon spread throughout western Europe and on to North America. But it was the work of British inventors and capitalists in the late eighteenth and early nineteenth centuries that provided the strongest argument in favour of private enterprise. Through a series of inventions, especially the steam engine, British inventors created new methods of large-scale production. British capitalists invested vast sums of money in order to purchase these machines and create factories in which large-scale production could take place. In addition, improvements in agriculture made it possible to feed the large numbers of factory workers, while changes in transportation and communication opened up new markets for manufactured goods. These changes transformed Great Britain during the nineteenth century, bringing about an Industrial Revolution.

Belgium was the first country to follow Great Britain's example. Then, between 1840 and 1860, France, the United States, and various German states began to industrialize. Sweden, Russia, and Japan followed suit after 1870.

▶ LAISSEZ-FAIRE CAPITALISM

The new science of political economy, founded near the end of the eighteenth century by such men as Adam Smith and David Ricardo, preached that the world's economy was controlled by natural economic laws regulating production and distribution. An **invisible hand** ensured that the common good would be enhanced if all people sought to serve their own personal self-interests. These natural laws operated efficiently only if government did not interfere in the economy. When this doctrine of *laissez-faire* was combined with the ideas of Thomas Malthus, the ''logical'' conclusion was that the state should not distribute charity to the poor. In his now famous book, *Essay on Population*, published in 1798, Malthus wrote that the world's population was advancing at a faster rate than the world's ability to produce food.

Population growth in the past had been checked by wars, disease, and famine. According to Malthus, poverty was nature's way of limiting population, and any interference would disrupt nature's plan. Charity would interfere with nature's way of killing off the weak and leaving the fit to carry on the race. Economist David Ricardo

Thomas Malthus (1766–1834)
The Bettmann Archive

used Malthus's ideas to argue that poverty was inescapable. Higher wages, he stated, led to larger families, an over-abundance of workers, and even lower wages than before. He believed that poverty was a law of nature that governments should not challenge.

▶ NATURAL SELECTION

These ideas were provided with additional support when Charles Darwin published his *Origin of the Species* in 1859. The laws of science, Darwin concluded, applied to plants and animals. Through the process of natural selection (survival of the fittest), nature ensured that only those physical characteristics that were suited to the environment would survive. Darwin's theories were later modified by such men as Herbert Spencer and William Sumner. **Social Darwinism**, as their ideas came to be known, provided additional support for the belief that government should neither meddle in the lives of its citizens nor with the economic system. Competition among individuals was declared to be the best method of ensuring that only the fittest would survive. Because the most efficient producers would obviously win, competition would eventually result in the progress of the human race as a whole.

Such arguments were accepted by the economic elite because they provided justification for its business practices and for the vast differences in wealth between the rich and the poor. ''Big business,'' said American tycoon J.D. Rockefeller, ''is merely the survival of the fittest, the working out of the law of nature and the law of God.'' Many in the nineteenth century believed that people received what they were worth, based upon the demand for their talents. If labourers were paid two dollars a day, that was because they produced only two dollars' worth of goods, whereas the salaries of engineers were ten times larger because the value of their work was ten times higher than that of labourers. By the same reasoning, the company president's income of $50 000 per year reflected his worth to the company and the scarcity of the talents that he possessed.[2] Employers would violate natural economic laws if they paid employees more than they were worth. In fact many people believed that the entrepreneurs had done more than their share in contributing to the workers' welfare by providing them with jobs. True, some tinkering and adjustments to the system were necessary from time to time, but on the whole, businesspeople and politicians of the nineteenth century believed that the economic system was working well.

▸ [2]The masculine pronoun is used here because it was rare for a woman to be president of a company in the nineteenth century.

Charles Darwin (1809–1882)
The Bettmann Archive

▶ CHARITY AND LAZINESS

Every system has its problems. Poverty resulted from the struggle for survival. As the animal kingdom is unequal, so is the human race. The fault allegedly lay with the genes that were passed on from parent to child. In fact, most people believed that all moral, intellectual, and emotional qualities were inherited.

Poverty was thus viewed as a clear sign of biological and social inferiority. The doctrine of evolution implied that human society, like nature, must be harsh to its weaklings or the wheels of progress would be upset. Charity, in other words, would retard the evolution of humanity.

For many people at the time, the argument that poverty was inevitable did not offer sufficient justification to allow the poor to starve before their very eyes. If this was the best of all possible worlds, why were there so many hungry men and women, and why were the streets filled with beggars? The answer was simple. People were poor because they were lazy, immoral, ignorant, and improvident. They wasted their energies and threw away their earnings in the taverns. Individual weakness was therefore at fault—not the system or the employers. One had to work for what one got. ''If thou dost not sow,'' warned the Bible, ''thou shalt not reap.'' Idleness was a sin, whereas prosperity was the earthly reward for living a moral life. If people failed, it was their own fault. All people, it was argued, could be successful if they worked hard, saved their money, and lived respectable, moral lives. Authors wrote children's books about penniless orphans who were able to rise from rags to riches through hard work, ability, thrift, and good moral character — this was the gospel of work.

▶ POLITICS AND ECONOMICS

As capitalism evolved, a supportive body of political ideas emerged to accompany its growth. Private enterprise came to be seen as the most democratic way to organize the economy. Rather than rely upon government decisions about what was best for everyone, capitalism allows individuals to decide for themselves, and the combination of their decisions determines what will be produced and who will get what. Inequality of wealth is considered normal and even desirable. Capitalists believe that wealth gravitates to those people who serve society's needs the best. Since private

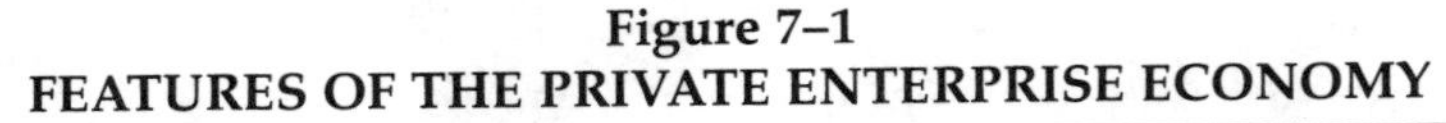

Figure 7–1
FEATURES OF THE PRIVATE ENTERPRISE ECONOMY

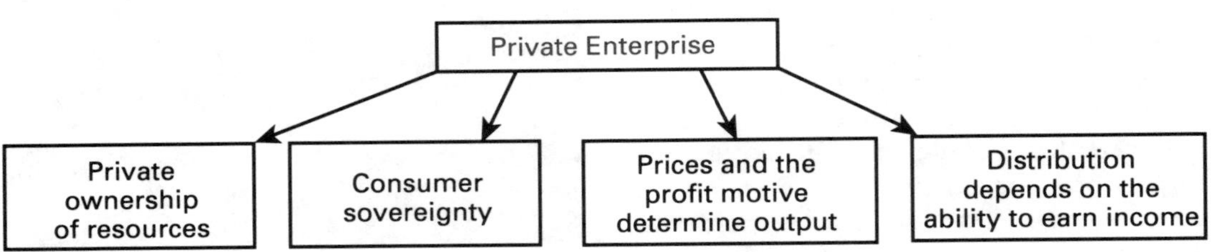

property is both a source and a result of wealth, it should remain free from government controls.

The **private enterprise system** (capitalism) stresses freedom — freedom of trade (no monopolies or government regulations) and freedom of choice (where to work, what to produce, what price to charge, and what to buy). The private enterprise system also stresses the importance of the individual, yet the individual is not idealized. People are portrayed neither as self-seeking beings interested only in their own welfare nor as enlightened, rational human beings. Individual goals are emphasized over the needs of society because the free enterprise system assumes that when each person carries out these goals, the society as a whole will also benefit.

Finally, the system is based upon a belief in the virtues of self-reliance, initiative, hard work, progress, and production—the more, the better. The following list summarizes the major characteristics of the private enterprise system:

- Private property
- The price system
- **Competition**
- Freedom to buy and sell
- The **profit motive**
- No government interference

FOCUS

1. Reread the ideas of John Locke in Chapter 2 and explain how his ideas could be used to support private enterprise.
2. How important were changing ideas to the growth of capitalism?
3. Explain why proponents of private enterprise oppose government involvement in the economy.
4. Is it desirable to entrust important economic decisions to private individuals and firms who in theory are motivated solely by profit? Explain. If you believe that it is undesirable, what are the alternatives?
5. "It has always seemed strange to me," said Doc. "The things we admire in man, kindness and generosity, openness, honesty, understanding, and feeling are [symbols of] failure in our system. And those traits we detest, sharpness, greed, acquisitiveness, meanness, egotism, and self-interest are the traits of success. And while men admire the quality of the first, they love and produce the second." To what extent is this excerpt from John Steinbeck's novel *Cannery Row* applicable to the private enterprise system? Explain your point of view.
6. Explain why very little was done in the nineteenth century to prevent poverty. Charity was considered detrimental to the human race, yet the poor were sometimes given aid. Explain this apparent paradox.
7. One of the major beliefs of capitalism is that all individuals can become an economic success as long as they have the ability and the proper attitude. Almost everyone can name someone who rose from "rags to riches." Are they the exceptions to the rule, or is this a normal occurrence? Explain.
8. While capitalism assumes that society benefits when individuals are free to do what they think best, socialists believe that society benefits when each person suppresses selfish objectives for the greater good. Prepare for a debate on this topic.

9. To what extent have nineteenth-century attitudes towards poverty and the poor changed? To ascertain the answer to this question, design and administer your own questionnaire. Questions should explore popular attitudes towards the extent of poverty in Canada, the ideas of survival of the fittest, charity, heredity, personal character faults, hard work, and ''rags to riches.''

▶ THE MARKET ECONOMY

Allowing business people to do what they want does not seem like a ''system,'' and freedom from government interference is not much of an economic plan. To discover how the private enterprise system is supposed to work, let us examine how it determines what is produced, how it is produced, and to whom the goods are distributed.

The private enterprise economy is sometimes described by its supporters as a miracle because it coordinates the decisions and activities of millions of individuals and enterprises in a reasonably orderly and efficient manner, without the help of a central coordinating authority. Nobody designed it—it just evolved.

The system can best be understood by examining how traditional marketplaces were organized. In pre-industrial villages, an open space was set aside where sellers presented their goods for sale. When buyers wished to purchase an item, they bargained with the seller until a mutually agreeable price was established. If the seller charged too much, the buyer went to another merchant; if the buyer was not willing to pay what the seller believed was fair, the merchant sold to someone else. The selling price, therefore, was usually a compromise between what the buyer was willing to pay and what the seller considered a fair return. The theory of the private enterprise economy is an extension of this mechanism. Each buyer attempts to buy at the lowest possible price, and each seller tries to sell at the highest possible price.

It is naturally more advantageous to make and sell commodities that people are interested in purchasing. If there is little demand for a particular item, its producers will stop making it and turn to manufacturing goods that people want to purchase. If an enterprise is not able to adjust to people's shifting demands, it will go out of business, whereas its more adaptable competitors will survive. In order to sell its products and make a profit, each enterprise will try to produce goods more cheaply and offer them for sale at a lower price than its competitors. To do this, the businessperson must either cut costs by producing more efficiently or accept a smaller profit. The system thus ensures that the economy is both responsive to the demands of consumers and uses the most efficient means of production.[3]

The mechanism that coordinates the multitude of economic decisions carried out in the marketplace is the price system. Prices perform three interrelated functions: they transmit information about consumer demands and the available supply of goods; they provide an incentive to produce those goods that are in demand, and to do so by the least costly methods; and they determine the distribution of income. The following examples illustrate how the price system performs these functions:

▸ [3]This section was adapted from J.P. Wogaman, *The Great Economic Debate*, Philadelphia: Westminster Press, 1977, p. 78.

▶ 1. Hamburgers Versus Fried Chicken

Imagine what would happen if a fast food hamburger chain devised a catchy new advertising campaign that persuaded a large number of teenagers to switch from buying fried chicken to eating hamburgers. As the number of people wanting to buy hamburgers increases (the demand), the number of available hamburgers (the supply) will decrease until there will be a shortage of hamburgers. On the other hand, there will be more chicken available than there will be people wanting to buy it. This situation will allow the hamburger chain to increase the price of hamburgers, while those restaurants selling chicken will be forced to lower prices in order to sell their surplus supply of chicken. The increase in the price of hamburgers might:

- reduce the number of people willing to buy hamburgers at the new price;
- encourage farmers to raise cattle rather than chickens;
- lead to the production of substitutes for hamburger meat, such as soybeans or minced pork;
- encourage other firms to enter the hamburger business and share in the high profits.

In the long run, these four changes would combine to reduce the shortage of hamburgers and lower the price. The same circumstances would influence the production of chicken — only in reverse. As the supply of chickens fell below the demand for them, their price would increase, and ultimately more chickens would be raised.

In this way, the price system determines what will be produced (hamburgers or chicken); how human and natural resources will be allocated (the farmer's land and labour), and who will get what (those who can afford hamburgers will buy them). In short:

- An increase in price removes shortages by reducing the demand and increasing the supply.
- A decrease in price removes a surplus by discouraging production and encouraging people to buy more.

The price system thus creates a balance between supply and demand. If there is a scarcity of one particular item and consumers want it badly enough, they will be willing to pay such a high price that others will be encouraged to supply it. This system of rewards (profit) and punishments (losses) ensures that the wants of consumers are taken into account, and that unwanted items will not be produced.

▶ 2. Lead Pencils

Suppose that there is an increased demand for lead pencils, perhaps because a baby boom increases school enrolment. Retail stores will find that they are selling more pencils and will order more pencils from their wholesalers. The wholesalers will order more pencils from the manufacturers and the manufacturers will, in turn, order more wood, more brass, more graphite — all the products used to make a pencil. In order to encourage the suppliers to produce more of these raw materials, the manufacturers will have to offer higher prices for them. Higher prices will induce suppliers to increase their work force to meet the higher demand. To hire more workers, they will have to offer higher wages or better working conditions. In this way, ripples spread out over ever-widening circles, transmitting the message to people all over the world that there is a greater demand for pencils — or, to be more precise, for the materials needed to produce pencils.

Prices not only transmit information from prospective buyers to retailers, wholesalers, manufacturers, and owners of resources, they also transmit information the other way. Suppose that a forest fire or a labour strike reduces the availability of wood. The price of wood will increase. This will inform pencil manufacturers that it will be wise to use less wood, and it will not profit them to produce as many pencils as before, unless they can sell them for a higher price. Lower production of pencils will enable the retailer to charge a higher price for them, and the higher price will inform consumers that it would be economical to wear pencils down to a stub before discarding them or to switch to pens.

The price system also operates with respect to workers and owners of resources. An increase in demand for wood will tend to produce higher wages for loggers; this is a signal that labour of that type is in greater demand than before. Higher wages give workers the incentive to act on that information, with the result that some workers, who were indifferent to the type of job they had, may now choose to become loggers, and more young people entering the labour market may also become loggers.

▶ PROFIT AND COMPETITION

The belief in private property and competition is central to the private enterprise system. Profit, whether measured in terms of land, money, happiness, or factories is the reward (or incentive) for those who are successful in the business world. Without private ownership, there would be no incentive for individuals to do their best. By permitting people to accumulate private wealth, the economic system encourages them to save money and invest it in profitable areas of the economy. Although the profit motive may appear selfish, it promotes research and savings and leads ultimately to greater productivity and wealth for all. Those who provide these services receive their reward based upon their ability to satisfy the people's desires.

Personal income in a private enterprise economy is largely determined by the demand for one's talents and possessions. People with abilities or resources that are in great demand receive higher incomes than those without such property or talents. A chef will earn more than a supermarket cashier. Similarly, the owner of a lot in a busy downtown city will make more money than the owner of a lot of the same size in the country. The poor in a private enterprise economy are people without highly-valued talents and resources.

The private enterprise system is based on the apparent near-universality of humanity's materialistic nature. In the desire to accumulate goods, people have unconsciously created the mechanisms of private enterprise. Although some people may have more ability to acquire material wealth than others, the system ensures that even the most selfish people serve society by trying to get ahead. The market economy, however, does not put any moral pressure on people to be either selfish or unselfish. The same price is established whether the buyer's motives are selfish or altruistic. Whatever the motive, the system translates individual economic actions into the greater good.

For private enterprise to function smoothly, individual enterprises must seek to maximize their profits, consumers must know the different prices of each item offered for sale, both must make buying and selling decisions based upon self-interest, and no individual or group of buyers (or suppliers) should be able to control or manipulate the price of any item. Automobile firms, it follows, should attempt to make as much money as possible, and no one company should be allowed to convince the other firms to agree upon a set price—otherwise the consumers would be forced to pay more than they should. At the same time, if prospective automobile buyers do not "shop around" to compare the price and quality of each car, and if they do not base their decisions upon the merits of each automobile, then there would be little reason for the companies to compete with each other by lowering prices or by manufacturing more efficient automobiles.

The system also requires a great deal of competition for jobs, customers, and goods. If, for example, there was only one hockey stick manufacturer, that company could simply increase the price and everyone who wanted a stick would have to pay the higher price. In a competitive situation with several dozen manufacturers all producing a similar product, each company attempts to sell more hockey sticks by lowering the price or improving the quality. This competition ensures that hockey players are charged a "fair" price for their sticks, and that the manufacturer will produce them in the most efficient way possible. The company that fails to make the best use of the available human and natural resources will be forced into bankruptcy, because the high costs of production will increase the price of its products. Similarly,

In the 1930s, drought in the prairies and low prices for foodstuffs prevented most western Canadian farmers from meeting their mortgage payments. Banks and loan companies threatened to foreclose and remove farmers from the land they had tilled for generations. In 1981, high interest rates led to another spate of foreclosures. Bankers and farmers have traditionally supported private enterprise. How might this situation change farmers' support of private enterprise? Can you think of anything that might cause the banks to modify their position on private enterprise?
Miller Features Syndicate Inc.

if large numbers of workers are looking for jobs — and they have not made an agreement among themselves—the competition for work will prevent wages from rising above an "acceptable" level.

The private enterprise system thus solves the three basic economic problems in the following manner:

- WHAT goods are produced is determined by the demands of consumers. If consumers will pay enough money for chocolate bars, then chocolate bars will be produced. If consumers shift their preferences to popsicles, then more popsicles and fewer chocolate bars will be produced.
- HOW goods are produced is determined by competition among producers to sell their goods. To earn the greatest possible profit, producers will select the cheapest possible method of production. If it is cheaper to dig a tunnel using labourers equipped with picks and shovels than to use a bulldozer, then this is how it will be done. However, if the cost of gasoline drops and the wages of labourers increase, then bulldozers will replace the picks and shovels.
- WHO gets what share of the goods that are produced is determined by supply and demand. If the demand for a person's skill is greater than the supply of that skill, then the person will command a larger income than someone whose skill is in less demand relative to its supply. By skill, we mean such talents as singing and playing tennis, as well as the ownership of property (rents) and money (interest rates).

FOCUS

1. If a three-dimensional television was invented, how would the private enterprise system decide the answers to the following questions?
   a) How many three-dimensional television sets should be manufactured?
   b) Should they be built mainly by hand or by automation?
   c) How much should they cost?
2. What would happen to the supply of T-bone steaks if their price suddenly increased
   a) in the short run?
   b) in the long run?
3. Define the following terms: marketplace; supply and demand; *laissez-faire*.
4. Many Marxists believe that people in a private enterprise society are selfish because their economic system has made them that way. Do you agree? Explain.
5. If all the workers in the margarine industry received a large pay increase, what might happen to
   a) the demand for butter?
   b) the supply of margarine?
   c) the price of margarine?
6. Explain why competition and private property are crucial to the private enterprise system.
7. In the market economy, the price of one item is dependent upon the prices of many other goods. As a result, a change in the price of one product can affect the prices of many other products. Explain how each of the following examples could have occurred.
   a) A war in the Middle East increases the cost of firewood in Nova Scotia.

b) Large forest fires in northern Ontario cause the price of books to increase.
c) A coffee labourers' strike in Brazil increases the price of tea.
d) Heavy migration of people to Alberta raises rents in that province.
e) Higher interest rates cause unemployment in the automobile industry.
f) Sales of wheat to the U.S.S.R. cause higher hamburger prices in Canada.

8. How does the market economy ensure that the country's resources will be used efficiently?
9. Based upon the following chart, debate the advantages of the private enterprise system.

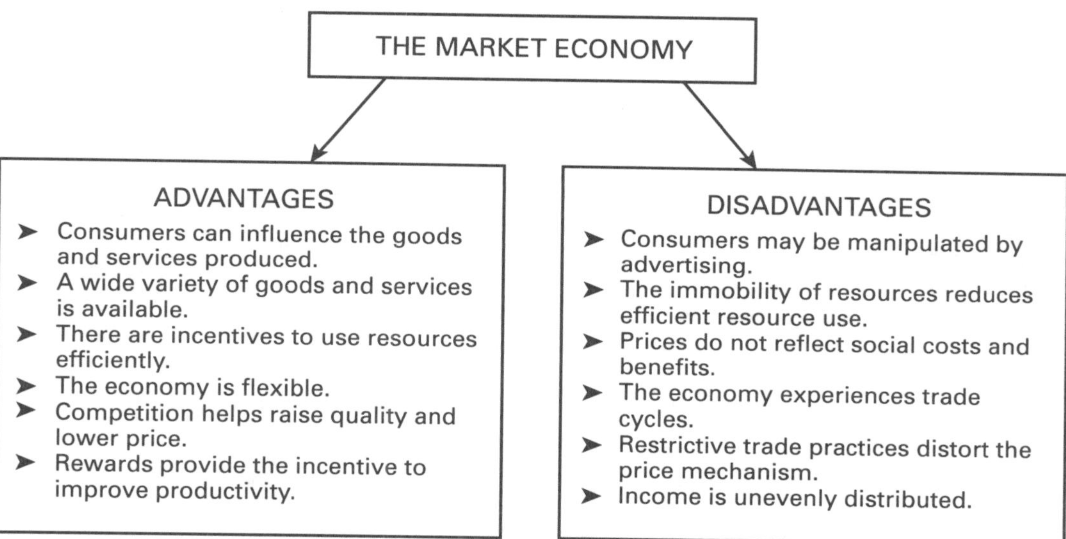

▸ Source: E.D. Shade et al., *Fundamentals of Economics*, Vol. I, 3rd ed. Permission granted by McGraw-Hill Book Company Australia Pty. Ltd.

▶ DEFENDING PRIVATE ENTERPRISE

Socialists and communists have accused capitalism of undermining society's values. The profit motive, some critics declare, creates an abnormal interest in competition and materialism at the expense of morality. The scramble for the "all mighty dollar," they argue, encourages unethical business practices and tasteless advertising. Critics claim that human worth is all too often measured in terms of a person's wealth; that the search for profits has led to ecological disasters; and that while some people are millionaires, many families live in poverty.

Supporters of private enterprise base their praise of the system upon both its economic benefits and its political and moral merits. Ironically, its detractors condemn capitalism under similar headings but reach opposite conclusions. The purpose of this section is to examine the theoretical merits of private enterprise as defended by its supporters. Criticisms of the system, which are only briefly outlined here, will be developed more fully in subsequent case studies.

▶ Claim 1: Equitable Incomes

Opponents of the private enterprise system claim that if we relied solely upon supply and demand for our incomes, the country's wealth would soon be owned by a small number of people. Given differences in ability, ambition, inheritance, and luck, capitalism would inevitably create a society in which a few extremely wealthy families controlled the destinies of the poverty-ridden majority.

Supporters of capitalism disagree. Some people, they argue, contribute more to society than do others. The inventors of insulin, for example, were more important than the doctors who administered it; the physicians, in turn, were more significant than the nurses who cared for the diabetic patients. Average people add very little to civilization, yet they benefit greatly from advances made by a relatively few people in such fields as medicine, technology, and the arts. These geniuses actually receive very few rewards in relation to their contribution to society.

To the complaint that such rock music groups as the Rolling Stones earn much more than they contribute to society, such supporters of capitalism as Ayn Rand claim that people are entitled to spend their money on whatever they wish—including expensive rock concert tickets. Those who don't like rock music do not contribute to the Rolling Stones' income.

Milton Friedman is the most prominent advocate of *laissez-faire* capitalism within the ranks of professional economists. His view is as follows:

Industrial progress, mechanical improvement, all of the great wonders of the modern era have meant relatively little to the wealthy. The rich in ancient Greece would not have benefited very much from modern plumbing because servants brought all the water the rich needed. The same is true for television and radio, since the wealthy could bring the leading musicians and actors to their homes. Other advances would have added very little to their life that they did not already possess. Modern capitalism has thus benefited the poor much more than it has aided the wealthy. It has brought conveniences that were the sole preserve of the rich to everyone. . . .

Industrial production, technological advances, and just plain hard work are dependent upon the desire for profit. What incentive does a producer have to make goods as efficiently as possible if it will not result in some sort of personal reward? If a hockey player's salary would be the same whether he skated hard or not, why should he try? He might do so for a while, but why would he work hard for nothing? Would you?

Why should you make the effort to start a new business, invent a new manufacturing process, or invest your money, if there was no reward? Human beings need the incentive provided by the private enterprise economy.[4]

▸ [4]Excerpt from *Free to Choose: A Personal Statement*, copyright © 1980 by Milton Friedman and Rose D. Friedman, reprinted by permission of Harcourt Brace Jovanovich, Inc., p. 23, pp. 146-148. Abridged and modified for this study.

FOCUS

1. If you were a hockey player, would you agree with Friedman's statements? Explain.
   a) What criteria do capitalism's supporters use to evaluate a person's worth to society?
   b) What other methods of evaluation could be employed?

▶ Claim 2: Coercion Versus Free Will

Critics of capitalism point out that the system relies heavily on the belief that the people know what is in their own best interest. But do consumers in fact have enough knowledge to make intelligent decisions? Few people, for example, possess the technical know-how to decide upon the best medicines to take. By the time the harmful effects of some drugs are known, it can be too late. The solution would seem to be government regulation—only government control, some critics state, can cure the abuses of capitalism.

Friedman and his supporters disagree. The evils and abuses that are normally blamed on capitalism, they state, are not caused by the market economy, but by government intervention in the economy. Let us once again turn to the ideas of Friedman:

Fundamentally, there are only two ways of co-ordinating the economic activities of millions. One is central direction involving the use of coercion by the modern totalitarian state. The other is voluntary cooperation of individuals by the market place.

Many intellectuals, even in our democratic societies, take for granted that free enterprise capitalism exploits the masses, whereas central economic planning is the wave of the future that will set their countries on the road to rapid economic progress.

The facts themselves are very different. Wherever we find any large degree of individual freedom and wide-spread hope of further progress in the future, there we also find that economic activity is organized mainly through the free market. Wherever the state undertakes to control the economic activities of its citizens, ordinary citizens have little political freedom, a low standard of living, and little power to control their own destiny.

The most obvious example is the contrast [that existed] between East and West Germany. People of the same blood, the same civilization, the same level of technical skill and knowledge [inhabited] the two parts. Which . . . prospered? Which had to erect a wall to pen in its citizens? Which [protected it] with armed guards, assisted by fierce dogs, minefields, and similar devices of devilish ingenuity in order to frustrate brave and desperate citizens who were willing to risk their lives to leave their communist paradise for the capitalist hell on the other side of the wall?

On one side of that wall the brightly-lit streets and stores were filled with cheerful, bustling people. Some [bought] goods from all over the globe. Others [went] to the numerous movie houses or other places of entertainment. They [could] buy newspapers and magazines expressing every variety of opinion. They [spoke] with one another or with strangers on any subject and [expressed] a wide range of opinions without a single backward glance over the shoulder. A walk of a few hundred feet, after an hour spent in line, filling in forms and waiting for passports to be returned, [would have taken] you, as it took us, to the other side of that wall. There, the streets [appeared] empty; the city, gray and pallid; the store windows, dull; the buildings, grimy. One hour in East Berlin [was] enough to understand why the authorities put up the wall.[5]

▸ [5]Milton Friedman, *Capitalism and Freedom*, Chicago: University of Chicago Press, 1962, pp. 69–70; *Free to Choose*, pp. 54–55. Text has been changed to reflect altered conditions in Germany.

FOCUS

1. What are Friedman's objections to government planning?

2. What connection does Friedman make between economic and political systems?
3. Outline Friedman's attitude towards totalitarianism, as revealed in the preceding selection.
4. a) Is Friedman's comparison between East and West Germany a valid method by which to evaluate the advantages of capitalism versus state planning? Explain.
   b) What additional information would you like to know about East and West Germany? Why?

▶ Claim 3: Freedom

One of the most frequent criticisms of the capitalist system is that money creates power — not only economic power but political power. Through the use of skillful lobbying, expensive lawyers, contributions to political parties, and control of the media, businesspeople are able to influence, if not dictate, government legislation. Supporters of private enterprise disagree. They believe that political freedom, even with all its flaws, is probably the most important benefit of capitalism. Ayn Rand, for example, stated that capitalism is the only system that allows people to be free. All human relationships are voluntary and, most important, because everyone has private property, all are free to disagree.

Milton Friedman expands upon Rand's ideas:

It is widely believed that politics and economics are separate and largely unconnected; that individual freedom is a political problem and material welfare an economic problem; and that any kind of political arrangements can be combined with any kind of economic arrangements. But such a view is a delusion. There is an intimate connection between economics and politics, and only certain combinations of political and economic arrangements are possible. A society which is Marxist cannot also be truly democratic.

In addition to providing economic freedom, capitalism promotes political freedom by separating economic power from political power and in this way enables the one to offset the other. This prevents power from being concentrated in only a few hands. . . .

A free society releases the energies and abilities of people to pursue their own objectives. It prevents some people from arbitrarily suppressing others. It does not prevent some people from achieving positions of privilege, but so long as freedom is maintained, these positions of privilege are subject to continued attack by other able, ambitious people. Freedom preserves the opportunity for today's underprivileged to become tomorrow's privileged and, in the process, enables almost everyone, from top to bottom, to enjoy a fuller and richer life.[6]

▸ [6]Friedman, *Capitalism and Freedom*, pp. 65–67; *Free to Choose*, pp. 148–149.

APPLYING YOUR KNOWLEDGE

1. Explain how capitalism might promote political freedom.
2. To what extent do you agree with the views of Rand and Friedman on capitalism and freedom? What is their definition of freedom? What is your definition?

FURTHER RESEARCH

1. Prepare for a debate on one of the following topics:
   a) Government planning is dangerous because it combines political power with economic power.
   b) Economic planning and political freedom are perfectly compatible.
   c) Economic freedom is necessary for political freedom.
2. Critics of *laissez-faire* capitalism argue that the period of the ''robber barons'' in the United States, just before 1900, illustrates what happens when a ''pure'' capitalist system is allowed full play. Their opponents counter that this period saw a perversion of ''pure'' capitalism into a very ''impure'' monopoly capitalism, and that it must not be taken as an example of what capitalism can really do. Using appropriate inquiry techniques (see Chapter 1), prepare a report on this period that discusses the power of these robber barons, the extent of political and economic freedom, and the advantages and disadvantages of *laissez-faire* capitalism.
3. Read Ayn Rand's novel *Atlas Shrugged* (New York: Random House, 1957) and outline the author's view of the ideal businessperson and the role of government.
4. Read the following case studies on the economies of Great Britain, Japan, U.S.S.R., Canada, Sweden, Peru, and Ivory Coast. Redraw the graph below in your notebook and locate these countries on it.

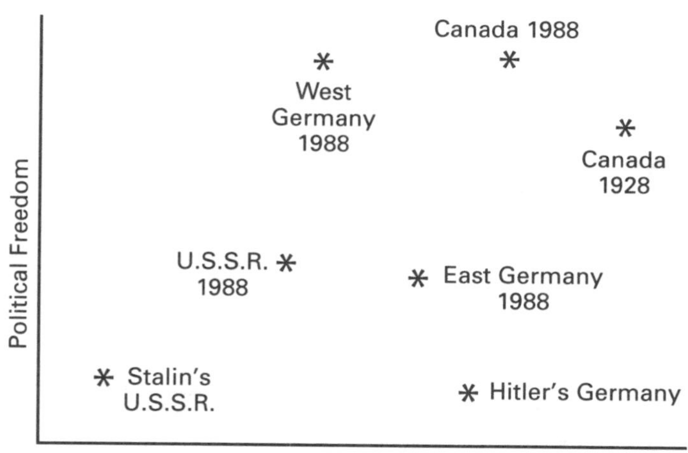

▸ Source: Paul Samuelson et al., *Economics*, 6th Cdn. ed. Toronto: McGraw-Hill Ryerson Limited, 1988, p. 786.

Case Study 17 Overview

Thatcherism and Reaganomics

This case study examines the merits of the supply-side economic theories employed by Ronald Reagan in the United States and Margaret Thatcher in Great Britain. The case study compares how both the supply-siders and the Keynesian economists respond to unemployment, inflation, taxes, and government spending and intervention in the economy. In general, supply-siders dislike government involvement in the economy and emphasize greater production. The case study examines the economic measures adopted by Reagan and Thatcher, including their goals, values, successes, and weaknesses, and concludes with an analysis of the benefits of supply-side economics.

▶ OBJECTIVES

After reading this case study, you should be able to:

- ▶ compare supply-side economic theories with demand-side theories
- ▶ evaluate the values of supply-side economics
- ▶ debate the advantages of supply-side economics
- ▶ analyse economic data
- ▶ outline the policies adopted by Thatcher and Reagan and describe their similarities and differences
- ▶ determine whether Canada should adopt supply-side methods

▶ KEY TERMS

Thatcherism
Reaganomics
supply-side economics
Keynesian economics
demand-side economics
recession
depression
privatization
inflation
deficit

Case Study

17 Thatcherism and Reaganomics

It is probably quite safe to say that neither former British Prime Minister Margaret Thatcher nor former U.S. President Ronald Reagan ever imagined that their names would someday be used to represent an economic theory. What has commonly become known as **Thatcherism** or **Reaganomics** is really just the economic theory previously known as **supply-side economics**. Some proponents claim that Adam Smith, in his book *An Inquiry into the Nature and Causes of the Wealth of Nations* (1776) was really describing supply-side economics. This case study examines how this theory operates and why it is supposed to be better than the demand-side theory that has dominated economic thinking since the Great Depression of the 1930s.

All industrial economies strive for full employment, price stability, and economic growth. The problem is how to achieve these goals. Past governments have employed a variety of economic theories to strengthen their economies. These theories have included **Keynesian** or **demand-side economics**; the monetarist school, which believes that societies' economic ills can be cured by controlling the money supply; and supply-side economics, which is the subject of this discussion.

▶ HOW DEMAND-SIDERS DEAL WITH RECESSION

It is often easier to understand a process if it is compared with another. We will therefore compare demand-side and supply-side theories.

Keynesian or demand-side economics emphasizes the amount of spending in the economy. When consumers, business people, and government spend, they create a demand for goods and services. This demand encourages business firms to increase production. The result is that more goods and services become available and more employment is created. A reduction in the amount of spending causes the econ-

Figure 1
THE KEYNESIAN PERCOLATOR—SOLVING A RECESSION

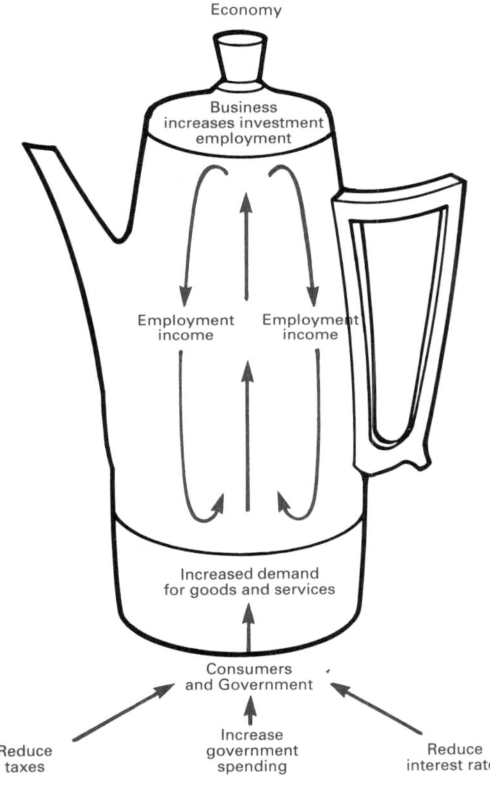

How could Keynes's theory be used to justify welfare payments to the disadvantaged?

omy to enter a **recession**, which is just another way of saying that employment and production have been reduced. According to demand-siders, during a recession or **depression**, government should intervene in the economy to increase spending. Such policies as reducing taxes, increasing government expenditures, and lowering interest rates are strategies the government may use to increase the purchasing power of its citizens. The renewed spending will increase the demand for goods and services, which in turn will encourage businesses to produce more goods and services, and employment will rise. As more people are employed, they will have additional money to spend. As spending increases, the cycle starts again.

▶ HOW SUPPLY-SIDERS DEAL WITH RECESSION

Supply-siders insist that government intervention is heresy. They emphasize the production side of the market (the producer). According to this theory, during a recession, government should stimulate the goods and services sector of the economy by reducing taxes (both corporate and personal), lowering interest rates, and selling government-owned enterprises.

Supply-siders view any form of government regulation as harmful to the economy. Regulation may be minor such as laws requiring fans in employee lunchrooms or major such as mandatory holidays, expensive safety equipment, or minimum wages. Reducing the number of rules and the amount of paperwork provides not only more cash to plow back into the company but also allows more flexibility in running the business.

Reducing corporate taxes creates more profits for business firms and acts as a carrot to encourage others to enter that business. Reducing personal income taxes increases the public's incentive to work and provides more earnings to spend. Lower interest rates make borrowing money less expensive, thus encouraging business expansion.

Privatization (the sale of government managed or owned companies to the private sector) removes "unfair" government competition with private companies and reduces the tax burden on the public. (See Case Study 22.)

Figure 2
THE SUPPLY-SIDE "DRIP-DOWN" THEORY

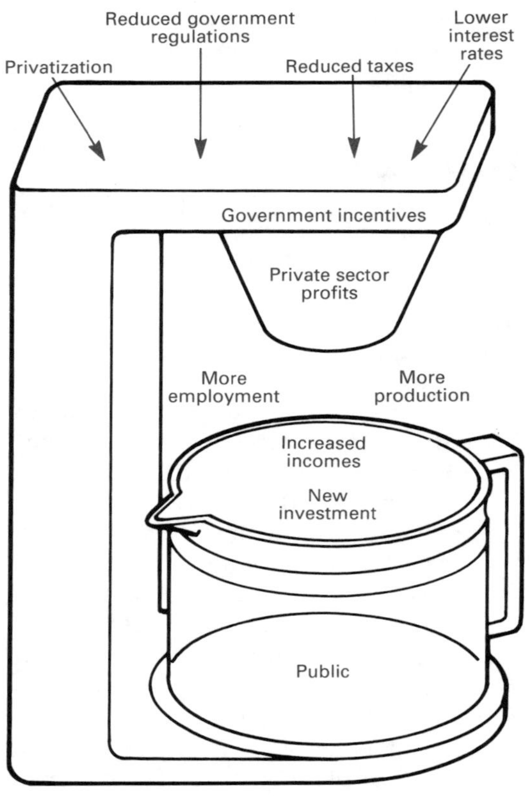

Supply-side theory states that if the private market is free to operate, then wealth will "trickle down" to the general public. Do you agree? Explain.

As the private sector produces more goods, employment levels increase. This results in additional spending and a greater demand for goods and services. Supply-siders thus argue that increased production creates its own demand. They insist that increased demand for goods and services must come from the private sector, not from government spending. For this theory to be successful, individuals must act as the theory states, that is, they must use the incentives to invest and increase production instead of employing the extra profits for speculative investments such as the stock market.

▶ DEALING WITH INFLATION

Inflation is a general rise in prices. An increase in the price of a ticket to the movies does not by itself constitute an inflation. If, however, the price of transport to the movie, the popcorn you eat at the movie, the clothing you wear to the movie, and so on, all experience a price rise at the same time, this is inflation. During an inflationary period, the demand-siders suggest that the government remedy the situation by introducing such policies as high interest rates, reduced expenditures, and tax increases. The supply-sider, on the other hand, believes that the unrestricted market will bring inflation under control.

Now that we have discovered how the system of supply-side economics is supposed to operate in theory (and this is a very simplified explanation), let us examine how well it functioned for its two most famous practitioners, Ronald Reagan and Margaret Thatcher.

▶ SUPPLY-SIDE ECONOMICS IN THE U.S.A.: REAGANOMICS

Ronald Reagan claimed that he was elected to cut taxes, limit government spending on social programs, establish a stable money policy, reduce government interference in the marketplace, and balance the budget. As history reveals, he was successful with all but balancing the budget. He created the highest deficit in American history.

Like other economic theories, Reaganomics has its supporters and detractors. As you read the following documents, try to separate fact from opinion.

A FAVOURABLE VIEW

When Reagan took office in 1981, most serious economists said he couldn't get away with boosting defense spending while cutting taxes. The resulting deficits, it was said, would fuel inflation and raise interest rates. Private investment and economic growth would be crushed. The experts also argued that inflation was so high (then 13 percent) that trying to bring it down with Friedmanesque tight-money policies might create not only a recession but another Great Depression. The cure, they said, would be worse than the disease.

Reagan happily defied that wisdom. He . . . applied a tourniquet to the money supply. The resulting squeeze produced a deep recession that lasted a year. But in that time inflation fell from 13 percent to 4 percent. And in the six years since then, the United States has enjoyed the longest expansion in postwar history—without a major resurgence of inflation.

Reagan's determination to cut taxes also stemmed from a mixture of anecdote and theory. Reagan says he first understood the folly of high marginal tax rates when he was making Army training movies during World War II. At the time, the top personal income tax rate was 90 percent. Reagan was shocked that top stars would make only four movies for the Army a year. Getting paid for additional movies would have pushed them into the top bracket. Even in the middle of a world war, the stars refused to work for 10 cents out of every dollar.

Reagan's encounters with Friedman reinforced his wartime experience. Friedman also teaches that high marginal taxes are bad. The more tax rates rise, the more they whittle away the incentive for workers to produce more and capitalists to invest. As a result, the economy can't grow as fast as it should. That simple principle underpinned Reagan's dramatic 1981 tax cuts and his support for the colossal Tax Reform Act of 1986.

Source: From *Newsweek*, December 26, 1988,

FOCUS

1. Reagan was not only a supply-sider but a monetarist. What evidence is there of this assertion in this document?
2. What two supply-side policies are discussed here?
3. Why does the author suggest that these were good policies?
4. Can you see any disadvantages emerging from Reagan's policies as they are described in this article? Explain.

A LESS FAVOURABLE VIEW

Of all Reagan's policies, perhaps none have generated more controversy than those concerned with the redistribution of income. The effects of the new policies are likely to be felt in American life far into the future.

Central to supply side economics is for the

government to take less money. Thus, one of the first actions of the Reagan Administration was to cut income tax by 25% across the board. This sounds like it should be a good thing for all, but a 25% tax cut doesn't mean quite the same thing to everyone.

Families earning less than $10 000 a year pay about $120 less in taxes; families earning between $20 000 and $40 000 average about $800 less in taxes; and families earning over $80 000 save an average of $15 000 a year in taxes. It is estimated that between 1983 and 1985, families with incomes over $80 000 will gain more than $55 *billion* in tax savings. Setting an example, President Reagan himself, thanks to tax changes that he signed into law, saved $90 000 in income tax in 1982.

If one side of the redistribution issue is to take less from those who have it, the other side is for the government to give less to those who don't. The Reagan Administration says that this is not happening; however, a close look reveals that this is exactly what's happening.

The Congressional Budget Office reports that in 1981, money set aside for 20 programs that helped the poor totalled $101 billion. For 1983, Reagan reduced the funding to $84.5 billion; and in 1984, the Administration intends to cut the amount to $71 billion.

Today, poverty is again on the rise in the United States. According to the Census Bureau, in 1979 11.1% of the population—23.6 million people—were below the poverty line. In 1981 this had risen to 14% (31.8 million people). In 1982, it rose again, and 34.4 million people (15% of the population) were living in poverty, the largest percentage since 1964. Yet, even this understates the problem, for the Census Bureau bases the poverty line on what is needed for subsistence living; for an urban family of four in 1982, this was $9290 a year. The Bureau of Labor Statistics, on the other hand, says that the average family needs $15 000 to maintain even a "low" standard of living, and $25 000 to live "moderately." Thus, in addition to the 34 million people who are "officially" poor, there are at least another 30 million who are "near poor."

How is the Reagan Administration addressing this growing problem of real human need and suffering?

- The food-stamp program, which was all that enabled many families both to pay the bills and to eat, was cut by more than $2 billion (almost 20%) in 1982; cuts of another $2.3 billion were proposed for 1983. Over 800 000 people have been cut from the program; several million more are scheduled to be eliminated, and most of the rest will have their benefits reduced. For example, a family of four living on $100 a week currently receives $34 in food stamps, but Mr. Reagan proposes to cut that to $30 a week—one dollar a day per person for food.
- Three million children were cut from the school-lunch program; the school-breakfast program was chopped by 20%; the school-milk program by 80%; the summer-feeding program by 50%. Funds for a special nutrition program for low income, pregnant women and infants were reduced by 35%.
- Medicaid, which 22 million poor people depend on to pay their medical bills, was cut by $2 billion dollars. Many people will lose their coverage, and the rest will have to pay more for health care; money that they simply don't have.
- Job-training and job-creation programs, which enabled many people to work and therefore get off welfare, were slashed nearly in half.

The Administration hopes that the benefits of a healthy economy will "trickle down" and help the poor more than welfare handouts. There is little evidence that this will ever be the case. It has long been recognized that those whose needs are the greatest require very specific assistance, not some vague hope of something trickling down to them. As Bernard Anderson of the Rockefeller Foundation puts it, "A rising tide will lift all boats, but a rising tide has never done a thing to lift shipwrecks from the bottom of the sea."

Source: Reprinted with the permission of *Canada and the World* Magazine, Oakville, Ontario, February 1984, pp. 18–20.

FOCUS

1. How has tax reform affected American society?
2. What is the argument offered against social programs? How is it supported?
3. Explain why the authors of these two documents disagree.
4. "The administration hopes that the benefits of a healthy economy will "trickle down" and help the poor. . . ." What is meant by "trickle down"? Is this possible? Explain.

▶ THE NATIONAL DEBT

Before further examining Reaganomics, we have to understand the national **deficit** and the debt. Just like any household, a country must have income in order to meet its expenses. A country derives its income through various taxes, be they direct such as income tax or indirect such as excise taxes and some sales taxes. When a government spends as much as it takes in, it has a "balanced budget." If the government spends less than its revenue, it has a "budget surplus," and if more is spent than received, it has a "budget deficit."

In the 1930s, British economist John Maynard Keynes suggested that a deficit was not necessarily bad during periods of slow economic growth. Increased government spending, he stated, would allow people to buy more goods and services. This increased demand would spur increased production and higher employment levels. Monetarists are also willing to tolerate a deficit as long as monetary policy is sound. It is the supply-siders who argue most adamantly against deficit budgeting. They support balanced budgets and consider deficit budgets as inflationary and the cause of national debt. If a country has a deficit, it must borrow money in order to pay its bills. The country must then pay interest on its loans, known as servicing the debt.

Table 1
FOR BETTER OR FOR WORSE

UP AND DOWN
Which of these groups are better off economically as a result of Reagan's policies?

Better off		Worse off
46%	You and your family	30%
75%	The wealthy	9%
41%	Middle class	47%
26%	Low income	60%
31%	The elderly	52%
35%	The young	45%
31%	Blacks	43%

Have Reagan's economic policies been good for the country?

Yes	No
56%	33%

▸ Source: "Are You Better Off?" *Time*, October 10, 1988, pp. 26–27. Copyright 1988 Time Warner Inc. Reprinted by permission.

The following document illustrates the impact of Reaganomics on the American national debt.

REAGANOMICS AND THE NATIONAL DEBT

The steeply dropping stock markets of Monday, October 19 [1987] and the days of chaos that followed are history. The questions now are: why did the stock markets fall? Will it cause a recession? How can the damage be controlled?

The market boom was like a house of cards built on a slippery table top. That slippery base was U.S. President Ronald Reagan's ideas about economics. He believed that by spending freely and lowering taxes demand would be stimulated. Increased production, higher employment, and prosperity would follow. The theory has been called supply-side economics, or Reaganomics.

For a while, Reaganomics seemed to work. Interest rates and inflation dropped. Lower taxes left more money in consumers' pockets, and they went on a spending spree.

Then, doubts began to creep in. Each year Washington spent billions more than it took in. The U.S. national debt topped the one trillion mark. As in Canada, much of the money the government collected went to pay the interest on the debt. The U.S. dollar no longer looked attractive to foreigners; it began to drop in value measured against the Japanese yen or the West German mark. Reaganomics had produced budget deficits that were out of control.

Along with this went another kind of deficit. The boom in consumer demand meant that spending on imports was jumping far ahead of the income from exports. Each year the U.S. was importing about $150 billion more than it sold abroad. The country was living on credit, and its trade deficit was paid for by borrowing from other countries.

It looked as though the United States was heading for economic disaster. Interest rates started to edge up. Higher inflation threatened. Reaganomics, as a few experts had predicted all along, was turning out to be a recipe for short-term gain and long-term pain.

People everywhere had looked to the U.S. for economic leadership. Now, confidence in the governing skills of the White House was fading. Nervous investors were in the mood to panic as they finally did on 19 October.

Source: Reprinted with the permission of *Canada and the World* Magazine, Oakville, Ontario, December 1987, pp. 12–13.

FOCUS

1. Outline the steps that caused the collapse of the American stock market in October 1987.
2. What is the relationship between
   a) interest rates and consumer spending?
   b) lower taxes and consumer spending?
   c) national debt, value of the dollar, and foreign investment?
3. a) How did the Americans solve their trade deficit?
   b) What was the result?

Figure 3
RICHER AND POORER
Percent Decrease or Increase in Average Family Income after Taxes from 1977 to 1988, Adjusted for Inflation
(All figures in 1988 U.S. dollars)

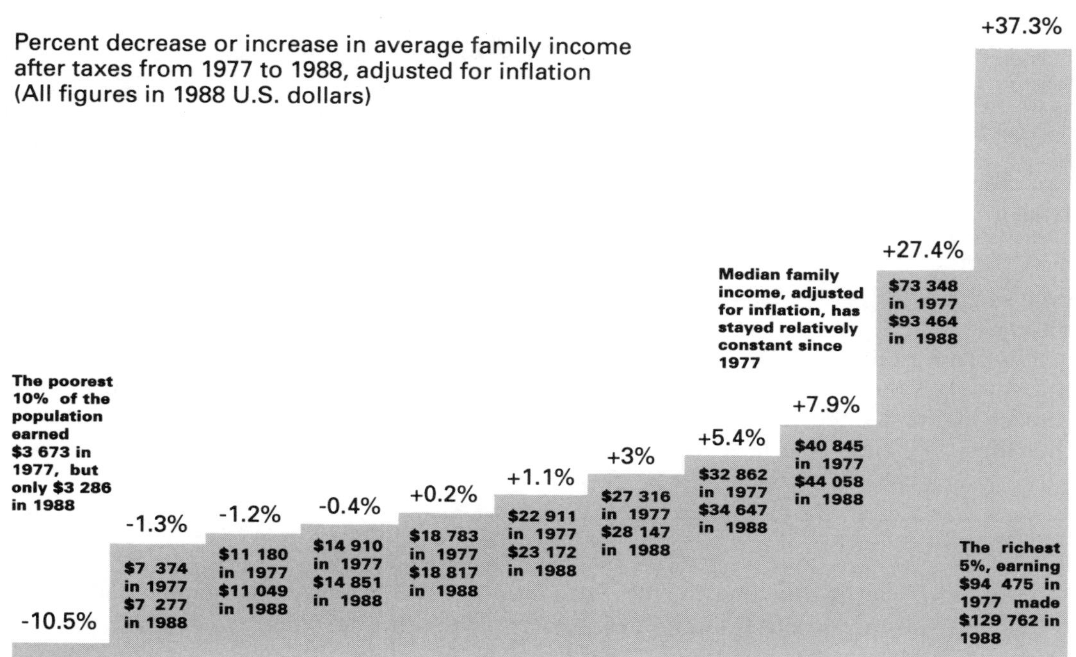

▸ Source: Adapted from "Are You Better Off?" *Time*, October 10, 1988, pp. 26–27. Statistics from Congressional Budget Office. Copyright 1988 Time Warner Inc. Reprinted by permission.

FOCUS

1. Compare Table 1 to Figure 3.
   a) What is the apparent inconsistency?
   b) How do you explain this inconsistency?
2. a) Explain how the middle class is "shrinking."
   b) Why should this be a concern for a government?

▶ REAGANOMICS: AN EVALUATION

The controversy over the American experiment with supply-side economics persists. Its critics claim that it has been a failure because Reagan left the American people with the highest debt in the country's history and his policies created an explosive social situation in the U.S.A. The critics also state that deregulated markets cause "boom and bust" cycles and that Reagan's

Doonesbury BY GARRY TRUDEAU

What is the message of this cartoon?

policies have led to the decline of the middle class.

The proponents of Reaganomics claim that supply-side economics has been successful in the United States. They argue that these policies have reduced inflation and unemployment, while increasing production. They also claim that a larger portion of the world, including the Soviet Union, is moving towards freeing the private market, which is further evidence of the soundness of Reaganomics.

FOCUS

1. Compare supply-side theory with Reaganomics. Did President Reagan actually practise supply-side economics or just parts of the theory? Was he actually practising more than one theory? Explain.
2. What do Reagan's policies and their apparent popularity reveal about the American peoples' view of personal freedom compared to economic or social justice?
3. To what extent is a government responsible to the less fortunate members of its society?
4. There are two sides to every story, and every decision has a cost. Explain the cost for each of Reagan's successes in the areas of:
   a) lowered taxes
   b) lowered unemployment
   c) reduced inflation

▶ SUPPLY-SIDE ECONOMICS IN GREAT BRITAIN: THATCHERISM

Since no two economies are alike, it is not surprising to find that the application of supply-side economics in Great Britain took a different form than Reaganomics. The basic principles applied are similar, but their application and, in some cases, the responses are different.

Since World War II, Great Britain has been strongly influenced by the policies of the British Labour party. The governments formed by this socialist party nationalized

The political relationship of former U.S. President Ronald Reagan and former British Prime Minister Margaret Thatcher helped form a Western alliance.
Canapress Photo Service

the coal industry, rail transportation, parts of the automobile industry, airlines, telephones and other utilities, and petroleum. Also, Labour administrations introduced a "cradle to grave" welfare system. Prime Minister Margaret Thatcher and her Conservative party argued that these policies were responsible for the stagnation of the British economy in the 1960s and 1970s.

Table 2
EMPLOYMENT IN GREAT BRITAIN: 1961–1981

	1961 (000's of people)	1971 (000's of people)	1981 (000's of people)
Agriculture, forestry, fishing, mining, quarrying	1 577	828	692
Manufacturing	8 381	8 013	6 199
Services (incl. construction)	13 050	13 075	14 468
Total	23 008	21 916	21 359

▸ Source: Stewart Dunlop, *Towards Tomorrow: Canada in a Changing World: Geography*. Toronto: Harcourt Brace Jovanovich, 1987, pp. 188–189.

Table 3
JOB LOSSES BY INDUSTRY IN GREAT BRITAIN: 1971–1981

	000's of people		% decline
1. Engineering and electrical	−298	1. Textiles	−41.6
2. Textiles	−259	2. Metal manufacture	−41.5
3. Metal manufacture	−231	3. Leather goods	−34.0
4. Vehicles	−180	4. Clothing and footwear	−31.2
5. Other metal goods	−148	5. Bricks, pottery, glass	−29.6
6. Clothing and footwear	−142	6. Shipbuilding	−25.4

▸ Source: Stewart Dunlop, *Towards Tomorrow: Canada in a Changing World: Geography*. Toronto: Harcourt Brace Jovanovich, 1987, pp. 188–189.

FOCUS

1. Using Tables 2 and 3, determine in which economic areas Great Britain's stagnation was felt the strongest and the weakest.
2. In which area is employment increasing? Why might this be?

When Margaret Thatcher took office in 1979, she began to implement supply-side economics. According to Dr. Madsen Pirie, she turned the economy around.

GREAT BRITAIN'S PRIVATIZATION REVOLUTION

The following is a summary of a speech by Dr. Madsen Pirie on "The Privatization Revolution" before 1200 guests at a dinner in Regina on October 2, 1987. Dr. Pirie is the president and founder of the London-based Adam Smith Institute, a free market think tank, and is an advisor to Prime Minister Margaret Thatcher on privatization.

Since last April we've privatized Rolls Royce and the British airports, we've sold off the Royal Ordinance factory which manufactures ammunition, we've sold off 25 component companies of the National Bus Corporation, we've privatized Leyland Truck, Leyland Bus, we've just announced the first contracts for catering at British Rail stations and at the end of this month we have the last shares of British Petroleum being sold. We've also announced the privatization of water, electricity and the municipal sports centres.

When the last shares of British Petroleum are sold, which will be on October 28, we'll have in Britain more people owning shares than are members of labor unions. When Mrs. Thatcher took office there were six times as many people who belonged to unions as owned shares.

Two and one-half million more families now own their own homes than they did in 1979. Before, they used to rent them at a subsidized rate from Labour local authorities so Mrs. Thatcher started selling them at discounted rates which varied from 20% to 80% of the market price. The people who buy them become property owners and acquire a stake in the country and change their voting habits. The target is to sell another million in the next two years.

We now have three quarters of a million more self-employed because when we privatize industries and we have to trim down the workforce to make it more efficient and more productive, we never fire anybody. We always offer sums of money sufficiently attractive that enough will take voluntary *redundancy*. The workers use that money to leave the state firm and start up in business for themselves. We have more small businesses and more self-employed than ever in the nation's history.

There are two thirds of a million fewer state employees and there are 20% fewer civil servants. None of them were fired. They are now the managers of highly successful private firms where they're making a lot more money.

The firms which were losing money under state ownership are now making money in the private sector. Some of the firms sold were making profits. However, we're now making more in the taxation of those firms than we did when we had 100% of their profits.

Britain now has the fastest growth rate in Europe, our strikes are at the lowest level in 40 years and our taxes are down. During the last 12 months, unemployment in Britain has gone down every single month. Privatization, during that period, has been at a higher level than ever.

Privatization has produced so many benefits in Britain that we know it's going to continue there and expand there.

The result is a changed society. We are rolling back the frontiers of the state. We are giving power and property back to the people. It's been a revolution in our own time.

Source: *Parkland Consumer (Alberta)*, November 2, 1987, p. 12.

FOCUS

1. Considering Dr. Pirie's background, why would you expect him to support Thatcher's economic policies?
2. a) List some of the industries affected by privatization.
   b) Using Tables 2 and 3, explain why certain industries were taken over by the government in the first place?
   c) List some of the results of privatization that Dr. Pirie mentions. How does he support his statements? Should taxpayers' money be given to individuals to start private businesses? Explain.

▶ THE BENEFITS OF THATCHERISM

There is no doubt that Prime Minister Thatcher took the slack out of the British economy. Her administration was characterized by a strong emphasis on self-help (self-reliance), individual initiative and enterprise, and efficiency and productivity. To achieve these targets, the administration first attacked organized labour. The Thatcher government prohibited wildcat strikes and secondary picketing and required that strikes be called only with approval by a secret ballot of a majority of the workers. Partly as a result, union membership fell from fifty-four percent in 1979 to forty percent in 1988. This loss of membership reduced the economic and political strength of the labour movement. Other achievements from a supply-side perspective were a decline in inflation from eighteen percent in 1979 to around three percent in 1988, and a reduction in income tax rates and corporate tax rates. Great Britain's share of world trade showed signs of improvement and productivity in manufacturing has increased at the rate of five percent per year since 1980 (see Figure 4).

This improved production picture has stimulated such investment from abroad as the new and successful Nissan plant at Newcastle. Great Britain has also become the second largest exporter of capital. This resurgence in the British economy has strongly affected the economic condition and the attitude of the average Briton.

For those who still have jobs, real wages have risen by seventeen percent. Approximately twenty-one percent of the population owns stocks, and 2.5 million more people possess their own homes. It is no wonder that many Britons feel more "middle class." In 1972, only sixteen percent of working-class Britons believed that they were middle class; now over twenty-five percent do. The political manifestations of such a shift in attitude kept Margaret Thatcher in office as Great Britain switched allegiance from the Labour party to the Conservative party. This does not mean, however, that Thatcherism was without its costs and critics.

Figure 4

ECONOMIC GROWTH RATES **MANUFACTURING PRODUCTIVITY**

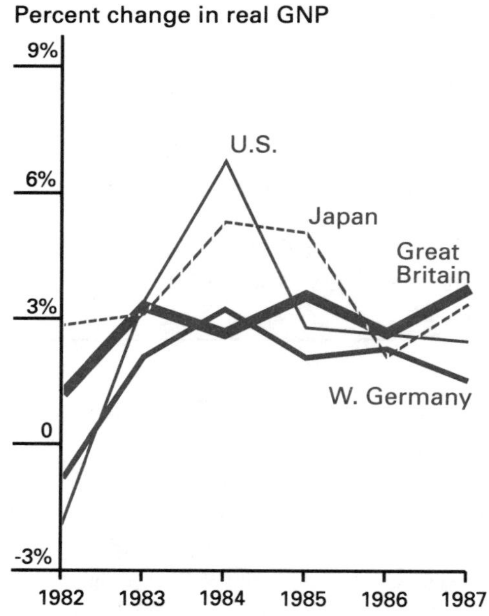

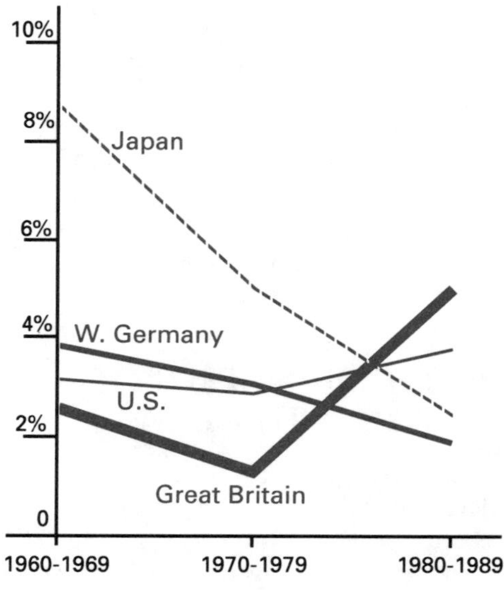

‣ Source: Courtesy of *Fortune Magazine*, May 9, 1988, p. 116.

Figure 5
BRITAIN'S RISING PROSPERITY

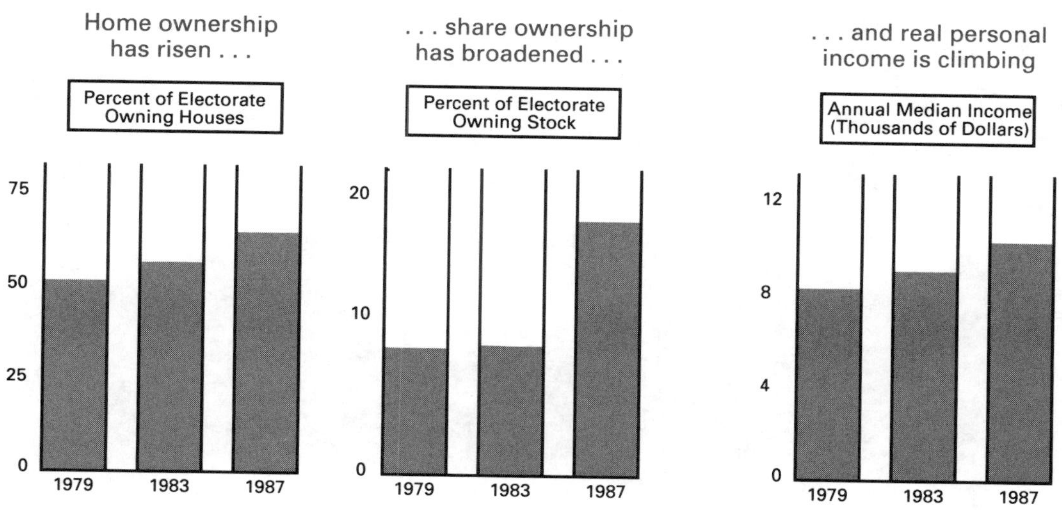

Source: Reprinted from September 26, 1990 issue of *Business Week* by special permission, copyright © 1987 by McGraw-Hill, Inc.

THE COSTS OF THATCHERISM

Prime Minister Thatcher was able to control government spending, so she was not attacked in that respect. But in the realm of unemployment, she received as much criticism as President Reagan did. As the British publication the *Economist* stated, "Thatcherism and Reaganomics. . . . were willing to accept a previously unthinkable level of unemployment — arguing, when pressed, that this was the price of longer-term economic success." For Great Britain this meant a steady unemployment rate of eleven percent. The following newspaper account identifies additional criticisms.

BRITISH BOOM HAS ITS HIDDEN CASUALTIES

by JIM SHEPPARD The Canadian Press

LONDON— . . . There's no doubt that, overall, the British economy is booming after almost a decade of market-oriented government by Prime Minister Margaret Thatcher. Growth is strong, investment and profits up, inflation down.

But there's a dark underside to that story— a world mostly hidden from view where millions of people are far worse off than before the advent of Thatcherism, a world where despair, cynicism and even death are accepted in a way that seems inconceivable to a North American mind.

The cradle-to-grave welfare state once renowned around the world is being dismantled in favor of varying degrees of user-pay health care, education and social services.

Critics say Thatcher is creating new divisions between the rich and the poor, and between the prosperous south around London and the poverty-stricken north and west.

However, bolstered by a third consecutive electoral majority in 1987 and disarray among the political opposition, the woman who revels in her Iron Lady nickname has made revamping of social policy her crusade of the late 1980s.

Last year, as Thatcher embarked on a lengthy campaign to outline the religious and moral basis for the social revolution she seeks, she quoted with approval St. Paul's Epistle to the Thessalonians:

"If a man will not work, he shall not eat," she said before a gathering of Scottish clerics.

That's fine, the critics say, if everyone is given the chance to work.

But not everyone is. Some are too old, some too young, some inhabit the wrong areas. . . .

In Liverpool, at the other end of the age scale, Darlington and his mates at the run-down, graffiti-strewn Childwall Valley Youth Club say they've got only one option now that the government is cutting off welfare to teenagers who have left school without a job lined up in advance.

"Rob, burgle," he says bluntly.

Source: The Canadian Press.

APPLYING YOUR KNOWLEDGE

1. List the "casualties" of Thatcher's policies.
2. What are the similarities between the effects of Reaganomics and Thatcherism?
3. Debate the advantages of supply-side economics versus demand-side economics.
4. Prepare for a mock debate among Thatcher, Reagan, and J.M. Keynes.

CHAPTER 8 OVERVIEW

THE WORLD'S ECONOMIES: CENTRALLY PLANNED SYSTEMS

This chapter describes the operation of the centrally planned economy. It begins with a discussion of the origins of central planning, evaluates the role of the Industrial Revolution in its growth, and examines the ideas of such early socialists as R. Owen, C. Fournier, and L. Blanc. Karl Marx played a central role in the development of socialist thought, and his ideas and contributions to central planning are outlined in considerable detail. The chapter then explains how a centrally planned economy would operate in theory and outlines its values, merits, and disadvantages. It concludes with brief vignettes of the planned economies of China, Cuba, and Yugoslavia.

▶ OBJECTIVES

After reading this chapter, you should be able to:

- ▶ explain the origins of central planning
- ▶ evaluate the role of the Industrial Revolution and the ideas of the Utopian Socialists in the growth of socialist thought
- ▶ critique the ideas of Karl Marx
- ▶ discuss the values of central planning
- ▶ outline how central planning operates
- ▶ debate the merits of central planning
- ▶ compare the economies of Cuba, China, and Yugoslavia

▶ KEY TERMS

centrally planned economy
socialism
Utopian Socialists
public ownership
Communist Manifesto
Das Kapital
Marxism
Industrial Revolution
bourgeoisie

CHAPTER 8 THE WORLD'S ECONOMIES: CENTRALLY PLANNED SYSTEMS

Adam Smith, you will recall, stated that government should not intervene in the economy. The best way to ensure the economic well-being of a country, he suggested, was for the government to stand aside and let the forces of the marketplace take control. As we have seen in the preceding case studies, actual free enterprise economies do not operate in such an ideal manner. Even so, the ideal free enterprise system as described by Adam Smith stands at one extreme of several possible ways of organizing an economy.

At the other end of the spectrum is the ideal **centrally planned economy**, in which government plans every aspect of the economy and maintains constant control over it. This chapter examines the origins, the ideals and values, the advantages and disadvantages, and the operation of centrally planned economies.

▶ ORIGINS OF THE PLANNED ECONOMY

Planned economies go back a long way. Two millennia before the birth of Christ, the Sumerian society in the Middle East was state-controlled. In ancient Egypt, agriculture and the gathering of important natural resources were controlled and administered by the priesthood under the direction of the Pharaohs. China has had at least three periods in its long history during which its rulers imposed sweeping controls over the country's economy. Other examples include the Incas of Peru and several religious sects in the Middle Ages.

The idea that property is owned by an entire people, not by private individuals, is also very old. Some historians have traced this idea back to the Old Testament and to the writings of the Greek philosopher Plato. The first modern political movement that favoured common ownership of property, rather than private ownership, was an English group in the mid-seventeenth century called the Diggers.

Economic planning on a country-wide basis, however, was generally not possible until the Industrial Revolution of the eighteenth and nineteenth centuries, when the invention of machines and the creation of the factory system made it possible to produce goods on a large and efficient scale. The economic advantages of mechanization, power-driven machinery, and factory production led to an unprecedented leap in output. For the first time in history it appeared that hunger and poverty could be eliminated. At the same time, advances in transportation and communications made it possible for industrialized countries to organize their economies on a national scale.

The early forms of capitalism created extreme income inequalities and deplorable living conditions. Men, women, and children worked twelve hours a day, six days a week, or longer. Working in smoke-filled, cramped, and unsanitary rooms crippled or deformed many workers. Children were chained to machines, and those who did not conform to the harsh discipline of factory life were fined, beaten, or cast out to join the crowds of beggars in the city streets. Workers returned home at night to slum conditions of an appalling nature. Houses were severely overcrowded, badly ventilated, and poorly lit; garbage and sewage were dumped in the streets; the smell was overpowering. Vice and crime flourished, and drunkenness and prostitution grew at an alarming rate. The terrible conditions, combined with the tremendous increase in production, led to the emergence of **socialism** as a major political force in the Western world.

▶ THE EMERGENCE OF SOCIALIST IDEALS

The first response to the Industrial Revolution came from so-called **Utopian Socialists** (approximately 1770–1850). Moved by humanitarian ideals, Christian principles, and an optimistic view of human nature, they demanded that these terrible conditions be improved.[1] Led by Robert Owen in Great Britain, Charles Fourier and Claude Saint-Simon in France, and Horace Greeley in America, the Utopian Socialists experimented with different forms of communal living that stressed co-operation, self-help, religion, and education. They thought that if the environment were improved, an ideal society could be established in which all people were happy and prosperous. These changes were possible, the Utopian Socialists stated, through education and peaceful democratic methods, and they sought to convince businesspeople to adopt more enlightened practices. Robert Owen, for instance, attempted to set a good example for other industrialists. He reduced the work day for his cotton mill labourers in New Lanark, Scotland, from twelve hours daily to ten and one-half hours; improved housing and working conditions; refused to hire children under the age of ten; and provided education for the young. Universal education, he argued, would eliminate crime and lead to prosperity for all. If other employers

▸ [1]The term "Utopian" was derived from a book written by Sir Thomas More in the sixteenth century, which described his fantasy of a perfect society where everyone lived in harmony and mutual co-operation. When Marx used the word "Utopian" to describe the socialists, he meant it as a derogatory remark.

could be persuaded to adopt similar practices, the evils of industrialization could be ended forever. The Utopian Socialists did not want to destroy the capitalist system, they merely wanted to remove some of its more blatant evils.

Although some experiments in communal living flourished for a while, the Utopians were unable to win many converts, and by the mid-nineteenth century the movement had lost its vitality. The next step in the development of socialist thought was provided by Louis Blanc of France. He popularized the idea of large-scale **public ownership**, combined with labourers' control over the workplace, and the distribution of goods according to individual need. When this attempt at government-initiated socialism also failed, the stage was set for Karl Marx's more radical and violent brand of socialism.[2]

Karl Marx (1818–1883)
The Bettmann Archive

▶ KARL MARX

The impact of Karl Marx (1818–1883) upon the socialist movement has been unparalleled. ''No thinker in the nineteenth century,'' claimed one of his biographers, ''has had so direct, deliberate, and powerful an influence on mankind as Karl Marx.'' Marx was a brilliant scholar, economist, and philosopher. After studying law and philosophy in Prussia (now Germany), Marx became a journalist. His radical ideas, however, led to successive exiles in Paris, Brussels, and finally London. Here, Marx spent years reading, researching, and writing in the British Museum. With his close friend Friedrich Engels, he wrote the ***Communist Manifesto*** in 1848, followed by numerous other works, and concluding with ***Das Kapital***, the last two volumes of which Engels wrote from Marx's rough notes and manuscripts. Although Marx did not invent socialism, he developed his ideas from earlier thinkers and soon dominated the movement. His theories came to be known as Marxism.

The name **Marxism** has different meanings for different people. It has been called the salvation of the future, the battle cry for revolutionaries, a religious dogma, and a harebrained scheme. To some people it is a system of ideas; to others it is a political movement. Although we are treating Marxism as an economic system in this chapter, you should bear in mind that it is both a political and an economic ideology that attempts to provide an overall interpretation of human life.

▸ [2]As minister of public works in 1848, Blanc established a system in which the workers managed their own factories. However, his system was quickly disbanded by the industrialists when they returned to power.

▶ Marxist Thought

Like earlier socialists, Marx was greatly moved by the inhumane conditions created by the **Industrial Revolution**. However, he disagreed with the Utopians' explanation of these conditions and with their solution to the problem. Life for the poor would never improve, he insisted, until the ruling class had been replaced by the workers.

The Industrial Revolution had spread from England to Belgium, to France, and then to Germany. Its abuses were worse on the continent than they were in Great Britain, and it was here that the young Marx first came into contact with the harshest features of *laissez-faire* capitalism. As he matured, he observed the failure of the Utopians to solve industrial evils and Marx witnessed the failure of Louis Blanc to convince the French government to remedy the situation. *The Communist Manifesto*, urging the overthrow of capitalism, was the result of his disillusionment. In fifty years, socialist thought, spurred by worsening conditions in the cities, had moved from urging mild reforms in the system to advocating a complete overthrow of government.

According to Marx, all aspects of a person's life were determined by the individual's relationship to the means of production (land, tools, factories). Although the way in which a person made a living was not the only criterion in determining human behaviour, Marx believed that it was the most important factor. People's relationship to the means of production was the foundation upon which each society in history had erected its culture, laws, government, and artistic endeavours. The story of humanity, Marx wrote, had been a history of class conflict between the owners of the means of production and the workers, between the exploiters and the exploited, and between the ruling class and the oppressed classes. In every case, the struggle was between classes that represented opposing economic interests, and each time the struggle resulted in the betterment of conditions for the majority — if only slightly.

In Marx's view, the classes themselves arose from their relationship to the means of production. The governing class owned the means of production, and the oppressed classes did not. In a nomadic society, for example, those who owned the most horses were the chiefs, whereas in an agricultural society, landowners were the ruling class. As each new class achieved power, it revised the law, education, religion, art, media, and government structures in order to justify and reinforce its dominant position in society.

▶ CLASS ANTAGONISMS

The kernel of Marxist thought was the belief that capitalism was only a stage in the historical progress of humankind. Capitalism, said Marx, arose when the feudal medieval society became a hindrance to the economic growth of Europe's merchants and manufacturers. The new emerging class of traders and industrialists overthrew the existing agriculturally based economic structure and a new era of capitalism was born. The ideology of this new ruling class, which Marx termed the **bourgeoisie** (literally, town-dwellers), emphasized freedom from economic restrictions and freedom from the political domination of the old land-based aristocracy.

According to Marx, the Industrial Revolution, which accompanied the capitalist era, created two economic classes. The ruling class (or bourgeoisie) consisted of wealthy financiers, large-scale merchants, and factory owners. It controlled the means of producing goods (factories, machines). The other class consisted of the workers who had to sell their labour to the highest bidder, and without whom the bourgeoisie could not survive. The existence of this class, which Marx termed the proletariat, showed that bourgeois freedom was not freedom at all for the great majority of people.

The central feature of the capitalist system, according to Marx, was that the workers must "sell" their labour power to those who owned the means of production. The bourgeoisie exploited the proletariat by forcing it to create goods, the value of which was greater than the wages the workers received for their labour. It was this difference between the value of goods produced and the wages of the workers that enabled the bourgeoisie to become wealthier than the proletariat. Marx condemned both the profit motive and private property — which he believed were the major sources of conflict between the two economic classes.

The capitalist system exploited and degraded workers, Marx insisted. It alienated people from themselves and from each other. Marx believed that human nature was essentially creative and that the work people perform was an expression of themselves. Artists, for instance, fulfill themselves through paintings, just as shoemakers do through shoemaking. When workers have to sell their labour like an object, and the creation of their labour is taken from them at a negligible price, they become alienated from themselves, from others, and from their work. Capitalism thus prevents humanity from ever fulfilling its potential.

Marx believed that the capitalist system, like the other economic systems that had preceded it, contained economic, social, and psychological forces within it that would ultimately bring about its ruin. These forces would cause wages and prof-

The cartoonist was commenting on the plight of workers in Poland in the early 1980s. What is the message of the cartoon?
Raeside, Victoria Times-Colonist

its to decline and would lead to the gradual emergence of class consciousness among the proletariat as the workers sank deeper and deeper into poverty. At the same time, the bourgeoisie would become wealthier as the means of production fell into fewer and fewer hands. These inevitable changes would lead to depressions, imperialism, wars, and finally to a revolution by the proletariat.

▶ The Revolution and Afterwards

Ultimately, Marx believed, the exploited class would rebel as it had always done in the past. It was possible that the capitalist system would be so weakened by this time that violence would be unnecessary. It was much more likely, however, that the bourgeoisie would fight to retain its power and wealth, as had every other ruling class in history. Because the bourgeoisie controlled the police, the government, the law courts, and the media, violence was almost inevitable. It was not so much that the bourgeoisie as a class was selfish (although many individuals were), it was just that they were blinded by their ideology from seeing the injustices created by the capitalist system.

The revolution would be the final struggle between the exploiters and the exploited. Instead of creating a new form of class domination, as had all previous revolutions, the proletariat would establish a classless society. In fact, there would be only one class left.

Marx's writings on capitalism and its evils were very detailed and thorough, but on the post-revolutionary period he spoke only in vague and general terms. Following the revolution, Marx envisioned a brief period in which the dictatorship of the bourgeoisie would be replaced by a dictatorship of the proletariat. Now the many (the workers) rather than the few (the bourgeoisie) would control the government. This was to be a transitional period during which time both the bourgeoisie and the capitalist system would be converted to proper socialist behaviour. Under the dictatorship of the proletariat, the state would have the following characteristics:

- a centrally planned economy
- increasing economic production
- distribution of income according to work performed
- increasing economic equality
- a gradual disappearance of classes
- increasing desire to work for the good of society rather than for personal profit

After this short transition period, Marx believed that the state would ''wither away,'' poverty and crime would disappear, and ''human history'' would replace ''class history.''[3] In this final stage of pure communism, as Marx called it, not only would class differences disappear but so also would national differences. After a series of revolutions, capitalism would be eliminated, and all people would live as one family.

On the specific economic details of the communist state, Marx was extremely vague. Society's production would be distributed according to the motto, ''From each according to his ability, to each according to his need.'' At first, individuals might tend to be greedy, but as they discovered that there would always be sufficient goods to meet their basic needs, such feelings would disappear. People would no longer go to work in order to survive and make a

▸ [3]Presumably, Marx meant that the coercive powers of society would wither away, not that all government and administration would cease. In a classless, egalitarian society, there would be no need to coerce anybody.

profit, as they did under capitalism. Instead, they would work because they wanted to work. In fact, according to Marx, human beings were dominated by the need to create and produce. Under communism, their creative abilities would be released, and the material and social accomplishments of society would prosper as never before.

▶ The Ideal Marxist Society

Bearing in mind that not every Marxist or non-Marxist will agree with the following discussion, let us conclude our description of Marxism by examining the values and principles of the ideal Marxist state. Marxist thought proceeds from an assumption that all people share certain minimum requirements—food, shelter, health, and physical and psychological security. Society should be organized to ensure that everyone's basic needs are met. At the same time, because all commodities are the result of a joint pooling of intelligence, skills, and labour, the country's resources should be shared to match the needs and interests of all the people. This does not mean strict mathematical equality, but enough for a decent standard of living, personal fulfillment, and self-respect. Individual differences would continue to exist, but they would no longer enable some people to amass enormous wealth, while others lived in dismal poverty.

Economic production would be directed to creating a humane, democratic society in which everyone would have equal opportunity. The economy would be administered by people who would be elected periodically to collect information about everyone's needs and to decide what should be produced in order to meet these needs.

With private property and the profit motive abolished, and with the existence of a surplus of goods for everyone, crime and greed would not exist. Freedom from exploitation and economic insecurity would allow people to develop their creativity and cultivate their talents and interests. According to Karl Marx:

> *A being does not regard himself as independent unless he is his own master, and he is only his own master when he owes his existence to himself. A man who lives by the favour of another [his boss or employer] considers himself a dependent being.*

The interests of the individual, many Marxists argue, are best served when the whole country benefits. Society should be based upon co-operation, not upon competition. Because they believe that self-centred, acquisitive people are developed and nurtured by such capitalist institutions as schools, media, law, and government, Marxists argue that the opposite type of personality can be developed by a "socialist education." Individual attitudes and the economic basis of society must be altered to create mutual trust and an identification with common goals. Only then can the ideal society be achieved.

▶ CENTRAL PLANNING

How, in theory, does a centrally planned economy operate? Because everything is planned, rather than leaving economic decisions to market forces, it may seem that it is a much simpler system. After the government (whether democratically elected or not) decides upon its priorities, it appoints a committee of economic experts to ensure that these priorities are met. Making these decisions is a complex task in an industrialized economy.

As in any economic system, the law of scarcity has to be addressed. Scarcity means that choices have to be made. The economic questions of what to produce, how the goods are to be produced, and who gets what, have to be answered. The distinction between a private enterprise economy and a centrally planned economy is how they answer these questions. In solving the question of what to produce, the committee of economic experts must consider many factors. First, what is the overall policy of the government? For example, if the government is concerned about an attack by a neighbouring country, it may decide to produce tanks rather than automobiles. If, on the other hand, the government is under pressure from the people to provide consumer goods, it may decide to produce automobiles rather than tanks. However, the government can only request that so many automobiles and/or tanks be produced. It cannot ask for two million vehicles if the resources (human, capital, and natural) can only produce one million vehicles. And if one million vehicles are produced, there will be less material (rubber, steel, glass, etc.) for other products.

The committee must also determine how these goods will be produced and what resources (human, capital, and natural) will be used. But again, economic and political forces will complicate the decision-making process. Politically, if the government decides that full employment is important, the committee might use human resources (labour) rather than machines, even if the former method is less efficient. If the country lacks the needed natural resources, then more expensive imported materials would have to be purchased.

Who will receive the goods that are produced is the final decision to be made. Prices for goods may be set to achieve government goals rather than to reflect the forces of supply and demand. For example, if the goal is to provide adequate housing for all citizens, then the government would have to set housing prices so that everyone could afford to rent or buy a house. However, by ignoring the actual housing costs, the government may create a serious economic problem. Charging a lower price for the lumber used in housing construction could hurt the economy if timber is in limited supply. The law of scarcity should be reflected in how prices are determined, and if using up the forests creates a scarcity of timber as well as problems of pollution from mills, then the country may eventually pay a "price" for having ignored economic reality.

The same principle can be applied to wages. If government policy decrees that everyone will be paid the same amount of money regardless of the type of work performed, this can be accomplished. However, some undesirable jobs may never be filled. The committee establishing wages may thus have to make some pay adjustments to provide an incentive for some people to take less desirable jobs. (See Figure 8-1.)

▶ Disadvantages of Central Planning

Critics of the centrally planned economy believe that because such economic decisions as income distribution and the choice of employment are controlled by the government, the motivation of workers will be reduced, and their efficiency will therefore decline. In addition, the emphasis on state planning and national goals unduly restricts individual freedoms and forces everyone to conform. The enlarged bureaucracy needed to manage the economy gives the government tremendous power over the lives of the citizens. Without economic freedom, some critics believe, there can be no political liberty.

A more pragmatic problem is the difficulty of coordinating the millions of decisions needed to carry out the central plan. Each economic decision, like a ripple in a pool of water, affects other parts of the

Figure 8–1
CENTRAL PLANNING—WHAT, HOW, AND FOR WHOM GOODS ARE PRODUCED

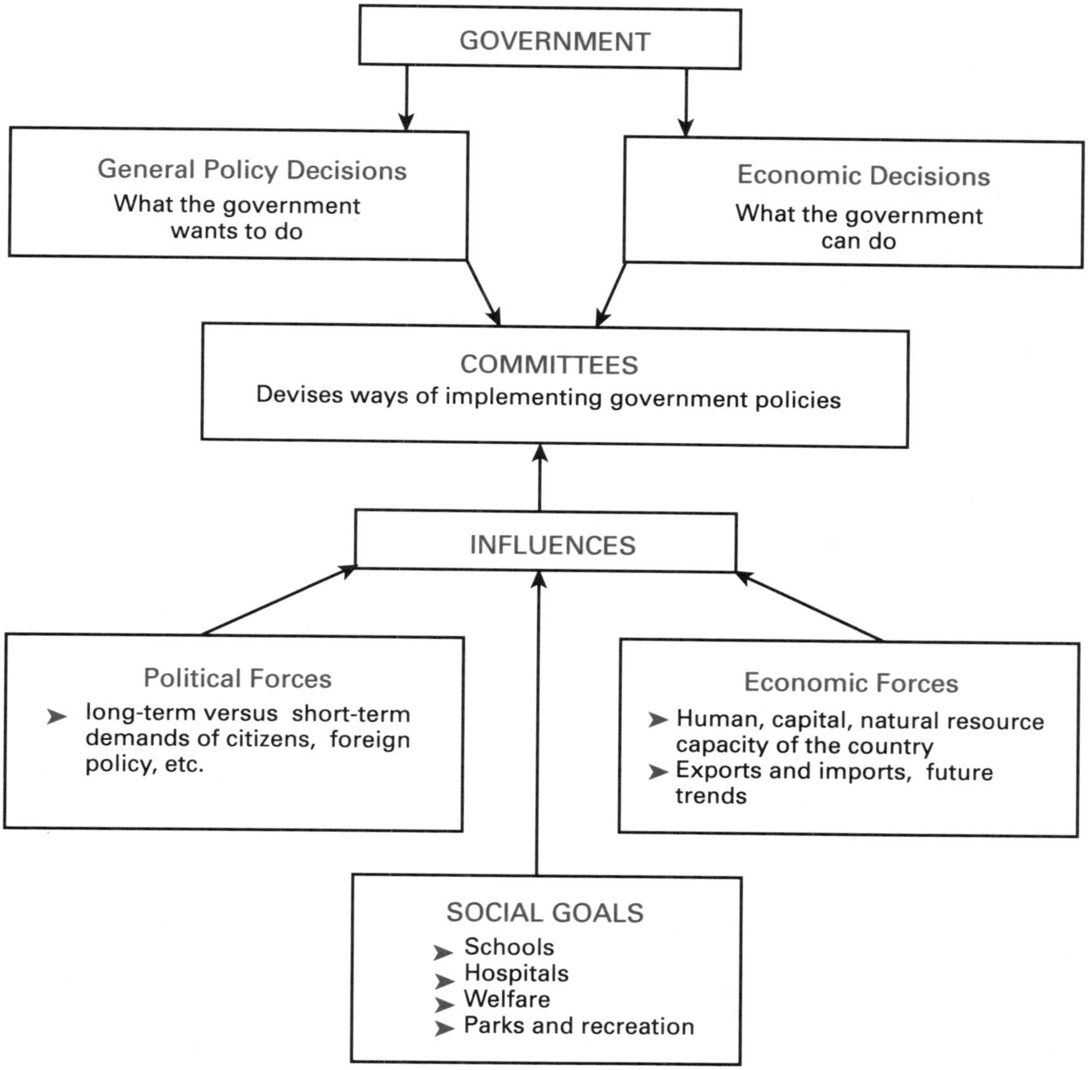

GOVERNMENT

General Policy Decisions
What the government wants to do

Economic Decisions
What the government can do

COMMITTEES
Devises ways of implementing government policies

INFLUENCES

Political Forces
- long-term versus short-term demands of citizens, foreign policy, etc.

Economic Forces
- Human, capital, natural resource capacity of the country
- Exports and imports, future trends

SOCIAL GOALS
- Schools
- Hospitals
- Welfare
- Parks and recreation

economy. In its efforts to solve one problem, a government may create another. An extreme case of such a situation took place late in 1981, when the government of Poland, faced with a food shortage, decided to reduce the consumption of other products, and announced that the price of cigarettes would double. Members of the

Polish workers' union, Solidarity, were enraged and the government was faced with violent objections to its entire economic policy.

The following hypothetical case illustrates how an attempt to change one aspect of an economy through planning can have widespread economic effects. Do not minimize the seemingly "minor" problem presented; as the Polish example illustrates, "minor" changes can have a snowballing effect, posing a serious dilemma for all planned economies.

Corkscrews Versus Bottle Openers

You have just been appointed head planner of the third division in the western section of Ungawa. Your division is in charge of manufacturing corkscrews and bottle openers. It is not a very important position, but you are determined to do a good job.

The first problem is to decide how many corkscrews and bottle openers should be manufactured this year. It soon becomes apparent that this decision is not nearly as easy as it seems. Your superintendent reports that last year the people bought 10 000 corkscrews at $2.00 each and 5000 bottle openers at $1.00 each. But this still has not solved the problem of how many bottle openers will be needed this year.

To answer this question, you decide to ask the consumers. Your first idea to conduct a nation-wide poll is rejected by the central planning committee as too expensive, and your imaginative scheme of having every television linked to a giant computer is not yet feasible. It now appears that you will have to rely upon last year's sales figures and the priorities set by the central committee. Because the government's plan is to reduce the amount of liquor consumed by the people, the planning committee has cut your supply of steel in half and has transferred fifty of your best factory workers to another sector of the economy. The best solution, it appears, is to manufacture 4000 corkscrews and 2000 bottle openers at last year's price.

Less than a month later the trouble began. When the government increased the price of wine in order to reduce consumption, wine drinkers switched from wine to beer. As a result, there are not enough bottle openers for sale, and most of the corkscrews are still sitting in the stores. By now, the people are lining up in front of the shops, and some merchants are reserving the bottle openers for their friends. As a temporary measure, you distribute ration coupons, but this creates a blackmarket ring that, it is rumoured, is selling bottle openers for $7.00 each.

What can you do? You are caught between the long-range goals of the planners and the immediate needs of the people. Your spouse suggests that you raise the price of bottle openers and lower the price of corkscrews. Resignation is also an attractive option, yet this choice is not really acceptable because you remember the time when there were no plans and people were free to buy what they could afford—a time when a few individuals were rich and the rest were poor. If this were the case today, there would be no limitations upon the consumption of alcohol, except its price. A country must have priorities!

There is a possibility of convincing the planning committee to give you additional steel supplies, but this means cutting back production in another area of the economy. There are some workers available in the mid-western section, but they do not have the proper skills, and your former bottle opener workers have just learned their new jobs. Each sector of the economy is so interrelated that it is impossible to change one operation without affecting everything else.

The beer drinkers will just have to wait a couple of months until you can convert the corkscrew factories into bottle opener plants. You can only hope that in the meantime they do not switch back to wine!

If only problems could be as easily solved as those of your husband. Sergei is in charge of a nail factory. Every year he is able to outwit the central planning committee that is always trying to make him work harder and produce exactly the types of nails it requires. Two years ago the government set a target of one million nails, so Sergei manufactured only small nails. Last year the target was ten tonnes of nails, so Sergei concentrated on producing large, heavy nails. This year he is supposed to manufacture $100 000 worth of nails. Sergei is now planning to make only the fancy, expensive type.

▶ Advantages of Central Planning

Supporters of the centrally planned economy believe that this system is best designed to meet the needs of the people and the state. Whereas production in a private enterprise economy reflects the business person's guess about future individual demands, the planned economy reflects government decisions about future national needs. If, for example, a country's priorities are to eliminate unemployment, pollution, poverty, and wasteful duplication of consumer products, this can be achieved by using the country's resources in a well-devised plan.

The principal assumption of the centrally planned economy is that government is capable of choosing suitable goals for the country and of selecting proper methods to implement them. The country's economic objectives and the methods employed to achieve these goals will therefore reflect the ideas of the country's leaders. Theoretically, a democratic government will design the economy to carry out the wishes of the elected representatives. The economic objectives and methods of a non-democratic country will depend upon the desires of that country's leaders. No matter what political system is in power, the advocates of central planning believe that planning can meet national economic goals more effectively than the private enterprise system does.

As our technology expands, particularly in computers, many of the technical problems associated with an overabundance of information can be overcome. In the past, planners failed simply because they were unable to exchange enough information to get the job done. Computers have the potential to handle the requests of millions of users so that fast, accurate, and efficient data can be utilized. This means that central planning, even with an expanding advanced economy, would be technically possible. The following three examples illustrate how China, Cuba, and Yugoslavia have employed central-planning techniques to answer the three basic economic questions.

▶ CHINA

China is the most densely populated country in the world. There are well over one billion people in an area of 9 450 000 square kilometres. Attempting to control the economy of China through central planning is extremely difficult.

After the Chinese Revolution in 1949 (see Case Study 11) the Communist party controlled the country and established a Marxist state under Mao Zedong, whose economic goal was to transform China into an industrial society. In the first stage, Mao rid China of the landlords and gave their land to the peasants, or formed co-operatives. This was followed in the mid-1950s by state farms (land controlled by the government). The final step was to be the ''Great Leap Forward'' in 1958. Self-sufficient communities of 5000 peasants were to produce both crops and steel in order to begin the process of industrialization. However, not enough food and inferior steel led to the termination of this plan in 1961, and China soon found itself in a period of political turmoil. As Mao fought to maintain control of the country, economic planning remained on hold.

It was not until moderate communists gained control of China after Mao's death in 1976 that significant changes in the economy occurred. Peasants were given the opportunity to practise a form of private enterprise. If they produced more than their quota of food, they could sell a portion of the surplus and keep the profits. This provided incentives for peasants to produce more, which resulted in them buying more consumer products.

Political moderation at home also meant a more moderate policy towards the rest of the world, and in the 1980s China welcomed more international involvement. By the end of the decade, a third of China's national income came from foreign trade. This opening up of China to international trade introduced more elements of private enterprise into certain areas in China. The southern coastal provinces near Hong Kong became relatively prosperous as commercial and industrial companies from the United States, Japan, Taiwan, and Hong Kong established plants and offices in an environment of decentralized economic conditions.

In China, as in every other country, economic and political events are inevitably

The southern coastal provinces of China have become more ''Westernized,'' with closer associations with Hong Kong, Japan, Taiwan, and the United States.
Consulate General of Japan

The 1989 action by the Chinese government on students had an immediate economic effect on China. What has been the long-term effect?
Durand/Langevin—SYGMA

linked. The Chinese government's action against the pro-democracy students in Tiananmen Square in Beijing, June 1989, produced increased attempts at economic as well as political control throughout China. Nonetheless, remarkable differences in the degree of economic planning and the amounts of economic reform can still be found in parts of China.

▶ CUBA

In direct contrast to China, which has gone through major periods of fluctuation, in Cuba communism has remained relatively stable over the last thirty years. It is one of the few countries that embraced central planning in the 1950s that continues to practise the same principles into the 1990s.

In 1959, Fidel Castro and his group of revolutionaries overthrew the Cuban government and shortly afterwards established a communist regime. (See Case Study 11.) He quickly took control of the army and the government, banning political parties and private businesses, and establishing close ties with the Soviet Union.

Economically, this meant the development of a centrally planned economy that included providing such basic necessities as food and low rents for all Cubans. Castro emphasized full employment, mass education, and free health care. He achieved these objectives through state control of prices and wages. After relinquishing control over some parts of the economy in the early 1980s, Castro re-established almost total control over the economy by the end of the decade.

Cuba thus moved against the trend towards less government control of the economy in communist states. Instead, Castro placed economic power back in the hands of central committees under his direct rule and appealed to Cuban workers to work for moral incentives rather than monetary ones. The name Ché Guevara, a leader of the 1959 revolution, was invoked and workers were urged to emulate Ché's ideals and revolutionary principles. Posters encouraged people to *Seamos como el Ché* (let's be like Ché). Even as other countries using central-planning methods (U.S.S.R., Poland, and Hungary) adopted certain capitalistic ideas, Castro asked the Cuban Congress in 1990 if it wanted capitalist bourgeois reforms. The delegates in the Congress shouted back, "No!"

▶ YUGOSLAVIA

Yugoslavia was one communist country that adhered neither to the central planning nor to the capitalist system. In 1950, Yugoslavia challenged the view that an economy must be organized either by a predetermined plan or by market forces. Instead, it enacted a series of reforms that combined elements of both a planned economy and a market economy, thereby creating a novel socialist market economy.

Yugoslavia emerged from World War II in a devastated condition. One out of every ten citizens had been killed; some 3.5 million people were left homeless; and approximately forty percent of the country's manufacturing capacity had been destroyed. Politically, the Communist party of Yugoslavia, under Marshall Josip "Tito" Broz, had gained control of the government. Although Tito had achieved power without the aid of the Soviet Union, Yugoslavia adopted the economic system of the largest Marxist state and its best trading partner. Industrial, mining, wholesale, and retail enterprises were taken over by the state (nationalized), and private ownership was restricted to small businesses employing no more than five workers. State farms and agricultural collectives were established, and private land holdings were limited to thirty-five hectares. Under the direction and control of the Communist party, a comprehensive five-year plan was developed to put the economy back on its feet.

▶ Relations with the U.S.S.R.

In 1948, Yugoslavia abandoned centralized economic planning and embarked on a new course that would eventually lead to workers' self-management. The immediate cause of this radical change in direction was Yugoslavia's disagreements with the Soviet Union.

This break with the Soviet Union forced Yugoslavia to reconsider its own economic and political ideologies. Tito's government was compelled to criticize the Soviet system in order to justify its defiance of the U.S.S.R. Yugoslavia described state planning as an authoritarian method of planning that left the economy at the mercy of a few politicians. Furthermore, it declared that nationalization and state ownership of the means of production (factories, people, and land) had not prevented Soviet workers from being exploited and dehumanized.

This controversy led Yugoslavia to closer contact with Western economic thought and institutions. At the same time, Tito broadened his base of political support. In addition, internal divisions prevented unanimous agreement on any central plan. These combined forces produced a different brand of socialism.

From 1949 to 1953, Yugoslavia searched for an alternate solution. Central planning was rejected because the government believed it reduced workers' initiative and prevented the development of social responsibility. However, the market economy, said Tito, was no better because it exploited the great majority of workers for the benefit of the few. True socialism, he decided, required direct political *and* economic democracy. All citizens should participate in decisions that concerned their lives—*both* in the political sphere and in the workplace.

In 1950, Yugoslavia began to develop a new type of socialist economy that it hoped would achieve social justice. The central planning apparatus was dismantled, and control over the country's enterprises given to the workers. Profit was re-established to serve as an economic incentive, and the market forces of supply and demand were used to guide the allocation of resources. These changes were instituted over a number of years, and it was not until 1965 that Yugoslavia's new economy fully emerged.

In recent years, Yugoslavia had been hard hit by a number of serious problems. Since the death of Tito in 1981, leadership of the country has rotated according to a system designed to reflect the multi-ethnic six republics and two autonomous regions that compose Yugoslavia. Without the ability of a leader like Tito to unify these ethnic groups, feuding has occurred among the republics that threatens both the hold that the Communist party has on the state and the state itself. Strikes and annual hyperinflation rates of up to 500 percent have made Yugoslavia less competitive and more vulnerable to economic and political collapse.

▶ MARX AND COMMUNISM

Today, communism is enduring a great deal of turmoil. Until the late 1980s, approximately one-third of the world's population lived under a form of communist government. Marxist leaders in Eastern Europe, who seemed unshakable only a few years ago, have gone through major political and economic changes. Poland, Czechoslovakia, and Hungary have moved towards a form of free enterprise. Even the Soviet Union has moved away from the highly centralized economic system of Lenin, Stalin, Khrushchev, and Brezhnev.

If it seems that central planning has not stood the test of time, it is important to note that many of the theories and ideas of Karl Marx have not been practised in any of the world's Marxist countries. Although it is impossible to fully understand contemporary communism without studying the central ideas developed by Marx, each communist state has interpreted his writings to suit its own specific economic, political, social, cultural, and military needs. The communism of the Soviet Union can, therefore, only be understood by examining the ideas of Lenin, Stalin, and Gorbachev. The same is true for Mao in China, Castro in Cuba, and Tito in Yugoslavia.

It is thus inappropriate to speak of *a* communist or *a* Marxist ideology. There are many communist ideologies: there is a Marxist-Leninist ideology, a Marxist-Leninist-Stalinist ideology, a Marxist-Leninist-Maoist ideology, and so on. Towards the end of his life, when there were already many different groups calling themselves Marxists, Karl Marx wrote: "Of one thing I am certain; I am no Marxist."

APPLYING YOUR KNOWLEDGE

1. Explain how a centrally planned economic system would determine whether or not to manufacture badminton racquets, how they would be made, how many would be produced, and who would get them.
2. How might these decisions be implemented?
3. Select one specific example (such as preparing for war, massive crop failures, anti-pollution measures, or more equitable income distribution) and decide whether the centrally planned economy or the private enterprise system could best manage the problem. Explain your reasoning.
4. Construct a chart illustrating the essential differences between an ideal private enterprise system and an ideal centrally planned economy.
5. If a country with a planned economy was governed by a dictatorship rather than by a democracy, how might the objectives and the techniques of the central planning committee differ?
6. a) Make a list of the advantages and disadvantages of the planned economy as illustrated in the fictional story about corkscrews.
   b) How would the private enterprise economy have dealt with the problems described in the fictional story?
7. Explain why the Industrial Revolution was important to the development of socialist thought.
8. Outline the major differences between Marx and the Utopian Socialists.
9. Construct a chart that compares the ideas of Adam Smith (Chapter 7) with those of Karl Marx, under the following topics: human nature, the Industrial Revolution, profits, the relationship between politics and economics, freedom, planning, and economic equality.
10. a) What criteria does Marx use in determining the class to which a person belongs?
    b) Using Marx's criteria, to what class does your family belong?
    c) What other methods might be used to divide people into classes?
    d) Do different economic classes exist in Canada? Explain.
11. Write an essay evaluating the ideas of Karl Marx. What are the merits and the weaknesses of his theories?

FURTHER RESEARCH

1. Prepare for a debate on one of the following topics:
   a) It is a part of human nature to be self-centred and acquisitive.
   b) Centrally planned economies provide the best quality of life for the most people.
2. Research and write an essay on one of the following topics:
   a) Lenin's contributions to Marxism
   b) the communal experiments of either Robert Owen in Great Britain or Charles Fourier in France
   c) why capitalism has not destroyed itself as Marx had predicted
3. Working in groups, use the following chart to help prepare for a debate on the merits of central planning.

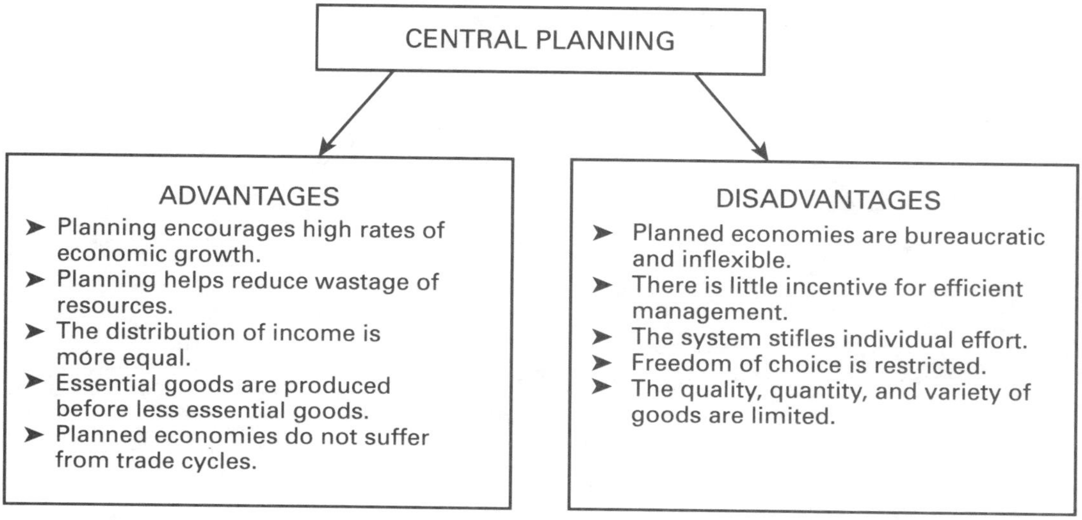

CENTRAL PLANNING

ADVANTAGES

- Planning encourages high rates of economic growth.
- Planning helps reduce wastage of resources.
- The distribution of income is more equal.
- Essential goods are produced before less essential goods.
- Planned economies do not suffer from trade cycles.

DISADVANTAGES

- Planned economies are bureaucratic and inflexible.
- There is little incentive for efficient management.
- The system stifles individual effort.
- Freedom of choice is restricted.
- The quality, quantity, and variety of goods are limited.

Case Study 18 Overview

The First Soviet Five-Year Plan: Central Planning in an Authoritarian Country

This case study analyses the Soviet Union's adoption of central planning in the late 1920s and 1930s and asks to what extent should national needs and goals take precedence over individual freedoms and well-being. The case study begins with an examination of the country's economic problems following the Communist Revolution of 1917 and discusses Lenin's adoption of a mixture of planning and private enterprise to remedy the situation. In 1928, Stalin adopted a five-year plan designed to industrialize the Soviet Union as rapidly as possible. The remainder of the case study examines the methods used to force industrial labourers to produce more and to convince farmers to grow more and accept less in return and to embrace the concept of state and collective farms.

▶ OBJECTIVES

After reading this case study, you should be able to:

- ▶ explain the reasons why Lenin adopted his New Economic Policy
- ▶ understand why Stalin was intent on rapid industrialization
- ▶ evaluate Stalin's values and methods
- ▶ debate the benefits of central planning
- ▶ discuss the delicate balance between individual rights and national needs
- ▶ devise an alternative plan to achieve similar goals

▶ KEY TERMS

New Economic Policy (N.E.P.)
kulaks
Five-Year Plan
collective farms
state farms

Case Study 18

The First Soviet Five-Year Plan: Central Planning in an Authoritarian Country

In a centrally planned economy, there is no doubt about who makes decisions. The government, whether democratic or non-democratic, determines its most important goals and orders its economic planners to achieve them. Every aspect of the economy, in theory, is regulated to carry out the government's overall objectives. Whereas private enterprise reflects a business estimate of future needs, the planned economy is centred around government decisions about the future needs of the state.

The argument in favour of planning was described by the former chair of the State Planning Commission of the U.S.S.R., Nikolai Baibakov:

Planning makes possible effective controls over the national economy on a nationwide scale and the national distribution of productive forces. Socialist planning has proved itself historically; it has served as the most important tool for the solution of the major tasks of each step of communist development. The fifty-year experience of the economic growth of the Soviet Union has established conclusively the overwhelming superiority of planning to guide national production. As a result of the systematic development of the economy, our country has transformed itself in a historically short period of time into a mighty industrial power with advanced agriculture and a high standard of living for the people. . . .[1]

[1]Nikolai Baibakov, "Economic Planning—The Fundamental Advantage of Socialism," trans. Daniel R. Brower, *Planovoe Khoziaistvo*, November 1967, p. 5.

This case study examines the validity of this quotation by analysing the Soviet Union's first comprehensive attempt to plan the country's economy. As you read the following discussion, keep these basic questions in mind: How well does the centrally planned economy manage the problems of what is produced, how it is produced, and to whom it is distributed? To what extent should national, political, and economic needs take precedence over individual freedom and well-being?

▶ THE U.S.S.R. AFTER THE REVOLUTION

World War I pitted France, Great Britain, and Russia against Germany and Austria-Hungary. After 1915, the war began to go from bad to worse for the autocratic and repressive government of Tsar Nicholas II. Corruption and incompetence combined to leave the Russian army desperately short of munitions and supplies. Unrest grew as the war intensified the terrible conditions existing in Russia prior to 1914. Peasants rioted. Many workers went on strike. When soldiers joined the strikers, the Tsar abdicated in March 1917, and a democratic government was established.

Unfortunately for the war-torn country, the new government decided to continue the war against Germany. In the meantime, a small group of "Bolshevik" revolutionaries led by V.I. Lenin continued their efforts to overthrow the government and establish communism. They promised to give control of the factories to the workers, to divide the land among the peasants, and to bring peace. Lenin's slogan, "Peace! Land! Bread!" struck sympathetic chords among the Russian people. In November 1917, the Russian troops mutinied, and a second revolution installed a communist regime that had strong support within the country's factories.

During the next few years, Lenin attempted to apply many of the principles of Marxian socialism to the Soviet Union. He nationalized private property, factories, natural resources, and land; gave the workers control of the factories; and asked the peasants to give their surplus food to the workers.

These wholesale changes failed to accomplish their purpose. The peasants wanted their own land and refused to surrender their excess grain when they were offered little in return. When the government began to seize the grain by force, the peasants merely planted fewer crops. By 1920, the amount of land under cultivation was twenty-nine percent less than it had been in 1913. The next year, the Soviet Union suffered a severe famine. In the cities, workers, whose numbers had been decimated by war and revolution, were unprepared either by education or by training to successfully run the factories. Industrial production declined drastically. Throughout most of this period, the Soviet Union also had to contend with both a civil war and a concerted attempt by foreign troops to drive the government from power. Foreign opponents included, among others, Japanese, British, French, Polish, American, and Canadian troops, whose governments refused to trade with or lend money to the Soviet Union.

Faced with these disruptions, the first major communist experiment in history seemed headed for disaster. Once the civil war was won and foreign troops forced out, Lenin devised a **New Economic Policy (N.E.P.)**, designed to stimulate both industrial and agricultural production and to help the Union of Soviet Socialist Republics (U.S.S.R.) recover from the effects of the revolution. The state retained its control over important industries and natural resources, but it now permitted small-scale private enterprise and allowed peasants to sell their crops in the open market. The new

V.I. Lenin (1870–1924)
Tass from Sovfoto

policy was a combination of private enterprise and state socialism.

▶ THE FIRST FIVE-YEAR PLAN

After Lenin's death in 1924, a split opened within the Communist party between those who believed that the country should industrialize slowly and those who wanted to quicken the pace of both industrialization and socialism.

At this time, there were approximately twenty-five million farms in the Soviet Union. Five to eight million peasant families were so poor that they tilled their land with wooden ploughs and had to hire farm implements and animals from rich farmers. These more prosperous farmers **(kulaks)** numbered approximately one million. The state relied upon kulaks to supply the cities with food, but they refused to deliver their surplus grain because of the low prices set for agricultural produce. Moreover, the government had very little money to import the machinery it needed to industrialize, and Western countries refused to give the U.S.S.R. financial help. The Soviet Union needed an agricultural surplus to pay for imported goods and to feed industrial workers. But most of the farms were so small (2.02 ha per family) or so poor that they were only able to produce enough for themselves. The kulaks were the only people who could provide the necessary surplus for export, but they wanted higher prices for their produce and cheaper manufactured goods. However, industries were just getting started and were unable to manufacture a wide variety of inexpensive products. If the struggling country was to feed its workers and industrialize rapidly, more reliable methods of agriculture and factory production would have to be adopted. But how could this be done?

In 1928, the new leader of the U.S.S.R., Joseph Stalin, declared that the rate of industrialization had to be increased at all costs. The new policy was designed to revitalize the spirit of the Communist party. An industrial country, he believed, would free the people from the bonds of poverty, but even more important, it would enable the Soviet Union to defend itself against Western European countries in a war that Stalin considered inevitable. Industrialization, Stalin argued, was essential for socialism and for the country's preservation:

The problem of heavy industry is more difficult and more important. It is more difficult *because it demands colossal investments of capital, and, as the history of industrially backward countries has shown, heavy industry cannot be developed without extensive long-term loans. It is* more important *because, unless we develop heavy industry, we can build no industry whatever, we cannot carry out any industrialization. And as we have never received, nor are we receiving, either long-term loans or credits for any lengthy period, the acuteness of the problem becomes more than obvious. It is precisely for this reason that the capitalists of all countries refuse us loans and credits; they believe that, left to our own resources, we cannot cope with the problem of accumulation, that we are bound to fail in the task of reconstructing our heavy industry, and will at last be compelled to come to them cap in hand and sell ourselves into bondage.*[2]

In October 1928, the State Planning Commission prepared a **Five-Year Plan** to implement Stalin's policy. The fundamental aims of the Five-Year Plan were to expand the country's heavy industry sector so that it could provide industrial machinery, transportation facilities, and military weapons; to introduce modern technology; to eliminate most privately owned farms and create state and co-operative farms in their place; to eliminate private enterprise; and to make the U.S.S.R. self-sufficient.

The plan was declared completed after only four years and three months, and a second Five-Year Plan was initiated to continue the Soviet Union's drive towards industrialization. By the end of the decade, a firm industrial base had been created and the U.S.S.R. ranked fourth in the world in terms of industrial output. Within four years, the number of industrial workers rose from three to six million. Illiteracy rates declined from eighty percent to ten percent. By 1934, the Soviet Union was producing more pig iron and steel than Great Britain. During the first Five-Year Plan the production of oil doubled, electric power increased by 550 percent, machinery production grew by 400 percent, and such new industries as synthetic rubber, plastics, and aviation were established. The percentage of farmers on state and co-operative farms grew from 1.7 percent in 1928 to 61.5 percent in 1932, and to 93.5 percent at the end of 1938. According to Nikolai Baibakov, the early Five-Year Plans transformed the Soviet Union into a major industrial power:

The country was [placed] firmly on the path of industrial development. The success of socialist industry created the prerequisites for the planned control of agriculture and prepared the basis for the widespread introduction of collectivization. . . . The success of socialism in all economic sectors permitted the growth of the standard of living of the population; unemployment, the scourge of labourers in capitalist countries, disappeared.[3]

This tremendous industrial growth was not achieved without some sacrifices. The concentration on steel, tractors, railways, and hydro-electricity meant that consumer needs were largely ignored. The production of sufficient shoes, clothing, and housing was left for a later date. Even food had to be rationed. Present shortages were justified on the grounds of future gains.

▶ Impact of the First Five-Year Plan

Nothing appeared to matter to Stalin as long as his plan succeeded. As a result, factory labourers were cruelly overworked, safety precautions were ignored, and housing conditions were miserable. Those who suggested caution and recommended more humane conditions were branded as spies or saboteurs, and were exiled or imprisoned. Factory managers feared for their lives if they failed to fulfill their production

▸ [2]From J.V. Stalin, "A Year of Great Change (On the Occasion of the Twelfth Anniversary of the October Revolution)" and "Problems of Agrarian Policy in the USSR (Speech Delivered at the Conference of Marxist Students of the Agrarian Question, December 27, 1929)," in *Problems of Leninism*, Moscow: Foreign Languages Publishing House, 1940, pp. 294-298, 302-305, 308-309, 325-326. Quoted in Daniel R. Brower (ed.), *The Soviet Experience: Success or Failure?*, New York: Holt, Rinehart and Winston, 1971, p. 28.

▸ [3]Baibakov, "Economic Planning," p. 46.

quotas. Private enterprise merchants were declared aliens and deprived of their civil rights — including housing facilities, food rations, and medical services.

Most of the three million new industrial workers were created by forcing the peasants off their farms and into the cities. They were not prepared for this new way of life and frequently vented their frustrations by ruining machinery, working slowly, or breaking the law. To produce better workers and more social uniformity, Stalin relied on both coercion and persuasion. Newspapers, radio, films, books, and posters publicized Stalin's goals. They praised the "heroes of the production front," agitated for the success of production quotas, exposed the unsatisfactory performance of "laggards," and told the people that it was their patriotic duty to work hard. Factory schools were created to teach good work habits and to improve the labourers' skills. Soviet schools were ordered to emphasize such "Communist virtues" as devotion to hard work, conformity, sobriety, nationalism, and the infallibility of the country's leaders. Each teacher was expected to indoctrinate the young, spread official information, and create efficient workers and managers. Those who refused were dismissed.

To prevent absenteeism, local superintendents deprived factory workers of their food cards and their housing facilities if they were absent for even one day without sufficient reason. These punishments, however, were infrequently imposed. Labourers who worked slowly, or produced goods of low quality, were punished — often brutally. They were broken to the habits of factory work and kept under control by ruthless drill and discipline. Pensions were made dependent upon performance, and the workers were paid for each item they produced. More positive incentives included better food and accommodation and longer vacations. Such measures, the Communist party believed, were essential in a country where the labour force was unused to industrial conditions. For most workers, however, the 1930s were a period of hardship and bitter experience.

▶ THE KULAKS AND COLLECTIVIZATION

Industrialization was to have been financed by surplus produce from the farms. However, as we have already seen, most peasants were too poor to produce a grain surplus, and the prosperous kulaks were unwilling to sell their crops for the low prices set by the state. Stalin's solution was to create large-scale **collective farms** where peasants would work together under state direction. Larger farms could afford to use modern machinery, which would help increase agricultural production. The mechanization of farming techniques would also release thousands of peasants to work in the newly developing industries in the cities. Collectivization would remove the well-to-do kulaks, whom Stalin viewed as the last remnant of capitalism and represented a threat to the principles of communism. Finally, the collective farms had an important military objective; in time of war, they would provide the basis for organized resistance.

Two types of farms were established. **State farms** were created to test new methods in mechanized agriculture. These farms were financed and operated by the government, which hired workers on a wage basis and kept the produce for state use. Collective farms were created by combining a number of peasants' holdings into one large farm. The peasants were allowed to keep their homes and animals, but all land and machinery was owned collectively by the group. An elected managerial board made all the important farming decisions about what to grow, what machinery to use, and how much money to put aside

A collective farm in the Stavropol region of Russia
Canapress Photo Service

for future use. The remaining income was divided among the farmers in proportion to their property and to the work they had performed.

At first, collectivization was voluntary. Special inducements in the form of lower taxes, easier borrowing facilities, and the use of tractors and modern machinery were offered to encourage the peasants to join the collectives. Because only the poorer peasants joined, Stalin soon came to the conclusion that the richer farmers would have to be forced into entering the state farms. In 1930, he inaugurated an all-out offensive against the kulaks. ''We must smash the kulaks, eliminate them as a class,'' Stalin proclaimed. ''We must strike at the kulaks so hard as to prevent them from rising to their feet again. . . . ''

Peasant was set against peasant. Committees of poor peasants were formed to denounce hoarders, and the government encouraged them to confiscate the kulaks' machinery and livestock for the benefit of the collective farms. Search parties were sent into the countryside to seize hidden supplies of grain. Village authorities received permission to treat the kulaks in their own way, and the villages that resisted were surrounded by soldiers carrying machine guns. The kulaks were forced to surrender; some had the shoes taken from their feet, and their clothing—including warm underwear—confiscated. Men were sent to prison on circumstantial evidence, or even without evidence. Some of the middle-income and poor peasants lost their belongings. Many rich farmers divorced their wives so that the women and children would be spared. The government was reluctant to curb even the worst abuses because it did not want to undermine the authority of the villages.

Rather than allow their property to fall into the hands of the state, the kulaks destroyed their machinery, burnt their crops, and killed their cattle. By 1931, one-third of the cattle, one-half of the sheep and goats, and one-quarter of the horses had been slaughtered. Agricultural production was lower in 1933 than it had been in 1928. Famine stalked the land in 1931 and 1932.

Within a few short years, more than 100 million people had been forced to radically change their lifestyles. The number of deaths reached unimaginable proportions—estimates vary between five and ten million. Tens of thousands of kulaks were deported to unpopulated regions in Siberia, thrown into prison, or sent to work camps. The Russian countryside glowed red, as the flames of burning peasant huts lit the sky. The ground was darkened with the blood of slaughtered cattle. Much of the agricultural produce was seized by the government and used to pay for needed industrial machinery. The Russian people were forced to live on short rations while millions of tonnes of grain were exported to other countries.

Out of this chaos and destruction the collective farm system began. Huge state farms, averaging about 40 000 hectares to 80 000 hectares, were established on previously unused land. Thousands of tractors and combines were put into operation. Some twelve million hectares of land were organized into state farms and, by 1937, over ninety percent of these farms were collectivized. The harvests of 1933, 1934, and 1935 were the largest in Russian history. Soviet agriculture had been made more efficient—but at what cost?

APPLYING YOUR KNOWLEDGE

1. Explain why Stalin was determined to collectivize agriculture.
2. Using the Five-Year Plan (1928–1932) as an example, make separate lists of the advantages and the disadvantages of a centrally planned economy.
3. Explain why the centrally planned economy is sometimes called a ''command economy.''
4. The Soviet experience indicates that central planning can accomplish industrialization—although not necessarily more effectively than other economic systems. Do you think the costs (deferred consumption and low priority on individual freedoms) are worth it? Explain. How do your values differ from Stalin's? Why?
5. Re-read the statement by Nikolai Baibakov at the beginning of this case study and comment on the validity of his conclusions.
6. Do you think that the aims of the Soviet educational system were much different from the goals of our system? Explain.

FURTHER RESEARCH

1. Bearing in mind that the Soviet Five-Year Plan illustrates an extreme example of government coercion and that a centrally planned economy can exist within democracies as well as dictatorships, prepare for a debate on this statement: ''Because national needs should take precedence over individual needs, a centrally planned economy is a superior economic system.''
2. Before condemning the brutality of the Soviet Five-Year Plan, it is useful to examine the conditions in Great Britain and Canada during their industrial revolutions. Research and report on one of the following topics:
   a) industrial conditions in Great Britain in the eighteenth century
   b) factory conditions in Canada during the late nineteenth and early twentieth centuries
3. Role-play a debate on the economy among Stalin, Lenin, and Gorbachev. (See Case Study 21.)

CHAPTER 9 OVERVIEW

THE WORLD'S ECONOMIES: MIXED ECONOMIC SYSTEMS

The economy of every industrial country combines features of both private enterprise and centrally planned economies. Such "mixed" economies are the subject of this chapter. It outlines the origins of welfare capitalism and explains the contributions of the Great Depression of the 1930s and the ideas of J.S. Mill and J.M. Keynes. The chapter then describes the origins of democratic socialism, the role of the Fabians in its growth, and the process of nationalization of key industries. It compares socialism to communism before evaluating the merits of market socialism as an alternative to welfare capitalism in Eastern Europe.

▶ OBJECTIVES

After reading this chapter, you should be able to:

- ▶ explain the influence of the Industrial Revolution in the growth of socialism and welfare capitalism
- ▶ evaluate the ideas of J.S. Mill, the Webbs, and J.M. Keynes
- ▶ debate the ideas of Marx and Mill
- ▶ discuss the differences between socialism and communism
- ▶ situate various countries on an economic continuum based upon the amount of government involvement in the economy
- ▶ compare market socialism to welfare capitalism
- ▶ debate the merits of nationalization

▶ KEY TERMS

mixed economy
democratic socialism
Fabian movement
market socialism

CHAPTER

9 THE WORLD'S ECONOMIES: MIXED ECONOMIC SYSTEMS

So far, we have examined the nature and values of *laissez-faire* capitalism and centrally planned economies. You will have noticed, however, that the Canadian economy does not fit into either category. It is not centrally planned—the existence of private companies is proof of that. But it is not *laissez-faire* capitalism either, as the presence of government-operated liquor stores and the Canadian Broadcasting Corporation (CBC) proves.

In order to understand the economic structure of our modern world, it is essential to know the basic concepts of *laissez-faire* capitalism and planned economies, since it is from these concepts that most countries derive their economic philosophy. Nonetheless, in the real world, there are no economies that are either entirely centrally planned or completely *laissez-faire*. Not even the economies of Cuba and China are entirely planned; they rely to some extent upon the market economy.

The economy of every major country in the world is really a combination of the two systems. In some, the market system is dominant; in others, central planning is supreme. This makes it difficult to categorize contemporary economic systems. The problem is further complicated by the interrelationship between economic and political ideologies.

One method of analysing economic systems is to arrange them along a continuum, according to the extent of government involvement in the economy. Figure 9-1 illustrates this distinction.

If we define a **mixed economy** as one in which most of the country's resources are privately owned, and the state usually intervenes in the economy only to promote economic growth or to remedy blatant defects in the system, then Canada, the United States, Sweden, Great Britain, and many other countries have mixed economies. Although the economic systems of Cuba, the U.S.S.R., China, and several other countries also employed some features of the market economy, they could not in the past be described as mixed economies because the state owned most of the natural resources and determined how the economy operated. In some countries (Hungary, Czechoslovakia, and Yugoslavia) the state owned most of the natural resources but allowed limited amounts of private enterprise until recently. This is called **market socialism**.

▶ ORIGINS OF WELFARE CAPITALISM

Liberal reformers in Great Britain appeared at approximately the same time in history as did Karl Marx. Like Marx, they were appalled at the evils of the Industrial Revolution, but unlike Marx, they wished to preserve the basic institutions of capitalism. Initially, they had supported Adam Smith's economic theories. They agreed that the role of the government should be kept to a minimum. They feared that the laws of supply and demand would be upset by government intervention and that the well-being of society would be destroyed. The views of John Stuart Mill (1806–1873) represented a transitional period in the development of liberalism, in which the liberals abandoned their unconditional support of *laissez-faire* capitalism and began to advocate that the government take an active role in correcting the abuses of the free enterprise system.

Initially, Mill had supported Adam Smith's ideas. However, as the abuses of industrialization multiplied, and as the industrialists showed little concern for the plight of their workers, Mill gradually came to believe that government should play a more active role in the economy. Mill sympathized with the desire of socialists for economic equality, yet he also admired the productivity of the capitalist system. And unlike Marx, he did not think that the market system inevitably led to class conflict. Capitalism, he felt, could be improved. As a result, he began to advocate government action to correct the abuses of capitalism without altering its essential features.

Figure 9–1
GOVERNMENTS AND ECONOMIC SYSTEMS

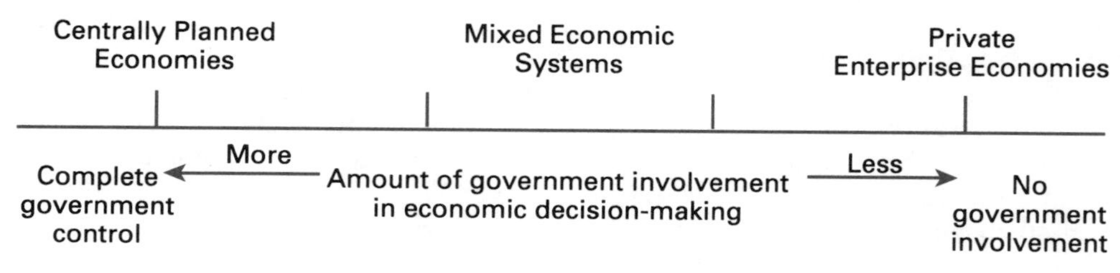

In Great Britain in the late nineteenth century, the ideas of Mill and his fellow liberal reformers influenced the passage of several factory acts and laws that improved working-class conditions. As the Industrial Revolution spread to the continent and to North America, so, too, did these reform ideas.

The Great Depression of the 1930s — in which millions of people found themselves homeless and unemployed — increased popular demand for government involvement in the economy and led to a general acknowledgement that the state had a responsibility for the welfare of its citizens. British economist John Maynard Keynes (1883–1946) argued that the state could reduce unemployment and economic depressions by adjusting its policies on taxation, spending, and banking. The goal of an economy, he stated, was to achieve the greatest possible amount of production and employment. In his classic work, *The General Theory of Employment, Interest, and Money* (1936), Keynes urged government to stimulate the economy during a depression by constructing public works and by lowering taxes and interest rates. Instead of attempting to balance the budget by restricting its spending, government should begin deficit financing. Then, as the economy improved, government could reduce its spending. Keynes, who became the most influential economist of the twentieth century, argued that through government intervention it was possible to remove the worst evils of capitalism.

These attempts to save capitalism from the destruction that Marx predicted resulted in the creation of mixed economies in such countries as Canada, Japan, and the United States. These mixed economies have attempted to correct the faults of the private enterprise system, to provide a fairer distribution of income, and to improve working conditions, rather than to replace the entire system. The role of government in these mixed economies expanded to include responsibility for unemployment, economic growth, poverty, and disease. Because of its concern for greater equality, the mixed economy included a welfare system designed to aid the poor, the sick, people who are disabled, and the aged.

Privately owned enterprises in North America are now affected by a complex maze of government regulations. For example, individual firms must conform to laws that prevent unfair business practices and control working conditions. These regulations also include pension funds, minimum wages and maximum hours, anti-discrimination laws, pollution regulations, labour laws, and advertising restrictions—the list is almost endless. The emphasis, however, is upon regulation rather than upon government ownership. Most property is still owned by individuals or private companies or corporations. Wealth is somewhat limited by taxation and other government policies, but huge fortunes can still be accumulated. Individuals are largely free to make their own economic decisions based upon their wants.

▶ ORIGINS OF DEMOCRATIC SOCIALISM

Democratic socialism also has its origins in the Industrial Revolution. By the time Karl Marx died, many people realized that capitalism was not about to collapse. Legislation passed at the encouragement of liberal reformers in numerous countries had much to do with the stabilization of the capitalist system. As a result, several groups of socialists, influenced by the writings of Eduard Bernstein (1850–1932) and Jean Jaurès (1859–1914), returned to the peaceful and gradual ideas of the Utopian Socialists.

The ideas of these social democrats formed the basis for nearly every major non-Marxist socialist movement in existence today, from the powerful social democrats in Scandinavia to the New Democratic party in Canada.

The specific ideas of democratic socialists vary from country to country. However, an analysis of the beliefs of Great Britain's social democratic offshoot, the **Fabian movement**, provides a good introduction to the theories of the early democratic socialists. In 1884, a small group of British intellectuals, led by Sidney and Beatrice Webb, George Bernard Shaw, and H.G. Wells, formed the Fabian Society. They rejected Marx's emphasis on class conflict and revolution and sought to change the system through gradual, democratic reforms.

The Fabians placed great faith in the power of human reason and concentrated upon preparing a series of pamphlets designed to educate the upper and middle classes in Great Britain about the benefits of socialism. Each pamphlet contained a detailed critique of the existing capitalist system, along with practical plans for correcting these evils. They knew that people could not be persuaded overnight, and they were prepared to continue their educational program until the public was converted. Reform, they believed, must come from within the democratic system, not through revolution.

Like Marx, the Fabians were outraged at the capitalist system for creating both immense wealth and crippling poverty. Unlike Marx, however, the Fabians believed that the major conflict in the existing society was not between the bourgeoisie (the owners of the means of production) and the proletariat (the wage earners), but between a small group of bourgeois financiers and the entire community. The Fabians' solution was to gradually return the country's land and the means of production (factories and equipment) to the entire community, not just to the proletariat (as Marx demanded). This could be achieved by nationalization. Slowly, as society became prepared for it, the government would take over the country's industrial firms and administer them in the best interests of the community. When nationalization was combined with social welfare legislation and a taxation system designed to distribute wealth more equitably, humanity would be able to reach its true potential.

Although the Fabians were not immediately successful, many of their ideas were later adopted by the British Labour party. Following World War II, the Labour party was elected to power. It immediately extended state welfare services; used income and estate taxes to redistribute income more equitably (and to pay for the welfare services); and began an extensive program of nationalization starting with coal, electric power, and railways.

Similar events occurred in a number of other European and Commonwealth countries after World War II, where democratic socialist parties nationalized their country's important industries. In actual practice, the degree of nationalization varied considerably from country to country and was determined largely by pragmatic needs. In Great Britain, for example, the coal industry, which was vital to the country's welfare, was doing poorly. It was nationalized when it appeared to be on the verge of collapse. In France, Renault was having financial problems and was nationalized, but the more economically stable Citroën remained in private ownership. In general, only those industries that were considered crucial to the functioning of the economy — such as transportation, steel, energy, communications, and utilities — were taken over by the government. Most businesses were left in private hands.

Nationalization was based on several arguments: its supporters believed that state ownership would modernize backward industries or save dying companies, thus providing continuing employment for the workers in these industries. Human welfare, not private profit, was the goal. Government ownership and planning, they also argued, would provide more orderly industrial development than the chaos of unrestricted capitalism. Finally, workers' morale (and therefore productivity) would presumably improve if the employees knew that the firm was managed for everyone's benefit.

The process of nationalization slowed down in the 1950s. This was due partly to political opposition and partly to the mixed results of nationalization. In general, publicly owned industries operated no better than privately owned firms, and whereas some did better, some did worse. In addition, the theories of John Maynard Keynes seemed to provide a method of regulating employment and economic growth without nationalization. Today, most democratic socialists no longer believe that all means of production should be state-owned but continue to follow policies that attempt to control employment and economic growth.

Maintaining a balance between government control in the economy and allowing private enterprise to function is always difficult. If there is too much control, private enterprises complain that government regulations do not permit enough competition and freedom in the marketplace. They demand "deregulation" (which means abolishing laws that restrict competition so that private companies can operate in greater freedom).

▶ IDEALS OF DEMOCRATIC SOCIALISM

The fundamental belief underlying democratic socialism is equality. Democratic socialists believe that while everyone may not be born with equal abilities, all are equal as human beings and should therefore be equal in income distribution as well as before the law.

This means that the economic system should be operated in the best interests of society as a whole. If we believe that citizens in a democracy should control their political lives by contributing to political decision-making, then why should they not also control their economic lives? Instead of relying upon the profit motive to organize the economy, society should seek to define its objectives and then achieve them through rational planning. This planning would not be executed by self-appointed elites, but by a democratic government responsible to the people. Democratic socialists argue that elected representatives of the people should decide such questions as what industries should be nationalized and how the country's production should be distributed. The important fact is that the people have a say in their economy. Only in this way can the problems of poverty, unemployment, and terrible working conditions be solved.

Strikes, unheard of in the Soviet Union prior to the Gorbachev era, began to occur in the late 1980s.
The Bettmann Archive

▶ COMMUNISM VERSUS SOCIALISM

It should be obvious from the preceding discussion that democratic socialism differs substantially from Marxism or communism. Yet democratic socialists are often associated with communists. Sometimes capitalist government and business leaders encourage this belief in order to defeat socialist parties at election time. On other occasions the misunderstanding is due to ignorance. Proponents of the two ideologies do have some beliefs in common: both favour public ownership and central planning; both dislike the profit motive and the emphasis on competition that is such a large part of capitalism; both sympathize with the working class; both desire equal economic opportunities combined with relatively modest differences in individual incomes; and finally, both socialists and communists believe that people must be re-educated so that they work in the best interests of society rather than solely for personal profit.

Despite such similarities, democratic socialists and communists have usually been arch-enemies. This has been especially true since the Russian Revolution of 1917, and each now views the other as the major threat to its own future. Table 9-1 illustrates some of the major differences between the beliefs of communism and socialism.

▶ A THIRD WAY?

In 1989, the surprising economic and political changes in Eastern Europe led some people to consider the possibility of combining free enterprise with central planning into what they called ''market socialism.'' As Case Study 24 will illustrate, Third World countries are also looking for a ''third way'' to organize their economies. The following article written by *Time* reporter John Borrell examines some of the possible economic options Eastern European countries are attempting to implement and the problems associated with each of them.

Table 9-1
COMMUNISM VERSUS SOCIALISM

	Communism	Socialism
Motto	From each according to ability, to each according to needs.	From each according to ability, to each according to work.
Source of Beliefs	The writings of either Marx, Lenin, or Mao	No guiding body of writing
Method of Gaining Power	Violent revolution	Democratic elections; peaceful persuasion
Type of Government	One-party democracy	More than one-party democracy
Degree of Public Ownership	Extensive, if not complete	Limited to essential industries
Means of Acquiring Public Ownership	Expropriation without compensation	Nationalization with compensation
Private Property	None. State-owned	Most individually owned
Dominant Influence on Human Actions	The relationship to the means of production	Conscience and rational reasoning

‣ Note: It is especially difficult to make specific statements about socialist beliefs, because socialists vary from country to country and from time to time. The beliefs listed here represent their most frequently held ideas.

Which Way to the Free Market?

. . . The 1989 revolutions swept away one ideology in Eastern Europe without replacing it with another as clearly defined. Democracy and a free market economy may be common and desirable goals, but history, geography and national psyche will be influential factors in determining how quickly, if at all, they are achieved. Each country is struggling to construct its own version of the future; what works along the Baltic may not fly in the Balkans.

Whatever the final designs, there is no longer serious talk of a "third way"—something never really defined—between communism and capitalism. . . . In fact, there is no single blueprint for building capitalism out of the wreckage of communism, nor would the neophyte democracies welcome one. They realize that creating new systems is not a turn-key operation. "We don't want to take over any one model," says Sándor Keresztes, vice president of the Hungarian Democratic Forum, the winner of recent parliamentary elections. "We want to collect the best parts of many systems and put them together."

That may be a hit or miss process. In Hungary's case, for example, it will probably entail a smaller state role in the economy than exists in France or Italy, but provide less of a social safety net than, say, in Sweden. Agricultural land, nationalized in Hungary from 1947 on, is unlikely to be returned to those from whom it was confiscated because of fear that such a move could cause a disastrous fall in food production. Nor will such acreage be given back in Czechoslovakia or Romania, at least for the moment.

In Bulgaria, by contrast, all the major political parties, including the former Communists, support an immediate return of farm land to private ownership. "The revival of this country is not possible without the revival of agriculture," says Viktor Vulkov, leader of the Agrarian Party. "And that means private ownership."

Some of the most fundamental differences focus on the pace and methods employed to overhaul creaking economies. Since January [1990], Poland has been applying a cold-shower treatment, plunging directly into the harsh realities of competitive capitalism. As a result, an internal free market has opened up in many commodities, prices have skyrocketed, wage increases have been pegged to productivity—and living standards have dropped at least 20%. For the first time in years, there is also plenty of food in the shops. While sharing in that newfound abundance is beyond the means of many Poles, the government receives surprisingly high marks in opinion polls. Says Prime Minister Tadeusz Mazowiecki: "The majority are accepting the changes with patience and understanding."

Other East European leaders have moved more cautiously, perhaps afraid of damaging their electoral prospects through unpopular economic measures. "Poles have suffered so much that they are prepared to accept anything," says Prime Minister Andrei Lukanov of Bulgaria. "Bulgarians would be less accepting." While the Czechoslovak government is sketching out a new economic program, subsidies remain in place for a wide range of goods, and opening a private business remains a cumbersome process.

The trickiest problem for all the countries is how to transfer state enterprises, which make up 80% to 90% of the economy in most, to private hands. Who owns factories, mines, airlines? The people as a whole? The government? The employees? The answer: all of them and none of them. The Polish government stepped in this year to prevent the *nomenklatura*, the managing élite under the

Communists, from snapping up at bargain prices the factories they once ran. Hungary has banned "spontaneous" privatization, which allowed local managers to sell off property cheaply, often to their personal advantage. Even worker buyouts are under a cloud because they favor employees in viable businesses and penalize those in run-down ones.

The most innovative scheme so far has been proposed by Václav Klaus, Czechoslovakia's Finance Minister. He would give ownership vouchers to every Czechoslovak citizen; as state companies were put up for sale, citizens could use the vouchers to bid for them. The system, Klaus suggests, would not only create a nation of shareholders but also establish a capital market.

Democratic Forum representatives in Hungary say they hope to reduce state ownership from 90% to 30% in just five years. That seems decidedly optimistic: though Hungarians lack the capital to purchase state enterprises themselves, the Forum wants to restrict foreign ownership.

How well the East Europeans manage economic reform will in large measure shape their political structures. While democracy is the espoused ideal everywhere and all five countries have had or are planning free elections, few have real experience at running a pluralistic system. . . .

One way of putting the effects of economic change beyond casual manipulation by ambitious politicians is to form grand coalitions. Hungary's two main political parties have rejected that option, but it remains a possibility in Bulgaria. "Regardless of who wins, we need a government of national accord," says Mladenov. "The coming two or three years will not be plain sailing, and we need people's support for profound and radical changes."

If a grand coalition is something that Western democracies generally resort to only in time of war, that is exactly the situation in which Central Europe and the Balkans find themselves. Communism may have been defeated, but its replacement has yet to take shape.

APPLYING YOUR KNOWLEDGE

1. Explain the meaning of the sentence: "The free market economy is a useful servant, but a bad master." Support or refute this position.
2. Explain why the Canadian economy is described as "mixed."
3. Discuss the similarities and the differences between Marxism and democratic socialism.
4. Explain the economic theories of John Maynard Keynes.
5. List ten government regulations that restrict your economic freedom.
6. Discuss the reasons for the growth of government involvement in the economy.
7. a) Which Canadian industries do you consider essential to the proper functioning of the economy?
   b) What would be the advantages and disadvantages of nationalizing one of them?
   c) Should they be nationalized? Explain.

8. Explain why communists and democratic socialists view each other as a major threat to their own existence.
9. Construct a table comparing the ideas of the liberal reformers to those of the democratic socialists in the following topics:
   a) amount of government intervention
   b) control of resources
   c) role of the individual
10. Winston Churchill is alleged to have said that he would be suspicious of the character of any person under thirty who was not attracted to socialism, but that he would be equally suspicious of the intelligence of any person over thirty who continued to be a socialist. Explain what you think he meant by this statement and comment on its validity.

FURTHER RESEARCH

1. Research the history of the federal New Democratic Party of Canada and explain why it has never won a federal election.
2. Choose a country mentioned in the *Time* article and research how well the country is performing economically.
3. Using appropriate inquiry techniques, research and report on the success of an industry after it was nationalized. Choices might include coal in Great Britain, the CNR in Canada, or Renault in France.
4. Working in groups, construct an economic continuum similar to Figure 9-1 and place the following countries on it: Mexico, Canada, Cuba, China, Great Britain, Hungary, the United States, the U.S.S.R., Sweden, Peru, Ivory Coast, and Japan.

Case Study 19 Overview

Sweden's Economy: The Middle Way?

This case study examines the economy of Sweden and asks if there is anything Canada can learn from Sweden's experiences. It begins with a discussion of the similarities between Sweden and Canada before describing Sweden's form of welfare capitalism in the 1970s. Although the Swedish government left the production of goods to the marketplace, the state had considerable influence over the allocation of these goods. Incomes, not production, had been socialized. The case study then examines how Sweden succeeded in extricating itself from a severe depression, outlines the recent changes to Sweden's welfare policies, and discusses Sweden's attitude to the environment.

▶ OBJECTIVES

After reading this case study, you should be able to:

- ▶ discuss Sweden's major economic and social goals and values
- ▶ compare Sweden's and Canada's welfare programs
- ▶ debate the benefits of Sweden's economic system
- ▶ evaluate what Canada might learn from Sweden's experiences
- ▶ discuss the merits of currency devaluation
- ▶ decide how a country's economic competitiveness can be improved
- ▶ detail the weaknesses of the Swedish system
- ▶ debate the merits of full employment versus high inflation
- ▶ compare the environmental policies of several countries
- ▶ analyse economic charts

▶ KEY TERMS

state monopoly

five-year plans

Co-determination Act of 1977

Case Study

19 Sweden's Economy: The Middle Way?

An examination of the experiences of other countries can illustrate the strengths and weaknesses of a variety of economic policies. Sweden and Canada share many similarities. As a result, a study of Sweden's economic past can provide Canadian economic planners with many useful insights. Each country has a northern location with a relatively small population compared to its large land mass. Both are well-endowed with natural resources, including fisheries, agriculture, forestry, water power, and mineral deposits (although Sweden is dependent upon imported oil), and each relies heavily upon exports for its economic growth. Both states have high living standards and democratic governments.

Sweden thus provides an excellent measuring stick with which to compare Canada's economic and social policies. What can we learn from Sweden's experiences, both positive and negative? Before examining Sweden's economy, it is important to note that the two countries do have several important differences.

Sweden has a history of low tariffs, whereas until very recently, Canada consistently placed high tariffs on most imported goods. Partly as a result of these different tariff policies, Canadian exports have traditionally been concentrated in the natural resources sector, whereas Sweden has diversified into manufactured products. In addition, Canada sells about two-thirds of its exports to one country (the United States), whereas Sweden's six major markets (the United Kingdom, Germany, Norway, Finland, France, and Denmark) account for only one-half of its exports.

Politically, Sweden is a unitary state that is accustomed to peaceful and extensive consultation among government, business, and labour organizations. Canada's federal system and the frequent antagonistic relationship among business, government, and labour have tended to hinder the evolution of consistent economic policies. Sweden is also an ethnically homogeneous society with only one official language. The only sizeable ethnic group is the Lapps, a nomadic people in the north, and only about seven percent of the population was not born in Sweden.

▶ A BRIEF ECONOMIC HISTORY TO 1982

Following World War II, Sweden gradually shifted its priorities from being primarily a supplier of natural resources (timber, iron ore) to becoming a producer of manufactured goods requiring skilled technology (transport and electrical equipment). In the early 1970s, Sweden had the second highest level of Gross Domestic Product (GDP) in the world. It was a pioneer in industrial technology, an innovator in labour-management relations, and a leader in social welfare policies. Inflation was low and employment rates were high.

Sweden's economy was such a complex blend of government and private enterprise that it was difficult to describe it in terms of socialism or capitalism. Although production of goods and services was generally left to the marketplace, the state had considerable influence over the allocation and distribution of these goods and services. Incomes, not production, had been socialized. The following section describes Sweden's economic and social policies from the 1960s to the early 1980s. Most of the welfare policies are still intact today.

▶ Private Ownership

Agriculture is almost totally directed by private enterprise. Individual firms, which employ ninety percent of all industrial workers in Sweden, produce ninety-five percent of the country's manufactured goods. As in Canada and other Western countries, in Sweden the industrial sector is dominated by a small number of very large firms. In fact, Sweden has more multinational firms per person than does the United States. One study revealed that almost ninety percent of Swedish households did not own stock (ownership) in any of the country's industries, whereas 2.6 percent controlled eighty-six percent of the total stock available. This overwhelming concentration of economic power is higher in Sweden than in any other Western European country.

▶ Government Controls

The Swedish government does, however, play an important role in the economy. This is especially true with regard to natural resources, transportation, and energy. Atomic energy is a **state monopoly**; Sweden owns one quarter of the country's forests, one-half of its waterpower, eighty-five percent of its iron ore, ninety-five percent of its railways, and twenty-one percent of its buses are publicly controlled. In addition, the government operates the telephone system and the liquor and tobacco businesses. Some of this nationalization has been a direct result of social policy — atomic energy and telephones, for example. Others, such as the government takeover of the steel and shipbuilding industries resulted from company bankruptcies and the desire to maintain high employment, not as the result of socialist ideology. Profit is not regarded as inherently bad—if it can be directed to the common good.

Although relatively few industries have been nationalized, the government still exerts a strong influence over the economy through its fiscal and monetary policies (loans, interest rates, subsidies, and taxes), and by direct intervention. A good example

The economic growth of modern Sweden can be gauged, at least in part, by this photograph of Stockholm.
Canapress Photo Service

of the latter is the government's pollution regulations. Certain chemicals, such as D.D.T., are prohibited. Limits are placed upon polluting activities, and the state directs private research into anti-pollution equipment. Similarly, in housing, private initiative is hampered by building subsidies and rent controls. The government also decides how many homes can be built each year.

▶ GOVERNMENT PLANNING

The purpose of most government regulations is to allow free enterprise to run more smoothly. Sweden's **five-year plans** are a good example of this. Unlike the Soviet Union's long-term plans, they are not considered official government policy, but are forecasts or projections for the future, designed to communicate information to private firms in every sector of the economy. The five-year plans provide guidance and help to reveal problems in the market economy, but they do not fix production goals. There is less long-range planning in Sweden than there is in France, Norway, or Great Britain, but more than in Canada or the United States. The success of these plans is aided by a great deal of voluntary co-operation among Swedish leaders of business, labour, and government — most of whom know each other personally.

Direct government planning is largely confined to social problems. The main targets are full employment and freedom from poverty. Powerless individuals are no longer obliged to fend for themselves in a

Over 400 000 Swedish children participate in the free lunch program run by the government.
Canapress Photo Service

ruthlessly competitive economic system, because the state provides them with jobs, housing, adequate incomes, and medical care. The burden of raising children, for example, has to a certain extent been transferred from the family to society as a whole. Mothers are given free pre-natal care and a substantial family allowance for each child under sixteen. Either parent is eligible for a year's maternity/paternity allowance. Nursery schools are free, lunches and medical care are provided by the schools, and higher education is funded by the government. The state also provides low-cost day care centres for working parents.

All employees are guaranteed five-week vacations. Old age pensions, which begin at age sixty-five, are tied to the cost-of-living index. By granting retired workers two-thirds of the average salary of their most productive fifteen years of work, the government provides them with sufficient income to enable them to maintain their standard of living.

The health of the citizen is regarded as a social good. As a result, medical care is almost completely free. Sweden's infant mortality rate is among the lowest in the world. Although there are large income differences in Sweden, there are no slums, no starvation, and little destitution. Swedes also have one of the highest longevity rates in the Western world.

The basis of Sweden's policies is the belief that freedom can be achieved only in a proper social and economic environment. The better the social programs, the more freedom there is. Government has thus assumed a position of watchful supervisor over all "significant" aspects of national life.

▶ Union Participation

Over eighty percent of the Swedish work force is unionized. The goal of Swedish labour unions has not been to destroy private ownership but to abolish the negative aspects of capitalism without destroying the system itself. Instead of demanding public ownership and nationalization, labour emphasized social welfare policies in the 1950s and 1960s, leaving the management of industry to individual firms. During the 1970s, however, trade unions began to fight for economic as well as political democracy. The result was a series of reforms culminating in the **Co-determination Act of 1977**, which gave trade unions an important voice in the actual operation of Swedish industry. Union representatives were guaranteed the right to sit on each company's board of directors and to participate at all levels of corporate decision-making. The employer's power to decide on matters of hiring, firing, and the placement of workers was abolished. In these situations, as in discussions on the nature and methods of production undertaken by each firm, all decisions are negotiated between the union and the company.

▶ The Economic Crisis, 1974 to 1982

In the late 1970s, much of this harmony faded as the economy spiralled downward. The national deficit rose alarmingly, inflation increased, unemployment grew, and the good relations among government, business, and labour evaporated. During this crisis period (1974 to 1982), the government attempted to remedy the situation by increasing its control over the economy. Sweden granted massive subsidies to firms that were in trouble, or nationalized ailing industries. Nothing seemed to work, and Sweden's ability to compete with the other industrialized countries continued to decline.

Then, in 1982, the Social Democratic party of Olof Palme returned to power and embarked upon a new industrial program. Within two years the country emerged from the doldrums, and in 1986 *Business Week* referred to Sweden as the new "industrial powerhouse" of Europe.

▶ THE NEW INDUSTRIAL STRATEGY

Despite considerable opposition, the Palme government decided to devalue the Swedish krona in relation to the American dollar. Ultimately the krona was devalued to fifty percent of the American currency. The government then adopted a plan designed to bring Sweden out of the depression. It did so by making Swedes save more of their incomes and by encouraging them to produce more goods per person. The socialist government discouraged the consumption of consumer goods by individuals; instead it sought to persuade Swedes to invest their surplus cash in the country's economy. For the first time since World War II, the government reduced its spending. To further encourage industrial growth and investments, the govenment kept interest rates at a low level.

Equally important, the Social Democratic party reversed its earlier industrial policies. Instead of supporting chronically bankrupt firms with subsidies, the government gradually reduced its support for such businesses and adopted a new plan designed to promote industrial growth based upon innovation and competitiveness with the rest of the world.

The devaluation of the krona lowered the price of Swedish export goods abroad, increased Sweden's national income, and enhanced the competitiveness of the country in world trading markets. To encourage industry, the government offered financial support and tax benefits to companies that were willing to invest funds in research and development into new products, or improved the use of technology. It also generously subsidized the creation of new businesses. Palme created a more positive atmosphere for economic growth by reducing government regulations and "red tape," adopting a more co-operative relationship between government and business, and deregulating (privatizing) some industries.

The results were spectacular. Exports of goods and services grew by twelve percent in the first year, and Sweden's trade balance rebounded from a deficit of six billion krona in 1982 to a surplus of eleven billion the next year. Labour agreements to limit wage increases to five percent further improved Sweden's international competitiveness, and by 1986, inflation and unemployment had been reduced to acceptable levels (3% and 2.7%, respectively).

Rather than using the traditional method of high unemployment and reduced public expenditures to fight inflation, Sweden increased exports, and by working hard, it literally saved its way out of the crisis. Another positive result of this economic growth was that the government was able to reduce the deficit without imposing tax increases.

This new industrial strategy succeeded in restructuring Sweden's economy. The emphasis on technology caused a decline in the number of labour-intensive industries, such as textiles, steel production, and shipbuilding, and an increase in knowledge-intensive (high technology) industries. In other aspects of the economy, such as in pulp and paper, specialization and innovation allowed Sweden to capture a major section of the American newsprint and magazine paper market. Sweden became one of the largest developers of industrial robots, and its major exports now included automobiles, telecommunications equipment, electrical machinery, and pharmaceuticals.

▶ MULTINATIONAL CORPORATIONS

Sweden's continued growth in multinational firms has also played a significant role in its economic growth. These companies have allowed Sweden to keep abreast of technological developments throughout the world. Sweden is now one of the few net exporters of technology.

▶ THE THIRD WAY

Political conditions also played a part in Sweden's recovery. Rather than continuing to argue over ideologies and personal benefits, various labour and political groups showed a new willingness to co-operate for the national good. Following the assassination of Olof Palme in 1986, the Social Democratic party under Ingvar Carlsson enjoyed great popularity and public confidence. More willing to compromise than Palme, the new prime minister developed a spirit of harmony with industry and the other political parties. As a result, the pre-1974 society of shared values, co-operation, and stability was partially restored.

Sweden's method of recovery has been termed the "Third Way." The main elements of this new strategy were a devaluation of the krona to regain international competitiveness, a reduction of government controls over the economy, a concentration on promoting research and development, incentives for high technology businesses, more emphasis on supply and demand in determining business decisions, and the creation of a favourable climate for business expansion. Sweden has used capitalist policies to maximize production, and socialist methods to redistribute wealth.

Table 1
WHO'S TAXED THE MOST

Government tax revenues as % of 1989 GDP	
1. Sweden	56.8
2. Denmark	50.8
3. Netherlands	46.1
4. Norway	45.5
5. France	43.9
...	
11. Great Britain	36.5
12. Spain	34.4
13. Canada	33.4
14. Switzerland	31.9*
15. Japan	31.3*
16. United States	29.8

*1988

Source: Organization for Economic Co-operation and Development.

▶ SOCIAL POLICIES

After being returned to power in 1982, the Social Democratic party sought to revise the country's welfare policies. The financial burden of high taxes on the Swedish people had become crushing, especially with the downturn in the economy. As Table 1 indicates, Swedes are still the most heavily taxed people in the world. As a result, many wealthy individuals, such as tennis star Björn Borg, leave the country to avoid paying taxes.

Equally important was the growing unhappiness of Swedes with a system that sought to control all aspects of their daily lives. The Swedish welfare state was designed for everyone, not just for the poor. It affected everyone's entire lives. Government homes and apartments were relatively drab in their uniformity because occupants were not allowed to paint their dwellings without approval. The most publicized example of the government's intrusion occurred in mid-1970s, when huge posters all over Sweden declared: "The Social Welfare Board wants us to eat 6-8 slices of bread per day." No one complained about the government's desire to have people consume the proper amount of fibre in their diet, but they did resent the fact that the government appeared to be commanding everyone to eat a set number of slices of bread. The posters were quickly removed, yet this incident convinced many Swedes that the government had gone too far in trying to control people's lives.

Following the economic crisis of the late 1970s, the government began to emphasize self-reliance and placed greater emphasis on reducing the costs of welfare programs. In several jurisdictions, such as kindergartens and medical practices, the government permitted private initiatives. Parents were now free to organize their own kindergartens, and doctors could establish their own clinics. Sweden thus began to re-examine some of its fundamental policies.

The government still offers first priority to full employment. Job creation schemes, retraining programs, grants to relocate workers, and employment information services ensure that Swedes consistently enjoy some of the highest rates of employment in the world. On the other hand, government involvement in the distribution of income has become more muted.

The Swedish welfare state, however, is not crumbling. Swedes still accept the necessity of paying high taxes for their welfare programs. Early in 1990, for example, Deputy Prime Minister Odd Engstrom explained: "The children, the sick, the hanidcapped, the old, and the unemployed—that's the five main groups. They always come first. If the welfare state can't show again and again and again that it has the best and most efficient way of taking care of us all in those periods of life, then the welfare state will be in trouble."[1]

▶ RECENT ECONOMIC CHANGES

In the last few years, labour shortages and higher wages have pushed costs and prices up and hurt international competitiveness. The government's centralized wage bargaining process has not worked as well as was hoped, and labour-government problems have prevented agreement on wage increases.

Other problems included a lack of competitiveness in the public sector of the economy and a subsequent waste of resources. In addition, the industrial sector is very narrow and is thus very sensitive to international changes. The high tax rate continues to limit savings, which has led to widespread tax evasion, as well as an underground service industry in which one service is traded for another service, whereby people avoid paying taxes.

In order to improve productivity, the government has renewed its efforts to promote high technology, research and development, and higher education.

▶ LESSONS

Sweden provides one example of how an intermediate-sized economy can alter its economic and industrial policies in response to international changes and successfully compete in international markets. Although there is no single path to industrial development, human resource policies appear to matter more than immense natural resources in achieving economic success. The Swedish example indicates that effective management and an appropriately educated and trained work force are essential for industrial progress.

The degree of private ownership in Sweden is still much higher than in most European economies. It is the combination of private ownership and social control over the distribution of wealth that constitutes Sweden's version of the mixed economy.

▸ [1]Gunnar Pettersson, "Is the Swedish Welfare Model Dead," *Scandinavian Review*, Autumn 1990, p. 20.

APPLYING YOUR KNOWLEDGE

1. Explain why, from an economic standpoint, a professional hockey player might prefer to play for an American rather than a Swedish team.
2. List those aspects in which Sweden's economy resembles Canada's, and those in which the two countries differ.
3. Write an essay discussing whether Sweden is closer to capitalism or socialism.
4. a) What values would a person who dislikes Sweden's economic system have? Be specific and give examples.
   b) Do the same for a person who admires Sweden's system.

5. a) In your opinion, does Sweden have an enlightened economic system or not? Support your decision.
   b) What, then, are your values?
6. Prepare for a debate on the advantages of Sweden's economic system.
7. Do you think wealthy athletes or businesspeople should be allowed to move to other countries where income taxes are low or non-existent? Explain.
8. What could Canada learn from Sweden and vice versa?
9. What are the advantages of being a country that produces manufactured products compared to providing natural resources for the world market?
10. Explain why Sweden has recently reduced its expenditures on social welfare policies?
11. Write an essay explaining how the government of Sweden pulled the country out of the 1974 to 1982 depression.

Case Study 20 Overview

The Japanese Economy

This case study examines the reasons behind Japan's economic success and asks what Canada can learn from Japan's example. Following World War II, Japan's economy prospered from a combination of American help and Japanese economic strategies. The Japanese government played a major role in fostering the country's growth. It provided economic incentives to businesses, encouraged research and development, and established a positive climate for business. Also important in this success were the Japanese conglomerates, the *keiretsu*. The case study points to Japan's educational system, production methods, employer-employee relations, and Japanese culture as additional reasons for the country's economic success. It concludes with an analysis of some of the negative features of Japan's methods and success.

▶ OBJECTIVES

After reading this case study, you should be able to:

▶ explain the major reasons for Japan's economic success
▶ discuss the role of the government in this success
▶ compare the Canadian and Japanese economies
▶ decide what Canada could learn from Japan's methods
▶ debate the merits of Japan's educational system
▶ outline the prerequisites for economic growth
▶ compare the business methods of Japanese and Canadian companies

▶ KEY TERMS

Meiji dynasty
zaibatsu
MITI
shilken jigoku
bosozoku
nyuu puaa
nyuu ritchi

Case Study

20 The Japanese Economy

Japan's economic success since 1945 is legend. One of the world's strongest economies has emerged from the ashes of a nuclear war. This study examines the extent of this success, evaluates how Japan attained this state of affairs, assesses some of the costs of this achievement, and considers whether Canada might be able to follow a similar route to economic prosperity.

▶ THE ACHIEVEMENT

We would have to return to the days of the British Empire to find a comparison for such a small land area that has had such a dramatic economic effect on the world. The statistics are impressive and improving. Japan is the world's largest creditor. Foreigners owe it $130 billion. Japan has only three percent of the world's population but commands eleven percent of the world's economy. Eight of the globe's ten largest banks are Japanese, and Tokyo is now competing with New York as the financial capital of the world. By the year 2000, Japan's economy might well exceed that of the United States, the yen might replace the American dollar as the currency of choice for international transactions, and more than one-third of world trade could occur on the Japan-Australia axis.

Table 1
JAPAN AT A GLANCE

Population: 122.7 million
Life expectancy: 75.1 male, 80.8 female
Literacy rate: 99%
Religion: Shintoism, Buddhism
Gross Domestic Product: $1.9 trillion
Per capita annual income: $12 923
Key economic activities: electronics, electrical equipment, autos
Major trading partners: United States, Saudi Arabia, Indonesia, China
Cities: Tokyo (capital) 8 354 615, Yokohama 2 992 926, Osaka 2 636 249
Area: 372 313 km² (one-third the size of Ontario)

▸ Source: *Canada and the World*, September 1989, p. 6.

Figure 1
JAPAN

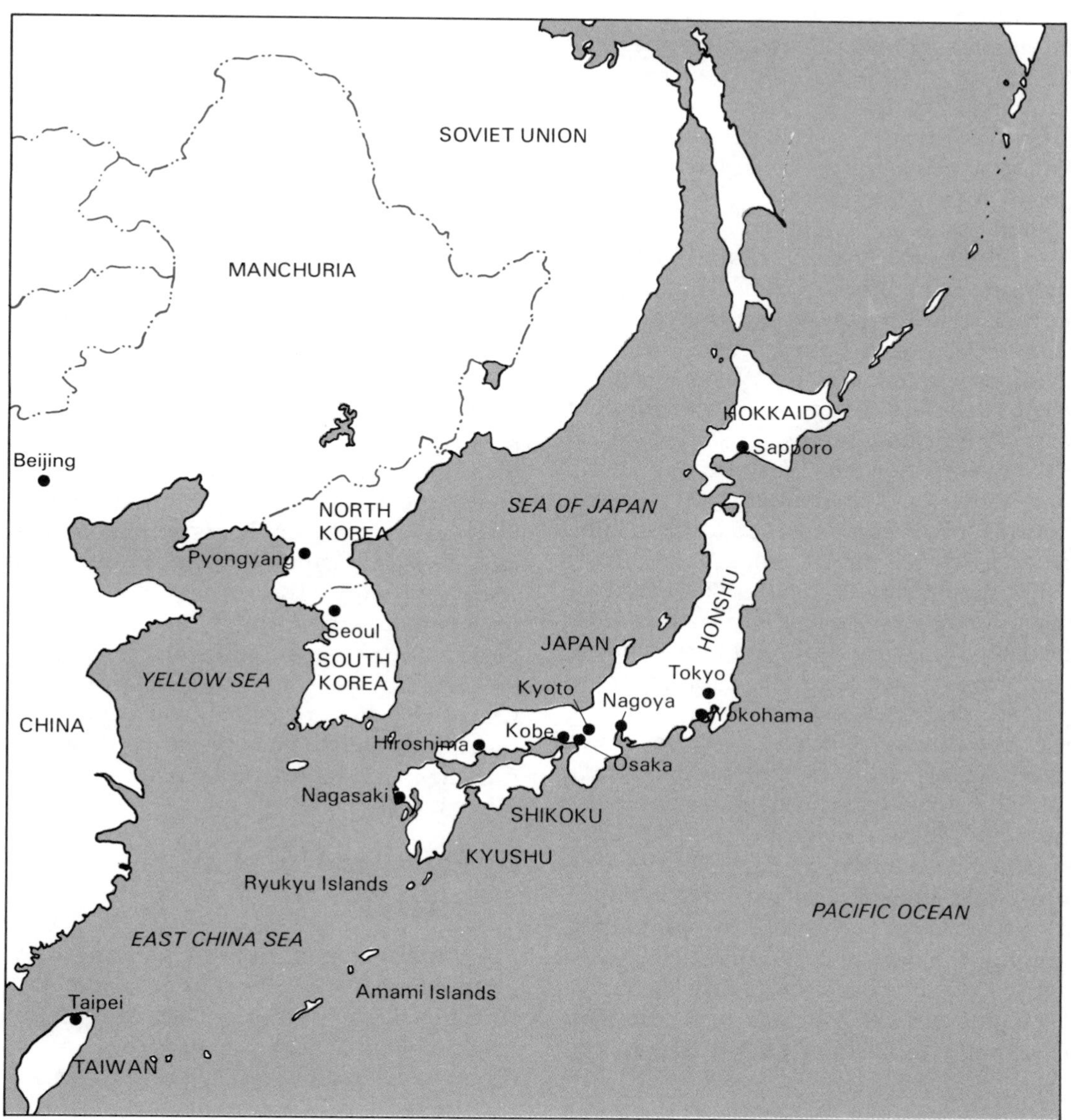

▶ HOW JAPAN DID IT

Even before World War II, Japan led all other Asian countries in the transition to an industrial economy. This change appears to have been a reaction to the Western intrusion begun in 1853 by American Commodore Matthew C. Perry, who "opened up" Japan by threatening to use naval force if Japan refused to do business with the United States.

In 1867, the newly installed **Meiji dynasty** immediately began to develop the infrastructure necessary for the construction of a modern industry as a means of avoiding exploitation by Western imperialists. Business interests and government officials found themselves willing partners in a race to develop Western technology and industry. Government intervention became the accepted method for launching Japanese development projects.

The government helped to build or improve railways, telegraph systems, and port facilities. It even developed model companies in order to teach the Japanese people how to conduct a business. Later, the government handed these companies over to the private sector. Central to this new industrial entrepreneurship were the ***zaibatsu.*** These monopolies, usually dominated by one family, concentrated the power of Japanese industry in the hands of a powerful few. The *zaibatsu* controlled mining, finance, and manufacturing. Mitsubishi was one such *zaibatsu*. In the 1930s, an aggressive militarism supported by rapid industrialization pushed Japan into World War II.

Despite defeat in this conflict, Japan possessed the ingredients for recovery after 1945. The infrastructure for an efficient industry was still in place, although it was in need of repair. Two factors shaped economic development after World War II: American policy and the Japanese government's political and economic strategy.

Following World War II, American policy in East Asia reflected a fear of regional communist expansion. After Mao's Communists marched into Peking in 1949 and took over mainland China, the United States helped the Japanese to re-industrialize. It provided raw materials, arranged investment capital and training, and supplied markets. Many of Japan's products were designed for export to the United States. During the American occupation from 1945 to 1949, intervention created a climate in Japan akin to Western capitalism. For example, the Americans discouraged the traditional *zaibatsu* and insisted that the large corporations have boards of directors.

Since World War II, the *zaibatsu* has been replaced by the *keiretsu.* This is a form of industrial organization in which private companies cluster around a major firm, forming a diverse family of enterprises that include manufacturing, finance, and even their own stock trading company. This form of organization demands a high degree of discipline and loyalty from individual employees as well as the member firms. It is a form of industrial organization that has proven to be very competitive and durable in the international marketplace.

▶ Postwar Government Strategy

The Japanese government continued to intervene in the economy after World War II. It developed a form of state capitalism, or guided capitalism, which is the type of economy frequently associated with fascist political systems. In these economies, the means of production are left in private hands, but the businesses themselves are subject to government supervision. The guiding hand of government, coupled with American policy, may be observed at work in the first prerequisite of modern industry —capital.

Life in Japan reflects the culture of both the East and the West. For example, many people wear Western-style clothing, but almost all the people dress in traditional kimonos during festivals and other special occasions.
Consulate General of Japan

Industry needs capital. Since 1945, Japan has existed under the protective umbrella of the American military establishment. Japan's constitution, which the United States imposed, limits Japanese military spending not to exceed one percent of the GNP. As a result, Japan has spent next to nothing on defence. In 1983, for example, Japan allocated $11.6 billion to defence, compared with the $21 to $24 billion spent by France, West Germany, and Great Britain, respectively, and the $239 billion spent by the United States. The average Japanese citizen pays only $98 annually for defence, compared with the average Briton's $439 and the average American's $1023. This surplus is channelled into such potentially productive investments as research and development.

Another source of investment capital has come from the characteristically high rate of Japanese personal savings. The Japanese government's income tax system encourages personal saving, and Japanese workers save over twenty percent of their wages. Also, since the government's pension schemes are inadequate, Japanese workers have to save money for their old age. These savings provide the funds that enable Japanese banks to lend money to entrepreneurs and industrialists.

More recently, capital has been pouring into Japan as the result of huge trade surpluses. The Korean War generated the initial export stimulus, especially because the Americans were thoroughly involved in the conflict.

THE JAPANESE BUSINESS ORGANIZATION

The origin of the Japanese industrial groups predates World War II, when four massive conglomerates controlled much of Japan's industry. . . . These formal clusters, or *zaibatsu,* were officially dissolved by the American military occupation after World War II. . . . As soon as the American occupation forces had left, however, the companies of these former conglomerates began to cluster back together again. . . . The main difference is that the members of today's groups are . . . independent companies, co-operating voluntarily with each other for important financial, commercial and strategic reasons.

. . . The Mitsui Group . . . is one of the eight or so such groupings that today dominate Japanese business. Others are the Mitsubishi Group, the Sumitomo Group, the Fuyo Group, the DKG Group, the Sanwa Group, the Tokai Group and the IBJ Group.

Each of these modern groups, or *keiretsu,* has at its core a commercial bank and usually one or two other firms, including a trading house. . . . Clustered closely around these core firms are other large companies from a wide cross section of industries. The Mitsui Group, for example, includes companies in fibre and textiles; foodstuffs; construction; retailing; finance and insurance; chemicals; pulp and paper; mining; steel and metals; transportation and warehousing; electricity and machinery; and automobiles. Farther afield are dozens of other companies more loosely affiliated with the group.

. . . Financial control remains closely held within the "family". Firms affiliated with a group may borrow widely, but their main bank relationship is always with the bank at the group's core. Both the bank and other firms within each group also own shares of the other member firms.

. . . The members of each group . . . conduct the bulk of their business activity within the group. For example, they procure their supplies and materials where possible from other members of the group, and they market their products through the group's trading company. It is estimated that as much as 50 per cent of the business transactions conducted by group members is with other affiliates of the same group.

Most importantly, the *keiretsu* co-ordinates planning and strategy formulation among its member firms. . . . In particular, the CEOs of the companies near the centre of each group meet periodically to discuss matters of common concern and to co-ordinate their business strategies. In the case of Mitsui, for example, the presidents of the 25 or so most strategically important firms . . . meet every second Thursday; hence the group is referred to as *Nimoku-kai,* or the "Second-Thursday Group".

It is difficult to overemphasize the importance of these meetings, at which the CEOs discuss candidly such matters as new product developments, competitive strategies and governmental policies. They may decide to provide . . . assistance to member companies that are launching new products [or] entering new markets.

The system . . . gives its member firms a large and stable in-house market base in which to develop and consolidate new products before attacking new markets. The individual firm in a *keiretsu* group can rely on the other members of the family of firms to do business with it wherever it may go, whether in Japan or abroad.

The *keiretsu* system also facilitates very rapid cross-fertilization of new technology across industry lines. Mitsui bank, for example, has immediate . . . access to new telecommunications technology developed by Toshiba and other firms within its group, in contrast to non-Japanese competitors, who must shop for comparable technology on the open market.

. . . It is largely these stable networks of business and financial relationships that enable Japanese firms to benefit from long-term planning. . . . In contrast with competitors elsewhere, Japanese managers need not pay excessive attention to short-term earnings. In a recent study in which American and Japanese managers were asked to indicate over what time period their performance was measured, 59 per cent of American managers responded that their performance is measured in periods of less than one year; only 2 per cent of the Japanese respondents said that their performance is measured in a span of a year or less.

Source: Adapted by permission of *Business Quarterly*, published by the Western Business School, The University of Western Ontario, London, Ontario, Canada.

▶ Ministry of International Trade and Industry

At the heart of government strategy is **MITI**, the Ministry of International Trade and Industry. Operating like a central planning bureau in a command economy, this government agency co-ordinates government, business, labour, and research, according to the government's policies and goals. It assists enterprises in potentially high growth areas by providing them with foreign exchange, raw materials, technology, loans, and tax incentives. MITI also discourages non-growth areas by withholding licenses, transferring resources and personnel to other sectors of the economy, and suspending other inducements. It was MITI that launched Japan into steel, ship building, automobile manufacturing, and other heavy industry just after World War II. These industries yielded large dividends for Japan and helped bring its economy out of the wartime recession. MITI also kept the Japanese currency, the yen, at an artificially low value so that Japanese goods would be less expensive on the international market.

Computers, microchips, and industrial robots offer three other examples where MITI played a role in advancing the competitive position of the Japanese economy. In the 1960s, Japan was distinctly inferior in the development of computers — to the West in general and to the United States in particular. Under MITI's guidance, Japan rectified this situation with spectacular results. In 1970, MITI published "The Vision for the 1970s," its overview of where the national economy should go. It stressed the crucial importance of knowledge-intensive industries and, in particular, of computers. Under MITI's guidance, Japan took the following steps:

- In 1971, Japan offered conditional loans to companies using or designing computers.
- For four years in the late 1970s, seventy-five billion yen, 40 percent of it contributed by the government, was spent on researching the semi-conductor industry.
- A MITI research association provided Japanese producers with the means to pool their research effort and share in its results.

- To support its computer technology, the Japanese public sector practised a policy of discriminatory purchasing, favouring domestic computers.

This daring and wide-ranging approach enabled Japan to advance from being a net importer to becoming a net exporter of computers in 1981. Progress continues to be very rapid. While 10.5 percent of Japanese computers were exported in 1980, by 1983, 34.7 percent of them were sold abroad.[1]

MITI has created a harmonious relationship among industry, labour, and government. This has enabled Japan to concentrate its national energies and resources in specific areas of the economy. The thrust of this economic nationalism has been directed towards encouraging exports and is best evidenced in the import restrictions imposed on foreign manufactured goods. These restrictions have created a protected market for domestic manufacturers.

[1] J. Laxer, *Decline of the Superpowers*. Toronto: James Lorimer, 1987, pp. 552–556.

▶ Education

The Japanese educational system reflects the order and planning that is characteristic of Japanese industry. The schools teach young people the skills and attitudes needed to assist industry. The employers augment this schooling with a systematic training program. The Japanese worker is always learning. Education is based upon two assumptions. First, that virtually all children have the ability to learn and master the regular curriculum. Second, that diligence and attention to detail can be taught.

Japanese students clean their school every day.
Consulate General of Japan

The course of studies is a tool for developing important attitudes in the pupil.

Respect for the work place, one's own work, as well as that of fellow workers, is developed quite early. Every day, the curriculum includes scheduled clean-up periods, during which time the students clean their school and its environs. Schools do not employ adult janitors. This practice also develops a feeling of responsibility and a sense of ownership.

Development of an industrious attitude is accomplished by a long school day (8:30–4:00) and school week (5½ days), as well as a rigorous homework load. Respect for the teacher (*sensei*), strict dress codes, and the absence of school dances and other social activities help foster the attitude that school is a work place and a learning place. This attitude is meant to be carried into the adult world. Once this mental set is in place, teachers in the higher grades can concentrate on instilling the specific skills and knowledge the students will need to compete in the industrial world.

At the secondary school level, education is intensely competitive, as is the industrial world. Entrance to all universities and upper secondary schools is based upon passing difficult examinations. There are few of these institutions and a great many students, and the pupils know that the best jobs in industry go to the people with the best marks. It is no wonder that the last year of high school is popularly called ***shilken jigoku*** (exam hell).

▶ Other Factors Affecting Success: Production Methods

Japan may have copied the West to begin its industrialization, but it has also been innovative. Innovation is the result of individuals having the time and incentive to think about a process or product and the problems associated with it. This process of investigation is more commonly called research and development. Government and private industry employ research scientists to accomplish this task. Japan takes research and development very seriously.

Figure 2
EXPENDITURES ON R & D AS A PERCENTAGE OF GDP

United States	2.74%
Japan	2.65%
Germany	2.54%
Sweden	2.46%
Switzerland	2.28%
United Kingdom	2.28%
France	2.24%
Netherlands	1.99%
Norway	1.53%
Finland	1.42%
Canada	1.40%

▸ Source: Adapted from Yvonne Van Ruskenveld, *About Canada: Innovation in Canada*. Minister of Supply and Services in Canada, 1988, p. 16.

▶ Employer-Employee Relations

Large Japanese firms provide a systematic training program for their employees as soon as they are hired. This is part of the "quality circle" concept in manufacturing. Unlike in North America, where workers are treated as parts of the production problem, in Japan, employers view their workers as components of the production solution. Workers are encouraged and trained to be multi-skilled. They work in

Figure 3
WILLINGNESS TO SERVE EMPLOYER AT EXPENSE OF PERSONAL LIFE

Are you willing to serve your employer even at the expense of your personal life?

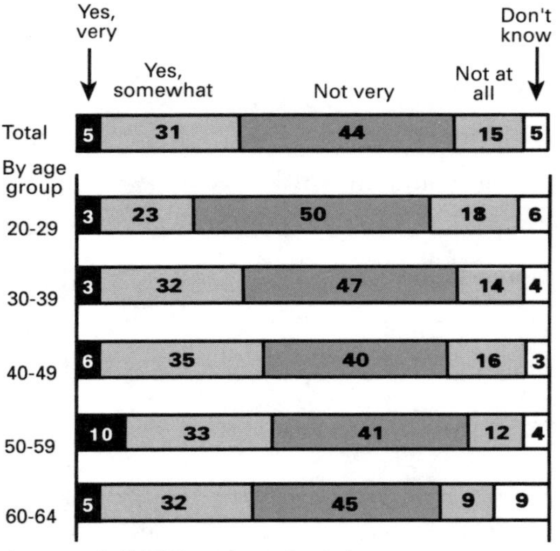

(percent; 1 729 respondents)

- Note: Survey was conducted in December 1982.
- Source: *Kinro ioshiki ni kansuru yoron chosa* (Survey of Attitudes Toward Work), Prime Minister's Office, June 1983.

teams that are involved in making production decisions. This practice creates varied job experience, and workers earn rewards such as transfers, rotations, and promotions.

The barriers that can arise between supervisory staff and line workers are always a concern in production. The Japanese believe that communication between workers and their superiors is critical in maintaining high productivity. In Japan, plant floor supervisors wear the same clothes as the workers; they eat in the same cafeteria; they exercise with the workers; and in some cases, the executive office is just a desk situated on the plant floor. This work-place democracy has kept employee morale and productivity high. It has enabled management to be instantly aware of problems as well as of worker-initiated new ideas.

Management trainees must gain ''hands-on'' experience. In Japan it is not surprising to find graduate engineers performing menial tasks on the plant floor. They are required to spend several years at this level, and they must learn all facets of the production process. Japanese firms generally recruit managers from the floor, rather than from the outside. This practice also contributes to company morale. Once an individual becomes an employee in a Japanese firm, the worker is hired until mandatory retirement at age fifty-five. This helps make the workers feel as if they are important

JAPANESE AND NORTH AMERICAN BUSINESSES COMPARED

Japanese Industries	**North American Industries**
Lifetime employment	Short-term employment
Slow evaluation and promotion	Rapid evaluation and promotion
Non-specialized career paths	Specialized career paths
Collective decision-making	Individual decision-making
Collective responsibility	Individual responsibility

members of the firm, and they develop a sense of ownership or responsibility for its success. As a result, Japanese workers tend to have a strong sense of loyalty and they work hard.

▶ Production Runs

A firm's relationship with suppliers is another production method contributing to Japanese success. The North American approach to business success is to deal with many different suppliers over time with competitive pricing being a key factor. The Japanese prefer to have one supplier per product or service. They expect a consistent level of quality and service that a more permanent business relationship may encourage. North American businesses with their emphasis on mass production tend to stockpile supplies in expensive warehouse space. The Japanese approach is to have smaller production runs and to allow for changes and market fluctuations.

Related to the smaller production runs are the shorter set-up times used in Japanese factories. In order to encourage their workers to shorten the time it takes to establish a production line, the firms offer wage incentives. For example, Toyota offers a basic wage, a productivity wage (amount of work produced per hour), and pay for the actual number of hours worked. At forty percent, the productivity wage is the largest pay component, and, therefore, the incentive for workers is to produce more.

The results tell the story. Western manufacturers are losing the productivity war with Japan. According to a recent Massa-

Figure 4
MEASURES OF COMPETITIVENESS IN MANUFACTURING, FOUR INDUSTRIALIZED COUNTRIES, 1980–1987

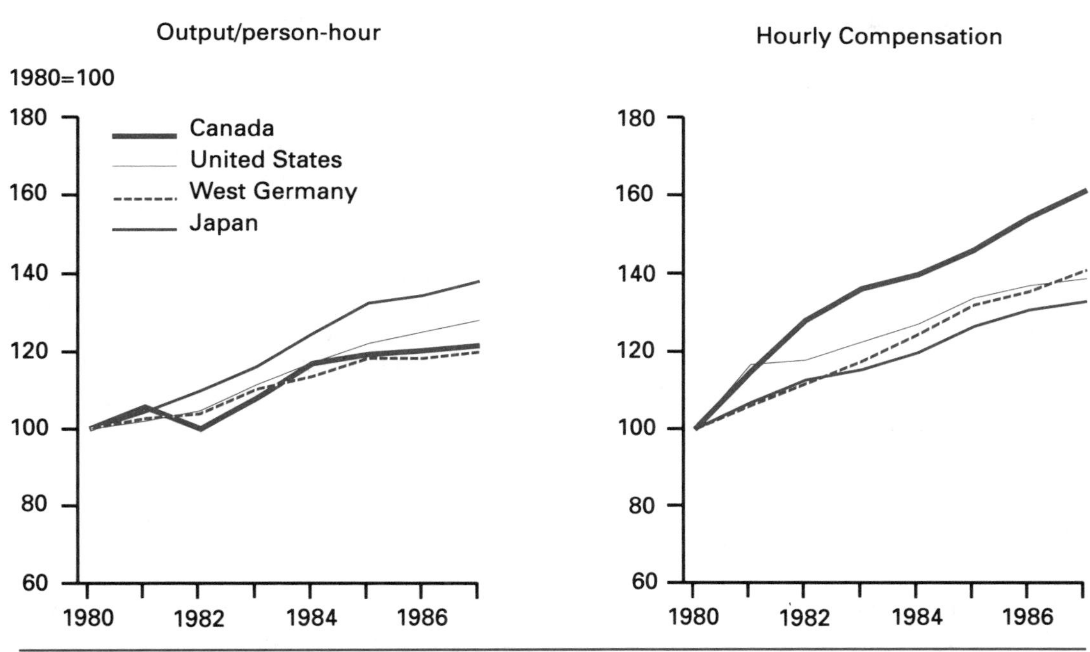

▸ Source: Economic Council of Canada, *Legacies*, Twenty-Sixth Annual Review, 1989, p. 14.

chusetts Institute of Technology study, Japanese workers are twice as productive as Westerners. The study found that to build a car, for example, it takes an American company twenty-five hours, a European manufacturer thirty-seven hours, and a Japanese company only seventeen hours. The Japanese can design and produce a car within forty-seven months. In the West, the process takes sixty months. Recently (1979–1988), the Ford Motor Company achieved a forty percent increase in productivity by adopting Japanese methods.

▶ Other Factors Contributing to Japanese Success: Culture

Japan has a homogeneous population, which enables the country to enjoy a social cohesiveness that fosters a strong sense of nationalism. The Japanese also have a tradition of respect for authority and social discipline, which makes it easier for the government and large firms to institute their policies. The Japanese have shown themselves to be a hard-working, loyal, easy to manage and train, self-confident people. They are willing and able to meet the challenges of a changing world.

▶ The Price of Success

It would be incorrect to assume that Japan's rapid rise as an industrial power was gained without costs. Japan and its people have been dramatically affected domestically, politically, economically, culturally, and environmentally. Japan's affluence has altered the balance in global economics and geopolitics. The country's affluence is fueled by a massive trade surplus, which by 1986 had reached $92 billion. This happened at the expense of Japan's trading partners. Japan's affluence raised the spectre of inflation if all that money remained at home. To prevent such a disaster, MITI has encouraged the Japanese to reinvest their funds throughout the world. Japan is now the world's largest creditor. Foreign countries owe Japan an estimated $500 billion. The world is increasingly tied to Japan's economy, much as it had been obligated to the American economy before 1929 and to the British economy in the nineteenth century. Any fluctuation or ripple in the Japanese economy is felt around the globe.

Table 2
TRADE WITH JAPAN BY CANADIAN REGIONS—1984
($ millions)

	Exports to Japan	Imports from Japan
Atlantic	218.4	86.0
Quebec	328.9	808.3
Ontario	416.9	1980.3
Prairies	444.9	385.5
Pacific	4219.7	2808.9
Total	5628.8	5710.8

▸ Source: *Canada/Japan: The Export Import Picture 1984*, Econolynx International Ltd., 1985.

Japan's triumph has encouraged other developing countries to emulate this success story. Some have been fairly successful. Taiwan, Singapore, Malaysia, South Korea, and Thailand are newly industrializing countries that are now successfully competing with Japan, because their labour costs are far lower. This is part of the reason why Japan has changed the emphasis in its export trade from machinery to high technology products.

More serious to Japan's stability is the negative reaction by the developed Western countries to Japan's invasion of their markets. The United States is the chief complainant. It has been demanding that Japan open its domestic market to more American and European goods, that it cease its protectionist policies, and that it allow the yen to float to its natural world price level. Some countries have warned Japan that they would oppose its fiscal and trade policies if Japan failed to respond to their pleas.

Western countries have also begun to demand that the Japanese assume responsibility for their own defence. This would mean a substantial increase in Japan's military spending. If Japan responded to these demands and increased its military budget to three to four percent of its GNP, the country would become the third-largest military power in the world. There is considerable global opposition to this move, particularly among Japan's militarily vulnerable neighbours. Domestically, the resistance to rearmament enjoys considerable support. Japanese businesspeople do not wish to see increased public spending, especially on armaments, because such a policy usually means higher taxes and more government intervention in the economy.

Figure 5
CANADA'S IMPORTS FROM JAPAN BY COMMODITY, 1984

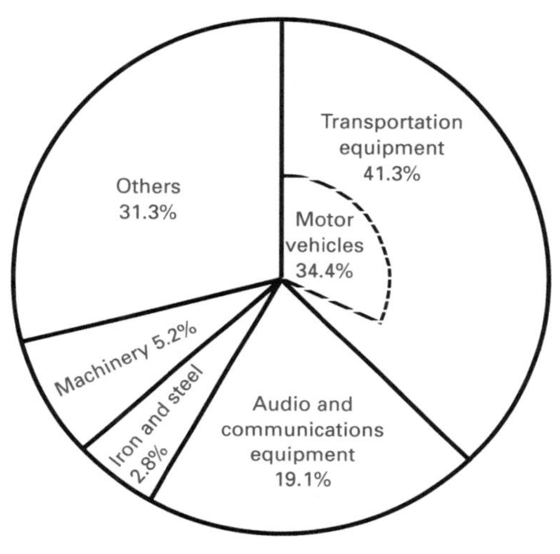

Source: Statistics Canada.

Table 3
CANADIAN EXPORTS TO JAPAN

	1980 Thousands of Dollars	%	1984 Thousands of Dollars	%	1985 Thousands of Dollars	%	1987 Thousands of Dollars	%
Live animals	6 374	0.2	2 925	—	2 056	—	1 642	—
Food, feed, beverages, and tobacco	764 747	17.4	1 077 512	19.1	1 017 836	17.7	1 191 842	17.0
Crude materials, inedible	1 959 171	44.7	2 645 986	47.0	2 886 158	50.2	2 812 404	40.1
Fabricated materials, inedible	1 536 800	35.0	1 727 561	30.6	1 653 530	28.8	2 668 776	38.0
End products, inedible	120 216	2.7	186 503	3.3	189 730	3.3	342 656	4.9
Special transactions	145	—	361	—	163	—	125	—
TOTAL	4 387 454	100	5 640 848	100	5 749 473	100	7 017 446	100

Source: Statistics Canada, *Summary of Canadian International Trade* (Dec. 1985), (Dec. 1987), pp. 46–51.

▶ The Impact of Industrialization

Japan is also experiencing the negative consequences of industrialization, with its pollution and rapid, unregulated growth. Japan has created some serious environmental problems for itself. The world is now aware of the horrors of the small fishing village of Minimata, and the disease that now carries that name. After decades of allowing a large industrial firm to pump raw sewage into the sea, the people of Minimata have suffered the effects of mercury poisoning in epidemic proportions. In the rest of Japan, air pollution is so devastating in most major cities that many citizens must wear masks on the streets.

Some critics believe that many Japanese companies have been successful at the expense of their employees. For example, sixty-four percent of the Japanese labour force works forty-five hours or more a week. There are increasing reports of *karoshi*-deaths resulting from severe overwork and fatigue. The suicide rate among Japanese students has increased, particularly during examination periods. Japan's success has caused a labour shortage. The best graduates are invariably hired by the large firms, which has resulted in intense competition and labour shortages at the middle management level.

Some young Japanese have started to rebel against the intensity they find in Japanese life and have begun to question Japan's definition of success. They are increasingly joining the ***bosozoku***, which are gangs of young people prepared to break the law in their rebellion even to the point of committing murder. In 1989, Japan recorded 107 889 arrests, an increase of twenty-two percent over 1988.

Another facet of the economic situation is the apparent disparity in the distribution of the country's wealth. For the most part, the Japanese middle class has benefited little from the country's prosperity. In order to foster domestic production, MITI created a pricing system in which the Japanese consumer pays more for Japanese goods than do the importing countries. A 1987 American government study demonstrated that on the average, the Japanese pay forty to sixty percent more for consumer goods.

These inflated prices are just one of the growing grievances of Japan's middle class. In fact, the existence of a Japanese middle class is becoming increasingly more questionable, and the Japanese now talk of the ***nyuu puaa*** (the new poor) and the ***nyuu ritchi*** (the new rich). The growing income gap between the rich and poor is determined by three factors. *Nyuu ritchi* are privileged enough to own land, play the stock market, and qualify for tax exemption status. In 1987, seventy-three percent of Japanese workers earned between $18 600 and $59 700 annually. This may appear to be a comfortable income level until the high cost of living is taken into consideration. Nearly fifty percent of the average worker's income is spent on rent and utilities. Most Japanese find it practically impossible to own a house. According to a 1988 article in *Business Week*,

> *With residential land in Tokyo now worth about $15 000 per square metre, a typical mortage of $308 000 requires a monthly payment of $2200, or 57 percent of the typical family's gross income. That buys a 65-square metre, three-room apartment situated in a drab Tokyo neighbourhood.*[2]

The affluence of the few and the success of the large *keiretsu* tend to hide what appears to be widespread poverty. Relatively few Japanese citizens have a share in the Japanese success in terms of such social facilities as public utilities, highways, and

▸ [2]"The Myth of Japan's Middle Class," *Business Week*, August 29, 1988.

parks. Only forty percent of Japanese homes have sewage connections. Highways, schools, parks, and streets have been neglected because the government has concentrated its efforts on capital accumulation for industrialization. Perhaps it is this disparity in rewards that is driving many young people to join the *bosozoku*. Some social critics predict a loss of enthusiasm for the work ethic and a decline in loyalty to country, firm, and Japanese traditions. Clearly, all is not perfect in Japan.

APPLYING YOUR KNOWLEDGE

1. While Japan rose from the ashes to become a major industrial power, Canada declined from the third largest industrial power in 1945 to nineteenth place in 1989. Compare Canada to Japan in the following categories:
   a) Canada's colonial past
   b) the extent of foreign ownership
   c) the effects of Canada's proximity to the United States
   d) the emphasis on consumption rather than production
   e) the attitude of the work force
   f) the adversarial labour-management relations
   g) the emphasis on the individual instead of the state
   h) the emphasis on *laissez-faire* capitalism opposed to government intervention
   i) an educational system that promotes individual expression rather than disciplined obedience
2. The seven prerequisites of industry are (1) a large pool of capital; (2) a large, cheap, well-educated labour force; (3) accessible and cheap natural resources; (4) domestic and foreign markets; (5) enterprising people; (6) transportation and communication facilities; and (7) a favourable political climate.
   a) Review this case study and identify which of these prerequisites Japan possesses.
   b) How did Japan compensate for the prerequisites it lacked?
3. a) Why do you think Canadian students do not clean their schools?
   b) What are the different attitudes towards school expressed in each country?
4. Explain the role of each of the following in Japan's success: *zaibatsu*, MITI, state capitalism, and export-oriented industries.
5. "The West treats workers as the problem, the Japanese view workers as the solution to the problem." Explain.
6. a) Explain what Figure 3 (page 394) shows.
   b) Why do you think young people feel the least loyalty?
7. List three examples of both planned economy and free enterprise in Japan.
8. Working in groups, determine whether the Japanese economic model would be successful in Canada.
9. Using Tables 2 and 3 and Figure 5, answer the following questions.
   a) Which Canadian region exports the most to Japan? Which imports the most from Japan?
   b) How might this affect the way these regions view relations with Japan?
   c) What appears to be the trend in Canada's trade with Japan?
   d) Categorize the nature of Canada's exports and imports with Japan.

e) Did Canada have a trade surplus or deficit with Japan in 1984? Explain.
f) Which country has the better productivity, Canada or Japan?
g) Which country pays its workers better? Explain.
h) Which country would have the competitive advantage on the world market? Why?

Case Study 21 Overview

Economic Planning in the U.S.S.R.

This case study examines how the Soviet Union handled the three basic economic questions both before and after Gorbachev's assumption of power. In the pre-Gorbachev period, the case study analyses the Soviet Union's central planning structure, the use of prices, and the problem of providing incentives for farmers and industrial workers. This section concludes with a discussion of the merits and disadvantages of the Soviet economic system. The drastic decline of the economy led to Gorbachev's policies of *glasnost* and *perestroika*. The remainder of this case study examines Gorbachev's economic reforms, including joint economic enterprises and the development of small private businesses, and concludes with an analysis of Gorbachev's economic policies.

▶ OBJECTIVES

After reading this case study, you should be able to:

- ▶ describe the operations of the Soviet economy prior to Gorbachev
- ▶ compare the Soviet and Canadian economic systems
- ▶ evaluate the merits of central planning
- ▶ devise your own central plan and prepare a solution to the Soviet Union's economic problems
- ▶ discuss Gorbachev's economic reforms
- ▶ hypothesize future directions of the Soviet economy

▶ KEY TERMS

Gosplan	self-financing	joint economic ventures
Gossnab		

Case Study 21

Economic Planning in the U.S.S.R.

The methods used by Joseph Stalin to meet the economic problems of the 1930s (as described in Case Study 18) could not be employed indefinitely. The people, for instance, could not be expected to forgo luxury items and essential goods while the Soviet Union built up its industrial and military might.

As Soviet industry became larger and more complex, planners in Moscow experienced greater difficulty in determining how the government's goals could be achieved. In fact, according to some critics of central planning, the planners will never have enough information to develop effective economic strategies, because there are too many economic facts for any one person or group of people to master.

Other theoreticians disagree. Oskar Lange, for example, believes that if a central planning board established prices for all goods and services, it would know what the people wanted by the amount of each item that was purchased. This case study examines the Soviet planning structure prior to the Gorbachev reforms, and speculates on the recent economic changes. How does the Soviet economy deal with the three basic economic questions: what, how, and to whom?

Article II of the Soviet Constitution states: "The economic life of the U.S.S.R. is determined and directed by the state economic plan." Prior to the Gorbachev regime, competition, as we know it in Canada, does not exist in the Soviet Union. The state owned virtually all the land, controlled transportation, finance, industrial production, and international trade and was responsible for over ninety percent of the country's retail stores. Although Soviet citizens owned as many clothes, televisions, automobiles, and other such consumer items as they could afford, they could not open their own store (beyond a retail level), own a farm, or purchase stock (part ownership) in a business enterprise. The Soviet economic system might be described as a gigantic government monopoly that embraced the entire country.

All major economic policy decisions were

made by the government, not by the individual firms themselves. For the most part, Soviet enterprises did not sell their products to other companies, as in Canada. Instead, government planning boards determined to which firms the products would be sold, in what quantities, and at what price.[1] Competitive consumer goods were sometimes produced by different companies, but if one company manufactured a better product than the other, the government ordered the less efficient firm to adopt the techniques of the more efficient factory. Business profits belonged to the state rather than to individual firms. Some factories continuously operated at a loss, but were supported from the profits of other enterprises.

Planners naturally found it difficult to determine exactly what items people would buy if they had their choice. Today, more emphasis is placed on providing such luxury goods as automobiles, televisions, and furniture. Because marketing surveys in the U.S.S.R. are still in their infancy, Soviet economists frequently observed the buying patterns of other European countries and then attempted to provide similar goods. All major decisions involving the distribution of scarce resources between consumer goods and military or industrial needs, however, were made by the Communist party.

▶ PRICES AND THEIR USES BEFORE GORBACHEV

Although consumers were free to buy whatever goods they could afford, demand only partly influenced supply. The Soviet government used its control over prices to help accomplish its goals. It set low prices, for instance, on school books in order to promote education, and on children's clothes to encourage large families; whereas high prices were used to curb the consumption of less socially desirable items such as vodka. Another objective was to reduce the gap between income levels. To do this, the government set a low price on such items as basic foods and clothing, which constituted a large proportion of the expenditures of the lower income groups, and fixed a higher price on luxury foodstuffs and automobiles that were more often purchased by people in the higher income groups. In this way, the Communist party influenced the buying practices of the citizens, based upon what was perceived as the best interests of the country. Soviet leaders were often discouraged from increasing the price of food and clothing because of the possibility that the people would hold a protest strike.

▶ PLANNING STAGES PRIOR TO 1985

The Soviet economy was controlled by an elaborate superstructure of economic plans. Long-term plans established general targets for up to twenty years ahead; five- to seven-year plans set more specific goals; annual, quarterly, and monthly plans were the most detailed. These plans underwent constant revision to correct original errors and to provide for unforeseen circumstances. The purpose of the long-range plans was to point planners in the "proper" direction. They set down broad objectives for the economy by weighing social, political, international, military, and scientific goals. Every plan ranked its priorities from most to least important. This ranking system was determined by the Communist party.

There were four stages to each plan. As their first step, planners used past perform-

▸ [1]This plan did not always work well in practice. As a result, many companies often traded among themselves with the help of individuals termed *expediters*. This trading was officially illegal, but the law was not enforced.

Figure 1
A SIMPLIFIED PLANNING MODEL

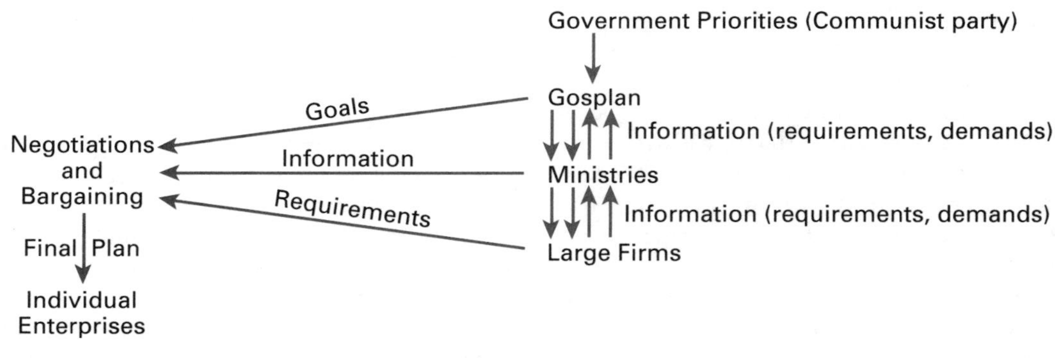

ances to calculate how much of the country's physical and human resources would be needed to fulfill the requirements of the most important targets. Moving on to less important targets, they went down the list of priorities until all resources were exhausted. The **Gosplan** (the central planning agency) then informed the regional ministries, which were in charge of specific sectors of the economy, of what commodities were needed, and in what amounts. Another planning body called the **Gossnab** determined how commodities were distributed. There were also separate agencies for determining prices, labour matters, technology, and foreign trade. In addition, each region and town had its own planning bodies.

In the second stage, the ministries and the larger firms determined whether they could meet these targets, drew up a list of all the resources (workers, money, equipment, natural resources) they required to fulfill these goals, and reported back to the Gosplan. In the third stage, the Gosplan co-ordinated all these demands. Heads of the ministries and large firms met with the Gosplan and from these negotiations, which often became quite heated, a national economic plan emerged that was much more detailed than the original directives. In the final stage, each firm was issued orders detailing production quotas. Physically, the five-year plan was a book of several hundred pages. The first chapter discussed the government's goals, and subsequent chapters described how these goals would be achieved in the areas of industry, agriculture, forestry, transportation, living standards, foreign trade, housing, and so on.

▶ MERITS AND DRAWBACKS

The Soviet economy, as mentioned previously, does not have an ideal centrally planned economic system. Approximately ten percent of the small retail stores were privately owned. More important were the tiny plots of land that farmers were allowed to do with as they pleased. Although these plots constituted less than three percent of the total arable land in the U.S.S.R., they produced approximately thirty percent of the country's food supply, and in some items the proportion reached almost ninety percent.

Compare this photograph of a Red Square parade in 1925 with the more recent photograph of a Moscow thoroughfare. What do the contrasts suggest about the success of economic planning in the U.S.S.R.?
Canapress Photo Service

The major advantage of central planning was that it allowed the government, rather than the market system of supply and demand, to determine what goods the country needed and who received these goods. If these decisions were poor, it was the fault of the political system, not of the economic system. Of course, there are also disadvantages to central planning. When the planners made a ''wrong'' decision, the effect could be disastrous because the plan was carried out on a national scale. Highly centralized plans were slow to respond to unforeseen changes. Because there was no built-in method of discovering consumer desires, huge inventories of unwanted goods often languished for years in warehouses or on store shelves. At the same time, shortages of desired consumer goods were a constant problem. Finally, when controls are highly centralized, individual initiative and innovation are frequently retarded. The Soviet Union, for example, imported foreign technology and established an underground smuggling network to procure such advanced technological data as computer microchips. It is partly because of this absence of initiative that the Soviet Union adopted a system of incentives.

▶ THE USE OF INCENTIVES PRIOR TO 1985

The desire for profits is the major motivating force in a private enterprise economy. Companies spend millions of dollars on research and development in the hope that they can develop a product that will outsell their competitors'. Individuals work hard not only to keep their jobs, but also to obtain a raise. Generally, the greater the production, the greater the profits. One of the most frequently heard complaints made by private enterprisers about socialism or government-operated industries is that there is no incentive for government employees to work hard or to ensure that the industry will operate efficiently.

Since almost all enterprises in the U.S.S.R. were government owned and operated, everyone was a public employee. Soviet firms strove, above all, to fulfill the directives of the Gosplan; profits, which went to the government, were incidental. The manager's goal was to fulfill the government's plans, rather than to search for the best production methods.[2] To solve this problem, the Soviet Union adopted a wide variety of different incentive plans.

Increased agricultural production from the Soviet collective farms was encouraged in two ways. At the end of the year, each farm distributed its profits among the farmers according to their work record. Each farmer's contribution was determined by assigning a money value to every task, based upon the difficulty of that task and the time needed to accomplish it.

Piece rates and bonuses were used to encourage greater efforts from the factory workers.[3] When the labourers' output reached a specific level, they received a bonus. Higher wages were given for dangerous and unattractive work, in order to induce people to enter these fields. Salaries were also based upon expertise—the more skill involved, the higher the rewards. As a further incentive, when an enterprise fulfilled the government's plan, it received a share of the profits for its ''enterprise fund.'' Enterprises expected to show a loss

▸ [2]One economist tells the story of a transportation firm that moved carloads of water back and forth on the railway tracks in order to meet its quota of having moved a specific volume of water for the year.

▸ [3]Piece rate workers receive a set amount of money for each item they produce. All workers, however, receive a guaranteed minimum salary.

for the year received part of any saving they might have achieved from reducing the expected loss. Production in excess of the government's plan increased the "enterprise fund," whereas under-production decreased the size of the fund. The "enterprise fund" might be used to pay annual bonuses to the workers and managers, to help needy employees, to improve working conditions, or to provide better housing.

Managers received bonuses of over thirty percent of their basic salaries for fulfilling the production goals set by the Gosplan. Other bonuses were given for introducing new technology and for producing consumer goods out of waste materials. In addition to these material incentives, the managers were given preferential housing, theatre tickets, special vacations, the use of a company car, or were allowed to shop in the prestigious stores that contained a wide variety of goods. Useful technological inventions were awarded with large cash grants, media coverage, and membership in such esteemed orders as the Badge of Honour or the Order of Lenin.

The following examples reveal that such measures were often not very successful. In the early 1980s, a Moscow newspaper reported that a factory manager in the Ukraine had been reprimanded for having produced 13 000 pairs of sunglasses so dark that the viewer could look straight at the sun without seeing any light. Other reports claimed that over half of all the Moscow milk sold in containers had spoiled because the packaging machinery had punched holes in most of the cartons. Elsewhere, a fully loaded freight train left Moscow carrying concrete roof beams to construction sites in Leningrad; it passed a train with a similar cargo on its way to building sites in Moscow.

On a collective farm, the workers' incentive was sharing the profits. On a state farm, the workers were paid wages and enjoyed few material incentives. The most frequently cited example of state farm inefficiency concerned the case of tractor drivers. They were paid per hectare ploughed and received bonuses for fuel savings and avoiding mechanical breakdowns. Clever drivers dug numerous but shallow furrows, and collected hefty bonuses. This angered fellow workers, as the farm produced a poor harvest and thus forfeited bonuses. Rural workers found it demoralizing that some people got rewarded for being tricky and performing shabby work, whereas the rest merely collected their guaranteed monthly salaries.

▶ THE POSTWAR ECONOMY

The planners of the First Five-Year Plan would not have dreamt that, over fifty years after their agonized efforts, the Soviet economy would suffer from such problems. In theory, communism is supposedly better, fairer, and more productive than capitalism. It ignores the profit motive and emphasizes the need for social utility of goods and services. But centralization undermined economic efficiency in the U.S.S.R.

The system became so unwieldy that central planners in Moscow had difficulty keeping track of the complex operations of each individual factory. In the early 1980s, the economy stagnated. The aging leadership refused to take radical steps to solve agricultural mismanagement, stop high-level corruption, and inspire a demoralized working force. Cynicism, sloppiness, and shabby performance flourished. Ordinary citizens became unhappy with standing in endless lines for food and consumer goods while senior party members received luxury goods at discount prices in special stores.

The queue (line-up) is a common feature of Soviet life. Soviet citizens spend several

What is the message of this cartoon?
©*Forth Worth* Star-Telegram

hours each day lining up in stores. This was because the Soviet economy operated as a seller's market rather than a buyer's market. Gosplan selected the consumer goods that would be produced with little or no input from consumers. Thus, production became a hit and miss affair. Unpopular or defective goods lay unsold, while popular items were quickly snapped up. One queue for rugs lasted two days and totalled over 10 000 people! Not surprisingly, these problems of supply spawned an underground black market economy that dealt in blue jeans, nylons, fertilizers, and services such as plumbing and legal aid.

Several complicated factors account for the decline in the Soviet economy. First and foremost was the conservatism of the Soviet leaders. A country that is so vast in size, so varied in terrain and climate, and so culturally diverse, needs innovation and imagination to prosper. The Soviet leaders feared, however, that the smallest crack in the Soviet Union's unified Marxist system would become a fatal chasm. Even minor innovations or deviations from the Marxian norms were rarely tolerated.

Following Brezhnev's death in 1982, Yuri Andropov made the first serious attempts since Lenin to reverse Soviet economic paralysis. But Andropov lacked the support to change the basic foundations of the Marxian economic system. Just like his predecessors, he merely tightened central control. He attempted to scare workers and managers into improving their job performance. For example, he had loafers, drunks, and poor workers openly arrested and punished. He fired dozens of elderly and inept high-level bureaucrats. He served notice on factory managers that their enterprises would be kept under close surveillance to monitor performance. This shocked the party into reluctant action.

After Andropov's untimely death, Chernenko, the second Soviet leader in three years, failed to pursue his predecessor's tough policy. Most likely, the Central Committee desired a rest period after Andropov's fire-breathing performance. Life in the Soviet Union, as in Tsarist Russia, moved slowly, and responded to the rhythms of old habits rather than to modern needs. Attempts by the authorities to make managers and workers toe the line through threats and intimidation had produced sullen resistance and even industrial sabotage.

Gorbachev is trying to publicize *glasnost* and *perestroika* among the leaders of the Soviet Union. How successful has he been since this picture was taken in 1985? What is your understanding of these two terms?
The Bettmann Archive

▶ GORBACHEV'S REFORMS

Since his election as General Secretary of the Communist party early in 1985, Mikhail Gorbachev has come out strongly in favour of imaginative production methods. He is determined to restructure the Soviet leadership, modernize the economy, eliminate the black market, and improve the image of the country at home and abroad.

Gorbachev has introduced reforms that strike at the heart of the country's production problems. Plant managers, not government ministers, now determine production needs, as they better understand the society's demands. Factories that produce unwanted merchandise will be phased out entirely. Some large state enterprises have been placed on a **self-financing** basis. This means that they can no longer disguise inefficiency and overspending by applying to the central government for subsidies. In a wage experiment in Estonia, workers are being paid a share of the profits.

Gorbachev has also encouraged the development of small private businesses, especially in the service industries. The Soviet Union has never expressly forbidden private enterprise, but conservative party officials never liked even small-scale "capitalism." Under Gorbachev, Soviet citizens may open up repair shops, beauty salons, and other convenience facilities.

Perhaps the most exciting economic development in Gorbachev's U.S.S.R. is the creation of **joint economic ventures** with Western companies. Three chief goals of this relaxation of Marxism are to improve the Soviet Union's export structure, to acquire currency to fund modernization ventures, and to stock the domestic market with high quality goods without having to import them. Such Soviet-foreign partnerships involve only products destined for export markets. Soviet ministries continue to control all domestic production.

▶ MOTIVES BEHIND ECONOMIC PERESTROIKA

By the early 1980s, a consensus was emerging among the Soviet elite that economic reform was needed. Some economists advocated radical changes. Siberian economist Tatiana Zaslavskaia, for example, stated that the weaknesses of the Soviet economy were not temporary, but inherent in the system and that no major changes had occurred in the economy since Stalin. This economic structure, she charged, was the real reason for the poor standards of work demonstrated by the labourers. The situation would improve only if the workers were granted greater freedom in the work place. She also criticized the overly centralized nature of economic decision-making, as well as the weak development of market mechanisms in the Soviet economy, and demanded that reforms be instituted to resolve both problems.

Although Zaslavskaia's proposals are widely believed to be behind the economic policies Gorbachev began implementing after assuming power in 1985, the General Secretary's record hardly supports the view that he has had a consistent, overall plan in mind. His speeches at times have advocated the somewhat contradictory policies of strengthening the authority of Gosplan, while simultaneously granting individual enterprises greater autonomy in the decision-making process. However, thanks to a traditional fear of assuming responsibility, many plant directors proved unwilling to act upon their own initiative. At the same time, a deeply rooted prejudice and suspicion of profits has hampered attempts to expand private enterprises. Bureaucratic red tape has prevented Soviet industries from reaping the full benefits of partnerships with foreign firms, which Gorbachev has encouraged.

The tentative measures of 1985–1987 did nothing to revive the stagnant economy, and by 1988 Gorbachev obviously recognized that a more far-reaching and integrated program was required. He also realized that this could be implemented only if a preliminary series of political reforms broke the power of his more conservative colleagues in both the Communist party and the Soviet government. As a result, he undertook a series of political measures that, by the spring of 1990, had transferred decision-making from the party to a governmental system. More important still, Gorbachev now headed the state administration by virtue of his election to the presidency. (See Case Study 10.)

Meanwhile, the economy continued to decline, and for most Soviet citizens, empty shop shelves and long line-ups were the norm. By the spring of 1990, Gorbachev reportedly had the outlines of an economic plan ready for presentation. Rumours that he planned to abolish price controls, however, immediately aroused widespread opposition. Nevertheless, Gorbachev now seems determined to introduce measures to create a "controlled market economy" within the U.S.S.R. Although the outlines of this program are still far from clear, most Soviet commentators accept that this transition is unavoidable. Only one fact seems clear: in the long run, the success of Gorbachev's whole program of *perestroika*, be it cultural, political, or economic, depends on Gorbachev's success in obtaining significant economic success within the next few years.

APPLYING YOUR KNOWLEDGE

1. In what ways did the Soviet economy resemble a monopoly?
2. Explain the differences and similarities between the use of prices in the U.S.S.R. and Canada.
3. Is there much difference between the Soviet's incentive system and the profit motive of private enterprise? Explain.
4. Do the advantages of the Soviet economic system outweigh their disadvantages? Write an essay explaining your answer to this question.
5. What do the recent economic changes in the Soviet Union imply about rigid government planning?
6. What does this case study reveal about the relationship between the economy and political power?
7. Describe the essentials of Zaslavskaia's critique and illustrate it with materials drawn from this case study.

FURTHER RESEARCH

1. Prepare for a debate on one of the following topics:
   a) The Soviet economic system is superior to the Canadian system.
   b) Government-owned companies cannot compete successfully with privately owned firms.
   c) The average person has less control over the economy in the private enterprise system than in a centrally planned economy.
2. a) Divide into small groups. Imagine that you are a committee in the Gosplan. Your task is to provide chairs for a new school that is presently under construction. Make a list of all the specific questions you would need answered before deciding upon how many should be manufactured, what design should be used, and what materials should be employed in their construction.
   b) Explain how these decisions would be made in Canada.
3. Keeping in mind the values and history of the Soviet Union, suggest possible economic reforms that might solve the country's problems.
4. Working in groups, devise a solution to the problem of incentive in the U.S.S.R.

Case Study 22 Overview

Canada's Mixed Economy: Competition and Regulation

This case study examines the Canadian mixed economy and the extent of government involvement in the economy. It outlines the four basic types of business competition (monopoly, oligopoly, perfect competition, and imperfect competition) and comments upon the merits of each. After discussing the extent of business concentration in Canada, the case study outlines the growth of government involvement in the economy. It concentrates upon the origins, motives, and growth of government owned and operated businesses. The case study concludes with a discussion of the recent trend towards privatization—the selling of state-owned companies to the private sector.

▶ OBJECTIVES

After reading this case study, you should be able to:

- ▶ explain the four different types of business competition
- ▶ evaluate the justifications for and against government-owned enterprises
- ▶ debate the necessity of government restrictions upon the economy
- ▶ decide whether Canada has too much or too little government involvement in the economy
- ▶ analyse the reasons behind the growth of privatization
- ▶ devise your own solutions to problems in the Canadian economy

▶ KEY TERMS

perfect competition
monopoly
imperfect competition
monopolistic competition
Combines Investigation Act
Competition Acts
Crown corporations

Case Study

22 Canada's Mixed Economy: Competition and Regulation

Most people acknowledge that capitalism has been extremely successful in promoting economic growth. Karl Marx, one of its harshest critics, wrote that capitalism "has accomplished wonders far surpassing Egyptian pyramids, Roman aqueducts, and Gothic cathedrals." It has, he said, "created more massive and more colossal productive forces than have all preceding generations together." As we have seen, the major stimulus behind this economic growth was the profit motive. Unfortunately, unrestricted competition among individuals struggling for the highest possible profits often created poverty, dangerous working conditions, and unhealthy accommodations for the victims of capitalism. It was largely to improve these conditions that governments intervened in the capitalist economy.

One of the most contentious areas of government involvement in the Canadian economy is the extent to which the state should control the policies and activities of individual business firms. Naturally, most businesspeople believe that they should be allowed to operate their companies without government interference. They argue that competition among entrepreneurs is the best guarantee that the consumers will receive quality goods at the lowest prices possible. The supporters of planned economies disagree—the only way for the state to ensure that a "just" economy is created, they say, is for the government to operate the economy. Ultimately, this implies government ownership of the country's resources and businesses.

Canada's mixed economy is somewhere between these two extremes. The actual amount (and type) of government intervention depends upon each country's historical experience, form of government, and objectives and values. To what extent and why does the Canadian government intervene in the economy? Does it intervene too much or too little? To help answer these questions, let us examine competition among individual business firms and assess the growth of government regulations in Canada.

▶ COMPETITION

There are hundreds of thousands of firms in Canada. Every day new companies are created and old firms declare bankruptcy. The average life expectancy of a Canadian business is only six years.

The size of firms within each sector of the economy varies tremendously. In the retail trade, for instance, there are approximately 150 000 companies, most of which sell less than $100 000 in goods annually. Retail chain stores, however, have sales totalling billions of dollars.

In an economy operating according to the ideal theory of free enterprise, all these firms would be in unrestricted competition for Canadian consumer dollars — a condition termed **perfect competition**. Its advantages for the consumer can be illustrated by examining the history of the invention and production of ball-point pens in the United States.

In 1945, Milton Reynolds acquired a patent on a new type of pen that used a ball bearing in place of the old nip-tipped fountain pens that had to be dipped into ink wells. He formed the Reynolds International Pen Company and began production on October 6, 1945.

The Reynolds pen was introduced with a good deal of fanfare by Gimbels, the New York department store, which guaranteed that the pen would write for two years without being refilled. The price was set at $12.50. Production costs were only about eighty cents per pen. Gimbels sold 10 000 pens on October 29, 1945, the first day they were on sale.

The Reynolds International Pen Company quickly expanded production. By early 1946 it was employing more than 800 people in its factory and was producing 30 000 pens per day. After six months, it had three million dollars in the bank. Not to be outdone, Gimbels' traditional business rival, Macy's department store, introduced an imported ball-point pen from South America that sold at $19.98. Other pen manufacturers also entered the field. Eversharp produced its first ball-point in April, and Sheaffer followed with its pen in July. So far, however, Reynolds still sold the cheapest pen on the market at $12.50, and its costs had declined to sixty cents per pen. The first signs of trouble emerged when the Ball-Point Pen Company of Hollywood (disregarding a patent infringement suit) put a $9.95 model on the market, and a manufacturer named David Kahn announced plans to introduce a pen selling for less than three dollars. A price war had begun.

Reynolds responded with a new model, priced at $3.85, that cost about thirty cents to produce. By Christmas of 1946, approximately one hundred manufacturers were in production, some of them selling pens for as little as $2.98. The next year, Gimbels decided to purchase its ball-point pens from the Continental Pen Company and reduced its price to ninety-eight cents. Reynolds had introduced a new model priced to sell at $1.69, but Gimbels sold it for eighty-eight cents in its continuing price war with Macy's. Reynolds then designed a new model listed at ninety-eight cents. By this time, ball-point pens had become economy items rather than luxury items, but they were still highly profitable.

In 1948, ball-point pens selling for as little as thirty-nine cents cost about ten cents to produce. In 1951, prices of twenty-five cents were common. Today, there is a wide variety of models and prices, ranging from nineteen cents upwards, and the market appears stable, orderly, and only moderately profitable.[1]

▸ [1]Adapted from R. Lipsey, Sparks, and Steiner, *Economics*, New York: Harper and Row, 1979, pp. 281–282.

FOCUS

1. What does the ball-point pen example illustrate about:
   a) the effect of competition in the business world?
   b) the benefits of competition for the consumer?
   c) the advantages of innovation for the innovating firms?

▶ Perfect Competition

The ball-point pen study is an excellent illustration of perfect competition. When many manufacturers are making an identical product and many people are willing to buy it, then no individual buyer or seller can control the price of the product. The resulting competition ensures that the product will be sold at a "fair" price.

Perfect competition does have its limitations. In situations of extreme competition, some sellers lower their costs by producing goods of such inferior quality that they are not worth the price. Manufacturers will also resort to frequent product changes ("new and improved," as their advertisements proclaim), in order to persuade customers to buy their product. Although these changes are usually minor, they involve unnecessary costs. Competition can also lead to secrecy. As we have seen in the ball-point pen example, the first firm to produce the new pens made fantastic profits. The Reynolds Pen company did not announce its new design until the pens were ready for sale. As a result, many customers bought the old fountain pens just before they became obsolete. At the same time, each pen company was conducting its own research — much of which was wasteful duplication. Perfect competition is clearly not "perfect."

But perfect competition rarely exists in practice: the consumer is not always well informed about the lowest price or the best quality available; there are not always enough firms in the same industry to ensure real competition; and it is unusual for companies to manufacture identical products. Competition is also restricted by the government. In Canada, hydro-electricity, education, nuclear power plants, and other important goods and services are owned and operated by the government. Minimum wage laws, health and safety regulations, restrictions on tobacco advertising, taxes on alcohol, and meat and milk inspections are only a few examples of government involvement in the economy.

Interestingly, too, business itself has frequently asked for government intervention to help reduce competition from abroad. In 1879, for instance, the federal government, at the request of many Canadian manufacturers, instituted a protective tariff to give certain Canadian products a price advantage over similar foreign products.

Competition is also limited by associations and unions that can manipulate the supply of their services. Law schools, for example, restrict the number of students they admit each year, thereby reducing lawyers' needs to compete for clients.

▶ MONOPOLY

A **monopoly** is the opposite of perfect competition. In Greek, *mono* means "single," and *polein* means "to sell." In a monopoly industry, there is a single seller for a product; the product has no close substitutes; and entry into the industry is restricted. When you turn on the light to read a book, you are using the output of the local monopoly power company. It is the only firm that sells electricity in your area. When you mail a letter at the post office, you have purchased the services of a monopoly.[2] The only drugstore in a small town is as much a monopolist as a corporate giant such as Bell Canada.

A description of the growth of Alcoa Aluminum Company in the United States illustrates how a monopoly can arise. The Alcoa Aluminum Company was established in the 1880s, when Charles Hall invented a new process for producing aluminum. The company was granted an American patent that allowed Alcoa to maintain a legal monopoly in the United States until 1909. By the time the patent expired, Alcoa had developed such a large degree of technical expertise in aluminum production that no other firm could successfully compete with it. The company was also able to maintain its monopoly of the industry because it controlled the natural resources — bauxite and hydro-electricity — needed to produce aluminum. With an eye on future sales and continued control of the industry, Alcoa offered reasonable prices for its product and constructed new factories to meet the future demand for aluminum. As a result, Alcoa's dominance was not challenged until the second half of the twentieth century. Today, there are still only a handful of aluminum-producing companies in North America.

The Alcoa story illustrates some of the factors that allow for the emergence and maintenance of a monopoly: government patents; technical knowledge; control over essential raw materials; and price policy designed to discourage other firms from entering the industry. The most obvious factor in the creation of monopolies is government legislation. A patent grants inventors the exclusive control of their new product for seventeen years. In the cases of electric utilities and telephone services, the government forbids other firms from entering the industry and competing for consumers. Other factors favouring monopolies are the high capital costs required to begin operations and a company's reputation for low prices and good services.

Monopolies are frequently depicted as the ogres of the capitalist system. Because monopolists have the power to restrict production, they can raise prices and earn enormous profits. A monopoly can also misuse a country's resources — free from the pressures of competition, the monopolist is neither forced to conduct research nor to use resources as efficiently as they might be utilized. In defence of monopolies, it can be argued that because they avoid wasteful duplication in advertising, research, and staffing, they can sell their products at lower prices than would be possible in a competitive market. More to the point, however, is the fact that in a mixed economy the government actually encourages the creation of some monopolies. Since it appears wasteful to have two sets of telephone wires or water pipes, the government grants the utility company a monopoly. Then, to protect the consumer from unfair prices and poor services, the

▸ [2]There are, of course, substitutes. Candles and flashlights could illuminate this page, and courier services will deliver letters.

government sets restrictions on the actions of this utility. The usual practice is to create a public commission to regulate the policies of the monopoly. Before increasing prices, the utility must get permission from the commission.

In fact, there are very few real monopolies, and those that do exist, face competition from alternate services. When railway companies set freight rates too high, for instance, shippers turn to trucks, buses, airplanes, and steamships. A hydro-electric utility can lose customers to natural gas or oil companies.

FOCUS

1. Explain why the Reynolds Pen Company lost its control over the ball-point pen market, while Alcoa maintained its control over the aluminum market. What were the most important differences between the two situations?

▶ THE REAL WORLD OF BUSINESS

The great majority of Canadian businesses falls somewhere between the extremes of perfect competition and monopoly. Although there are no cut-and-dried categories, most industries can be divided into **imperfect competition** (also called **monopolistic competition**), and oligopoly.

An imperfectly competitive industry has a large number of producers that manufacture similar, but slightly different products. An excellent example of imperfect competition is the soft drink industry. Each company produces a similar product that differs slightly according to taste, colour, and image. Other examples include furniture and clothing manufacturers, the retail industry, barbers, automobile service stations, and the publishing industry. Each individual firm has some control over the price of its product, and some companies earn large profits; however, the threat of new firms entering the same industry, and the availability of close substitutes usually serve to keep prices within reason.

Unlike an imperfectly competitive industry, an oligopolist industry has only a few leading firms that produce almost identical products. This allows the oligopolist companies more control over the prices of their products. Firms operating within this type of industry do not generally compete for customers by lowering their prices. Experience has taught oligopolists that price wars usually end up hurting everyone (except the consumer). Instead, they use advertising to create loyalty to their own brand or offer better service than the other firms within the same industry. At other times, the largest company will set its price based upon a predetermined level of sales and profits, and the other firms in the industry will adopt approximately the same price as the "price leader." Large corporations are often more interested in long-term security and "adequate" profits than in maximizing profits, which might result in a damaging price war.

In Canada, oligopoly is most common where huge amounts of capital are needed to begin operations — as in the automobile industry, for example. Many manufacturing and financial industries are oligopolies. Table 1 illustrates the extent to which a few large firms dominated specific Canadian industries in the mid-1980s.

Do the savings made through efficient marketing and production techniques offset the higher prices charged through co-operative pricing? The actions of the Cana-

Table 1
CONCENTRATION IN SELECTED CANADIAN INDUSTRIES
(percentage of output produced by four largest firms)

Industry	%
Tobacco products	99.4
Breweries	97.7
Motor vehicles	95.1
Aluminum rolling and casting	88.8
Asphalt roofing	86.1
Major appliances	85.0
Copper rolling	82.4
Cement	81.7
Fibre and filament yarn	79.4
Railroad rolling stock	78.8
Leather tanneries	77.4
Distilleries	77.0
Lubricating oils and greases	76.4
Shipbuilding and repair	71.4
Batteries	69.4
Wood preservation industry	68.9
Wire and wire rope industry	68.2
Petroleum products	64.0
Steel pipe and tubes	63.7

‣ Source: C. R. McConnell et al. *Economics*, 5th Cdn. ed. Scarborough: McGraw-Hill Ryerson Limited, 1990, p. 251. Statistics from Statistics Canada.

dian government (as well as British and American governments) indicate that politicians do not think so. Beginning in 1889 (1890 in the United States), the federal government attempted to foster greater competition in the economy by making it illegal for any producer to ''unreasonably'' raise prices by ''unduly'' lowering the supply of products. However, the wording (''unreasonably,'' ''unduly'') of the legislation was vague and no enforcement agency was established. In 1910, the **Combines Investigation Act** prohibited the formation of any monopoly or oligopoly that was ''likely to operate to the detriment of the public.'' Subsequent legislation in 1923 and 1960 forbade agreements to fix prices, reduce production, and restrict entry of other firms into the industry, but enforcement was sporadic and often depended upon public pressure rather than government action. Mergers ''not in the public interest'' were prohibited, as was misleading price advertising. Once again, however, the wording of this legislation was vague and imprecise,

Part of Imperial Oil's Strathcona Refinery in Edmonton. Supplying approximately one-third of the company's total refining capacity, this refinery helps to illustrate the large financial investment required by the oil industry, and the resulting dominance of a few huge companies.
Imperial Oil Limited Photo

and in some cases the fines imposed upon multi-million dollar corporations amounted to only a few thousand dollars. In 1977, new **Competition Acts** (notice the change in emphasis from "combines" to "competition") extended control over retail stores, hotels, banks, and brokerage firms that had been previously exempt.

Government legislation designed to stimulate and encourage competition has been far from perfect. Government patents, wheat boards, and state-regulated companies such as Bell Canada have further restricted competition. Before examining government involvement in the economy in greater depth, review the types of competition, as shown in Table 2.

▶ GOVERNMENT INVOLVEMENT IN THE ECONOMY

Despite the presence of an overwhelming number of private businesses in Canada, our economic system is best described as a mixed economy. Since the turn of the twentieth century, the state has played an increasingly important role in the economy. This is reflected today in massive government expenditures, social welfare legislation, government-operated businesses, and a welter of rules and regulations controlling our economic activities.[3]

The agricultural industry is a good example of the mixture of private enterprise and government regulations. Farmers are governed by the forces of supply and demand, and there is a high degree of competition within the industry. However, government-controlled marketing boards influence food prices by using crop controls and quotas to limit production. Food inspection, subsidies, and government-negotiated sales of wheat to foreign countries are just a few of the other means by which the agricultural industry is regulated.

In recent years, concern over ecology, health, safety, and poverty has created thousands of pages of new rules and regulations. Pollution controls, minimum wage acts, safety standards, old-age pensions, and food inspection are just a few such examples. Federal, provincial, and municipal governments all exercise a measure of control over the economy. The provinces regulate the activities of hairdressers, lawyers, doctors, barbers, morticians, and most other occupations. The province of Alberta regulates petroleum production. Language legislation in Quebec controls

▸ [3]Social welfare legislation will be examined in Case Study 23.

Table 2
TYPES OF COMPETITION

Type of Competition	Number of Producers	Product	Producers' Control Over Price	Selling Techniques	Ease of Entry
Perfect Competition	Many	Identical	None	None	Easy
Imperfect Competition	Many	Slightly different	Some, but not a great deal	Advertising; quality rivalry	Relatively easy
Oligopoly	Few	Few differences	Considerable, but not total	Advertising; price leader	Difficult
Monopoly	One	No close substitutes	Regulated only by the government	Advertising	Virtually impossible

Figure 1
TRENDS IN GOVERNMENT SPENDING, 1926–1985

The share of government spending grew in war and peace. Federal spending rose rapidly during World War II, and there was a much smaller blip in federal spending during the Korean War of the early fifties. But notice that the main reason for the rising share of government spending in the postwar period has been the steady rise in spending at the provincial and municipal levels. One statistical point: since federal transfers to the provinces show up as part of provincial spending, such transfers are excluded from our definition of federal spending. Otherwise we would be counting the same dollars of spending twice.

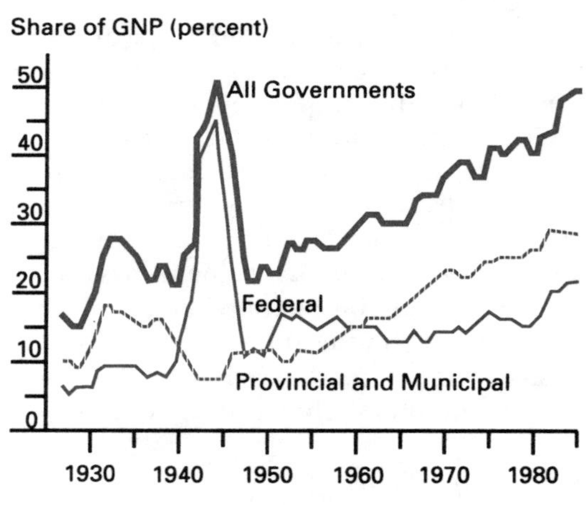

▸ Source: Paul A. Samuelson et al., *Economics*, 6th Cdn. ed. Toronto: McGraw-Hill Ryerson Limited, 1988, p. 736. Statistics from Statistics Canada.

the language to be used in work and school. City councils use their control over licensing to limit the number of taxis.

More indirectly, government spending also influences the direction of the economy. In fact, British economist John Maynard Keynes explained how government expenditures could be utilized to reduce unemployment and promote prosperity. Figure 1 illustrates the dramatic growth in government expenditures. Note that governments today spend as much as fifty percent of Canada's Gross National Product (GNP)—this alone has meant that governments play a key role in the economy.

▶ Government-owned Businesses

The most controversial area of government involvement in the Canadian economy has been the creation (or nationalization) of government owned and operated businesses. Although public ownership is considered somewhat exceptional in Canada (compared to many European countries), there is more public ownership in Canada than in the United States. The reasons for this are not always easy to determine, but one explanation links Canada's greater preference for state-controlled companies to a long connection with Great Britain. The British government's practice of making important political and economic decisions for its colonies is said to have accustomed Canadians to the idea of government involvement in the economy and caused the Canadian government to continue this practice following Confederation. Also, because Canada had neither the immense sources of wealth of the United States nor its large population, individual entrepreneurs could not finance such huge undertakings as the construction of canals in the

1820s and 1830s, or the building of railways in the 1850s and 1880s, without government aid.

The most significant growth of government intervention into the economy occurred after World War II. The government's success in organizing the economy during the war led many people (especially democratic socialists) to believe that it should continue to do so in peacetime. Socialists argued that central planning would make the economy more efficient and more responsive to human needs. Some politicians and economists believed that **Crown corporations** would generate large profits for the government. Control over such strategic industries as nuclear energy was also used to justify government ownership. In addition, Keynesian economists believed that the state could, and should, use its economic powers to create full employment. By the mid-1980s, there were about 300 federally controlled Crown corporations, 230 provincially owned firms, and another 300 companies that were jointly owned by private individuals and governments. Some Crown corporations rank among the largest companies in Canada.

Most of these public enterprises fulfill functions that private firms either would not provide or could not be trusted to oper-

Figure 2
REASONS FOR GOVERNMENT INTERVENTION

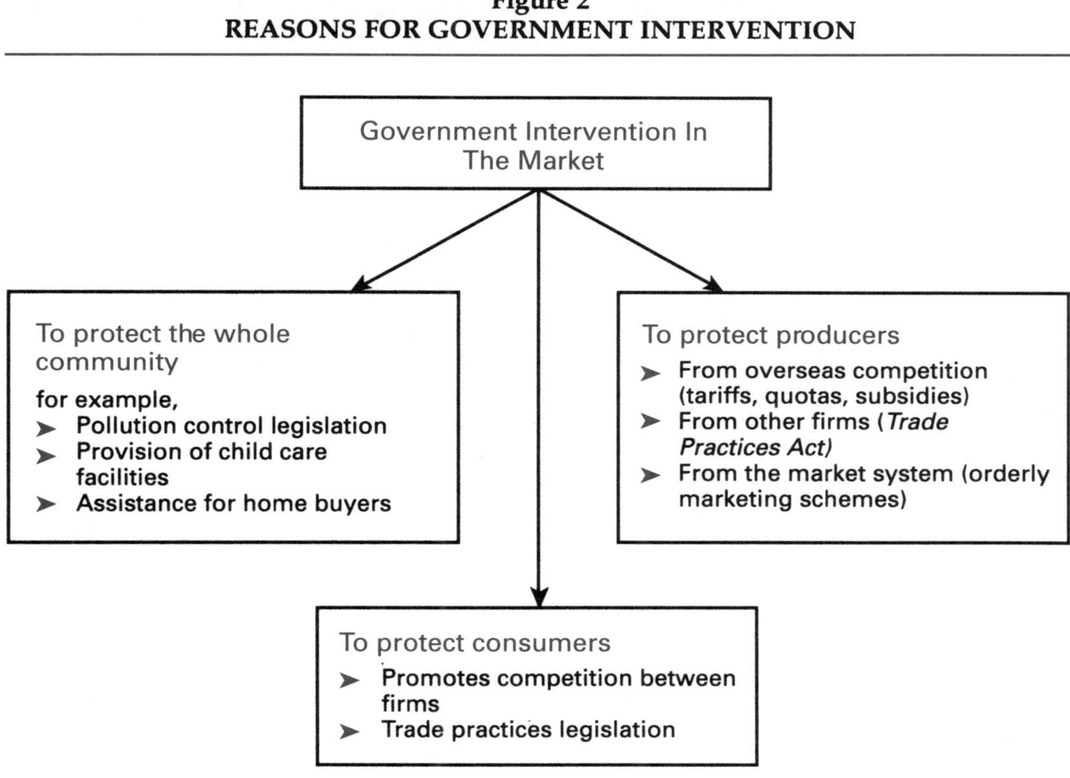

▸ Source: E.D. Shade et al., *Fundamentals of Economics*, Vol. I, 3rd ed. Permission granted by McGraw-Hill Book Company Australia Pty. Ltd.

The Mirabel Airport in Montreal is one example of a federal government-operated enterprise.
Transport Canada

ate fairly. Privately owned railways, for instance, would not build branch lines to out-of-the-way areas of the country because there would be no profit in doing so. Control over such "natural" monopolies as electrical power, telephones, and drinking water, could also not be left to profit-motivated private firms. The reasons for the growth of public enterprises can be divided into seven broad categories.

- **1.** To control an area of the economy necessary for the general welfare.
- **2.** To help stimulate regional development.
- **3.** To produce goods vital to the country's security.
- **4.** To provide services that private entrepreneurs are unable or unwilling to provide.
- **5.** To earn income for the government.
- **6.** To rescue a brankrupt firm that is essential to the economic well-being of a particular region.
- **7.** To maintain and influence public morality.

These categories are not rigid; in most cases, the rationale behind public ownership includes several categories. The creation of Petro-Canada, for instance, was a result of Canada's desire to increase the country's energy supplies, to provide revenue for the federal government, and to limit foreign control over such an important industry.

▶ PRIVATIZATION

When the economic history of the 1980s (and perhaps the 1990s) is written, privatization will be one of the major themes. Privatization is simply the selling of state-owned companies to the public—returning them to the private enterprise sector of the economy.

Privatization of state-owned corporations first gained prominence in Great Britain under Margaret Thatcher's leadership. The idea quickly spread to the newly elected conservative governments in many Western democracies during the late 1970s and early 1980s. Since then, developing countries have also embraced privatization, and the trend now appears to be worldwide. In 1987, for example, over 1400 state-controlled companies in some eighty countries were in the process of being privatized. As Figure 3 illustrates, private enterprises account for over ninety percent of Canada's production.

The popularity of privatization can be attributed to several factors. During the 1970s it became fashionable to criticize the growing size of government bureaucracies and the alleged inefficiency of government-owned companies. The ideological climate also reflected a renewed faith in private enterprise. According to the conservative ideology of Margaret Thatcher and Ronald Reagan, governments should stay out of the marketplace, especially if a natural monopoly was not involved. More important, however, was the drain on the government treasury that such companies, which seemed to lose money perpetually, often entailed. Worries about inflation and the mounting national deficit thus encouraged the state to sell its money-losing corporations. The airline business is an excellent example of the worldwide trend towards privatization. All British Airways' shares have been sold to private investors. European governments sold part ownership in Lufthansa, Finnair, KLM, and Air France. Elsewhere, the airlines of Malaysia, Singapore, Japan, Mexico, Argentina, Australia, and New Zealand have been completely or partially sold to the private sector.

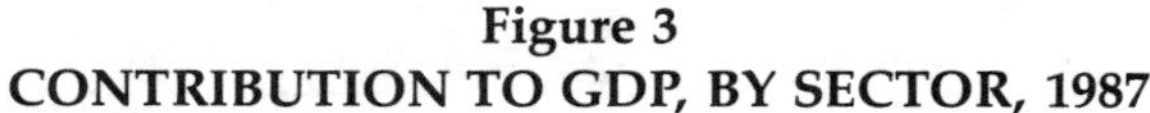

Figure 3
CONTRIBUTION TO GDP, BY SECTOR, 1987

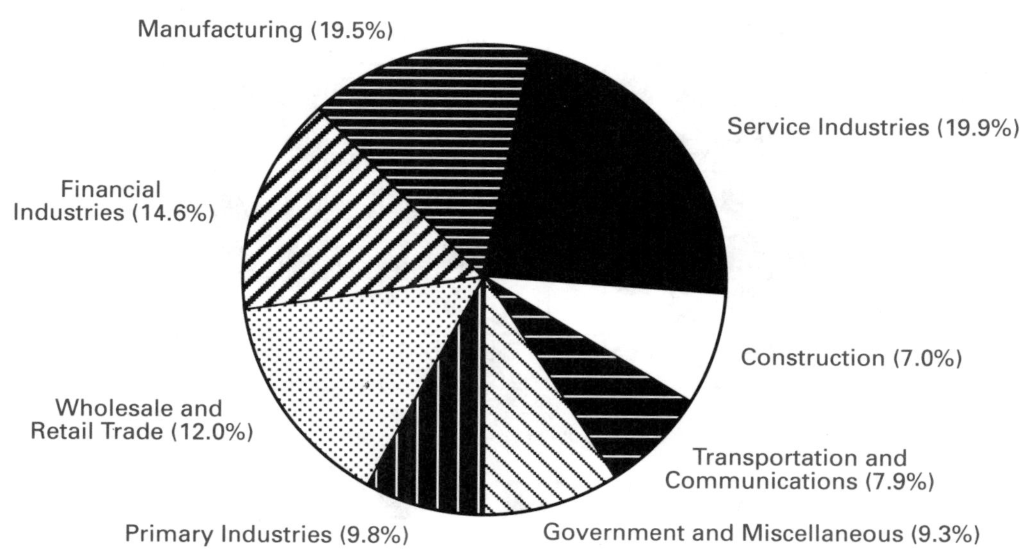

▸ Source: *1989 Corpus Almanac & Canadian Sourcebook*. Don Mills, Ontario: Southam Business Information and Communications Group, Inc., 1989.

Figure 4
PUBLIC ENTERPRISE IN TEN COUNTRIES, 1985

Who owns how much?	Posts	Telecommunications	Electricity	Gas	Oil production	Coal	Railways	Airlines	Motor industry	Steel	Ship building	
Australia	●	●	●	●	○	○	●	◔	○	○	na	Australia
Austria	●	●	●	●	●	●	●	●	●	●	na	Austria
Belgium	●	●	◔	◔	na	○	●	●	○	◑	○	Belgium
Brazil	●	●	●	●	●	●	●	◔	○	◕	○	Brazil
Britain	●	●	●	●	◔	●	●	◕	◑	◕	●	Britain
Canada	●	◔	●	○	○	○	◕	◕	○	○	○	Canada
France	●	●	●	●	na	●	●	◕	◑	◕	○	France
West Germany	●	●	◕	◑	◔	◑	●	●	◔	○	◔	West Germany
Holland	●	●	◕	◕	na	na	●	◕	◑	◔	○	Holland
India	●	●	●	●	●	●	●	●	○	◕	●	India
Italy	●	●	◕	●	na	na	●	●	◔	◕	◕	Italy
Japan	●	●	○	○	na	○	◕	◔	○	○	○	Japan
Mexico	●	●	●	●	●	●	●	◑	◔	◕	●	Mexico
South Korea	●	●	◕	○	na	◔	●	○	○	◕	○	South Korea
Spain	●	◑	○	◕	na	◑	●	●	○	◑	◕	Spain
Sweden	●	●	◑	●	na	na	●	◑	○	◕	◕	Sweden
Switzerland	●	●	●	●	na	na	●	◔	○	○	na	Switzerland
United States	●	○	◔	○	○	○	◔	○	○	○	○	United States

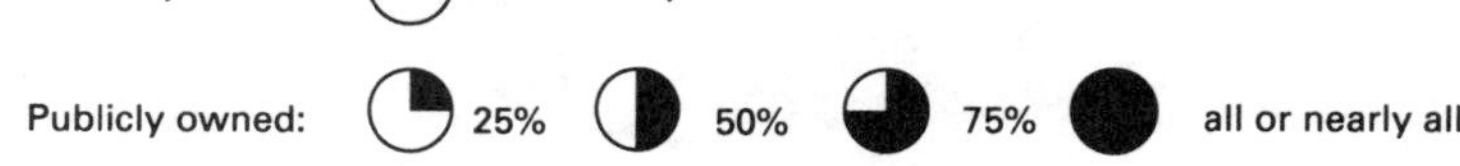

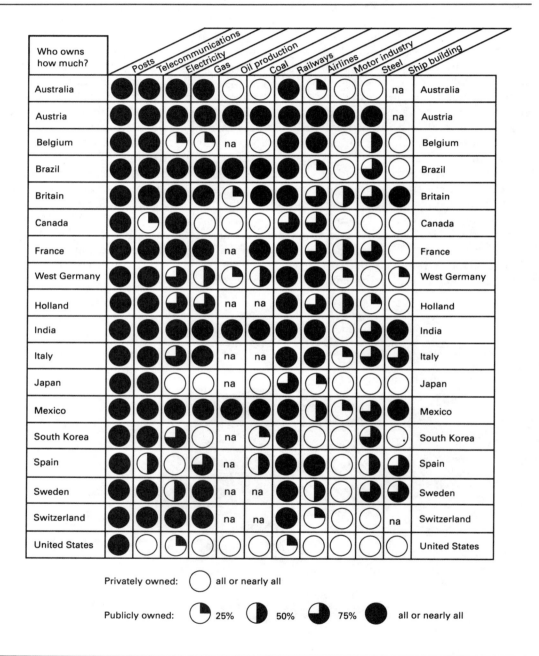

▸ Source: Paul A. Samuelson et al., *Economics*, 6th Cdn. ed. Toronto: McGraw-Hill Ryerson Limited, 1988, p. 561. Statistics from Statistics Canada.

In Canada, the Conservative government of Brian Mulroney followed the British example. Since 1984, the federal government has privatized thirteen Crown corporations, including Air Canada; and five Crown investments, including CNCP Telecommunications, have been sold to the private sector. So far, Canadian privatization has centred on the sale of enterprises that were not considered essential public services or were not competing directly with private corporations.

APPLYING YOUR KNOWLEDGE

1. Based on the evidence presented in this case study, give as complete an answer as you can to the question: Why does Canada have a mixed economy?
2. If monopolies are said to be detrimental to society, why does the government allow and even foster them? Choose one of the following monopolies and explain why it is protected by government: telephone, hydro-electricity, water, garbage collection, police, or the armed forces.
3. It might be argued that a monopoly can cater to consumer demands better than a competitive industry can. Consider a hypothetical case in which the potential radio audience in one town is divided by musical tastes into two groups. One audience, comprising eighty percent of the population, wishes to listen to popular music. The remaining twenty percent is interested only in classical music. Assuming that each radio station would seek to attract the largest possible listening audience:
   a) If there were only two equally competitive radio stations in the town, what type of music would each play? Why?
   b) If there were four radio stations, what type of music would each play? Why?
   c) Assuming there were only two radio stations, but both were owned by the same company, what music would each station play? Why?
   d) What do these two examples indicate about the possible advantages of monopolies?
   e) What would be the disadvantages of having both stations owned by the same company?
4. Explain why oligopolistic firms do not usually compete by cutting prices.
5. The automobile industry is oligopolistic. Explain all the problems that might be encountered if you attempted to establish your own automobile firm.
6. Referring to Table 1, explain why there was so much concentration in any *two* of the examples listed.
7. List two specific public enterprises for each of the seven rationales behind government-operated firms.
8. Using appropriate inquiry techniques (see Chapter 1), write an essay explaining how competition in the Canadian mixed economy ensures, or fails to ensure, that consumers are adequately served by business.
9. Explain the reasons for the decline of public corporations between 1970 and 1990.
10. Select one Crown corporation and prepare a case either for or against privatization.
11. Why would government-owned companies be any less or more efficient than private enterprise firms?

FURTHER RESEARCH

1. One type of company this case study has not discussed is the multinational firm. Such companies as Shell, General Motors, and Labatts operate on an international level. Explain why many such companies have recently emerged? What changes have taken place internationally to facilitate their growth?
2. a) Divide into small groups and design your own anti-combines legislation. Your proposal should include explanations as to how you would decide what companies to break up and which business practices restrain trade.
   b) If the bill was brought before the Canadian House of Commons, how successful do you think it would be? Explain.
3. Prepare for a debate on the topic: The Canadian economy has too many government-owned enterprises.
4. Conduct a survey of your community's attitude towards public enterprise and government regulations.
5. Examine Figure 4 and determine
   a) which country has the greatest and which has the least amount of government ownership.
   b) Select two countries and attempt to explain why they differ.

Case Study 23 Overview

Who Has What in Canada

This case study examines the distribution of wealth in Canada and the plight of Canada's poor people. The case study begins by discussing poverty in both absolute and relative terms before outlining the extent of poverty in Canada and what life for the poor is like. It then analyses who the wealthy people in society are and what factors most determine why some people are wealthier than others. The importance of education to full employment and high incomes is particularly stressed. The case study concludes with a discussion of the changing attitudes towards the poor, the growth of welfare capitalism in Canada, and government programs designed to redistribute the country's wealth.

▶ OBJECTIVES

After reading this case study, you should be able to:

- ▶ understand the differences between relative and absolute poverty and the extent of poverty in Canada
- ▶ analyse financial statistics and decide upon government spending priorities
- ▶ research alternative solutions to poverty
- ▶ examine your own values towards economic inequalities
- ▶ evaluate the importance of education, among other factors, to employment and high incomes
- ▶ debate the right of entertainers to high incomes

▶ KEY TERMS

relative poverty
income distribution
welfare capitalism
demogrants
social-insurance programs
transfer program
progressive taxes

Case Study

23 Who Has What in Canada

In a *laissez-faire* capitalist economy, personal income is dependent upon the ownership of society's resources (land, labour, and capital). The value of these resources is determined by their supply and demand. The rich are those people who own valuable resources. The poor are those individuals whose talents and resources are not in great demand, either because their skills are not considered important or because there is an over-abundance of people with similar abilities and resources. In theory, those who contribute the most to what society deems essential will earn the most money.

In a planned economy, on the other hand, the state is responsible for distributing wealth. If one group is wealthier than another, it is because the state has placed a higher value on the contribution of that group. In theory, a planned economy aims at distributing the country's resources so that those who help to produce wealth get a fair share of it.

A mixed economy lacks a clear-cut theory of distribution. Since government and private enterprise are both involved in the economy, and therefore in the production of wealth, how should wealth be distributed? This case study examines the distribution of wealth in Canada. It concentrates in particular on the plight of Canada's poor. To what extent should the government redistribute the country's wealth to aid Canada's poor?

▶ POVERTY IN ABSOLUTE TERMS

Throughout history, mass poverty had been generally accepted as inevitable. Following the Industrial Revolution, however, most countries in the Western world experienced sufficient economic growth to virtually eliminate mass poverty. Karl Marx's prediction that the modern labourer would become increasingly poorer did not come true in absolute terms. Since World War II,

A Vancouver newspaper investigated conditions among the homeless in that city. This man slept beneath an underpass, on an old mattress laid out beside a heated pipe.
Vancouver Sun *Photo*

for example, Canadians' real incomes (incomes with inflation taken into account) have grown at a yearly rate of more than 2.5 percent.

In absolute terms, then, mass poverty has virtually disappeared in Canada. Many of those Canadians whom we describe as poor live infinitely better than the vast majority of people in such Third World countries as India, Brazil, Haiti, and Nigeria. For more than one-half of the world's population, an income of three thousand Canadian dollars would represent undreamed-of wealth. Some poor families in Canada own a television, an automobile, or a washing machine. It is true that some Canadians suffer from inadequate food, clothing, and shelter. But as Table 1 illustrates, this is a drop in the bucket compared to the widespread famine that characterizes large parts of the world.

▶ RELATIVE POVERTY

Poverty is often defined in relative terms. Simply, this means, "How much income do I earn compared to my friends, or to the entire population?" One method of determining who is poor is to construct an arbitrary "poverty line" based upon the minimum amount of money needed to ensure adequate food, clothing, health care, and shelter. The National Council of Welfare, for example, declares any family to be poor if it spends more than fifty-nine percent of its income on food, clothing, and

Table 1
VARYING LIVING STANDARDS THROUGHOUT THE WORLD

Country	Per capita GNP, 1986 ($U.S.)	Life expectancy at birth, 1986	Infant mortality per 1000 live births, 1986	Daily per capita calorie supply, 1985
United States	$17 480	75 years	10	3 680
Canada	15 530	76	8	3 440
Japan	12 840	78	6	2 690
Brazil	1 810	65	65	2 650
Mauritania	420	47	127	2 070
Haiti	330	54	119	1 780
India	290	57	86	2 120
Bangladesh	160	50	121	1 800
Ethiopia	120	46	155	1 700

▸ Source: World Bank, *World Development Report, 1988*. New York: Oxford University Press, July 1988; used with permission.

housing. By this formula, approximately sixteen percent of all Canadians are below the ''poverty line.''

Another method of measuring poverty is to compare the income of one group in society with the income of other groups. In Table 2, each individual in Canada was ranked in ascending order according to total income. This list was then divided into five equal groups. If incomes were distributed equally, the lowest twenty percent of the population would receive the same proportion of the country's total income as the highest twenty percent. The extent of the difference between each group indicates the degree of economic inequality in Canada.

Table 2 illustrates the discrepancy between the wealthy twenty percent of the population and the poor twenty percent. Before we examine who the poor people are and why they tend to be poor, let us briefly discuss the rich.

Among the wealthy of our society are those whose talents or resources are in great demand. The majority of society's wealthy citizens acquire only a fraction of their wealth through wages and salaries.

Table 2
DISTRIBUTION OF INCOME IN CANADA
1975–1988

All Individuals Shares of Total Income	Percentage of Total Income						
	1975	1977	1979	1981	1983	1985	1988
Lowest 20%	3.9	3.8	4.6	5.0	4.8	5.2	5.3
Second 20%	8.9	8.4	8.9	9.5	9.5	10.2	10.1
Third 20%	15.5	15.4	15.8	15.7	14.5	15.0	15.3
Fourth 20%	25.6	25.8	25.1	25.1	24.2	24.2	24.3
Top 20%	46.1	46.5	45.6	44.7	47.1	45.4	44.9

▸ Source: Statistics Canada, *Income Distribution By Size in Canada*, Cat. 13-207, 1988; *Canada Year Book*, 1990, p.5-36.

Table 3
AVERAGE ANNUAL ASSESSED INCOME, 1986

Physicians and surgeons	$106 000
Dentists	$ 84 000
Lawyers	$ 74 500
Accountants	$ 59 600
Engineers and architects	$ 38 500
Fishers	$ 20 500
Salespeople	$ 19 400
Farmers	$ 15 700

▸ Source: Statistics Canada, *Canada Year Book*, 1990, p. 22-16.

Much of their income is derived from investments in bonds and in the stock market. Inheritance, royalties from inventions, and ownership of valuable land or companies also contribute to their fortunes. Corporate businesspeople such as the Irvings, the Bronfmans, the Reichmanns, the Eatons, the Sobeys, the Molsons, the Blacks, the McCains, the Steinbergs, and the Westons are among the wealthiest families in Canada.

Professional athletes comprise another group of wealthy Canadians. Their salaries are a product of spectators' demand to see them perform. These athletes command high salaries because their talents are in scarce supply, and the demand for these talents is high.

The following example indicates why professional athletes are able to command high salaries. In 1976, the Chicago Black Hawks hockey team signed Bobby Orr to an unconditional five-year contract, despite the fact that his knees had undergone numerous operations and there was a good chance that he would never play again. The following article from *Sports Illustrated* explains the team's decision.

What prompted Chicago to pay $3 million for a hobbling hockey player? The Black Hawks have been a dull defensive-minded team ever since they refused to re-sign Bobby Hull in the face of his $3 million offer from the WHA's Winnipeg Jets in 1972. Last season the most popular Black Hawk home attendance figure was ''12,000 estimated,'' some 8,000 short of the crowds that jammed Chicago Stadium in Hull's days. . . . To earn his annual salary of $600,000 Orr will have to attract only 1,500 extra paying spectators at $10 for each of Chicago's 40 home games.[1]

Since this was written, athletes' salaries have risen substantially. Ice hockey stars earn several million dollars a year. Golfers and tennis players capture millions of dollars annually in winnings alone (some athletes make more money in endorsements than they do from playing their sport). In 1991, the Toronto Argonauts signed Raghib Ismail for $26 million for four years. Table 4 illustrates the inflation in baseball earnings since 1973.

▶ Poverty and Happiness?

Some people believe that because the poor have less responsible jobs than the rich, they have fewer worries and are therefore happier. This is a misconception. A survey conducted in the United States asked a randomly selected group of people whether they would call themselves ''very happy,'' ''fairly happy,'' or ''not very happy.'' The responses were then analysed according to the respondents' income. The results were significant:

Highest Incomes	56% Very Happy	4% Not Very Happy
Lowest Incomes	29% Very Happy	13% Not Very Happy

In general, people with high incomes were happier than those who were poor. Of course, it was not the amount of money that made the people happy—it was what they could do with the money. This included providing a satisfactory diet, a

▸ [1]*Sports Illustrated*, June 21, 1976, p. 25.

Table 4
TWO BASEBALL DYNASTIES AND SALARY INFLATION

The last time Oakland was a perennial powerhouse — winning the World Series in 1972, '73 and '74 — the payroll was in the hands of penurious owner Charles O. Finley. Today, the A's are among the biggest spenders in baseball — and the salaries are going up (salaries listed are projected for the 1991 season). Walt Weiss, the lowest-paid of today's starting A's, could make a salary higher than the top 15 A's combined in 1973.

	1973 A's	Salary	1990 A's	Salary*
1B	Gene Tenace	$ 35 000	Mark McGwire	$ 3 000 0000†
2B	Dick Green	$ 42 500	Willie Randolph	$ 875 000†
3B	Sal Bando	$ 60 000	Carney Lansford	$ 2 200 000†
SS	Bert Campaneris	$ 65 000	Walt Weiss	$ 750 000†
LF	Joe Rudi	$ 62 500	Rickey Henderson	$ 3 000 000
CF	Bill North	$ 30 000	Dave Henderson	$ 1 000 000
RF	Reggie Jackson	$ 75 000	Jose Canseco	$ 4 750 000
C	Ray Fosse	$ 40 500	Terry Steinbach	$ 1 050 000
DH	Deron Johnson	$ 75 000	Harold Baines	$ 1 250 000†
OF	Angel Mangual	$ 25 000	Willie McGee	$ 2 500 000†
IF	Ted Kubiak	$ 35 000	Mike Gallego	$ 500 000
SP	Catfish Hunter	$ 75 000	Dave Stewart	$ 3 400 000
SP	Vida Blue	$ 50 000	Bob Welch	$ 2 500 000†
SP	Ken Holtzman	$ 55 000	Mike Moore	$ 1 200 000
RP	Rollie Fingers	$ 47 500	Dennis Eckersley	$ 3 000 000
TOTALS		$773 000		$30 975 000

**Figures are projected for 1991. †Players not currently under contract for '91; figures are estimated in accordance with market value; some players may not re-sign with A's.*

▸ Source: The article above is reprinted courtesy of *Sports Illustrated* from the September 10, 1990 issue. "The Rich Get Richer" by Steve Rushin.

good education, plenty of travel, and a great variety of cultural activities, as well as acquiring such material possessions as houses, clothes, and cars.

▶ Life of the Poor

In 1967, the government created a special Senate committee to examine poverty in Canada. Three years later, the committee reported that poverty was the gravest social issue of our time and stated that unless something was done immediately, five million Canadians would continue "to find life a bleak, bitter, and never-ending struggle for survival." Poverty, it concluded, had become a way of life for those who are poorly educated, unskilled, or sick; those who are disabled; and the one-parent family. (It is important to note, however, that not all people within these groups are poverty-striken.)

Many of Canada's poor are caught in a vicious circle of poverty that seems almost impossible to break. This problem was vividly described in the minority report issued by the Special Senate Committee on Poverty:

From the very beginning, when you are still a child, you must learn to undervalue yourself. You are told that you are poor because your father is too stupid or too shiftless to find a decent job, or that he is a good-for-nothing who has abandoned you to a mother who cannot cope. And as you grow up on the streets, you are told that your mother is dirty and lazy and that is why she has to take money from the welfare department. Because you are poor the lady from the welfare office is always coming around asking questions. She wants to know if your mother is living with a man, and why she is pregnant again. . . . By the time you are a teenager you accept without question your teacher's advice that you are not really good enough to go any further with your education. You know that it would be a waste of time even to think about it because your parents couldn't afford to send you anyway. From then on, as you go from one menial job to another, you come to know that machines are more important than you are. . . . As you move through a succession of crummy apartments, where the rents are always just too high, your kids start growing up the same way you did—on the street. And you suddenly realize there is no way out, that there never was a way out, and that the years ahead will be nothing but another long piece of time, spent with an army of other sick, lonely and desperate old people. For unless you are blessed with an exceptional stroke of good fortune or a driving natural talent that will get you out into the larger world of affluence and opportunity, then you will, like the majority of the poor, live on the street and die on the street—and very few will ever give a damn about you.[2]

[2]Ian Adams et al., *The Real Poverty Report*. Edmonton: Hurtig, 1971, pp. xi-xii.

There are more poor people than rich people in Canada, yet it is often stated that the government caters to the wealthy. What comment does this cartoon make?
Josh Beutel

▶ HOW INCOME IS DETERMINED

What determines a person's income? According to a variety of statistical studies, it is related to many variables such as a person's physical and mental capabilities, type of job, and location. Table 5, for example, illustrates the close relationship between years of schooling and income. A similar chart for employment statistics would reveal the same close correlation between unemployment and lack of education.

As the economy has become more complex and automated, the demand for unskilled workers has declined. Employers now require educated employees. A recent study, for example, discovered that an automotive technician must be able to read

Figure 1
FAILING GRADES

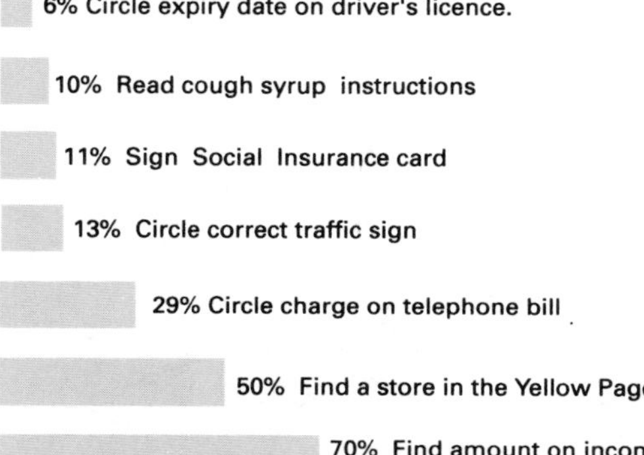

▸ Source: Adapted from the Southam Literacy Study, conducted by The Creative Research Group, *The Report on Business Magazine*.

over 90 000 pages of complex manuals in order to service the latest vehicles. The *Complete Oxford Shakespeare* contains fewer than 1500 pages. The average technical worker spends about 160 minutes per day reading memos, shipping orders, manuals, and other job-related materials. By contrast, the average high school student reads for less than 100 minutes per day. Unfortunately, about one in five Canadians is functionally illiterate. This means that they are unable to read, write, and compute well enough to perform the basic tasks of daily life.

Canadian children attend school approximately 180 days a year. In Japan, children attend classes 240 days annually. ''What's the magic about 180 days, anyway,'' argues Lee Iacocca, the president of Chrysler Corporation, ''the world has changed — . . . kids don't need three months off to plow, plant and take in the crops. This isn't an agricultural society anymore.''

Equally distressing is the fact that approximately thirty-five percent of Canadian high-school students fail to graduate (one-quarter of these drop-outs are functionally illiterate). Motorola, an electronics firm, estimated that it costs a North American company $200 to train a semi-skilled worker, whereas a Japanese firm will spend only forty-seven cents, because Japanese workers know how to read a manual before entering the work force. In Canada, only seventy-two percent of all seventeen year olds are still in school. In Japan, the corresponding figure is ninety-four percent, in Germany eighty-nine percent, in the United States eighty-seven percent, and in Sweden seventy-eight percent. Since the volume of scientific knowledge is expected

Figure 2
UNEMPLOYMENT RATE BY EDUCATION LEVEL: NOVA SCOTIA, 1987

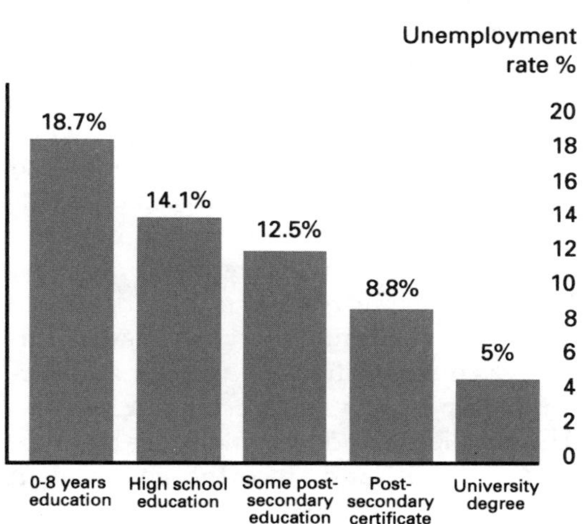

▸ Source: Adapted from *The Chronicle-Herald* (Halifax), September 19, 1990, p. i3. Statistics from Statistics Canada.

to double in the next fifteen years, workers will have to be literate enough to undergo extensive retraining.

Table 5
EDUCATION RELATED TO INCOME IN 1988

Education	Average Earnings in $ Men	Women
0—8 Years	20 700	10 200
High school	23 200	12 600
Some post-secondary	22 100	13 100
Post-secondary diploma	29 200	17 200
University degree	40 700	25 700

▸ Source: Computed from Statistics Canada, *Earnings of Men and Women*, 13-217, 1988.

▶ ATTITUDES TOWARDS INCOME DISTRIBUTION

In the nineteenth century, upper- and middle-class Canadians generally ignored the plight of poverty-stricken people because they believed that poverty was due to a failure of character. Poverty was thought to be the individual's own fault. When help was provided, its purpose was to re-shape the character of the poor by providing them with education, religion, discipline, and a belief in hard work and frugality. Anyone could become rich, it was thought, if he had a good character and worked hard. (Women were expected to stay at home.)

By the turn of the twentieth century, however, liberal reformers had begun to argue that environment, rather than heredity, was the most important factor in determining a person's future economic success. This implied that poverty was not the individual's fault, and since the government was partly responsible for shaping the environment, it was the state's moral duty to care for the poor and to improve the environment.

These ideas grew stronger as the twentieth century progressed. World War I increased the extent of government involvement in society. The economy was adjusted to war production. The government controlled fuel consumption and prices and established personal and corporate income taxes to help finance the

In the 1980s, western Canada flourished while many other parts of the country did not. The result was that many people came west seeking work. They could sometimes be seen in places like "The Corner" in Calgary, waiting for an offer of temporary employment.

It seemed to many westerners that the relative poverty of other areas was being transferred to the west, where it was becoming their problem. Why, they asked, should the surplus labour of other parts of the country become a western problem, since there were clearly only so many jobs to go around?

On the basis of further research, discuss this issue in relation to the concept of welfare capitalism.

Canapress Photo Service

war. The Great Depression of the 1930s provided even greater stimulus to government involvement. In 1934, one out of every three adult Canadians was unemployed, and it was obviously not their fault. Reluctantly, the government acted to help the poor. It established relief and government-sponsored make-work projects out of genuine humanitarian sentiments, and because many government and business leaders feared a revolution if nothing was done to help the unemployed. Finally, the tremendous growth of government involvement in all aspects of life during World War II led to the establishment of present-day government welfare programs.

▶ WELFARE CAPITALISM

Today, the concept of **welfare capitalism** is widely accepted in Canada. As its name implies, welfare capitalism conforms to most of the theories of free enterprise capitalism but adds to this the belief that government should take responsibility for the well-being of its citizens. In the last fifty years, the government has adopted numerous policies designed to make life more bearable for the poor. These programs can be divided into four major categories:

1. **Demogrants** are grants to people in specified population groups who *might* need financial help. All Canadians sixty-five years of age and over, for instance, receive money under the Old Age Security program. Families with children under eighteen years of age receive family allowance payments.
2. **Social-insurance programs** include unemployment insurance, welfare payments, mothers' allowance, veterans' pension, and workers' compensation. Their major purpose is to protect people against a total loss of income.
3. The **transfer program** bases its grants upon the recipient's needs. Examples include aid to the disabled, help for Canada's native people, and grants to underdeveloped and depressed areas of the country.
4. Taxes. Economic inequality has two basic sources—unequal earnings and inheritance. **Progressive taxes** such as the graduated income tax are meant to deal with unequal income by deducting more money from the rich than from the poor. The larger the income, the greater the proportion of the tax that is deducted.

APPLYING YOUR KNOWLEDGE

1. Discuss the merit of surveys such as the one on page 432. Can "happiness" be measured? Does money necessarily buy happiness?
2. a) Explain the difference between absolute and relative poverty.
   b) Is there an absolute standard by which we can judge whether people are poor? Explain.
3. a) What does Table 2 reveal about the extent of economic inequality in Canada?
   b) Karl Marx wrote that under capitalism, the rich would become richer and the poor would become poorer. Using the same table, determine whether this has been true on a relative basis since 1975.
   c) Construct your own table depicting how you think income should be distributed.
   d) What does this table reveal about your values?
4. a) Explain why doctors, dentists, and lawyers earn more money on the average than members of other occupations.

b) Do you think the high salaries of most professional athletes are justified? Explain.
c) Convert the information in Table 5 into a bar or line graph.

5. a) Explain why people in the Atlantic provinces are poorer than Canadians who live in Ontario or Alberta.
   b) Do you consider this just? Explain.
6. a) Identify some typical ''women's jobs'' and explain why, traditionally, women took these jobs.
   b) Should women earn equal pay for work equal to that performed by men? Explain.
7. Why is it difficult for the poor to escape from poverty?
8. To what extent do you think the government should use income and inheritance taxes to redistribute income?
9. Working in small groups, examine the table below and answer the following questions:

FEDERAL GOVERNMENT FINANCES, 1982 AND 1986 IN MILLIONS OF DOLLARS

	1982	1986
Total Revenue	72 500	89 300
Expenditures		
Health	4 700	7 100
Canada Pension Plan	2 500	4 900
Old Age Security	8 600	12 500
Unemployment Insurance	5 600	10 300
Family Allowances	2 000	2 500
Social Welfare Assistance	2 700	4 600
Education	2 700	4 000
Agriculture, Industry, Tourism	8 500	8 100
Environment	350	420
Recreation and Culture	620	850
Employment and Immigration	900	1 300
Housing	1 100	1 500
Foreign Affairs and Assistance	1 300	2 100
Research	1 100	1 100
Debt Charges	13 600	24 000
Police and National Defence	7 500	11 900
Transportation, Communication	4 200	3 500
Total Expenditures	81 700	120 400

▸ Source: Statistics Canada, *Canada Year Book*, 1990, p. 22-13.

a) What was the government's deficit in 1982 and 1986?
b) Which types of expenditures increased the most?
c) Using these figures, discuss government priorities in 1986 and explain to what extent they changed between 1982 and 1986. Do you agree with these priorities?
d) If you could balance the budget only by reducing expenditures, what cuts would you make in the 1986 budget?
e) Compare your answers to those of other groups and explain the reasons for any differences.

FURTHER RESEARCH

1. Obtain a copy of *The Real Poverty Report*. What was the basis for the excerpt on page 434 of this textbook? Analyse its validity. Would these findings hold true today?
2. Disparities in wealth are usually attributed to ability, education, age, gender, discrimination, luck, inheritance, unique talent, motivation, unfair practices, hard work, occupation, and geographical location. Divide into groups and rank these factors from the most to the least important in determining disparities in wealth in Canada. Be prepared to justify your answer.
3. Prepare for a debate on one of the following topics:
   a) Some professions are overpaid.
   b) Government aid to the poor destroys their incentive to work.
   c) Unemployment insurance should be abolished.
   d) Lee Iacocca's statement that the school year should be extended should be acted upon.
4. Several solutions have been proposed to deal with the problem of poverty. They range from destroying the existing sytem and establishing complete equality to accepting the idea that some people will always be poor and need welfare. Two popular solutions are the guaranteed annual income and a negative income tax. Prepare a report about one of these proposals.
5. Most of the material in this case study has focused on the weakness of the mixed economy, yet all around us there are signs of material progress. Do the positive results of the system outweigh the problems of poverty? Prepare for a debate on this question.

Case Study 24 Overview

Economic Systems in Developing Countries: Ivory Coast and Peru

This case study examines how two developing countries, Ivory Coast and Peru, answered the three basic economic questions (what, how, and to whom). It outlines the variety of economic, political, and social conditions in Third World countries and discusses the range of methods that have been adopted to promote economic development in the Third World. The majority of the case study concentrates on the economic solutions adopted by Ivory Coast and Peru and their successes. Separate sections discuss such matters as the national debt, guerrilla organizations, and the role of cocaine in the economy. The case study concludes with a summary of the unique problems facing Third World countries.

▶ OBJECTIVES

After reading this case study, you should be able to:

- ▶ understand the unique problems facing Third World countries
- ▶ discuss the economic solutions adopted by Ivory Coast and Peru
- ▶ research the economies of other Third World countries
- ▶ compare the economies of Peru and Ivory Coast
- ▶ devise solutions to the problems presented in this case study
- ▶ recognize that Third World countries vary greatly in their economic and political problems
- ▶ evaluate what Canada could do to help these countries

▶ KEY TERMS

developing countries
infrastructure
advanced technology
urbanization
French Community
World Bank
debtors' cartels
Sendero Luminoso

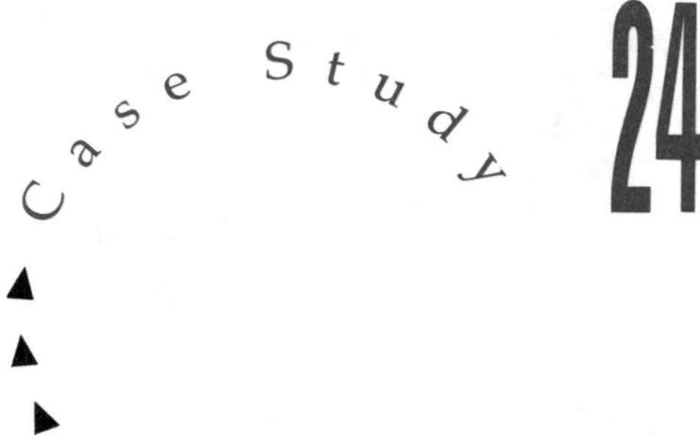

Economic Systems in Developing Countries: Ivory Coast and Peru

All countries, whether industrialized or less developed, need to consider the fundamental economic questions of what to produce, how to produce it, and who gets these goods. Before answering these questions, each state must decide how much emphasis it wishes to place on economic growth, to what extent the government will intervene in the economy, and how extensive its social welfare system will be. Many **developing countries** must also decide how to deal with such problems as widespread illiteracy, mass poverty, one-crop economies, high birth rates, mountainous debts, minimal technology, and an economy dominated by foreign businesses. Other names for less developed countries include the South, developing nations, and the Third World. It should be emphasized, however, that these countries vary widely in political, economic, and social conditions. Mexico developed its own brand of democracy, whereas dictators dominated Chile. Chad has virtually no rich mineral resources, but Gabon is well-endowed with minerals. Ethiopia is often drought-stricken, and Indonesia is located in the rain forests. Brazil and South Korea have experienced rapid industrialization, while Nepal and Afghanistan rely heavily on subsistence agriculture. In general, however, developing countries are poor. Although seventy-five percent of the world's population lives in these countries, these people account for only twenty percent of the world's income and ten percent of the industry.

The traditional choice between planned and free enterprise economies has not always been realistic for such countries. In the 1950s and 1960s, these countries tended to imitate the development models that had been used in the North, which emphasized rapid industrialization, economic growth, foreign aid and capital investment, development of an **infrastructure**, **advanced technology**, and **urbanization**. Some states sought to achieve these goals through private enterprise, whereas other countries chose public ownership and central planning. This case study examines how Ivory Coast and Peru answered the three basic economic questions.

▶ PROBLEMS WITH DEVELOPMENT APPROACHES

By the 1970s and 1980s, some countries had been successful in achieving rapid economic growth (South Korea, Taiwan, Singapore, and other newly industrialized countries). Most had not — especially in Latin America and Africa. In many countries, conventional development policies had resulted in massive rural poverty, urban problems, destruction of traditional cultures and values, massive population increases, huge debts, and greater dependency on the industrialized North.

Dissatisfaction with conventional development approaches led some states to reconsider their view of economic growth. Some suggested that satisfaction of people's basic needs (including adequate food, clean water, clothing, shelter, health care, education, and employment) should take precedence over economic growth. Other countries advocated alternative development approaches that emphasized the following:

- rural development (including land reform, provision of water, rural industry, and support systems)
- mass participation in decision-making (working "from the bottom up")
- appropriate technology (suitable to the special needs of developing countries)
- self-reliance (at individual, community, and national levels)

Some observers blamed the lack of development on the North, with its domination of the world's economy. To many people, this factor was a bigger barrier than were specific conditions within less developed countries. Protectionism prevented the South's manufactured goods from being sold in the North, resulting in a reliance on agricultural and mineral resources. Low prices for these natural resources made it difficult to earn a decent income, and price fluctuations made planning difficult. The South's debt to the North resulted in huge annual transfers of interest payments. Multinational corporations exploited the South, and patents for key products and processes were all held in the North.

In the mid-1970s, a group of 114 developing countries proposed fundamental reform in the global economy. Their proposals included improving access to markets by lowering the North's protective tariffs; stabilizing commodity prices; tying the prices of natural resources to the cost of manufactured goods; renegotiating debts; increasing foreign aid for development; expanding access to technology; and controlling the activities of multinational enterprises.

In analysing the economic systems of developing countries, students need to determine how each country, in the light of its own circumstances, has tried to solve the following issues:

- How much emphasis to place on private or public enterprise
- The extent to which equality or individualism should be pursued
- How much emphasis to place on rural versus urban development
- The degree to which it should pursue

basic needs or economic growth as goals
- The extent to which traditional values and customs should be preserved
- Whether to involve citizens in decisions
- Whether industry should be for export or for local consumption, and how to encourage industry
- The degree to which it should attempt to be self-reliant or to compete actively in the global economy
- How to deal with foreign debt

These questions should be kept in mind when analysing the following case studies of Ivory Coast and Peru.

▶ IVORY COAST (CÔTE D'IVOIRE)

Table 1
BASIC DATA—IVORY COAST

Geography	Area in Square Kilometres: 323 750 Capital (Population): Abidjan (economic) (1 686 100); Yamoussoukro (political) (n/a) Climate: tropical	**Labour Force**	over 80% in agriculture
		Military	Number of Armed Forces: 7140
People	Population: 12 million Ethnic Makeup of Population: over 60 tribes Languages: official: French; others spoken: Dioula, Agni, Baoulé, Kru, Senufo, Mandinka, others Religion(s): 66% traditional indigenous; 22% Muslim; 12% Christian Adult Literacy Rate: 41%	**Economy**	Currency ($ U.S. Equivalent): 286 CFA francs = $1 Inflation Rate: 4.3% Natural Resources: agricultural lands; timber Agriculture: coffee; cocoa; bananas; pineapples; palm oil; corn; millet; cotton; rubber Industry: food and lumber processing; oil refinery; textiles; soap; automobile assembly
Communication	Televisions: 625 000 (1987) Telephones: 87 700 Newspapers: 3	**Foreign Trade**	Imports: $4.6 billion (1987) (31% from France) Exports: $6.2 billion (1987) (17% Netherlands; 15% France)
Transportation	Highways—Kilometres: 53 736 Railroads—Kilometres: 657 Commercial Airports: 1		

▸ Sources: Jo Sullivan, *Global Studies: Africa,* 3rd ed. Guilford, Conn.: The Dushkin Publishing Group Inc., 1989.
The Canadian World Almanac and Book of Facts 1990. Global Press, 1989.

▶ Political History

A succession of relatively rich, powerful, and well-organized kingdoms dominated parts of pre-colonial Ivory Coast. Near the coast, a great variety of tribes controlled smaller areas. Europeans were attracted to this region by ivory and the slave trade and made some advances into the area as early as the fifteenth century. After establishing a series of protectorates, France made the area a colony in 1893. The French consolidated their power with the defeat in 1898 of Samory, the Malinke chief who had tried to prevent French expansion in West Africa. French reforms after World War II resulted in the founding of the first all-African political party in 1946 by Félix Houphouët-Boigny. After 1950, Ivory Coast's co-operation with the colonial

Figure 1
IVORY COAST

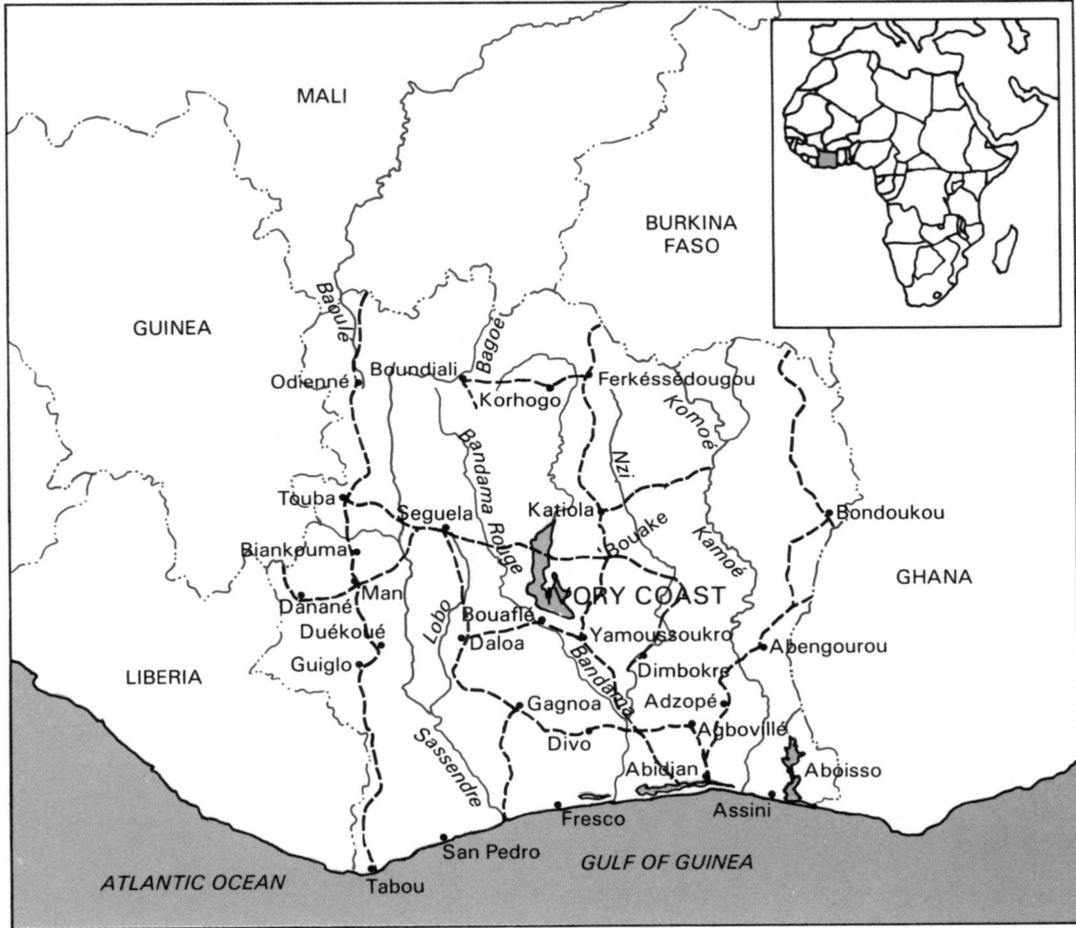

power resulted in a gradual move towards reform and self-government. In 1958, Ivory Coast joined the **French Community** (an organization that linked France with its overseas territories) as a self-governing republic.

In 1960, Ivory Coast declared itself fully independent. However, it has continued to keep close economic ties with France. Houphouët-Boigny was elected president in that year and continued to govern the country through its only political party, the Ivory Coast Democratic party (PDCI). In 1990, he agreed to begin to relinquish control and to establish a multi-party political system.

▶ The Economy

Until its recent problems, many people considered Ivory Coast to be one of the most productive countries in Africa.

Table 2
WEST AFRICA AND IVORY COAST: BASIC INDICATORS

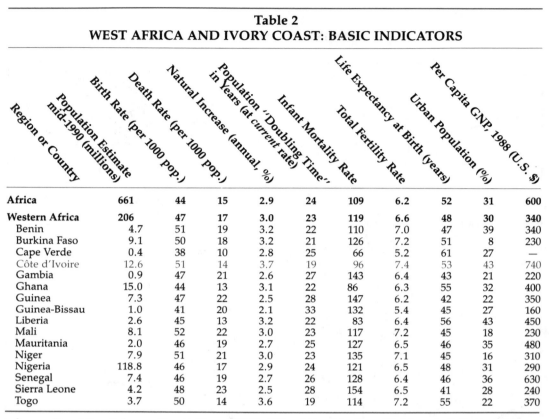

Region or Country	Population Estimate mid-1990 (millions)	Birth Rate (per 1000 pop.)	Death Rate (per 1000 pop.)	Natural Increase (annual, %)	Population "Doubling Time" in Years (at current rate)	Infant Mortality Rate	Total Fertility Rate	Life Expectancy at Birth (years)	Urban Population (%)	Per Capita GNP, 1988 (U.S. $)
Africa	**661**	**44**	**15**	**2.9**	**24**	**109**	**6.2**	**52**	**31**	**600**
Western Africa	**206**	**47**	**17**	**3.0**	**23**	**119**	**6.6**	**48**	**30**	**340**
Benin	4.7	51	19	3.2	22	110	7.0	47	39	340
Burkina Faso	9.1	50	18	3.2	21	126	7.2	51	8	230
Cape Verde	0.4	38	10	2.8	25	66	5.2	61	27	—
Côte d'Ivoire	12.6	51	14	3.7	19	96	7.4	53	43	740
Gambia	0.9	47	21	2.6	27	143	6.4	43	21	220
Ghana	15.0	44	13	3.1	22	86	6.3	55	32	400
Guinea	7.3	47	22	2.5	28	147	6.2	42	22	350
Guinea-Bissau	1.0	41	20	2.1	33	132	5.4	45	27	160
Liberia	2.6	45	13	3.2	22	83	6.4	56	43	450
Mali	8.1	52	22	3.0	23	117	7.2	45	18	230
Mauritania	2.0	46	19	2.7	25	127	6.5	46	35	480
Niger	7.9	51	21	3.0	23	135	7.1	45	16	310
Nigeria	118.8	46	17	2.9	24	121	6.5	48	31	290
Senegal	7.4	46	19	2.7	26	128	6.4	46	36	630
Sierra Leone	4.2	48	23	2.5	28	154	6.5	41	28	240
Togo	3.7	50	14	3.6	19	114	7.2	55	22	370

▸ Source: Population Reference Bureau, Inc., *1990 World Population Data Sheet*, Washington, D.C.: Population Reference Bureau, Inc., 1990.

FOCUS

1. Using the statistics above, rank the countries from the wealthiest to the poorest. Which facts did you consider the most important in ranking countries?

Ivory Coast's recent problems illustrate some of the economic problems and choices that many of the less developed countries encounter. For many years, consistent attempts to diversify the economy and to avoid relying on a few commodities helped to promote growth and stability. Pro-private enterprise, pro-Western, and pro-foreign investment policies also contributed to prosperity. Ivory Coast's emphasis on education (with innovative and effective use of television in remote villages); concentration on improving the infrastructure, especially its transportation systems; and broad social reforms also promoted economic growth. However, some government actions and the problems in the global economy in the 1980s caught up with Ivory Coast.

In the 1980s, there was a disastrous decline in the price of Ivory Coast's two biggest export commodities, cocoa and coffee. (It was the world's largest producer of cocoa and the third-largest producer of coffee.) The country tried to work through international agencies to control supply and prices, but the price collapse could not be prevented. Ivory Coast had steadfastly refused to sell below a break-even price and had continued to guarantee high prices to its farmers through subsidies, but in 1989 international pressure and mounting financial problems forced it to abandon both policies. As a result, its export earnings dropped dramatically, and its debts rose. In order to obtain new loans, the country had to adopt some of the tough policies advocated by the International Monetary Fund (IMF). These changes included increased taxes and cuts in government programs. When these policies and developments made the situation within the country worse, there were protests, and increasing numbers of workers joined the "informal economy" and avoided paying taxes. This further limited government revenue.

President Houphouët-Boigny's rule came under increasing attack. Charges of corruption and mismanagement accompanied criticism of the president's massive spending on the new capital city, Yamoussoukro (his birthplace), and its costly cathedral.

Read the following two articles and explain what happened to change Ivory Coast's economy and what impact these changes had on the people.

AFRICAN SUCCESS STORY

When she arrived in Abidjan, the palm-fringed capital of the Ivory Coast, the young American woman could hardly conceal her astonishment. "This is Africa?" she asked. "The street lights work; there are good roads, no potholes—and those skyscrapers!"

With its neatly cultivated plantations, its electrified villages and its efficient and stable government, the Ivory Coast is certainly not the Africa of its impoverished neighbors: Mali, Guinea, Liberia and Upper Volta. Its export performance outstrips that of Nigeria or Zaïre, which embarked upon political independence with much larger markets, and its domestic industry is far superior to that of Ghana or Zambia, which are more richly endowed with natural resources. Unlike those countries, the Ivory Coast has been able to sustain 21 years of carefully planned economic growth that has made the former French colony one of the richest nations in Black Africa. It also has become a model of the kind of development that the Reagan Administration hopes to foster throughout the Third World.

Wealth: In just two decades the Ivory Coast has tripled its agricultural exports. Per capita economic growth has raced ahead at a rate of more than 7 percent a year, and the government has ensured that the new wealth is fairly evenly distributed. A liberal investment code has attracted large amounts of foreign capital, allowing industry to flourish along with agriculture. As prosperity has spread, it has created a general sense of well-being among the people. "Odd as it is in the Third World, they've never known anything but political stability," says one European diplomat. "And that is their expectation for the future."

Behind the economic miracle is the benevolently autocratic—and highly respected—rule of President Félix Houphouët-Boigny. "The word 'revolution' has one 'r' too many," he once remarked, and since the beginning of his Presidency in 1960 he has stressed gradual change. His first task was to develop the agricultural sector, a task he accomplished by setting attractive domestic prices for farm products and sticking to those prices regardless of the fluctuations of the international markets. The result was a rapid growth of small farms—and steadily mounting agricultural exports. Meanwhile, the government's export profits were plowed back into a highway system that allowed farmers to bring even bigger crops to market.

At the same time, Houphouët-Boigny has maintained a healthy respect for foreign ideas—and foreign money. There are more Frenchmen in the Ivory Coast today than there were at the time of independence, and their influence is so great that the Ministry of Planning is occasionally referred to as the "Ministry of Whites." But there is little bitterness in the joke, because along with the French has come plenty of French investment. A steady inflow of private money has allowed the Ivory Coast to get by with remarkably little foreign aid. . . . Houphouët-Boigny avoids talking about oil when discussing his country's future. All that he will say is that it is lucky that oil was not discovered sooner; otherwise the Ivory Coast might not have had as much incentive to develop its agriculture.

With its network of roads and communications, there is an excellent chance the Ivory Coast will be able to use its new oil revenues to develop new export industries. Even without that bonanza, continued progress seems inevitable. The country may face a difficult time as it adjusts to earlier overspending, but the essentials of growth are there. The key assets, says one Western aid official, are "a combination of honest government, an open economy, rational prices and a willingness to accept foreign advisers and foreign help."

Source: From *Newsweek*, October 26, 1981,

STABLE NO MORE

Economic recession caused by stagnant prices for commodities exports is helping to lead the Ivory Coast, West Africa's most consistently stable country, toward a precipice of civil revolt. . . . Foreigners from France, Arab countries, and other African countries are seen as holding too many jobs. While some fear a bloody pogrom against foreigners, others see young people leading the attack on the government of Félix Houphouët-Boigny, who at 85 is often rumored to be ill and "seems to be too occupied" with the building of a huge Catholic basilica.

"One of the Ivory Coast's problems," Cros writes, "is the lack of job openings for its youth, who thought that going to school would guarantee them access to jobs in the civil service. This has not happened. Even worse, the serious recession because of the crisis in the cacao and coffee [export] markets—which support about two-thirds of all Ivorians—has affected everyone." In the view of a local journalist whom Cros quotes: "Young people are tired of not having work. They see corruption. They resent the older people hanging on to their jobs and keeping them from taking part. They are impatient. . . . One of these days they will [revolt], as they did in Algeria."

Source: Barry Shelby, *World Press Review*, November 1989, p. 50.

▶ Profile: Félix Houphouët-Boigny

Houphouët-Boigny has dominated Ivory Coast politics. He was born in 1905, the son of a plantation owner and chief of the Baoule tribe. He studied medicine and became an "African Doctor" (a position that required less than a full medical degree, but was as high as an African could achieve). Prevented from rising further in this profession, Félix became a cocoa grower, which led to his involvement in politics. In 1944, he founded the African Planters' Movement to obtain equality with European planters. It quickly became the basis for a political party.

The French allowed colonial representation in the French National Assembly at the end of World War II, and Houphouët-Boigny was elected from Ivory Coast in 1945. Here, he embarked on a path of close cooperation with France. Félix served as a cabinet minister in the French government from 1956–1959, while consolidating his power in Ivory Coast by serving as president of its Assembly and mayor of its capital, Abidjan. He consistently rejected outright independence and African federation and helped to bring about the French Community in 1958. His policies of close ties with France, capitalism, foreign investment, interdependence, and gradual reform can be seen in an essay he wrote in 1957:

President Felix Houphouët-Boigny of Ivory Coast
Bureau For Information

. . . We want to cooperate within this great aggregate which is the French Union [forerunner of the French Community], because it is there that we can safeguard the advantages and the interests of the black people of Africa.

. . . This outside capital assistance is needed by all countries undergoing rapid expansion, whether they are nominally independent or not. We wish to remain in the French Union because it furnishes us this assistance and does it by an arrangement which seems to us the surest and best adapted to further the social and technical progress of our peoples. . . .

Those arrangements which we have chosen, and which are going into effect now, offer assurance of stability and security—conditions that are indispensable to the creation of an economic and social environment in which the African people can attain a standard of living comparable to that of the peoples of the great modern nations. These institutional arrangements are such as to attract investments in all forms—imports of capital, technicians and methods—which are indispensable to our territories. They allow us to prove our maturity, within the forms and modes of thought to which our culture has accustomed us. . . .

Moreover, we have, in common with the French, qualities which have facilitated our relations with them: good sense, realism, discrimination, which are as widespread among the black peasants of Africa as in the rural sections of France. In difficult times these qualities have enabled us to establish distinctions between colonization and the abuses of colonization. They enable us to understand today that in a world where interdependence has become the supreme rule, outbreaks of fanaticism and nationalism accomplish nothing and run the risk of merely increasing misery.

. . . The modern world offers so many examples of barriers to race or class which pen in human beings that we cannot help but want to respond to France's loyalty and humane conduct in like fashion. It is important that the Franco-African community—egalitarian, humane and fraternal—appear to all nations not only as an example to be emulated but also as an element of international stability on which a sure future can be built.[1]

Throughout his decades in power, Houphouët-Boigny has survived strikes and attempted coups. While he has exercised a tight hold on power through the country's only political party, he has governed through a system of advisors, councils, and committees. He has portrayed himself as "the nation's grandfather" and has lessened tensions by including representatives of most ethnic groups in his cabinet and by giving government posts to some opponents of his regime. In the late 1980s, his rule became increasingly more unpopular as the economy continued to worsen, resulting in his promise in 1990 to relinquish power in the near future.

Figure 2
THE SOUTH'S DEBT GROWTH

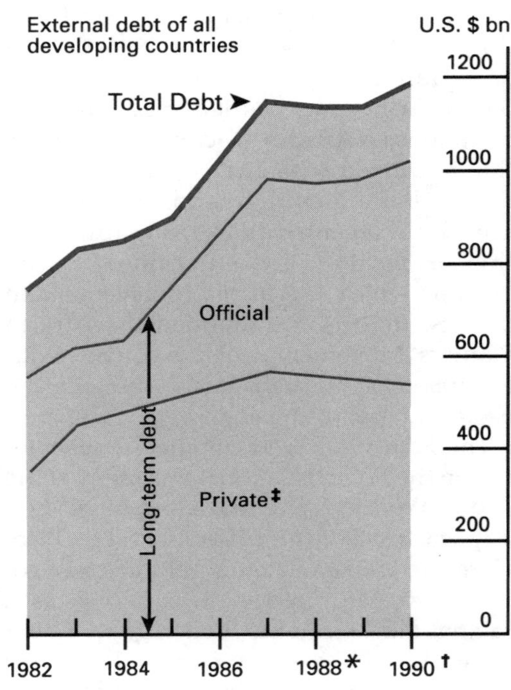

Source: Adapted from "The Debtors' Slow Progress," *South*, no. 112, February 1990, p. 30. Statistics from World Debt Tables.

THIRD WORLD DEBT

The 1980s witnessed an enormous increase in the debt owed by countries of the South to the North. Huge sums were transferred annually to the industrialized North from the less developed countries of the South in the form of interest payments, with devastating effects on the debtor countries' economies. According to the **World Bank**, the developing countries transferred a net of $51.6 billion (U.S.) in resources to the North in 1989, making a total outflow of $242.6 billion (U.S.) since 1982.

Less developed countries have found themselves using much of their export earnings simply to pay their debts. These huge debts literally have devoured some

[1] *Patterns of Civilization: Africa*. Institute for Contemporary Curriculum Development. New York: Cambridge Book Co., 1975, pp. 455-456.

national budgets and have contributed to an increase in poverty, rather than to the development that was hoped for in the 1980s. Argentina's former president, Raul Alfonsin, warned the industrialized countries that it was in their best interest not to ignore the problem of debt in the South. He stated, "On a plane there are different classes, but if there is a bomb on board no one can be safe."[2]

[2] *Latin American Index*, Vol. XIX, No. 5, March 5, 1990, p. 18.

The choices facing countries of the South seem cruel. Defaulting on loans results in no further loans. Cutting government spending, however, often devastates the country, particularly the poorest groups. Attempts at banding together by forming **debtors' cartels** have not been successful. At the same time, impoverished states cannot purchase the products of the North, so the world economy suffers. According to some observers, the problem of Third World debt will be the key issue of the global economy in the coming decade.

PERU

Table 3
BASIC DATA—PERU

Geography	Area in Square Kilometres: 1 280 000 Capital (Population): Lima (4 165 000) Climate: coast area, arid and mild; Andes, temperate to frigid; eastern lowlands, tropically warm and humid	**Military**	Number of Armed Forces: 135 000 Current Hostilities: unresolved long-smoldering dispute with Ecuador over 80 km stretch of border
People	Population: 18 million Ethnic Makeup of Population: 45% Indian; 37% *Mestizo*; 15% White; 3% Black, Asian, and other Religion: more than 90% Roman Catholic Adult Literacy Rate: 80% (est.)	**Economy**	Currency ($ U.S. Equivalent): 13 908 soles = $1 (1985) Natural Resources: minerals; metals; petroleum; forests; fish Agriculture: coffee; cotton; cocoa; sugar; wool; corn Industry: mineral processing; oil refining; textiles; food processing; light manufacturing; automobile assembly
Communication	Televisions: 1 600 000 Telephones: 544 000 Newspapers: 5 dailies	**Foreign Trade**	Imports: $3.0 billion (1988) (U.S. 25%, E.C. 23%) Exports: $2.6 billion (1988) (E.C. 23%, Japan 10%, U.S. 6%)
Transportation	Highways—Kilometres: 56 645 Railroads—Kilometres: 1876 Usable Airfields: 225		
Labour Force	38% agriculture; 17% industry and mining; 45% government and other services		

Sources: Paul B. Goodwin, Jr., *Global Studies: Latin America*, 3rd ed. Guilford, Conn.: The Dushkin Publishing Group Inc., 1988.
The Canadian World Almanac and Book of Facts 1990. Global Press, 1989.

FOCUS

1. Compare Peru to Ivory Coast in terms of televisions and kilometres of highways per person. In what areas of the economy are the two countries similar?

Figure 3
PERU

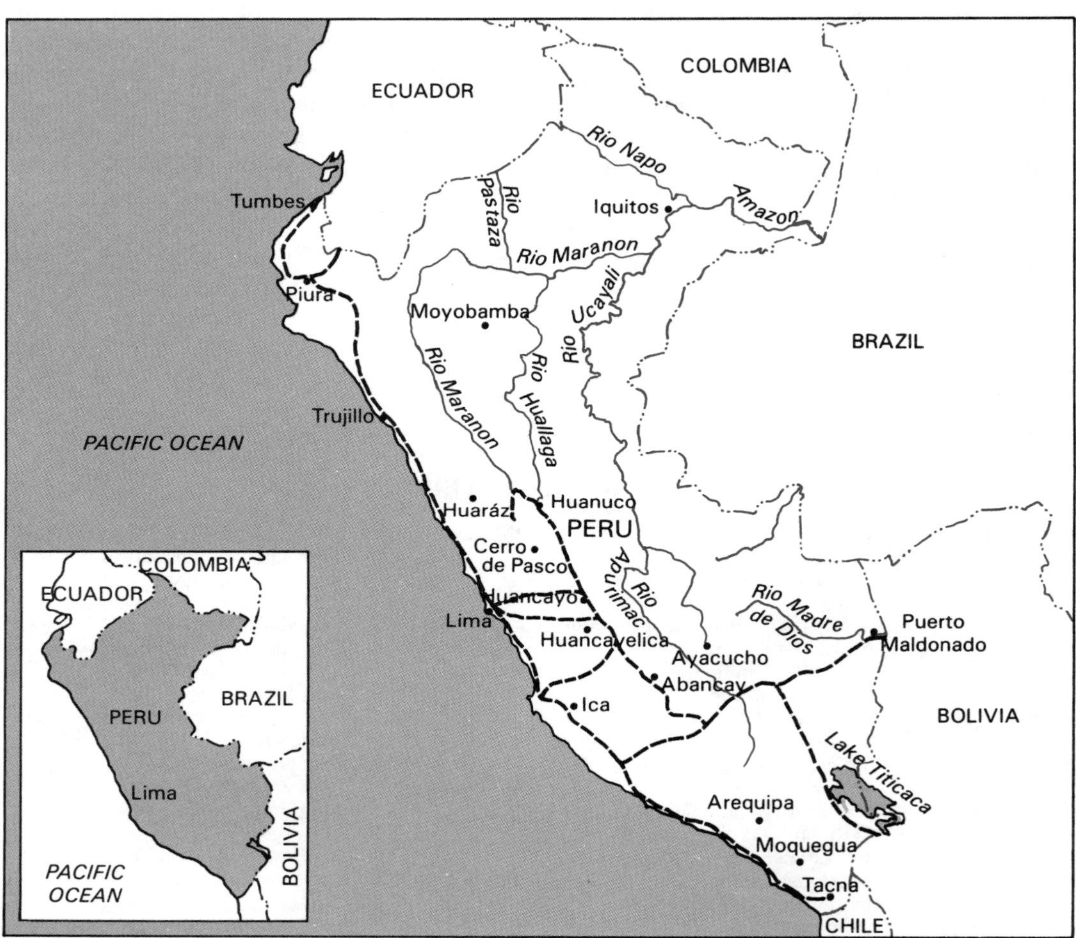

▶ Political History

Peru's early history was dominated by a series of sophisticated civilizations, culminating in the Incas, who began their empire in about 1200 A.D. This society had high levels of skill in architecture, astronomy, road building and engineering, farming, and social organization. Spanish adventurers, lured by gold and silver, conquered the Incas in the 1530s and began almost 300 years of harsh rule. Indians and *mestizos* engaged in frequent rebellions. In 1824, Peru achieved independence, partly through the efforts of South American liberators San Martín, Bolívar, and de Sucre. In the late 1800s, Peru and its neighbours warred over territory and resources.

As was the case in much of Latin America, for most of the first half of the twentieth century, Peru's governments were dominated by a succession of military and civil-

Table 4
TROPICAL SOUTH AMERICA AND PERU: BASIC INDICATORS

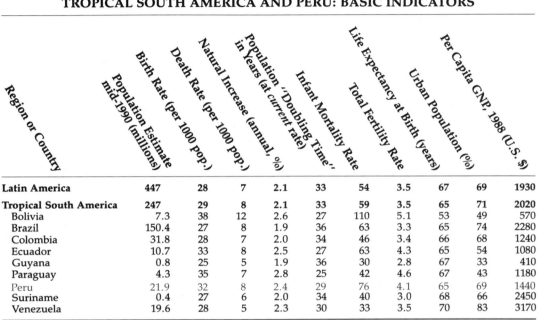

Region or Country	Population Estimate mid-1990 (millions)	Birth Rate (per 1000 pop.)	Death Rate (per 1000 pop.)	Natural Increase (annual, %)	Population "Doubling Time" in Years (at current rate)	Infant Mortality Rate	Total Fertility Rate	Life Expectancy at Birth (years)	Urban Population (%)	Per Capita GNP, 1988 (U.S. $)
Latin America	**447**	**28**	**7**	**2.1**	**33**	**54**	**3.5**	**67**	**69**	**1930**
Tropical South America	**247**	**29**	**8**	**2.1**	**33**	**59**	**3.5**	**65**	**71**	**2020**
Bolivia	7.3	38	12	2.6	27	110	5.1	53	49	570
Brazil	150.4	27	8	1.9	36	63	3.3	65	74	2280
Colombia	31.8	28	7	2.0	34	46	3.4	66	68	1240
Ecuador	10.7	33	8	2.5	27	63	4.3	65	54	1080
Guyana	0.8	25	5	1.9	36	30	2.8	67	33	410
Paraguay	4.3	35	7	2.8	25	42	4.6	67	43	1180
Peru	21.9	32	8	2.4	29	76	4.1	65	69	1440
Suriname	0.4	27	6	2.0	34	40	3.0	68	66	2450
Venezuela	19.6	28	5	2.3	30	33	3.5	70	83	3170

▸ Source: Population Reference Bureau, Inc., *1990 World Population Data Sheet*, Washington, D.C.: Population Reference Bureau, Inc., 1990.

ian dictators, who represented the interests of the country's wealthy elite. As well, the influence of the United States continued to increase. Gradually, a reformist party, the American Popular Revolutionary Alliance (APRA), began to have an impact and influenced the election of a number of presidents. In 1963, with military support, Fernando Belaunde Terry of the Popular Action party won election as president. His promises of democracy, progress, and reforms were hampered by economic and political problems.

In 1968, military leaders seized control of the government and formed a ruling junta. Twelve years of military rule followed, featuring the radical left-wing reforms of Juan Velasco Alvarado who headed the junta until 1975.

Latin American revolutions are often revolutions in name only and simply signify the passing of power from one military

General Juan Velasco Alvarado of Peru
The Bettmann Archive

group to another. Such was not the case in the revolution led by Alvarado in Peru from 1968 to 1975. Clearly, he meant what he said when he described the aim of his government as the "transformation" of Peruvian society.

Alvarado was born in 1910, the son of working-class parents. As a child, he played near the fenced compound of the American-owned International Petroleum Company (IPC), which he later described as "an enclave of the rich designed to keep Peruvians out forever." He joined the army as a private in 1929, went to cadet school, and after graduating first in his class, rose rapidly through the ranks. By 1968 he was Commander-in-Chief of the Army. Whereas the military officers in other Latin American countries are right-wing and upper class, Alvarado was typical of many of Peru's officers, who were of lower middle-class backgrounds and had little in common with ruling oligarchies.

The involvement of Alvarado in the 1968 revolution resulted in his being made leader of the ruling junta. His widespread social, economic, and cultural reforms were accompanied by an aggressively nationalistic foreign policy, which brought a hostile reaction from the United States. In particular, the takeover of the IPC by Peru and its extension of territorial waters to 125 km (to control fishing) caused relations to deteriorate drastically. Alvarado maintained that the United States had been exploiting Peru for years and that Peru was finally beginning to exercise control over what was rightfully hers. To threats of an American invasion, he replied, "Let them send in the marines . . . we will defend ourselves with rocks, if necessary."[3]

Although the revolution achieved some early successes and made broad social and economic changes, later problems (such as the lack of foreign investment) created serious financial difficulties. Alvarado was replaced in a bloodless coup in 1975 and died in 1977.

The military group that replaced Alvarado adopted more moderate policies and had the support of the middle class. Increasing problems in the economy convinced the military to relinquish its control of the country, and in 1980 Peru returned to civilian control with the election of Belaunde as president. His previous policies were replaced by conservative, free-market programs, which also failed to solve Peru's problems. These difficulties led to the election of the APRA candidate, Alan Garcia Perez, in 1985. After a promising first year in power, Peru's problems again multiplied; Garcia's (and APRA's) popularity deteriorated. The election in June of 1990 resulted in the rejection by the voters of all the main parties and in the choice of a political novice, Alberto Fujimori, as president.

▶ The Economy

Peru's economy has often been described as having enormous potential and overwhelming problems. In several ways, it reflects many of the problems facing Latin American countries in particular, and those of the South in general. The potential and the problems are reflected in the attempts by Peru's various governments to improve the economy.

Peru has many advantages. Partly as a result of its three very different regions (the coast, the Andean highlands, and the Amazon basin), it has diversified resources. Several of Peru's problems stem from enormous income inequalities. The country has one of the worst income distributions in the world and the society has deep divisions based on class and race. In addition, rural areas have long felt dominated and exploited by Lima and rejected in their development needs.

▸ [3]*Current Biography*, 1970, p. 428.

Calls for change, accompanied by rural violence, resulted in a few land reforms in the early 1960s, but the government made little progress. Dramatic changes occurred after the military seized power in 1968. The sweeping reforms of the Alvarado regime included government takeovers of large estates and their transfer to peasant collectives; nationalization of railroads, utilities, most banks, and many large foreign companies; protection policies for Peru's industries; and education and health care reforms. This "top-down" revolution produced a society that was neither capitalist nor socialist and was accompanied by a much more independent foreign policy, which earned the disapproval of the United States. After early successes, the reforms ran into a variety of problems, often characterized as a combination of bad luck, wasteful spending, mismanagement, and the difficult nature of Peru's fundamental problems. Faced with mounting financial difficulties, the new military regime in 1975 adopted austerity measures.

After the Revolution

President Belaunde's second term (1980–1985) was characterized by a further retreat from reform and an emphasis on free-market policies. However, the debt increased dramatically, the annual inflation rate passed 100 percent, and terrorism worsened. By 1985, sixty percent of Peru's industrial capacity was idle, real wages had plummeted, and per capita income had fallen to the level of the mid-1960s.

These problems led to the election of the APRA candidate Alan Garcia Perez as president in 1985, but they proved insurmountable for him as well. His policy of drastically limited payments on the foreign debt was popular in Peru, but angered the industrialized countries and was later abandoned. His policy of nationalizing the remaining banks led to less foreign investment and more pressure from the international banking community. Garcia's early enormous popularity vanished as "hyperinflation" reached over 2700 percent in 1989. (A television set that sold on January 1 for 1000 units of currency cost about 27 000 units by December 31.) In addition, the guerrilla war in the cities worsened. A return to austerity failed to turn the situation around, and people increasingly joined the "informal economy."

The 1990 Election

The 1990 presidential election featured a rejection of the mainstream parties and a run-off choice between two political novices. The famed novelist Mario Vargas Llosa had the support of Peru's traditional elite. He called for a "shock treatment" that included an open economy; free markets; privatization; and subsidy-cutting policies, which had become popular in Chile, Mexico, Brazil, and Argentina and were favoured by the IMF and the United States.

But he was rejected in favour of Alberto Fujimori (the son of Japanese immigrants), who received his support from poorer groups. He promised a balanced approach and an end to corruption and inefficiency. However, after taking office he instituted a harsh austerity program, which included several of Vargas Llosa's proposals.

▶ Sendero Luminoso

Peru's ***Sendero Luminoso*** ("Shining Path") guerrilla movement is often described in terms of fanaticism, ruthlessness, brutality, ideological dedication, and an absolute unwillingness to compromise. It began in the mid-1960s as a radical student organization in the remote highland area of Ayacucho. The leader is Abimael Guzman, a former university professor. Its armed struggle began in earnest in 1980 and has resulted in the deaths of about 20 000 Peruvians. The guerrillas' tactics are based on Mao Zedong's examples, and their goal is to create a Marxist state.

Their tactics have included selective assassinations of popular leaders and government workers, including foreign workers on government projects. The guerrillas achieve their goals by establishing a base in an area and killing those people who refuse to co-operate. They then focus their attention on recruiting young people. They consistently practice terrorism. In their first appearance in Lima in 1980, they hung dead dogs from lightposts to protest Deng Xiaoping's then-reformist government in China. They have often killed members of other left-wing revolutionary groups, whom they consider to be too moderate.

Their appeal is mostly to peasants, but they try to recruit urban workers as well. It is generally agreed that the factor that brings most support to the Senderos is the overwhelming poverty of so many of Peru's people, especially the Indians in the neglected mountain region. A priest who worked with the poor said of Indian children, "Those who survive have three choices — '*sendero, coquero,* or *ratero*' — meaning they can join the guerrillas, work with the drug traffickers, or steal.

The government in the late 1980s gave broad powers to the military to deal with the guerrillas. The military's tactics have resulted in charges of massacres and widespread human rights abuses. The Senderos maintain that they are prepared for a fifty-year struggle.

▶ Peru and Cocaine

While Colombia's drug wars have often dominated the news, more than half of the coca (the source plant for cocaine) grown in the world is produced in Peru, mostly in the Upper Huallaga valley. The coca leaf is made into coca paste and shipped to Colombia, where it is processed into cocaine. While it has been grown in the area for at least 1000 years, its production increased dramatically with the recent growth in demand for cocaine in the United States. It is estimated that at least 70 000 small farmers earn their living growing coca and that the net earnings for Peru are from $750 million to $1.2 billion per year in foreign exchange.

Peruvian governments have co-operated with U.S. efforts as part of a war on drugs, but their measures have had extremely limited success. The core of the American program is crop eradication, the physical destruction of the coca crop. *South Magazine* offered the following assessment of the program:

> *Despite evidence that simply destroying the coca crop does not work — 1300 ha were eradicated in the Huallaga in 1988, but another 5000 ha were sown — the US persists in its policy.*
>
> *Eradication is a losing battle. With so much empty land available and no other crop to match the price of coca, the peasants simply move on and start cultivating coca elsewhere.*[4]

Alternative approaches are more costly. For example, helping peasants switch to other crops requires guaranteed prices and other assistance in order to be successful. The eradication policy has also played into the hands of the Senderos, who have offered protection to the peasants who grow coca. Some Peruvians feel that the only policy that will end the problem is to eliminate poverty in Peru. Other observers feel that the drug problem is one more example of the wealthy North creating problems for the people of the South. In their view, the whole focus of the effort on lim-

▸ [4]*South*, No. 112, February 1990, p. 12.

iting supply is misguided, and until the demand for drugs in the affluent North is curtailed, all attempts are doomed.

▶ CONCLUSION

The major problem for most developing countries is mass poverty. Solutions are difficult. Poverty tends to create poverty. As the following diagram illustrates, countries stay poor because they are poor. Poverty-stricken families do not have the opportunity or the incentive to save money. Low income families cannot buy many consumer goods, which means that few commodities are produced (supply and demand) and employment remains low. Rapid population growth quickly absorbs any increases in income. High inflation rates wipe out any remaining gains and further reduce the incentive to save money.

During the 1980s, several Third World countries, such as Korea, Taiwan, and Singapore, broke out of the poverty cycle and experienced a period of rapid economic growth. Other countries, including Brazil and Peru, remained mired in poverty. Economist Jeffrey Sachs has examined the economies of these states and has concluded that the crucial difference between the successful and the non-successful countries was the extent to which income was equally distributed among the people.

When a country's income is relatively equally dispersed, the government can pursue economic policies that involve short-term sacrifices from the people, but lead to long-term economic stability. Where mass poverty exists, governments cannot ask the people to sacrifice, even for a short time, without facing threats of violence and actual starvation. Income inequality is particulary high in Latin America. In Peru, for example, one percent of the population controls fifty percent of the country's income. In such situations, the wealthy elite, which usually controls the govern-

Figure 4
THE VICIOUS CIRCLE OF POVERTY

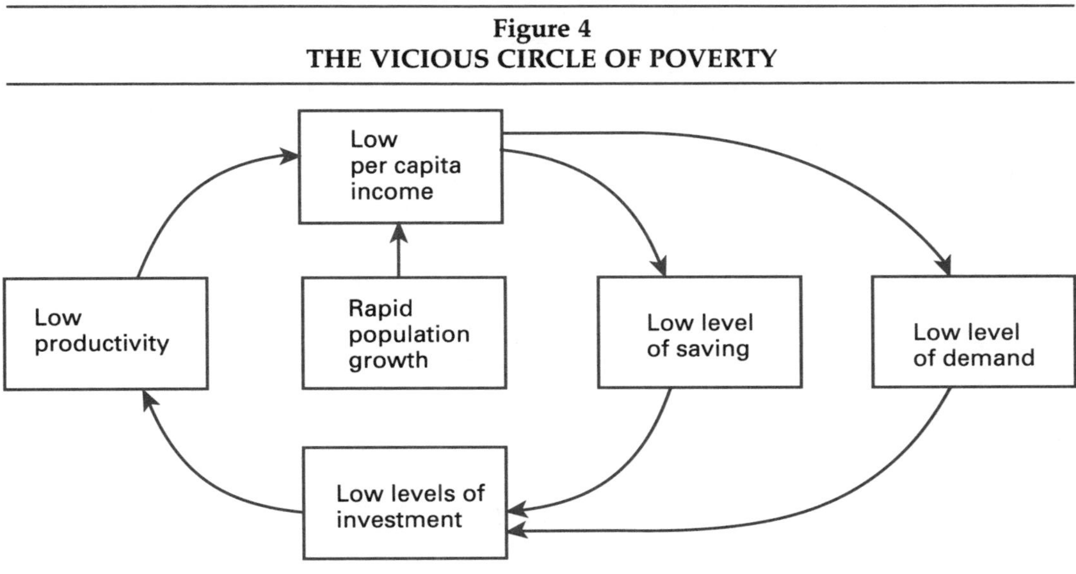

▸ Source: Campbell McConnell et al., *Economics*, 5th Cdn. ed. Toronto: McGraw-Hill Ryerson Limited, 1990, p. 944.

ment, prevents a fairer distribution of the country's resources.

Although the economies of Third World countries vary tremendously, they all must face the three fundamental economic questions (what/how/for whom). Less developed countries thus face similar economic decisions to those confronted by more developed states. The fact that Peru and Ivory Coast have chosen different paths and have altered their courses several times illustrates that Third World countries face differing problems than those normally encountered by more developed countries. Such obstacles include large informal economies, mass poverty, huge international debts, one-crop economies, a less educated population, and economic domination by the countries of the North. As a result, some economists suggest that Third World countries must find their own unique economic solutions. Peru, Ivory Coast, Zimbabwe, and Costa Rica (Case Study 16) illustrate four different attempts.

APPLYING YOUR KNOWLEDGE

1. a) How are countries of the South and the North similar and different in the kinds of economic decisions and problems that face them?
   b) What factors might affect the kinds of economic systems that have emerged in less developed countries?
   c) What factors (national and global) have limited economic development in the South, and what alternative approaches have emerged?
   d) Rank the questions on pages 443 and 444 in order of importance. Explain the reasons for your rankings.
2. a) Using the data in Table 2 (Basic Indicators), to what extent are conditions in Ivory Coast similar to those in the rest of Western Africa?
   b) How have historical factors helped to shape Ivory Coast's economic system?
   c) What factors led to Ivory Coast being seen as a ''model of development''?
   d) Compare the two descriptions of Ivory Coast's economy (1981 and 1989). What factors caused the changes?
3. a) Using the data in Table 4 (Basic Indicators), describe the degree to which conditions in Peru are similar to those in the rest of tropical South America.
   b) Describe Peru's two biggest economic problems and potentials. Present reasons for your selections.
   c) What is the relationship between GNP and life expectancy?
   d) What factors have contributed to the growth of the Senderos?
   e) Outline various courses of action that could be taken on the problem of cocaine. What are the drawbacks to each one?
4. Compare the economic systems of Ivory Coast and Peru. How are they similar and different? What factors might account for these similarities and differences?
5. a) What factors have led to the success of some Asian economies? To what extent could other countries copy them? Why? Should they? Why?
   b) How might the ''informal economy'' be used to advantage by countries? What might be some of the drawbacks?

FURTHER RESEARCH

1. a) Select three countries from each of Latin America, Asia, and Africa and compare them on the basis of the following categories: ethnic diversity, literacy, communications, transportation, military establishment, labour force, and foreign trade. What conclusions can you draw? What are the limitations on your conclusions? How do your conclusions compare with those of other students who have chosen other groups of countries?
   b) Choose another Latin American country, analyse its economic system, and compare it to Peru's. Or, choose another African country and compare its economic system to Ivory Coast's. Suggest reasons for similarities and differences.
   c) Choose an Asian country, analyse its economic system, and compare it to Ivory Coast's, Peru's, or both.
2. Research the recent situation with respect to drugs or terrorism in Latin America. What changes and approaches have emerged?
3. Choose a less developed country and analyse its economic system using the questions on pages 443 and 444 and the criteria in this case study as a guide.
   - Write an essay describing your findings.
   - Present your conclusions to the class.
   - Compare your findings with those of other students who have researched different countries.
   - Write an essay in which you identify the factors that lead countries of the South to develop similar and different economic systems.
4. Working in groups, devise a solution to Peru's economic problems.
5. Prepare for a debate on the benefits of defaulting on foreign loan payments.
6. Write a letter to your MP outlining what Canada should do to help less developed countries.

Case Study 25 Overview

Tropical Rain Forests, the Ecology, and the Multinational Corporation

This case study examines the threatened destruction of the world's tropical rain forests. It begins with a description of rain forests, including their locations, characteristics, life forms that inhabit them, and extent to which they are being destroyed. The major causes of the rain forests' decline include agriculture, logging, ranching, and population growth. Rain forests nurture an enormous number of different species of plants and animals, provide oxygen for the planet, and are the source of many medicines. The case study examines the role of multinational corporations in the destruction of the tropical rain forests and concludes with a discussion of some of the possible solutions to this problem.

▶ OBJECTIVES

After reading this case study, you should be able to:

- ▶ discuss the importance of tropical rain forests
- ▶ explain the role of multinational corporations in the destruction of the rain forests
- ▶ outline the reasons for the continuing destruction of the rain forests
- ▶ recognize the difficulties in arriving at a viable solution
- ▶ evaluate possible solutions and devise your own answer
- ▶ research and report on other environmental problems

▶ KEY TERMS

rain forests
deforestation
ranching
soil erosion
selective logging
ecosystems
supra-national

Case Study 25

Tropical Rain Forests, the Ecology, and the Multinational Corporation

One of the crucial environmental problems facing the world is the destruction of the **rain forests** by multinational corporations and by local inhabitants engaged in lumbering, agriculture, and grazing. Their operations are rapidly eliminating the rain forest, and in the view of many scientists, are causing severe economic and environmental hazards. At the current rate of **deforestation**, practically all remaining tropical rain forests will disappear within forty years. This case study explains what a rain forest is, how it contributes to the global economy, and what is happening to it and examines the repercussions of its destruction.

▶ WHAT IS A RAIN FOREST?

Tropical rain forests, with a few exceptions, are located almost entirely within the tropics and close to the Equator. The largest rain forest areas are in Central and South America, but rain forests are also prevalent in Indonesia, mainland Asia, and parts of continental Africa and Madagascar.

Rain forests depend on relatively constant rainfall and temperatures that are warm enough to allow plant life to grow all year long. Perpetual rainfall and warmth force trees to grow ever upward to compete for sunlight. These tall trees have long,

Figure 1
DISTRIBUTION OF TROPICAL RAIN FORESTS

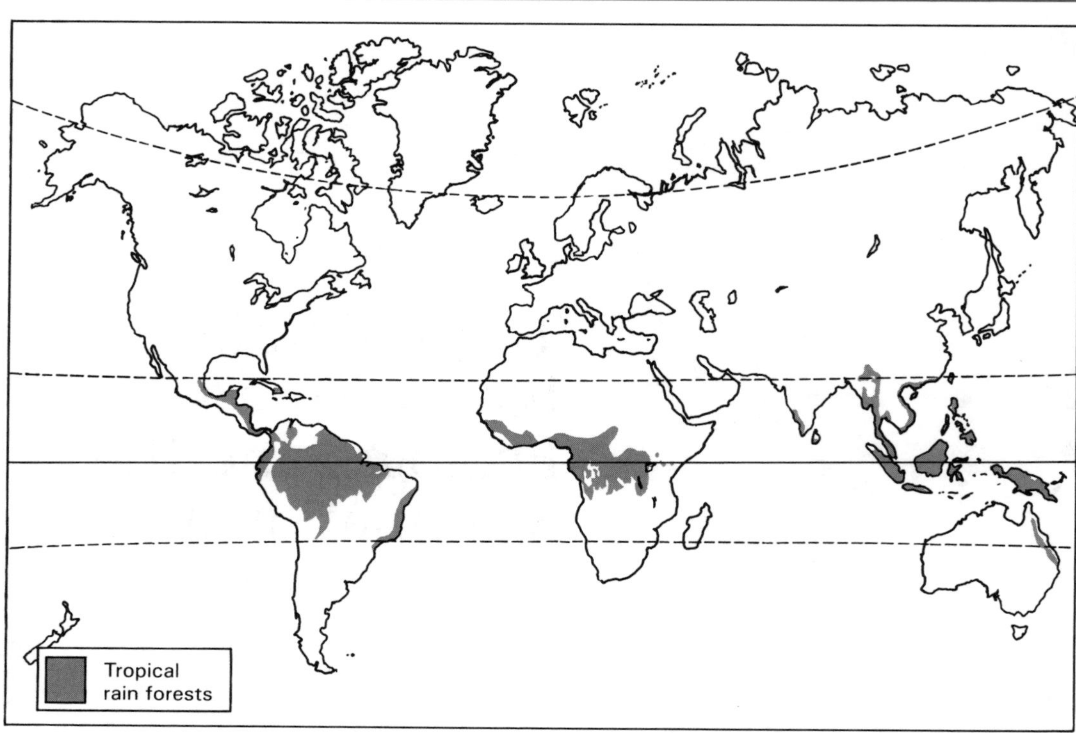

slender trunks, with branches only near the top. This dense, high canopy blocks out much of the sunlight from the forest floor. Only plants that can survive in dim light and high humidity can survive below the canopy.

The tallest trees form the main canopy, which shades everything below. Younger trees grow beneath, waiting for one of the giants to die and fall, before taking its place. Below, the smaller trees are seedlings, shrubs, and herbs. Since few plants can survive the dimness of the lower levels, the forest floor is fairly open. Without access to direct sunlight, plants cannot undergo photosynthesis, a process in which plants capture solar energy and use it to produce glucose from carbon dioxide and water that is necessary for their survival. The photosynthesis process also releases oxygen into the atmosphere. This oxygen produces the atmosphere's ozone layer, which screens the earth from most of the sun's damaging ultraviolet light.

Decomposing plants release carbon dioxide into the air, which the plants above the surface utilize. If the rain forest is cut down, this carbon dioxide will be released into the air without being utilized and will escape into the atmosphere. A build-up of carbon dioxide in the atmosphere caused by the destruction of the rain forest could have a dramatic effect on the world's climate. It should be noted, however, that all the fac-

Figure 2
TROPICAL RAIN FOREST

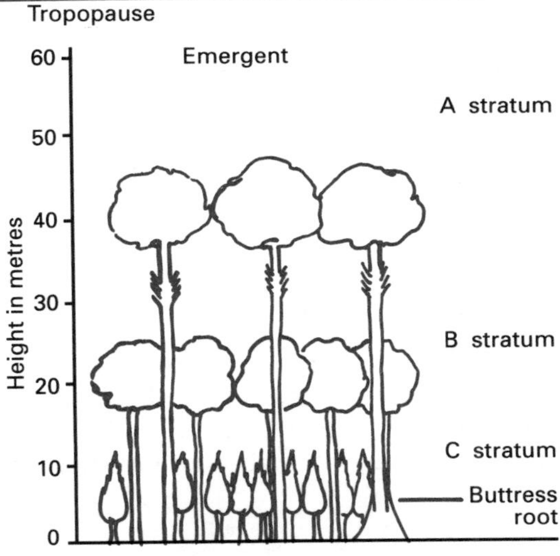

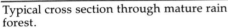

Typical cross section through mature rain forest.

tors affecting world climate and temperature are not fully understood and that there are various opinions concerning rain forest destruction and climate change.

Another characteristic feature of the tropical rain forest is its great diversity of plant and animal life. Indeed, some species may be found in one small area only, and nowhere else. The Amazon River has approximately 3000 species of fish. Panama has 1500 species of butterflies compared to 763 in the United States and 68 in Great Britain. The Malayan Peninsula, which encompasses an area approximately half the size of Great Britain, has almost 8000 species of flowering plants compared with the 1400 or so species found in the British Isles. A recent study estimated that a typical rain forest area of only six square kilometres may contain up to 1500 species of flowering plants, 750 species of trees, 400 species of birds, 150 species of butterflies, 100 species of reptiles, and 60 species of amphibians. The number of species of insects can only be approximated, but a single hectare may contain up to 42 000 species.

This great diversity of life might lead one to believe that the land upon which the rain forest rests is very rich in nutrients. This is not the case. The forests may be ancient, but so are the soils in which they grow. The living organisms in the rain forests, not the soil, contain most of the nutrients. Fallen leaves that would take a year to decompose in a temperate broad leaf forest decompose within six weeks in the rain forest. Since the nutrients are contained in the plants and not in the soil, the destruction of the forest leaves infertile land that is poor for growing crops. Deceptively lush tropical rain forests have misled ranchers and agriculturalists into believing that the land is exceptionally fertile.

▶ DEFORESTATION AND SOIL EROSION

Deforestation is the permanent clearing of forest land and its conversion into non-forest uses. According to many scientists, deforestation is the world's most serious land use problem. In the tropical rain forest, deforestation is caused by population growth, farming, **ranching**, logging, and the search for fuel wood. Such operations have caused **soil erosion** throughout the tropics.

▶ AGRICULTURE

Although tropical soils are not well suited to agriculture, with great care and the proper techniques, farming can be managed in these soils. Small groups of tribal people have been practising traditional methods of farming, called slash and burn agriculture, for countless generations. This type of agriculture involves clearing a small patch of forest by cutting the trees and burning the vegetation. The ashes from the burnt vegetation are added to the soil to act as a nutrient-rich fertilizer. This cleared patch of forest is farmed until the nutrients are depleted and the forest encroaches again. The people then abandon this land and move on to clear another small patch of forest. The depleted areas regenerate, and in a few decades are capable of producing food once again. Unfortunately, the land is often over-farmed and is not given enough time to recover.

Slash and burn agriculture is not suited to modern farmers who must till large tracts of land in order to make the purchase of heavy machinery profitable. These modern farmers do not understand the weaknesses of tropical soils the way the local farmers do, and modern farming in the rain forest has resulted in some huge agricultural catastrophes. Some of these failures involved huge American banana farms. The companies lost millions of dollars, and the rain forests suffered disastrous devastation.

▶ RANCHING

In South America, huge expanses of rain forest have been destroyed and turned into grassland for beef cattle. This beef is produced for a few cents cheaper per kilogram

The destruction of the world's rain forests is one of the most crucial environmental problems facing the world today.
World Wildlife Fund

than American cereal-fed beef. The landowners sell this beef to the United States, rather than use it to feed the natives who work on the ranches and live in the area. The United States imports 133 million kilograms of beef annually from Central America. One hamburger chain alone sells 3 billion hamburgers a year, the equivalent of 300 000 cattle. The imported beef causes a glut on the American market and pushes out the higher-priced American beef.

South American cattle ranches provide little employment for the native population because ranching, unlike manufacturing, is not a labour-intensive enterprise. It is ironic to note that these ranches were financed in the 1970s and 1980s by international agencies such as the Inter-American Development Bank, the World Bank, and the United Nations Development Fund in order to improve the world's food supply. The opposite has occurred. The beef produced on former rain forest land is too expensive for the local populace to afford. As a result, land that might have been put to local use is being depleted to produce crops for export. The local people are left with a desert wasteland on what was once a vibrant rain forest.

▶ LOGGING

Tropical hardwood is some of the finest wood on the planet and is in great demand throughout the world. Between 1950 and 1980, tropical timber imports to Japan, Europe, and the United States increased sixteen-fold. Japan buys the largest quantity of tropical hardwoods (fifty-three percent), followed by Europe (thirty-two percent), and the United States (fifteen percent). These countries import tropical hardwoods because their own forests grow mainly softwood trees. The demand, however, is for specific species of hardwood such as ebony, teak, and mahogany.

Trees are harvested by either **selective logging** or clear-cutting. In selective logging, only the most desirable trees are taken. This method need not cause extensive damage, but it often does. Equipment must travel into the forest and return with the felled trees. To improve efficiency, additional trees are cut down to create roads. Felled trees may also bring down neighbouring trees. Selective logging may injure up to seventy percent of the remaining forest. In Borneo, selective logging has increased river silt, destroyed fragile habitats, and opened remote areas to hunting and farming. Selective logging has also played a major role in sparking disastrous forest fires, killing thousands of birds and animals. If managed properly, logging experts contend, selective logging can maintain a forest as a sustainable resource.

The second method of logging is clear-cutting, in which entire areas of forest are cleared of all trees and vegetation. The felled vegetation is used to make chipboard. This logging method can be less destructive to the forest as a whole if it is restricted to limited areas. The cleared land, however, is left ravaged. Logging in Borneo's state of Sabah has depleted almost all of the first-growth rain forest. In neighbouring Sarawak, at the present rates of destruction, loggers will have harvested the last primary forest by 2001.

Logging provides developing countries with much needed capital. In the mid-1980s, tropical lumber provided the producing countries with $7 billion in annual export earnings. These Third World countries are desperate for funds to restructure and operate their economies, as well as to make repayments on crippling international loans. Rain forest lumber, therefore, provides cash for financing various national projects, often to the detriment of the rain forest.

Also contributing to the economic problem is the fact that rain forest lumber, compared to timber elsewhere, is quite inexpensive. A few developing countries have suggested imposing a tax on rain forest products that would help to pay for proper resource management, as well as provide revenue for the state. Conservation practices that would decrease the amount felled would cause prices to rise (supply and demand) and consequently lead to an increase in the money available for forest management. This would help the forest to become a sustainable resource and would further increase the monetary returns to the producing country.

▶ POPULATION GROWTH AND FIREWOOD

The human population in the tropical rain forest has more than quadrupled in the last fifty years. Many of these people rely almost entirely on firewood for energy, cooking, and heat. As a result, in many tropical rain forests the area for several kilometres around communities has been completely cleared in the search for fuel wood.

The firewood shortage has been hastened by several factors, including agriculture, logging, and urban demands for wood. The rising price of oil in the 1970s increased the demand for fuel wood by making kerosene prohibitively expensive. Kerosene, a petroleum product, is the main alternative to firewood in many poor countries. Four-fifths of the wood felled in the tropics is used as fuel or in the manufacture of charcoal. The demand for fuel wood results in severe soil erosion. The tropical rain forest area may one day face the same problem of famine that plagues Africa. The famine in Africa can be partly traced to the soil erosion caused by deforestation by local people searching for firewood.

This "Earth First" demonstration increased public awareness of potential rain forest destruction.
Canada Wide Feature Service Limited

▶ WILDLIFE AND PLANT DESTRUCTION

The diversity of animal life in the rain forest is greater than in any other ecosystem in the world. Scientists estimate that the rain forest is home to millions of species, most of which will be extinct before they are ever discovered, named, or described.

Extinctions have occurred throughout history, but those that have resulted since 1900 far outnumber all that have happened before. Modern extinctions are a direct result of the human population explosion and the development of technology enabling the spread of human beings into all of the earth's **ecosystems**.

Aside from the ethical and aesthetic reasons for preserving wildlife, there are many economic grounds for doing so. In purely practical terms, humans derive many household, medical, and technological products from tropical sources. Such products include latex, resins, dyes, rayons, plastics, fertilizers, ceramics, and emulsions. Lignin is useful as a rubber reinforcer, as an asphalt strengthener, and as a dispersant for oil spills. Many prescription drugs are derived from tropical substances. A recent study determined that one-quarter of all prescription drugs used in the United States during the last twenty years contained ingredients derived from tropical plants.

Researchers investigating a poison substance obtained from tropical tree frogs in Colombia discovered batrachotoxin. This substance is now a major tool for biologists studying the functions of the nervous system. With the rapid increase in deforestation, scientists may never get a chance to discover many potentially useful or life-saving substances.

The conservation of plant and animal species is also crucial in the development of new crops and livestock, and in the preservation of old ones. All our agricultural products and domesticated animals originated with wild species. Plants and animals existing in natural ecosystems can be viewed as a genetic bank, the members of which can be used to maintain disease-resistance and productivity in domesticated strains. For example, ancestral wheat plants are crucial in the development of new rust-resistant wheat plants. Since wheat rust fungus adapts to the old strain, new wheat strains must be developed every few years.

Scientists understand very little about how ecosystem destruction affects nature's ability to provide basic life-supporting functions. When humans destroy or endanger plant and animal species, they undermine natural systems and reduce the biosphere's capacity to sustain life. Scientists are unsure at what point nature will no longer be capable of carrying out its functions of filtering pollutants from the atmosphere and water, recycling nutrients in the soil, and preserving habitable climates. As yet, no human technology can assume these functions if nature fails. Thus, when we endanger or destroy the natural species that serve these functions, we also place ourselves in peril.

▶ MULTINATIONAL CORPORATIONS: BEYOND IDEOLOGY?

To a large extent, the economies of many tropical countries are controlled by multinational corporations. The multinational corporation is a large international or **supra-national** business organization that makes investments not only at home but also outside of its country of origin. It has strong corporate links with other countries and performs its manufacturing operations largely in countries of the Third World. Bankrupt governments grant them rights

Figure 3

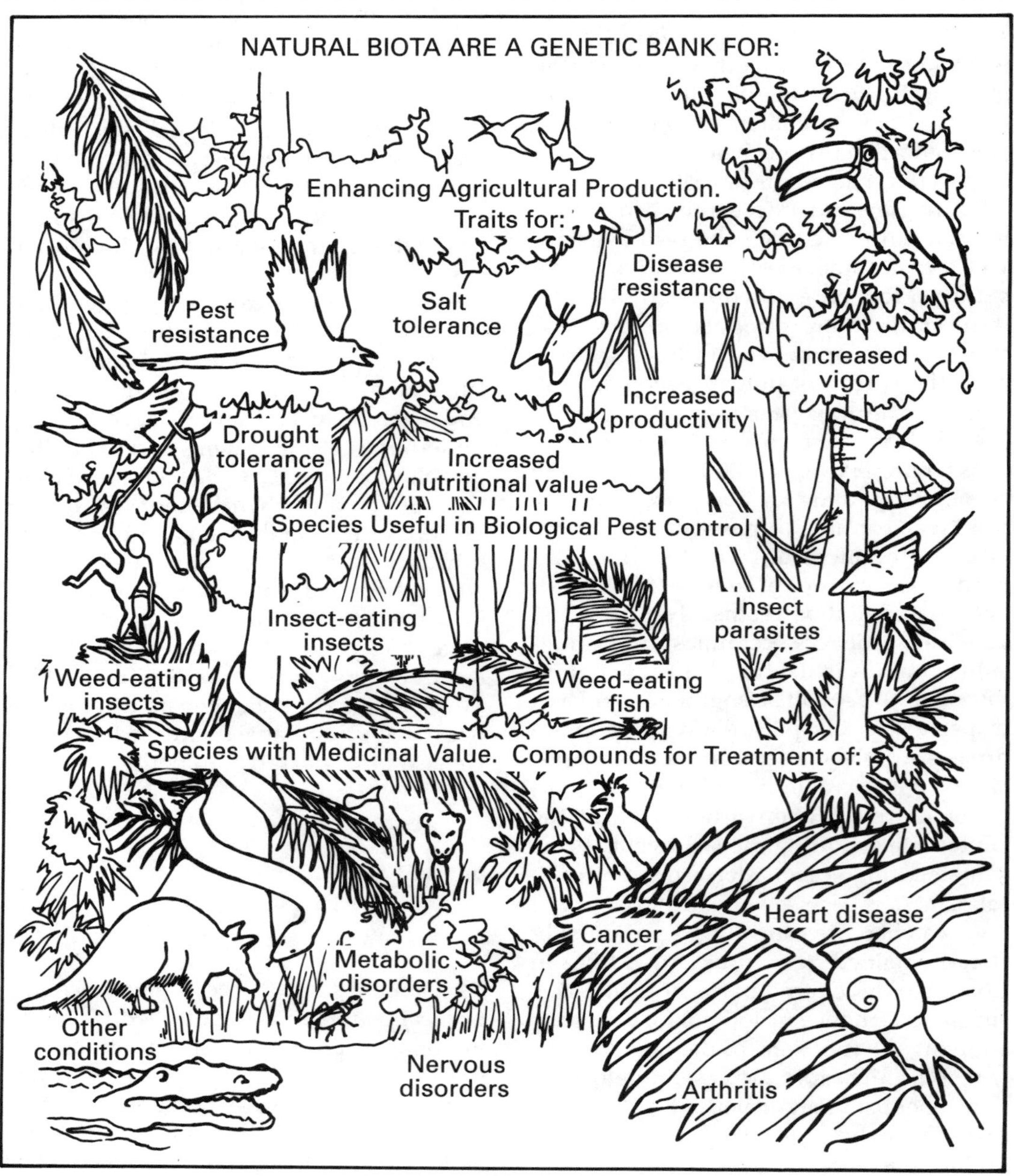

Natural biota serve as a "genetic bank." Wild species have many invaluable uses as depicted here. Hence, a healthy, diversified natural biota may be viewed as a genetic bank from which withdrawals for these uses can be made at any time. What will be the effects on the areas illustrated if natural biota are destroyed?

to hire labour at extremely low hourly rates to harvest and sell the countries' natural resources at bargain prices.

Many of these countries later discover to their dismay that what they believed were unlimited natural resources, such as water and wood, are in danger of disappearing. According to many political scientists, multinationals owe no particular loyalty to the countries in which they operate. As a result, they often may ignore the long-term dangers to the ecosystem and the often dire consequences for the local and global environment. This story is largely identical in dozens of Third World countries with rain forests, whether the country is capitalist, socialist, or Marxist.

Multinational corporatism seems to extend beyond the aims of socialism, Marxism, and capitalism. These three ideologies have always claimed to be interested in helping the people to attain a better life or standard of living, each by applying its own unique economic blueprint. The multinational corporation exists to serve, to a limited degree, the interests of its employees but considers mainly the higher objectives of its shareholders and board of directors.

Many examples point to multinational corporations taking seemingly deliberate economic advantage of less developed countries. Frequently, capital has been invested in large-scale commercial endeavours, such as cattle ranches, dams, railways, or sawmills, that benefit the multinational rather than the local populace. Some projects have had irreversible negative outcomes. For example, the introduction of cattle ranches in tropical rain forest areas has destroyed local agriculture and reduced vast areas of forest to virtual desert.

The problem is that Third World countries are so deeply in debt to international lenders that they have no bargaining power when multinationals come knocking at their door with "get rich quick" schemes.

Costa Rica seems to have found a possible solution to curb the power of multinationals. Scientists believe that Costa Rica contains five to nine percent of the world's known species in an area that constitutes barely 1/3000th of the world's land mass. The country has declared twelve percent of its territory as national parks or biological reserves. As a result, Costa Rica has received $36 million for conservation from various developed countries and has unburdened itself of $75 million in foreign debt through a process called "debt-for-nature-swap." The sums involved in these operations may be small, but the approach points the way to confronting multinationals with some hope of success.

Through a combination of regulations implemented by the less developed countries and a self-examination of priorities and methods on the part of multinational corporations, future development need not be as grim as the past and present have been. Governments are beginning to respond to the rising pressure of environmental concerns. In 1989, Indonesia suspended or cancelled eighty-five logging concessions, and levied $4 million in fines for logging violations. As well, the export of whole logs was suspended, and reforestation fees have been increased. Unfortunately, the Indonesian government has also made some major environmental blunders. Areas of the Kinabalu National Park have been turned into a copper mine, a golf course, and a cattle ranch. Half of the land belonging to one national park was appropriated, logged, and then returned to national-park status.

▶ CONCLUSION

The tropical rain forests are the world's richest ecosystems. They contain approximately fifty percent of the earth's animal and bird species and four-fifths of the world's vegetation. But, at the current rate of deforestation, practically all remaining tropical rain forest will disappear within an estimated forty years. This destruction will have severe economic repercussions that will be felt all over the world.

Agriculture and ranching in tropical areas damage the soil and hence the forests. These activities displace the local inhabitants, who have no alternative means by which to feed and house themselves. Agriculture and ranching often do not provide work or food for the local population, since these industries are not labour intensive. As well, logging deprives local natives of their land and their livelihoods and leaves them with useless former rain forests. Logging, agriculture, and ranching all magnify the problem brought on by the lack of firewood, which causes the poor populace to further denude the local resources in search of fuel wood.

These activities are often controlled by large multinational corporations. While the corporations may profit, the local economies of the host countries often suffer, and their limited national resources are destroyed in the process.

Multinational corporations may be seen as an outgrowth of capitalism, socialism, and Marxism—the major ideologies of the modern world. Multinational corporatism is the catalyst in the move towards a unified global economy and might well serve as the ideology of this new system in a way that capitalism, socialism, or Marxism no longer can. Multinational corporations and their host governments continue to recognize and evaluate the environmental and economic implications of their activities. It is hoped that these realizations will lead to the conservation of local resources and the betterment of the global economy.

APPLYING YOUR KNOWLEDGE

1. Explain why multinational corporations enjoy nearly unlimited power in less developed countries.
2. Explain how the poverty of Third World countries contributes to the power of multinational corporations.
3. Should the world's governments intervene to curtail the power of multinational corporations? Explain.
4. What choices do Third World countries have regarding their natural resources?
5. Explain why large-scale logging operations are harmful to the environment.

FURTHER RESEARCH

1. Prepare for a debate on the following topics:
   a) Exploitation of the rain forests must stop until the means are found to protect the ecology.
   b) The destruction of the rain forest is inevitable.
   c) The United Nations must stop the exploitation of the rain forests by multinational corporations.
2. The United Nations Commission on Environment and Development was held in 1987. Their report, *Our Common Future*, warned "that the time has come for a marriage of economy and ecology, so that governments and their people can take responsibility not just for environmental damage, but for the policies that cause the damage." Obtain a copy of the report. What recommendations were made by the Commission to achieve this marriage?

3. Consult current magazines and newspapers and write a report on the current status of the world's rain forests.
4. Multinational corporations are learning to treat rain forests and the ecology with greater care than ever before. Argue this point pro or con.
5. Begin a newspaper file of articles on an environmental problem such as the rain forests, the greenhouse effect, or water pollution.
6. Working in groups, prepare a viable solution to the tropical rain forest problem.
7. ''Sustainable development'' refers to economic development that does not deplete the earth's resources or disturb fragile ecosystems. Is ''sustainable development'' possible to achieve? Working in groups, prepare a viable solution to the tropical rain forest problem.

CHAPTER 10 OVERVIEW

THE WORLD'S ECONOMIES: SUMMARY PROJECTS

This concluding chapter provides an opportunity to develop your own values, opinions, and ideas and to hone your research and writing skills. The chapter briefly outlines each of the following four topics and provides suggested procedures to aid in answering the questions:

1. Which is the best economic system for the twenty-first century?
2. To what extent will economic systems around the world move closer together in some form of welfare capitalism or democratic socialism?
3. To what extent should countries work together to improve their mutual economic conditions?
4. To what extent can existing global organizations make a difference in improving economic conditions in the developing world?

▶ OBJECTIVES

After reading this chapter, you should be able to:

- ▶ integrate some of the ideas, values, and opinions that you have been developing thoughout the study of *Ideologies*
- ▶ formulate a research strategy and conduct in-depth research
- ▶ present your ideas in a convincing and well-written format

▶ KEY TERMS

interpreting information analysing information generalizations

CHAPTER

10 THE WORLD'S ECONOMIES: SUMMARY PROJECTS

The previous chapters and case studies outlined several different economic theories and systems. As well, a variety of issues has been discussed and case studies employed to show how various countries have dealt with these issues. Now it is your turn.

There are four issues presented in this chapter. The first two topics are based directly on the chapters and case studies you have read. The last two topics deal with additional global issues in which further research is required. Read all four projects and decide which one you find most interesting. Then follow the procedure and use this opportunity to develop your ideas, opinions, and values.

PROJECT #1 WHICH IS THE BEST ECONOMIC SYSTEM FOR THE TWENTY-FIRST CENTURY?

It is naïve to expect that organizations created by human beings—whether political, economic, or cultural—would or should be similar in every country. The fact that all countries face the problem of scarcity does not mean that identical solutions are suitable for everyone. As people differ, so do economic systems. Not only do capitalist economies differ from centrally planned ones, but mixed economies differ from each other as well. The economic systems of Yugoslavia, Poland, Cuba, and Hungary are quite unlike the Soviet Union's economy, while the systems of France, Sweden,

Holland, and Great Britain vary from the Canadian and American economies.

Which is the best economic system? There is no simple, straightforward answer to this question, because no two countries have the same needs, goals, values, political systems, or historical experience. The important decision is not between planning and *laissez-faire*, but how much control the government ought to exert over the economy and how this control should be used. It is now time for you to decide. Devise what you consider to be the best possible economic system. Your solution should take into account:

- the goals and values of your economic system;
- who will own the means of production;
- how it will determine what is produced and who will perform what tasks;
- how the goods will be distributed, and
- how people will be encouraged to work efficiently.

This project will be evaluated according to how well it promotes its goals and how practical it is.

Finding, Interpreting, and Analysing Information

The following are a few suggestions for research.

1. Review Chapters 6 to 9 and Case Studies 17, 19, 20, 21, 22, 23, and 24.
2. Extract those features you find desirable and feasible.
3. Compile a list of economic factors that are most important to you (such as high employment).
4. Examine how other countries have dealt with these issues.

You might want to make this a group project.

PROJECT #2 ECONOMIC SYSTEMS: NARROWING THE GAP

Since the end of World War II, many socialist principles have found their way into private enterprise economies and more individual freedom and incentives have led to modified public enterprise economics than ever before. In parts of the developing world, the economic success of countries such as Japan, Germany, and the United States have been held up as models for development by the supporters of private enterprise.

The most recent trend in economic systems has been a movement towards more capitalist principles. Eastern European countries have altered many of their economic principles of public enterprise and have moved (sometimes quite dramatically) towards capitalist ideals.

Is the trend towards capitalism continuing? What has happened to countries that have abandoned their public enterprise principles? Are developing countries attempting to follow the examples of private enterprise economics?

Finding, Interpreting, and Analysing Information

The following are a few suggestions for research:

1. Review Chapters 6 to 9 and Case Studies 18, 19, 20, 21, 22, 23, and 24.
2. Use comparisons of one or more Eastern European countries in the 1970s, 1980s, and 1990s to see what fundamental changes have occurred.
3. Examine what has happened to existing welfare capitalist countries (Canada and Great Britain) and democratic socialist countries (Swe-

den and France) to discuss if they are increasing or decreasing their socialist policies.

- **4.** Look at developing countries to see if they are accepting capitalist principles or relying on socialist ideals.

▶ Assessing the Present Situation

What is your assessment of the issue? Are countries coming closer together economically? Write a summary essay on this question and conclude with some **generalizations** as to the direction in which economic systems are moving.

▶ PROJECT #3 INTERNATIONAL ORGANIZATIONS: THE ANSWER TO THE WORLD'S ECONOMIC PROBLEMS?

Even if the trend in many parts of the world is to smaller political units (where people feel a greater degree of identification and security), economic organizations are becoming more popular. Countries see examples of economic co-operation such as the European Community as significantly improving the economic conditions for all its members. The number of associations and organizations have increased dramatically in the last forty years. Many countries see these larger economic units as necessary for free trade, a common currency, and the free movement of goods and labour—all of which they believe will increase their standard of living.

At the same time, some countries associate these organizations with the loss of political power, national security, and economic control. Many believe that regional economic organizations will lead to less trade among its non-members and higher tariffs between these larger economic groupings.

Are countries continuing to form closer economic associations? Is there a trend to closer political associations as well? Is the world becoming ''polarized'' around these regional organizations? Will the future world consist of a small number of large economic ''blocs''? Are countries in economic organizations becoming more prosperous? Are there any new trends in economic organizations?

▶ Finding, Interpreting, and Analysing Information

The following are a few suggestions for research:

- **1.** Review Chapters 5 and 6.
- **2.** Examine the state of affairs in the European Community. Has the organization moved towards even greater co-operation economically and/or politically? How well are its members doing?
- **3.** Compare economic statistics to determine economic growth rates among regional economic organizations.
- **4.** Examine the number of regional economic organizations compared to 1985. Find reasons for their popularity (or lack of popularity).

▶ Assessing the Present Situation

What is your assessment of regional economic organizations? Write a summary essay and conclude with some generalizations as to the success and future of these organizations.

▶ PROJECT #4 GLOBAL ORGANIZATIONS: CAN THEY MAKE A DIFFERENCE FOR DEVELOPING COUNTRIES?

One of the major objectives of the United Nations has been to improve economic conditions in the developing world. The United Nations established several organizations to provide better health (WHO), education (UNESCO), access to loans (The World Bank), and increased food production (FAO). These organizations are controlled by the developed countries through their financial contributions and policy decisions. There is no doubt that they have provided economic improvement for developing countries.

Has the economic gap increased or decreased between developed and developing countries? How effective has the United Nations been in helping to improve the standard of living in the developing world? Can significant changes occur within the existing structure of the UN's economic organizations or will new, more radical organizations be advocated by the developing world? What will be the consequences if developing countries fall even further behind the developed world?

▶ Finding, Interpreting, and Analysing Information

The following are a few suggestions for research:

- **1.** Review Chapters 5 and 6 and Case Studies 16, 24, and 25.
- **2.** Find out how effective the major UN organizations have been in improving developing countries' economic conditions.
- **3.** Examine different viewpoints about Third World development such as the New International Economic Order.
- **4.** Use graphs, charts, and other devices to make economic comparisons between developed and developing countries in such areas of concern as birth and death rates, standards of living, Gross Domestic Product, and daily calorie intakes. Use a computer to make projections about what may happen five, ten, or twenty-five years from now.

▶ Assessing the Present Situation

What is your assessment of the issue? Write a summary essay on the issue and conclude with some generalizations about the effectiveness of current global organizations; or role play a discussion among members from developed and less developed countries.

Glossary

▶ **Absolute poverty:** Poverty measured strictly in terms of low income, without taking into account the numerous existing private and governmental aids and subsidies designed to help the poor in Canada.

▶ **Absolute power:** The doctrine or system of government that bestows unlimited jurisdiction on a ruler.

▶ **Advanced technology:** Post-industrial development in communications such as FAX, in medicine such as lasers, in space travel, and in atomic research, among many others.

▶ **African National Congress:** The leading, predominantly non-White political party in South Africa founded in 1912. It advocates a racially unified South African state.

▶ **Afrikaner:** A White Christian resident of South Africa whose Dutch ancestors settled the Cape Horn area starting in the mid-seventeenth century. *See also* Boer.

▶ **Analysing information:** Scrutinizing the available information on a rational, objective, and logical basis.

▶ **Apartheid:** Apartness, in Afrikaans; a political approach under which Blacks must live in segregated Bantustans, or regions, where they are supposedly permitted to develop their own culture.

▶ **Authoritarian government:** A political system in which one person, either a monarch or a dictator, assumes total constitutional power under his or her authority.

▶ **Authoritarian personality:** A personal trait in which people are governed by the need to dominate everyone with whom they interact.

▶ **Authority:** The power or right to command, enforce obedience, or make final decisions.

▶ **Autocrat:** A person who rules as an authoritarian.

▶ **Autonomous:** Self-governing in all internal matters and concerns.

▶ **Balkans:** A large peninsula located in southeastern Europe, encompassing European Turkey, Greece, Albania, Bulgaria, Yugoslavia, and Romania.

▶ **Bantustan:** In South Africa, a racially determined political unit inhabited exclusively by members of the Black race.

▶ **Belief:** A subjective standard, such as a religion, considered as being valuable or desirable.

▶ **Bias:** Prejudice or discrimination.

▶ **Bicameral:** Having two houses of Parliament (for example, House of Commons and House of Lords).

▶ **Boer:** Synonym for Afrikaner.

▶ ***Bosozoku:*** Gangs of rebellious young people in Japan who are questioning their country's definition of success.

▶ **Bourgeoisie:** According to Marxian theory, the next-to-the-last social class on the eve of the Communist revolution, in which the middle class would lose their commanding position, especially of economic power. The owners of the means of production.

▶ **Bureaucracy:** A rationally organized system designed to administer the affairs of a government or business enterprise through officials who follow a set routine.

▶ **C.P.S.U.:** The Communist Party of the Soviet Union—until recently, the only legally sanctioned group in the U.S.S.R.

▶ **Capitalism:** In economics, a system that thrives on the accumulation and use of all assets that can be transformed into cash, including the labour of individual workers.

▶ **Caucus:** The plenary (full) meeting of a political party in which party policies are discussed and approved, often by a consensus.

▶ **Centrally planned economy:** An economic system in which a central body makes all the major economic decisions for the country.

▶ **Charismatic; charisma (n.):** Having the ability to capture the attention and gain the support of people through the force of one's personality.

▶ **Checks and balances:** A system of government in which the executive, legislative, and judicial branches of government are constitutionally vested with the right to check each other's actions in order to prevent violations of the constitution.

▶ **Civil disobedience:** The deliberate violation of the law(s) by groups of individuals devoted to a certain cause or opposed to various government practices or policies.

▶ **Civil liberties:** The enjoyment of all lawful freedoms of action and belief by citizens of a state.

▶ **Civil servant:** A government official charged with carrying out government policy; a member of the civil service.

▶ **Co-determination Act of 1977:** A reform law in Sweden that gave trade unions an important voice in the operation of Swedish business enterprises, involving hiring, firing, and production methods.

▶ **Coalition government:** A government that stays in power, that is, it enjoys the support of the legislature by combining with another political party or parties to form a majority.

▶ **Collective farms:** Under Stalin, *circa* 1929, many individual small farms were seized by the government and combined into large government owned and managed enterprises. Here, the peasants were able to keep their homes and farm animals, but all equipment was owned jointly by the entire group.

▶ **Coloured:** In South africa, anyone who is of mixed race.

▶ **Combines Investigation Act of 1910:** A Canadian law that prohibited the formation of any monopoly or oligopoly that was likely to be detrimental to the public good.

▶ **Communist:** Pertaining to a political system characterized by one-part dictatorship, government ownership of all the means of production, and a totalitarian approach to all problems.

▶ ***Communist Manifesto:*** An 1848 declaration by Karl Marx and Friedrich Engels in which they called upon all the workers of the world to unite and cast off the shackles that the exploitive bourgeois businesspeople used to hold them in captivity.

▶ **Competition:** In economics, the more or less free competition among entrepreneurs engaged in the same business enterprise, each of whom is trying to capture as large a share of the marketplace as possible.

▶ **Competition Acts of 1977:** A Canadian law that extended the government's policing powers over retail stores, hotels, banks, and brokerage firms.

▶ **Congress of People's Deputies:** Under Mikhail Gorbachev, the governmental body designed to wield full authority in the U.S.S.R.

▶ **Consensus:** A general opinion, informally arrived at.

▶ **Conservative:** A person who favours the retention of traditional values, especially in government, economics, religion, and morals, but who supports slow and cautious, organic reforms.

▶ ***Coup d'état:*** An attempt, whether successful or unsuccessful, to overthrow the government of a state.

▶ **Crisis theory:** The political science theory that all historical events in human society are triggered by various crises such as war and depression.

▶ **Critical thinking:** The ability to subject ideas and situations to a sound estimate of the problems involved.

▶ **Crown corporation:** In Canada, a business enterprise owned and operated by a government-appointed management team and regarded as essential for protecting the public's welfare.

▶ ***Das Kapital:*** ''Capital,'' one of the most influential books of economic theory in the nineteenth century, formulated by Karl Marx with the assistance of Friedrich Engels in 1847, which outlines the beliefs of Marxian communism.

▶ **De-Stalinization:** The process of dismantling the police state built by Joseph Stalin.

▶ **Debtors' cartels:** Attempts by developing countries in debt to international bankers to band together for their mutual benefit.

▶ **Deficit:** A situation in which the total annual expenses of a country surpass its total income.

▶ **Deforestation:** The permanent clearing of forest land and its conversion into agricultural and grazing areas.

▶ **Demand-side economics:** In economics, a system in which the government is expected to remedy a recession by introducing high interest rates, reduced expenditures, and tax increases.

▶ **Democracy:** A state ruled by the consent of its citizens (the people).

▶ **Democratic centralism:** According to the political doctrine practised in the U.S.S.R., a system under which the Communist party alone protects the interests of proletarians, who in turn delegate their democratic rights and power to the party.

▶ **Democratic socialism:** The non-Marxist branch of socialism, developed in the nineteenth century in response to clamourings in European societies for thorough reform. Democratic socialism evolved globally into Social Democratic parties, with programs emphasizing the importance of capitalism and the determination to effect social reforms through peaceful, constitutional action.

▶ **Democratization:** An attempt in the Soviet Union under Mikhail Gorbachev to dismantle the country's highly centralized and autocratic political and economic system in favour of more dispersed decision-making powers for the population of the U.S.S.R.

▶ **Demogrants:** Grants offered by the Canadian government to needy people in specified population groups such as the elderly and families with under-age children.

▶ **Depression:** In economics, the state of economic collapse that government action or activity by the business community cannot remedy.

▶ **Developing countries:** Countries with traditional, pre-industrial economies, located mainly in the South.

▶ **Direct democracy:** A state in which all political decisions are made directly by all the qualified voters, as in a referendum or plebiscite.

▶ **Economic system:** A rationally conceived plan for the production, distribution, and consumption of a country's wealth.

▶ **Ecosystem:** The totality of a region's human, mineral, and animal resources.

▶ **Electoral district:** A political sub-division served by only one person with the proviso that he or she won the majority vote (fifty percent plus one) during an election.

▶ **Electoral process:** The system of organizing and administering the voting process.

▶ **Electorate:** The body of citizens privileged to vote.

▶ **Ethnic origin:** The descent of an individual based on cultural characteristics.

▶ **Executive:** The group or person with constitutional power to carry out and enforce a country's law.

▶ **Fabian movement:** An elitist socialist group united in latter nineteenth century Great Britain by the determination to reform society through peaceful means and faith in the power of human reason and the power of education. The ultimate aim was nationalization of all large business enterprises as a means of ending greed in society.

▶ **Fact:** An actual occurrence, or a piece of information, presented as having objective reality.

▶ **Fascism:** A political system characterized by the leadership of a dictator with totalitarian powers in a one-party state.

▶ **Federal system:** A political system under which a federal government delegates certain legislative and administrative powers to sub-divisions such as provinces or territories (for example, Canada).

▶ **Federalism:** A political system in which political powers are divided between the central (federal) government and regional units such as provinces.

▶ **Five-Year Plan:** An economic program first attempted by Stalin in 1928 in order to hasten the quick industrialization of the Soviet Union.

▶ **Five-year plans:** Unlike in the Soviet Union, in Sweden five-year plans are not official government policy declarations but merely projections for the future to assist industry in arriving at rational decisions.

▶ **Formal democracy:** A state in which political decisions are made by a dictator or oligarchy that maintains the outward manifestations of being ruled by the consent of the governed.

▶ **French Community:** A political organization sponsored by France after World War II that links that country with its former colonies.

▶ **Führer:** Also fuehrer. ''Leader'' in German. Specifically, Adolf Hitler, leader of the National Socialist party and head of the government of Germany (1933–1945).

▶ **Generalizations:** Constructing general statements after having analysed and collated all the information at disposal.

▶ ***Glasnost:*** A public policy in the U.S.S.R. characterized by Mikhail Gorbachev as an open and frank approach to solve the Soviet Union's problems.

▶ **Gosplan:** In the Soviet Union, the central economic planning agency responsible for informing regional authorities of what commodities were needed and in what amounts.

▶ **Gossnab:** In the Soviet Union, an economic planning body responsible for determining how commodities were to be distributed.

▶ **Great Trek:** A mass migration into the interior of South Africa undertaken by the Boers in the nineteenth century to escape the effects of English settlements in the region.

▶ **Greens:** Politically and economically motivated activists functioning in many countries of the North. They wish to save the environment from industrial pollution and governmental neglect of the ecology.

▶ **Gross National Product:** In economics, the sum total of an entire country's annual economic output.

▶ **Guerrilla warfare:** Small-scale fighting, mostly hit-and-run raids, by small groups of highly trained and often politically indoctrinated non-professional soldiers.

▶ **Hereditary monarch:** Any ruler who occupies his or her throne by having the hereditary right to inherit his or her position, based usually on family (dynastic) affiliation.

▶ **Homelands:** Separate geographic areas allocated to all Blacks by South Africa's White government. *See* Bantustan.

▶ **Human right:** A belief that all people are born with the right to enjoy certain basic freedoms and protection against such dangers as hunger and disease.

▶ **Hungarian Uprising of 1956:** A temporarily successful revolt in Hungary directed against the Soviet and indigenous "Stalinist" communist leadership; revolt smashed by the Soviet army forces later in 1956.

▶ **Ideology:** A rationally conceived plan for the study or organization of ideas, their nature, source, and goals.

▶ ***Il Duce:*** Benito Mussolini, "the leader" of Fascist Italy between 1922 and 1945.

▶ **Imperfect competition:** A situation in which a few entrepreneurs control or own certain resources and prevent intruders from entering into competition with them.

▶ **Imperial rivalry:** A struggle involving large powers bent on world domination.

▶ **Individual freedom:** The constitutional or traditional right of individuals to be protected against illegal actions launched against them by their government.

▶ **Individual's rights:** The natural or lawfully delegated power of an individual to enjoy certain privileges or powers.

▶ **Industrial Revolution:** The transformation, first in mid-eighteenth century England, of a traditional agricultural economy into one dominated by steam-driven machinery and a regimented working class.

▶ **Inflation:** in economics, a condition under which a steady rise in prices is not matched by people's incomes.

▶ **Infrastructure:** The basic economic, political, and social network of a state.

▶ ***Inkatha:*** A Zulu cultural movement founded in the 1970s that has since assumed political importance as it wishes to liberate all of South Africa's Blacks.

▶ **Inquiry process:** An objective, rational, and logical system for an investigation into or examination of facts or principles.

▶ **Institutional Revolutionary party (P.R.I.):** The governing party in Mexico.

▶ **Interdependence:** In economics, the need for individuals and business firms to interact with one another for the mutual benefit of all parties involved.

▶ **Interest group:** An organized or informal group representing a certain political, social, or economic position in society.

▶ **Interpreting information:** Placing facts, observations, and statistics into a coherent, logical, analytical framework.

▶ **Invisible hand:** The expression used by Adam Smith to explain the fact that the selfish economically governed actions of all the individuals of a society ultimately combine to benefit society and the individuals in it.

▶ **Joint economic ventures:** A new economic system under Mikhail Gorbachev that permits the creation of joint economic ventures with Western businesses.

▶ **Judicial power:** The constitutional or traditional right to judge or cancel laws passed by the executive or legislative branch of government.

▶ ***Keiretsu:*** Successors to the *zaibatsu*, controlled by eight large industrial business firms. The *keiretsu* dominate contemporary Japan's business life.

▶ **Keynesian economics:** In economics, a system that attempts to counteract a depression by heavy governmental deficit spending and by launching public works projects, that is, "priming the pump."

▶ **Kulaks:** Rich peasants in the Soviet Union who refused to co-operate with Soviet authorities and were destroyed as a group in the 1930s under Stalin's orders.

▶ ***Laissez-faire* System:** In economics, a system proposed in the mid-eighteenth century, according to which entrepreneurs and farmers should be permitted to function freely without the intervention of government.

▶ **Legislative power:** The constitutional or traditional right to pass laws vested in a legislative body or bodies.

▶ **Liberal:** A person who favours reform, especially in government, economics, and religion, and who prefers democratic or republican forms of government in a constitutional state.

▶ **Lobbyist:** Usually a paid employee of various economic and political groups or business firms whose task is to influence governmental action or legislation.

▶ **Market economy:** An economic system in which the marketplace, that is, the combined effects of individual demands, determines what is to be produced.

▶ **Market socialism:** The latest development in socialist thought that advocated the judicious combining of free enterprise with central planning.

▶ **Marxism:** The economic and political theories of Karl Marx.

▶ **Meiji dynasty:** The dynasty that came to rule Japan in 1867, in the wake of a civil war. The new regime saw the introduction of wide-ranging reform of Japan's economic, political, and social structure and the pursuit of modernization and Westernization.

▶ ***Mein Kampf:*** *My Struggle*, Adolf Hitler's autobiographical and philosophical book, written in prison after the abortive Munich *Putsch* of 1923. The work outlines Hitler's distant objectives.

▶ **Mercantilism:** An economic system widely practised until the end of the eighteenth century, in which private enterprises were permitted to function only by submitting to detailed intervention and supervision in their business activities by the government.

▶ **Military junta:** A group of military personnel, usually of middle or high rank, who have taken over a country's government and who dominate that country's affairs.

▶ **Minority government:** A government mandated by the legislature to conduct the affairs of state without having a majority in that body.

▶ **MITI:** Ministry of International Trade and Industry, a government agency in Japan commissioned to function as a central planning bureau and to be equally responsive to government policies and business concerns.

▶ **Mixed economy:** An economic system in which government enterprises co-exist with privately owned businesses.

▶ **Moderate:** A political middle-of-the-roader, a centrist, neutral, or a compromiser.

▶ **Monopolistic competition:** Synonymous with imperfect competition.

▶ **Monopoly:** Exclusive ownership or control of certain industries by a limited number of business participants or government.

▶ **Multi-member constituency:** A political sub-division served by as many persons as are able to win a certain minimum percentage of the vote during an election.

▶ **Multi-party system:** A system in which more than two parties dominate politics and legislation, usually by means of coalition governments (for example, Italy).

▶ **Multinational corporation:** A sophisticated, wealthy, and influential business organization that functions on a global basis but is not subject or loyal to any particular government or state.

▶ **Natural right:** A political theory, according to which all people are born with certain inalienable (something that cannot be taken away) privileges.

▶ **Natural state:** A condition under which people are not organized under a social contract.

▶ **Nazi party:** The National Socialist Party that governed Germany under Adolf Hitler (1933–1945).

▶ **New Economic Policy (N.E.P.):** An economic plan (1921–1927) implemented by Vladimir Lenin in order to combat a major economic depression in the Soviet Union. Its chief features were the permissions granted to small entrepreneurs and farmers to function in the marketplace undisturbed by government.

▶ **Non-Aligned Movement:** A broad, informal movement, largely among the countries of the South, designed to maintain strict neutrality in the struggle between the United States and its allies and the Soviet Union and its allies.

▶ **Non-confidence vote:** A vote in the legislature on a major bill, mostly of financial nature, that brings down the government.

▶ **Non-violent protest:** A peaceful demonstration by individuals or groups to further a certain cause or to oppose the government on certain policies or practices.

▶ **North:** Generally refers to the highly industrialized and advanced countries of the Northern Hemisphere.

▶ ***Nyuu puaa:*** Literally, the "new poor"; certain members of the salaried Japanese middle classes whose incomes have not kept pace with inflation.

▶ ***Nyuu ritchi:*** Literally, the "new rich"; members of Japan's middle classes who have been keeping ahead of inflation due to incomes derived from high-yield investments.

▶ **Oligarchy:** A government conducted and controlled by a relatively few influential members.

▶ **One-party state:** A country governed by one entrenched political party. *See* one-party system.

▶ **One-party system:** A system in which only one political party, either by law or through subterfuge, wields all the constitutional power (for example, Mexico).

▶ **Opinion polls:** A rationally organized effort by a professional business organization to test the public's reaction to certain events or conditions.

▶ **Pan Africanist Congress:** A small, extremist Black organization that advocates the transformation of South Africa into a new ''Azania'' that would be governed by the Black majority.

▶ **Party discipline:** The status of obtaining and maintaining party loyalty.

▶ **Party loyalty:** The obligation of elected members of a political party to cast a vote in the legislature in their party's favour, even if they disagree with the bill.

▶ **Passive resistance:** The systematic, non-violent refusal by individuals or groups to obey the laws and regulations of a state, and their refusal to co-operate with government officials and their representatives.

▶ ***Perestroika:*** Restructuring of the political and economic institution of the U.S.S.R. under Mikhail Gorbachev.

▶ **Perfect competition:** A situation in which numerous entrepreneurs can enter a business field and be assured of having a market that enables them to reap satisfactory profits.

▶ **Platt Amendment:** A United States law of 1901 that made Cuba an American protectorate; abrogated by Cuban Treaty in 1934.

▶ **Plebiscite:** A direct ballot by all qualified voters on an issue of national importance.

▶ **Polis:** In ancient Greece, a city state, that is, a city and its surrounding countryside.

▶ **Politburo:** A leading committee of the Communist party of the Soviet Union, responsible for analysing events and determining policy between sessions of the larger Central Committee; replaced by the Presidium in 1952.

▶ **Political apathy:** A state of indifference regarding political issues.

▶ **Political equality:** The right of all citizens of a state to enjoy similar political rights.

▶ **Political party:** A political organization formed to represent certain stated goals and policies.

▶ **Political system:** A rationally conceived plan for the governance of a state.

▶ **Pollster:** A person employed by a public opinion firm or political party to canvass public opinion.

▶ **Prague Spring (1968):** A temporarily successful revolt in Czechoslovakia directed against the Soviet and indigenous communist party rule; revolt smashed by the Warsaw Pact intervention later that year.

▶ **Pressure groups:** Similar to interest groups, except that pressure groups are far more aggressive and activist in their efforts to achieve a certain objective (for example, Greenpeace).

▶ **Private enterprise system:** In economics, a system that permits individuals and business firms to function freely without unreasonable interference by governments in their lawful activities.

▶ **Privatization:** The sale of government run and owned enterprises to private industry.

▶ **Productivity:** In economic theory, the rate of labour output by individual workers and machinery.

▶ **Profit motive:** The desire of business entrepeneurs to engage in a commercial venture to accumulate capital.

▶ **Progressive taxes:** Taxes that are proportionately higher depending on the person's annual income.

▶ **Proletariat class:** According to Marxist theory, the class of industrial wage earners whose only capital is their labour.

▶ **Proportional representation:** A political system under which parties gain their seats in the legislature based on the percentage of the vote received in an election.

▶ **Protective tariff:** A levy imposed on imports by government to protect the market for native entrepreneurs.

▶ **Public order:** A state in which law and order are maintained by governments either by law or by extraordinary powers vested in them.

▶ **Public ownership:** In Marxian theory, the economic system under which a communist government seizes, maintains, and exploits all the means of production of the country on behalf of the proletarian working class. More generally, government owned and operated industries.

▶ **Puppet dictatorship:** A political system, under which a dictator secretly directs the activities of a highly visible and respected politician.

▶ ***Putsch:*** A *coup d'état* loosely translated into German. *See coup d'état.*

▶ **Radical:** A political extremist, mostly of the left, such as an anarchist (a person who does not believe in the need for organized government).

▶ **Rain forest:** Largely tropical forests located in regions with heavy rainfall and hot climates.

▶ **Ranching:** Intensive cultivation of herds of cattle.

▶ **Reactionary:** A person who favours a return to narrow, traditional values, especially in government, economics, religion, and morals.

▶ **Reaganomics:** A supply-side economic policy pursued by U.S. President Ronald Reagan, according to which the government can best ensure prosperity by fiscal restraint and by permitting private enterprises to be architects of a healthy economy.

▶ **Recession:** In economics, the state of a country's economy in which all economic indicators show a downward trend for three consecutive quarters (nine months).

▶ **Referendum:** The submission of a planned law to a direct vote of the people.

▶ **Reichstag:** The lower legislative chamber during the Weimar Republic.

▶ **Relative poverty:** Poverty measured in terms of comparison with the incomes of other people and taking into account the minimum amount of money needed to ensure all of a person's basic needs.

▶ **Representative democracy:** A state in which the legislative powers are delegated by qualified voters to their representative in a legislative body, such as parliament, senate, or congress.

▶ **Republican democracy:** A political system in which an elected official, usually the president, wields the constitutional power.

▶ **Responsible government:** A system of parliamentary government in which the executive functions at the will of the legislative body.

▶ **Riksdag:** The legislative body in Sweden.

▶ **Russianization (Russianized):** The attempt by the U.S.S.R. from time to time to induce non-Russian peoples in the country to adopt Russian linguistic and cultural norms.

▶ **Scarcity:** In economic theory, the shortage of a good or service that drives up its price.

▶ **Segregate:** To practise a policy of racial segregation. In South Africa, the act of denying Blacks and other non-Whites the use of the same facilities or services enjoyed by Whites, as well as the physical separation of the races.

▶ **Selective logging:** An operation in which logging companies seek to cut down only specific, financially lucrative, trees.

▶ **Self-determination:** The right of a people to determine its own government or way of life without interference by outsiders.

▶ **Self-financing:** A system whereby enterprises in the Soviet Union can no longer depend on the government to subsidize their losses; they must eliminate inefficiency and waste and cover their own debts.

▶ ***Sendero luminoso:*** Literally, ''Shining Path''; a highly active, ruthless, and effective Peruvian guerrilla force begun in the mid-1960s as a radical student organization.

▶ **Shiite Muslims:** A Muslim splinter group that seceded in the late seventh century from the main Sumni body of Islam, largely on doctrinal grounds.

▶ ***Shilken jigoku:*** The last year of high school in Japan, literally ''exam hell,'' owing to the extremely rigorous educational standards demanded of students in Japanese society.

▶ **Social contract:** The theory that a government cannot wield its authority by force alone but must have the tacit or written consent, such as a constitution, of the governed.

▶ **Social Darwinism:** The English naturalist Charles Darwin taught that survival of a species is ensured by overcoming various genetically governed challenges over long periods of time. Social Darwinists adapted Darwin's theory to individual human beings. Those who cannot endure stress succumb, those who can prevail and propagate the species.

▶ **Social-insurance programs:** Payments offered by the Canadian government to people in specific positions of financial want such as unemployment, disability, or sustained injury.

▶ **Socialism:** A socio-political and economic system of varying diversity of beliefs, ranging from government ownership of all businesses to benign government interference in business activities to ensure an equitable distribution of wealth among the population.

▶ **Societal norms:** The behavioural standards of a community, usually arrived at by consensus.

▶ **Soil erosion:** The gradual disappearance of topsoil due to deforestation and other abuses.

▶ **South:** Generally refers to the still developing and relatively less advanced countries of the Southern Hemisphere.

▶ **Sovereign:** A person who exercises supreme (but not necessarily unlimited) power (n.); independent of any other authority; free (a.).

▶ **Splinter party:** A group, comprising the membership of a party, from which it secedes and forms its own party.

▶ **Stalin's Russia:** The period in Soviet history during which Joseph Stalin ruled the U.S.S.R. with an iron hand as a virtual dictator (1924–1953).

▶ **State farms:** Government-owned mechanized farms in the Soviet Union begun by Stalin about 1929. Peasants shared in the income from the sale of farm products and they were permitted to keep their homes, small plots of lands, and farm animals for their private use.

▶ **State monopoly:** A commonly used economic policy whereby government owns, maintains, and operates vital facilities such as railways, airlines, postal systems, and similar facilities.

▶ **Storm troopers:** A paramilitary force of Brownshirts, also known as S.A., who enforced the will of Germany's National Socialist government.

▶ **Suffrage:** The right of qualified women to vote in an election.

▶ **Supply-side economics:** In economics, a system in which the private market is free to operate and the wealth thus created gradually trickles down to the lower echelons of the population to benefit the entire economy.

▶ **Supra-national:** Not limited to one country alone; engaging in operations across international frontiers.

▶ **Thatcherism:** A supply-side economic policy pursued by Prime Minister Margaret Thatcher in Great Britain, with similar principles that guided Reaganomics. Thatcherism emphasized privatization, self-help, efficiency, and increased productivity.

▶ **The Long March:** The historical northward trek by Chinese Communist armies under the leadership of Mao Zedong (1934–1935).

▶ **Third Reich:** The name given to Germany by the ruling National Socialist party after the collapse of the Weimar Republic.

▶ **Tolerance:** Permitting, though not condoning, particular actions or beliefs differing from or conflicting with one's own standards.

▶ **Totalitarian:** Relating to a political system in which the ruler or ruling body has established total control over all aspects of society.

▶ **Traditional economy:** An economic system largely practised by people in a pre-industrialized stage of development. It is based mostly on agricultural pursuits and on a division of labour decreed by custom and tradition.

▶ **Transfer program:** A federal plan designed to relieve the poverty of individual groups, such as indigenous peoples, or of depressed regions of Canada.

▶ **Tsarist Russia:** The period of Russian history during which the country was ruled by autocratic tsars, or emperors, until the overthrow of the Romanov dynasty in 1917.

▶ **Two-party system:** A system in which two political parties dominate the politics and legislation of a country (for example, the U.S.A.).

▶ **Tyranny of the majority:** A condition under which the ruling majority unlawfully oppresses minorities of any type.

▶ **Unitary system:** A political system under which all geographic regions are governed directly by the central government (for example, France).

▶ **Universal suffrage:** A political system that grants the right to vote to all qualified citizens, regardless of political belief, gender, race, or ethnic affiliation.

▶ **Urbanization:** The growth of urban centres due to the trend of abandoning village life to a better lifestyle in the cities.

▶ **Utopian Socialists:** Early socialists (eighteenth to nineteenth centuries) who advocated idealistic and romantic methods to achieve economic prosperity, and who believed in the power of education and the basic goodness of human nature to assist this process.

▶ **Value:** A subjective standard, such as a philosophy or principle, that is deemed valuable or desirable.

▶ **Weimar Republic:** The republican type of parliamentary democracy, with its capital located in Weimar, that the victorious Entente powers forced Germany to accept (1919–1933) after its defeat in World War I.

▶ **Welfare capitalism:** A capitalist's system that recognizes the necessity for government to intervene in the economy to curb violations and to ensure the welfare of the entire population by sponsoring various types of protective legislation.

▶ **World Bank:** A lending institution established by the United Nations in 1945, charged with the task of making loans available to member states.

▶ **Written constitution:** A document or charter that spells out in writing the basic laws and power relationships in a state.

▶ ***Zaibatsu:*** Japanese monopolies, each industry dominated usually by a single family, that jointly controlled the industrial life of Japan; dissolved by the American military authorities shortly after World War II.

Index